− 3 NOV 2016   346.074 G (R)

BPP University Library and
Information Service

Reference Use Only

Not to be removed from the library

BPP
UNIVERSITY

D1339747

L

Goode on Legal Problems of Credit and Security

Fifth Edition

Goode on Legal Problems of Credit and Security

Fifth Edition

Edited by

Professor Louise Gullifer

SWEET & MAXWELL

THOMSON REUTERS

First edition	1982
Second edition	1988
Third edition	2003
Fourth edition	2008
Fifth edition	2013

Published in 2013 by Sweet & Maxwell, 100 Avenue Road, London, NW3 3PF part of Thomson Reuters (Professional) UK Limited (Registered in England & Wales, Company No 1679046.
Registered Office and address for service: Aldgate House, 33 Aldgate High Street, London, EC3N 1DL)

Sweet & Maxwell ® is a registered trademark of Thomson Reuters (Professional) UK Limited.

For further information on our products and services, visit *www.sweetandmaxwell.co.uk*

Typeset by Letterpart Limited, Caterham on the Hill, Surrey CR3 5XL

Printed and bound by CPI Group (UK) Ltd, Croydon, CR0 4YY

No natural forests were destroyed to make this product; only farmed timber was used and re-planted.

A CIP catalogue record of this book is available for the British Library.

ISBN: 978-0-414-04802-7 (HB)
978-0-414-03343-6 (PB)

Thomson Reuters and the Thomson Reuters logo are trademarks of Thomson Reuters.

Crown copyright material is reproduced with the permission of the Controller of HMSO and the Queen's Printer for Scotland.

All rights reserved. No part of this publication may be reproduced or transmitted in any form or by any means, or stored in any retrieval system of any nature, without prior written permission, except for permitted fair dealing under the Copyright, Designs and Patents Act 1988, or in accordance with the terms of a licence issued by the Copyright Licensing Agency in respect of photocopying and/or reprographic reproduction. Application for permission for other use of copyright material, including permission to reproduce extracts in other published works, shall be made to the publishers. Full acknowledgement of author, publisher and source must be given.

© 2013 Thomson Reuters (Professional) UK Limited & Sir Roy Goode

Whilst Sir Roy Goode is no longer responsible for this or future editions of this work, the right of Sir Roy Goode to be identified as the author of the 1st—3rd Editions of this work has been asserted in accordance with the Copyright, Designs and Patents Act 1988.

Foreword

I am delighted to introduce the fifth edition of this book, the second to be published under the editorship of my friend and colleague Professor Louise Gullifer. This edition, like its predecessor, is no mere technical update. Louise shares my belief that there is no point in undertaking a new edition of a work based on a conceptual framework unless one has something new to say. And there is much to discuss and analyse since the previous edition appeared some five years ago. There have been substantial changes in the statutory provisions governing registration of company charges, where a closed list of registrable charges has been replaced by provisions making all charges by companies registrable unless they fall within one of a limited number of exceptions. Certain provisions of the Financial Collateral Directive continue to give rise to debate as to their meaning. The rules on set-off have been developed over a great many years, yet there is still no clarity as to the means by which transaction set-off has to be invoked. Again, the courts continue to be troubled by aspects of the floating charge, reinforcing the case for reform of personal property security law along the lines provisionally recommended many years ago in a Law Commissions consultative report, now picked up by the secured transactions law reform project of which Professor Gullifer has recently taken charge as Executive Director.

All these and many other issues are explored through rigorous analysis combined with a keen perception of the underlying policy issues, thus ensuring that this work, which originated as a series of public lectures over 30 years ago at Queen Mary College, University of London, is up-to-date not simply in a technical sense but in its focus on current and emerging issues. I have no doubt that it will receive as warm a welcome among both academics and practitioners as the previous editions.

Roy Goode
Oxford
November 11, 2013

v

Dedication of 4th and 5th editions

To my patient family: Robert, Emma and Hetty

Preface to the fifth edition

It is a continuing privilege to be entrusted with editing this volume, which started life as a series of lectures and which has grown into a text which is read by practitioners, judges, academics and students. It is characterised by not merely reporting the law as it is, but by exploring the theoretical background to it, and by discussion of issues which have not (yet) been the subject of consideration by the courts.

In the last edition I sought to change little of the structure and analysis of the book. This time, I have restructured and, to some extent, rewritten two major chapters to reflect not only changes in the law but to emphasise what is now important in legal practice. Thus, Chapter 6, which was originally included to consider security interests in investment securities, has been restructured as a chapter on the law relating to financial collateral, that is, not just securities but cash and credit claims as well. This is a highly technical area, which is of immense importance to the financial markets, and which engenders very considerable debate, not to say strong feeling, among those who practise in and regulate the area. Chapter 7 has also been rewritten and restructured, partly to reflect interesting case law developments in the law of transaction set-off, but also to bring up-to-date the discussion of netting and its critical role in managing risk on the financial markets. In both these chapters, and indeed throughout the book, the law of insolvency underlies the discussion. Although developments in insolvency law are referred to in context in this book, for detailed discussion the reader is referred to the fourth edition of Professor Goode's *Principles of Corporate Insolvency Law*. Thus, for example, the case of *Belmont Park Investments Pty Ltd v BNY Corporate Trustee Services Ltd* and the subsequent cases on the anti-deprivation and pari passu principles, are discussed only in the context of contractual set-off and netting.

The law of registration of company charges has recently been the subject of limited legislative reform. Of course, this has affected the discussion in the book, particularly in Chapter 2, but I have made no attempt to give a detailed and comprehensive account of the reforms, but rather have focused on their implications, particularly for issues of notice and priority. Discussion among academics and practitioners about further reform remains ongoing, and I have attempted to highlight areas where difficulties and uncertainties still remain.

There have, of course, been some important cases which have merited discussion. The litigation arising out of the insolvency of the Lehman companies has been a fruitful source of judicial discussion of some fundamental concepts. Thus, in *Lehman Brothers International (Europe) (In Administration)* [2012] EWHC 2997 (Ch) Mr Justice Briggs considered whether a valid security interest could be given to someone other than a person to whom the secured obligation was owed, or a trustee for that person. In this, and other Lehman cases[1] the courts have considered the legal structure of intermediated securities, repos and the effect of the right of use. In addition, the question of whether a charge falls within the Financial Collateral Arrangements (No.2) Regulations (which are now so ubiquitously referred to that they have their own acronym: the FCARs) has been considered in two first instance decisions: the *Lehman* decisions mentioned above and *Gray v G-T-P Group Ltd* [2010] EWHC 1772. Further, the scope of the FCARs was considered in the judicial review case of *R (on the application of Cukurova Finance International Ltd v HM Treasury* [2008] EWHC 2567 (Admin) and the remedy of appropriation has been considered in some detail by the Privy Council in that litigation in *Cukurova Finance International Ltd v Alfa Telecom Turkey Ltd* [2009] UKPC 19; *Cukurova Finance International Ltd v Alfa Telecom Turkey Ltd* [2013] UKPC 2; and *Cukurova Finance International Limited v Alfa Telecom Turkey Limited* [2013] UKPC 20.

Another area in which the courts have been busy is that of transaction set-off. The difficult question of what is meant by that type of set-off operating as a substantive defence was considered at first instance in *Fearns v Anglo-Dutch Paint and Chemical Co Ltd* [2010] EWHC 2366 (Ch), and the approach of the courts to the requirement that the claim and cross-claim be closely connected was considered by the Court of Appeal in *Geldof Metaalconstructie NV v Simon Carves Ltd* [2010] EWCA Civ 667. The distinction between a "see to it" and a conditional payment guarantee has been discussed by the Court of Appeal in *McGuinness v Norwich and Peterborough Building Society* [2011] EWCA Civ 1286; the effect of the rule against double proof on the rule in *Cherry v Boultbee* has been definitively settled by the Supreme Court in *Mills v HSBC Trustee (CI) Ltd* [2011] UKSC 48; and the distinction between fixed and floating charges has been considered further in *Re Harmony Care Homes Ltd* [2009] EWHC 1961 (Ch). Many other new cases have been the subject of footnotes and other references.

Cases in other jurisdictions have also been discussed where the reasoning provides an interesting opportunity to reflect on English law in the area. Two decisions, in particular, fall into this category. One is *Caisse Populaire Desjardins de l'Est de Drummond v Canada* [2009] S.C.C. 29 in which the Supreme Court of Canada decided that an agreement for set-of, coupled with negative pledge and flawed asset provisions, amounted to a security interest within the definition of a tax statute; and *Re JD Brian Ltd* [2011] IEHC 113; [2011] 3 I.R. 244, an Irish decision on the effect of an automatic crystallisation clause.

Over the past five years I have reflected further on some of the issues discussed in the book, and so I have redrafted the text accordingly. One example is the question of whether the appointment of an administrator by a floating charge holder crystallises the charge, another is the effect of security being held for a debt which is the subject of insolvency set-off (especially in the context of a charge-back). I have expanded the discussion of when a security interest over an

---

[1] *In the Matter of Lehman Brothers International (Europe) (In Administration)* [2009] EWHC 2545 (Ch), *Re Lehman Brothers International (Europe) (In Administration)* [2010] EWHC 2914 (Ch), *Lehman Brothers International (Europe) (In Administration)* [2010] EWCA Civ 917.

asset can be traced into the proceeds of sale of that asset, and I am greatly indebted to Magda Raczynska and Professor Lionel Smith for their assistance in clarifying my thoughts.

As with the last edition, I have greatly benefited from discussing the issues in the book with many colleagues, students and practitioners. As well as those already mentioned I am particularly indebted to those with whom I teach the Corporate Finance law course at Oxford: Jenny Payne of Merton College, Richard Salter Q.C. and Chris Hare of Somerville College, and also to Professor Hugh Beale of Warwick University, with whom I have debated many difficult points, particularly concerning financial collateral. Practitioners who have been especially helpful include Ed Murray from Allen and Overy and Matthew Dening from Sidley Austin, who have commented on drafts and discussed netting and financial collateral and Marisa Chan of Clifford Chance; however, I have also benefitted from discussions with many others. I have had very considerable help from four research assistants, three of whom, Harry Martin, Stuart Cribb and Sophia Hurst, worked on different chapters identifying potential new material and found all the updated references to textbooks, and one of whom, my daughter Emma Gullifer, applied the Sweet & Maxwell style guide to the footnotes with commendable rigour. My family, Robert, Emma and Hetty, have again been a source of inspiration, and have been stoic in the face of approaching deadlines. Yet again, though, I am principally indebted to Professor Sir Roy Goode, both for such an excellent book which it is a pleasure to edit and for all his help and encouragement over the years.

Louise Gullifer
Oxford
November 1, 2013

Preface to the fourth edition

I was enormously surprised and honoured to be asked by Professor Sir Roy Goode to edit the fourth and subsequent editions of this book, which has, in its first three editions, become essential reading for practitioners, academics and students. Roy Goode has, over many years, been a hugely valued mentor, colleague and inspiration to me, and it is a great honour to be entrusted with this book which, out of all his books, is the one which is most closely aligned with my research interests. I have known this book throughout my career, and its penetrating analysis as well as its exploration of fundamental questions have informed much of my thinking in the area of security interests and their place in English law.

As befits a first new edition by someone other than the original author, I have sought to change very little except as has been dictated by recent developments in case law, legislation, academic debate and proposals for reform. The book originated as a series of lectures, and, in the third edition, some parts were still written in the first person. I have sought to rewrite these in a more passive sense, without, I hope, losing the personal nature of some of the anecdotes and comments. I have also tried to continue Professor Goode's spirit of inquiry into difficult legal problems virtually untouched by case law, by introducing some of the thinking that went into the book on Personal Property Security that I recently co-wrote with Professors Hugh Beale, Michael Bridge and Eva Lomnicka. For example, I have attempted to analyse in some detail what it means to take property "subject to a floating charge", as where a floating charge disposes of charged property outside the ordinary course of business or in breach of a restriction in the charge agreement to someone who has notice of this. This was an attempt to take up the challenge laid down by Lord Phillips in the Court of Appeal decision in *Re Spectrum Plus* [2004] Ch. 337.

I have also introduced some further discussion on academic debates originally engendered by the views expressed in previous editions, for example, the question of the validity of a provision for automatic attachment of a security interest in a negative pledge clause, which is now the subject of dicta by the Singapore Court of Appeal in the case of *The Asiatic Enterprises (Pte) Ltd v United Overseas Bank* [2000] 1 S.L.R. 300, and of a significant amount of international scholarship.

In terms of recent development in case law, pride of place must go to the House of Lords' decision in *Re Spectrum Plus* [2005] 2 A.C. 680, which is the final chapter in the long-running saga of characterisation of charges over book debts. Even with such a definitive decision, there are still areas of doubt, which I have attempted to identify: this is an area of such importance that discussion will

xiii

never completely die and, indeed, there have already been a number of important cases on floating charges since *Spectrum*. Other cases which have necessitated discussion have been *Re SSSL Realisations (2002) Ltd* [2004] EWHC 1760 (Ch); [2006] EWCA Civ 7 (subordinated debt and turnover trusts); *Barbados Trust Co Ltd v Bank of Zambia* [2007] EWCA Civ 148 (effect of non-assignment clause and trust of a promise); *Buchler v Talbot* [2004] 2 A.C. 298 (priority of costs of liquidation, now the subject of s.176ZA of Insolvency Act 1986); *Burton v Melham* [2003] EWCA Civ 173; [2006] UKHL 6; and *IATA v Ansett Australia Holdings Ltd* [2008] H.C.A. 3 (two out of a host of new cases on set-off); and *Stotter v Equiticorp Australia Ltd (In Liquidation)* [2002] 2 N.Z.L.R. 686 (effect on creditor's proof on part payment by surety). Many other new cases have been the subject of footnotes and other references.

Legislation relating to companies has recently been reformed and consolidated in the Companies Act 2006. Sadly, there has been very little substantive reform of the law relating to the registration of company charges, despite the excellent report produced by the Law Commission in 2005. However, what used to be Pt XII of the Companies Act 1985 has been replaced by Pt 25 of the new Act, and not only the section numbers but the order of the sections has changed. This edition refers almost exclusively to the 2006 Act numbers (except where a previous section has been referred to in a case that is discussed) despite the fact that the new sections do not come into force until October 1, 2009. The few changes that have been made, or are proposed to be made, to this area of law are discussed in the text.

Although the reform of insolvency law brought about by the Enterprise Act 2002 was already underway at the time of the last edition, this edition addresses its ramifications in more detail, such as the operation of the "ring-fenced fund" for unsecured creditors (already the subject of one decision: *Re Airbase Ltd* [2008] 1 B.C.L.C. 436). I have also included discussion of the more recent legislative reforms to specific areas of insolvency, such as the reform of Insolvency Rule 4.90 in relation to set-off, and the extension of Insolvency Set-Off to distribution in administration, in r.2.85. However, for a more definitive and systematic discussion of the new Insolvency regime, the reader is referred to the third edition of Professor Goode's seminal book, *Principles of Corporate Insolvency*. Among the many interesting and informative discussions in that book, is some detailed consideration of the difficulties raised by Arts 2(g), 5 and 13 of the EU Regulation on Insolvency Proceedings (Ch.13). As a result, I have not thought it appropriate or necessary to take up the invitation of one reviewer of the third edition of *Legal Problems of Credit and Security* to discuss these issues in this book.

The law relating to intermediated securities has been the subject of attention from both national and international law reform bodies, and reference has been made in Ch.6 to these recent developments. I have included a number of references to the draft UNIDROIT Convention on Substantive Rules regarding International Securities, largely by way of comparison to the current UK law. At the time of writing the book, the final draft was to have been determined at a Diplomatic Conference finishing on September 13, 2008. I have just heard that, despite huge strides having been made in reaching agreement on many extremely difficult issues, there is still need for further drafting and for a final final conference, which will take place in mid-2009. The Financial Collateral Arrangements (No.2) Regulations 2003 have spawned their first case, albeit in the Court of Appeal of the British Virgin Islands (*Alfa Telecom Turkey Ltd v Cukurova Finance International Ltd* HCVAP2007/027), which I was able to include at proof stage, although sadly there has been no judgment yet in the application for judicial review brought by Cukurova in respect of the Financial Collateral Directive.

Many of the issues addressed in this book have been the subject of discussion with colleagues and students, particularly in the Principles of Commercial Law and Corporate Finance courses which I teach at Oxford, and I am grateful to everyone who has helped to form and refine my views. Particular thanks are due to two supervisees, Woo-Jun Jon, for many discussions on the assignment of receivables, and Simon Duncan, for discussions on the floating charge point mentioned earlier. Among my colleagues, I am particularly indebted to Jenny Payne of Merton College, Oxford and Professor Hugh Beale of Warwick University for their patience in reading drafts and discussing particular points. I am also grateful to John Trundle, of Euroclear, for his help on the CREST parts of Ch.6. Although I had no formal research assistance in preparing this edition, I had some invaluable help at the beginning of my task from my daughter, Emma, who downloaded all the footnoted cases so that they were at my fingertips. I have had enormous help and support from James Douse and Fiona MacLeod of Sweet & Maxwell both for their detailed work and their patience in relation to deadlines. I am also greatly indebted to my family, Robert, Emma and Hetty, for their patience and understanding. Most of all, I am hugely indebted to Professor Roy Goode, for writing such a superb book in the first place, for allowing me to prepare this edition, for his help and support in discussing particular points and for all his help and encouragement throughout my career as an academic.

Louise Gullifer
Oxford
September 22, 2008

Preface to the third edition

To my astonishment it is now 15 years since the appearance of the second edition of this little book. In that time much has happened. There have been a great many decisions on security interests, from the High Court to the House of Lords. Issues of characterisation, to which much space was devoted in the previous editions, have continued to feature prominently as courts wrestle with the question whether the contractual arrangements have created a security interest and, if so, whether it is in the nature of a fixed charge or a floating charge. An illuminating example is the series of decisions in the *Cosslett* case culminating in *Smith (Administrator of Cosslett (Contractors) Ltd) v Bridgend County Borough Council* [2002] 1 A.C. 336. Happily the clarity of *Re Brightlife* [1987] Ch. 200, temporarily blurred by decisions such as *Re New Bullas Trading Ltd* (1993) B.C.L.C. 1389, has been restored by the decision of the Privy Council in *Agnew v Commissioners of Inland Revenue* [2001] 2 A.C. 710. Priority issues also remain a regular feature of case law, throwing up a division of judicial opinion as to whether a negative pledge clause in a charge affects subsequent incumbrancers or is purely contractual in effect and continuing debate as to the resolution of the circularity problem which arises where a company that has given a fixed charge expressed to be subordinate to a floating charge goes into liquidation owing preferential debts.

There have also been some significant cases on the effect of an assignment in breach of a no-assignment clause, in particular the decision of the House of Lords in *Linden Garden Trust Ltd v Lenesta Sludge (Disposals) Ltd* [1994] 1 A.C. 85.

The legislature has not been idle either, with further restrictions on the enforcement of security given by a small company where the directors obtain an automatic moratorium under the Insolvency Act 2000 by filing prescribed documents with the court and, more dramatically, the almost total abolition of the institution of administration receivership, as well as the elimination of what remained of Crown preference, by the Enterprise Act 2002, though both of these sets of provisions are more relevant to the companion volume in this series, *Principles of Corporate Insolvency Law* (2nd edn), than to the present volume.

This shift in the balance of power from secured creditors to general creditors and the potential beneficiaries of reorganisations of insolvent companies appears to represent a belated reflection of the sympathies of the incomparable Ambrose Bierce, whose *Enlarged Devil's Dictionary* defines a (secured?) creditor as:

> "One of a tribe of savages dwelling beyond the Financial Straights and dreaded for their desolating incursions",

while "debtor" receives the beneficent definition of:

"A worthy person, in whose interest the national debt should be so managed as to depreciate the national currency."

This seems particularly appropriate for inclusion in a preface written on Budget day!

A subject that has assumed enormous importance in recent years is the taking of security and quasi-security interests in corporate investment securities. The move from paper-based to electronic issue and transfer systems (e.g. CREST) and, even more significantly, from directly held investment securities to securities held through accounts with intermediaries, has thrown up a complex of problems which in the United States have been largely resolved in the revised Article 8 of the Uniform Commercial Code but with which English law has yet to grapple, including some basic questions as the nature of an account holder's rights in securities credited to his account and whether an account holder can look through his own intermediary to assert claims against higher-tier intermediaries. Of great significance also is the warmly welcomed 2002 EC Directive on Financial Collateral Arrangements, which is designed to protect financial collateral against various possible grounds of avoidance under insolvency law. Finally, in December 2002 there was concluded the Hague Convention on the law applicable to certain rights in respect of securities held with an intermediary, addressing an important conflict of laws question, yet one which there has hitherto been no reported English case. These developments have led me to provide a substantial new chapter on security interests in investment corporate securities, which I hope will shed some light on dark places. In addition to the above matters I have taken the opportunity to examine the characterisation of transactions such as repos and sell buy-backs and stock loans.

Apart from these developments, the interval since the second edition has given me time for further reflection on a number of issues, leading to a substantial revision and expansion of the text, including a treatment of security interests by attornment and novation and a rewriting of the chapters on set-off and guarantees. And in relation to charge-backs, the hare which I started in the first edition has now run its course and I have felt compelled to accept that conceptual purity must give way to commercial needs and practices! But my modest suggestion way back in 1982 that charge-backs were conceptually impossible has at least served to stimulate jurisprudential debate, engaging the attention of numerous academic and practising specialists here and abroad and leading to the decision of a High Court judge (now in the Lords), who adopted the suggestion, obiter dicta by judges in two Court of Appeal cases (in one of which serious doubt was expressed as to the earlier ruling while the other, which supported the ruling, was on behalf of a court which included the quondam High Court judge himself) and an obiter dictum of the House of Lords disapproving of the obiter dictum of the second Court of Appeal! How the doctrine of stare decisis is to be applied in this situation remains unclear!

I have benefitted over the years from many helpful discussions with fellow academics, practitioners and students, I am indebted in particular to a number of friends and colleagues mentioned below for their assistance. The new chapter on security interests in investment securities was considerably improved as the result of comments by Philip Wood, Catherine Beahan and Nick Segal of Allen and Overy, Guy Morton of Freshfields, Professor Dan Prentice of Pembroke College,

PREFACE TO THE THIRD EDITION

Oxford, Professor Jim Rogers of Boston College, Jack Wiener, managing director and deputy general counsel of The Depository Trust and Clearing Corporation, Kristin Geyer, managing director and general counsel, and Diego Devos, director and deputy general counsel, of Euroclear. Robert Stevens of Lady Margaret Hall, Oxford, and Richard Hooley, currently at Fitzwilliam College, Cambridge, but shortly to take up his appointment to a chair at King's College, London, were kind enough to read through the proofs and saved me from a number of errors and omissions. I should also like to express my thanks to my former research assistants, Rafal Zakrzewski and Bushra Razaq, for their help with literature searches. My last but not least expression of appreciation is to Kate Hayes, Senior Publishing Editor, and Melanie Pepper, Senior Project Editor, of Sweet & Maxwell, for all their expertise and support in the production of this new edition, which I hope will be found of assistance both to practising lawyers and to students.

Roy Goode
Oxford
April 9, 2003

Preface to the second edition

This book began as a series of public lectures delivered at the Centre for Commercial Law Studies, Queen Mary College, in 1982, the purpose of which was to explore a range of fundamental legal concepts relating to security and quasi-security interests, with particular reference to security in personal property. The large attendance at those lectures and the kind welcome given both by academic and by practising lawyers to the first edition of this book revealed a widespread recognition of the practical value of a conceptual approach in this complex field, and an awareness of the problems that can result from a purely mechanical application of a set of detailed rules.

This new edition is not merely a technical update but is in many respects a new book. I have now devoted two distinct chapters to the nature and forms of consensual security and concepts of attachment and perfection. The treatment of negative pledges has been substantially expanded, an analysis offered of the legal nature of sub-participations in loan agreements and the chapter on priorities has been enlarged to include an examination of twelve typical priority problems and their solution. I have elaborated the discussion of the vexed question whether a bank can take a charge over its own customer's credit balance, reinforcing the negative view expressed in the first edition which received judicial vindication in *Re Charge Card Services Ltd* [1986] 3 All E.R. 289. The chapter on set-off has been totally rewritten and substantially extended. Dr. Rory Derham's excellent new book *Set off*, which I had the pleasure of evaluating as an external examiner when it was presented in its earlier form as a doctoral thesis at Cambridge University, reached me too late to be reflected in the above chapter except by way of footnote reference. It is the first modern monograph on the subject and is required reading for anyone interested in set-off.

By concentrating on fundamentals rather than on the minutiae of English law I have sought to provide a text which will be of assistance to lawyers throughout the Commonwealth. In this new edition I have drawn on many Commonwealth decisions, particularly those from courts in Australia, Canada and New Zealand, which have shed light on a number of complex issues and which will, I believe, be as helpful to judges in this country as their own decisions are to courts elsewhere in the Commonwealth.

I am indebted to all those who over the past few years have helped to clarify my thinking or have drawn my attention to cases and problems of which I might otherwise have remained unaware. They are too numerous to mention by name but include my academic colleagues, my students and friends in the practising profession. I owe a particular debt to Philip Wood of Allen and Overy, who has allowed me freely to draw on his encyclopaedic knowledge of finance and security in general and of set-off in particular; to David Weed of Victor Mishcon & Co, who helped me with a practical point on searches in the Companies Register; and to the various banks and firms of City solicitors who invited me to present in-house seminars on *Charge Card* and related problems and helped me to sharpen the argument, even at the expense to them of an inconvenient conclusion! I should also like to express my thanks to the editorial team at Sweet & Maxwell, and to Sheila Aked for preparing the index. Finally, I am indebted to Queen Mary College for granting me sabbatical leave to complete a new edition of this and other works.

The law is stated on the basis of the materials available to me at February 1, 1998.

R. M. Goode
Centre for Commercial Law Studies,
Queen Mary College,
London
February 17, 1988

Preface to the first edition

My purpose in delivering the lectures reproduced in this book has been to explore some of the fundamental legal conceptions underlying the more important types of commercial security and to suggest that a number of conventional propositions relied on in everyday practice are conceptually unsound. In some cases the analysis leads to the conclusion that a particular form of security is less effective that previously supposed. Examples are the provision for equal and rateable security in negative pledge causes; arguments purporting to create a charge in favour of a bank over its customer's credit balance; the registration of details of restrictions in a floating charge; and the use of automatic crystallisation clauses and the mistaken assumption that crystallisation necessarily establishes priority over a subsequent security interest. In other cases, my task has been the more agreeable one of seeking to show that apparent weaknesses in a creditor's security do not in fact exist—for example, the so-called "flawed" asset created when restrictions are imposed on the withdrawal of a deposit; the use of a provision in a guarantee which, far from prohibiting the surety from proving in competition with the creditor, requires him to do so and to hold any dividends on trust for the creditor.

That the practitioner is keenly interested in legal theory, however abstract, affecting commercial transactions was amply demonstrated by the large number of lawyers, bankers and businessmen who attended these lectures. I am indebted to my audience for several thought-provoking questions and illuminating comments, and in preparing the written text I have revised and slightly expanded the material to take account of some of the more important points made. I have also taken the opportunity to update the treatment of the law, which is believed to be correctly stated as at September 14, 1982.

R. M. Goode
Centre for Commercial Law Studies,
Queen Mary College,
London
1982

TABLE OF CONTENTS

CONTENTS

CONTENTS

CONTENTS

CONTENTS

TABLE OF CASES

TABLE OF CASES

TABLE OF CASES

TABLE OF EC INSTRUMENTS

TABLE OF STATUTES

TABLE OF STATUTORY INSTRUMENTS

TABLE OF STATUTORY INSTRUMENTS

TABLE OF INTERNATIONAL TREATIES AND CONVENTIONS

CHAPTER 1

The Nature and Forms of Consensual Security

1. THE PURPOSES OF SECURITY

A financier taking security for an advance[1] is concerned to see that if the debtor's **1–01** assets are insufficient to meet the claims of all his creditors the financier will at least be able to look to his security to obtain total or partial payment. So the primary purpose of security is to reduce credit risk and obtain priority over other creditors in the event of the debtor's bankruptcy or liquidation. However, there is no necessary connection between security and priority. For policy reasons the law allows certain classes of unsecured claim priority over certain classes of secured claim. For example, in a winding up preferential creditors have priority over a floating charge,[2] while the secured claims of directors of a company may in certain circumstances be subordinated to the claims of general unsecured creditors.[3] Nevertheless it remains the general principle that a secured creditor has priority over an unsecured creditor.

A secondary, but important, consideration is that security gives the creditor a certain measure of influence or control over events. This is particularly true of a creditor holding a fixed and floating charge covering substantially the whole of a debtor company's assets. The priority enjoyed by the chargee is likely to deter unsecured creditors from precipitate enforcement action which might inhibit the orderly reorganisation of the company or the sale of the company as a going concern or effective realisation of its assets. Moreover, a creditor holding a charge of the kind described above until fairly recently had as one of its most powerful remedies the appointment of an administrative receiver, empowered to assume the management of the company in place of its directors, to carry on the business with a view to sale, hiving down of the company to a newly formed subsidiary, or disposal of the assets. Administrative receivership, a widely used

---

[1] The term "security" should not be confused with securities such as shares and bonds. It would be preferable to adopt the term "collateral" for the former, widely used in international finance, at the risk of offending traditionalists who do not care to see English adjectives converted into American nouns! However, the terms are not entirely interchangeable, since in relation to dealings in investment securities the provision of collateral is taken to include sale and repurchase agreements because these serve a security function even though not constituting security agreements in law. See para.6–27, below.

[2] Insolvency Act 1986 s.175(2)(b). See para.5–68, below.

[3] For example, one of the sanctions for fraudulent or wrongful trading by a director of a company in liquidation is subordination of his debt, wholly or in part, to all other debts of the company (Insolvency Act 1986 s.215(4)).

mode of enforcing security, has now been replaced by administration,[4] with certain exceptions related to the capital and financial markets. The holder of a fixed and floating charge still, however, has considerable influence and control in the event of the debtor's insolvency: it can appoint an administrator out of court,[5] and is often the main force behind the use of a pre-packaged administration.[6]

1–02   There are other reasons too for taking security. The holding of security is relevant to the risk-weighting of capital for capital adequacy purposes under Basel III[7]; and where the collateral consists of investment securities held with a right of "use" (including sale) this enhances the creditor's ability to raise funds itself and engage in market operations.

From the viewpoint of the borrower, the ability to furnish security may give it access to funds which might not otherwise be available or might be offered on more expensive terms. Historically the most important subjects of security were tangible assets: land and goods. With the development of documentary intangibles[8] the pledge could be extended to embrace documents of title to goods, negotiable instruments and negotiable securities. Pure intangibles, such as receivables and securities, also became increasingly important as security, a move sharply accentuated when paper-based securities were increasingly replaced by electronic securities and direct holdings from the issuer by indirect holdings through a securities account with a bank or other securities intermediary.[9] The position now is that intangible property is far and away the most significant form of collateral, and in the securities field alone some billions of pounds of value are transferred every day. Yet physical collateral continues to play a significant role in finance, and this is particularly true of cross-border dealings in mobile equipment of high unit value or economic importance. Hence the potentially huge impact of the 2001 Cape Town Convention on International Interests in Mobile Equipment, which provides an international regime governing security, title retention and leasing interests in aircraft objects, space assets and railway rolling stock.[10]

The secured creditor's protection against competing interests predicates at least three distinct legal facts: first, that his security has attached, in the sense that it has fastened on the asset so as to give the creditor rights over the asset vis-à-vis the debtor; secondly, that it has been perfected, i.e. all steps have been taken to preserve its validity against third parties; thirdly, that it will have priority under the relevant priority rules.

---

[4] By the reforms introduced by the Enterprise Act 2002. See Ch.4, below; and L. Gullifer, "The Reforms Of The Enterprise Act 2002 And The Floating Charge As A Security Device" (2008) 46 C.B.L.J. 399.

[5] Pursuant to Insolvency Act 1986 Sch.B1 para.14.

[6] For discussion of the "pre-pack" see R. Goode, *Principles of Corporate Insolvency Law*, 4th edn (London: Sweet & Maxwell, 2011) paras 11–37 et seq.

[7] Agreed in December 2010 and revised in June 2011, and implemented by the Capital Requirements Directive (2013/36/EU). The bulk of the rules will apply from January 1, 2014.

[8] See para.1–48, below.

[9] See paras 6–02 et seq., below.

[10] For a comprehensive analysis, *Convention on International Interests in Mobile Equipment and Protocol Thereto on Matters Specific to Aircraft Equipment: Official Commentary,*see R. Goode, 3rd edn (Rome: UNIDROIT, 2013). The Convention has been ratified by 58 States, but not yet by the UK.

2. THE CONCEPT OF SECURITY

Attachment and perfection of security interests are discussed in the next chapter. **1–03**
But first we must explore the different kinds of security and the legal nature of a
security interest. The ingenuity of financiers and their legal advisers has given
rise to many forms of agreement which are intended to provide security but do
not in law create a security interest. Among such quasi-security devices are the
reservation of title under a contract of sale, contractual set-off and the imposition
of restrictions on the withdrawal of a cash deposit, as well as title transfer
arrangements, which are particularly important in relation to receivables[11] and
financial collateral.[12]

The problem is to distinguish true security from quasi-security, a matter on
which legal opinion is at some points acutely divided. The problem is not purely
of theoretical interest, for where an agreement creates a security interest in law
the debtor has a right to redeem and an interest in any surplus resulting from
repossession and sale by the creditor, the security agreement may be registrable
by statute and the tax and accounting treatment of the transaction may turn on the
fact that it constitutes a security transaction.

The very concept of security varies widely from jurisdiction to jurisdiction, **1–04**
depending as it does on concepts of ownership and possession which are
inherently fluid. It appears to be recognised everywhere that a security interest
involves the grant of a right in an asset which the grantor owns or in which he has
an interest, but legal systems differ in their concept of ownership for this purpose.
The most fundamental divide is between the formal and the functional approach.
The formal approach is one which sharply distinguishes the grant of security
from the retention of title under conditional sale, hire-purchase and leasing
agreements, on the basis that the buyer, hirer or lessee has merely a possessory
interest, subject to which the seller, owner or lessor continues to enjoy absolute
ownership by virtue of the agreement between the parties. The functional
approach treats a conditional buyer, a lessee with an option to purchase and, in
many cases, a lessee under a finance lease, as the owner and the interest of the
conditional seller or lessor as limited to a security interest, so that the reservation
of title is equated with a purchase-money chattel mortgage. The functional
approach is that adopted throughout the US under art.9 of the Uniform
Commercial Code,[13] throughout Canada under the Personal Property Security
Acts based on art.9,[14] in New Zealand under its Personal Property Securities Act

---

[11] See Ch.3, below.
[12] See Ch.6, below.
[13] Though art.9 has undergone radical changes over the years, the classic text remains the two
volumes of G. Gilmore, *Security Interests in Personal Property,* (Boston: Law Book Exchange, 1999).
[14] There are two basic models: the Ontario Personal Property Security Act and the Model Personal
Property Security Act of the Canadian Conference on Personal Property Security Law adopted, with
local variations, by the Western Provinces. For a penetrating treatment of the whole subject in the
context of the Ontario Act, see J. S. Ziegel and D. L. Denomme, *The Ontario Personal Property
Security Act: Commentary and Analysis,* 2nd edn (Ontario: Butterworths & Company (Canada) Ltd,
2000).

1999,[15] which came into force in 2002, and in Australia under its Personal Property Securities Act 2009, which came into force in 2012.[16] The legal systems of other countries, including the United Kingdom,[17] and legal systems belonging to the common law family outside North America, New Zealand and Australia[18] and to the civil law family, adhere to the formal approach.[19]

This does not mean that English law looks always to the form of a transaction and not to the substance. If, for example, a document is a sham designed to disguise the true nature of the agreement reached by the parties, the court will look behind the document to ascertain the real character of the transaction.[20] Again, if the document is a true record of the agreement but its terms indicate that its legal character is not that ascribed to it by the parties—as where a transaction described as a lease is in fact a conditional sale—the court will disregard the label attached by the parties and look to the legal substance. The nature of the rights intended to be conferred by the parties is to be ascertained from the terms of their agreement; the characterisation of such rights is a matter of law and is to be determined by the court.[21] But it is the legal substance to which the court has regard, not the economic effect. English law recognises that the parties are free to structure their transaction as they wish, and that there is nothing objectionable to their selecting, say, conditional sale or hire-purchase instead of a purchase-money

---

[15] As amended in 2001. For excellent analyses see L. Widdup and L. Mayne, *Personal Property Securities Act: A Conceptual Approach,* 3rd edn (Wellington: Butterworths, 2012); and M. Gedye, R. Cuming and R. Wood, *Personal Property Securities in New Zealand*, (London: Sweet & Maxwell, 2002).

[16] See A. Duggan and D. Brown, *Australian Personal Property Securities Law* (Lexis Nexis Butterworths, 2012).

[17] There are, however, marked differences between English law and Scots law.

[18] Note that Jersey (though not wholly a common law jurisdiction) has started the process of reform of its law of personal property security, although so far the legislation is limited to security over intangibles, see Security Interests (Jersey) Law 2012. Reform of the law relating to taking security over tangibles is under way, see *http://www.gov.je/Government/Consultations/Pages/SecurityInterestsStage2.aspx* [accessed September 18, 2013].

[19] A number of bodies have considered reform of the law in England and Wales along the lines of art.9: see the The Crowther Committee, *Report of the Committee on Consumer Credit* (1971), Cmnd.4506 Ch.5.5. This recommendation was endorsed by the Insolvency Law Review Committee in its report, *Insolvency Law and Practice* (1982), Cmnd.8558, paras 1620–1623; and by the report of Professor A. Diamond, *A Review of Security Interests in Property* (HMSO, 1989). Following a recommendation by the Company Law Review Steering Group in its Final Report, the Law Commission examined the current system and possible reform. In its Consultative Report No.176 (2004), *Company Security Interests*, the Law Commission set out a possible scheme for England and Wales based on the Personal Property Securities schemes of Canada and New Zealand. Following further consultation, it set out a modified version of this scheme in its final report: Law Commission, *Company Security Interests* (2005) Law Com. No.296; see para.2–33, below. The Scottish Law Commission is considering reform of the law of security at the moment, and published a Discussion Paper in June 2011; Scottish Law Commission, *Discussion Paper on Moveable Transactions* (June 2011) DP 151. See further; http://www.scotlawcom.gov.uk/law-reform-projects/security-over-corporeal-and-incorporeal-moveable-property/ [accessed September 18, 2013].

[20] See *Welsh Development Agency v Export Finance Co Ltd* [1992] B.C.L.C. 148, 186; and, for an exhaustive analysis, W.J. Gough, *Company Charges*, 2nd edn (London: Butterworths, 1995), Ch.21.

[21] *Welsh Development Agency v Export Finance Co Ltd* [1992] B.C.L.C. 148; and see the decision of the Privy Council in *Agnew v Commissioners of Inland Revenue* [2001] 2 A.C. 710; para.1–36, below.

chattel mortgage in order to avoid the application of the Bills of Sale Acts.[22] So in determining the substance of the transaction the court looks to what the parties have actually agreed.[23]

There is also a divergence between legal families in the concept of possession. In common law systems possession denotes either physical possession or control through a physical possessor or means of physical access such as a key,[24] so that pure intangibles cannot be given in pledge as this requires the delivery of possession. Civil law systems likewise require possession for a pledge but by a legal construct treat intangibles as notionally delivered if certain formalities are complied with, for example, registration in a public register. A striking example is the fact that most securities issued in France in dematerialised form are characterised by French law as bearer securities.

3. THE CLASSIFICATION OF SECURITY

The only forms of consensual security known to English law are the mortgage, **1–05** which is a security transfer of ownership; the pledge, which creates a limited legal interest by the delivery of possession; the contractual lien, which differs from the pledge only in that the creditor's possession was acquired otherwise than for the purpose of security, as where goods are deposited for repair and the repairer then asserts a lien for unpaid repair charges; and the chargee. Except in the case of land, where statute provides for a charge by way of legal mortgage,[25] all charges are equitable.

Security may be classified in a number of different ways.

Real and personal security

Real security means security in an asset, whether of the debtor or of a third party. **1–06** The asset may be tangible or intangible. Real security is to be contrasted with personal security, that is, security in the form of a personal undertaking which reinforces the debtor's primary undertaking to give payment or other performance. Typically the personal undertaking is given by a third party, for example, as a surety under a suretyship guarantee or a guarantor under a demand guarantee.[26] But the debtor too can provide a personal undertaking in a stronger or more easily assignable form than his primary undertaking, as, for example, by giving a negotiable instrument as security for payment. The greater part of this

---

[22] i.e. the Bills of Sale Acts 1878–91.

[23] *McEntire v Crossley Brothers Ltd* [1895] A.C. 457, per Lord Herschell L.C. at 462–463. See further paras 1–36 et seq.

[24] Note that "possession" may have a different meaning in the context of the Financial Collateral Arrangements (No.2) Regulations 2003 (FCARs) which enact the Financial Collateral Directive 2002 (FCD); see *In The Matter Of Lehman Brothers International (Europe) (In Administration)* [2012] EWHC 2997 (Ch) at [131]–[136] and paras 6–33 et seq.

[25] Law of Property Act 1925 s.85(1); Land Registration Act 2002 s.51.

[26] A demand guarantee is one which, though intended as between the account party (or principal) and the beneficiary to be called only upon the account party's default, is not dependent on default, only on presentation of a written demand and other specified documents. In other words, the requirement of default is confined to the internal relationship between account party and beneficiary and does not constitute a term of the guarantee itself. See para.8–02, below.

book, including the present chapter, is concerned with real security. However, there are separate chapters on set-off, which is a form of quasi-security,[27] and guarantees.[28]

Tangible and intangible security

1–07   Real security may be over tangible or intangible property.[29] The major difference between the two relates to the mode of creation, in that possessory security (the pledge and the contractual lien) may only be taken over tangibles. Security over pure intangibles[30] may be created only by way of mortgage or equitable charge.[31] A mortgage may be effected by assignment, novation or negotiation, depending on the type of intangible[32]; an equitable charge may be created by agreement with the debtor.[33]

Possessory and non-possessory security

1–08   Where the security relates to tangible property, it may be either possessory or non-possessory. There are two forms of possessory security, the pledge and the contractual lien.[34] The pledgee or lienee has a limited legal interest in the asset.[35] Pure intangibles do not lend themselves to possession.[36] By contrast documentary intangibles are treated as goods and may be pledged in the same way.[37] Events may result in a possessory security becoming converted into a non-possessory security. For example, where documents of title pledged to a bank are released to the pledgor to enable the goods to be sold and a sale takes place, the proceeds become subject to an equitable charge.[38] Similarly if a pledgee in possession of bearer securities has them converted into registered securities, he becomes a mortgagee or chargee.[39]

Security over existing assets and security over future assets

1–09   As we shall see,[40] while the common law insisted that security could be given only over assets currently owned by the debtor, equity facilitated the grant of security over future property by treating the agreement for security as effective to

---

[27] Ch.7, below.

[28] Ch.8, below.

[29] Documentary intangibles are equated with tangible property. See para.1–48, below.

[30] That is, intangibles which are not documentary intangibles. See para.1–48, below.

[31] It was conceded in *In The Matter Of Lehman Brothers International (Europe) (In Administration)* [2012] EWHC 2997 (Ch) that a security interest labelled "general lien" could not be a lien in relation to intangible property: in that case the security interest created was held to be a charge, see [34]–[48].

[32] See paras 1–48 and 3–03, below.

[33] See para.3–21, below.

[34] See paras 1–47 et seq., below.

[35] See paras 1–47 and 1–53, below.

[36] This proposition, while correct as a matter of English law, is not necessarily true in relation to the term "possession" used in the FCARs.

[37] See para.1–48, below.

[38] See para.1–71 fn.327, below.

[39] See paras 6–38 and 6–40, below.

[40] See para.2–12, below.

confer a security interest on the creditor immediately on acquisition of the asset by the debtor, without need of any new act of transfer.

Fixed and floating security (security in specie and security in a fund)

Security is of two kinds, fixed and floating. Under a fixed charge the asset is appropriated to satisfaction of the debt immediately or upon the debtor acquiring an interest in it. Under a floating charge appropriation is deferred; the chargee's rights attach in the first instance not to specific assets but to a shifting fund of assets, the debtor company being left free to manage the fund in the ordinary course of business. It is only when the debtor's management powers are brought to an end that the charge crystallises and fastens on the specific assets then comprised in the fund or subsequently acquired by the debtor.[41] The floating charge is the only kind of floating security encountered in practice, but there seems no theoretical objection to a floating mortgage, by which the mortgagee acquires ownership of the fund by way of security and, upon crystallisation, ownership of the individual components of the fund.[42] The mortgage would, of course, take effect in equity only, there being no present transfer of ownership of identified assets. There is, however, no such thing as a floating pledge, for a pledge requires actual or constructive possession, which can only be taken of assets *in specie*, not of a fund. The distinction between fixed and floating security has important priority implications both at common law and under the Insolvency Act 1986.[43]

1–10

Title transfer[44] and charge

Leaving aside the limited legal interests created by pledge or lien, the grant of security may take the form either of a security transfer of title (mortgage) or an encumbrance (charge, or hypothecation) which leaves the debtor as owner but imposes a clog on his ownership in favour of the creditor.[45]

1–11

---

[41] See paras 4–07, 4–31 et seq., below.

[42] See P. Giddins, "Floating mortgages by individuals: are they conceptually possible?" (2011) J.I.B.F.L. 125. The distinction between a charge and an equitable mortgage is not clear-cut, and, arguably, many security documents which purport to create a floating charge actually create a floating (equitable) mortgage, see H. Beale, M. Bridge, L. Gullifer and E. Lomnicka, *The Law of Security and Title-Based Financing,* 2nd edn (Oxford: Oxford University Press, 2012), paras 6.54 et seq.

[43] See paras 4–09 et seq., below.

[44] Note that this term is also used in a different context, namely the absolute transfer of title to an asset. This can be used in order to provide collateral for a transaction: examples are title transfer financial collateral arrangements (see paras 6–27 et seq.) and receivables financing (see paras 3–04 et seq.).

[45] See paras 1–55 et seq., below.

Legal and equitable security

(1)   Nature of the distinction

1–12   A security interest may be either legal[46] or equitable. We have seen that a limited legal security interest arises from a pledge or a lien. To take effect at law in the hands of the creditor any other form of security interest must be a present transfer of an existing asset, the transfer must be to the creditor himself and must be made in conformity with any statutory formalities and the transferor's title to the asset must be a legal title, not merely an equitable interest. Accordingly a security interest may be equitable for any one of six reasons, namely that: (a) it relates to future property; (b) there is no transfer or agreement for transfer at all, merely a charge; (c) there is no present transfer, merely an agreement for transfer or a declaration of trust by the debtor; (d) the transfer is not made in accordance with the formal requirements for the transfer of legal title; (e) the transfer is made not to the creditor but to a third party as trustee for the creditor; or (f) the transferor's title to the asset is equitable, not legal (one example of this is where a legal mortgage has already been granted over the same asset). The essential difference in effect between a legal mortgage and an equitable mortgage or charge is that a legal mortgage has priority over subsequent interests whereas an equitable mortgage or charge may be overreached by a disposition to a bona fide purchaser for value of the legal title without notice of the equitable interest.[47] The significance of the distinction has been substantially reduced by statutory provisions for the registration of mortgages and charges created by companies[48] and the fact that registration sometimes constitutes constructive notice.[49] In such cases registration is in the nature of a statutory perfection requirement[50] and does not affect the characterisation of the security interest as legal or equitable. However, in the case of certain specialist registers, such as those relating to intellectual property rights[51] and ship and aircraft mortgages[52] registration is a prerequisite of legal title and an unregistered interest takes effect only as an equitable interest.

(2)   Mode of creating a legal mortgage

1–13   This varies according to the subject matter of the mortgage:

(a)   A legal mortgage of land may be effected by a charge by way of legal mortgage.[53] The mortgage must be by deed[54] and in the case of registered land must be registered in the Land Registry.[55]

---

[46] The word "legal" is also used in a different sense to denote a security interest created by law (e.g. a repairer's lien) as opposed to consensual security interest.
[47] See paras 5–09 et seq., below.
[48] See Ch.2, below.
[49] See paras 2–25 et seq., below.
[50] See paras 2–16, 2–21, below.
[51] See paras 1–13, 2–32, below.
[52] See paras 1–13, 2–32, below.
[53] Law of Property Act 1925 s.85(1). Mortgages by demise for a term of years absolute, which are also provided for in this section, are in practice obsolete (Law Commission, *Land Registration for the*

(b)   A legal mortgage of goods may be created orally,[56] but if it is in writing and is given by an individual it must be made by deed and in accordance with the form and in conformity with the other requirements of the Bills of Sale Acts 1878 and 1882, and if by a company it is registrable under s.859A of the Companies Act 2006. Moreover, for certain types of goods the mortgage must be in accordance with a prescribed form and registered in a special register to take effect at law, e.g. in the case of registered ships the mortgage must be registered in the register of ship mortgages,[57] in the case of registered aircraft, in the register of aircraft mortgages.[58]

(c)   A legal mortgage of registrable intellectual property rights is effected by entry in the relevant register.[59]

(d)   A legal mortgage of a debt or other chose in action is effected by assignment in writing under the hand of the assignor and written notice of the assignment to the debtor[60] or alternatively by novation.[61]

(e)   A legal mortgage of registered securities is effected by novation through entry of a transfer on the issuer's register[62] or the CREST register[63] and of negotiable securities and negotiable instruments by endorsement and delivery and by delivery of possession with intent to transfer ownership in the case of bearer securities. It is not possible to create a legal mortgage of intermediated (indirectly held) securities.[64]

Security for fixed indebtedness and continuing security

Just as personal security—such as a guarantee—may be given either for a specific advance, so that it terminates on repayment, or as a continuing guarantee, which covers the ultimate debit balance due on closure of the account between debtor and creditor and is not satisfied by any intermediate payment,[65] so also real security—such as a mortgage or charge—may secure a specific debt or be a continuing security for an ultimate debit balance. The latter is the common situation where the credit extended to the principal debtor is revolving credit,

1–14

Twenty-first Century, a Conveyancing Revolution (HMSO, 2001), Law Com. No.271, para.4.7); and an owner of registered land has no power to create such an interest (Land Registration Act 2002 s.23(1)(a)).

[54] Law of Property Act 1925 ss.52(1), 85, 86. A registered charge under the Land Registration Act 2002 takes effect as   if it were a charge by deed by way of legal mortgage (s.51) and if effected electronically is also to be treated as made by deed (s.91(5)).

[55] Under the Land Registration Act 2002.

[56] *Newlove v Shrewsbury* (1888) 21 Q.B.D. 41; *Flory v Denny* (1852) 7 Exch. 581; *Reeves v Capper* (1838) 5 Bing. N.C. 136.

[57] Under s.16 of and Sch.1 to the Merchant Shipping Act 1995 and the Merchant Shipping (Registration of Ships) Regulations 1993.

[58] Under the Mortgaging of Aircraft Order 1972 (SI 1972/1268).

[59] i.e. the register of patents (Patents Act 1977 ss.30–33), the register of trade marks (Trade Marks Act 1994 s.25), or the register of designs (Registered Designs Act 1949 s.19). There is no registration of copyright.

[60] Law of Property Act 1925 s.136.

[61] See para.3–03, below.

[62] See para.6–38, below.

[63] See para.6–41, below.

[64] See para.6–42, below.

[65] See para.8–05, below.

such as a bank overdraft. While the quantum of the security can never exceed what is due to the bank at any particular time, the security is not discharged merely because the debit balance is reduced to zero or the account goes into credit. This form of credit is a continuing facility, the debtor being free to draw on it as and when he chooses within the terms of the facility, not fixed-sum credit, which is granted at the outset for a specified amount and is discharged when that amount is paid. Security for a continuing facility itself continues at least until such time as the facility is ended and the debtor's ultimate obligation is discharged. In practice, security agreements, like guarantees, frequently prolong the duration of the security to cover the possibility that payments made to the secured creditor are recovered by the debtor's trustee in bankruptcy or liquidator as preferences[66] or on some other ground, so that if the secured creditor has to make a repayment the debt thus revived will continue to be secured.

Security for the debtor's obligation and security for third-party indebtedness

1–15   A person may give an asset in security not only for his own indebtedness but also for that of a third party. For example, A, without itself incurring any personal obligation, may mortgage or charge its property to secure a debt due to the creditor from B. Despite the absence of any personal liability on the part of A, this is considered in law to constitute a guarantee.[67] Not uncommonly the same security agreement secures both the primary indebtedness of a third party and a secondary liability of the debtor. The typical case is that of companies forming part of a corporate group which give cross-guarantees, each guarantee covering the indebtedness of other members of the group and being secured over property of the guarantor which also directly secures the indebtedness of the other companies. Here the security agreement has a dual aspect, in that it secures both the primary obligation of the other companies and the secondary obligation of the grantor of the security as guarantor. This cross-collateralisation is a common feature of modern financing, though it may in certain circumstances be vulnerable as a transaction at an undervalue in the event of the debtor's insolvency.[68]

Security for an obligation owed to someone other than the security taker

1–16   It is very common for a debtor to grant a security interest to a person who is acting as trustee for the actual creditors. This has the advantage, where there are a number of creditors, such as in a syndicated loan or bond issue, of one person having the ability to enforce the security interest and hold the proceeds on trust for all the creditors, the identity of whom may change from time to time.[69]

---

[66] Insolvency Act 1986 ss.239, 238, 240–241.

[67] *Re Conley* [1938] 2 All E.R. 127.

[68] See Insolvency Act 1986 ss.238, 240, 241; para.8–37, below; and Goode, *Principles of Corporate Insolvency Law* (2011) paras 13–33 to 13–38.

[69] For a recent case analysing the duties of a security trustee in the context of enforcement of security; see *Saltri Iii Ltd v MD Mezzanine Sa Sicar* [2012] EWHC 3025 (Comm).

Although sometimes the debtor will enter into a direct obligation to pay the debt to the trustee,[70] this is not essential for the trust to operate, since a security interest can be granted to someone to hold on trust for the actual creditor. However, can a security interest be granted to A to secure an obligation owed to B, when A is not a trustee? This question was considered by Briggs J. in a recent case which was part of the *Lehman* insolvency litigation.[71] He decided that the grant of such a security interest was possible, saying:

> "In my judgment, it is not inherent in the nature of a charge that the chargee must be, or be a trustee or fiduciary for, the creditor. All that is necessary is that the chargee has a specifically enforceable right to have the relevant property appropriated to the payment or discharge of the relevant debt or other obligation.... That being so, I can see no good reason why A should not confer a specifically enforceable right on B to have A's property appropriated towards the discharge of a debt which A (or someone else) owes C, without any requirement that B be C's trustee or fiduciary. B may have good business or personal reasons to wish to ensure that A pays his debt to C, and I cannot see why the law should prevent B taking an enforceable (and therefore proprietary) interest in A's property so as to give himself the power to achieve that objective, without making himself a trustee or fiduciary for C. In truth, it seems to me that the relationship between B and C is irrelevant to the enforceability of A's promise to B, if it derives from a specifically enforceable contract between them."[72]

Briggs J. relied on the definition of a charge given by Lord Wrenbury in *Palmer v Carey*[73] discussed later in this chapter,[74] and reached a similar conclusion that the crucial feature was that the parties had agreed that the asset should be appropriated to the discharge of the debt.[75] To whom the debt was owed was irrelevant, provided that the parties' agreement was genuine. Obviously, in most cases the chargee will be the creditor,[76] and this explains the terms in which a charge (or any security interest) is usually defined.[77]

4. WHAT CONSTITUTES A SECURITY INTEREST

The nature of a security interest

A security interest is a right given to B in the asset of A to secure payment or performance by A or C to B (or to another party). This last qualification is necessitated by the discussion in the last paragraph, but from now on, for ease of

1–17

---

[70] This is a parallel covenant to the main covenant to pay the creditors, and is common in a bond issue, see G Fuller, *The Law and Practice of International Capital Markets,* 2nd edn (London: LexisNexis Butterworths, 2012) para.9.101.

[71] *In The Matter Of Lehman Brothers International (Europe) (In Administration)* [2012] EWHC 2997 (Ch).

[72] *In The Matter Of Lehman Brothers International (Europe) (In Administration)* [2012] EWHC 2997 (Ch) at [43] and [44].

[73] *Palmer v Carey* [1926] A.C. 703.

[74] See para.1–28, below.

[75] See the discussion at paras 1–28 et seq., below.

[76] Or the creditor's trustee.

[77] See, for example, the definition from *National Provincial & Union Bank of England v Charnley* [1924] K.B. 431 at 449 set out in para.1–55, below.

exposition, we will focus on the typical case where A (the person giving the security interest) is the debtor and B (the person to whom the security interest is given) is the creditor. A fixed, or specific, consensual[78] security interest possesses the following characteristics:

(1)   it is a right given by a debtor to a creditor in an asset[79];
(2)   the right is by way of grant of an interest in the debtor's asset, not by way of reservation of title to the creditor[80];
(3)   the right is given for the purposes of securing an obligation[81];
(4)   the asset is given in security only, not by way of outright transfer[82]; and
(5)   the agreement restricts the debtor's right to dispose of the asset free from the security interest.[83]

After the decision of the House of Lords in *BCCI (No.8)*, where the point, though obiter, was dealt with very specifically, it appears that a debtor can give security over its own obligation, so that a bank can take a charge over its customer's credit balance.[84] This, despite some conceptual difficulties, represents widespread commercial usage.

A floating security, such as a floating charge, differs from a fixed security in that it relates not to a specific asset but to an identifiable fund of assets, the debtor being authorised by the terms of the security agreement to dispose of all or any of the assets comprising the fund free from the security interest.[85]

(1)   Fixed security interest is a right given by a debtor to his creditor in an asset

1–18   It is inherent in a security interest that an asset is appropriated to the debt. Where the debtor is to pay out of his general assets, none of which is earmarked to the debt, there can be no security interest. A good example is provided by the decision in *Swiss Bank Corp Ltd v Lloyds Bank Ltd*,[86] in which the House of Lords, affirming the decision of the Court of Appeal,[87] held that a covenant by a borrower in a loan agreement to observe all exchange control requirements, one of which was that the proceeds of the borrower's securities were to be applied in discharge of the loan, did not create a security interest, since the loan agreement did not itself require the loan to be paid out of the proceeds, and the requirement

---

[78] That is, a security interest created by agreement, as opposed to one conferred by law, such as the unpaid vendor's lien.
[79] See para.1–18, below. The ingredients for attachment (i.e. creation) of that right and of its perfection to give it efficacy against third parties are examined in Ch.2, below.
[80] See paras 1–31 et seq., below.
[81] See para.1–36, below.
[82] See para.1–36, below.
[83] See para.1–43, below.
[84] See paras 1–44, 3–12, below.
[85] See paras 4–03 et seq., below.
[86] *Swiss Bank Corp Ltd v Lloyds Bank Ltd* [1982] A.C. 584. See also *Flightline Ltd v Edwards* [2003] EWCA Civ 63; [2003] 1 W.L.R. 1200; *Re TXU Europe Group Plc* [2003] EWHC 1305; [2004] 1 B.C.L.C. 519.
[87] *Swiss Bank Corp Ltd v Lloyds Bank Ltd* [1982] A.C. 584.

was simply a stipulation by the Bank of England when granting exchange control consent. As Buckley L.J. had pointed out in his judgment in the Court of Appeal,[88] it had been conceded that if the Bank of England had waived or rescinded the requirement the lender would have had no right to require the proceeds to be utilised in discharge of the debt.

Even where the creditor is to be given rights in respect of an asset, it is necessary to distinguish real rights from personal rights. A real right is a right in an asset (right in rem) as opposed to a personal right to an asset (right ad rem). A personal claim to delivery or transfer of an asset does not survive the debtor's bankruptcy but becomes converted into a right to prove for a dividend in the debtor's estate in competition with other creditors. By contrast a security interest is a right in rem[89] and in principle the secured creditor is entitled to remove the asset from the general body of creditors.[90] In distinguishing security interests from personal rights the following deserve particular mention[91]:

Agreement to give security   The maxim that equity treats as done that which   **1–19**
ought to be done has the effect that most agreements to give security in an asset will be treated in equity as if they were actual transfers,[92] thus blurring the distinction between real and personal rights. The requirements of equity in relation to such uncompleted transfer agreements are considered below.[93] Moreover, even in equity a mere agreement for security is not sufficient to create a security interest unless the agreement relates to an asset or fund which at the time of the agreement or on subsequent acquisition by the debtor can be identified as falling within the agreement. So an obligation by the employer under a building contract to set aside as a separate fund retention monies deducted from interim payments as provided in architects' certificates does not make the contractor a secured creditor until the fund has in fact been established. The deductions themselves simply amount to withholding of payment and do not create any res to which a security interest can attach, so that if the employer goes into liquidation before the fund has been set up the contract is merely an unsecured creditor and the court will not grant a mandatory injunction to establish the fund after the employer has gone into winding-up.[94]

---

[88] *Swiss Bank Corp Ltd v Lloyds Bank Ltd* [1982] A.C. 584 at 596–597.

[89] More accurately, a particular type of right in rem. Rights in rem are those available against third parties generally, and include, for example, some rights in tort. Civilian writers refer to rights *in re*, or real rights, to distinguish rights in an asset from other in rem rights. It is, of course, a necessary prequisite of a security interest that the subject matter is both identifiable (see para.2–05, below) and capable of being transferred or otherwise given in security (paras 2–07, 3–38 et seq., below).

[90] In relation to a debtor who is a company, the Insolvency Act 1986 imposes restrictions on the secured creditor's right to enforce his security where an application for an administration order has been made, pending the coming into effect of an out-of-court appointment of an administrator, during the period of administration, as well as where the terms of an approved company voluntary arrangement provide for such restrictions, and, for small eligible companies, while a meeting to consider a CVA is pending. See Sch.B1 paras 42, 43, 44 and Sch.A1; and for more detail, Goode, *Principles of Corporate Insolvency Law* (2011) paras 11–51 et seq.

[91] See also R. Goode, *Commercial Law*, E. McKendrick (ed.) 4th edn (London: Lexis Nexis, 2010), pp.645 et seq.

[92] *Tebb v Hodge* (1869) L.R. 5 C.P. 73.

[93] See para.2–11, below.

[94] *Re Jartay Developments Ltd* (1983) 22 Build. L.R. 134; *Mac-Jordan Construction Ltd v Brookmount Erostin Ltd* [1991] B.C.L.C. 350. The distinction between a trust (or security interest)

1–20 **Contractual set-off**   A deposits money with B Bank under an agreement which empowers B Bank to set-off against its deposit liability any claim it has against A on any other account. Exercise of this contractual right of set-off will, of course, result in B Bank being paid its claim up to the amount of the deposit. The set-off thus fulfils an important security function. But is it a security in law? We can answer this question only by going back to fundamentals. A security interest is a real right in the asset given in security. A right of set-off, even if given by contract, is a purely personal right to set one claim against another. The party asserting it never acquires rights in the other's monetary claim at all; he merely asserts a countervailing claim which operates in pro tanto extinction of his monetary liability. It follows that a contractual set-off does not create a security interest.[95] However, the distinction between contractual set-off and security has become blurred by the decision of the House of Lords in *Re Bank of Credit and Commerce International SA (No.8)*[96] to the effect that there is no conceptual barrier to a person charging back to its creditor the obligation owed to it by that creditor. But since the only method of realising the charge is by a book-entry debit to the account recording the chargee's indebtedness, which is the self-same method utilised to effect a contractual set-off, it seems that the only way of distinguishing a charge over the debtor's obligation from a contractual set-off is by the label given to the agreement by the parties, a point to which we shall return.[97] When the chargor is insolvent, however, it may well be that the existence of the charge prevents the operation of insolvency set-off, unless the chargee chooses to prove in the liquidation or administration, although the chargee will have taken the charge subject to any contractual rights of set-off.[98] When the chargee is insolvent, there is a danger that insolvency set-off will not apply, and that the chargee's insolvency officer will have the choice of enforcing the security by book entry or suing the chargor for the debt, leaving him to prove for his debt in the chargee's insolvency proceedings.[99]

1–21   Interestingly, the Supreme Court of Canada has recently considered whether a contractual right of set-off was a "security interest" within the meaning of s.224(1.3) of the Income Tax Act 1985, which gave priority to the revenue over a "security interes".[100] In one sense, this decision is about the meaning of a particular term in a statute which is part of a very different system of personal

---

over part of a specific fund, which is potentially valid if intended, and an attempt to create a trust (or security interest) where there is no fund at all, which is not valid, is made clear in *Re Lehman Brothers International (Europe) (In Administration)* [2010] EWHC 2914 (Ch) at [225]–[235]; [2011] EWCA Civ 1544 at [69]–[72].

[95] This passage was cited with approval by the Singapore Court of Appeal in *Electro-Magnetic (S) Ltd v Development Bank of Singapore Ltd* [1994] 1 S.L.R. 734. However, it was distinguished in the decision of the Supreme Court of Canada, *Caisse Populaire Desjardins de l'Est de Drummond v Canada* [2009] S.C.C. 29 discussed in para.1–21, below.

[96] *Re Bank of Credit and Commerce International SA (No.8)* [1998] A.C. 214.

[97] See below and para.3–12, below.

[98] See para.7–100, below.

[99] For further discussion, and for suggested counter-arguments to this unsatifactory state of affairs, see para.7–100, below.

[100] *Caisse Populaire Desjardins de l'Est de Drummond v Canada* [2009] S.C.C. 29 Sup Ct (Can). For comment in the Canadian and Australian contexts, see R. Wood, "Journey to the Outer Limits of Secured Transactions Law" (2010) 48 C.B.L.J. 482; Duggan and Brown, *Australian Personal Property Securities Law* (2012), paras 3.52–3.57.

property security law from that operating in England and Wales,[101] and concerned the very specific terms of the contract between the parties. However, it raises more wide-ranging issues about the relationship between personal rights and rights in rem. The agreement in question[102] concerned a line of credit made available by a bank to a debtor, and a deposit made by the debtor with the bank. The deposit was for a fixed term, and the debtor was not permitted to withdraw the money before the end of the term (the fixed term obligation), or at any time until all amounts due under the credit line were repaid (a flawed asset[103]), could not transfer or charge the deposit (a negative pledge clause[104]). The majority took the view that, although these provisions individually created personal obligations, collectively they amounted to the creation of a security interest, that is, a right in rem.[105] The minority, however, took the view that the mere combination of a number of personal rights could not create an interest in property (a right in rem).[106]

Under English law the issue is whether there is a contractual appropriation of an asset of a debtor (A) to payment of the debt owed by A to B. It has already been made clear that a mere agreement for set-off is not such an appropriation of the asset represented by B's debt to A which arose on the making of the deposit. Instead, it confers on B a right to extinguish or reduce its debt to A by asserting its own claim. Is that (personal) right changed by contractual provisions entitling B to refuse to extinguish or reduce that debt by any other means than set-off (the fixed term obligation and the flawed asset provision)? As discussed below, this right to withhold repayment cannot be seen as an appropriation of the asset to the debt: it merely defines the nature and scope of the payment obligation. Is the personal nature of the right of set-off changed by a provision prohibiting A from charging or assigning the debt due from B to A (the negative pledge)? As discussed below, a covenant not to encumber gives B no rights in the asset at all: it is a purely contractual obligation which can only attract personal remedies.[107] Although these contractual rights have the economic effect of preserving B's ability to extinguish its obligation by set-off when, if the obligations were differently constituted, that ability could easily be lost, this does not make the combination of rights a security interest.[108]

The Canadian case also raises the issue as to whether the label the parties give to the rights and obligations created by an agreement can make a difference to the characterisation of that agreement. The majority followed the functional approach

---

[101] The case related to the law of Quebec, which is both a PPSA system (see para.1–04, above) and a civil law system.

[102] Or, at least, the part of it that was relied upon. Another part of the decision was that, although the Bank also had a charge-back, it could choose not to rely on it if it wished.

[103] See para.1–23, below.

[104] See paras 1–24, 1–76, below.

[105] *Caisse Populaire Desjardins de l'Est de Drummond v Canada* [2009] S.C.C. 29 Sup Ct (Can) at [36], [39].

[106] *Caisse Populaire Desjardins de l'Est de Drummond v Canada* [2009] S.C.C. 29 Sup Ct (Can) at [121]–[125].

[107] See para.1–24, below.

[108] In a different context, the right to restrain misapplication of assets has, in a line of cases, been held not to constitute a security interest as it is negative rather than a positive right to be paid out of those assets, see para.1–28, below.

which governs the personal property security legislation regime,[109] in that it looked at the rights and obligations created by the agreement and held that they amounted to the creation of an interest in the debtor's property (the debt that is owed to the debtor by the bank as a result of the deposit)[110] despite the fact that the label "security interest" was not used. Despite the fact that English law looks to the legal substance of an agreement, and is prepared, on occasion, to ignore the label used by the parties,[111] the parties are entitled to structure their transaction in the form they wish, and the English courts will determine their intention from the words they use. Thus, if the parties intend to create a security interest (for example, by using the word "charge") the courts will give effect to this,[112] but if the rights and obligations they intend to create are purely personal in form, the courts are likely to give effect to this and not recharacterise the transaction as a security interest.[113]

1–22   **Balance on a current account**   We have seen from the above that a right of set-off does not constitute a security interest. A fortiori this is true of an offset effected through the operation of a single current account, since the only credit balance is the ultimate balance on the account, which forms a single indivisible fund. This is well illustrated by the decision of Millett J. in *Re Charge Card Services Ltd*.[114] This case concerned an invoice discounting arrangement with recourse.[115] The financier was obliged to maintain a current account to which would be credited (inter alia) the purchase price of each receivable before deducting the discounting charge and debited (inter alia) certain contingent liabilities of the company under the agreement and the discounting charge; further the factor was to remit to the company any balance for the time being standing to the credit of the current account less any amount which the factor in its absolute discretion decided to retain as security for claims against the company. The company went into insolvent liquidation and contended that the factor's right of retention was taken as security for rights of set-off and constituted a charge which was void against the liquidator for want of registration:

> "It was held that the amount payable by the factor for a receivable was not the purchase price as such but the balance standing to the credit of the company's

---

[109] *Caisse Populaire Desjardins de l'Est de Drummond v Canada* [2009] S.C.C. 29 Sup Ct (Can) at [25], [41].

[110] *Caisse Populaire Desjardins de l'Est de Drummond v Canada* [2009] S.C.C. 29 Sup Ct (Can) at [29]–[30].

[111] See para.1–04, above, paras 1–36 et seq., below.

[112] See above and paras 3–04 et seq., below. Note that even where such words are not used, if it is clear that the "essential nature" of a transaction is that it creates a security interest, the courts will give effect to this, and will not enable the parties to avoid the registration regime, see *In The Matter Of Lehman Brothers International (Europe) (In Administration)* [2012] EWHC 2997 (Ch) at [48].

[113] See R. Derham, *The Law of Set-Off*, 4th edn (New York: Oxford University Press, 2010), paras 16.93–16.107, who takes the view that some set-off agreements are charges, although many are not. Broadly speaking, he agrees with the majority reasoning in the *Caisse Populaire* case that when a right of set-off is combined with a flawed asset, commenting that there seems to be little if any difference between a provision for set-off and for appropriation or application of the credit balance to the payment of the debt.

[114] *Re Charge Card Services Ltd* [1987] Ch. 150.

[115] See para.3–05, below.

account after the relevant debits had been made and subject to the right of retention. Accordingly the case was not one of set-off at all but of account, for there were no mutual but independent obligations capable of set-off, merely a right to payment of a single balance remaining after exercise of the right of retention.[116] It followed that the right of retention was not a charge on money due to the company, for what was due was arrived at after deducting the sum retained, so that there was no relevant property capable of forming the subject matter of the charge."

Condition of repayment   A security interest is also to be distinguished from a   1–23
contractual condition of repayment. An example is the so-called "flawed asset" created where company A deposits money with a bank upon terms that the deposit is to be repayable only when company A and company B (which is typically a member of the same group) have discharged their indebtedness to the bank on other accounts. Such an agreement does not of itself constitute a security, for the bank acquires no rights over the deposit,[117] merely a right to withhold repayment. The case is thus similar to that of contractual set-off except that A's deposit is not extinguished; it remains intact as A's asset but can be withdrawn only on fulfilment of the condition.

Negative pledge   A negative pledge is an agreement by the debtor not to   1–24
encumber his assets in favour of a third party, or not to encumber them by way of a security which would rank ahead of or pari passu with the security given to the creditor. Negative pledges are dealt with later in the present chapter.[118]

Subordination agreement   A subordination agreement is an agreement by   1–25
which a creditor agrees to subordinate his claim against the debtor, or alternatively a security taken by him from the debtor, to the claim or security of another creditor. The characterisation of subordination agreements is discussed later in the present chapter.[119]

Sale of sub-participation in loan assets   The sale of a sub-participation in a   1–26
loan or other financial asset does not usually create a security interest.[120]

Lien on sub-freights   There are several first instance decisions holding that a   1–27
shipowner's lien on sub-freights is an equitable charge and as such is registrable under the relevant Companies Act either as a charge on book debts or as a floating charge.[121] The authority of these decisions was weakened by the statement of Lord Millett in delivering the decision of the Privy Council in *Agnew v Commissioner of Inland Revenue*[122] that the better view, as expressed by

---

[116] See further para.7–11, below, as to the distinction between set-off and account.

[117] The efficacy of the flawed asset concept was recognised by the Court of Appeal in *Re Bank of Credit and Commerce International SA (No.8)* [1996] Ch. 245; and, on appeal, by the House of Lords [1998] A.C. 214, per Lord Hoffmann at 227. For a case considering whether a charge or a flawed asset was created by the agreement between the parties, see *Fraser v Oystertec Plc* [2004] EWHC 1582 (Ch).

[118] See paras 1–76 et seq., below.

[119] See paras 1–84 et seq., below.

[120] See para.1–87, below.

[121] *Re Welsh Irish Ferries Ltd* [1986] Ch. 471; *Itex Itagrani Export SA v Care Shipping Corp* [1990] 2 Lloyd's Rep. 316; *The Annangel Glory* [1988] 1 Lloyd's Rep. 45.

[122] *Agnew v Commissioner of Inland Revenue* [2001] 2 A.C. 710; [2001] UKPC 28.

Dr Fidelis Oditah some years previously,[123] is that a lien on sub-freights is not a charge at all, merely a personal right to intercept freight before it is paid to the owner, and thus a right analogous to stoppage in transitu. Despite the great persuasive value of Lord Millett's view, it has been rejected in recent cases, where a lien of sub-freights has been held to be an equitable charge.[124] Although none of the cases concerned the priority of the lien or its validity on the insolvency of the debtor, it does appear that a lien on sub-freights is registrable under the wider registration provisions now in s.859A of the Companies Act 2006[125]: it is perhaps a shame that this point was not directly addressed in the 2013 reforms.

1–28   **Directions as to the application of assets, including proceeds**   Where a person borrows money in order to purchase an asset the loan agreement may provide that if the asset is later sold the proceeds are to be applied in or towards discharge of the debt. There may also be a stipulation that the proceeds are to be paid into a designated bank account in the creditor's name. Suggestions that contractual provisions of this kind are sufficient to confer a security interest on the creditor have usually been robustly rejected by the courts except where the asset from which the proceeds are derived was itself the subject of a security interest in favour of the creditor. Thus in *Palmer v Carey*,[126] money was lent to a trader to enable him to purchase goods as stock in trade for his business and the agreement provided that when the goods were sold the proceeds were to be paid to the credit of the lender's account at the lender's bank, and he was to deduct the amount of the loan and one-third of the gross profit and pay the balance to the borrower. Subsequently, the borrower agreed to transfer his unsold stock in trade to the lender in discharge of all obligations under the earlier agreement. The borrower then became bankrupt and in the bankruptcy the transfer of the stock in trade was held void. The lender asserted that if this was the case his rights under the original agreement were restored, and by virtue of that agreement he had an equitable charge over the goods and their proceeds.[127]

The claim was rejected by the Privy Council in the following terms:

> "An agreement for valuable consideration that a fund shall be applied in a particular way may found an injunction to restrain its application in another way. But if there be nothing more, such a stipulation will not amount to an equitable assignment. It is necessary to find, further, that an obligation has been imposed in favour of the creditor to pay the debt out of the fund. This is but an instance of a familiar doctrine of equity that a contract for valuable consideration to transfer or charge a subject matter passes a beneficial interest by way of property in that subject matter if the contract is one of which a Court of equity will decree specific performance. Under

---

[123] F. Oditah, "The Juridical Nature of a Lien on Sub-Freights" [1989] L.M.C.L.Q. 191.

[124] *Western Bulk Shipowning III A/S v Carbofer Maritime Trading ApS* [2012] EWHC 1224 (Comm) [32]–[52]; *Dry Bulk Handy Holding Inc v Fayette International Holdings Ltd* [2012] EWHC 2107 (Comm) at [51] (upheld on appeal at [2013] EWCA Civ 184 but this point was not considered).

[125] See Ch.2, below.

[126] *Palmer v Carey* [1926] A.C. 703, reversing the decision of the High Court of Australia (1924) 34 C.L.R. 380 and restoring the decision of the trial judge.

[127] The proceeds appear to relate to the sale of some goods which took place as part of the handing over of the stock-in-trade pursuant to the agreement which was later declared void, and were not proceeds that had ever been paid into the lender's account at the lender's bank, see *Re Gillott's Settlement* [1934] Ch. 97, 110 referred to below.

[the] agreement the money when borrowed is the borrower's money, and the lender becomes a creditor. The goods when purchased are the borrower's goods. The proceeds of sale when the goods are sold belong to the borrower. They arise from the sale of goods belonging to him. Under art.3, however, the proceeds are to be paid to the lender's credit at his bank. This gives the lender a most efficient hold to prevent the misapplication of the proceeds, but there is nothing in that article to give him a property by way of security or otherwise in the moneys of the borrower before or after he, the lender, has them in his charge."[128]

In short, there must be a contractual appropriation of the asset to the debt, which was held to be lacking in *Palmer v Carey*, as it was in the subsequent House of Lords case *Swiss Bank Corp v Lloyds Bank Ltd*.[129] A similar result was reached in *Flightline Ltd v Edwards*,[130] where a freezing order against a company was discharged by agreement on the condition that the parties' solicitors opened a joint bank account into which the company paid £4.2 million and the company undertook not to withdraw, encumber or deal with funds from that account up to £3.3 million. The Court of Appeal held that no charge was created: while F had a right to restrain misapplication of the assets, and while the assets were, during the currency of the agreement, under the control of the court, F had no right, without more, to be paid any judgment debt out of the assets in the joint account.[131] Further, in *Re TXU Europe Group Plc*,[132] a company agreed with its senior executives that they would continue to be entitled to final salary pensions, and, in order to give the executives some comfort, the company established a fund which would match the extent to which the pensions were not funded by Inland Revenue approved arrangements. Although it was clear that the fund was intended as the source from which the pension obligations would be met, it was held that the senior executives had no right to have recourse to the fund to satisfy their claims to pension benefits, and so did not have a charge over the fund. Blackburne J. identified two criteria from the cases already mentioned as to whether a security interest has been created: first whether there was contractual appropriation of the asset to the debt and secondly whether the chargee has a specifically enforceable right to look to the asset (or class of asset) or its proceeds for the discharge of the liability. The question is governed by the intentions of the parties, but this includes both express and implied intention, so that express words may not be determinative if upon a proper understanding of the admissible evidence, the transaction has a different legal effect.[133]

A similar objective approach[134] was followed in the *Cosslett* litigation, both in **1–29** the Court of Appeal[135] and the House of Lords,[136] although a diametrically opposite result was reached. In that case, the employer under a building contract was given power, on default by the contractor, to take possession of and use plant

---

[128] *Palmer v Carey* [1926] A.C. 703, per Lord Wrenbury at 706–707. But see below.

[129] *Swiss Bank Corp v Lloyds Bank Ltd* [1982] A.C. 584. See para.1–17, above.

[130] *Flightline Ltd v Edwards* [2003] EWCA Civ 63; [2003] 1 W.L.R. 1200.

[131] This reasoning has been followed in *Masri v Consolidated Contractors International Co SAL* [2007] EWHC 3010 (Comm); *Tradegro (UK) Ltd v Charles Price* [2011] EWCA Civ 268; *Withers LLP v Langbar International Ltd* [2011] EWCA Civ 1419 at [37]–[39].

[132] *Re TXU Europe Group Plc* [2003] EWHC 1305; [2004] 1 B.C.L.C. 519.

[133] *Re TXU Europe Group Plc* [2003] EWHC 1305 at [35]; [2004] 1 B.C.L.C. 519 at [35].

[134] For example, by Lord Hoffmann at [2002] 1 A.C. 336 [42] and by Lord Scott at [53].

[135] *Re Cosslett (Contractors) Ltd* [1998] Ch. 495.

[136] *Smith v Bridgend County BC* [2002] 1 A.C. 336; [2001] UKHL 58.

and machinery on the site belonging to the contractor[137] and to sell it and apply the proceeds towards discharge of the contractor's obligations to the employer. It was held that the provision for possession and use of the plant and machinery did not create a security interest since its purpose was not to provide security but to enable the employer to complete the contract works. By contrast, the power of sale was not attached to any possessory security (i.e. a pledge or a lien) but derived solely from the contract and was given for the purpose of security, so that the right of sale and application of the proceeds given to the employer constituted an equitable charge.

The significant difference between *Palmer v Carey* and *Cosslett* is that in the former case the sale was to be effected by the borrower, to whom the goods belonged, so that the proceeds were those of the borrower, whereas in *Cosslett* the agreement created a charge in favour of the employer over the plant and materials,[138] who was empowered to sell them and pay itself the debt owing to it out of the proceeds of sale. This right, however it was described in the agreement, clearly created a security interest.[139]

1–30   Nevertheless *Palmer v Carey*, which though referred to in argument in the Court of Appeal was not mentioned in any of the judgments in *Cosslett* in the Court of Appeal or any of the speeches in the House of Lords, is not an altogether easy case. That decision had been explained in *Re Gillott's Settlement*[140] as turning on the fact that the time of the bankruptcy there was no credit balance in the lender's account, which was substantially overdrawn. This explanation itself is not free from difficulty, for the passage from the opinion of the Privy Council quoted above states that the lender would acquire no security interest in the proceeds even after he had them in his charge in the account. But on this point the reference to moneys in the account can be regarded as obiter, since in the absence of such money any question of their appropriation to the debt was moot. The decision could then be explained, as it was in *Re Gillott's Settlement*, on the basis that the only security interest that could be asserted was to the goods themselves, there was no manifested intention to appropriate the goods to the debt, and it was unnecessary to decide whether there was an appropriation of the proceeds.

This seems to be the true ratio decidendi. It is significant that in the courts below the claim was merely to the goods, since there were no longer any proceeds in the bank account. The majority decision of the High Court of Australia had been based on the view that a provision for the application of proceeds of an asset in discharge of a debt constituted a charge on the asset. That was plainly wrong, for as will be seen[141] a security interest runs forward from an asset to its proceeds, not backwards from proceeds to the asset. The Privy Council rightly held that no intention had been manifested to create a charge over the goods. That was sufficient to dispose of the case. It was unnecessary to consider whether, independently of any interest in the goods, the lender acquired a charge over moneys in the bank account, because there were no longer any such moneys.

---

[137] There was a provision in the contract deeming such plant and materials to become the property of the employer but this was held not to indicate an intention to transfer legal ownership to the employer.

[138] So that, for example, the employer owed a duty to the contractor to take care to obtain a reasonable price on sale, see [2002] 1 A.C. 336 at [57] and [71].

[139] *Smith v Bridgend County BC* [2002] 1 A.C. 336 at [53].

[140] *Re Gillott's Settlement* [1934] Ch. 97, per Maugham J. at 109–110.

[141] See para.1–72, below.

If there had been, then it is submitted that they would have been subject to a mortgage in favour of the lender,[142] not because he had any prior charge over the goods which produced the proceeds but because he was plainly given control of the account by way of security, otherwise such control would have served no purpose. The borrower would then have had an equitable proprietary right to the return of any part of the fund remaining after discharge of the debt, or to the whole of the fund if the debt was discharged from other sources.[143] If, as the Privy Council accepted, a charge is created when a debtor agrees to pay the creditor from a fund held by the debtor, then a fortiori a debtor's conferment on the creditor of a right to withdraw money from a fund under the creditor's control should be effective to create a security interest. This would be an application of the objective approach to characterisation referred to earlier, and is in distinction to the *Flightline* and *TXU* cases where there was no right on the part of the creditors to be paid out of the particular fund.

At the end of the day, of course, it all comes down to a question of construction of the parties' agreement and the legal effect of what they have agreed.[144] The moral is that the creditor should expressly provide for the creation of a charge or for appropriation of the asset and its proceeds to the debt, if that is what he wants, and should provide clearly for merely personal rights if he does not want a security interest to be created.[145]

(2)   Security is by way of grant of an interest in the debtor's asset, not by way of reservation of title to the creditor

The debtor cannot give security over an asset in which he has no interest or of which he has no power to dispose. We shall examine in the next chapter what constitutes an interest or power of disposal for this purpose.[146] We have previously noted that, in contrast to legal systems in North America and many Commonwealth jurisdictions, English law distinguishes reservation of title under a conditional sale, hire-purchase or leasing agreement from a mortgage or charge, treating the conditional seller, owner or lessor as absolute owner subject only to the possessory interest of the conditional buyer, hirer or lessee. It follows that a provision in such an agreement empowering the seller, etc. to repossess upon default by the buyer, does not make the agreement a security agreement, for the seller is not taking rights over an asset of the buyer but is simply reserving the right to recover his own property. Similarly, the lessor's right of re-entry on forfeiture of a lease of land, though sometimes described as designed to secure performance of the tenant's covenants,[147] is not a true security interest, for the lessor is merely reserving the right to re-enter his own property, not taking a

1–31

---

[142] Not a mere charge because the account was in the lender's name so that legal title to the claim on the bank was vested in him.

[143] The mortgage would be by novation, as with other cases of cash collateral, the only difference being that the cash comes from the third-party purchaser, not from the debtor direct.

[144] See, for example, *Palette Shoes Ptry Ltd v Krohn* (1937) 58 C.L.R. 1; *Federal Commissioner of Taxation v Betro Harrison Constructions Pty Ltd* (1978) 20 A.L.R. 647.

[145] See para.1–21, above.

[146] It may be noted at this point that an agreement to give security over future assets creates an inchoate security interest which attaches automatically upon the debtor's acquisition of the asset and then takes effect as from the time of the agreement. See paras 2–12 et seq., below.

[147] See, for example, *Shiloh Spinners Ltd v Harding* [1973] A.C. 691.

security interest in property of the lessee.[148] Expressed in a more general form, the principle is that security in the legal sense derives from grant or declaration of trust by the debtor, not from reservation of title by the creditor. It is for this reason that the reservation of legal title under a sale, hire-purchase or leasing agreement does not constitute a security interest.[149]

However, English property law does not recognise the possibility of reserving equitable ownership whilst transferring the legal title. This is because equitable ownership in one person presupposes legal ownership in another. If legal and beneficial ownership are combined in the same person, he is not the holder of a legal title and a separate equitable interest, he is simply the full owner.[150] It follows that when transferring the legal title he cannot exclude equitable ownership from the transfer for at that stage there is none. An attempt to reserve equitable ownership will be construed as a grant back by the transferee; and if the "reservation" is for the purpose of securing an obligation, it will constitute a security interest.[151]

The distinction between reservation and grant is not always clear-cut. Particular problems have arisen in relation to reservation of title clauses in contracts of sale of goods. Four cases deserve particular examination:

1–32   **Simple reservation of title to goods under contract of sale**   S sells goods to B under a contract which reserves title until B has paid the price. As previously stated, no security interest is created in favour of S, for B is not granting rights in an asset in which he has an interest. The effect of the contract is that B does not acquire an interest in the goods until he completes payment. S is simply retaining legal ownership pending payment, and under the Sale of Goods Act the time when the property is to pass from seller to buyer is a matter for agreement between them.[152]

1–33   **Reservation of title securing other indebtedness**   The character of the transaction is not affected by the fact that the seller's reservation of title is

---

[148] See *Christopher Moran Holdings Ltd v Bairstow (also referred to as Re Park Air Services Plc)* [2000] 2 A.C. 172, per Lord Millett at 186.

[149] *McEntire v Crossley Bros* [1895] A.C. 457.

[150] *Commissioner of Stamp Duties (Queensland) v Livingston* [1965] A.C. 694, per Viscount Radcliffe at 612; *Re Bond Worth Ltd* [1980] Ch. 228; *Westdeutsche Landesbank Girozentrale v Islington London BCl* [1996] A.C. 669, per Lord Browne-Wilkinson at 706.

[151] *Re Bond Worth Ltd* [1980] Ch. 228. It has been suggested that doubt is thrown on this reasoning by the decision of the House of Lords in *Abbey National v Cann* [1979] 3 A.C. 629 on the grounds that it was there held that where a buyer bought a house using money lent by a bank which was secured by a mortgage, there was no *scintilla temporis* when the buyer owned the entire legal estate in the house before the bank's mortgage attached (see para.5–63, below). However, this argument was rejected by Judge John Newey Q.C. in *Stroud Architectural Systems Ltd v John Laing Construction Ltd* [1994] 2 B.C.L.C. 276, 283 on the grounds that Slade J.'s argument in *Bond Worth* worked equally well if the transfer of title and the grant of a security interest were seen as happening simultaneously. This must be right: for the purposes of analysing whether there is a valid grant back of an equitable interest, it makes no difference whether this is done at the same time as the transfer of title to the buyer, or afterwards.

[152] Sale of Goods Act 1979 ss.17 and 19.

expressed to secure payment not only of the price of the particular goods sold but of the buyer's other indebtedness to the seller under prior or subsequent transactions.[153]

Claims to proceeds of goods supplied under reservation of title The position here is a little more complicated. If a person contracts to sell goods, reserving title until payment but giving the buyer the right to resell them on condition that he accounts for the proceeds of sale, does the stipulation as to proceeds constitute merely an undertaking to make over to the seller that which already belongs to him in equity or does it constitute a grant by the buyer of rights over proceeds which belong to him? The point is of some practical importance because if in the latter case the grant is construed to be by way of security and the buyer is a company, the security interest will be void against a liquidator, administrator and creditors if not registered.[154] In the famous *Romalpa* case[155] the Court of Appeal held that the proceeds belonged to the sellers in equity and the clause requiring the buyers to account for the proceeds did no more than require the buyers to make over to the sellers that which in equity was already their property. However, this was on the basis that the buyers held the goods as bailees for the sellers (which was conceded) and that therefore the buyers were in a fiduciary relationship with the sellers. The question of whether the clause created a registrable charge was not considered by the Court of Appeal, although it was discussed briefly by Mocatta J. at first instance who held that it was not.[156]

1–34

Subsequently, courts have doubted whether a bailment, or even an agency, relationship necessarily gives rise to a fiduciary relationship between the parties in relation to the proceeds of sale.[157] Instead, where the contract is silent as to the proceeds of the sub-sale the court will consider whether a duty to account for the proceeds can be implied, and is almost certain to hold that it should not.[158] Where, as is common, the contract does provide that the proceeds of any sub-sale belong to the seller, this is invariably seen as a grant of an interest to the seller by the buyer,[159] and, moreover, as a (registrable) security interest, since it will be limited in scope to the amount outstanding between the parties, and will also be defeasible on payment of that amount by the buyer from another source.[160]

---

[153] *Armour v Thyssen Edelstahlwerke AG* [1991] 2 A.C. 339.

[154] Under ss.859A and 859H of the Companies Act 2006.

[155] *Aluminium Industrie Vaassen BV v Romalpa Aluminium Ltd* [1976] 1 W.L.R. 676.

[156] *Aluminium Industrie Vaassen BV v Romalpa Aluminium Ltd* [1976] 1 W.L.R. 676, 682–683.

[157] See *Re Andrabell Ltd* [1984] 3 All E.R. 407 at 413–414; *Hendy Lennox (Industrial Engines) Ltd v Grahame Puttick Ltd* [1984] 1 W.L.R. 485, 498–499. A relationship of bailment could in any event be seen as inappropriate in the context of a sale on retention of title terms, see *E. Pfeiffer Weinkellerei-Weineinkauf GmbH & Co v Arbuthnot Factors Ltd* [1988] 1 W.L.R. 150, 159.

[158] *Re Andrabell Ltd* [1984] 3 All E.R. 407 at 413–414; *Hendy Lennox (Industrial Engines) Ltd v Grahame Puttick Ltd* [1984] 1 W.L.R. 485, 498–499. There is no prima facie implication of such a term, the normal implication being that the buyer sells for his own account, see *E. Pfeiffer Weinkellerei-Weineinkauf GmbH & Co v Arbuthnot Factors Ltd* [1988] 1 W.L.R. 150. 159.

[159] cf. K. Loi, "Quistclose trusts and Romalpa clauses: substance and nemo dat in corporate insolvency" (2012) 128 L.Q.R. 412.

[160] *Tatung (UK) Ltd v Galex Telesure Ltd* (1989) 5 B.C.C. 325, 333; *E. Pfeiffer Weinkellerei-Weineinkauf GmbH & Co v Arbuthnot Factors Ltd* [1988] 1 W.L.R. 150, 160–161; *Compaq Computer Ltd v Abercorn Ltd* [1993] B.C.L.C. 602, 614–615; *Modelboard Ltd v Outer Box Ltd* [1992] B.C.C. 945, 949–950.

1–35   **Claims to products of goods supplied under reservation of title**   Contracts of sale commonly provide that where goods supplied under reservation of title are commingled with other materials, belonging to the buyer or third party, to form a new product, ownership of the product is to vest in the seller. Such a provision will almost invariably be treated as creating a mortgage or charge.[161] If a new product has been formed, this will usually belong to the manufacture (the buyer) under the doctrine of specificatio.[162] Any interest the seller has pursuant to the agreement will therefore be by way of grant.

However, judges in a number of cases have said that the parties can agree that the new thing should belong, from the moment of its creation, to the seller rather than the buyer.[163] Even if this is possible, it is very unlikely to be what the parties have intended, since the resultant product will include materials not previously owned by the seller but contributed by others which can therefore vest in the seller only by way of grant, not by way of reservation,[164] and will also usually have involved work by the buyer which increases the value of the product above the value of the goods, so that the buyer will only intend the seller to have an interest in the product to the extent of the value of the goods, that is, a security interest. If the goods have simply become commingled without losing their identity, the seller becomes co-owner of the mixture.[165]

(3) & (4)   The right is given for the purpose of securing an obligation and in security only, not by way of outright transfer

1–36   So far we have considered the requirement that a security interest must be a proprietary interest, and that it must be an interest in an asset of the grantor, as opposed to an asset of the secured party or anyone else. It is, of course, possible for a person to grant an interest in his asset which is not a security interest but an absolute interest. The difference between the two types of interest has two aspects. First, a security interest is always granted to secure an obligation, whereas an absolute interest may be (but need not be[166]) transferred in fulfilment of an existing or future indebtedness or other obligation. Thus, if an interest is to be a security interest, it is necessary to identify a separate obligation which is secured by the grant.[167] Secondly, the security interest is limited to its security function, so that it is defeasible if the secured obligation is paid,[168] and only

---

[161] See *Re Bond Worth Ltd* [1980] Ch. 228; *Borden (UK) Ltd v Scottish Timber Products Ltd* [1981] Ch. 25; *Clough Mill Ltd v Martin* [1985] 1 W.L.R. 111.

[162] *Clough Mill Ltd v Martin* [1985] 1 W.L.R. 111, 119; *Hendy Lennox (Industrial Engines) Ltd v Grahame Puttick Ltd* [1984] 1 W.L.R. 485, 494. See also D. Webb, "Title or Transformation: Who Owns Manufactured Goods?" [2000] J.B.L. 513.

[163] *Clough Mill Ltd v Martin* [1985] 1 W.L.R. 111, 119; *Trading International Inc* [2001] 1 Lloyds' Rep. 284, 322; *Bacardi-Martini Beverages Ltd v Thomas Hardy Packaging Ltd* [2002] 1 Lloyds Rep. 62 [47]–[49]; upheld on appeal without consideration of this point, [2002] EWCA Civ 549.

[164] *Re Bond Worth Ltd* [1980] Ch. 228; *Clough Mill Ltd v Martin* [1985] 1 W.L.R. 111; *Ian Chisholm Textiles Ltd v Griffiths* [1994] B.C.C. 96.

[165] *Glencore International AG v Metro Trading International Inc* [2001] 1 Lloyd's Rep. 284, 321–323.

[166] For example, an absolute interest can also be transferred by way of gift or bequest.

[167] For a recent statement of the principle, see *Hughmans Solicitors v Central Stream Services Ltd* [2012] EWCA Civ 1720 at [25].

[168] The method by which it is defeasible will vary according to the type of security interest, see paras 1–46 et seq., below.

extends as far as is necessary to secure the obligation, so that on enforcement the grantor is entitled to any surplus value. Further, if, on enforcement, the amount realised is less than the obligation secured, the balance remains payable. These three "indicia of a charge" were set out clearly by Romer L.J. in *Re George Inglefield Ltd*,[169] and are frequently relied upon by courts when deciding whether an interest is granted absolutely or by way of security, an exercise in characterising the transaction between the parties.

In characterising any transaction the court has to perform two tasks. The first is to ascertain the intention of the parties from the terms of their agreement. The second is to determine the legal effect of what they have agreed. Whether what they have agreed produces a given legal effect is a matter of law and does not depend on intention. Thus in deciding whether or not an agreement has created a security interest the court looks not to whether that was intended by the parties but whether the nature of the rights they intended their agreement to confer is such as to constitute the agreement an agreement for security.[170] The point was well put by Lord Millett in *Agnew v Inland Revenue Commissioners*,[171] where the dispute was not whether a charge had been created but whether it was a fixed or floating charge:

> "The question is not merely one of construction. In deciding whether a charge is a fixed charge or a floating charge, the court is engaged in a two-stage process. At the first stage it must construe the instrument of charge and seek to gather the intentions of the parties from the language they have used. But the object at this stage of the process is not to discover whether the parties intended to create a fixed or a floating charge. It is to ascertain the nature of the rights and obligations which the parties intended to grant each other in respect of the charged assets. Once these have been ascertained, the court can then embark on the second stage of the process, which is one of categorisation. This is a matter of law. It does not depend on the intention of the parties. If their intention, properly gathered from the language of the instrument, is to grant the company rights in respect of the charged assets which are inconsistent with the nature of a fixed charge, then the charge cannot be a fixed charge however they may have chosen to describe it."

When the question is whether a security interest has been created at all, the relevant intention is the intention to confer on the creditor an interest in the debtor's property by way of security which will cease when the debt has been discharged. If that is the intention, the fact that the parties have chosen to label the transaction in some other way, for example as an outright transfer, is, in theory, irrelevant. Conversely, no security interest is created where the asset is made available to the creditor for purposes other than security or is intended to be paid or transferred to the creditor absolutely, so that though it is paid or transferred as "security" for the debt, the debtor is to have merely a personal claim to repayment of any excess received by the creditor over what was due to him.[172] However, in the context of whether a security interest is created, the

---

[169] *Re George Inglefield Ltd* [1933] Ch.1.

[170] For a similar approach to the question of whether there has been contractual appropriation of the asset to the debt, see para.1–28, above, in particular in relation to the more recent cases discussed.

[171] *Agnew v Inland Revenue Commissioners* [2001] UKPC 28 at [32]; [2001] 2 A.C. 710, 725.

[172] See, for example, *Orion Finance Ltd v Crown Financial Management Ltd* [1996] 2 B.C.L.C. 78. This is discussed at para.1–38, below.

courts do take account of the language used by the parties in order to decide what rights and obligations are created by the agreement, so long as the agreement is internally consistent, and there is no evidence of a sham.[173] This approach,[174] which is consistent with the parties' freedom under English law to structure their transaction in the legal form that they choose, is rather different in emphasis from that applied in the characterisation of charges as fixed or floating.[175]

1–37   If a security interest is held to have been created, this has various consequences, stemming from the protection given by the law to the grantor and to its other creditors (particularly on its insolvency). First, depending on the type of interest created, it is likely to be registrable under s.859A of the Companies Act 2006 if it is created by a company, and may be registrable under the Bills of Sale Acts if created by a person who is not a company.[176] This is of considerable significance, since if it is not registered it will be void against other secured creditors, and the liquidator or administrator on insolvency of the debtor.[177] The registration requirements are designed to give notice to other creditors of interests which affect the assets of the debtor so that they can adjust accordingly,[178] but are, in general, limited to security interest rather than absolute interests.[179] Further, if an interest is enforced, the grantor will have a proprietary interest in any surplus proceeds,[180] and any restriction on its right to redeem mortgaged or charged assets may be challengeable.[181] A good example of assets made available otherwise than for the purpose of security is provided by the decision of the Court

---

[173] *Orion Finance Ltd v Crown Financial Management Ltd* [1996] 2 B.C.L.C. 78, 84, per Millett L.J.; *Welsh Development Agency v Export Finance Co Ltd* [1992] B.C.L.C. 148, 162, per Dillon L.J. See also Staughton L.J. at 187. In interpreting a commercial contract, especially where a contract is in the standard form of a particular market, the court will interpret it in the light of the business market in which it transacted and will not necessarily give words their natural meaning if this is inconsistent with the plain commercial intention of the parties, *Re Sigma Finance Corp (In Administrative Receivership)* [2009] UKSC 2 at [37]; where the parties have used unambiguous language, the court must apply it but where there is more than one possible construction, the court is entitled to prefer the construction which is consistent with business common sense (*Rainy Sky SA v Kookmin Bank* [2011] UKSC 50 at [21]).

[174] For discussion of the application of this approach to structures used in receivables financing, see paras 3–04 et seq., below.

[175] See paras 4–03 et seq., below; and Beale, Bridge, Gullifer and Lomnicka, *The Law of Security and Title-Based Financing* (2012), para.4.36 for discussion of possible policy reasons for the difference in approach.

[176] See paras 2–22 et seq., below.

[177] Companies Act 2006 s.859H.

[178] See para.2–16, below.

[179] An exception is the requirement that a non-corporate trader register an absolute assignment of book debts, Insolvency Act 1986 s.344. See para.3–29, below.

[180] See para.1–40, below.

[181] This could be on the grounds of unconscionablity, or that the provision is a penalty, or that it is inconsistent with the nature of a mortgage (*Kreglinger v New Patagonia Meat and Cold Storage Co Ltd* [1914] A.C. 25, 54; *Jones v Morgan* [2001] EWCA Civ 995 at [99]). Whether the last of these should continue to be a separate ground for striking down a contractual provision (in the absence of unconscionability or penalty) has been questioned, see *Jones v Morgan* [2001] EWCA Civ 995 at [86], per Lord Phillips; A. Berg, "Clogs on the equity of redemption—or chaining an unruly dog" [2002] J.B.L. 335; Law Commission, *Working Paper on Land Mortgages* (HMSO, 1986) Law Com. No.99, at para.3.36; Beale, Bridge, Gullifer and Lomnicka, *The Law of Security and Title-Based Financing* (2012), paras 6.45–6.46.

of Appeal in *Cosslett*[182] to which reference has already been made. Again, where title to an asset is transferred and the intention is that the transfer shall be absolute, so that the transferor will have neither the right nor the obligation to reacquire it in specie, no security interest arises. Four groups of cases deserve particular mention:

Transfer in or towards reduction of an existing indebtedness The assignment of a debt or transfer of another asset in reduction or discharge of the assignor's own indebtedness to the assignee does not constitute a security interest but an outright transfer. The principle was long ago applied in *Re Garrud Ex p. Newitt*,[183] where a provision in a building contract entitling the building owner, upon default by the builder, to take the builder's materials towards discharge of the builder's liability for damages was held not to create a security interest, for the materials were taken not as security for the builder's obligation but towards discharge of it.[184]

1–38

Another illustration is the decision in *Siebe Gorman & Co Ltd v Barclays Bank Ltd*[185] in which A, who owed B money, made an outright assignment of bills of exchange to B "as security for the aforementioned debt". The bills were held by A's bank, who used the proceeds to reduce A's overdraft. A went into liquidation, and B sued the bank for recovery of the proceeds of the bills. The bank argued that the assignment of the bills to B was a charge, void for non-registration. It was held by Slade J. that whilst the assignment was not by way of sale it was equally clear that it was not intended as a mortgage either but was an outright transfer towards payment of A's indebtedness. The words "as security for the aforementioned debt", though prima facie indicating a mortgage or charge,[186] had to be construed in context as denoting an assignment in payment of the debt. The assignment was therefore not registrable.

In *Siebe Gorman* the value of the bills transferred was less than the assignor's indebtedness to the bank, so that commercially there was no point in the assignor being given a right to redeem the bills. Suppose, however, that the collectable value of the debt due to the intending assignor exceeds what he owes to the intended assignee. In this situation, it is unlikely that the assignor intends to make a gift of the excess to the assignee, and the court will normally infer an intention to mortgage the debt instead of assigning it outright. But let us imagine that the assignor is willing to make an outright transfer of the debt due to him, with no

1–39

---

[182] *Re Cosslett (Contractors) Ltd* [1998] Ch. 495; and *Smith v Bridgend County BC* [2001] UKHL 58; [2002] 1 A.C. 336, in relation to the provision for possession and use of the plant and machinery. The position was held to be otherwise as regards a power in the same contract to sell the plant and take from the proceeds payment of the sums due to the employer. See para.1–29, above.

[183] *Re Garrud Ex p. Newitt* (1881) 16 Ch.D 522. See also *Ashby Warner & Co Ltd v Simmons* [1936] 2 All E.R. 697; distinguished in *Coakley v Argent* Unreported June 4, 1998, per Rimer J.

[184] The distinction between this case and the creation of a security interest over building materials was pointed out by Lord Scott in *Smith v Bridgend*, who said that in the latter case, "if there were a deficiency, the contractor would still owe the amount of the deficiency. If there were a surplus, the employer would have to account for it to the contractor" [2001] UKHL 58; [2002] 1 A.C. 336 at [57]. See para.1–37, above.

[185] *Siebe Gorman & Co Ltd v Barclays Bank Ltd* [1979] 2 Lloyd's Rep. 142; see to the same effect *Carreras Rothman Ltd v Freeman Mathews Treasure Ltd* [1985] Ch. 207.

[186] See, for example, *In Re Kent and Sussex Sawmills Ltd* [1947] Ch. 177; *Orion Finance Ltd v Crown Financial Management Ltd* [1996] 2 B.C.L.C. 78.

right of redemption, provided that the assignee for his part undertakes to repay the amount by which the sum he collects from the account debtor (the assignor's debtor) exceeds the debt due from the assignor. At first sight this seems a mortgage disguised as an outright assignment to evade the registration requirements.[187] However, if it be the case that the assignor is genuinely giving up all his interest in the debts due to him, with no intention to reacquire the debts by paying off his own indebtedness but merely a reliance on the assignee's personal undertaking to repay the excess, the assignment cannot be faulted as a mortgage and escapes the registration provisions. We should see no difficulty in the matter if the subject matter of the assignment were not debts but a motor car. What causes us to hesitate in the case of assignment of debts is that money is being exchanged for money, and it is a matter of indifference to the assignor whether he mortgages the debts or sells them outright against the assignee's undertaking to pay him the surplus. But such considerations have not in the past led the courts to disregard the distinction between an outright transfer of debts and a loan on the security of debts.[188] Moreover, the outright transfer of the proceeds differs in substance in another way from a mortgage of the proceeds in that the assignor, whose claim to repayment of the excess is a purely personal claim, bears the risk of the assignee's insolvency before repayment has been made.

In short, the position is exactly the same as that described in para.1–40 below except that the payment or transfer is made in or towards satisfaction of an existing indebtedness rather than a prospective indebtedness.

1–40   **Transfer to cover future indebtedness**   Similar reasoning applies where money is paid not towards discharge of an existing indebtedness but as cash cover for a future indebtedness to the payee. Examples are the payment of margin by an investor to his broker to cover future indebtedness arising from share dealings on the investor's behalf, payment of money by an importer to his bank to cover the bank's prospective liability under letters of credit issued to pay for the goods being imported, and payment of a deposit by the buyer under a contract of sale as security for completion of the purchase or by a tenant as security for dilapidations.[189] In each case the intention is to provide security in the sense of assurance to the payee but it is necessary to distinguish a special-purpose payment which must be held and applied exclusively for the purpose of satisfying any indebtedness of the payer, any surplus being returned and meanwhile being held on trust for the payer, from an outright payment which becomes part of the payee's free assets, so that his only obligation if the sum paid exceeds the later indebtedness is a personal repayment obligation. In the former case the payee is the legal mortgagee of the fund, the payer having an equity of redemption which

---

[187] Under the Companies Act 2006 s.859A.

[188] See, for example, *Olds Discount Ltd v John Playfair Ltd* [1938] 3 All E.R. 275; *Chow Yoong Hong v Choong Fah Rubber Manufactory* [1962] A.C. 209; *Lloyds and Scottish Finance Ltd v Cyril Lord Carpet Sales Ltd* (1979) reported at [1992] B.C.L.C. 609. See also para.3–05, below.

[189] This structure is also used on the financial markets as a title transfer collateral arrangement, see para.6–30, below. The collateral taker is protected economically by close-out netting provisions which convert any repurchase obligation into a money obligation, which can be netted or set off against that owed by the collateral provider. The collateral provider is exposed to the credit risk of the collateral taker since the obligation to return surplus collateral is purely personal.

is not subject to rights of set-off by third parties against the payee[190] or by the payee himself against the debtor in respect of other indebtedness of the debtor,[191] and which can be asserted against the payee's creditors in the event of his insolvency[192]; in the latter there is no security interest at all, and the payment is an outright transfer of funds in which the payer has no equity of redemption.[193]

Sale and lease-back; sale and repurchase   The third category of outright   **1–41** transfers involves, as an integral part of the transaction, an agreement by the transferor to take the asset back on lease or hire-purchase or to repurchase it. It is well established that so long as the initial transfer is genuinely intended to confer full ownership on the transferee, as opposed to a mere security interest, the transaction will be characterised according to its description and will not be recharacterised as a security agreement. So a genuine sale of land or goods does not constitute a borrowing on security even if it is followed by a lease back or a letting on hire-purchase,[194] and a sale of debts does not become a mortgage of debts merely because the seller gives recourse.[195] Similarly, the raising of overnight or other short-term funds by the sale and repurchase of investment securities ("repos") does not as a rule involve the grant of a security interest, for the intention is that the original sale shall pass a full title and the buyer has a mere contractual obligation to retransfer the securities. Accordingly the seller runs the risk of the buyer's failure to effect the promised resale, though if the retransfer obligation is collateralised a security interest may then come into existence.[196] Again, stock lending, which involves the transfer of securities upon terms that at a later date the recipient is to retransfer equivalent securities,[197] does not constitute a security agreement, though it is common for the obligations of one or both of the parties to be secured by cash or securities collateral.[198] Hence the commercial treatment of repos and stock loans as collateral reflects the economic rather than the legal effect; the seller or lender transfers outright title, which exposes it to a credit risk, but the risk that the buyer or borrower will not honour its repurchase or reacquisition obligation is covered by contractual provisions

---

[190] *Re Pollitt Ex p. Minor* [1893] 1 Q.B. 455.

[191] *Talbot v Frere* (1878) 9 Ch.D. 568; *Re Gedney* [1908] 1 Ch. 804; *Lloyds Bank NZA Ltd v National Safety Council of Australia Victorian Division (in liq)* (1993) 10 A.C.S.R. 572; Derham, *The Law of Set-off* (2010) paras 10.50–10.53. See para.1–73, below.

[192] *Re City Equitable Fire Insurance Co Ltd* [1930] 2 Ch. 293.

[193] See para.3–06, below.

[194] *Yorkshire Wagon Co v Maclure* (1882) 21 Ch.D. 309; *Welsh Development Agency v Export Finance Co* [1992] B.C.C. 270. The position is otherwise where the agreement recording the purported sale and transfer back is a sham, as in *North Central Wagon Finance Co Ltd v Brailsford* [1962] 1 All E.R. 502; *Polsky v S. and A. Services* [1951] 1 All E.R. 185; affirmed [1951] 1 All E.R. 1062; or where, though the agreement is genuine, its overall legal effect is that of a security agreement, as in *Re Curtain Dream Plc* [1990] B.C.L.C. 925. See generally Goode, *Commercial Law* (2010), pp.645 et seq.; Beale, Bridge, Gullifer and Lomnicka, *The Law of Security and Title-Based Financing* (2012), paras 4.28–4.29.

[195] See cases cited at para.3–05, below.

[196] See further para.6–27, below.

[197] See para.6–27, below.

[198] See paras 3–08 and 6–27, below.

which entitle the seller or lender to close out the transactions in the event of default and net the obligations of the parties.[199]

1–42   **Establishment of common fund as payment mechanism**   Finally, a security agreement must be distinguished from an arrangement in which a fund in common beneficial ownership is established as a means of payment to the beneficial owners of the sums respectively becoming payable to them. An instructive decision is *Lovell Construction Ltd v Independent Estates Plc*.[200] In that case, the plaintiffs entered into an agreement with the defendants to carry out certain construction work for them. The parties entered into an agreement by which an escrow account was to be opened on the plaintiffs' behalf in the names of their solicitors to receive moneys payable by the defendants and third parties. Such moneys were to be deemed impressed with a trust in favour of the plaintiffs, to whom sums would be payable from the account against architects' certificates, while in certain circumstances moneys might be payable to the defendants, e.g. for liquidated and ascertained damages for breach of the construction contract. The defendants went into liquidation and the liquidator alleged that the escrow agreement created a registrable charge which was void for want of registration. The court held that the escrow account was established not for the purpose of giving security but as a mechanism of payment and created a trust of the moneys paid into the account in which both parties had a beneficial interest. The escrow agreement was therefore not registrable as a charge.[201]

(5)   A fixed security interest implies a restriction on the debtor's dominion over the asset

1–43   A creditor cannot claim a fixed security interest in an asset and at the same time allow the debtor the right to continue to treat the asset as his own, so that any right of the debtor to dispose of or encumber the charged assets is likely to result in a charge being characterised as floating, even if it is labelled as fixed.[202]

The grant of security by a debtor over his own obligation: charge-backs and pledge-backs

1–44   Since a person cannot sue himself, it was until fairly recently thought conceptually impossible for a debtor to take from his creditor a charge or other security over the debtor's own obligation and that a "security" of this kind took effect as a contractual set-off. But the House of Lords has now decided that there is no conceptual impossibility in a debtor taking a charge over his own

---

[199] For further discussion of the advantages of title transfer arrangements, see paras 6–30 and 6–31, and for discussion of close-out netting see para.7–21, below.

[200] *Lovell Construction Ltd v Independent Estates Plc* [1994] 1 B.C.L.C. 31.

[201] Whether money held on trust is held absolutely or by way of charge depends on the facts of the case. For cases where a charge was held to exist, see *Re ILG Travel Ltd (in administration)* [1995] 2 B.C.L.C. 128; and *Obaray v Gateway (London) Ltd* [2004] 1 B.C.L.C. 555.

[202] *Agnew v Commissioners of Inland Revenue* [2001] UKPC 28; [2001] 2 A.C. 710; *Re Spectrum Plus Ltd* [2005] UKHL 41; [2005] 2 A.C. 680. This technical area of law is discussed in detail in Ch.4, below.

obligation.[203] It is, however, not clear whether Lord Hoffmann's reasoning, which appears to rely on the fact that a charge does not involve a transfer of title, can apply to mortgage-backs.[204] The issue of charge-backs is examined in later chapters in the context of a charge taken by a bank over its own customer's credit balance, by a company over its own shares, or by a securities intermediary over its customer's securities account with that intermediary.[205] Suffice to give a reminder at this stage that the debtor's equity of redemption is a property right, not a mere money entitlement, so that any surplus remaining when the mortgagee has taken what is due to him is not available for set-off against other, unsecured indebtedness of the mortgagor to the mortgagee.[206] So the prudent creditor will reinforce his charge-back with a general set-off clause.

Security in a fund of assets

Hitherto the discussion has been concerned with specific (or fixed) security, that is, security which attaches to identified or identifiable assets or classes of asset in the sense that there is an immediate appropriation of the assets to satisfaction of the debt and the debtor loses the right to deal with them free from the security interest. However, it is also possible to take security in an identifiable fund of assets by way of a floating mortgage or floating charge which leaves the debtor free to continue managing and dealing with the assets in the ordinary course of business, so that no specific assets are appropriated to the debt until the fund closes through crystallisation of the security. It is also possible to have a floating sub-security in a floating security interest, and this probably occurs more often than is realised. Despite voluminous literature devoted to floating security some of the underlying concepts remain elusive. They are examined in some detail in Ch.4, below.

1–45

5.   THE FORMS OF CONSENSUAL SECURITY

The four consensual security devices

There are only four types of consensual security known to English law: the pledge, the contractual lien, the mortgage, and the charge.[207] Each of these is capable of being given in security so as to create a derivative, or sub-security, interest.[208]

1–46

---

[203] *Re Bank of Credit and Commerce International SA (No.8)* [1998] A.C. 214.

[204] See para.3–12, below; and discussion in Beale, Bridge, Gullifer and Lomnicka (2012), para.6.24.

[205] See paras 3–12, 6–38 and 6–42, below.

[206] See para.1–40, above and para.1–73, below. The enforcement of a security interest over financial collateral can be by sale or appropriation, with the value of the collateral being set-off against the relevant financial obligations. However, these only include obligations which are secured or otherwise covered by the financial collateral arrangement, and so it would seem that the surplus is not available to set off against other, unsecured, obligations, but must be accounted for to the collateral giver (Financial Collateral Arrangements (No.2) Regulations 2003 (SI 2003/3226) reg.18(2)(a)). See para.6–50, below.

[207] This is disputed by some scholars, who maintain that there is no numerus clauses of security interests. This is true in the sense that English law does not formally limit the permissible categories of security interest, but the four categories designated appear to cover every case, and the critics have

Pledge[209]

(1) Nature of pledge

1–47 The pledge, the oldest security device, is the actual or constructive delivery of possession of the asset to the creditor by way of security. As possessor the pledgee enjoys a "special property"[210] or limited legal interest in the asset, but ownership remains with the pledgor. The pledgee's interest goes beyond a mere right to detain the asset. It encompasses the right to use the asset at his own risk so long as this will not impair it; to sell his interest as pledgee or assign it by way of gift; to deliver the asset to another for safekeeping; to sub-pledge the asset on the same conditions as he holds it and for a debt no greater than his own; and to sell the asset in the event of default in payment by the pledgor.[211]

(2) Assets susceptible to pledge

1–48 Since a pledge depends on possession, an asset is not pledgeable unless it is reducible to possession. It may still be theoretically possible to have a pledge of land,[212] but such a security has not been encountered for centuries. In practice, pledges are confined to goods and to documentary intangibles, that is, documents embodying title to goods, money or securities such that the right to these assets is vested in the holder of the document for the time being and can be transferred by delivery of the document with any necessary indorsement. Put another way, the obligor's delivery or payment obligation is owed not to the original obligee as such but to whoever is the holder of the document and presents it for delivery or payment. Documentary intangibles are thus to be distinguished from pure intangibles, where the entitlement may be evidenced in or recorded in a document but it is not a document which represents the right.

What constitutes a documentary intangible has never been exhaustively determined in English law; indeed, the class is not closed, for it is liable to expansion through mercantile usage. We can say with confidence that a pledge

---

not been able to identify any new kind of interest. The proposition in the text, advanced in successive editions of this work, receives support from the judgment of Millett L.J. (as he then was) in *Re Cosslett (Contractors) Ltd* [1998] Ch. 495 at 508. cf. the view of Briggs J. that "there may be rare cases in which security rights fall wholly outside the recognised categories of lien, pledge, mortgage or charge, and into a residual, purely contractual, category sometimes categorised as turning the grantor's property into a form of 'flawed asset'": *In The Matter Of Lehman Brothers International (Europe) (In Administration)* [2012] EWHC 2997 (Ch) at [47]. However, it is not clear that the judge had in mind that such a "flawed asset" would be a security interest as defined in this chapter, since he refers to it as a "purely contractual" category of security right.

[208] See para.1–74, below.

[209] See generally N. Palmer, *Bailment,* 3rd edn (London: Sweet & Maxwell, 2009), Ch.22; Beale, Bridge, Gullifer and Lomnicka, *The Law of Security and Title-Based Financing* (2012), paras 5.01 et seq.

[210] *Donald v Suckling* (1866) L.R. 1 Q.B. 585, where the nature of the pledge is exhaustively examined.

[211] See *Donald v Suckling* (1866) L.R. 1 Q.B. 585 and authorities there cited; *The Odessa* [1916] A.C. 145 at 158–159; and below. The pledgee is not entitled to foreclosure, for he lacks the ownership which this remedy makes absolute (*Carter v Wake* (1877) 4 Ch.D. 605).

[212] The pledge was the earliest form of security over land known to English law. See A.W.B. Simpson, *A History of the Land Law,* 2nd edn (Oxford: Clarendon Press, 1986), p.141.

may be taken of bills of lading and other documents of title to goods,[213] and of negotiable instruments[214] and negotiable securities,[215] but that it is not possible to pledge ordinary written contracts such as building contracts or hire-purchase agreements, the production of which is not a condition of the obligor's duty of payment or other performance. Between these are documents and commercial papers which are not negotiable in the ordinary sense but are commonly deposited with banks by way of security. Examples are non-negotiable transport documents, non-negotiable instruments, certificates relating to registered shares and debentures, and insurance policies. Some of these are normally required to be produced before the obligor will perform and to this extent they differ from ordinary written contracts. However, their possession does not of itself confer rights against the obligor and there is therefore little doubt that they too are non-pledgeable,[216] but they deserve somewhat closer examination:

Non-negotiable transport documents   A document of title to goods, such as a   **1–49**
bill of lading, embodies an undertaking by the carrier to surrender the goods to whoever is the holder of the document and presents it at the destination. Delays in the arrival of bills of lading have led increasingly to the use of non-negotiable transport documents, such as sea waybills, which constitute a receipt by the carrier and evidence the terms of the contract of carriage but do not require to be produced by the consignee in order to obtain possession of the goods. Delivery of such a document to a bank by way of security does not of itself confer on the bank any right to delivery of the goods. Accordingly it is not effective to create a pledge of the goods and at most evinces an intention to create an equitable mortgage or charge. Delivery could, however, create a pledge of the document itself which would have some effect if the pledgee is named as consignee as it can call for delivery of the goods.[217]

Non-negotiable instruments   A bill of exchange marked "Not negotiable" is   **1–50**
incapable of transfer[218] and is thus non-pledgeable. By contrast a cheque crossed "Not negotiable" remains transferable and the only effect of the crossing is that a transferee acquires no better title than his transferor and thus takes subject to equities.[219] There is therefore no legal obstacle to the pledge of such a cheque. However, a cheque is not transferable (and therefore not pledgeable) if it is

---

[213] e.g. warehouse and dock warrants or receipts which by statute or custom are negotiable.

[214] The term "negotiable instrument" is here used in its broad sense to denote an instrument capable of transfer by delivery and indorsement, whether or not it is of a kind such that a transferee is capable of taking as a holder in due course free from equities. Among such instruments are bills of exchange, cheques, promissory notes and Treasury bills.

[215] Including bearer shares, share warrants, bearer bonds and debentures and negotiable certificates of deposit.

[216] It should be pointed out that in all the cases discussed the pieces of paper themselves can be pledged, but that they have little value since entitlement to the piece of paper does not entail entitlement to the underlying contractual rights. Such pieces of paper can also be the subject of a lien, which is, perhaps, more likely to occur.

[217] For further discussion of how the "pledge" can be protected where it is not named as consignee, see Beale, Bridge, Gullifer and Lomnicka, *The Law of Security and Title-Based Financing* (2012), para.5.40.

[218] Bills of Exchange Act 1882 s.8(1).

[219] Bills of Exchange Act 1882 s.81.

crossed and marked "not transferable".[220] A cheque crossed and bearing the words "account payee" or "a/c payee", either with or without the word "only", was formerly transferable but this is no longer the case,[221] so that a cheque so crossed is no longer capable of being pledged.

1–51 **Share and debenture certificates** Whilst share warrants and bearer shares and debentures, being transferable by delivery, are clearly capable of being pledged, it would seem that English law does not recognise a pledge of registered securities.[222] The modern trend towards dematerialisation of securities or the issue and immobilisation of global notes[223] has greatly reduced the significance of investment securities as pledgeable assets. However, it should be noted that in international finance the term "pledge" is often used as a generic term for the grant of security and thus as encompassing intangibles.[224] The analysis in this chapter is based on the English law concept of pledge as delivery of possession by way of security.

1–52 **Insurance policies** Certain types of insurance policy, such as endowment policies, are commonly deposited by way of security. Nevertheless they are not pledgeable, since whilst their production may be called for as a condition of payment their possession does not of itself confer rights against the insurer.[225]

Contractual lien

1–53 Whilst a possessory lien is generally described as a right conferred by law to detain goods until money owed to the detainee has been paid, a possessory lien may also be created by contract. It differs from a pledge in that the goods are deposited not for the purpose of security but for some other purpose, e.g. custody or repair. The addition of a contractual power of sale might convert a contractual lien into a pledge,[226] but this is likely to make little practical difference and is rarely argued in English cases.[227] It would be more significant were such a lien to

---

[220] Bills of Exchange Act 1882 s.8(1).

[221] Bills of Exchange Act 1882 s.81A.

[222] Even where the delivery of the certificate to the creditor is accompanied by a completed or blank transfer the interest of the transferee is purely equitable until the transfer has been registered, *Harrold v Plenty* [1901] 2 Ch. 314; *Re Lin Securities Pte* [1988] 1 S.L.R. 340, 350; *Re City Securities Pte* [1990] 1 S.L.R. 468, 474.

[223] Discussed in Ch.6, below.

[224] The word "lien" is also similarly used, resulting in a recharacterisation of an "extended lien" as a floating charge in *In The Matter Of Lehman Brothers International (Europe) (In Administration)* [2012] EWHC 2997 (Ch).

[225] Again, the position is otherwise in the US. See Gilmore, *Security Interests in Personal Property* (1999), §1.3.

[226] N.S.W.R. 1229, although this might be said to depend upon the extreme width of the power of sale in that case; *Osborne Computer Corp Pty Ltd v Airroad Distribution Pty Ltd* (1995)17 A.C.S.R. 614; cf. *Re Rick Cobby Haulage Pty Ltd (In Liquidation); Jackson v Esanda Finance Corp Ltd* (1992) 7 A.C.S.R. 456 Sup Ct SA.

[227] For example, the following cases involved a contractual lien with a right of sale, although in none of the cases had the right of sale been exercised: *London Flight Centre (Stansted) Ltd v Osprey Aviation Ltd* [2002] B.P.I.R. 1115; *Re Hamlet International Plc (In Administration)* [1999] 2 B.C.L.C. 506 CA; *Chellaram & Sons (London) Ltd v Butlers Warehousing & Distribution Ltd* [1978] 2 Lloyd's Rep. 412; *Jarl Tra AB v Convoys Ltd* [2003] 2 Lloyd's Rep. 459.

be recharacterised as a charge, but the courts so far seem unwilling to do so.[228] However, in a case where the word "lien" was used in relation to intangible property, probably reflecting market practice, the security interest was recharacterised as a charge.[229]

Mortgage

A mortgage is a transfer of ownership of the asset (or of any lesser interest held   **1–54**
by the transferor) by way of security upon the express or implied condition that ownership will be re-transferred to the debtor on discharge of his obligation. A mortgage thus involves the acquisition of an existing interest, not the creation of a new one, a fact which distinguishes it from an equitable charge. It does not require the delivery of possession so that any kind of asset, tangible or intangible, is capable of being mortgaged. Since a mortgage constitutes a form of appropriation of the asset to the discharge of the debt it encompasses a charge.[230] A mortgage may be legal or equitable.[231]

Mortgages of intangibles raise distinct considerations in the variety of forms they may take. A mortgage of almost any kind of intangible may be effected by assignment[232] or novation[233]; and in the case of documentary intangibles, a further option is negotiation by delivery with any necessary indorsement.[234] These are examined in Ch.3, below in the particular context of security over receivables.[235]

It is not clear whether a mortgage can be granted to a creditor over his own obligation, and this may be one of the situations in which the distinction between a mortgage and a charge is of practical significance.[236]

Charge

A good description of the nature of a charge is to be found in the judgment of   **1–55**
Atkin L.J. in *National Provincial and Union Bank of England v Charnley*[237]:

---

[228] *Great Eastern Railway Co v Lord's Trustee* [1909] A.C. 109; *Re Hamlet International Plc (In Administration)*[2000] B.C.C. 602; [1999] 2 B.C.L.C. 506; *Online Catering Ltd v Acton* [2010] EWCA Civ 58; *Waitomo Wools (NZ) Ltd v Nelsons (NZ) Ltd* [1974] 1 N.Z.L.R. 484 CA, Wellington; *Re Cosslett (Contractors) Ltd* [1998] Ch. 495 CA; *Young v Matthew Hall Mechanical & Electrical Engineers Pty Ltd* (1988) 13 A.C.L.R. 399 SC Western Aust; *Seka Pty Ltd (In provisional liquidation) v Fabric Dyeworks (Aust) Pty Ltd* (1991) 4 A.C.S.R. 455 Queensland District Registry. For further discussion see Beale, Bridge, Gullifer and Lomnicka, *The Law of Security and Title-Based Financing* (2012), para.5.83.
[229] *In The Matter Of Lehman Brothers International (Europe) (In Administration)* [2012] EWHC 2997 (Ch) at [34]–[46].
[230] See para.1–56, below.
[231] See paras 1–12, 1–13, above and para.2–04, below.
[232] See para.3–03, below.
[233] See para.3–03, below.
[234] See para.1–13, above.
[235] See also discussion in paras 6–38 et seq., below in relation to creation of mortgages over securities and cash in bank accounts.
[236] See para.1–44, above; and, for a discussion of such "charge-backs", para.3–12, below.
[237] *National Provincial and Union Bank of England v Charnley* [1924] K.B. 431 at 449.

"The first question that arises is whether or not this document does create a mortgage or charge, and to determine that it is necessary to form an idea of what is meant by a 'charge.' It is not necessary to give a formal definition of a charge, but I think there can be no doubt that where in a transaction for value both parties evince an intention that property, existing or future, shall be made available as security for the payment of a debt, and that the creditor shall have a present right to have it made available, there is a charge, even though the present legal right which is contemplated can only be enforced at some future date, and though the creditor gets no legal right of property, either absolute or special, or any legal right to possession, but only gets a right to have the security made available by an order of the Court. If those conditions exist I think there is a charge. If, on the other hand, the parties do not intend that there should be a present right to have the security made available, but only that there should be a right in the future by agreement, such as a licence, to seize the goods, there will be no charge."

Thus a charge (also sometimes termed hypothecation) does not depend on either the delivery of possession or the transfer of ownership, but represents an agreement between creditor and debtor by which a particular asset or class of assets is appropriated to the satisfaction of the debt, so that the creditor is entitled to look to the asset and its proceeds to discharge the indebtedness, in priority to the claims of unsecured creditors and junior incumbrancers. The charge does not transfer ownership to the creditor[238]; it is merely an incumbrance, a weight hanging on the asset which travels with it into the hands of third parties other than a bona fide purchaser of the legal title for value and without notice. Thus in contrast to a mortgage, an equitable charge entails the creation of a new interest in the property of the debtor, so that while a mortgagee acquires a right in re sua by virtue of the transfer to him the interest of a chargee is a right in re aliena.[239] A mere contractual right to take or retain possession, without a right of appropriation, does not constitute a charge.[240] Apart from the special case of the consensual maritime liens such as bottomry bonds and respondentia, which have their roots in Admiralty law, the charge is the creature of equity; there is no such thing as a legal charge, except as provided by statute. Land is a special case, by virtue of the Law of Property Act 1925. In the first place, the Act provides,

---

[238] *Carreras Rothmans Ltd v Freeman Mathews Treasure* [1985] Ch. 207, 227. In consequence it cannot be created by novation. Moreover, the chargee, unlike a mortgagee, has no right to obtain foreclosure, nor can he avail itself of the self-help remedies of sale or appointment of a receiver, though he may apply to the court for one of these remedies or alternatively, in the case of a charge on a debt, for an order directing the chargor to execute an assignment in his favour (*Burlinson v Hall* (1884) 11 Q.B.D. 347, per Day J. at 350). Many documents purporting to create a charge in fact include the right to take such self-help remedies or to call for an assignment. This may mean that the interest created should properly be characterised as an equitable mortgage, see J. Armour and A. Walters, "Funding Liquidation: a functional view" (2006) 122 L.Q.R. 295, 303; Beale, Bridge, Gullifer and Lomnicka, *The Law of Security and Title-Based Financing* (2012) para.6.58.

[239] It has been argued that the decision of the House of Lords in *Buchler v Talbot* [2004] UKHL 9; [2004] 2 A.C. 298 ignores this distinction; see R. Mokal, "Liquidation Expenses and Floating Charges—The Separate Funds Fallacy" [2004] L.M.C.L.Q. 38, in that the House of Lords say that charged assets "belong" to the chargeholder and are not part of the "assets of the company". This decision was essentially one of statutory interpretation, concerning some slightly unclear sections of the Insolvency Act 1986 and the position of secured creditors in liquidation, not before (see Gullifer, "The Reforms of the Enterprise Act 2002 and the Floating Charge as a Security Device" (2008) 46 C.B.L.J. 399) and the ratio has now been statutorily overruled. It is thus submitted that the decision does not throw doubt on the basic distinction discussed in the text.

[240] *Re Cosslett (Contractors) Ltd* [1998] Ch. 495, per Millett L.J. at 507–508.

somewhat confusingly, for a charge by way of legal mortgage.[241] Secondly, a mortgage of land is by demise for a term of years absolute (i.e. a lease) or by legal charge, not by assignment.[242]

Whilst a mere charge does not transfer ownership, either at law or in equity, the agreement to appropriate the asset to discharge the debt may be reinforced by an agreement to give a mortgage, which equity treats as itself a mortgage. In such a case the mortgage (which itself entitles the creditor to appropriate the asset in satisfaction of the debt) encompasses the charge. Hence the saying that "every charge is not an equitable mortgage, though every equitable mortgage is a charge".[243] In other words, a mortgage is a right of appropriation (i.e. a charge) plus a transfer of ownership, at law or in equity, as security for payment. Since a mortgage is a broader security and includes a charge it is often referred to as a charge, and this is unobjectionable so long as it is borne in mind that the converse is not true. An equitable charge which is neither created as an incident of a mortgage nor accompanied by an agreement for a mortgage is a mere charge and does not operate to transfer ownership to the creditor either at law or in equity.[244] Whether a security is a mere charge or a charge with a superadded agreement for a mortgage depends on the intention of the parties.[245]

1–56

It has to be said that courts and writers have not been consistent in their use of terminology. The terms "charge" and "mortgage" have often been treated as interchangeable or used in combination.[246] This is particularly true in relation to security over a debt or fund. Thus it has been said that a charge on a fund operates as a partial assignment[247] and that a direction by a debtor to a person holding a fund on his behalf to pay a sum from the fund to the creditor amounts to "an

---

[241] Law of Property Act 1925 ss.86(1), 87(1).

[242] Law of Property Act 1925 s.86(1), (2). A mortgage by demise of registered land is in effect obsolete and is no longer possible in relation to registered land (Land Registration Act 2002 s.23(1)(a)).

[243] *Shea v Moore* [1894] I.R.158, per Walker L.C. at 18.

[244] In consequence the chargee is not entitled to possession or foreclosure, merely to an order for sale or the appointment of a receiver, with an alternative right to sell or appoint a receiver out of court where the charge is by deed (Law of Property Act 1925 ss.101(1), 205(1)(xvi)). See fn.238, above. For the position of a debenture holder under a debenture creating a floating charge see paras 4–06 et seq., below.

[245] This can have practical effects, see *Re ELS Ltd* [1995] Ch. 11 in relation to distress for rates. However, significant practical effects of the distinction are few, see Beale, Bridge, Gullifer and Lomnicka, *The Law of Security and Title-Based Financing* (2012), para.6.67.

[246] This is not helped by the fact that s.861(5) of the Companies Act 2006 provides that, in that chapter of the Act, "charge" includes a mortgage and s.205(xvi) provides that "mortgage" includes a charge. Examples of cases where the terms have been used interchangeably in the same judgment are *In Re Richardson* (1885) 30 Ch. D. 396; *In Re Regent's Canal Ironworks Co, Ex p.Grissell* (1876) L.R. 3 Ch. D. 411; *In Re Yorkshire Woolcombers Association Ltd* [1903] 2 Ch. 284, 293 and 298; *Re Crompton & Co Ltd* [1914] 1 Ch. 954, 967; *London County and Westminster Bank Ltd v Tompkins* [1918] 1 K.B. 515 at 528–529 CA.

[247] *Colonial Mutual General Insurance Co Ltd v ANZ Bank Group (New Zealand)* [1995] 1 W.L.R. 1140 at 1144; citing *Durham Bros v Robertson* [1898] 1 Q.B. 765, where, however, the charge was accompanied by an assignment. The crystallisation of a floating charge is often described as an assignment, see *Biggerstaff v Rowatt's Wharf Ltd* [1896] 2 Ch. 93, 106 CA, per Kay L.J.; *Evans v Rival Granite Quarries Ltd* [1910] 2 K.B. 979, 1000 CA, per Buckley L.J.; *NW Robbie & Co Ltd v Witney Warehouse Co Ltd* [1963] 1 W.L.R. 1324, 1337 CA; *Rother Iron Works Ltd v Canterbury Precision Engineers Ltd* [1974] Q.B. 1, 5 CA; *Business Computers Ltd v Anglo-African Leasing Ltd* [1977] 2 All E.R. 741, 745; *Supercool Refrigeration and Air Conditioning v Hoverd Industries Ltd* [1994] 3 N.Z.L.R. 300, 321 High Court; *Re ELS Ltd* [1995] Ch. 11, 17.

equitable assignment by way of charge".[248] The explanation for this rather loose use of language lies in the fact that in contrast to charges on tangibles, under which the creditor looks to the proceeds of the charged asset, a charge on a debt or fund is enforced by collecting payment out of the fund from the fund holder in the same way as under a partial assignment, and in construing the statutory provisions governing the assignment of choses in action[249] the courts focused on the question whether the assignment was to be considered absolute or "by way of charge only," a phrase taken to include partial assignment. Certainly in practical terms the difference between a partial assignment by C to A of a debt owed to C by D and a charge of the debt by C to A is of little significance, since in both cases D is entitled to make payment to A of the sum assigned or charged, in neither case can D safely pay C after notice of A's rights, and in neither case can D be compelled to pay A except in proceedings to which C is a party.

As discussed above, a charge can be granted to the creditor over his own obligation.[250]

The trust not an independent security device

1-57   The pledge, the contractual lien, the mortgage and the charge encompass all the forms of consensual security known to English law. The trust, if created for the purpose of securing an obligation, is not an independent security device, merely a form of equitable mortgage, which may be effected either by the debtor declaring himself to be a trustee of the asset for the creditor or by his transferring the asset to a trustee to hold it on trust for the creditor.[251]

Attornment not an independent security device

1-58   We have seen that in the case of goods and documentary intangibles[252] a pledge may be created by the delivery of actual or constructive possession. A common form of constructive possession is by attornment, where the debtor or a third party agrees to hold the goods or documents for the creditor instead of the debtor.[253] Attornment in relation to goods or documentary intangibles is therefore simply a mode of constructive delivery, not a distinct form of security interest, and thus simultaneously creates and perfects a pledge.

The cases also indicate that where a third party holds a fund, whether of money or of securities, on behalf of the debtor, the third party can attorn to the creditor by agreeing to hold the fund for him instead of for the debtor.[254] But there are important differences between an attornment in respect of goods or documents and an attornment in respect of a fund. Goods and documents are

---

[248] *Rodick v Gandall* (1851, 1852) 1 De G. M. & G. 763, 777–778; *Walter & Sullivan Ltd v J. Murphy & Sons Ltd* [1955] 2 Q.B. 584, per Parker L.J. at 588.

[249] Law of Property Act 1925 s.136, see para.3–14, below.

[250] See paras 1–12 and 1–13, above and para.3–12, below.

[251] For examples of where a trust has been characterised as a security interest, see *Re ILG Travel Ltd (In Administration)* [1995] 2 B.C.L.C. 128; and *Obaray v Gateway (London) Ltd* [2004] 1 B.C.L.C. 555.

[252] See para.1–48, above.

[253] *Dublin City v Doherty* [1914] A.C. 823.

[254] See para.3–32, below.

tangibles and are therefore susceptible to pledge, but this requires actual or constructive delivery; mere agreement is not sufficient. Attornment in respect of a fund presupposes that the fund remains the property of the debtor and is therefore consistent only with a charge, not a mortgage. The creation of the charge is not, however, brought about by the attornment but stems from the agreement between the debtor and the creditor, which suffices without more. Accordingly attornment in respect of a fund constitutes neither a distinct form of security interest nor a mode of attachment of a charge; its sole function is to give the chargee control of the fund, in that the fund holder will act only on the chargee's instructions and the chargee has the right to appropriate the fund to satisfaction of the debt due to him. The requirement of perfection under the US Uniform Commercial Code can be satisfied by control, namely an undertaking by the fund holder to comply with instructions by the secured party (in other words, what we would call an attornment); for example, in relation to security interests in investment securities held with a securities intermediary,[255] commodity contracts held with a commodity intermediary,[256] and even deposit accounts.[257] In this country, control is now relevant in that one requirement for a security financial collateral arrangement[258] is that the collateral is in the possession or control of the collateral taker.[259] However, the term "control" means something very different from that under the UCC: the latter means "positive control" while it appears that "negative control" is required under the FCARs.[260]

6. THE PERMISSIBLE OBJECTS OF SECURITY

We have previously seen that a pledge cannot be taken over pure intangibles.[261] **1–59**
Subject to this, a security interest may in principle be taken over any kind of property or class of property, tangible or intangible, present or future,[262] including land, goods, negotiable and non-negotiable instruments, documents of title, securities (whether held directly from the issuer or through a securities account with an intermediary),[263] intellectual property rights of various kinds, policies of insurance, transferable licences and quotas, bank deposits and letters

---

[255] Uniform Commercial Code §§ 8–106, 9–106(a), 9–314.

[256] Uniform Commercial Code §§ 9–106(b).

[257] Uniform Commercial Code §§ 9–104, 9–314. This probably goes beyond the purview of attornment in English law, where the better view is that it is available only in respect of a fund, not a mere debt, despite the controversial decision in *Shamia v Joory* [1954] 1 Q.B. 448, a decision not followed by the Queensland Supreme Court in *Rothwells Ltd v Nommack* (1988) 13 A.C.S.R. 421, which preferred the view expressed in R. Goff and G. Jones, *Law of Restitution* (London: Sweet & Maxwell, 2006), para.28-003, that there cannot be an attornment to a mere debt. See to the same effect R. Goode, "The Right to Trace and its Impact in Commercial Transactions-I" (1976) 92 L.Q.R. 360 at 387–388. For a contrary view see Oditah, "The Judicial Nature of a Lien on Sub-Freights" [1989] L.M.C.L.Q. 191.

[258] Under the Financial Collateral Arrangements (No.2) Regulations 2003 (SI 2003/3226) (FCARs).

[259] See paras 6–32 et seq., below. The term "financial collateral" covers cash, securities and credit claims.

[260] See paras 6–35 et seq., below.

[261] That is, intangibles not embodied in a negotiable document of title, instrument or security.

[262] Though in the case of future property the security interest is nascent and cannot attach until the property has been acquired. See below.

[263] See Ch.6, below.

of credit, drawing rights under facility agreements with banks, subscription agreements with underwriters, rights under construction contracts, transferable membership rights, carbon trading allowances[264] and indeed anything which is identifiable[265] and transferable, whether in gross or as appurtenant to land or other property.[266] Moreover, security interests may themselves be given in security, so that a pledgee may grant a sub-pledge, a chargee may grant a sub-charge and a mortgagee a sub-mortgage or a charge.[267]

As we have seen, the focus has shifted sharply from tangibles to intangibles as the subject matter of security in commercial and financial transactions. There are, however, certain categories of property which, by reason of their personal nature, considerations of public policy or a contractual prohibition against assignment, are incapable of transfer, though this will not preclude an assignment of the income or proceeds received by the assignor.[268] Among the types of property not capable of being given in security are: contract rights which are made non-assignable by the terms of the contract[269] or by rules incorporated into the contract; property and rights which are made non-assignable by statute, such as future property under a bill of sale,[270] occupational pension rights,[271] social security benefits,[272] various categories of statutory licence, and the rights of a participating charity in a common investment scheme which makes no provision for assignment,[273] and rights the assignment of which is contrary to public policy, such as an assignment which would deprive the debtor and his family of all means of support,[274] an assignment of the salary of a public officer,[275] and an assignment of a bare right of litigation.[276] There are also rights which can be assigned in equity but not at law because they are recorded in a register and are transferable at law only by novation, that is, substitution of the creditor for the debtor. These include registered securities[277] and ship and aircraft mortgages.[278] Finally, there are certain categories of mortgage which cannot be effected without judicial or administrative approval. For example, land held by a charity, other than an exempt charity, may not be mortgaged without an order of the court or the Charity Commissioners.[279]

---

[264] These were accepted as "property" in recent cases, see *Armstrong DLW GmbH v Winnington Networks Ltd* [2012] EWHC 10 (Ch); and *Deutsche Bank AG v Total Global Steel Ltd* [2012] EWHC 1201 (Comm).

[265] See paras 2–05 et seq., below.

[266] *Swift Dairywise Farms Ltd* [2001] 1 B.C.L.C. 672 (agreement for transfer of milk quota by way of security and retransfer on redemption). As to legal impediments to assignment, see below.

[267] See para.1–74, below.

[268] See para.3–39, below.

[269] See paras 3–38 et seq., below.

[270] Bills of Sale Act 1878 (Amendment) Act 1882 s.5.

[271] Pensions Act 1995 s.91.

[272] Social Security Administration Act 1992 s.187.

[273] Charities Act 2011 s.103(1)(a).

[274] *King v Michael Faraday & Partners* [1939] 2 K.B. 753; *Horwood v Millar's Timber & Trading Co Ltd* [1917] 1 K.B. 305.

[275] *Palmer v Bate* (1821) 2 B. & B. 673.

[276] *Trendtex Trading Corp v Credit Suisse* [1982] A.C. 679. See para.3–38, below.

[277] See paras 6–38, 6–41, below.

[278] See para.1–13, above and para.2–32, below.

[279] Charities Act 2011 s.124(1).

Money, in the sense of a claim on a bank as opposed to notes and coin, may be given in security in two different ways. One way is by assignment of the claim, as where a customer charges his bank deposit account to secure an advance from a third party.[280] The other is by novation, that is, by transfer of funds to the creditor or a third party by way of a special-purpose payment, to be held as a segregated fund and used only to discharge the debt due to the creditor, any balance being returnable to the debtor, whose interest is thus a proprietary interest in the shape of an equity of redemption.[281]

7.   ACCRETIONS TO THE SECURITY

In principle, accretions to the asset given in security, such as fixtures, accessions and improvements, enure for the benefit of the secured creditor. It is a separate question whether the income from intangibles, such as interest and dividends, forms part of the security or belongs to the debtor.[282]

1–60

8.   DERIVATIVE SECURITY INTERESTS

A security interest may be derivative either because it is in an asset derived from other assets as their product or proceeds or because it is a sub-security interest carved out of a larger interest held by a secured creditor of higher degree, as in the case of a sub-mortgage or sub-pledge.

1–61

Security in derivative assets

Security in an asset and its product

We have seen that a retention of title to goods which is expressed to carry through to a new product formed by the commingling of those goods with others will almost invariably be treated as creating a mortgage or charge.[283] Security in a product may also arise as a matter of law from the fact that goods over which a security interest has been taken become commingled with the goods of others.[284] Where goods of a similar kind are mixed together, so as to form a divisible mixture, the secured creditor's interest will extend over the whole bulk (if all the goods involved belong to the debtor) or to the debtor's co-ownership share in the

1–62

---

[280] Or even from the bank itself. As to such charge-backs, see para.3–12, below. See also para.6–44, below.

[281] See para.1–40, above.

[282] See para.1–61, below.

[283] See para.1–35, above. It is therefore likely to be void for non-registration.

[284] The subject is complex, involving consideration of principles of *confusio, commixtio* and *specificatio* as well as equitable rules governing tracing into mixed substitutions. For analyses, see P. Birks, *"Mixtures" in Interests in Goods,* N. Palmer and E. McKendrick (eds) (London: LLP Professional Publishing, 1998); and L. Smith, *The Law of Tracing* (Oxford: Clarendon Press, 1997), Ch.2; Palmer, *Bailment* (2009) Ch.8; M. Smith and N. Leslie, *The Law of Assignment,* 2nd edn (Oxford: OUP, 2013), Ch.28.

bulk, if some of the goods are owned by others.[285] Where goods subject to a security interest are mixed with other goods to form a new product, the position is more complicated. A new product is a "new thing" and so prima facie belongs to the maker, according to the Roman law doctrine of *specification*; this, however, is subject to two exceptions. The first is where the parties have agreed a different result. Thus, where goods subject to a fixed charge are used, with the chargee's consent, to make a new product, the parties are likely to agree expressly or impliedly that the new product shall be subject to the charge. If the goods are subject to a floating charge, then the chargor is authorised to dispose of them: this has been done by the creation of the new product, which will therefore, in theory, be free from the floating charge.[286] The second exception is where the creation of the new thing is unauthorised by the secured party, that is, wrongful. In the analogous situation where A's goods are mixed by B with B's goods to make a new thing without A's authority, English law gives A an interest in the new thing.[287] Therefore, where goods are subject to a fixed charge, and the chargor uses them to make a new thing without authority, the chargee will have a security interest in the product in the proportion which the value of the original goods bears to the value of the product.

Security in an asset and in its proceeds[288]

1–63 Security in an asset will almost invariably carry through to the proceeds of an unauthorised disposition by the debtor or a third party[289] and will also extend to proceeds of an authorised disposition where it is effected on behalf of the creditor rather than for the debtor's own account.[290] But where the debtor sells subject to the security interest the creditor has no claim to the proceeds, for the subject of the sale is the debtor's equity of redemption, not any asset of the creditor.[291]

---

[285] It is clear that mixed goods of the same type are co-owned by the owners of the goods, *Indian Oil Corp v Greenstone Shipping SA* [1988] Q.B. 345, and since a co-ownership share is identifiable, there is no reason why the security interest should not continue to apply. A similar analysis would apply to securities which are placed in an omnibus account, see paras 6–17 et seq., below.

[286] In fact, it is quite likely that the charge agreement will expressly provide that the product falls within the scope of the floating charge, see para.1–69, below.

[287] *Glencore International AG v Metro Trading International Inc* [2001] 1 Lloyd's Rep. 284 at [178]. This can be seen as an example of tracing (rather than following, which is the exercise performed when goods of the same type are mixed together) see L. Smith, *The Law of Tracing* (Oxford: Clarendon Press, 1997), pp.112–115. For a view that only a personal remedy should be available, see Smith and Leslie, *The Law of Assignment* (2013), para.28.104.

[288] In making the changes to this section for the 5th edition, the editor has much benefited from discussions with Magda Raczynska, in the context of the examination of her doctoral thesis on "Security interests in derived assets" and with Lionel Smith.

[289] This whole statement was approved by the Court of Appeal in *Buhr v Barclays Bank Plc* [2001] EWCA Civ 1223.

[290] *Buhr v Barclays Bank Plc* [2001] EWCA Civ 1223 at [45]–[50], despite the fact that that case concerned only an unauthorised disposition. A disposition of property subject to a fixed security interest which is specifically authorised by the creditor is likely to be on behalf of the creditor, while a disposition by a floating chargee (authorised by the nature of the charge) is likely to be for the debtor's own account.

[291] See *Buhr v Barclays Bank Plc* [2001] EWCA Civ 1223 where the argument that the mortgagors were selling only their equity of redemption was rejected, the purchasers having contracted to buy the full unencumbered title. See also para.5–35, below.

Proceeds may result not only from the act of the debtor but from other events outside the debtor's control, including exercise by the creditor or another creditor of a power of sale on default.[292]

The relationship between a security interest in an asset and a security interest in its proceeds has not been fully developed in English law. Numerous issues require examination.

(1) What is the theoretical basis of the claim to proceeds of an unauthorised disposition?

Professor Lionel Smith's work on *The Law of Tracing*[293] has done much to clarify **1–64** both thinking and terminology in this complex subject. First, a distinction is drawn between following the original asset and tracing its proceeds. When an asset subject to a security interest is disposed of, the recipient may or may not take free from that security interest: this depends on the rules of priority which are discussed in Ch.5, below. If the recipient takes subject to the security interest, the secured creditor can enforce it against him. This is an example of following, since it is enforcement against the original asset. If the recipient is a bona fide purchaser who acquires legal ownership without notice of an equitable security interest, he will take free of the security interest. The proceeds received by the debtor as a result of the disposition is an entirely new asset: the original asset has, for our purposes, disappeared and the secured creditor cannot follow into it. The process which links the new asset (the proceeds) with the former asset is tracing. It is wrong to regard proceeds as the original asset in a changed form, since the original asset continues to exist, and the proceeds represent the exchange value of the asset to the parties to the transaction which produces them. It follows that there is no need to show any physical correlation between the asset the claimant lost and the asset the defendant received, merely a loss of value by the claimant and a receipt of value by the defendant. Accordingly an improper transfer of value by novation[294] is just as traceable as a transfer of value by assignment. These concepts have now been endorsed by the highest authority.[295]

Secondly, Professor Smith shows us that tracing is not itself a remedy, merely a legal technique to establish that value received by the defendant can be identified as resulting from value formerly held by the claimant. Assuming that this is demonstrated, it is then for the law to determine, according to rules of claiming, whether the claimant has a proprietary claim to what the defendant received or whether this is barred by an available defence. One view, which has been espoused by the House of Lords in *Foskett v McKeown*[296] as well as by some academics[297] is that the claimant has an automatic proprietary right to the

---

[292] See para.1–73, below.

[293] L. Smith, *The Law of Tracing* (1997).

[294] See para.3–03, below.

[295] See *Foskett v McKeown* [2001] 1 A.C. 102, per Lord Millett at 128.

[296] *Foskett v McKeown* [2001] 1 A.C. 102.

[297] G. Virgo, *The Principles of the Law of Restitution,* 2nd edn (Oxford: Oxford University Press, 2006), pp.12–14 and Ch.20; R. Grantham and C.E.F. Rickett "Property Rights as Significant Events" [2003] C.L.J. 717, 744–748. See also Lord Millett, 'Proprietary Restitution' in S. Degeling and J. Edelman (eds), *Equity in Commercial Law* (Sydney: Thomson LBC, 2005), Ch.12; and Smith and Leslie, *The Law of Assignment* (2013), Chs 28 and 29.

"new" asset as a result of the proprietary right it had in the "old asset", which was disposed of without authority, so that the claim to the new asset is a vindication of proprietary rights. Others take the view that the claim to the new asset must be a new claim, and must be justified separately. Although the claim is causally related to the proprietary interest that the claimant had in the old asset, its justification is in the unjust enrichment of the defendant, which, in these circumstances, gives rise to a proprietary remedy (here, the security interest over the proceeds).[298] An attractive middle way, espoused by Professor Smith,[299] is to accept that the interest in the new asset is a new interest, but that the reason that it is imposed is not the unjust enrichment of the defendant, but the unauthorised interference with the claimant's property.[300] Even though, where the claimant is a secured creditor, it will not be the absolute owner of the asset, the fact that it has a proprietary interest by way of mortgage or fixed charge (which, without more, has the effect that any disposition of the asset is unauthorised) means that an unauthorised disposition triggers this interest in the new asset.

Whichever view of the basis of the claim to the proceeds is taken, all agree that it is a proprietary claim. The "vindication" view, including Professor Smith's version, would mean that the secured creditor had a security interest of the same nature as before, but in a different asset,[301] arising automatically at the moment of receipt of the proceeds by the defendant. The "unjust enrichment" view would seem to require the imposition of a proprietary remedy, probably an equitable lien, that is, a non-possessory security interest imposed by the operation of law. The other practical consequence of the difference in theoretical justification discussed above is the availability of defences. On the "unjust enrichment" view, a defence of change of position would be possible, while the House of Lords in *Foskett* specifically deny that such a defence is available on the "vindication" view.[302] However, it is difficult to see when such a defence would be applicable in the current context.

---

[298] P. Birks, "Property and Unjust Enrichment: Categorical Truths" [1997] N.Z.L.R. 623; A. Burrows, *The Law of Restitution*, 3rd edn (Oxford: Oxford University Press, 2011), Ch.8. Some other forms of unjust enrichment only give rise to personal remedies.

[299] L. Smith, "Unravelling Proprietary Restitution" (2004) 40 C.B.L.J. 317, 326–331; L. Smith, "Tracing" in *Mapping the Law: Essays in Memory of Peter Birks*, A. Burrows and A. Rodger (eds), (Oxford: Oxford University Press, 2006); "Simplifying the claims to traceable proceeds" (2009) 125 L.Q.R. 328. See also R. Calnan, "Proprietary Remedies for Unjust Enrichment" in *Commercial Remedies* (eds A. Burrows and E. Peel, 2003).

[300] This in fact telescopes Professor Smith's reasoning, which starts by considering the case where the defendant is a trustee, so that the breach of the trust obligation gives rise to the imposition of a trust obligation on the new property, and then moves to consider the case where the defendant is not a trustee, which must be explained on the basis of unauthorised interference.

[301] See Lord Millett in *Foskett v McKeown* [2001] 1 A.C. 102 at 128: "He will normally be able to maintain the same claim to the substituted asset as he could have maintained to the original asset. If he held only a security interest in the original asset, he cannot claim more than a security interest in its proceeds".

[302] *Foskett v McKeown* [2001] 1 A.C. 102 at 129. Note that Smith seems to support some limited change of position defence, L. Smith, "Unravelling Proprietary Restitution" (2004) 40 Canadian Business Law Journal 317, 331.

(2) What constitutes proceeds?

1–65 The parties may themselves agree that a security interest in an asset is to carry through to its proceeds, and what constitutes proceeds is then a question of construction of the agreement. In other cases, what counts as proceeds depends on the context of the secured creditor's claim. If it is a claim to proceeds of an authorised disposition, then, again, the scope of "proceeds" subject to a security interest depends on the agreement between the parties. If it is a claim to proceeds of an unauthorised disposition, the proceeds of an asset are anything which is traceable as a direct or indirect substitute for the asset. Proceeds thus cover money, goods, or anything else received in exchange for the asset and traceable as such into the debtor's hands, as well as the traceable proceeds of proceeds. Whether something is traceable is to be determined by rules of equity which define the conditions in which property held by the defendant can be considered causally linked to property lost by the plaintiff.[303] So if an asset subject to a security interest is wrongfully sold by the debtor, who receives a cheque in payment, the cheque constitutes traceable proceeds. When the cheque is collected and the amount of the cheque is credited to the debtor's account, the resultant claim on the bank constitutes traceable proceeds.

Thus, what counts as proceeds is context specific and it is not particularly helpful or even possible to generalise. Whether assets which do not derive from a disposition by the debtor are included in the scope of the charged assets is to a large extent a question of construction of the charge document. A good example concerns the proceeds of insurance taken out by the debtor in relation to charged assets.[304] There is a considerable body of authority establishing that such proceeds will not be held to be within the scope of the charge in the absence of express or implied inclusion.[305] Where, however, the agreement includes a covenant to insure, the court may hold that this implies a grant of a charge over the proceeds of insurance to the secured creditor.[306]

Proceeds do not include income derived by the debtor from an asset (e.g. rentals, share dividends), or natural produce (e.g. milk from cows) or natural increase (e.g. progeny of livestock), for these are not given in exchange for the asset, which remains in place. Whether, in the absence of agreement to the contrary, they belong to the debtor or the creditor depends on the circumstances. Where the debtor is lawfully in possession of a tangible asset, such as land or goods, it will normally be assumed that the fruits belong to the debtor in the absence of any agreement to the contrary.[307] Income received by the debtor from an asset given in security to the creditor of which the debtor had no right to possession or had lost such right, or in respect of which he had no right to enter

---

[303] See *Foskett v McKeown* [2001] 1 A.C. 102; and, for an extended analysis, Smith, *Law of Tracing* (1997).

[304] See R. Calnan, *Taking Security: Law and Practice,* 2nd edn (London: Jordan Publishing, 2011) paras 3.153 – 3.159.

[305] *Lees v Whiteley* (1866) L.R. 2 Eq. 143, 149; *Sinnott v Bowden* [1912] 2 Ch. 414, 419; approved in *Halifax Building Society v Keighley* [1931] 2 K.B. 248, 256; and *Re CCG International Enterprises Ltd* [1993] B.C.C. 580, 586. The position of the mortgagee may be ameliorated by s.108 of the Law of Property Act 1925.

[306] *Colonial Mutual General Insurance Co Ltd v ANZ Banking Group (New Zealand) Ltd* [1995] 1 W.L.R. 1140 PC.

[307] See as to livestock *Tucker v Farm & General Investment Trust Ltd* [1966] 2 Q.B. 421.

into the transaction producing the income, belongs to the creditor—not, however, as proceeds but as the fruits of the creditor's property.[308] The same applies to income derived from proceeds of the creditor's asset resulting from the debtor's unauthorised disposition.[309] In the case of intangibles, such as bank deposits and investment securities, the same principle should apply. In relation to investment securities market usage considers it fair that dividend income and other distributions should enure for the benefit of the debtor. Since in many cases the securities account is in the name of the creditor it is customary for the agreement between debtor and creditor to provide that so long as the debtor is not in default the creditor will pass over all such benefits.[310]

(3)   Can the creditor enforce a security interest both in the asset and in its proceeds?

1–66   Suppose that C has taken a specific mortgage of D's motor car and D wrongfully sells the car to E. In the absence of any applicable exception to the nemo dat rule C can recover his vehicle from E. Alternatively he can treat his security interest as attaching to the proceeds received by D. But can he enforce security in both the car and the proceeds at the same time? No, because the remedies are inconsistent. C cannot have his cake and eat it. He must elect which right to pursue and having made his election he is bound by it.

(4)   What is C's position prior to his election?

1–67   Two alternative views have been propounded.[311] The first, advanced by the late Professor Peter Birks,[312] is that where C still has rights to the original asset he has no vested interest in the proceeds but merely a power, or equity, which crystallises only upon C's electing to take the proceeds rather than the original asset. The alternative view, put forward by Professor Lionel Smith,[313] is that C acquires a vested interest in the proceeds as soon as they come into existence but that he must elect whether to claim the original asset or the proceeds and upon electing for one remedy he loses the other.[314] The two approaches produce different results. Under the former, C's right to the proceeds is displaced if, before he has made his election, the debtor disposes of the proceeds to a bona fide purchaser for value and without notice, even if the purchaser's interest is purely

---

[308] The distinction between a claim to proceeds and a claim to fruits is admirably explained by Smith, *Law of Tracing* (1997), pp.21–24.

[309] Smith, *Law of Tracing* (1997), pp.23–24, 144.

[310] This is the case whether the arrangement is by way of security or title transfer. See, for example, International Swaps and Derivatives Association (ISDA), *Master Agreement Credit Support Annex* (1995), para.5(c); International Securities Lending Association (ISLA), *Global Master Securities Lending Agreements (GMSLA),* 2010, para.4.4; and International Capital Markets Association (ICMA), *Global Master Repurchase Agreement (GMRA)* 2011, para.5.

[311] For further analysis, see C. Davis, "Floating Rights" (2002) 61 C.L.J. 423, 447.

[312] P. Birks, *An Introduction to the Law of Restitution* (Oxford: Clarendon Press, 1989), pp.70, 92, 393; P. Birks (ed.), *Laundering and Tracing* (Oxford: Clarendon Press, 1995), pp.307–311.

[313] Smith, *The Law of Tracing* (1997), pp.356–361; 380–383. See also *Marsh v Keating* (1834) 1 Bing. (New Cases) 198; 131 E.R. 1094.

[314] It has also been argued that the claimant has the right to pursue multiple claims until one or the other is actually paid; see Smith and Leslie, *The Law of Assignment* (2013) para.31.06.

equitable, for this will override a mere equity, whereas under the latter approach C would win since his vested equitable interest is first in time. It would seem from the speech of Lord Millett in *Foskett v McKeown*[315] that the latter approach is correct:

> "A beneficiary of a trust is entitled to a continuing beneficial interest not merely in the trust property but in its traceable proceeds also, and his interest binds everyone who takes the property or its proceeds except a bona fide purchaser for value[316] without notice."[317]

The question of election does not, of course, arise where C loses title to the car by virtue of some exception to the nemo dat rule.

(5) One security interest or two?

Here it is important to make a distinction between authorised and unauthorised dispositions. Where a disposition of an asset subject to a fixed security interest is authorised (by consent of the chargee) the disposition is (usually) on behalf of the creditor. The proceeds will be held subject to a charge, but this arises by agreement between the parties. If the proceeds are, expressly or impliedly, included in the secured assets as defined in the original charge agreement (as would be the case were assets of the same kind as the original charged assets to be substituted for the original assets) and if the charge, expressly or impliedly, covers future assets, then the charge over the new assets will be the same charge as the original. Otherwise, it will be a new charge arising by, and at the time of, the agreement to dispose and will be registrable under s.859A of the Companies Act 2006 as it is "created" by the debtor. A lender taking a fixed charge should therefore ensure that any proceeds are included within the scope of the original charge.[318] If the assets disposed of are subject to a floating charge, then the disposition is likely to be for the account of the debtor, and so the proceeds will not be subject to any charge, unless they are of a type of assets which falls within the original charge agreement. So far in this discussion, disposition has meant sale or other substitution. Where receivables are collected in, the position is different, and the "proceeds" (which are just another form of the receivables) are subject to the same charge as covered the receivables.[319]

Where assets subject to a fixed charge are disposed of without authorisation,[320] the secured creditor's interest in the new asset arises automatically by operation of law.[321] Although it is a new security interest, it will not be registrable under s.859A of the Companies Act 2006 since it is not "created" by the company. However, priority may well date from the date of creation of the "new"

1–68

---

[315] *Foskett v McKeown* [2001] A.C. 102.

[316] Semble, a bona fide purchaser of the legal title; on general property principles, the purchaser of an equitable interest is postponed to the holder of a prior equitable interest. See paras 5–03 et seq., below.

[317] *Foskett v McKeown* [2001] A.C. 102 at 128.

[318] See Calnan, *Taking Security: Law and Practice* (2011), para.3.167.

[319] See R. Goode, "Charges over Book Debts: A Missed Opportunity" (1994) 110 L.Q.R. 592 at 603–605.

[320] The same applies where assets subject to a floating charge which includes a negative pledge clause are disposed of in breach of that clause.

[321] See para.1–64, above.

interest rather than the date of the original charge, so again a chargee would be well advised to include after-acquired proceeds in the scope of the original charge.

(6) What if C expressly bargains for security both over an asset and over its proceeds?

1–69   Two situations have to be considered. The first is where the security agreement, in covering both the asset and its proceeds, indicates that the security rights are to apply consecutively rather than concurrently, as where D is authorised to dispose of the asset free from C's security interest, so that this subsists in the goods until sale to E and in the proceeds thereafter. In such a case C, having authorised resale, plainly cannot trace the goods into E's hands. The second situation is where the security agreement, while containing no such authorisation, is expressed to confer on C a security interest in the proceeds concurrently with his security interest in the original asset. Such an agreement cannot of itself entitle C to cumulative remedies so as to avoid the need for him to make an election. The case is not one where the proceeds can also be picked up as original collateral,[322] for they do not fall within a separate category of collateral but are simply whatever results from disposition of the original asset.

It may also be noted that it is not possible to have a concurrent interest in a debt and its proceeds, for upon collection the debt ceases to exist.

(7) Security in an asset both as proceeds and as original collateral

1–70   One and the same asset may, however, constitute both proceeds and original collateral where it is covered by a description which is independent of its status as proceeds. For example, C takes a fixed charge over D's business equipment and book debts to secure an advance. D wrongfully sells equipment for £10,000 to E, who buys with notice of the charge. D has agreed to give E three months' credit. C can assert concurrent security rights over the equipment and the book debt resulting from the sale to E. This does not involve the assertion of mutually inconsistent rights, for C's claim to the book debt does not depend on the right to trace in equity from the equipment to its proceeds but derives from the fact that the book debts are a separate category of collateral under the security agreement.

Proceeds may also be picked up concurrently as original collateral by virtue of an after-acquired property clause in the security agreement. For example, C takes a charge over D's equipment and any equipment D may subsequently acquire. At the time the charge is given D owns a lathe which, in breach of the security agreement, he exchanges for a new lathe. C has a security interest in the new lathe both as proceeds of the original lathe and as after-acquired equipment.

(8) Relationship between security in an asset and security in its proceeds

1–71   Where the security interest in the proceeds derives from agreement, there is no necessary correspondence between that interest and the interest in the original asset; indeed, the agreement may not confer a security interest in the original

---

[322] See below.

asset at all.[323] So a creditor may take a floating charge over stock in trade but a fixed charge over proceeds, or a fixed charge over equipment—requiring the chargee's consent to a sale free from the charge—but a floating charge over the proceeds of an authorised sale. There is, however, an exception which derives from the nature of the subject matter of the charge. In the case of a charge on debts, as opposed to a security interest in tangible assets, it is not possible to have a fixed charge over a debt when the charge over the proceeds is only a floating charge.[324] This is because, if the chargor is left to collect the debts, the only way in which the chargee can assert his security interest as a fixed interest is through the proceeds, for collection extinguishes the debt, so that the original asset given in security is destroyed.[325]

Where a proprietary interest in proceeds arises by operation of law—for example, on the defendant's wrongful disposal of the claimant's asset—it will not normally be different in quantum from the interest enjoyed over the original asset, so that if the interest in the original asset was only a security interest, the interest in the proceeds will likewise be a security interest.[326] However, the character of the security interest in proceeds is dependent on the nature of the proceeds and is not necessarily the same as in the original asset. For example, if imported goods are pledged to a bank by deposit of a bill of lading which is then released to the pledgor under a trust receipt by which the pledgor agrees to hold the goods and their proceeds on trust for the bank, then if the pledgor sells the goods and receives payment into his bank account the proceeds, in the form of the pledgor's claim on his bank, are intangible and so cannot be the subject of a pledge but only of a mortgage or charge, which in this case will be equitable in nature.[327]

(9) Security interests run forward to proceeds, not backwards to the original asset

There are dicta which on a superficial reading suggest that an obligation on the debtor to apply the proceeds of his asset towards discharge of the debt, and not for any other purpose, creates an equitable charge not merely over the proceeds but over the asset itself.[328] But the dicta must be taken in context and are not, it is

1–72

---

[323] See further para.1–72, below.

[324] *Re Spectrum Plus Ltd* [2005] UKHL 41; [2005] 2 A.C. 680. See para.4–16, below.

[325] See para.4–16, below.

[326] See *Foskett v McKeown* [2001] A.C. 102, per Lord Millett at 128.

[327] Astbury J. in *Re David Allester Ltd* [1922] 2 Ch. 211 said that the pledgee's interest in the proceeds was not a charge, but rather in the nature of a trust as the pledgor had sold as agent of the pledgee. However, this reasoning clearly depended on the words of the trust receipt, whereby the pledgor undertook to account to the pledgee for the whole proceeds of sale. If the pledgor was only liable to account to the pledgee for that part of the proceeds necessary to redeem the pledge, the pledgee's interest would surely be by way of charge. Apart from this case, there seems to be a curious dearth of authority as to the metamorphosis undergone by a possessory security interest when tangible property subject to the security interest is converted into intangible property, but there can be no doubt that the erstwhile lienee or pledgee does have a security interest in the proceeds, albeit in a different form. If the position were otherwise, any right of sale given to the holder of a possessory security by agreement or custom (in the case of a lien) and by implication of law (in the case of a pledge) would be valueless.

[328] See, for example, the judgment of Browne-Wilkinson J. in *Swiss Bank Corp v Lloyds Bank Ltd* [1979] Ch. 548 at 566.

submitted, intended to lay down any such rule, which would cause great confusion. To the extent discussed above, a security interest in an asset carries forward to proceeds; a security interest in proceeds does not run backwards to the asset from which they derive. If it did, a creditor taking a charge over book debts would automatically acquire a charge over the trading stock the sale of which produced the book debts. What is necessary to create a security interest in an asset is that the asset itself, and not merely its proceeds, is appropriated to the debt.[329]

(10)   Surplus proceeds on realisation by a creditor

1–73   An important method of enforcing a security interest in the event of the debtor's default is sale of the asset given in security and application of the proceeds in discharge of the debt. Where no other creditor has a security interest in the asset, any surplus proceeds remaining after the creditor has taken what is due to him have to be handed over to the debtor and meanwhile are held on trust for him,[330] so that if the creditor becomes insolvent while the surplus is still in his hands it does not form part of his estate but belongs to the debtor. It follows that the creditor has no right to set off some other debt owed to him by the debtor against the surplus, for a money claim cannot be set off against a property claim.[331] Where the sale is by a junior incumbrancer and takes effect subject to the interest of a prior incumbrancer, the latter has no claim to the surplus proceeds, since his security interest continues in the original asset. By contrast, an incumbrancer ranking after the selling mortgagee has an interest in the surplus ahead of the debtor, and the mortgagee, if having notice of such incumbrancer's rights, is obliged to hold the surplus on trust for him, and to make it over to him.[332] Where the selling mortgagee is a junior incumbrancer and the sale is not made subject to the senior incumbrancer's interest, this then attaches to the proceeds of sale and must be satisfied from those proceeds in priority to the claim of the junior incumbrancer.[333]

---

[329] See para.1–28, above; and *Re Sikorski v Sikorski* (1979) 89 D.L.R. (3d) 411.

[330] *Talbot v Frere* [1878] 9 Ch. 568, 575–574. This is so whether the mortgagee sells under his statutory power (Law of Property Act 1925 s.105) or under the express provisions of the mortgage (*Charles v Jones* (1887) 35 Ch. D. 544; *Banner v Berridge* (1881) 18 Ch. D. 254). The mortgage instrument may, of course, make express provision for a trust of the surplus proceeds, but if it does not the mortgagee is a constructive trustee (*Banner v Berridge*, above).

[331] See para.1–40, above. The position is otherwise where the parties have agreed that the mortgagee is to be a mere debtor for the proceeds (or the set-off is against a money claim secured on property (see paras 7–66 and 7–83, below)).

[332] *Charles v Jones* (1887) 35 Ch. D. 544. It appears that where there are several mortgages ranking after that of the selling mortgagee, his duty is to hand over the entire surplus to the next in line, leaving it to him to pass over any remaining surplus to the next mortgagee, rather than the selling mortgagee having to distribute the surplus among all junior incumbrancers in order of priority. See *Fisher & Lightwood's Law of Mortgage,* 13th edn (London: Butterworths Law, 2010), para.30.47; and para.5–35, below.

[333] See Law of Property Act 1925 ss.105, 107(2).

Sub-security

The holder of a security interest may himself give that interest in security except   1–74
so far as the security agreement otherwise provides. Thus a mortgagee may grant
a sub-mortgage, a chargee a sub-charge and a pledgee a sub-pledge. In each case
what is involved is the security transfer of or charge on the security interest
coupled with an assignment of the debt secured by that interest. However, the
holder of the security interest may not grant a sub-security interest greater than
his own. So a chargee under an equitable sub-charge can give a sub-charge but
not a sub-mortgage, since he has merely an incumbrance, not ownership. On the
other hand, there is nothing to prevent a mortgagee from charging his mortgage
interest instead of granting a sub-mortgage. A pledgee cannot sub-pledge for an
amount exceeding that secured by the pledge to him.[334]

In general the law governing sub-security is reasonably clear. The main area of
difficulty in financial transaction relates to the right of the holder of a security
interest in investment securities to deal with them, whether by way of
sub-security or otherwise. This is dealt with in Ch.6, below.

9.   THE SCOPE OF SECURED OBLIGATIONS

As mentioned earlier, there must be an obligation secured by the security   1–75
interest.[335] However, a security interest can only secure an obligation owed to the
creditor[336] if the obligation falls within those specified in the security
agreement.[337] It is common for security agreements to define the secured
liabilities very widely, covering "all monies" due to the secured creditor. There
are, however, dangers in permitting such clauses to range too widely. A secured
creditor with an "all monies" clause could, in the run-up to, or even after, the
debtor's insolvency, acquire debts owed by the debtor to unsecured creditors at a
discount: if these debts were included within the security agreement it would
have the effect of turning previously unsecured debts into secured debts, which
would have a very detrimental effect on other creditors.[338] At present, the English
courts' response to widely drafted definitions of obligation is to construe them
against the debtor. Thus, in *Re Quest Cae*[339] such a clause was construed only to
apply to "dealings or transactions between the Company and the lender" and not
to "dealings and transactions between the Company and some third party in
whose shoes the lender may later happen to stand".[340] This approach has been
followed in a case concerning the interpretation of both a guarantee and the

---

[334] *Donald v Suckling* (1866) L.R. 1 Q.B. 585.

[335] See para.1–36, above.

[336] Or to anyone else, see para.1–16, above.

[337] Note that even then there may be restrictions on the extent to which the lender has priority over
other secured creditors in relation to future advances, see paras 5–10 and 5–17 et seq., below.

[338] See R. Wood, "Turning Lead into Gold: the Uncertain Alchemy of 'All Obligations' Clauses"
(2004) 41 Alta. Law Rev. 802.

[339] *Re Quest Cae* (1985) 1 B.C.C. 99389. See also *Re Clark's Refrigerated Transport Pty Ltd* [1982]
V.R. 989.

[340] *Re Quest Cae* (1985) 1 B.C.C. 99389 at 99393–99394.

charge supporting it.[341] In both these cases, the courts took the view that it would be inconsistent with the commercial nature of the transaction for the clause to be interpreted more widely.[342] However, it is not clear that this approach would be followed if very clear and unambiguous words were used,[343] and policy consideration, such as those raised but not considered in *Re Quest Cae*[344] may have to be addressed.

10.   THE NEGATIVE PLEDGE

1–76   We will now turn to a new topic, on which there has been relatively little English case law, namely the negative pledge. For further discussion of negative pledge clauses in international loan transactions and analysis of typical forms of the clause, see Professor Philip Wood's excellent six-volume work *Law and Practice of International Finance*.[345] For a detailed conceptual analysis of the negative pledge we have to turn to the works of our American colleagues, and in particular to Ch.38 of the late Professor Grant Gilmore's brilliant book *Security Interests in Personal Property*, which after many years remains the *locus classicus* for the legal treatment of security interests.

Common forms of negative pledge

(1)   Domestic transactions

1–77   The typical negative pledge clause in a domestic financing transaction is that which is to be found in the standard form of floating charge, by which the debtor company undertakes that it will not, without the prior written consent of the debenture holder, grant any subsequent security ranking in priority to or pari passu with the floating charge. Such a stipulation may also be contained in a fixed charge, though it is not strictly necessary for priority purposes, since a fixed charge has priority over subsequent interests except a bona fide purchaser for value of the legal title without notice. However, the covenant in a fixed charge tends to be more stringent, since it typically prevents the borrower from granting even subordinated security without the consent of the prior lender. Such a covenant goes beyond mere preservation of the first lender's priority; the grant of a subsequent security interest to another financier is a breach of the negative pledge clause and thus a default event attracting various rights and remedies. Whether the covenant not to incumber is restricted or absolute, in domestic transactions the traditional form of covenant does not involve any commitment by the debtor to give security to the first financier, whether on breach of the covenant not to incumber or as a condition of its relaxation.

---

[341] *Kova Establishment v Sasco Investments Ltd* [1998] 2 B.C.L.C. 83.
[342] In this the approach more recently endorsed in *Rainy Sky SA v Kookmin Bank* [2011] UKSC 50 at [21] was followed.
[343] *Rainy Sky SA v Kookmin Bank* [2011] UKSC 50
[344] *Re Quest Cae* (1985) 1 B.C.C. 99389, 99391, 99394.
[345] P. Wood, *International Loans, Bonds, Guarantees and Legal Opinions*, 2nd edn (London: Sweet & Maxwell, 2007), paras 5–008 et seq.

(2) International transactions

In international loan finance, the negative pledge is commonly taken by an **1–78** unsecured lender and is often designed to secure equality rather than priority. In such cases the objective is sometimes not to prohibit the borrower from giving security to another financier but to ensure that if the debtor does so then the prior (unsecured) lender will either have equal and rateable security over the same asset or be given security over other assets of the debtor to at least the same value. The negative pledge clause may be expressed as a purely negative covenant or as an affirmative covenant. In its negative form the covenant is that the borrower will not give security over the asset without giving equal and rateable security over that asset (or alternatively security over another asset of equal value) to the earlier financier. In the affirmative form of covenant the borrower agrees that if it gives security over an asset it will give equal and rateable security over that asset (or over another asset of equal value) to the same financier.[346] This may seem a distinction without a difference but the effect of the two formulations is not quite the same. In its purely negative form the covenant does not involve a promise by the borrower to give equal and rateable security (or security of equal value); the provision of such security is simply a condition of the borrower's licence to encumber the asset. By contrast the affirmative covenant obliges the borrower to give security to the first financier upon the occurrence of the designated contingency, i.e. the grant of security to the second financier.

Juridical nature of the negative pledge

(1) Covenant not to incumber

Is the negative pledge a mere contract an equity or a full-blooded security **1–79** interest? In attempting an answer to this question so far as English law is concerned it should be emphasised that this is necessarily speculative, there being no English case law containing any conceptual analysis of the question. It seems reasonably clear that a pure negative pledge—that is, a covenant not to incumber, with no requirement to furnish security to the first financier if security is given to another financier—cannot of itself amount to a security interest, for it does not purport to give the creditor any rights, even contingently, over the debtor's present or future assets,[347] although breach is invariably an event of default which will usually give the first financier powers to accelerate the loan and terminate the agreement.[348] In this respect, it makes no difference whether the negative pledge is given in favour of a secured or an unsecured creditor. However, where

---

[346] Such a clause can also be combined with a negative covenant not to give security, so that the affirmative clause only applies if the debtor is in breach of the negative covenant.

[347] *Pullen v Abalcheck* (1990) 20 N.S.W.L.R. 732. As to the effect of the covenant on a subsequent financier who takes with notice of it where the covenantee is an unsecured creditor, see para.1–78, above.

[348] In practice these are often combined with "cross default" clauses making an event of default on one agreement a default on all: the seriousness of the consequences of breach has a very significant deterrent effect on borrowers, see L. Gullifer and J. Payne, *Corporate Finance Law: Principles and Policy* (Oxford: Hart Publishing, 2011), p.160.

the creditor holds a floating charge, what the negative pledge does do is to limit the scope of the debtor company's dealing powers and thereby ensure the priority of the floating charge, once crystallised, over a subsequent incumbrancer in favour of a third party taking with notice of the negative pledge.[349] So in this case the negative pledge, though not a security interest in itself, firms up the security given by the floating charge, and constitutes an equity binding a third party with notice.

(2) Provision for matching security

1–80 Let us now take the case where the negative pledge clause allows the debtor to grant subsequent security provided that matching security is given to the creditor. Where this covenant is given in negative form the debtor does not undertake to furnish security to the first creditor on granting security to the second; the furnishing of security is merely a non-promissory condition of the debtor's right to incumber the asset.[350] Accordingly the first creditor is not entitled to security, even if the covenant is broken, as he has not bargained for it. The position is otherwise in the case of an affirmative covenant; the debtor undertakes that if an asset is given by way of security to a subsequent creditor security in another asset of at least equal value will be given to the first creditor. The occurrence of the stipulated event triggers the debtor's promise to give security. So the question in this case is not whether, on security being given to the second creditor, the first creditor is entitled to security—for at the very least he has a personal right to call for it—but whether he acquires a security interest without any further act on the part of the debtor. The contention by the first creditor that he automatically acquires a security interest falls at the first hurdle, for the assets prospectively offered as future security are not identifiable without an act of appropriation by the debtor after the contingency has occurred.[351] This makes it unnecessary to proceed to the second question, whether a contingent agreement for security constitutes a security in equity so as to attach automatically to an identified asset upon the occurrence of the contingency. Such a question does, however, arise where the covenant is to provide equal and rateable security in the same asset, or where the relevant assets are otherwise identified in the agreement.

(3) Provision for automatic attachment to same asset

1–81 Where the agreement provides that on the grant of security over an asset a security interest in favour of the earlier creditor shall automatically attach to that asset so as to constitute the creditor a secured creditor over the asset equally with the later incumbrancer, the problem of identifiability is removed. The grant of security to the third party fixes the asset to which the negative pledge clause is to

---

[349] See para.5–41, below.

[350] It is, of course, a question of construction whether the covenant is negative or affirmative. A covenant which appears at first sight to be negative may, when the instrument is construed as a whole, be read as importing a promise, not simply stating a condition.

[351] The law is not very demanding, however, in relation to certainty so long as it is possible to identify the assets which are to be the subject of the security interest and the problem can easily be overcome by good drafting, see J. Stone, "The Affirmative Negative Pledge" (1991) 6 J.I.B.L. 364, 368.

apply, without the need for any act of appropriation on the part of the debtor. At first sight, therefore, the creditor's rights attach to the incumbered asset by virtue of the negative pledge clause, and the only question remaining is whether those rights rank equally with those of the incumbrancer or whether the latter has priority.

However, there are a number of difficulties which are likely to result in the creditor failing to obtain an enforceable security interest, let alone one with priority over the later incumbrancer. At the time it is made, an agreement for automatic attachment of a security interest to an asset upon the debtor subsequently charging this to a third party gives the first creditor nothing at all beyond a mere contract right. It does not constitute even an inchoate security, capable of retrospective attachment later on,[352] for it is merely contingent on the occurrence of a future uncertain event.[353] The next question is whether the provision for automatic attachment has effect as a security interest at the time when the debtor gives security to the third party. There are differing views on this question, focusing on whether fresh consideration is required at the time of attachment. One view[354] is that an agreement for security takes effect automatically in equity only if the consideration is executed, by actual advance of the money. For this purpose, the money must be furnished at or after and in consideration of the security. But in the case of a purely contingent agreement for security, the security interest cannot come into existence, even in equity, until the contingency has occurred. Money advanced by the creditor prior to that date does not count as new value; on the contrary, it represents no more than an advance by an unsecured creditor who may, at some unspecified time, be able to call on the debtor for security in the future. So the mere occurrence of the contingency does not produce automatic attachment. The opposite view[355] is that the consideration given by the creditor at the time of the agreement is sufficient to support the creation of the security interest once the contingency occurs. Two of the cases relied upon by both sides of the argument[356] seem inconclusive: neither of them deal overtly with automatic attachment since in both cases the security interest was expressly executed on the occurrence of the contingency and appeared to

---

[352] See paras 2–13, 2–15, below.

[353] See para.2–09, below. The Singapore Court of Appeal approved this view in *The Asiatic Enterprises (Pte) Ltd v United Overseas Bank Ltd* [2000] 1 S.L.R. 300 at [16] although, as will be seen below, they disagreed with the view about consideration expressed in the text. The position is otherwise if the security interest is to attach on a specified future date or the expiry of a stated period or the occurrence of some other future event which is bound occur. For a view that, at least in relation to land, a negative pledge clause in this form does create an immediate security interest which is registrable as a floating charge, see G. Hill, "Negative Pledge with Provision for 'Automatic Security' on Breach: a Form of Floating Charge?" (2008) 23 J.I.B.F.L. 528. This view has some support from an obiter dictum of Lord Scott in *Smith v Bridgend County BC* [2001] UKHL 58; [2000] 1 A.C. 336 at [61]–[63].

[354] This is the view put forward in previous editions of this book, and supported by J. Maxton, "Negative Pledges and Equitable Principles" [1993] J.B.L. 458; P. Ali, *The Law of Secured Finance* (Oxford: Oxford University Press, 2002), paras 3.20–3.24; A. McKnight, "Restrictions on dealing with assets in financing documents: their role, meaning and effect" (2002) 17 J.I.B.L. 193, 203.

[355] P. Gabriel, *Legal Aspects of Syndicated Loans* (London: Butterworths, 1986), pp.86–90;. Stone, "The affirmative negative pledge" (1991) 6 J.I.B.L. 364; Beale, Bridge, Gullifer and Lomnicka, *The Law of Security and Title-Based Financing* (2012), para.8.81; T. C. Han, "Charges, Contingency and Registration" (2002) 2 J.C.L.S. 191.

[356] *Re Jackson & Bassford Ltd* [1906] 2 Ch. 467; *In Re Gregory Love & Co* [1916] 1 Ch. 203.

have been made by deed, so that consideration was irrelevant.[357] Much depends on the interpretation of dicta[358] relating to the agreement itself, which could either refer to enforcement of the agreement by the grant of security or by other routes. There is now, though, dicta from the Singapore Court of Appeal in support of the view that fresh consideration is not required,[359] but again this is not part of the ratio of the case. It is submitted that the automatic attachment of the security interest is not possible without fresh consideration. There are two possible arguments to avoid this result. One is that fresh consideration is not required if the original agreement is made by deed, since no consideration is required for the attachment of a security interest granted pursuant to a deed. However, this argument involves two difficulties: first, if the attachment of the security interest cannot be referable to the consideration provided under the original agreement, it is unlikely that it can be referable to the fact that the original agreement was made by deed. Secondly, the argument would only work in relation to assets owned by the debtor at the time of the original agreement, and not in relation to future property for which executed consideration is required.[360] The second argument is that, since the giving of security to the later incumbrancer is likely to be an event of default under the loan agreement which makes the entire amount immediately payable, it could be argued that any forbearance from demand by the creditor is sufficient fresh consideration for the attachment of the security interest.[361] However, it might be difficult to show forbearance if, as is likely to be the case, the creditor is unaware that the event of default has occurred.[362]

Even if the consideration problem can be overcome, there are other difficulties which are likely to prevent the creditor obtaining an enforceable security interest. It seems reasonably clear that any interest, if it does arise, is only created at the date when the security is given to the later incumbrancer.[363] Unless exempted by the FCARs, the interest will be registrable under s.859A of the Companies Act 2006 within 21 days of that date. However, if the provision in the clause is for automatic attachment, the creditor is unlikely to know that the contingency has

---

[357] *Re Jackson & Bassford Ltd* [1906] 2 Ch. 467, 470; *In Re Gregory Love & Co* [1916] 1 Ch. 203, 205.

[358] *Re Jackson & Bassford Ltd* [1906] 2 Ch. 467, "It seems to me that in the present case the promise—which was certainly made and, I agree, for value—was a promise to which effect could not legally be given by calling for performance at a time when, in the absence of the promise, the security would have been a fraudulent preference" (at 479); and *Re Gregory Love & Co* [1916] 1 Ch. 203, "The agreement contains no present charge, but merely a right to the plaintiffs' testator to have a charge of a certain kind on the occurrence of either of two events. And an enforcement of the agreement would result in the plaintiffs getting a floating charge—not as at the date of the agreement, but as at the date when the first of the two events happened, which cannot on the evidence be put earlier than the actual issue of the third debenture" (at 211).

[359] *The Asiatic Enterprises (Pte) Ltd v United Overseas Bank Ltd* [2000] 1 S.L.R. 300 [18]: "Where it is part of the agreement that the debtor will in certain event provide a certain security or further security, then upon the happening of that event, the debtor will be obliged to provide such security and no fresh consideration from the creditor is called for".

[360] Ali, *The Law of Secured Finance* (2002), para.3.57.

[361] Han, "Charges, Contingency and Registration" (2002) 2 J.C.L.S. 191, 199.

[362] McKnight, "Restrictions on dealing with assets in financing documents: their role, meaning and effect" (2002) 17 J.I.B.L. 193, 203.

[363] *Re Gregory Love & Co* [1916] 1 Ch. 203: in that case the charge was registered at the time of creation; cf. Hill, "Negative Pledge with Provision for 'Automatic Security' on Breach: a Form of Floating Charge?" (2008) 23 J.I.B.F.L. 528.

arisen, and therefore will not know to register the charge.[364] The creditor could, of course, monitor the register very closely to see if another charge is registered, or could monitor the operations of the debtor very closely,[365] but this is cumbersome and rather defeats the object of an automatic attachment clause. The argument that the original agreement constitutes a registrable charge is unlikely to succeed in this country.[366] Even if it were to succeed, a requirement to register the original agreement is unlikely to be welcome to those lending unsecured on the basis of a negative pledge clause.

In order to obtain priority, it would also be necessary for the creditor's interest to arise before that of the later incumbrancer. If the trigger for the attachment of the creditor's interest is the grant of a security interest to someone else, then logically the latter interest would have priority. The situation is somewhat similar to when the automatic crystallisation of a floating charge is triggered by the grant of security in breach of a negative pledge clause, and it should be possible, with appropriate drafting, for the original agreement to provide that the security interest arises immediately before that of the later incumbrancer.[367]

Finally, even if all these hurdles were overcome, there is the danger that the creditor's interest would be vulnerable as a preference if it arose within the prescribed time prior to the onset of insolvency of the company.[368] The time runs from when the interest is created, which here is the time the contingency arose, and is likely to be at a point when the debtor is in some financial difficulty. Even if the consideration given at the time of the original agreement is said to be sufficient to support the attachment of the security interest, it will not count as new value, which would prevent the interest being a preference.[369] Further, the lack of new value will mean that the security interest is likely to be set aside under s.245 of the Insolvency Act 1986 if it is, or could be characterised as, a floating charge.[370]

---

[364] The charge could be registered late, with leave of the court under s.859F, but leave will only be given subject to any charges already created, see para.2–24, below.

[365] Stone, "The affirmative negative pledge" (1991) 6 J.I.B.L. 364, 369.

[366] cf. the rather enigmatic dictum of Lord Scott in *Smith v Bridgend County BC* [2000] 1 A.C. 336 at [61], [63] to the effect that a charge arising on a contingency would be registrable as a floating charge, discussed in para.2–15, below; Hill, "Negative Pledge with Provision for 'Automatic Security' on Breach: a Form of Floating Charge?" (2008) 23 J.I.B.F.L.528. The registration provisions in Australia and Singapore are different and provide for registration of an "agreement to make a charge", so it is arguable that the original agreement would be registrable there; see Han, "Charges, Contingency and Registration" (2002) 2 J.C.L.S. 191, 208–211. This view is supported by the decision at first instance in the *Asiatic Enterprises* case, but not by the Court of Appeal decision.

[367] See, in the context of automatic crystallisation, *Re Manurewa Transport Ltd* [1971] N.Z.L.R. 909; *Fire Nymph Products Ltd v The Heating Centre Property Ltd* (1992) 7 A.C.S.R. 365. Whether this analogy would be accepted by the courts has been doubted by some writers (J. Arkins, "'OK—So You've Promised Right?' The Negative Pledge Clause and the 'Security' It Provides" 15 J.I.B.L. 198).

[368] *Re Jackson & Bassford Ltd* [1906] 2 Ch. 467, a case on what was termed fraudulent preference under the former insolvency legislation. The position under the present law is that a preference may be set aside by the court where it is given in favour of a person connected with the company in the period of two years ending with the onset of insolvency or, where given in favour of any other person, in the period of six months ending with the onset of insolvency (s.239 of the Insolvency Act 1986).

[369] T.C. Han, "The Negative Pledge as a Security Device" (1996) S.J.L.S. 415, 440. For a discussion of new value in the context of preferences, see Goode, *Principles of Corporate Insolvency Law* (2011), paras 13–83 et seq.

[370] Goode, *Principles of Corporate Insolvency Law* (2011), paras 13–112 et seq.

So the pro rata clause, insofar as it is designed to produce automatic security, is likely to fail to achieve that objective. It merely gives the creditor a contractual right to call for security on the grant of the charge to the third party and may constitute a default event triggering other remedies.

(4) Provision entitling the first creditor to call for equal and rateable security

1–82   If a stipulation for automatic creation of equal and rateable security in an asset upon its being incumbered by the debtor does not suffice to create a security interest when that event occurs, then a fortiori a provision which merely entitles the first creditor to call for equal and rateable security does not give rise to a security interest in equity. Such a provision introduces a second contingency, the demand for security by the first creditor, whose position is thus weaker than under the form of negative pledge previously described.[371] Obviously, if the debtor grants a security interest to the creditor, and either fresh consideration is given, or is not required (for example, where the interest is granted by deed and does not cover future property) then, subject to registration requirements being fulfilled, such an interest will be enforceable, although it will not have priority over the later incumbrancer.

Enforcement of the negative pledge by the unsecured creditor

1–83   Given that a negative pledge clause is not effective by itself to create a consensual security interest in favour of the original creditor, what remedies does he have against the later incumbrancer? One possibility is an injunction to restrain breach of the negative covenant but this depends for its efficacy upon the creditor becoming aware of the intended breach in time.[372] Further, although there are no reported cases, there has in the past been much discussion of the possibility of an action in tort against the later incumbrancer for inducing breach of contract or interference with contractual relations.[373] However, following the recent exposition by the House of Lords[374] of the torts of inducing breach of contract and causing loss by unlawful means, there appears to be no such tort as interference with contractual relations, and the requirements of knowledge and intention for the tort of inducing breach of contract to be established are so restrictive, it is unlikely that a successful tort action against a later incumbrancer would succeed in the absence of special circumstances.[375]

---

[371] In *Williams v Burlington Investments Ltd* (1977) 121 S.J. 424 it was argued that an agreement for the execution of a charge on demand by the creditor gave rise to an equitable security when the demand was made. The House of Lords, while not finding it necessary to rule on the point, appears to have treated the proposition with appropriate scepticism.

[372] A mandatory injunction to undo a breach already committed is unlikely to be granted. For two Australian cases on the availability of negative injunctions, see *Pullen v Abelcheck Pty Ltd* (1930) 20 N.S.W.L.R. 732; *Bond Brewing v National Australia Bank* (1990) 1 A.C.S.R. 445; D. Allen "Negative Pledge Lending" (1990) J.I.B.L. 330.

[373] Stone, "Negative Pledges and the Tort of Interference with Contractual Relations" (1991) 8 J.I.B.L. 310; Han, "The Negative Pledge as a Security Device" (1996) S.J.L.S. 415; L. Wo, "Negative pledges and their effect on a third party" (1999) 14 J.I.B.L. 360.

[374] *OBG v Allen* [2007] UKHL 21; [2008] 1 A.C. 1.

[375] See T. Matsuda and S. Thompson, "He who procures the wrong is a joint wrongdoer: tortious liability for inducing breach of contract in the context of a bond restructuring" (2012) 7 J.I.B.F.L. 442.

Can the creditor invoke any equitable real right against a subsequent incumbrancer who takes his security with notice of the negative pledge? The matter does not appear to have been the subject of any reported case in England, and in such few cases as have surfaced in the United States the courts have been divided,[376] with the cases deciding that the creditor had an equitable lien[377] on the assets concerned probably being explicable on the particular circumstances of those cases.[378] It is unlikely that an English court would decide that such a real right should be granted as a remedy, particularly as the party invoking the negative pledge cannot be put in a better position than he would have had if the covenant had not been broken. If the claimant is himself unsecured and thus has no real rights in the debtor's assets, what meaning, in property terms, is to be given to the proposition that the subsequent creditor takes his security subject to the negative pledge? Such a proposition surely has significance only where the claimant holds a floating charge and the negative pledge is used to secure priority for that charge over a subsequent incumbrance.[379]

11. THE SUBORDINATION AGREEMENT

A party to whom money is owed may accept subordination either of a security **1–84** interest he holds or of unsecured indebtedness owed to him.[380] A creditor holding security may agree to subordinate his security interest to that of a third party over whom he would otherwise have priority; an unsecured creditor may agree with a third party not to take payment from the debtor until any debts owed by the debtor to the third party have been paid. Does either of these forms of subordination constitute the grant of a security interest by the subordinated creditor to the party in whose favour the subordination is made?

Subordination of security

The holders of successive security interests are free to vary the priority of their **1–85** interests inter se without the consent of the debtor, who has no right to insist on the order in which successive mortgage debts are satisfied.[381] This does not result

---

[376] *Coast Bank v W. J. Minderhout*, 392 P. 2d. 265 (1964); *Kelly v Central Hanover Bank & Trust Co*, 11 F.Supp. 497 (1935); reversed 85 F.2d 61 (1936) (the first instance judgment in this case which rejects the imposition of an equitable lien is more generally approved, for example, see Gilmore, *Security Interests in Personal Property* (1999), pp.1006–1007).

[377] In English law terms, an equitable charge.

[378] *Commercial Co v New York NH & HHR Co* 94 Conn. 13 107; *Kaplan v Chase National Bank* 156 Misc. 471, 281 N.Y.S. 825, both referred to in P. Wood, *International Loans, Bonds, Guarantees and Legal Opinions* (2007), para.5–025.

[379] See para.5–41, below.

[380] See generally P. R. Wood, *Project Finance, Securitisations, Subordinated Debt* (London: Sweet & Maxwell, 2007), Chs 10–14; Gough, *Company Charges*, Ch.40; Beale, Bridge, Gullifer and Lomnicka, *The Law of Security and Title-Based Financing* (2012), paras 8.100 et seq.; B. MacDougall, "Subordination Agreements" (1994) 32 Osgoode Hall L.J. 225. Subordination may also be by agreement between the debtor and the junior creditor.

[381] *Cheah v Equiticorp Finance Group Ltd* [1992] 1 A.C. 472. It is advisable for the debt to be subordinated as well as the security interests, in case the security turns out to be deficient, see Wood, *Project Finance, Securitisations, Subordinated Debt* (2007), para.10–031.

in an exchange of the security interests, which could affect the ranking of the subordinated interest in relation to an intermediate security interest in favour of a third party. All that happens is that the priorities are reversed—so that if the subordinated creditor enforces his security he holds what he receives on trust for the senior creditor up to the amount due to the latter or any lower sum fixed by the subordination agreement—but that in other respects each of the two mortgagees retains exactly the same interest as he had before. No exchange of security interest is intended to result from the subordination and none is effected. It follows that if there are successive mortgages in favour of M1, M2 and M3, and M1 agrees to subordinate his security interest to M3, this does not give M3 priority over M2, for M3 is not taking over M1's mortgage in exchange for his own, merely acquiring a priority over M1.[382] Subordination differs, of course, from release of the asset to the debtor in that the subordinated interest retains its priority against interests other than that to which the subordination relates, and when the latter is discharged attaches to any surplus. Contractual subordination also differs from waiver in that the former is given for consideration whereas the latter is voluntary. Subject to this, subordination produces the same consequences as waiver in constituting an equity in favour of the senior creditor[383] which will bind an assignee from the junior creditor who takes with notice of it or without giving value.[384]

Subordination of unsecured debt[385]

1–86   A creditor who merely agrees to subordinate his unsecured claim to that of another creditor by not collecting his debt or any dividend payable in the debtor's liquidation until the senior debt has been paid does not, on the face of it,[386] give security over anything. His subordination (commonly termed a contractual subordination) is a particular form of negative covenant, i.e. a covenant not to collect the debt due to him before the senior creditor has been paid. The question is whether, if he collects payment in breach of that covenant, he holds the amount collected on trust for the senior creditor. If so, then indirectly his covenant is secured. It is thought that subordination of this kind gives the senior a purely personal contractual right to require an accounting, not a proprietary claim. The position is not analogous to, say, the assignor of a debt who collects it on behalf of the assignee and holds it on trust for the assignee,[387] for what the assignor collects belongs to the assignee, who has bought it, whereas the subordinated debt belongs to the subordinated creditor. In the case of the "turnover" subordination, where the subordinated creditor expressly agrees to account for collections, it is a question of construction whether this is a purely personal

---

[382] There appears to be no English authority on the point, but it is well-established in pre-Uniform Commercial Code decisions in the US. See, for example, *AmSouth Bank NA v J & D Financial Corp*, 679 So. 2d 695 (1996); *Shaddix v National Security Co*, 221 Ala. 268, 128 So. 20 (1930).

[383] i.e. the creditor in whose favour the subordination is given.

[384] See para.5–57, below.

[385] For a description of the different types of subordination see *Re SSSL Realisations (2002) Ltd* [2004] EWHC 1760 (Ch) at [25]–[27].

[386] Where the subordination is not immediate but is triggered only by specified events, such as default in payment of the senior debt or the debtor's winding-up, it is commonly referred to as contingency subordination.

[387] See para.3–34, below.

undertaking or a declaration of trust.[388] The most common form of turnover subordination is the subordination trust, in which the junior creditor expressly undertakes to hold on trust for the senior creditor payments received in respect of the junior debt. So long as the trust is limited to the amount of the senior debt, this trust will not be recharacterised as a charge.[389]

12. SALE OF PARTICIPATION IN LOAN ASSETS[390]

As part of the process of disintermediation[391] that began many years ago in the financial markets, both in England and overseas, banks and other financial institutions have become extensively engaged in the securitisation[392] of financial assets. There are three main methods for "selling" financial assets: assignment, novation, and sub-participation. An assignment is a transfer by the lender to a third party of the whole or part of his rights under the loan agreement. Unless otherwise provided by the loan agreement this may be done without the borrower's consent. A novation is the substitution of a third party as lender under the loan agreement, the original lender giving up his rights and being relieved of his obligations. This requires the assent of the borrower unless provided for in the loan agreement.[393] A funded sub-participation[394] involves an agreement by a third party (known as the buyer or sub-participant) to deposit with the original lender

1–87

---

[388] See further paras 5–60 and 8–24, below.

[389] *Re SSSL Realisations (2002) Ltd*; sub nom. *Squires v AIG Europe (UK) Ltd* [2004] EWHC 1760 (Ch) at [54], approved by the Court of Appeal [2006] EWCA Civ 7; [2006] Ch. 610 at [122]. See further para.8–24, below.

[390] See Gullifer and Payne, *Corporate Finance Law: Principles and Policy* (2011), Ch.8 for an account of the different methods of transfer of financial assets. The law in this area is extremely complex, and the reader is referred to specialist texts, e.g. Wood, *Project Finance, Securitisations, Subordinated Debt* (2007); S. Henderson, *Henderson on Derivatives*, 2nd edn (London: LexisNexis, 2010); P. Jeffrey, *Practitioner's Guide to Securitisation* (London: City and Financial Publishing, 2006); A. Mugasha, *The Law of Multi-Bank Financing* (Oxford: Oxford University Press, 2007), Chs 6 and 7.

[391] Disintermediation is the inelegant term given to the process by which banks and other holders holders of financial assets (receivables due from borrowers, lessees, etc. whether secured or unsecured) move out of borrowing and on-lending by way of loans held to maturity and instead of acting as intermediate parties between borrowers and lenders adopt ancillary roles such as brokerage, underwriting, initiation and disposal of loan agreements. Several factors have brought about this process, in particular, the discovery by commercial borrowers that they could obtain funds more cheaply than from banks by issuing commercial paper directly to the market, and by investors that they could obtain a greater return on their funds than from deposits with the banks, and the desire of banks to reduce their financial assets, and thus remove them from the balance sheet, in order to reduce exposure and to avoid having to inject more capital to meet increasingly stringent capital to primary assets ratios introduced by regulatory authorities.

[392] That is, the packaging of receivables of a given class (which may be secured or unsecured) and their sale to a special-purpose vehicle, the price being either borrowed from banks or raised by issue of a bond or note on the securities market, repayment being secured on the purchased assets. It is important to bear in mind the distinction between "security" in the sense of conferment of rights in assets as security for payment and "securities," a term used to denote stocks, shares, debentures, notes, etc. issued on a market (see fn.1, above). "Securitisation" refers to the conversion of non-marketable into marketable financial assets; it does not denote security for payment, though as stated above the obligations of the purchaser are secured.

[393] The mechanism for novation can be agreed in advance, e.g. by an agreement that registration of an executed transferable loan certificate will result in an automatic substitution of the new lender.

(known as the seller, or lead bank) a sum of money representing an agreed proportion of the amount advanced or to be advanced by the lead bank, the sub-participant acquiring in exchange the right to receive from the lead bank a sum equal to the same proportion of the amount repaid by the borrower. Sub-participation agreements usually make it clear that the sub-participant's relationship is solely with the lead bank and that he acquires no interest in the underlying loan, whether by assignment or otherwise. Hence the "sale" of a participation refers not to the transfer of an interest in the loan as such but to the conferment on the sub-participant of a right to payment from the lead bank measured by the agreed proportion of its receipts from the borrower. It follows that under such an agreement there is no trust in favour of the sub-participant who bears the double risk of insolvency of the borrower and of the lead bank, and in either case is merely an unsecured creditor, with no right in rem either to sums payable by the borrower or to sums received by the lead bank.[395]

The purpose of sub-participation is to transfer the risk of the debtor defaulting from the lead bank to the sub-participant. The credit default swap, which has developed in recent years, is another, hugely popular, method of shifting credit risk from a creditor either to another person or, through a synthetic securitisation structure, to many investors.[396] In the credit default swap, what is purported to be "sold" is not the original loan, but "protection", so that the protection seller agrees to assume the risk of default on stipulated obligations, for a periodic fee. If there is a "credit event", usually either the insolvency of the obligor or non-payment, then the protection seller has to pay a "settlement amount" to the protection buyer. If there is no credit event, the protection buyer just continues to pay the fee throughout the currency of the swap. Again, this is a merely contractual arrangement, which does not involve any transfer of the underlying assets, which performs the same function as a security interest in terms of protecting the creditor against the risk of default.[397]

---

[394] Also termed a participation, a term which is avoided here because it is also used to embrace any arrangement by which the lender disposes of an interest in his financial assets, whether by assignment, novation or otherwise. The term "sub-participation" helps to make the essential point that the agreement between lead bank and sub-participant is a sub-agreement, that is, a back-to-back (and non-recourse) transaction not legally derived from the underlying loan agreement with the borrower.

[395] *Lloyds TSB Bank Plc v Clarke* [2002] UKPC 27; [2002] 2 All E.R. (Comm) 992. See also Wood, *International Loans, Bonds, Guarantees and Legal Opinions* (2007), Ch.9.

[396] For a detailed account see P. Ali, "Credit Derivatives", in P. Ali (ed.), *Secured Finance Transactions: Key Assets and Emerging Markets* (London: Globe Law and Business, 2007); Dr Ali points out that, at the end of 2006, outstanding credit default swaps totalled a notional value of $34 trillion.

[397] Ali, *Secured Finance Transactions: Key Assets and Emerging Markets* (2007), p.241.

CHAPTER 2

Attachment and Perfection of a Security Interest: General Considerations[1]

Priority rules governing fixed and floating security cannot be properly understood without a grasp of the concept of attachment. As we shall see, this apparently straightforward concept possesses a number of subtleties which we ignore at our peril. A mechanical application of priority rules which takes no account of the manner in which a security interest attaches or the time from which attachment takes effect is likely to lead to erroneous solutions.

2–01

1. PRINCIPLES OF ATTACHMENT

The concept of attachment

Attachment denotes the creation of the security interest as between debtor and creditor. The effect of attachment is that the security interest fastens on the asset so as to give the creditor rights in rem against the debtor himself, though not necessarily against third parties. Attachment of a security interest is thus to be distinguished from perfection of a security interest, the latter usually involving a further step (possession, registration, notice, or attornment) which constitutes notice of the security interest to third parties and must be taken if they are to be bound.[2] This is using the concept of perfection in a broad sense, to mean any steps to give public notice of the interest which have the effect of making the interest enforceable against one or more (but not necessarily all) third parties, and which can, on occasion, be confused with steps required to give the security interest holder priority over holders of other interests.[3]

2–02

There is admittedly something odd in the notion of a right in rem available only against the debtor, for that which distinguishes real rights from personal rights is supposed to be that the former affect not only the obligor but the world at large. True, we can speak of the secured party's right vis-à-vis the debtor to restrict the debtor's use or disposition of the goods, to take possession or to sell,

---

[1] See generally R. Goode, *Commercial Law*, E. McKendrick (ed.), 4th edn (London: Lexis Nexis, 2010), Ch.23. For attachment and perfection of security interests in non-documentary receivables see Ch.3, below; and in corporate investment securities, Ch.6, below.

[2] The conversion of an equitable interest into a legal interest may also be regarded as an aspect of perfection in that it confers stronger rights against third parties, but some further act of perfection such as registration may still be required.

[3] See paras 2–16 et seq., below.

but precisely the same rights could be exercised by mere contract. The fact is that a real right enforceable only against the debtor is scarcely distinguishable in its effects from a mere personal right. A similar conundrum is posed by the sub-heading to Pt III of the Sale of Goods Act 1979, which speaks of "transfer of property as between seller and buyer". What sort of transfer can it be that is effective solely inter partes?

In fact, of course, even an unperfected security interest, like a transfer of property "as between seller and buyer", is likely to bind at least some categories of third party, in particular an unsecured non-insolvency creditor. The purpose of the concept is to demonstrate that the debtor cannot dispute the conferment of real rights on the creditor,[4] and the consequent restriction on the debtor's own dominion over the asset, but that the same is not necessarily true of all third parties, some of whom may, in the absence of perfection, be able to contend that the grant of the security has no impact on them.

The rules governing attachment apply equally whether the security interest is being granted to the creditor himself or a trustee on his behalf. The only difference in legal effect is that the legal owner (in the case of a legal mortgage) is the trustee, not the creditor, who is the beneficial owner of the mortgage and thus an equitable mortgagee. Mortgages and charges to secure syndicated loans or issues of bonds, notes or debentures (often in the context of a securitisation) are invariably made in favour of security trustees for the holders, who hold their entitlements subject to the terms of the trust deed. This has the effect of coordinating the holders' fractional interests so that while they are the legal owners of the securities registered in their name[5] their rights are enforced by the security trustee pursuant to the irrevocable authority conferred by the trust deed, not by the holders directly.

The ingredients of attachment

2–03   In order for a security interest to attach otherwise than by operation of law the following conditions must co-exist:

(1)   there must be an agreement for security conforming to statutory formalities;
(2)   the asset to be given in security must be identifiable;
(3)   the debtor must have an interest in the asset or a power to give it in security;
(4)   there must be some current obligation of debtor to creditor (or to another)[6] which the asset is designed to secure;
(5)   any contractual conditions for attachment must have been fulfilled; and
(6)   in the case of a pledge, actual or constructive possession must be given to the creditor.

---

[4] These rights will bind third parties if perfected, and the debtor cannot prevent this.

[5] Whether the holders are legal owners will depend on the method of holding the securities. Many bond issues are issued as a global note; the holders then hold through the intermediary who is the legal owner of the note. See further paras 6–07 et seq., below; and L. Gullifer and J. Payne, *Corporate Finance Law: Principles and Policy* (Oxford: Hart Publishing, 2011), pp.334–339.

[6] *In The Matter Of Lehman Brothers International (Europe) (In Administration)* [2012] EWHC 2997 (Ch) at [43]–[44]; see para.1–16, above.

Each of these elements will now be examined in turn.

(1) Agreement for security conforming to statutory formalities

Mere unilateral action by the creditor against the asset does not suffice to give him a security interest. There must be an agreement to create a security interest. The agreement may be to create a pledge, which as we will see requires delivery of actual or constructive possession, or a mortgage (which is a security transfer of ownership or of such lesser interest as the transferor possesses), or an equitable charge, where there is a mere incumbrance on the debtor's continuing ownership. Leaving aside pledge for the moment,[7] we can say that so long as the agreement is valid it suffices to create a security interest in equity so long as conditions (2)–(5) are fulfilled. If a mortgage is to take effect as a legal mortgage there must be an actual transfer by way of security[8] and compliance with any statutory requirements as to form, but these are not conditions of attachment of a security interest, merely additional steps needed to convert an equitable security into a legal security. An equitable charge, not being a transfer of ownership, rests in contract; there is therefore no distinction between a charge and an agreement for a charge.[9] The essential point is that there must be an agreement for security. A debtor who deposits deeds or documents of title with his bank by way of safe custody does not thereby create a charge, or any other form of security, in favour of his bank to secure his indebtedness, nor does he by implication confer on the bank the right to take unilateral action to bring a security interest into existence.[10] The creation of security by actual transfer is relatively simple; and in the case of intangibles the transfer may be effected in one of several different ways, depending on the nature of the intangible.[11] But where the creditor relies not on an actual transfer but on a mere agreement for security—as in the case of an equitable charge or an agreement for a mortgage—equity requires certain conditions to be satisfied before it will recognise the contract as giving rise to real rights. So we shall shortly return to the efficacy of the security agreement itself constituting an equitable security. This is not possible in the case of pledge, which depends on actual or constructive possession; mere agreement is not sufficient.[12] Nor can a contractual lien subsist without possession as against the debtor.[13]

2–04

An equitable charge or mortgage may be reinforced by a document or book entry which enables the chargee or mortgagee to strengthen his security interest. For example, an equitable mortgage or charge of paper-based shares is usually accompanied by execution of a blank transfer in favour of the chargee or mortgagee which enables him, in the event of default, to be registered as the holder,[14] whilst in the CREST system for dematerialised securities the same effect is produced by transfer into an escrow account which is a sub-account of

---

[7] See para.2–10, below.

[8] Land is a special case. See para.1–55, above.

[9] Again, the position is otherwise in the case of a charge of land by way of legal mortgage. See para.1–55, above.

[10] The bank may, of course, have a lien by operation of law.

[11] In particular, whether it is a documentary or a pure intangible. See para.1–48, above.

[12] See para.2–10, below.

[13] See para.2–10, below.

[14] See para.6–38, below.

the mortgagor under the control of an escrow agent.[15] But the blank transfer and the escrow account are not constitutive elements of the equitable mortgage or charge, which takes effect solely by virtue of the agreement. A security interest cannot attach unless the agreement providing for it is a valid and enforceable agreement.[16] So an agreement for a mortgage of land is devoid of legal effect, and thus incapable of creating a security interest in the land, unless it is in writing and the document incorporates all the agreed terms and is signed by or on behalf of both parties.[17] There is a similar requirement for a mortgage of a patent,[18] copyright,[19] a design right[20] or a registered trade mark.[21] However, an agreement for security which is fully binding but requires only that the consideration be executed[22] before it can be enforced is an inchoate security which, upon the consideration being executed, as by the making of the advance, becomes attached as from the time of the agreement.[23]

(2) Identifiability of the subject matter

2–05   A security interest cannot exist in an asset which is neither identified at the time of the security agreement nor identifiable as subsequently falling within its terms. The point may seem an obvious one but it is regularly overlooked.

The requirements for identification of the subject matter of tangible security are the same as those for the identification of goods as the subject of a contract of sale.[24] The asset to be given in security must either be identified by the security agreement or, in the case of fungibles[25] ascertained subsequently as the result of an unconditional act of appropriation of the asset to the agreement. So a purported mortgage of 100 tons of potatoes amounts to no more than an agreement for a mortgage, and until a particular group of potatoes is earmarked to

---

[15] See para.6–41, below.

[16] It is, of course, possible to have an agreement which is valid and unenforceable and thus a security interest which is valid and unenforceable, but with the enactment of the Law of Property (Miscellaneous Provisions) Act 1989 s.2 (see fn.17, below) this is rarely likely to arise. In any event, enforceability is included as an element of attachment since a security interest which cannot be enforced in any manner is a theoretical abstraction. It is not without interest that art.9 of the American Uniform Commercial Code requires as a condition of attachment that the security interest is enforceable against the debtor, which requires (inter alia) that the security agreement be in writing or otherwise authenticated. See §§9–203(b)(3)(A), and §9–102(73).

[17] Law of Property (Miscellaneous Provisions) Act 1989 s.2. Previously the agreement was merely required to be evidenced in writing signed by or on behalf of the party to be charged and, if not, was merely unenforceable, not wholly void (Law of Property Act 1925 s.40), and even this requirement could be dispensed with if there was a sufficient act of part performance, an equitable doctrine abolished by the 1989 Act.

[18] Patents Act 1977 s.30(6).

[19] Copyright, Designs and Patents Act 1988 s.90(3).

[20] Copyright, Designs and Patents Act 1988 s.222(3).

[21] Trade Marks Act 1994 s.24(3).

[22] See para.2–13, below.

[23] Whether this gives the secured creditor priority over a subsequent incumbrancer who acquired his interest while the first security interest was still inchoate is a separate question discussed in para.2–13, below. See also Goode, *Commercial Law* (2010), pp.676–678.

[24] See Goode, *Commercial Law* (2010), pp.227 et seq., 255–257; *Benjamin's Sale of Goods*, M. Bridge (ed.), 8th edn (London: Sweet & Maxwell, 2008), paras 5–068 et seq.

[25] That is, consisting of two or more units which, in terms of the delivery or transfer obligation, are legally interchangeable.

the agreement the creditor has no security interest of any kind. The same is true of an agreement to give security in an unidentified part of an identified bulk. A purported pledge of 12 cases of 1966 Chateau Montrose wine from a larger quantity of such wine in a warehouse is a mere agreement for a pledge, for without an act of appropriation we could not tell which cases are the subject matter of the security,[26] nor is the position altered where several creditors each hold purported pledges of undivided interests in a bulk to a quantity totalling the entirety of the bulk.[27]

However, in the case of contracts of sale the position was altered by the Sale of Goods (Amendment) Act 1995, which introduced new provisions into the Sale of Goods Act 1979 to make the prepaying buyer of goods forming part of a bulk a proportionate co-owner of the bulk.[28] One effect of this is to enhance the security of banks advancing money against bills of lading. Bulk cargo, such as oil and grain, is frequently shipped under a multiplicity of bills of lading without segregation as between one bill and another; indeed, such segregation would in most cases both be unnecessary and impracticable. Hence all that the bank as holder of an individual bill of lading previously acquired against the carrier was a personal right to delivery of a given quantity or volume of the cargo upon its arrival at the port of destination. Now, its advance of the purchase price results in the buyer becoming a co-owner of the bulk, so that the bank acquires a valid pledge of the buyer's share of the bulk.[29] The provisions do not apply (and are not needed) where the contract itself identifies the goods, for which purpose a contract of sale of a given share of the bulk (as opposed to a stated number of units of the bulk) suffices at common law.

It should, of course, be borne in mind that providing the mortgagor owns the entire bulk, there is no problem with giving a security interest over the whole bulk to secure an obligation of a far lower value than that of the bulk. Thus issues of identification are often of less significance than where an absolute interest is being transferred, since all that is required is that the subject matter of the security interest is identified.

Security in intangible property remains governed by the common law requirement of identification. It is, however, necessary to bear in mind that the problem of identification, whether in relation to tangibles or intangibles, arises only where the subject matter of the transaction is susceptible to division into units capable in law of being separately owned and transferred.[30] In the case of goods this depends on whether they are capable of physical segregation. A charge of a share in a racehorse is a charge of a single, identified asset, for a racehorse

2–06

---

[26] *Re London Wine Co (Shippers) Ltd* [1986] P.C.C. 121; also reproduced in R. Goode, *Proprietary Rights and Insolvency in Sales Transactions*, S. Mills (ed.), 3rd edn (London: Sweet & Maxwell, 2009), Appendix.

[27] *Re London Wine Co (Shippers) Ltd* [1986] P.C.C. 121.

[28] See Sale of Goods Act 1979 ss.20A and 20B.

[29] This does, however, depend upon the bank obtaining constructive possession of the pledged assets, see L. Gullifer, "Constructive possession after the Sale of Goods (Amendment) Act 1995" [1999] L.M.C.L.Q. 93; Goode, *Commercial Law* (2010), p.249. It may be that transfer of the bill of lading, or an equivalent attornment, takes effect by transferring shared constructive possession to the pledgee. N. Palmer, *Palmer on Bailment*, 3rd edn (London: Sweet & Maxwell, 2009), paras 8–021 to 8–022; M.Bridge, L. Gullifer, G. McMeel, S. Worthington, *The Law of Personal Property* (London: Sweet & Maxwell, 2013), para.11–031.

[30] See R. Goode, "Are Intangible Assets Fungible?" [2003] L.M.C.L.Q. 379.

cannot be divided without loss of identity and it is impossible to hold a share in a racehorse otherwise than by co-ownership of the racehorse itself. In the case of intangibles the test is not whether they are capable of physical division (obviously they are not) but whether are legally divisible into units capable of separate ownership, as opposed to ownership in common. Legal ownership of shares would be impossible if it were necessary to separate shares owned by A from shares owned by B as there is no way to identify one share from another. However, A's shareholding can be seen as sufficiently identified if it is seen as a fractional interest in the whole share capital, which is owned in common by all the shareholders. Thus, shares represent co-ownership of a single, identified asset, and as such there is no problem with identification of a shareholder's interest, either at law or in equity.[31] The same applies to debt securities and to a credit balance in a bank account. The argument advanced by some writers that an assignment of £100 forming part of a £500 credit balance in the assignor's account is void for want of identification, is misconceived, because there is only one, indivisible asset, the credit balance, and the sole effect of the partial assignment is to make the assignee co-owner of the credit balance with the assignor.

Precise identification of the asset at the time of the agreement is not required; it suffices that it is or becomes identifiable as falling within the terms of the security agreement. So a debtor can effectively charge all his existing and future book debts[32] or, indeed, all his assets.[33]

(3) Debtor's interest or power to dispose

2–07   The third prerequisite of attachment is that the debtor[34] has a present interest in the asset intended to comprise the security or alternatively has, by virtue of some exception to the nemo dat rule, a present power to dispose of the asset or grant a charge over it. The debtor cannot normally give a valid security over someone else's asset, though there are exceptions to this rule, both at common law (e.g. where the owner has held out the debtor as having a power of disposal) and by statute (e.g. where the debtor is a mercantile agent).[35] But whilst the grant of security over future property does not create a security interest until the debtor has acquired an interest in the property, the security agreement does create an inchoate interest which is legally significant. This will be dealt with later.[36]

It is not necessary for the debtor to be the owner of the asset given in security. Any interest suffices, including a security interest granted by the debtor's own debtor (so that the debtor is giving a sub-security to his own creditor),[37] and a possessory interest, for example, that enjoyed by a lessee in possession under an

---

[31] See further para.6–14, below.

[32] *Tailby v Official Receiver* (1888) 13 App. Cas. 523.

[33] *Re Kelcey* [1899] 2 Ch. 530; *Syrett v Egerton* [1957] 3 All E.R. 331. The last case left open the question whether an assignment of all future property by an individual would be held contrary to public policy if its effect were to deprive the debtor of all means of support.

[34] The word "debtor" here includes anyone who grants security to secure an obligation: it is not necessary that the grantor owes the obligation himself, see para.1–16, above.

[35] Factors Act 1889 s.2. For non-assignable rights, see para.1–59, above.

[36] See paras 2–12 et seq., below.

[37] See para.1–74, above.

equipment lease. Of course, in the absence of some applicable exception to the nemo dat rule the debtor cannot grant by way of security an interest greater than that which he himself holds. One such exception is where the grantor is authorised by the owner of the asset to grant security over it.[38] One example is where a trustee, holding assets for a debtor, grants security over those assets to secure an obligation owed by the debtor: the security interest will extend to the beneficial interest in those assets.

(4)   Subsistence of current obligation

No security interest can exist in an asset at any time when there is no current obligation of debtor to creditor[39] which is secured on the asset. Security may be given for a past advance, and can then attach on the making of the agreement for security, but if it is for an advance to be made after execution of the security agreement then until it has been made the creditor has merely an inchoate security interest, of much the same kind as that of a purchaser of land on exchange of contracts who has not yet paid the purchase price, the interest relating back to the time of the agreement once payment has been made.[40] As a corollary, a security interest can never be greater in quantum than the value of the debtor's current obligation. Suppose that the debtor company mortgages its premises to secure a loan of £10,000. The premises may be worth £500,000, but the creditor's security interest is still no more than £10,000, for on payment of this sum (if we ignore interest) the debtor is entitled to have the mortgage discharged. The same applies to a charge to secure a fluctuating balance, e.g. an overdraft. Unless there is a debit balance on the account, the chargee, even if holding a charge by way of legal mortgage, has no security interest, but the interest will automatically arise as soon as an advance is made and will date back to the date of the grant of the interest.[41]

2–08

(5)   Fulfilment of contractual conditions for attachment

Attachment does not take place unless the conditions for attachment specified in the security agreement have been fulfilled. This does not, however, imply that the parties may, consistently with the equitable rules for creation of a security interest by agreement, stipulate any event they choose as producing attachment. On the contrary, where the designated event is a mere contingency—an event which may or may not occur—then unless the contingency is simply the debtor's acquisition of an interest in the asset the agreement will not by itself be effective to create a security interest, even on the occurrence of the contingency.[42] The rule is otherwise where the agreement provides for the grant of security on a specified

2–09

---

[38] See para.5–05, below.

[39] Note that it is possible to grant security to secure an obligation owed to someone other than the grantee of security, see *In The Matter Of Lehman Brothers International (Europe) (In Administration)* [2012] EWHC 2997 (Ch) at [43]–[44]; and para.1–16, above.

[40] *Rayner v Preston* (1881) 18 Ch.D. 1, per James L.J. at 13; *Shaw v Foster* (1872) L.R. 5 H.L. 322; *Lysaght v Edwards* (1876) 2 Ch.D. 499.

[41] See also para.2–11, below in relation to the requirement for executed consideration for an equitable mortgage or charge over future property.

[42] See para.1–81, above; para.2–15, below.

date or after the lapse of a stated period or on the occurrence of some other future event which is bound to occur, or on the debtor's acquisition of property falling within the description in the security agreement, for in all these cases attachment of the security interest is not dependent on a contingency other than (in the case of security in future property) the debtor's acquisition of the property.

The rule concerning contingent interests does not apply to a provision in an agreement for the conversion of a floating security, such as a floating charge, into a fixed security; the parties are free to designate any event they choose as causing the charge to crystallise and fasten on the assets then owned or subsequently acquired by the chargor. This is because a floating charge is not a mere contract for future security; on the contrary it creates a present security in a fund of assets.[43]

(6)   In the case of pledge or contractual lien, delivery of possession

2–10   The sixth requirement for attachment is confined to pledges and contractual liens. A pledge requires delivery of possession; an agreement for a pledge which is not accompanied or followed by delivery of possession is a mere contract conferring no real right on the intended pledgee.[44] The delivery of possession to the creditor may be actual or constructive. A pledge of goods may be created by delivery to the creditor of the documents of title to the goods.[45] Another common form of constructive possession arises where a third party holding physical possession on behalf of the debtor agrees to attorn to (i.e. hold possession for) the creditor instead. There is authority to indicate that even the debtor in possession may create an effective pledge by declaring that he holds the goods to the creditor's order,[46] in which case his possession is in law the creditor's possession. This is consistent with long-established case law on delivery and receipt in the sale of goods[47] and with decisions upholding continuance of a pledge where the pledgee redelivers the goods to the pledgor to hold on the pledgee's behalf, e.g. under a trust receipt.[48] Under the previous registration regime,[49] such a pledge, if in writing, was probably registrable under s.860(7) of the Companies Act 2006.[50] Although s.860(7)(b) referred only to a "charge", in this context a charge included a pledge.[51] It is not entirely clear whether a pledge created in this way would fall within the new s.859A. An early draft of the section expressly included such a pledge,[52] but this was omitted in the final draft, as was a clause expressly

---

[43] See para.4–03, below.

[44] *Dublin City Distillery Ltd v Doherty* [1914] A.C. 823.

[45] See Goode, *Commercial Law* (2010), p.751.

[46] *Marin v Reid* (1862) 11 C.B.N.S. 730; *Meyerstein v Barber* (1866) L.R. 2 C.P. 38; *Dublin City Distillery Co Ltd v Doherty* [1914] A.C. 823, per Lord Parker of Waddington C.J. at 852; *Askrigg Pty Ltd v Student Guild of the Curtin University of Technology* (1989) 18 N.S.W.L.R. 738.

[47] *Michael Gerson (Leasing) Ltd v Wilkinson* [2001] Q.B. 514; *Marvin v Wallace* (1856) E. & B. 726.

[48] *North Western Bank v Poynter* [1895] A.C. 56; *Re David Allester Ltd* [1922] 2 Ch. 211.

[49] For discussion of the reform to the registration regime, see paras 2–18 et seq., below.

[50] This subsection made registrable any charge created or evidenced by an instrument which, if is had been executed by an individual, would require registration as a bill of sale.

[51] *Dublin City Distillery v Doherty* [1914] A.C. 823, 854.

[52] Department for Business, Innovation and Skills (BIS), *Revised Scheme for Registration of Charges created by Companies and Limited Liability Partnerships: proposed revision of Pt 25 of the Companies Act 2006*, BIS/10/697 (August 2011), s.860B.

exempting pledges from registration. While the line between pledges and charges is usually easy to draw (rendering such an exemption unnecessary) the situation under consideration here, that is, a pledge created by attornment by the debtor, is one area where there is a potential overlap. It is suggested that such a pledge should be registrable as a charge under s.859A. If this is correct, then the main policy objection to permitting a pledge to be created in this way, that of false wealth, falls away.

A third party in physical possession may agree to attorn to the creditor subject to discharge of a lien or other interest held by the third party itself. For example, where the debtor's goods are held in a warehouse and on the debtor's instructions the warehouseman undertakes to the creditor to hold them on the latter's behalf subject to discharge of the warehouseman's lien for warehousing charges, the pledge is inchoate and becomes operative as soon as the lien is discharged. In such a case the debtor's bankruptcy before discharge of the lien does not affect the efficacy of the pledge, for the goods have been subject to a continuous possessory interest, first in favour of the warehouseman and then, without any interval, in favour of the pledgee.[53]

Similar considerations apply to a contractual lien, which differs from a pledge only that it arises from the creditor's possession of goods which were delivered to him for some purpose other than security.[54]

The security agreement

We must now look more closely at the first of the prerequisites of attachment, a security transfer or agreement. If the security has actually been given, by pledge or mortgage, no problem arises. Our concern is with the effect of an agreement for security. At this point, it will occur to the property lawyer to ask: how can a mere agreement for security, as opposed to an actual transfer by way of security, give rise to an immediate security interest? The answer at common law was quite clear: it could not. The creation of proprietary rights, whether absolute or by way of security, required a completed transfer, by deed or bill of sale or delivery of possession, except where the contract was for the sale of goods[55] or related to potential property, such as future crops or identified, future young of identified livestock, etc.[56] Save in these cases a mere agreement to transfer constituted at best a contract, creating a mere obligation, not a proprietary right.

2–11

Equity, however, treating as done that which ought to be done, considers that the agreement to give security takes effect as an immediate security interest if this is consistent with the agreement between the parties and the subject matter is identifiable. This is subject to the qualification that the security interest remains inchoate, or incomplete, until the consideration is executed. That is to say, the creditor cannot enforce his security against the debtor, or assert it against third parties, until he has actually advanced his money; his commitment to advance it

---

[53] The same principle applies to a buyer's rights to identified goods subject to a lien. See Goode, *Proprietary Rights and Insolvency in Sales Transactions* (2009), pp.17–18.

[54] See para.1–53, above. A power of sale is also implied (or express) in a pledge, whereas a lien usually includes no such power.

[55] This common law exception, now embodied in s.17 of the Sale of Goods Act 1979, is of long standing. See *Cochrane v Moore* (1890) 25 Ch.D. 57, per Fry L.J. at 70–71.

[56] *Grantham v Hawley* (1615) Hob. 132.

does not suffice, for equity does not decree specific performance of a contract to borrow or lend money[57] and the court will therefore not treat the debtor as one who could be compelled to execute the security instrument.[58] But once the creditor has advanced his money the contract ceases to be executory and equity treats the transfer as perfected, so that the matter is no longer considered to rest in contract and specific performance in its narrow sense[59] is unnecessary. Perfection of the transfer by making of the advance takes effect as from the date of the security agreement,[60] in much the same way as a charge over future property has retrospective effect once the property has been acquired.[61]

In order for the existence of the security interest to be consistent with the agreement between the parties the following conditions must be satisfied:

(a)   the agreement must manifest an intention to confer a security interest on the creditor, not a mere contractual right[62];

(b)   it must reflect the intention of the parties that the interest should attach to the asset immediately or on the debtor's acquisition of an interest in it or at an agreed time or on the occurrence of some future event which is certain to occur, and that attachment is not to be dependent on some contingent event (other than the debtor's acquisition) such as the execution of a security instrument on demand by the creditor[63]; and

(c)   the asset over which the security is claimed must be shown to fall within the description in the security agreement—a not very stringent requirement, amounting, as we have seen, to little more than that ascertainment of the subject matter of the security must be apparent from the terms of the security agreement itself and must not be made to depend on some act of appropriation by the debtor.

Security over future property

2–12   At common law, an agreement to give security over future property created no proprietary rights even after acquisition of the property by the debtor. This was consistent with the common law rule that only an immediate transfer would do.

---

[57] *Rogers v Challis* (1859) 27 Beav. 175.

[58] It is only in this sense that the susceptibility of the contract to specific performance—a requirement described in somewhat infelicitous terms by Lord Westbury in *Holroyd v Marshall* (1862) 10 H.L. Cas. 161 and subsequently explained away in *Tailby v Official Receiver* (1888) 13 App. Cas. 523— is relevant to the recognition of the security interest.

[59] i.e. an order compelling performance of an executory contract. Though secured in equity because the contract has become executed, the creditor whose debtor has promised to execute a security instrument is entitled to specific performance in its broader sense of compelling performance of any contractually stipulated act, even though it is not necessary for the establishment of his proprietary rights but merely perfects rights already acquired in equity. See G. Jones and W. Goodhart, *Specific Performance*, 2nd edn (Haywards Heath: Tottel Publishing, 1996), p.1, fn.1; and, for the two meanings of specific performance, I.C.F. Spry, *Equitable Remedies*, 8th edn (Sydney: Law Book Co, 2009), pp.51 et seq.

[60] *See Rayner v Preston* (1881) 18 Ch.D. 1, per James L.J. at 13, when discussing the position of the purchaser under a contract of sale of land.

[61] See para.2–13, below.

[62] *Palmer v Carey* [1926] A.C. 703, 706–707; *Swiss Bank Corp Ltd v Lloyd's Bank Ltd* [1982] A.C. 584, 595. See further para.1–28, above.

[63] See para.1–81, above and para.2–15, below.

The common law therefore usually required some new act of transfer, after acquisition by the debtor, to vest a proprietary interest in the creditor.

Had the common law rule retained its full vigour, financing against future assets would have remained seriously inhibited, for the creditor has no ready way of knowing that his debtor has acquired a new asset, and the debtor may become insolvent before the creditor has the chance of obtaining the performance of the required new act of transfer.

Fortunately, equity came to the rescue. In the great case of *Holroyd v Marshall*,[64] machinery in a mill was mortgaged upon terms requiring the mortgagor to hold the machinery for the mortgagee, with liberty to substitute new machinery, which would then itself become subject to the mortgage, together with any additional machinery brought on to the premises. It was held that the mortgage attached to new and additional machinery from the moment of its acquisition by the debtor, without any new act of transfer, and had priority over the claims of an execution creditor. Though the principle had been established well before, the authoritative effect of *Holroyd v Marshall* as a decision of the highest tribunal has been to place a most powerful security device in the hands of a creditor, who can literally secure a monopoly of the debtor's non-purchase-money financing[65] by taking security over all his property, present and future. Whether an interest such as that upheld in *Holroyd v Marshall* is a fixed or floating interest is now a matter of some debate: it may well be that, following the decision in *Re Spectrum Plus*,[66] the interest would now be held to be floating.[67]

As from what time does a security interest in future property attach?

We now come to the crucial question, when does the security interest in future property attach? This seems clear enough. We have already seen—indeed, it is almost too obvious to require stating—that a security interest cannot attach in an asset before the debtor has acquired an interest in it (we exclude for this purpose cases where the debtor has a power to give security over someone else's property). In addition, *Holroyd v Marshall* tells us that, unless the arrangement otherwise provides, the debtor's acquisition is sufficient without more. For example, a debtor executes a charge in favour of X over future property on April 1 and acquires a new asset on August 1. The charge attaches on August 1. There appears to be no problem. But suppose that on May 1 the debtor had executed a second charge, in favour of Y, over the same classes of future asset. Who wins, X or Y? The answer is simple enough: X wins, as he is the first in time. The problem is to know how this result is arrived at, because, of course, the security interest does not attach until the debtor has acquired the asset, so that the competing interests of X and Y attach simultaneously. How, then, does X get priority?

2–13

---

[64] *Holroyd v Marshall* (1862) 10 H.L. Cas.191.
[65] The position is otherwise as to purchase-money finance, in that there are certain techniques available to a financier who is second in time to obtain priority, such as devices based on retention of title, discussed at paras 1–32 et seq., above. See also paras 5–63 et seq., below.
[66] *Re Spectrum Plus* [2005] 2 A.C. 680.
[67] See para.4–23, below.

Here we have a striking example of the intellectual subtlety of the law. In a number of cases the courts have ruled that whilst, in a sense, an agreement for security over after-acquired property cannot attach to that property prior to acquisition, yet the agreement constitutes a present security.[68] In other words, it creates an inchoate security interest which is waiting for the asset to be acquired so that it can fasten on to the asset but which, upon acquisition of the asset, takes effect as from the date of the security agreement. Acquisition of the asset produces the situation in which the security is deemed to have continuously attached to the asset from the time of execution of the security agreement.[69] This may seem metaphysical but has its counterpart in other branches of law. Take the case of the unborn child. Until birth, a child has no separate legal existence and no action can be brought on its behalf. But once born it acquires the right to sue even for injuries caused to it before birth.[70] Legal existence is, so to speak, attached to the child at birth as from the moment of its conception.[71] So also with a security interest in future property. There are some consequences of this continuous attachment, which have considerable practical advantages. First, the time for registration of the security interest runs from the date of its creation,[72] even if there are no assets falling within in at that time. Second, the relevant time for the application of priority rules is the date of the agreement creating the interest.[73] Further consequences are considered in the next paragraphs.

A corollary is that once value has been given for the grant of the security, each asset coming in under the after-acquired property clause is deemed to have been given for new value. Let us take an extreme case. A lends B £1 and takes security over B's after-acquired property. B acquires a new asset to the value of £1,000. A has security over that asset for the £1 advance. B acquires a further asset, to the value of £100,000. The further asset is likewise deemed to have been charged to A for new value. A can go on stacking up more and more security without injecting any additional funds. Indeed, the expansion of his security is not halted even by B's bankruptcy. A new asset falling in after the commencement of B's bankruptcy becomes instantly caught by A's security interest,[74] provided that the consideration for the security was already executed before the commencement of the bankruptcy.[75] Indeed, we can go further. Even the debtor's discharge from bankruptcy does not affect the force and priority of the after-acquired property clause. However, the value of the security interest can never exceed £1 and accrued interest.

---

[68] See *Holroyd v Marshall* (1862) 10 H.L. Cas.191, per Lord Chelmsford at 220; *Tailby v Official Receiver* (1888) 13 App. Cas. 523, per Lord Watson at 533.

[69] See also *Hadlee v Commissioner of Inland Revenue* [1991] 3 N.Z.L.R. 517, where it was held that the assignment passed the beneficial interest automatically to the assignee without any intermediate vesting of that beneficial interest in the assignor, and so the asset was not chargeable to tax in the hands of the assignor (approved on appeal to the Privy Council without consideration of this point ([1993] 2 N.Z.L.R. 385)); see also *Norman v Federal Commissioner of Taxation* (1963) 109 C.L.R. 9; *Federal Commissioner of Taxation v Everett* (1980) 54 A.L.J.R. 196.

[70] *Watt v Rama* [1972] V.R. 353. There is no reported English decision, but the right of action is expressly given by the Congenital Disabilities (Civil Liabilities) Act 1976.

[71] *Kelly v Gregory*, 125 N.Y.S. (2d) 696 (1953).

[72] See para.2–23, below. The date of creation of a charge for the purposes of registration is now defined in s.859E(1) of the Companies Act 2006.

[73] See Ch.5, below.

[74] *Re Reis* [1904] 2 K.B. 769; *Re Lind* [1915] 2 Ch. 345.

[75] *Re Collins* [1925] Ch. 556.

A good example of the principle, and of the underlying conceptual rationale, is **2–14**
Re Lind[76]:

> "L assigned his expectant share in his mother's estate to the N. Society by way of
> mortgage to secure an advance, and subsequently executed a further mortgage of
> the same expectancy to A, subject to the first mortgage. L later became bankrupt,
> and eventually received his discharge. He then assigned the same expectant share to
> the I. Syndicate. His mother then died. It was held that the first two mortgages were
> unaffected by the bankruptcy or the discharge and therefore had priority over the
> third mortgage, even though the asset had not fallen into possession until after the
> discharge."

Particularly significant are the words of Bankes L.J.:

> "It is true that the security was not enforceable until the property came into existence,
> but nevertheless the security was there, the assignor was the bare trustee of the
> assignee to receive and hold the property for him when it came into existence."[77]

This principle of continuous existence applies equally to the winding up of a
company. So an after-acquired property clause in a charge given by a company is
effective to catch property coming into the company's hands after the
commencement of the winding up of the company despite s.127 of the Insolvency
Act 1986. That section (re-enacting prior legislation) renders void any disposition
of a company's property made after the commencement of the winding up. If
security in future property had no inchoate existence prior to the acquisition of
the asset, then a post-liquidation acquisition would fall foul of s.127. But once it
is seen that the security interest relates back to the time of the security agreement,
any problem with s.127 disappears. The cautionary comment should be added
that it appears that this point has not yet arisen for decision by the courts.[78]
Nevertheless, the conclusion must, it is submitted, follow from the principle.

Re Lind and the earlier decision in *Re Reis*[79] which it applied, have been
trenchantly criticised as running counter to the policy of bankruptcy law.[80]
Insofar as the principle in *Re Lind* allows the chargee to increase his security
margin during the six months run-up to liquidation, the point is, it is submitted,

---

[76] *Re Lind* [1915] 2 Ch. 345.

[77] *Re Lind* [1915] 2 Ch. 345 at 374. For recent support for the views expressed by the Court of Appeal
in *Re Lind* and rejection of the view espoused by the Court of Appeal in *Collyer v Isaacs* (1881) 19
Ch. D. 342 (that a contract to assign future property gave rise to a mere contractual right which was
released on the assignor's discharge in bankruptcy), see *Peer International Corp v Termidor Music
Publishers Ltd* [2002] EWHC 2675 at [79]; and *Performing Right Society Ltd v B4U Network
(Europe) Ltd* [2012] EWHC 3010 (Ch) (which dealt with the specific provision in s.91 of the
Copyright, Designs and Patents Act 1988 that copyright in future works vests in an assignee when the
copyright comes into existence).

[78] It is, however, well established that exercise of a power of sale by a mortgagee or receiver after
commencement of the winding up does not contravene the section, for to the extent that the asset is
subject to the security interest it is not the property of the company at all. See *Sowman v David
Samuel Trust Ltd* [1978] 1 W.L.R. 22, per Goulding J. at 30; *Re Margart Pty Ltd* (1984) 9 A.C.L.R.
269.

[79] *Re Reis* [1904] 2 K.B. 769.

[80] P. Matthews, "The effect of bankruptcy upon mortgages of future property" [1981] 1 L.M.C.L.Q.
40.

well taken.[81] But an enhancement of the security margin outside this period seems to be unobjectionable. The creditor bargained at the outset for security over future property; he ought not to be deprived of the basis of his bargain. He is entitled to say that in asserting security rights over future property without putting in fresh value he is not taking out of the estate a penny more than he put into it, for without the debtor's acceptance of the after-acquired property clause the money would never have been advanced in the first place.

Equitable security distinguished from mere contract

2–15   An agreement for a mortgage or charge is treated in equity as a security interest only if it is not subject to any contingency other than the debtor's acquisition of an interest in the asset.[82] An agreement to give security on any other contingency, whether the contingency be a demand by the creditor to do so, default by the debtor or the occurrence of some other uncertain event, is a mere contract, not an equitable charge.[83] It might be thought that the dicta of Lord Scott in *Smith v Bridgend County BC*,[84] where he says that "a charge expressed to come into existence on the occurrence of an uncertain future event and then to apply to a class of assets that cannot be identified until the event has happened would, if otherwise valid, qualify for registration as a floating charge", throws doubt on this analysis. However, the cases supporting the view put forward in this paragraph were not cited to the House of Lords, and Lord Scott's view was not discussed in the other opinions, since the security interest was viewed as a floating charge created at the time of the contract, rather than a security interest that only arose on the occurrence of a future event.[85] Even on the occurrence of the designated event the security interest will not attach in equity merely by virtue of the earlier agreement, for in order to be specifically enforceable so as to constitute an equitable security the agreement must be supported by an executed consideration, i.e. the making of the advance; whereas an unqualified agreement for security over future property creates an inchoate security, so that a payment made on or after the agreement constitutes value in equity, an agreement for security contingent on a future uncertain event is a mere contract.[86] It follows that

---

[81] See R. Goode, "The Death of Insolvency Law" (1980) 1 Co. Law 123 at 125–126.

[82] See para.1–81, above.

[83] *Re Jackson & Bassford Ltd* [1906] 2 Ch. 467; *Re Gregory Love & Co Ltd* [1916] 1 Ch. 203; *Williams v Burlington Investments Ltd* (1977) 121 S.J. 424. It is therefore not registrable under s.860 of the Companies Act 2006. In general a contingent agreement for security, being a mere contract and not a security interest, has no priority effect, and a subsequent incumbrancer whose interest is created after the contingent agreement and before the grant of security pursuant to that agreement has priority. However, an agreement to give a charge over unregistered land if so requested by the creditor is registrable as an estate contract under the Land Charges Act 1972, and the House of Lords has held that this suffices to give a subsequent charge made pursuant to the agreement priority over an intervening incumbrance even though the agreement, being for contingent security, does not itself create a security interest (*Williams v Burlington Investments Ltd*, above).

[84] *Smith v Bridgend County BC* [2001] UKHL 58; [2000] 1 A.C. 336 at [61], [63].

[85] *Smith v Bridgend County BC* [2000] 1 A.C. 336 at [44], per Lord Hoffmann, and see also the Court of Appeal decision in the first round of litigation: *Re Cosslett (Contractors) Ltd* [1998] Ch. 495, 509–511, per Millett L.J. Lord Scott also did not consider the issue of consideration discussed in the text.

[86] J. Maxton, "Negative Pledges and Equitable Principles" [1993] J.B.L. 458; for a contrary view, see P. Gabriel, *Legal Aspects of Syndicated Loans* (1986), Vol.2, pp.85–90; J. Stone, "The 'Affirmative'

a security interest cannot attach by virtue of that agreement even on the occurrence of the designated event. There must be either a completed security transaction, by pledge or mortgage, or a new security agreement accompanied or followed by the payment of money; and in the latter case, the security interest will be limited to the amount so paid.[87] It is for this reason that provisions for equal and rateable security in negative pledge clauses are of little value as security devices.[88]

The floating charge is a special case, standing midway between a mere contract for future security and an attached security interest. The floating charge is a present security, not a mere agreement for security on a contingency,[89] but it is security in a shifting fund of assets, not in the specific assets from time to time comprising the fund.[90]

Nature of perfection

When a security interest attaches it becomes enforceable against the debtor himself. But the existence of the security interest will not necessarily be known to a third party who is himself proposing to acquire an interest in the asset, or to other unsecured creditors, particularly where the debtor remains in possession of the asset, or where the asset is intangible. To safeguard such people the law usually requires the secured party to give some form of public notice designed to bring the security interest to the notice of subsequent purchasers or incumbrancers, or unsecured creditors. This requirement of public notice can be called a perfection requirement. A perfection requirement is not a necessary step to render the security enforceable against the debtor himself, for of course as the grantor of the security interest he needs no notice of it.[91]

2–16

The methods by which a security interest can be drawn to public notice vary according to the type of interest created. It is possible to call them all methods of "perfection"[92] but it must be remembered that they do not all operate in the same

---

Negative Pledge" [1991] 9 J.I.B.L. 364. See also T. Cheng-Han, "Charges, Contingencies and Registration" [2002] J.C.L.S. 191, who relies on Australian and Singaporean authority in support of the view that fresh executed consideration is not required. However, the question of consideration was not considered in any of the Australian cases cited, and, although the Singaporean Court of Appeal rejected the view expressed in the text that fresh executed consideration was required to create a new charge (at para.18) this was not part of the ratio of the case as they held that no charge was created for other reasons.

[87] The security interest thus created will require to be registered under s.859A of the Companies Act 2006.

[88] See para.1–81, above. In *Williams v Burlington Investments Ltd* (1977) 121 S.J. 424, it was argued that an agreement for the execution of a charge on demand by the creditor gave rise to an equitable security when the demand was made. The House, while not finding it necessary to rule on the point, appears to have treated the proposition with appropriate scepticism.

[89] *The Annangel Glory* [1988] 1 Lloyd's Rep. 45 which applies the principle that a floating charge is a present security, not a mere agreement to provide security upon a contingency.

[90] See para.1–10, above; para.4–03, below.

[91] A remarkable exception to this rule is to be found in the Bills of Sale Act (1878) Amendment Act 1882, s.8 of which renders an unregistered security bill of sale void as to the security even as against the debtor himself.

[92] For further discussion of the concept of "perfection" see H. Beale, M. Bridge, L. Gullifer and E. Lomnicka, *The Law of Security and Title-Based Financing*, 2nd edn (Oxford: Oxford University Press, 2012), Ch.9.

way, nor is the reasoning behind their effect always the same. The most important method of perfection is where there is a requirement laid down by statute for registration of the security interest in the Company Charges Register (if the interest is created by a company) or in the Bills of Sale Act register (if the interest is created by a person who is not a company). Failure to comply with such requirement means that the security interest will be ineffective against other secured creditors and in the debtor's insolvency.[93] However, in some situations a security interest is not required to be registered in this way. It could then be said that this is because the interest is "perfected" by some other means: this is the analysis that is used in UCC art.9 and the various Personal Property Security Acts.[94] However, this does not really describe the current state of English law: there is no express "requirement" of perfection which can be fulfilled by registration or by some other means. Until recently, there were a number of disparate reasons for there being no registration requirement for certain security interests created by companies. This was due to the fact that the registration requirement in s.860 of the Companies Act 2006 applied to the list of charges in that section, and to nothing else. Reforms brought in in April 2013 have replaced this list with a requirement that all charges created by a company be registered, with two specific (policy driven) exceptions[95] and an exception for charges excluded by any other enactment: this chiefly relates to those charges excluded by the Financial Collateral Arrangements (No.2) Regulations 2003 (the FCARs).[96] It is now easier than before to list security interests created by a company which are not registrable[97]; the chief reason why registration is not required is because public notice is given by other means, for example, where the secured creditor has possession,[98] or control,[99] of the asset, but there are also policy reasons for other exclusions.[100] Unlike under a PPSA regime, it cannot be said that these interests fulfil some sort of requirement of perfection. Indeed, possession is necessary for the creation of a pledge[101] so it is difficult to see this as a separate perfection requirement. The same can be said for security interests created by debtors who are not companies. Unless these are required to be

---

[93] An unregistered Bill of Sale is void as regards everyone, including the debtor, see fn.91 above. Note that, in relation to security interests created by companies, an unregistered interest is not void against a purchaser of the asset, but that the purchaser will normally have priority under the priority rules, see Ch.5.

[94] Such as the Canadian PPSAs, the New Zealand PPSA (Pt 4) and the Australian PPSA (s.21).

[95] See para.2–19, below.

[96] Discussed in detail in Ch.6. Another exempt category are charges created in favour of the Bank of England or any other central bank, see s.252 of the Banking Act 2009.

[97] See para.2–19, below.

[98] For example, in the case of a pledge.

[99] Control by the chargee is a criterion for a charge over financial collateral to be a security financial collateral arrangement, in relation to which any registration requirements imposed by the Companies Act are disapplied, see para.2–19 and para.6–32, below.

[100] See, for example, the exclusion of charges granted in favour of central banks (fn.96, above) and charge granted by members of Lloyds to secure underwriting obligations (s.859A (6)(b)).

[101] See para.2–10, above.

registered as Bills of Sale[102] or as a general assignment of book debts,[103] there is no general requirement of perfection for such interests.

The concept of perfection needs to be kept distinct from the rules of priority, but there is considerable overlap between methods of giving public notice and methods of obtaining priority. Take, for example, the distinction which English law draws between legal and equitable interests. The latter may be displaced by transfer of the legal title to a bona fide purchaser for value without notice. Thus the conversion of an equitable interest into a legal interest affects the priority position of that interest, but does not displace any separate perfection requirement such as registration. In the case of certain types of asset, notably registrable ship and aircraft mortgages and intellectual property rights, a legal interest is obtained only by registration in the relevant specialist register,[104] but such registration will not perfect it so that it is enforceable in the debtor's insolvency and against other secured creditors. If the interest is registrable under the Companies Act or the Bills of Sale Act, then to gain such enforceability it must be duly registered in the Company Charges register or the Bills of Sale register. Further, in order to create a legal mortgage of securities, the transfer of title must be registered on the company's register (for registered certificated securities)[105] or on the CREST register (for uncertificated securities).[106] However, unless the mortgage falls within the FCARs and is thus exempt from the registration requirements, it must also be registered in accordance with s.859A of the Companies Act 2006. In relation to a security interest over a debt or fund, the giving of notice by the security holder to the account debtor[107] could be said to be a means of giving some form of public notice of the security interest and therefore a means of "perfection". This has the effect of securing priority for the notice giver over any purchasers or incumbrancers who have not given this notice.[108] There are also other advantages of giving notice to the account debtor, which are discussed in Ch.3, below.[109] However, this method of giving notice is independent of any registration requirements which may apply: unless the security interest falls under the FCARs, or is otherwise exempt from registration, if it is not registered notice to the account debtor will not prevent it being void against secured creditors and in the debtor's insolvency. Therefore, although giving notice to the account debtor can be seen as a form of perfection, it is very different from perfection by registration.

---

[102] See para.2–32, below. The registration will not show that the transfer is by way of security interest.

[103] See para.3–29, below. The registration will not show that the transfer is by way of security interest.

[104] See para.1–13, above and para.2–32, below.

[105] See para.6–38, below for the effect of this.

[106] See para.6–41, below for the effect of this.

[107] i.e. the person who owes the debt obligation.

[108] *Dearle v Hall* (1828) 3 Russ. 1. It should also be noted that a registered security interest over a debt will have priority over a second security interest over that debt, even if the holder of the second interest is first to give notice, since the latter will have notice of the first security interest because it is registered. This is an example of the operation of the so-called "second limb" of the rule in *Dearle v Hall* (see para.5–08, below) which says that only a second assignee who at the time of taking his assignment has no notice of the previous assignment can gain priority by being the first to give notice to the account debtor.

[109] See para.3–30, below.

Despite the examples of overlap between perfection and priority discussed above, perfection by registration does not guarantee priority over subsequent incumbrancers; that is a matter to be resolved by the priority rules we shall examine later. All that perfection of a security interest does is to give maximum efficacy to the security interest. So an unperfected security interest will usually be invalid against other secured creditors and against unsecured execution and insolvency creditors regardless of any other priority rule[110]; and a perfected security interest will bind other secured creditors and execution and insolvency creditors unless displaced by a particular priority rule.

2–17   This chapter will consider perfection by registration, and also the situations in which registration is not required. Further details of perfection by registration and other means of giving public notice in relation to security interests in intangible property are considered in Ch.3, below.

Registration of security interests created by companies

2–18   As discussed later on, a few years ago the Law Commission proposed considerable changes to the registration system for company charges.[111] Some of the proposals proved to be controversial, and only a very few changes were made at the time of the Companies Act 2006.[112] However, that Act included a power to make amendments to Pt 25 of that Act (which dealt with the registration of charges, and which largely re-enacted Pt 12 of the Companies Act 1985).[113] In 2010 the Department for Business, Innovation and Skills (BIS) started a consultation process regarding more widespread amendments to the registration process: after a number of consultations, new regulations were brought into force applying to all charges created after April 6, 2013.[114] The previous law continues to apply to charges created before that date.

The new regime addresses several shortcomings in the previous law. First, it replaces the list of registrable interests with a provision making all charges registrable, with limited exceptions. Secondly, it abolishes the criminal sanction for non-registration.[115] Thirdly, it provides for a new scheme enabling registration to be done electronically. There are a number of other more detailed amendments to the registration scheme. In this chapter we will consider certain aspects of the new scheme, in the context of the general law. No attempt will be made to give a comprehensive account of the new scheme.[116]

---

[110] See para.2–22, below.

[111] See para.2–33, below.

[112] In particular, in relation to registration of overseas companies' charges, see para.2–22, below.

[113] Companies Act 2006 s.894. A more general power is also included in s.1292 of that Act.

[114] The Companies Act 2006 (Amendment of Pt 25) Regulations 2013 (SI 2013/600).

[115] The other consequences of non-registration are retained, see para.2–23, below.

[116] For this, see Tolley's Company Law Service, "Company Charges III: Registration of Charges, Overseas Companies, and Scotland" (Issue 130, August 2013) ed. M. Evans, J. Walsh, D. Peel, S.Buckingham; also (2013) 28 B.J.I.B. & F.L. 326.

Security interests which are not required to be registered

There is no doubt that the change from a list of registrable charges to a provision   **2–19**
that all charges are registered is to be warmly welcomed. The difficulties of
identifying which charges fell within the list and which did not were
considerable, as evidenced by the discussion in the previous editions of this book.
There are now only a few categories of security interests not required to be
registered. These are:

(1)   Charges in favour of a landlord over a cash deposit as security for
obligations owed by a tenant.[117]

(2)   Charges created by Lloyds' members in connection with their underwriting
business.[118]

(3)   Security interests which arise by operation of law. Most of these are
possessory liens, which involve possession by the secured party and
therefore also fall within the category discussed below, but non-possessory
equitable liens are also included.[119]

(4)   Security interests which are security financial collateral arrangements
within the meaning of reg.3 of the Financial Collateral Arrangements
(No.2) Regulations 2003.[120]

(5)   Security interests granted in favour of the Bank of England or another
central bank.[121]

(6)   Security interests where the holder is in possession of the assets, that is,
pledges and liens.

It will be seen that these exceptions cannot be rationalised under one principle.
Some are the result of policy considerations based largely on convenience (such
as (1) and (2) and maybe (5)). Exception (3) is probably because it would be
impractical to require registration of interests arising by operation of law, since
the parties may not know that this has occurred. One might rationalise the
exception for possessory interests (6) on the basis that possession gives sufficient
notice to the outside world that the security interest exists. This point is discussed
in the next paragraph. For a security interest to be a security financial collateral
arrangement under the FCARs it is necessary for the collateral taker to have
possession or control of the collateral.[122] It might be thought that the purpose of
this requirement was also to give some sort of notice of the interest to the outside
world. However, this does not seem to be the case, or at least not the only reason
for the requirement, since it is reasonably clear that that not only practical control

---

[117] Companies Act 2006 s.859A(6)(a).

[118] Companies Act 2006 s.859A(6)(b).

[119] *London and Cheshire Insurance Co Ltd v Laplagrene Property Ltd* [1971] Ch. 499, 514. For
discussion of equitable liens see Beale, Bridge, Gullifer and Lomnicka, *The Law of Security and
Title-Based Financing* (2012), paras 6.140–6.163.

[120] Financial Collateral Arrangements (No.2) Regulations 2003 (SI 2003/3226). See para.6–32,
below.

[121] Banking Act 2009 s.252. There is likely to be considerable overlap between this category and
category (4).

[122] See paras 6–32 et seq., below.

but legal control is required. Legal control refers to the rights and obligations between the two parties themselves, and so cannot be relevant to the issue of notice.[123]

Possession by the security interest holder

2–20   Registration has never been a requirement where the security interest holder is in possession of the assets subject to the security interest. This is usually rationalised on the basis that possession is sufficient notice of the interest and so registration is not necessary. Even under the UCC art.9 and PPSA regimes, where the scope of registration of interests which have the function of security is much wider, possessory interests are not required to be registered. However, especially where possession is transferred to the creditor by attornment rather than by an actual transfer of possession, it is hard to see that the creditor's possession constitutes very effective public notice. There is one particular situation, in which a pledge is created by attornment by the debtor, where there is no public notice of the security interest, and the attornment is in writing. As discussed above,[124] it seemed that this security interest was registrable under s.860(7)(b) of the Companies Act 2006[125] and should also be registrable under the new regime.

Another situation where registration would be desirable, is where pledged goods are released to the pledgor under a trust receipt. Under the previous regime, the interest of the pledgee in the proceeds under the trust receipt was not registrable as it was said to derive by operation of law from the pre-existing pledge.[126] However, the interest is clearly a security interest (in that it only extends to the amount of the proceeds required to redeem the pledge). Further, the pledgor is in possession of the goods, so the same false wealth arguments apply as to the pledge created by the pledgor's attornment. There are therefore good reasons for such an interest to be registrable.[127] The only argument against this is that trust receipts interests tend to be of very short duration, and registration is then likely to be impractical. For this reason, the Law Commission suggested that registration would be required within 15 days of creation but would not be required if the goods were returned to the pledgee before the expiry of that time.[128]

Perfection by registration

2–21   As mentioned above, all charges created by companies are registrable under s.859A of the Companies Act 2006, except for those listed above.[129] This registration requirement is a perfection requirement as described above, and lack

---

[123] For more discussion, see paras 6–35 et seq., below.
[124] See para.2–10, above.
[125] *Dublin City Distillery Ltd v Doherty* [1914] A.C. 823, 854–857.
[126] *Re David Allester Ltd* [1922] 2 Ch. 211.
[127] See Beale, Bridge, Gullifer and Lomnicka, *The Law of Security and Title-Based Financing* (2012), para.5.30; Law Commission, *Company Security Interests*, Law Com. No.296 (2005), paras 3.22–3.25; and Yung, "Pledge by constructive delivery in Hong Kong" (2013) 24 I.C.C.L.R. 273, 276–277.
[128] Law Commission, *Company Security Interests*, Law Com. No.296 (2005), para.3.25.
[129] See para.2–19, above.

of registration renders the security interest void in the debtor's insolvency. Perfection by registration is sometimes complicated by the ability to register in a specialist register in addition to registration under the Companies Act.[130] Registration in a specialist register is not a perfection requirement in the sense that that registration is compulsory, nor is an unregistered security interest void in the debtor's insolvency.[131] However, registration in the appropriate specialist register is necessary in order to create a legal mortgage,[132] although in some registers equitable mortgages and charges can also be registered. Further, in many cases the order of registration determines the order of priority, for example, in relation to interests over land, registered ships and aircraft[133] and agricultural charges,[134] and a registered interest has priority over an unregistered one.[135] Where, as with mortgages over registered ships, equitable mortgages can also be registered, this priority rule has the effect of breaking down the distinction between legal and equitable mortgages, so that the type of mortgage that is created is a sui generis statutory mortgage.[136]

2. REGISTRATION UNDER SECTION 859A OF THE COMPANIES ACT 2006

Registrable charges

This paragraph will address two aspects of the scope of the reformed scheme which have not already been covered[137]: charges created by overseas companies, and trustee companies. Subsequent paragraphs will discuss the registration regime in outline, focusing particularly on the issue of notice. 2–22

One of the major changes brought about by the BIS reforms is that there is now one regime applying to charges created by companies registered in any part of the United Kingdom, whereas before there was a separate scheme for charges created by companies registered in Scotland.[138] This harmonisation process has many obvious benefits, although it has made the drafting of the provisions a little

---

[130] As to the specialist registers, see para.2–32, below.

[131] When electronic conveyancing becomes compulsory, registration of mortgages and charges over registered land will be compulsory, Land Registration Act 2002 s.93, however, this is unlikely to happen soon, see para.5–27 fn.120, below.

[132] See para.1–13, above.

[133] Land Registration Act 2002 s.48 (registered mortgages of registered land), Law of Property Act 1925 s.97 (puisne mortgages of unregistered land which are registered as land charges) (although in relation to the interrelation between this section and s.4(5) of the Land Charges Act 1972 see para.5–16, below), Merchant Shipping Act 1995 Sch. 1 para.8. (registered mortgages and charges of registered ships), Mortgaging of Aircraft Order 1972 (SI 1972/1268) art.14 (registered mortgages and charges of registered aircraft).

[134] Agricultural Credits Act 1982 s.8(2).

[135] Land Registration Act 2002 s.30, Land Charges Act 1972 s.4(5), Merchant Shipping Act 1995 Sch. 1 para.8, Mortgaging of Aircraft Order 1972 (SI 1972/1268). The position in relation to mortgages of patents and trade marks is slightly different, see para.5–16, below.

[136] A. Clarke, *Interests in Goods*, N. Palmer and E. McKendrick (eds), 2nd edn (London: Lloyd's of London Press, 1998), p.683.

[137] The question of what charges are now registrable is discussed at para.2–19, above.

[138] Companies Act 2006 Pt 25 Ch.2.

more complex.[139] If a company is registered in the United Kingdom, any charge it creates is registrable even if created outside the United Kingdom and comprising property situated outside the United Kingdom. Charges created by overseas companies are no longer registrable in the Companies Register,[140] so that the so-called "Slavenburg register"[141] has been abolished.[142]

In the past, there has been considerable doubt about the application of the registration provisions to charges granted by a trustee company. One view has been that these are not registrable at all: not against the trustee company, since it was not the beneficial owner of the charged assets, and not against the beneficial owner, since it had not created the charge. Reinforcing this conclusion was the fact that in relation to unsecured creditors in a winding up the sanction of invalidity for non-registration had no meaning, since the charged assets, being trust assets, could not be claimed by the liquidator anyway. Further, s.874 of the Companies Act, which established the sanction of invalidity referred to "any security on the company's property", which could be said not to include property which the company did not own beneficially.[143] Another view is that a trustee company, which unlike a bare trustee has management powers, is to be considered the full owner of the charged assets and that the charge should therefore be registered against it. In practice, chargees usually do register against the trustee company *ex abundante cautela*. The Law Commission proposed legislative provisions requiring registration against the trustee company.[144] While such a provision was not included in the BIS reforms, the new scheme does enable a trustee company registering a charge to deliver a statement to the registrar stating the position.[145] This reflects current practice. The new equivalent to s.874 is unchanged,[146] so that residual doubt about whether charges created by a trustee are required to be registered still remains. However, the better view both from a policy and practical view is that they are, and any difficulties flowing from this are ameliorated by the new provision.[147]

What will now be discussed are a number of questions relating to the effect of registration of charges in general and floating charges in particular.

---

[139] Note that the Scottish Law Commission is considering more radical reform to the law relating to assignment and security over moveable property. It issued a discussion paper (DP 151) in 2011 and intends to report back in 2014.

[140] This reform was brought into force earlier than the other reforms (Overseas Companies (Execution of Documents and Registration of Charges) (Amendment) Regulations 2011 (SI 2011/2194)) after some temporary changes enacted in 2009.

[141] Named after the decision in *NV Slavenburg's Bank v Intercontinental Natural Resources Ltd* [1980] 1 All E.R. 955.

[142] It is still necessary, however, for an overseas company to keep available for inspection a register of charges over land in the UK, ships, aircraft or intellectual property registered in the UK or any floating charge over property situated in the UK (Overseas Companies (Execution of Documents and Registration of Charges) (Amendment) Regulations 2011 (SI 2011/2194) regs 23 and 24).

[143] Beale, Bridge, Gullifer and Lomnicka, *The Law of Security and Title-Based Financing* (2012), para.10.31.

[144] Law Commission, *Company Security Interests*, Law Com. No.296 (2005), paras 3.112–3.115.

[145] Companies Act 2006 s.859J(1).

[146] Companies Act 2006 s.859H.

[147] Companies Act 2006 s.859J(1).

Registration is a perfection requirement

At the risk of restating the obvious, it should be emphasised that registration within 21 days of creation of a charge[148] is a perfection requirement, which has to be complied with in order to make the charge effective against a liquidator, an administrator and creditors. By "creditors" is meant creditors having an interest in the charged assets, and thus a locus standi to complain of want of perfection, i.e. secured[149] and execution creditors[150] and lienees and, if (but only if) the company has gone into liquidation or administration, unsecured creditors.[151] An unregistered charge is not, as the law currently stands, void against outright purchasers of the charged assets. This lacuna was pointed out in the Diamond Report,[152] and the ill-fated Companies Act 1989 included a provision that an unregistered charge was void against "any person who for value acquires an interest in or right over property subject to the charge".[153] At one point, BIS proposed to include a provision dealing with this point,[154] but this was dropped, maybe because of concern that the power in s.894 is not wide enough to include it. This is one of a number of opportunities missed by the reforms.[155]

2–23

With the abolition of the criminal sanction by the BIS reforms, registration of charges is no longer compulsory in the sense that it was before, but is a commercial decision for the chargee,[156] who must decide whether to risk invalidity on the chargor's insolvency. Thus short term charges may not be registered in practice, even though they are registrable. Registration is not a requirement for attachment; an unregistered charge is good against the company itself, so long as it is not in winding up or administration. Nor is registration a priority point.[157] Priority of competing charges is governed by the rules described in Ch.5, below, not by the order of registration. So an intending lender who advances money to a company in reliance on a clear search should not assume that he is protected; there may well be an earlier charge granted within the preceding 21 days that has not yet been registered, but that will be duly registered and will therefore have priority as the first in time. Unfortunately there is no provision in the Companies Act comparable to that of the property legislation by which protection is given to one who makes a pre-completion search and then completes his own transaction within 14 days.[158] Similarly, registration does not

---

[148] Companies Act 2006 s.859A(4).

[149] *Re Monolithic Building Co* [1915] 1 Ch. 643.

[150] *Re Ashpurton Estates Ltd* [1983] Ch. 110, 123.

[151] Companies Act 2006 s.859H.

[152] Diamond Report (Ch.1 fn.19) para.24.3. See also *Re Overseas Aviation Engineering (GB) Ltd* [1963] Ch. 24, 38; *Stroud Architectural Services Ltd v John Laing Construction Ltd* [1994] 2 B.C.L.C. 276; cf. *E. Pfeiffer Weinkellerei-Weineinkauf GmbH & Co v Arbuthnot Factors Ltd* [1988] 1 W.L.R. 150, 155 where the issue is ignored and a purchaser is treated as a creditor.

[153] Companies Act 1989 s.94, new s.399.

[154] *Government Response – Consultation on Registration of Charges created by Companies and Limited Liability Partnerships* (December 2010) (proposal F).

[155] See L. Gullifer, "Personal Property Security, Where Next? (Part 1)" [2012] B.J.I.F.L. 465.

[156] See *Revised Scheme for Registration of Charges created by Companies and Limited Liability Partnerships: proposed revision of Pt 25, Companies Act 2006*, comments to s.860.

[157] However, failure to register may have priority effects. See paras 3–28 and 5–28, below.

[158] Priority issues were not addressed by the BIS reforms. This is mainly because of the view taken by BIS of the scope of the power in s.894(1), see BIS, *Registration of Charges created by Companies and Limited Liability Partnerships: Proposals to amend the current scheme and relating to specialist*

guarantee priority against subsequent interests. This is so even where registration constitutes notice of the charge, for notice is not necessarily in all cases a determinant of priority.[159]

The new registration scheme

2–24   Before considering whether, and to what extent, registration is notice, it is necessary to consider the new scheme in a little more detail. In order to register, the chargor or any person with interests in the charge (usually the chargee or its agent) must deliver to the registrar a statement of particulars and a certified copy of the charge instrument within 21 days of the creation of the charge. It is possible to obtain an extension to this period on application to the court.[160] Section 859E sets out in some detail the date on which a charge is taken to be created[161]; these largely reflect current English law[162] and, although expressed only to be for the purposes of calculating the period for registration, are likely to apply for other purposes (such as priority) since any disjunction would be most unfortunate. The particulars and the certified copy can be delivered electronically, in which case the filer has to obtain an authorisation code, which then applies to all filings it makes.[163] On delivery of the relevant document, the registrar includes both the certified copy of the charge instrument[164] and the particulars on the register,[165] and gives a certificate of registration to the person who registered the charge[166]: this is merely conclusive evidence of delivery of the necessary documents. Under the previous regime, the registrar's department checked the particulars against the charge instrument, so the certificate issued was conclusive as to the accuracy of the particulars, and any risk of inaccuracy was borne by those searching.[167] Under the new regime, no such check takes place, but searchers are able to check the particulars themselves against the registered

---

register' BIS/10/1319 (March 2010), para.7. Compare the position in Ireland, see N. McGrath, "The company charge register in Ireland: some reflections on the reform proposals in the Companies Consolidation and Reform Bill 2012" [2013] J.B.L. 303.

[159]   See paras 5–15 and 5–40, below.

[160]   Companies Act 2006 s.859F. The grounds for the granting of such extension are identical to those in s.873 for the extension of time or the rectification of the register, and it is likely that the previous practice, which was to make grants of extension of time conditional on being without prejudice to the rights of parties acquired during the period between creation and registration, see *Re Kris Cruisers Ltd* [1949] Ch. 138, 141.

[161]   This was included mainly in order to achieve uniformity with the existing Scottish law, see *Revised Scheme for Registration of Charges created by Companies and Limited Liability Partnerships: proposed revision of Part 25, Companies Act 2006*, comments to s.860A.

[162]   Where the charge is created by an instrument, it is taken to taken to have been created on the date on which the instrument is intended to have effect (the provisions relating to deeds are more complicated and this is a broad summary). This, then, is consistent with the view expressed above, para.2–13, that a charge over future property is continuously attached even when there is no property falling within the charge.

[163]   See information on *http://www.companieshouse.gov.uk/pressDesk/news/eCharges.shtml* [accessed September 20, 2013].

[164]   Provision is made for the redaction of sensitive personal information, see s.859G of the Companies Act 2006.

[165]   These two documents are linked electronically by a unique reference code.

[166]   Companies Act 2006 s.859I.

[167]   *National Provincial and Union Bank of England v Charnley* [1924] 1 K.B. 431; *Re Advantage Healthcare (T10) Ltd* [2000] 1 B.C.L.C. 661.

charge instrument. Thus searchers still take the risk that the particulars are inaccurate, but they are at least able to find out inaccuracies for themselves. This may not be the case where a negative pledge clause is included in an agreement other than the charge agreement.[168]

Section 859D sets out what particulars are required to be included. As well as identifying the chargor and chargee, these include whether the charge is fixed or floating, and, if floating, whether the terms include a negative pledge clause, and, if fixed, whether the charged assets include any land, ship, aircraft or intellectual property required to be registered in the United Kingdom.[169] It might be wondered why particulars are required, since the charge document appears on the register. According to BIS, there are two purposes in requiring the registration of particulars. The first is so that an informed decision can be taken whether to inspect the filed instrument and the second is for the benefit of those who do bulk downloads of information or broad-brush analyses.[170] These people require information in a form which is easier to manipulate than the PDF form of the copied instrument, and are, it is said, less concerned about possible inaccuracies in the particulars.

Registration as notice[171]

It has commonly been said that registration of a charge constitutes notice to the outside world. But this formulation raises three questions: notice of what?; by what means?; and to whom? We should now add the question whether the previous law has been changed by the new registration regime. At various stages in the drafting process provisions clarifying the law on constructive notice were included in the new legislation, but in the end no such provisions were included. As a result, not only is the existing law unclear, but it is unclear precisely what is the effect of registration under the new regime on those who do not check the register. The following discussion considers the three questions mentioned above in relation to both the previous regime and the new regime.[172]

2–25

Of what facts does registration constitute notice?

(1) Pre-2013 regime

Registration of a charge is not notice of its contents

Under the pre-2013 regime it was well established that registration of a charge, though notice of the existence of the charge, was not notice of the contents of the

2–26

---

[168] I am indebted to Marisa Chan of Clifford Chance for this point.

[169] Companies Act 2006 s.859D(2). If there is no charge instrument, more information is required (s.859D)(1)(d) and (3)).

[170] *Revised Scheme for Registration of Charges created by Companies and Limited Liability Partnerships: proposed revision of Part 25, Companies Act 2006*, comments to s.860A.

[171] For an exhaustive treatment of this subject under the pre-2013 regime, see J. de Lacy, "Constructive Notice and Company Charge Registration" (2001) 65 Conv. 122.

[172] It should be borne in mind that, at the moment, there are many charges registered under the old regime still on the register to which, presumably, the old law on constructive notice applies.

instrument of charge,[173] despite the fact that a party searching the register and obtaining details of a registered charge[174] was then entitled to inspect a copy of the charge instrument at the company's registered office.[175]

This rule had little impact on the rights of a fixed chargee. In the case of a fixed charge, the debtor has neither actual nor ostensible authority to dispose of the charged asset free from the charge. Hence notice of the existence of the charge suffices to preserve the chargee's priority over a subsequent legal mortgagee. The position was otherwise in the case of a floating charge, where a third party dealing with the debtor company was entitled to assume that it has freedom to dispose of its assets, in the absence of notice of restrictions on the debtor's powers of disposition, that is, a negative pledge clause.

Particulars to be filed

2–27   Under the pre-2013 regime, it was clear that as regards all particulars which were required to be filed under the Companies Act, the filing of those particulars constitutes notice of them, at any rate as regards third parties who could reasonably be expected to make a search. If certain particulars were omitted, although the grant of the conclusive certificate had the effect that the registration requirements had been complied with, the better view was that registration did not constitute notice as regards those particulars which ought to have been filed and were not, and that a searcher was entitled to rely on the accuracy of the particulars filed. So if he was misled by the omission of a part of the security or by any other material mis-description of the assets comprising the security, he was not fixed with notice of the matters omitted or misstated.

Particulars filed voluntarily (negative pledge clause)

2–28   Where a floating charge created restrictions on the debtor's powers of disposal—typically, by providing that the debtor should not create any subsequent charge ranking in priority to or pari passu with the floating charge or sell any of its assets outside the ordinary course of business (a negative pledge clause)—it was customary to record brief details of these restrictions in the filed particulars. It was reasonably clear that this constituted notice of the negative pledge clause to those who actually searched the register, but not to those who did not, even though they might have been expected to do so.[176] Thus, filing was

---

[173] *English & Scottish Mercantile Investment Co v Brunton* [1892] 2 Q.B. 700; *Wilson v Kelland* [1910] 2 Ch. 306; *Siebe Gorman & Co Ltd v Barclays Bank Ltd* [1979] 2 Lloyd's Rep. 142.

[174] The only documents of which copies could be obtained from Companies House were the form containing the particulars for registration, and the certificate of registration. Thus the only way a creditor could see the charge instrument was by asking the debtor or the secured party for a copy, or by inspection at the company's offices. Of course, this is changed under the new regime.

[175] Companies Act 2006 s.877. It should be noted that the requirement to register charges in company's own register, and to make such charges available for inspection, included all charges created by the company over its property and not just those registrable at Companies House under s.860.

[176] *English & Scottish Mercantile Investment Co v Brunton* [1892] 2 Q.B. 700; *Standard Rotary Machine Co Ltd* (1906) 95 L.T. 829; *Wilson v Kelland* [1910] 2 Ch. 306, 313; *G & T Earle Ltd v Hemsworth Ltd* (1928) 154 T.L.R. 605; *Welch v Bowmaker (Ireland) Ltd* [1980] I.R. 251; *Re Salthill Properties Ltd* (2004) I.E.H.C. 145.

constructive notice as regards those matters for which it is required but not as regards optional extras. An argument had been made that such restrictive provisions are now so common that a third party has inferred knowledge of them at common law once he has acquired notice of the existence of the floating charge.[177] However, it was argued in previous editions of this book that this view did not represent the law.[178]

(2) The New Regime

Applying these principles to the new regime, one might have thought that someone searching the register would have actual notice of everything in the charge instrument as well as everything in the particulars, since all these matters appear on the register. Furthermore, a person for whom registration is constructive notice[179] would have such notice of the same material, on the grounds that they are required to be registered. However, it is necessary to examine what is meant by "required to be registered" under the old law. When non-registration was a criminal act, registration of registrable charges could reasonably be said to be compulsory. Under the new regime, since the criminal sanction has been abolished, whether to register is a commercial decision and registration is no longer compulsory. It is at least arguable that registration under the new scheme does not constitute constructive notice of anything registered: this would, of course, be an unfortunate consequence and it is a shame that this uncertainty was not remedied by an express provision (for the avoidance of doubt) as to whether and of what registration constituted constructive notice. After all, one reason for including, in the required particulars, an indication of whether there is a negative pledge clause was to overcome the restriction discussed above.[180]

2–29

It is also unclear what the position is if the registered particulars do not reflect the charge instrument accurately. Suppose, for example, the "negative pledge" box is not ticked, even though a negative pledge clause is included? Does this mean that the statement of particulars is not a "s.859D statement of particulars" within s.859D(1), so that the charge is not properly registered under s.859A? Although this is arguable, it would be unfortunate if registration could be invalidated by a mistake and so it is more likely that the registration is valid, and that searchers take the risk that the particulars are not accurate.[181] Of what, though, would someone not searching have constructive notice? Would it be of the (accurate) charge instrument or of the (inaccurate) particulars? Although it could be said that the registered charge instrument, as the definitive document, "trumps" the particulars so that the person has constructive notice of its contents, there is nothing in the regulations to make this clear.[182]

2–30

---

[177] J. H. Farrar, "Floating Charges and Priorities" (1974) 38 Conv. (N.S.) 315, at 319 et seq.

[178] Some support for this was to be found in the judgment of Deputy Judge Kwan in *ABN Amro Bank NV v Chiyu Banking Corp Ltd* [2001] 2 H.K.L.R.D. 175.

[179] See para.2–30, below.

[180] See para.2–28, above.

[181] See para.2–26, above.

[182] I am indebted to Professor Hugh Beale for discussion on this particular point, as well as more on this topic. Again, the problem is even more difficult when the negative pledge clause is not included in the charge agreement but in another agreement, see para.2–24, above.

To whom is registration notice?

2–31   Even as regards those matters of which registration constitutes notice—i.e. the existence of the charge and those obligatory particulars which are in fact filed—it does not follow that the whole world is affected. It has been held in several cases that the doctrine of constructive notice does not apply to chattels or to commercial transactions.[183] But those decisions must be read in their context and should not be taken to lay down any absolute rule. In particular, a distinction must be drawn between those buying goods from a supplier selling in the ordinary course of business and those lending money on the security of goods or other assets. What can be said with some confidence, having regard to the underlying purpose of the doctrine of notice, is that registration is notice only to those who could reasonably be expected to search.[184] This would normally exclude a buyer of goods in the ordinary course of business,[185] for it would be quite impracticable to expect a purchaser from a manufacturer or dealer to search in the Companies Registry every time he wishes to consummate a purchase; and since the buyer of goods comprised in a floating charge is not bound by the charge merely because he knows of it, but only if he is on notice that the sale to him is in breach of the terms of the charge, such a buyer will usually take free from the chargee's rights regardless of any registered restriction on dealing.

However, it is less clear that this argument applies to an absolute assignee of receivables, who takes the assignment as part of a financing transaction. Further, should those taking unregistrable security interests, such as possessory security interests[186] or security financial collateral arrangements, be expected to search? It is a shame that the 2013 Regulations do not deal expressly with the question of to whom registration is constructive notice. The issue was dealt with in the Companies Act 1989,[187] and was also included in the earlier papers produced by BIS[188]; one of the very latest drafts before the Regulations came into force included a provision identical to that in the Companies Act 1989, but this limited constructive notice to anyone taking a charge over the company's property. This is both too narrow (it did not include receivables financiers or pledgees) and probably too wide in that it potentially included those taking security financial collateral arrangements, who, since their own charges were not registrable, might reasonably be expected not to check the register. It is therefore to be welcomed that this provision was not included in the final Regulations. It would, however,

---

[183] *Manchester Trust v Furness* [1895] 2 Q.B. 539; *By Appointment (Sales) Ltd v Harrods Ltd* Unreported 1977 CA (Bar Library transcript No.465); *Feuer Leather Corp v Frank Johnstone & Sons* [1981] Comm. L.R. 251.

[184] A different view is taken by Gough, *Company Charges*, 3rd edn (London: LexisNexis Butterworths, 1996), Ch.32. For a detailed rebuttal of the view express in Gough see Beale, Bridge, Gullifer and Lomnicka, *The Law of Security and Title-Based Financing* (2012), paras 12.04–12.14.

[185] *Feuer Leather Corp v Frank Johnstone & Sons* [1981] Comm. L.R. 251.

[186] Lord Hacking in the House of Lords debate on the 1989 Companies Act (1989 *Hansard*, HL Vol.505, 1217) argued that it would not be reasonable to expect a pledgee who is not himself registering to check the register. Cotton L.J. in *Joseph v Lyons* (1884) 15 Q.B.D. 280, 286 was of the opinion that a pawnbroker was not expected to search the Bills of Sale register.

[187] Companies Act 1989 s.103, new s.416.

[188] BIS, *Government Response – Consultation on Registration of Charges created by Companies and Limited Liability Partnerships*, BIS/10/1319 (December 2010) (proposal F).

have been useful to have legislative clarity in this area, even though, in practice, most persons taking an interest in company's property will search the register, and so constructive notice is irrelevant.

3.   THE SPECIALIST REGISTERS[189]

Apart from the register maintained by the Companies Registry for charges by companies falling within s.859A of the Companies Act 2006 there are at least ten specialist registers providing for registration of security interests in particular types of asset, namely registers for bills of sale,[190] charges over registered land,[191] charges over unregistered land,[192] agricultural charges,[193] ship mortgages over registered ships or shares therein,[194] aircraft mortgages over registered aircraft,[195] mortgages of patents,[196] trade marks,[197] and registered designs,[198] and charges granted by an industrial and provident society.[199] When granted by a company most of these categories of charge are concurrently registrable under the Companies Act 2006 and if not so registered will be void against secured creditors and against a liquidator or administrator and creditors generally in a winding-up.[200]

2–32

Certain features common to a number of these specialist registers may be noted. First, in most cases a mortgage or charge on an asset is registrable only if ownership of the asset has been registered. Secondly, though a security interest can still be created without registration it will generally take effect in equity only. Thirdly, registration is usually a priority point, so that priority is determined by the order of registration. This is not changed by notice of the prior interest or by the fact that the security interest is also registrable under the Companies Act, where the order of registration is irrelevant to priorities.[201]

---

[189] See para.2–16, above.

[190] Established under the Bills of Sale Acts 1878 and 1882 and located in the Filing Department of the Royal Courts of Justice. These provide for registration of both absolute and security bills of sale (written chattel mortgages) and also require a general assignment of book debts by an unincorporated trader to be registered as it were a bill of sale.

[191] i.e. land registered under the Land Registration Act 2002.

[192] Maintained in the Land Charges Registry under the Land Charges Act 1972.

[193] Which must be registered in the Land Registry under the Agricultural Credits Act 1928 s.9.

[194] Merchant Shipping Act 1995 Sch.1 and Merchant Shipping (Registration of Ships) Regulations 1993 (SI 1993/3138).

[195] Maintained under the Mortgaging of Aircraft Order 1972 (SI 1972/1268).

[196] Patents Act 1977 s.33.

[197] Trade Marks Act 1994 s.25.

[198] Registered Designs Act 1949 s.19.

[199] Registrable in the central office established under the Industrial and Provident Societies Act 1896 s.1 and exempt from the Bills of Sale Acts if an application is lodged within 14 days (Industrial and Provident Societies Act 1965 s.1).

[200] Companies Act 2006 s.859H.

[201] The position in relation to mortgages of patents, registered designs and trade-marks is slightly different, see para.5–16, below.

4.   PROPOSALS FOR REFORM

2–33   It has been suggested by the Law Commission that registration be made a priority point, not merely a perfection requirement.[202] This would have several advantages. First, it would remove the problem of the invisibility period and makes the grant of security transparent. Secondly, it would obviate the need to require registration within a stated period,[203] and the consequent expense of obtaining leave to register out of time; a secured creditor would have every incentive to register as quickly as possible in order to avoid the risk of subordination to another secured creditor who registered first. Indeed, the proposals go further and advocate[204] the adoption of the "notice filing" system embodied in art.9 of the Uniform Commercial Code, as well as the Canadian, New Zealand and Australian Personal Property Security Acts,[205] which dispenses with the filing of transaction documents and even the need for transaction details and permits the filing of a simple financing statement specifying the asset or description of asset in which the registrant has acquired or may acquire a security interest. In contrast to the system under the Companies Act 2006, notice-filing is not transaction-based; a single filing can cover all future secured transactions between the parties, obviating the need for a separate filing for each security interest. A consequential feature is that the steps to perfection (agreement, value, filing) can be taken in any order, so that a financing statement may be filed before the security agreement has been concluded and no further filing is required when the agreement has been made and value given. Priority goes back to the time of filing, so that a subsequent secured creditor who took and perfected his security interest first will nevertheless be on notice from the financing statement that his priority is liable to be displaced.

The Law Commission's proposals in its final report were limited to traditional types of security[206] and did not include quasi-security interests, since proposals to include the latter in the scheme had met with a great deal of dissent. Despite this, the proposals in the final report were thought by some to be controversial[207] and, as has been discussed, reform so far has been very limited. Various research

---

[202] Law Commission, *Company Security Interests*, Law Com. No.296 (2005), para.3.155. Note that a similar regime is being introduced in Ireland, see Companies Bill 2012 s.413 and N. McGrath, "The company charge register in Ireland: some reflections on the reform proposals in the Companies Consolidation and Reform Bill 2012" [2013] J.B.L. 303.

[203] A requirement the Law Commission logically proposed should be abolished (*Company Security Interests*, para.3.82). The abolition would be subject to an extension of s.245 of the Insolvency Act 1986 (avoidance of floating charges created in the run-up to insolvency) to floating charges registered in the run-up to insolvency even though created earlier, see ibid. para.3.85.

[204] *Company Security Interests*, para.3.91.

[205] A similar regime is being introduced in Jersey in two stages. The first, dealing with intangible property, has been enacted in the Security Interests (Jersey) Law 2012. See Gullifer, "Personal Property Security, Where Next? (Part 2)" [2012] B.J.I.F.L. 541. See also the UNCITRAL Legislative Guide to Secured Transactions, and book XI of the Draft Common Frame of Reference (DCFR) produced in 2009 by the drafting team of the Study Group on a European Civil Code and the Research Group on EC Private Law (Acquis Group).

[206] Although some outright assignments of receivables were also included.

[207] See, for example, the comments of the Financial Law Committee of the City of London Law Society (August 31, 2005).

groups are continuing to examine the idea of further reform.[208] It is hard to overstate the importance of the law relating to secured transactions to the economic wellbeing of the economy, and it is vital to continue to examine critically the present law and consider improvement.

---

[208] These range from the Scottish Law Commission, who produced Discussion Paper 151 in 2011 and will report in 2014 to Secured Transaction Law Reform Project (set up by Professor Sir Roy Goode and chaired by Lord Savile of Newdigate) and City of London Law Society Secured Transaction Reform Project, chaired by Richard Calnan.

CHAPTER 3

Attachment, Perfection and Effects of Fixed Security in Non-Documentary Receivables

1. INTRODUCTION

Intangible property is today the most valuable object of security for the financier, and pure intangibles[1] possess several advantages over tangible assets. They are not susceptible to physical loss, damage or deterioration; they can be stored on and transferred by computer and turned over in huge volumes without constraints of size or physical delivery requirements; and they may be notionally shifted from one country to another at the press of a button. This does not mean that they are free from risk. Intellectual property rights may be attacked as invalid or lose their value because of superior competing products; debtors may become insolvent; and supposed debtors may assert against a mortgagee or chargee defences based on non-performance or defective performance by the mortgagor or chargor or rights of set-off in respect of cross-claims against the mortgagor or chargor.[2] But the ease with which intangibles may be given in security makes them an ideal form of collateral.

Intangibles are also distinctive in that, depending on their nature, they may be mortgaged in up to three different ways: by assignment, by novation, and by negotiation.[3]

The particular form of intangible examined in the present chapter is the account receivable (abbreviated to "receivable"), by which is meant the right to payment of a sum of money, whether presently or in the future, for goods supplied, services rendered or facilities made available, being a right not embodied in a negotiable instrument.[4] The discussion is concerned with fixed security interests.[5] Floating charges, and the particular problems of distinguishing

3–01

---

[1] As distinguished from documentary intangibles. See para.1–48, above.

[2] The subject of set-off is discussed in Ch.7, below.

[3] See paras 3–03 et seq., below as to assignment and novation.

[4] In other words, debts. But "receivables" is a convenient term, first, because it makes it clear that the perspective is that of the creditor, not the debtor, and secondly, because it avoids confusion with book debts, which constitute a narrower category. See also the definition of "receivables" in reg.2(3) of the draft Regulations included in the Law Commission, *Company Security Interests*, Law Com. No.296 (2005). For a comprehensive treatment of the subject, see F. Oditah, *Legal Aspects of Receivables Financing* (London: Sweet & Maxwell, 1991). As to documentary intangibles, which are susceptible to pledge as well as mortgage or charge, see para.1–48, above.

[5] Fixed security interests over receivables have become more difficult to create as a result of the *Spectrum* decision [2005] UKHL 41; [2005] 2 A.C. 680, see para.4–16, below. It has been argued that

a fixed charge of receivables from a floating charge, are analysed in Ch.4, below. Priority issues are the subject of Ch.5, below. The special problems arising in connection with security interests in investment securities, and particularly in investment securities held indirectly with an intermediary, are examined in Ch.6, below.

3–02   Receivables financing cannot be viewed in isolation but must be seen in the context of a life cycle of assets. Money is invested in raw materials which are made up into the finished product, becoming stock in trade. The stock is sold, producing receivables. The receivables crystallise into cash which is reinvested in new raw materials. Security may be taken over an asset at any stage in its life cycle—from chrysalis to butterfly, as well as over all the assets of the borrower (as in a typical bank debenture). There are potential clashes between those financing assets at different stages of the life cycle, for example, between a seller on retention of title terms and a receivables financier. These have largely been resolved under the current law,[6] but could arise in future if any aspect of the law were to be changed.

But first, some preliminary remarks about characteristics of security over receivables.

2.   CHARACTERISATION AND FORMS OF SECURITY

Mortgage by assignment and mortgage by novation

3–03   It is necessary to draw a clear distinction between a mortgage by assignment and a mortgage by novation. A mortgage by assignment does not change the identity of the contracting parties; the mortgagor retains his contractual relationship with the account debtor,[7] and the account remains in the mortgagor's name. The assignment merely entitles the assignee to payment in place of the mortgagor

---

this led to a rise in invoice discounting arrangements, in situations where the financier is unwilling to risk the statutory consequences of a charge being floating (J. Armour, "Shall we redistribute in insolvency?" in J. Getzler and J. Payne (eds), *Company Charges: Spectrum and Beyond* (Oxford: Oxford University Press, 2006), p.204). The rise in invoice discounting is demonstrated by the statistics produced by the Asset Based Finance Association (see *http://www.abfa.org.uk/members/ statistics.asp* [accessed September 20, 2013]) which show that domestic invoice discounting rose from just over £4bn in 1995 to £61bn at the end of 2012. However, the growth over this period has been reasonably gradual, indicating that the difficulties created by the *Spectrum* decision were not the only cause. It is likely that advances in information technology have enabled receivables financiers to keep firmer and more fine-tuned controls over receivables, with the result that the cost of such financing has been reduced. Further, when bank lending became less available during the financial crisis, asset based financing, and particularly invoice discounting, went some way to fill the gap. Innovative forms of financing, such as that offered by *http://marketinvoice.com* [accessed September 20, 2013] are also being developed; see para.3–43, below for discussion of the difficulties caused to such financing by prohibition of assignment clauses. Much of the discussion in this chapter is applicable to invoice discounting arrangements, which are effected by equitable assignments of receivables.

[6] See L Gullifer, "Retention of title clauses: a question of balance" in A Burrows and E Peel (eds), *Contract Terms* (Oxford, Oxford University Press, 2007); see also Ch.5 fn.150, below.

[7] The account debtor is the debtor of the person assigning or charging the debt by way of security. The assignor is, of course, himself a debtor to the assignee. To avoid confusion the term "debtor" will be used to refer to the account debtor, his creditor as the mortgagor or intending mortgagor and the latter's creditor or intended creditor as the mortgagee or intended mortgagee.

upon giving notice of the assignment to the account debtor. Accordingly an assignment does not in principle require the consent of the account debtor. By contrast a mortgage by novation entails a change of parties through a transfer of funds which are to be held by the mortgagee as a segregated fund, separate from the mortgagee's own moneys, to which the mortgagee may resort in the event of default but must otherwise hold on trust for the mortgagor[8] and return to him if the debt for which the fund is security is discharged from other sources.[9] The provision of such cash collateral[10] is an everyday occurrence, for example, to provide margin deposits to a broker or cash cover to a bank by its customer for an anticipated liability to be incurred by the bank to a third party on the customer's behalf.[11] So in contrast to an assignment, which preserves the original debt and results in the mortgagee taking over whatever claim the assignor had against the debtor, a novation replaces an existing debt in which the creditor was the mortgagor with a new debt which is owed to the mortgagee in his own right, not as assignee.[12] Novation produces a change of parties and requires the consent of all parties involved.[13] In the straightforward case where mortgagor and mortgagee bank with same bank, all that is involved is an in-house transfer in the books of the bank, so that there is a novation solely by change of creditor. In the more complex case where the mortgagor and mortgagee hold their accounts with different banks the novation is not direct but takes place through the books of a higher-tier bank with whom the banks of both parties hold their accounts and transfer funds by an in-house transfer.[14] In this case there is a change of both creditor and debtor; the debtor's claim against its bank as the paying bank is replaced pro tanto by the creditor's claim against its bank as the transferee bank. The same principle applies where the funds provided as cash collateral come not from the debtor directly but from a third party at the debtor's direction, including a third party buying goods from the debtor and paying them into the creditor's account.[15]

Both methods of mortgage—assignment and novation—allow tracing.[16] The difference between them may, however, be significant in that as assignee the mortgagee takes subject to equities, including any rights of set-off the debtor may

---

[8] The mortgagee is not, of course, a trustee to the extent that he holds for an interest of his own, but he is a trustee to the extent of the mortgagor's equity of redemption.

[9] It is thus to be distinguished from an outright funds transfer by way of payment, which is by far the more common type of funds transfer, where the transferee becomes outright owner of the claim on its bank.

[10] "Cash" here refers not to physical notes or coin but, typically, to the chose in action represented by a claim on a bank.

[11] See further paras 6–04 and 6–44, below.

[12] It follows that a mere charge, which creates no new debt, cannot be created by novation.

[13] The same novation technique is used in relation to securities, whether held directly from the issuer (in which case the mortgagee replaces the mortgagor on the company register or the CREST register) or indirectly through a securities account with a bank or other securities intermediary, in which case there will be a book-entry transfer in the books of the intermediary if common to the parties or, if not, in the books of a common higher-tier intermediary. See further Ch.6, below.

[14] If the parties' banks themselves hold their accounts with different higher-tier banks, it is necessary to go further up the chain until one reaches a common bank, which in the case of the clearing banks is the Bank of England.

[15] For an example of such a fact situation, see *Palmer v Carey* [1926] A.C. 703. See para.1–28, above.

[16] See paras 1–63 et seq., above and para.3–35, below.

have against the mortgagor, whereas as recipient of a new right by way of novation the mortgagee is not concerned with equities available to the debtor against the assignor, only with those available against the mortgagee himself, e.g. a right of set-off against the mortgagee's credit balance, and then only if the debtor is not on notice that its creditor holds the credit balance as mortgagee.[17] The rest of this chapter is devoted to security transfers by assignment except where otherwise stated.

Security distinguished from purchase

3–04 It is necessary at the outset to distinguish a loan on the security of receivables from a purchase of receivables. A transaction described by the parties as purchase and sale may be characterised as a secured loan either because the document evidencing the transaction is a sham in that it does not represent the true intention of the parties or because, though it is genuine, its provisions viewed as a whole show that, contrary to the description given by the parties, its legal effect is that of a mortgage or charge.[18] A loan on security postulates a repayment obligation and a right to redeem the security by repayment. A purchase involves an outright transfer, in which the transferor has no duty to repay and no right to redeem. In practice, the distinction is not always so clear cut. The following deserve particular mention.

(1) Sale with recourse

3–05 The transferor of receivables (who is referred to hereafter as the assignor, to distinguish him from the account debtor) may dispose of them by way of sale but guarantee payment by the debtors and, by way of convenient implementation of his guarantee, furnish an instalment note, or series of bills of exchange, covering the amount of his recourse liability. In this type of transaction, there is an exchange of money for money, so that in terms of cash flow and economic effect it is virtually indistinguishable from a mortgage of receivables. Yet in law the character of the transaction as a sale is not altered by the giving of the guarantee, for the assignor's liability is not to repay an advance but to pay a sum in discharge of a recourse obligation.[19] Provided that the transaction is genuine and

---

[17] Thus where the mortgage is effected by transfer of funds from the mortgagor's bank account to an account in the name of the mortgagee the bank may exercise a right of set-off in respect of moneys due from the mortgagee on another account so long as it is not on notice that the mortgagee is a mortgagee and not the beneficial owner of the account. But if it is on notice the bank cannot, it is thought, exercise a right of set-off even for the amount of the mortgagor's indebtedness in respect of which the mortgagee has a right of recourse to the credit balance, for this would erode the mortgagor's equity of redemption if it were to discharge its indebtedness from other sources. See further para.1–73, above; paras 7–66 and 7–69, below.

[18] Re Curtain Dream Plc [1990] B.C.L.C. 925; Welsh Development Agency v Export Finance Co Ltd [1992] B.C.L.C. 148 (where the transaction was upheld as producing its intended legal effect). See generally H. Beale, M. Bridge, L. Gullifer and E. Lomnicka, The Law of Security and Title-Based Financing, 2nd edn (Oxford: Oxford University Press 2012), Ch.4.

[19] Olds Discount Co Ltd v John Playfair Ltd [1938] 1 All E.R. 275; Chow Yoong Hong v Choong Fah Rubber Manufactory [1962] A.C. 209; Lloyds & Scottish Finance Ltd v Cyril Lord Carpet Sales Ltd [1982] B.C.L.C. 609.

not a sham,[20] the courts will uphold it as a sale, even if the parties use commercial language which to the legal mind would suggest a loan on security.[21]

(2) Outright transfer of debt with creditor's personal obligation to repay excess of proceeds over amount of debt

Again, an agreement by which a debtor assigns to his creditor a debt exceeding the amount he owes the creditor, the latter agreeing to repay any excess he receives, is not a security agreement, for the debtor has parted with the debt due to him unconditionally and with no right of redemption.[22]

3–06

(3) Non-recourse loan

A non-recourse loan on the security of receivables, in which the assignor undertakes no personal repayment obligation and the financier agrees to look exclusively to the receivables to secure recoupment, looks very much like a sale disguised as a mortgage. But the concept of non-recourse lending is well established in English law. The transaction remains a loan transaction even though the parties have agreed that the assignor is to make repayment only from an identified fund, not from his own resources.[23] The transaction is in fact distinguishable from sale in that once the financier has recouped his advance with stipulated interest, any remaining value in the receivables belongs to the assignor.

3–07

(4) Sale and repurchase; sale and lease-back; stock lending[24]

A provision by which the seller of a debt is given a right of repurchase may be an indication that the transaction as a whole is a mortgage and the right of repurchase a right to redeem, particularly when it is accompanied by language suggestive of a loan, such as a line of credit and a rate of interest.[25] But it should not be too readily assumed that a right of repurchase indicates an intention to create a mortgage. Sales and lease-backs of land and goods are common transactions, and while they are frequently utilised as a means of raising capital they are not on that account to be characterised as other than what they purport to be.[26] Sale and repurchase transactions in securities ("repos"), where the seller is

3–08

---

[20] There appears to be no reported case in which a purported sale of receivables has been struck down as a disguised loan on security, but the cases on chattel mortgages disguised as outright sales would be equally in point here. See, for example, *Polsky v S&A Services* [1951] 1 All E.R. 185; affirmed [1951] 1 All E.R. 1062; *North Central Wagon Finance Co Ltd v Brailsford* [1962] 1 All E.R. 502.

[21] *Lloyds & Scottish Finance Ltd v Cyril Lord Carpet Sales Ltd* [1982] B.C.L.C. 609.

[22] See paras 1–36 and 3–04, above.

[23] *Mathew v Blackmore* (1857) 1 H. & N. 762; *De Vigier v Inland Revenue Commissioners* [1964] 1 W.L.R. 1073; *Levett v Barclays Bank Plc* [1995] 1 W.L.R. 1260; H. Beale (ed), *Chitty on Contracts*, 31st edn (London: Sweet & Maxwell/Thomson Reuters, 2012), para.38–258.

[24] For discussion of the detail and purpose of repos and stock lending, see para.6–27, below.

[25] *Re Curtain Dream Plc* [1990] B.C.L.C. 925.

[26] *Yorkshire Railway Wagon Co v Maclure* (1882) 21 Ch.D. 309; *Staffs Motor Guarantee v British Wagon Co Ltd* [1934] 2 K.B. 305. Cases where such arrangements have been recharacterised as creating security interests can be explained as based on the fact that the arrangement was a sham, and that the consumer "borrower" did not fully understand the nature of the transaction, see *Cochrane v Matthews* (1878) 10 Ch.D. 80; *Re Watson* (1890) 25 Q.B.D. 27; *Madell v Thomas* [1891] 1 Q.B. 230;

required to buy back the securities at the original sale price plus a finance charge calculated by reference to a notional interest rate occur daily, and there is no reason to suppose that such transactions are other than genuine sales with provision for repurchase, entered into for perfectly good commercial reasons, including but not limited to the raising of funds.[27] The same considerations apply to the repo's close relation, the sell/buy-back[28] and also to stock lending.[29] Such title transfer transactions have a number of features which are not consistent with security. First, the buyer or transferee in the "on-leg" (sale or loan) has the freedom to use the securities as it pleases.[30] Secondly, the redelivery obligation of the buyer or transferee is to deliver "equivalent" securities and not identical securities, so that the transferor has no equity of redemption.[31] Thirdly, the netting arrangements on default, which form part of standard repo and stock lending agreements, would not operate effectively if there was not a transfer of title in the "on-leg".[32]

Significance of the distinction between purchase and secured loan

3–09 Quite apart from the presence or absence of repayment obligations and rights of redemption, the distinction between a purchase of receivables and loan on the security of receivables is legally significant in a number of respects. The sale of receivables is usually not registrable, the mortgage of receivables usually is.[33] The treatment of the transaction for tax and accounting purposes will vary

---

British Railway Traffic & Electric Co v Jones (1931) 40 Lloyds Rep. 281; *Polsky v S&A Services* [1951] 1 All E.R. 185; *North Western Central Wagon Finance Co Ltd v Brailsford* [1962] 1 W.L.R. 1288; and Beale, Bridge, Gullifer and Lomnicka, *The Law of Security and Title-Based Financing* (2012), para.4.28.

[27] See generally Beale, Bridge, Gullifer and Lomnicka, *The Law of Security and Title-Based Financing* (2012), paras 7.58–7.71. There are international standard-term master agreements for repos, such as the Global Market Repurchase Agreement of IBMA/ISMA . See further para.6–27, below.

[28] The sell/buy-back produces effects similar to the classic repo but differs from it in instead of a sale back at the original purchase price plus a charge or interest the resale is at a forward price which is higher in order to cover what would otherwise have been interest. There are also other differences which need not be discussed here. See generally M. Choudhry, *The REPO Handbook*, 2nd edn (Oxford: Butterworth-Heinemann, 2010), pp.121 et seq. See further para.6–27, below.

[29] Stock lending is generally carried out under the Global Master Securities Lending Agreement issued by ISLA, see para.6–27, below.

[30] *Re Lehman Brothers International (Europe) (In Administration)* [2010] EWHC 2914 (Ch) at [79]; *Beconwood Securities Pty Ltd v ANZ Banking Group* [2008] F.C.A. 594 at [45] Fed Ct Aust; *Primebroker Securities v Fortis Clearing Sydney Pty Ltd* [2009] V.S.C. 364 at [60] Sup Ct (Vic).

[31] *Beconwood Securities Pty Ltd v ANZ Banking Group* [2008] F.C.A. 594 at [50] and [56]–[57] Fed Ct Aust. This reasoning is consistent with the view of securities as fractional interests put forward in para.6–14, below, since each fractional interest acquires a different "history" meaning that different fractional interests are equivalent and not identical.

[32] *Beconwood Securities Pty Ltd v ANZ Banking Group* [2008] F.C.A. 594 at [45] and [50] Fed Ct Aust.

[33] Under s.859A of the Companies Act 2006 unless the mortgage falls within the Financial Collateral Arrangements (No.2) Regulations 2003 as a security financial collateral arrangement over credit claims, see para.6–45, below. But a general assignment of book debts by an unincorporated trader is registrable as if it were a bill of sale (Insolvency Act 1986 s.344), whether the assignment is by way of security or outright sale, see para.3–29, below.

according to whether it is done by way of sale or security.[34] Where receivables are transferred by an equitable assignment, if that assignment is absolute the assignor is not able to bring an action against the debtors, whereas if it is by way of charge, the assignor is able to sue the debtor.[35]

Forms of security

There are two types of security that can be taken over receivables, namely   3–10
mortgage and charge. As stated previously, a mortgage involves a security transfer of ownership, whereas a charge is a mere incumbrance, ownership being left in the chargor. The distinction is in practice of limited significance. In both cases the giving of notice of the secured creditor's interest to the account debtor protects the secured creditor both against the risk of payment to the mortgagor/chargor and against loss of priority to a subsequent incumbrancer. It is true that in the absence of agreement a chargee, lacking legal ownership, does not have certain remedies available to a mortgagee, such as a right to sue in his own name or to sell or appoint a receiver without leave of the court. But a well-drawn charge will in practice provide for all the remedies the chargee may require, including a provision for the execution of a legal mortgage and a power of attorney to do so in the name of the chargor.[36]

Existing and future debts

Security may be given over existing debts, future debts or both. The difference   3–11
between existing and future debts is legally material in that a mortgage of the latter can take effect only in equity, whereas a present debt can be assigned under s.136 of the Law of Property Act 1925 so as to take effect at law. However, the distinction between a statutory and an equitable assignment has little practical impact, beyond the fact that a statutory assignee can sue in his own name[37] whereas an equitable assignee may be required to join the assignor.[38] A sum

---

[34] On sale of an asset, it disappears from the balance sheet and is replaced by the proceeds of sale. Where the asset is mortgaged, it continues to be shown as an asset of the mortgagor, the repayment obligation being recorded as a liability. Some transactions will, however, be caught by Financial Reporting Standard 5 which requires accounts to reflect the "substance" of the transaction. However, for the purpose of value added tax there is no distinction between a sale of receivables and a mortgage of receivables; both are exempt supplies within item 1 of Group 5 of the 9th Schedule to the Value Added Tax Act 1994.

[35] *Hughes v Pump House Hotel Co* [1902] 2 K.B. 190 at 193; *Bexhill UK Ltd v Abdul Razzaq* [2012] EWCA Civ 1376.

[36] It may well be that the provision of such remedies means that the charge is actually an equitable mortgage, see J. Armour and A. Walters, "Funding Liquidation: a functional view" (2006) 122 L.Q.R. 295, 303. However, this makes very little difference in practice, see Beale, Bridge, Gullifer and Lomnicka, *The Law of Security and Title-Based Financing* (2012), paras 6.59–6.67.

[37] Law of Property Act 1925 s.136(1).

[38] A requirement which has been frequently ignored in practice. Non-joinder of the assignor was not a ground for dismissing the action under the old Rules of the Supreme Court (RSC Ord.15 r.6(1)). The effect of the Civil Procedure Rules 1998 is that the assignee may bring proceedings in his own name and the assignor may be added as a party if this is desirable to resolve the issues in dispute (CPR Pt 19 r.2). The requirement of joinder is seen as a rule of practice, which will not be insisted upon where there is no need: *Central Insurance Co Ltd v Seacalf Shipping Corp (The Aiolos)* [1983] 2 Lloyd's Rep. 25, 32; *Three Rivers District Council v Governor and Co of the Bank of England* [1996] Q.B.

growing due under an existing contract is regarded in law as a present debt, even though the right to payment has not yet matured, e.g. because this is dependent on performance of the work which is to generate the payment obligation.[39]

Charge-backs

3–12   In the first two editions of this book Professor Goode argued that the giving of security over receivables necessarily involved three parties: the debtor; the creditor; and the creditor's assignee or other incumbrancer; and that it was conceptually impossible for the debtor to be given a security interest over his own obligation to his creditor, e.g. for a bank to take security over its own customer's credit balance. The reason was that as between creditor and debtor a debt is not a species of property, merely an obligation, and since the creditor purporting to take the security interest cannot sue himself, appoint a receiver to collect from himself or sell his own obligation the so-called security interest is in reality a contractual set-off. That view, which divided the legal profession, was adopted by Millett J. in *Re Charge Card Services Ltd*,[40] and by the Court of Appeal in *Re Bank of Credit and Commerce International SA (No.8)*,[41] but when the latter decision was appealed to the House of Lords, Lord Hoffmann opined that there was no conceptual reason why a bank should not be able to take a charge over its own customer's credit balance, which is a charge like any other except that it was enforceable only by book-entry.[42] Lord Hoffmann's statement, though obviously of great persuasive value, was obiter, so the point remains open. It is also unclear whether Lord Hoffmann's reasoning can apply to an equitable mortgage.[43] Professor Goode has addressed elsewhere[44] both the conceptual problems of charge-backs and the policy issues which deserved consideration but appear never to have been argued.[45] But the force of business practice cannot be denied. Lord Hoffmann himself drew attention to legislation in Hong Kong and Singapore giving statutory effect to charge-backs. There was in fact a good example at home in the shape of s.215(2)(a) of the Insolvency Act 1986, which empowers the court, when making a declaration of wrongful trading under s.214 of the Act, to direct that the defendant's liability be charged on any debt or

---

292 313; *Sim Swee Joo Shipping Sdn Bhd v Shirlstar Container Transport Ltd* Unreported February 17, 1994 QBD; *Raiffeisen Zentralbank Österreich AG v Five Star Trading LLC* [2001] 1 Q.B. 825; [2001] EWCA Civ 68 at [60]; *Charnesh Kapoor v National Westminster Bank Plc* [2011] EWCA Civ 1083; *Bexhill UK Ltd v Abdul Razzaq* [2012] EWCA Civ 1376 at [58]. For a view that the difference between a legal and equitable assignment is substantive rather than procedural, see G. Tolhurst, *The Assignment of Contractual Rights* (Oxford: Hart Publishing, 2006), Ch.5; see also M. Smith and N. Leslie, *The Law of Assignment*, 2nd edn (Oxford: OUP, 2013), paras 11.19–11.47.

[39] *G&T Earle Ltd v Hemsworth RDC* (1928) 140 L.T. 69.

[40] *Re Charge Card Services Ltd* [1987] Ch. 150.

[41] *Re Bank of Credit and Commerce International SA (BCCI) (No.8)* [1996] Ch. 245.

[42] *Re BCCI (No.8)* [1998] A.C. 214 at 226–228.

[43] See discussion in Beale, Bridge, Gullifer and Lomnicka, *The Law of Security and Title-Based Financing* (2012), para.6.24. It is therefore advisable for a charge-back to be drafted as a mere charge, without the provisions as to enforcement referred to in para.3–10, above, which would, in any event, be unnecessary since the charge can be enforced by book entry, *Re BCCI (No.8)* [1998] A.C. 214 at 226–227.

[44] R. Goode, *Commercial Law in the Next Millennium (the 1997 Hamlyn Lectures)* (London: Sweet & Maxwell, 1998), pp.69–71.

[45] Indeed, Lord Hoffmann expressly stated (at 228) that there was no objection of public policy.

obligation due to him from the company. Article 9 of the American Uniform Commercial Code provides for perfection of a security interest in a deposit account by control,[46] and states that a secured party has control of a deposit account if (inter alia) it is the bank with which the deposit account is maintained.[47] The provision of cash collateral to banks and brokers is commonplace: although this is often done by title transfer collateral arrangement,[48] it could also be done by creation of a security interest over a credit balance held with the collateral taker.[49] Further, where a bank takes a fixed charge over a borrower's receivables, on terms that the proceeds of those receivables must be paid into an account with that bank,[50] the charge that the bank has over those proceeds is a charge-back. Accordingly conceptual problems such as the blurring of the distinction between property and obligation, and policy problems such as the fact that the only method of distinguishing a charge-back from a contractual set-off is by the label given to the transaction by the parties, must yield to business practice and legislative developments designed to accommodate it.

3. ATTACHMENT OF SECURITY INTEREST IN RECEIVABLES

Mortgage

As stated above a mortgage of receivables is effected either by assignment or by novation. An assignment may be a statutory assignment taking effect at law or an equitable assignment. The difference between the two is of little practical significance in relation to priority, since the normal rule giving priority to a subsequent purchaser of a legal title in good faith and without notice of a prior equitable does not apply to successive dealings in receivables, which are governed by the rule in *Dearle v Hall*.[51] Unless the security interest falls within the Financial Collateral Arrangements (No.2) Regulations 2003 (the FCARs),[52] it will be registrable.[53] The relevance of this in relation to priority is discussed below.[54] **3–13**

(1) Statutory assignment

To constitute a statutory assignment, so as to vest the receivable in the assignee at law and enable him to sue solely in his own name, the assignment must be effected in accordance with the requirements of s.136 of the Law of Property Act **3–14**

---

[46] American Uniform Commercial Code §9–312(b)(1).

[47] American Uniform Commercial Code §9–104(a)(1).

[48] See para.6–28, below.

[49] See para.6–44, below.

[50] One method of taking a fixed charge over receivables, identified by Lord Hope in *Re Spectrum Plus Ltd* [2005] UKHL 41; [2005] 2 A.C. 680 at [54], see also para.4–16, below.

[51] *Dearle v Hall* (1828) 38 E.R. 475. See paras 3–30 and 5–08, below.

[52] See Ch.6, below.

[53] Under s.859A of the Companies Act 2006.

[54] See Ch.5, below.

1925. The assignment itself must be in writing under the hand of the assignor, it must be absolute and not by way of charge,[55] it must relate to the whole of the debt[56] and it must be notified to the debtor in writing.[57] As mentioned above,[58] only present debts can be assigned by statutory assignment. An assignment which fails to meet any of these conditions takes effect in equity only. A statutory assignment is not possible where the account debtor or other counterparty is not obliged, and may not even be entitled, to receive notice of the assignment—for example: (a) on a transfer of securities,[59] which to take effect in law must be done by novation, i.e. substitution of the transferee for the transferor in the books of the issuer or in the CREST register[60]; or (b) where the claim is embodied in a negotiable instrument, in which case the acceptor's duty is to pay the holder on presentation, regardless of notice of assignment from someone else[61]; or (c) where the contract to which the assignment relates prohibits assignment.

(2) Equitable assignment

3–15   The rules for an equitable assignment by way of mortgage are very much more relaxed. All that is necessary is that the intending mortgagor shall manifest a clear intention to make an irrevocable transfer of the receivable. The assignment will be effective as between mortgagor and mortgagee even if no notice is given to the debtor,[62] though the debtor will not, of course, be affected by the assignment himself unless and until he has notice of it. There are four methods by which a receivable may become vested in equity in the intended mortgagee:

3–16   **Transfer or agreement for transfer**   The most common is for the intending mortgagor either to sign a written transfer and send this to the intended mortgagee or to make a binding agreement for assignment to which equity will give effect, either immediately, in the case of a present receivable, or upon its

---

[55] But an assignment by way of mortgage is within the section (*Tancred v Delagoa Bay & East Africa Railway* (1889) 23 Q.B.D. 239).

[56] *Forster v Baker* [1910] 2 K.B. 636; *Re Steel Wing Co Ltd* [1921] 1 Ch. 349; *Charnesh Kapoor v National Westminster Bank Plc* [2011] EWCA Civ 1083.

[57] The notice of the assignment is not required to contain any explicit direction to the debtor to pay the assignee. He is expected to infer this from the fact that the debt has become vested in the assignee. All that is required for a valid notice is one which tells the debtor that the assignment has been made, which identifies the debt and which sufficiently identifies the assignee (*Van Lynn Developments Ltd v Pelias Construction Co Ltd* [1969] 1 Q.B. 607, 615). There is much to be said for a rule along the lines of ss.9–318(3) of the Uniform Commercial Code authorising the debtor to make payment to the assignor unless the notice to him requires payment to the assignee. Article 8(1)(b) of the 1988 UNIDROIT Convention on International Factoring is to the same effect. It is by no means uncommon for the purchaser of a receivable, e.g. a factor, to agree with his assignor that despite notice of the assignment to the debtor the assignor will continue to collect, as agent of the assignee, until otherwise directed. It is important that the debtor should be left in no doubt as to whom payment is to be made, and notice of the assignment, though sufficient under s.136 of the Law of Property Act, is not necessarily informative enough to achieve its commercial purpose.

[58] See para.3–11, above.

[59] See para.6–38, below.

[60] See para.6–41, below.

[61] See para.5–08, below.

[62] If the assignor becomes bankrupt, his trustee in bankruptcy stands in his shoes. It follows that the trustee cannot secure priority over the assignee by being the first to give notice to the debtor (*Re Wallis* [1902] 1 K.B. 719; *Re Anderson* [1911] 1 K.B. 896).

coming into existence, in the case of a future receivable.[63] But neither writing nor signature is necessary. An assignment is equally effective in equity if made by word of mouth or by conduct; all that is necessary is an intention, manifested to the intended mortgagee, to make a present assignment by way of mortgage.[64]

Declaration of trust   The second method is for the intending mortgagor to declare himself a trustee of the receivable for the intended mortgagee. Such a trust may be express or implied from the agreement between the parties, as where the intending mortgagor undertakes to account to the intended mortgagee for sums paid by the debtor to the intending mortgagor.[65] Such an undertaking is common in a master invoice discounting agreement, where a trade supplier discounts its debts to a factoring company or invoice discounter on terms that the supplier's customers will not be given notice of the assignment in the absence of special circumstances and the supplier will continue to collect the receivables, account for the collections to the factor or invoice discounter and meanwhile hold them on trust.[66]

3–17

Transfer to trustees   A third method, which is a variant of the second, is for the debt to be transferred to a trustee or nominee to hold on behalf of the mortgagee. The use of a security trustee is widespread in syndicated loans and bond issues. It is used in the securitisation of secured receivables, where the originator, i.e. the creditor, transfers the receivables (and the mortgages or charges securing them) to a special-purpose vehicle which issues loan notes against them and grants a sub-mortgage or sub-charge to trustees on behalf of the note holders, assigning to the trustees by way of additional security all relevant contracts, including rights under the sale agreement, insurances and credit enhancement contracts.

3–18

Direction to make payment to the intended mortgagee   The fourth method is for the intending mortgagor to communicate with the debtor directing him to

3–19

---

[63] See paras 2–12 et seq., above.

[64] *William Brandt's Son & Co v Dunlop Rubber Co* [1905] A.C. 454; *Dry Bulk Handy Holding Inc, Compania Sud Americana de Vapores SA v Fayette International Holdings Ltd* [2012] EWHC 2107 (Comm) at [56].

[65] *GE Crane Sales Pty Ltd v Commissioner of Taxation* (1971) 126 C.L.R. 177, 183. This case equates a declaration of trust with an assignment, but this seems wrong, as pointed out by Waller L.J. in *Barbados Trust Co Ltd v Bank of Zambia* [2007] EWCA Civ 148 at [43], since an equitable assignment in writing can be converted into a statutory assignment, and this is not true of a declaration of trust; although see Rix L.J. in the same case at [111], who says that he recognises that a declaration of trust of rights of suit under a contract is akin to an equitable assignment of those rights. Despite this, the view of Waller L.J. appears to be settled law; see also R. Marshall, *The Assignment of Choses in Action* (Pitman, 1950) who lists three types of assignment: by trust, by contract and informal assignments, the first two being mutually exclusive; see M. Bridge, L. Gullifer, G.McMeel, S. Worthington, *The Law of Personal Property* (London: Sweet & Maxwell, 2013), paras 27–037 et seq.; L. Gullifer and J. Payne, *Corporate Finance Law: Principles and Policy* (Oxford: Hart Publishing, 2011), p.384. For further discussion see G. Tolhurst, "Prohibitions on Assignment and Declarations of Trust" [2007] L.M.C.L.Q. 278, 285; Smith and Leslie, *The Law of Assignment* (2013), Ch.11 which takes the view that an equitable assignment by contract takes place by a constructive trust (para.11.16) and this is contrasted with a transfer by way of express trust (paras 11.48 et seq.).

[66] *International Factors Ltd v Rodriguez* [1979] 1 Q.B. 351. However, in that case, and in most agreements, there is an agreement to assign the relevant debts.

make payment to the intended mortgagee. But this by itself is not enough.[67] In order for the direction to be effective it must either be given pursuant to prior agreement between the intending mortgagor and the intended mortgagee[68] or be communicated to the latter afterwards.[69] A direction to the debtor which has neither been previously arranged with the intended mortgagee nor subsequently communicated to him is merely a revocable authority to pay, even if it is expressed to be irrevocable.[70] Moreover, the direction itself must be couched in such language as to convey to the debtor that he is required to pay the intended mortgagee not merely as a matter of convenience to the intending mortgagor but because the right to receive payment has become vested in the mortgagee. If the direction does not make this clear, the debtor will be entitled to assume that the intending mortgagor is still entitled to receive payment.[71]

(3) Novation

3–20   As stated earlier,[72] a mortgage by novation is effected by a transfer in which the mortgagee replaces the mortgagor as creditor. The question of notice to the debtor therefore does not arise.

Charge

3–21   Whereas a mortgage of receivables transfers ownership to the secured creditor, either at law or in equity, a charge is a mere encumbrance. Nevertheless, most of the effects of a mortgage apply to a charge. Notice of the charge to the debtor precludes him from making payment to the chargor, preserves the chargee's priority against subsequent incumbrancers and cuts off the debtor's right of set-off in respect of cross-claims arising from future dealings with the chargor.[73] The one major difference, in theory at least, relates to enforcement. A charge (otherwise than on land) is purely the creation of equity; it does not exist at common law, nor does it come within s.136 of the Law of Property Act 1925 so as to be capable of conferring on the chargee a right of action solely in his own name against the debtor. Accordingly the chargor may need to be joined as a party to any proceedings by the chargee for recovery of the debt, and a chargee has no power of sale otherwise than under an order of the court.[74] In practice a well-drawn charge over receivables will confer on the chargee all the powers it needs, including power to convert the charge into a mortgage, for which purpose

---

[67] *Bell v London & North Western Railway Co* (1852) 15 Beav. 248; *Curran v Newpark Cinemas Ltd* [1951] 1 All E.R. 295.

[68] As in *Re Kent & Sussex Sawmills Ltd* [1947] Ch. 177; and *Winn v Burgess*, *The Times*, July 8, 1986.

[69] *Curran v Newpark Cinemas Ltd* [1951] 1 All E.R. 295; *Alexander v Steinhardt, Walker & Co* [1903] 2 K.B. 208.

[70] *Curran v Newpark Cinemas Ltd* [1951] 1 All E.R. 295.

[71] *James Talcott Ltd v John Lewis & Co Ltd* [1940] 3 All E.R. 592.

[72] See para.3–03, above.

[73] See *Business Computers Ltd v Anglo-African Leasing Ltd* [1977] 2 All E.R. 741 and para.7–70, below.

[74] See para.1–55 fn.238, above. See also *Bexhill UK Ltd v Razzaq* [2012] EWCA Civ 1376.

the charge should incorporate a power of attorney to the chargee to execute an assignment in the name of the chargor.[75]

Since a charge leaves ownership of the debt with the chargor it cannot be effected by novation. All that is required for attachment is an agreement for a charge.

4. PERFECTION OF SECURITY INTEREST IN RECEIVABLES

Hitherto we have been concerned with attachment of a security interest in receivables, that is, its efficacy as between assignor and assignee. It is now necessary to see what steps have to be taken to make the security assignment enforceable against third parties. As discussed in Ch.2,[76] the giving of public notice of a security interest can be done by a number of different methods, and has a number of different consequences. The following discussion will consider both the methods and the consequences, some of which relate to the validity of the security interest in the debtor's insolvency, and some of which relate to the priority of the security interest over other incumbrancers and purchasers.

3–22

Perfection by registration under the Companies Act 2006

A charge on receivables is registrable under s.859A of the Companies Act 2006[77] unless it falls within the FCARs.[78] Before the 2013 reforms, fixed charges over receivables were only registrable if the receivables constituted book debts: thus the previous editions of this book included considerable analysis of what was included in the category of book debts. This is now omitted.

3–23

(1) The registration requirement

Section 859A applies only to charges created by the company, not to charges arising by operation of law.[79] Accordingly, a security interest in receivables which arises not by agreement but by virtue of an equitable tracing right—e.g. as the proceeds of an unauthorised disposition of stock or equipment—is not registrable. The same applies where the agreement, though specifying a duty to account for receivables as proceeds, is merely spelling out rights which would in any event vest in the chargee in equity.[80] The position is otherwise where it is

3–24

---

[75] It is possible that the inclusion of such a power, together with the right to appoint a receiver, and for that receiver to have power to take possession of and sell the charged assets, means that the security interest is an equitable mortgage anyway, see fn.36, above.

[76] See paras 2–16 et seq., above.

[77] Note that the regime put in place by s.859A only applies to charge created after April 6 2013, see para.2–18, above.

[78] Companies Act 2006 s.859A(6). For the scope of the FCARs see Ch.6, below.

[79] Companies Act 2006 s.859A(1). See also *Capital Finance Co Ltd v Stokes* [1969] Ch. 261.

[80] In relation to clauses covering the proceeds of goods sold on retention of title, the position is not clear. At first instance in *Aluminium Industrie Vaassen BV v Romalpa Aluminium Ltd* [1976] 1 W.L.R. 676, 682–683, Mocatta J. held that the interest of the sellers in the proceeds was not registrable. The question of registration was not argued in the Court of Appeal, and Mocatta J.'s view was doubted in

apparent from the security instrument that the receivables resulting as proceeds of other security are to be regarded as the property of the chargor, but subject to a charge created by the instrument.

(2) What is a charge?

3–25   The term "charge" includes a mortgage.[81] The registration requirement applies whether the mortgage is effected by assignment or by novation.

(3) Negotiable instruments

3–26   One form of receivable is a negotiable instrument, however, being tangible property this can be the subject of either a pledge or a non-possessory security interest such as a mortgage or a charge. The latter would be registrable under s.859A; the former would not. Under the previous registration regime the deposit of negotiable instruments given to secure payment of a book debt was specifically exempt from registration, in order to avoid interfering with the concept of negotiability.[82] This provision was not included in the 2013 reforms, since such a deposit would normally be a pledge and pledges are not required to be registered.

(4) The effect of registration

3–27   Registration perfects the security and constitutes notice to those who could reasonably be expected to search, but not otherwise.[83]

(5) The effect of failure to register

3–28   Failure to register a charge on book debts renders the charge void against a liquidator or administrator and creditors,[84] by which is meant creditors in a winding up or administration and secured creditors, as opposed to unsecured creditors where no winding up or administration has occurred. Non-registration does not avoid the charge as against a subsequent outright purchaser of the debt,

---

by Phillips J. in *Tatung (UK) Ltd v Galex Telesure Ltd* (1989) 5 B.C.C. 325, 335–336. A concession to the opposite effect, however, was made by the floating chargee in *Compaq Computers Ltd v Abercorn Group Ltd* [1993] B.C.L.C. 602, 613. It has been held that a trust receipt by which pledged documents of title to goods are released by the pledgee to the pledgor to enable him to sell them as the pledgee's trustee-agent upon terms that the proceeds are to be held in trust for the pledgee did not constitute a charge over those proceeds as book debts, since these are vested in the pledgee in equity from the beginning as the proceeds of his original security (*Re David Allester Ltd* [1922] 2 Ch. 211). However, there are good arguments that a charge is created, and that it should be registrable, see Beale, Bridge, Gullifer and Lomnicka, *The Law of Security and Title-Based Financing* (2012), para.5.30; Law Commission, *Company Security Interests*, Law Com. No.296 (2005), paras 3.22–3.25; P. Yung, "Pledge by constructive delivery in Hong Kong" (2013) 24 I.C.C.L.R. 273, 276–277; and para.2–20, above.

[81] Companies Act 2006 s.859A(7)(a). But it would seem that for the purposes of s.670 of the Companies Act 2006 "charge" bears its narrower meaning. See para.6–38, below.

[82] Companies Act 2006 s.861(3).

[83] See para.2–31, above.

[84] Companies Act 2006 s.859H(3).

but if he acquires the legal title without notice of the unregistered charge he has priority under the normal priority rules.[85]

The effect of non-registration is exhausted if the debts are collected before anyone has acquired a locus standi to complain of non-registration, i.e. before winding up or administration or the grant of specific security.[86] When a charge becomes void under s.859H the money secured by it immediately becomes payable.[87]

Registration of assignment of book debts by unincorporated trader[88]

The Bills of Sale Acts, which require the registration of written chattel mortgages granted by individuals, do not apply to choses in action.[89] However, s.344 of the Insolvency Act 1986 provides that a general assignment by a trader of his existing or future book debts, or any class thereof, shall be void against his trustee in bankruptcy as regards book debts not paid before the presentation of the bankruptcy petition unless registered as if it were an absolute bill of sale.[90] But the section does not apply to an assignment of book debts due at the date of assignment from specified debtors, or debts growing due under specified contracts, or any assignment of book debts included in a transfer of a business made bona fide and for value or in any assignment of assets for the benefit of creditors generally.[91] For the purpose of the section, "assignment" includes an assignment by way of security and other charges on book debts.[92] Registration merely perfects the assignment so as to prevent it from being impeached by the assignor's trustee. It does not constitute notice to the outside world or guarantee the priority of the assignment over subsequent interests.[93]

3–29

Notice to the account debtor

Where the security is created by assignment or charge (as opposed to transfer by novation), notice to the account debtor[94] may be important for at least five different reasons:

3–30

[85] This is subject to the application of the rule in *Dearle v Hall*. See para.5–08, below.

[86] *Mercantile Bank of India Ltd v Chartered Bank of India, Australia and China and Strauss & Co (in liquidation)* [1937] 1 All E.R. 231; *Re Row Dal Constructions Pty Ltd* [1966] V.R. 249; *NV Slavenburg's Bank v Intercontinental Natural Resources Ltd* [1980] 1 W.L.R. 1076.

[87] Companies Act 2006 s.859H(4).

[88] For suggestions for reform, see G. McBain, "Repealing the Bills of Sale Acts" [2011] J.B.L. 475.

[89] Which are excluded from the definition of "personal chattels" in s.4 of the Bills of Sale Act 1878.

[90] i.e. under the procedure in the Bills of Sale Act 1878, not the Bills of Sale (1878) Amendment Act 1882, which applies to security bills.

[91] Insolvency Act 1986 s.344(3)(b).

[92] Insolvency Act 1986 s.344(3)(a).

[93] See cases cited in fn.100, below. Registration could, however, constitute constructive notice to those expected to search the register, which might be relevant to the operation of the second limb of *Dearle v Hall* (1828) 3 Russ. 1. Priority of other registered bills of sale is by date of registration (s.10 of the Bills of Sale Act 1878). The Register of Assignment of Book Debts, which is kept at the Royal Courts of Justice, is handwritten and not in a readily searchable state, see McBain, "Repealing the Bills of Sale Acts" [2011] J.B.L. 475, 506.

[94] That is, the person who owes the receivable.

(1) To prevent him from making payment to the assignor. If he does so despite the notice of assignment, he can be made to pay again, to the assignee.[95]

(2) To stop new equities arising in favour of the debtor.[96]

(3) To prevent modification of the agreement between assignor and debtor under which the debt arose.[97]

(4) To secure priority over another incumbrancer. Under the rule in *Dearle v Hall*,[98] a later incumbrancer taking without notice of the earlier assignment and giving notice to the debtor first would obtain priority.

(5) To obtain the benefit of a statutory assignment, and thus the right to sue for the debt in the assignee's own name without joining the assignor.[99]

It should be observed that registration of the assignment, assuming it to be registrable, does not dispense with the need to give notice to the debtor, for he is not required to search a register for encumbrances before settling the debt,[100] although registration does have the effect of preserving priority over subsequent assignees who are expected to search the register, under the second limb of *Dearle v Hall*.[101] Giving notice to the debtor has no effect where the debtor or other obligor is not obliged to have regard to the notice, for example, where it relates to a non–assignable debt or to registered securities or negotiable instruments.[102]

Novation

3–31   As an alternative to assignment, a receivable may be mortgaged by novation, that is by transfer of the receivable into an account in the name of the mortgagee.[103] This has the effect of giving public notice of the mortgagee's interest in the receivable, although registration is still required.

---

[95] *Brice v Bannister* (1878) 3 Q.B.D. 569; *Yates v Terry* [1902] 1 K.B. 527.

[96] *Roxburghe v Cox* (1881) 17 Ch.D. 520. By contrast, defences arising out of the transaction giving rise to the debt (e.g. where the debt is for goods sold, that they are defective) are available regardless of the date of receipt of the notice of assignment, for the assignee cannot acquire greater contractual rights than those possessed by his assignor. See further para.7–70, below.

[97] *Brice v Bannister* (1878) 3 Q.B.D. 569. In practice, an assignee usually finds it necessary to allow some leeway to the assignor in regard to modifications, particularly in the case of a contract involving continuing performance, such as a construction contract. Art.11:308 of the Principles of European Contract Law provides that a modification made without the consent of the assignee after notice of assignment does not bind the assignee "unless the modification is provided for in the assignment agreement or is one which is made in good faith and is of a nature to which the assignee could not reasonably object". A construction contract is given as an illustration in Comment E to art.11:204 of the Principles.

[98] *Dearle v Hall* (1828) 3 Russ. 1. See para.3–13, above para.5–08, below.

[99] Law of Property Act 1925 s.136(1). See para.3–11, above. However, joinder will not be required even in the case of an equitable assignment where there is no need, see fn.38, above.

[100] *Snyder's Ltd v Furniture Finance Corp* (1930) 66 D.L.R. 79; *Re Royal Bank of Canada* (1979) 94 D.L.R. (3d) 692.

[101] See para.5–08, below.

[102] See further paras 3–39, 5–08 and 5–29, below.

[103] See para.3–03, above.

Attornment

If a third party receiving a fund as trustee of the debtor acknowledges the **3–32** creditor's interest and agrees that until that interest has been discharged the third party will act in accordance with the instructions of the creditor, not the debtor, the creditor can enforce his interest against the third party.[104] The effect of this attornment is to give the creditor control of the account[105] and therefore gives a sort of public notice of the creditor's interest. Since this can only properly be done by agreement of the debtor the charge is to be treated as created by the debtor, and differs from an ordinary charge only in that the third party's attornment produces the same effect as receipt of a notice of assignment, the third party in both cases becoming bound to respect the creditor's interest in the fund.

Where the debtor holds a cash or securities account with a bank or securities intermediary, a common method of setting up the control is by transfer of the required amount of cash or securities to a "pledge" or escrow account in the name of the debtor but under the control of a third party, such as an escrow agent.[106]

5. RIGHTS ACQUIRED BY THE ASSIGNEE

Assignee takes subject to equities

The assignee of a receivable takes subject to equities, i.e. to all defences available **3–33** by the debtor against the assignor and all rights of set-off open to the debtor against the assignor in respect of claims arising prior to the debtor's receipt of notice of assignment.[107]

---

[104] *Griffin v Weatherby* (1868) L.R. 3 Q.B. 753, 758.

[105] The concept of control is an important feature of arts 8 and 9 of the Uniform Commercial Code. See §§8–106, 9–104 to 9–107, where it constitutes automatic perfection, so that no filing is required. The nearest English law equivalent is attornment. Under English law, unless it falls within the FCARs (see Ch.6, below) the charge will have to be registered under the Companies Act 2006 s.859A. If the trustee is a company, it, or any person interested in the charge, may deliver a statement to that effect to the registrar (s.859J). This was introduced by the 2013 reforms to reflect current practice.

[106] As to escrow balances in CREST accounts, see para.6–41, below.

[107] *Roxburghe v Cox* (1881) 17 Ch.D 520; *Re Pinto Leite & Nephews* [1929] 1 Ch. 221; Law of Property Act 1925 s.136(1). See further para.7–70, below. However, if the receivable is embodied in a document which provides that it is to be transferrable free from equities the court will give effect to this provision (*Hilger Analytical Ltd v Rank Precision Industries Ltd* [1984] B.C.L.C. 301). In relation to debt securities which are held and traded through CREST, the rules provide that they must be "transferable free from any equity, set-off or counter-claim between the issuer and the original or any intermediate holder of the security" (r.7.3.2); see also *Newcastle Building Society v Mill; Re Kaupthing Singer and Friedlander Ltd (Isle of Man) Ltd* [2009] EWHC 740 (Ch); [2009] 2 Lloyd's Rep. 154.

Assignor is trustee of sums received by him

3–34   Where the account debtor, whether or not it has notice of assignment, makes payment of a receivable to the assignor, the latter holds the sum received, whether in cash or in the form of a cheque or other instrument, on trust for the assignee.[108] In the latter case, wrongful appropriation of the instrument, e.g. by paying it into the assignor's bank account, constitutes a conversion,[109] with an alternative liability to account for the proceeds of the instrument in an action for money had and received.

Tracing receivables into proceeds[110]

3–35   A security interest in receivables normally attaches to any proceeds received in exchange for them, except where the assignor has been given freedom to deal with the receivables and to mingle the proceeds with his own moneys, that is, where the security interest is a floating charge. A distinction should be made between proceeds of sale and collections. If receivables are disposed of by the assignor without the assignee's authority, the security interest will normally attach to the proceeds by operation of the rules of tracing based on the unauthorised disposition.[111] This tracing right is available against the assignor and the assignee's trustee in bankruptcy or liquidator. Whether it is equally available against a subsequent purchaser or incumbrancer is a priority question which will be examined a little later.[112]

Where the assignor collects the receivables and it is evident that the assignor is required to keep such collections as a separate fund for the assignee, the latter's security interest will automatically attach to them. This is not a tracing right as such but arises from the agreement of the parties in creating a fixed charge (or mortgage) over the receivables. If the chargor is authorised to dispose of the proceeds of collection, then the charge is floating in the first place.[113] The security interest over the proceeds of collection is, therefore, created by the original charge agreement and its priority position will stem from that fact.[114] Thus, if the proceeds are paid into a bank account held by the chargor, over which the chargor has created another charge, the priority position (in the absence of any other factors) will depend on the date of creation of the two charges.[115]

---

[108] *GE Crane Sales Pty Ltd v Commissioner of Taxation* (1971) 46 A.L.J.R. 15; *Barclays Bank Ltd v Willowbrook International Ltd* [1987] 1 F.T.L.R. 386; *Northern Bank v Ross* [1991] B.C.L.C. 504.

[109] The measure of damages is the face value of the cheque *Morison v London County & Westminster Bank* [1914] 3 K.B. 356; *International Factors Ltd v Rodriguez* [1979] 1 QB 351. Note that pure intangibles cannot be converted, see *OBG v Allen* [2007] UKHL 21; [2008] A.C. 883.

[110] See the treatment of this issue in detail at paras 1–63 et seq., above.

[111] See paras 1–64 et seq., above.

[112] See para.5–36, below.

[113] See paras 4–13 et seq., below.

[114] In virtually all cases the charge agreement will make it clear that the fixed charge over the receivables extends to the proceeds of collection.

[115] See Ch.5, below.

6. LEGAL IMPEDIMENTS TO THE CREATION OF SECURITY OVER A RECEIVABLE

In an earlier chapter we have listed the principal types of property which are incapable of being given in security.[116] Two of these need to be examined in more detail, namely bare rights of action, on grounds of public policy, and debts made unassignable by contract.[117]

3–36

Bare right of action not assignable[118]

The law views with disfavour those who seek to support another's litigation without just cause (maintenance) or to exact as the price of such support a right to share in the fruits of the litigation (champerty). An agreement by which a party purports to assign a bare right of action, unconnected to any legitimate interest of the assignee, savours of maintenance and champerty and is unenforceable as being contrary to public policy,[119] for its effect would be to enable the assignee to intervene in an action in which he had no proper interest. The law of champerty has attracted considerable attention recently in two areas: the assignment of a right of action for personal injury[120] and conditional fee agreements.[121] Since champerty is, essentially, a matter of public policy, not surprisingly it operates differently in different contexts.[122] Thus, in relation to conditional fee agreements, the fact that Parliament has legislated in this area is a good reason for not extending, or even restricting, the scope of the doctrine.[123] However, in relation to an action for personal injury, the test is whether the assignee has a sufficient interest to support the assignment of what would otherwise be a bare cause of action.[124]

3–37

These areas are somewhat removed from that under consideration in this chapter. It is reasonably clear that the assignment of a debt carries with it the right to sue for its recovery, and an assignment is not open to attack as champertous merely because the debt is disputed or it is clear that it will be recovered only through proceedings by the assignee.[125] There is no objection to the assignment of the fruits of an action under an agreement which does not involve either financial support for the litigation or the assignment of a right to intervene in the

---

[116] See para.1–59, above.

[117] An impediment to assignment contained in a negative pledge clause is not discussed here, for it is not inherent in the obligation itself; the question is simply one of priorities. See para.5–41, below.

[118] For a detailed discussion see Smith and Leslie, *The Law of Assignment* (2013), Ch.23; and A. Tettenborn, "Assignment of Rights to Compensation" [2007] L.M.C.L.Q. 392.

[119] *Trendtex Trading Corp v Crédit Suisse* [1980] Q.B. 629 CA; [1982] A.C. 679 HL, the facts of which are given below.

[120] *Simpson v Norfolk & Norwich University Hospital NHS Trust* [2011] EWCA Civ 1149.

[121] *Sibthorpe v Southwark London BC (Law Society intervening)* [2011] EWCA Civ 25.

[122] See the approach of the Court of Appeal in *Sibthorpe v Southwark London BC (Law Society intervening)* [2011] EWCA Civ 25; and Smith and Leslie, *The Law of Assignment* (2013), para.23.12.

[123] *Sibthorpe v Southwark London BC (Law Society intervening)* [2011] EWCA Civ 25 at [47].

[124] *Simpson v Norfolk & Norwich University Hospital NHS Trust* [2011] EWCA Civ 1149 at [22]–[24].

[125] *Camdex International Ltd v Bank of Zambia* [1998] Q.B. 22, 32–33; *Zabihi v Janzemini* [2009] EWHC 3471 (Ch) settled, however, see Tettenborn, "Assignment of Rights to Compensation" [2007] L.M.C.L.Q. 392, 399–400.

proceedings.[126] Again, the assignment of a right of action itself is unobjectionable where, looking at the totality of the transaction, the assignment is one in which the assignee had a genuine commercial interest,[127] as where the action concerns property held by the assignee as principal or agent[128] or where the assignor will be able to reduce his indebtedness to the assignee from the fruits of the action[129] or to assign the claim in satisfaction of the debt.[130]

A good illustration of what is and is not permitted is furnished by the decision of the House of Lords in *Trendtex Trading Corp v Crédit Suisse*[131]:

The plaintiff owed money to its bankers, the defendants. The plaintiff had a substantial claim against the Central Bank of Nigeria for dishonour of a letter of credit, and the action was financially supported by the defendants, whose only hope of recouping their advances lay in the successful outcome of the proceedings. Subsequently the plaintiff assigned its right of action to the defendants, who almost immediately resold it to an unidentified third party for a substantially higher figure.

In an action by the plaintiff for a declaration that the assignment to the defendants was void as constituting an assignment of a bare right of action, the House of Lords, affirming the decision of the Court of Appeal, held that the assignment in itself was unobjectionable, in that the defendants had a legitimate interest in the success of the action; that the arrangements for sub-sale of the right of action to the third party, who had no legitimate interest in the proceedings, were champertous; but that by virtue of an exclusive jurisdiction clause in the agreement the dispute fell within the jurisdiction of the Swiss courts and was governed by Swiss law.

Contractual prohibition against assignment or charge[132]

3–38   A more serious threat is posed by the common practice on the part of large customers of inserting in their purchase orders a clause prohibiting the supplier from assigning his right to payment under the supply contract. The reasons for such a clause are, first, to avoid the risk of the debtor having to pay twice by inadvertently overlooking notice of assignment and paying the assignor; secondly, to preserve its right to set up new equities notwithstanding receipt of notice of assignment; thirdly, to avoid exposure to an assignee whom it does not know and who may have a more severe approach to delay in payment or a less amenable attitude to the handling of complaints about the performance for which

---

[126] *Camdex International Ltd v Bank of Zambia* [1998] Q.B. 22 at 33.

[127] *Massai Aviation Services Ltd v Attorney General* [2007] UKPC 12.

[128] *Ellis v Torrington* [1920] 1 K.B. 399; *Kaukomarkkinat O/Y v Elbe Transport Union GmbH: The Kelo* [1985] 2 Lloyd's Rep. 85.

[129] *Trendtex Trading Corp v Credit Suisse* [1980] Q.B. 629 CA; [1982] A.C. 679 HL.

[130] *Re Timothy's Pty Ltd and the Companies Act* [1981] 2 N.S.W.L.R. 706.

[131] *Trendtex Trading Corp v Credit Suisse* [1980] Q.B. 629 CA; [1982] A.C. 679 HL.

[132] See the latest discussion on this subject by Professor Goode in "Contractual Prohibitions Against Against Assignment" [2009] L.M.C.L.Q. 300. In the discussion in this section the assignor and the assignee are referred to as such for ease of exposition, despite the fact that the assignment is of limited validity.

the payment is exacted; and fourthly, to avoid a situation where the debtor is contractually obliged to make a payment to an assignee in a country where such a payment is illegal.[133]

It is clear that the debtor is not obliged to recognise the title of an assignee under an assignment in breach of a no-assignment clause. It is equally clear that a contractual provision against assignment entitles the debtor to refuse to deal with the assignee and to continue making payment to the assignor, so that the assignment is not capable of taking effect as a statutory assignment. The debtor can therefore safely disregard any notice of assignment by the assignee or any person to whom the assignee itself assigns the debt, and, contrary to the usual rule,[134] he can continue to assert against the assignor rights of set-off arising from mutual dealings concluded after receipt of the notice of assignment. Further a purported assignment by the original creditor would place him in breach of contract and entitle the debtor to exercise any remedies for breach of contract given him by the agreement or by law, although if the assignment is ineffective against the debtor, any damages are likely to be nominal.[135] In short, the prohibition is effective as between debtor and assignee, and if the assignee brings proceedings his claim will be dismissed. Such was the outcome of *Helstan Securites Ltd v Hertfordshire CC*.[136]

Assignments in breach of a no-assignment are commonly described as void, invalid or ineffective.[137] Such statements, however, do not refer to the proprietary effects of such an assignment as between assignor and assignee but rather to the ineffectiveness of the assignment against the debtor, who is not bound to recognise it. This is made clear in the speech of Lord Browne-Wilkinson in *Linden Gardens Securities Ltd v Lenesta Sludge Disposals Ltd*, in which the assignee sought to recover from the debtor despite a prohibition against assignment in the contract. Rejecting the argument that such a prohibition was of no effect even against the debtor Lord Browne-Wilkinson said:

> "Therefore the existing authorities establish that an attempted assignment of contractual rights in breach of a contractual prohibition is ineffective to transfer such contractual rights. I regard the law as being satisfactorily settled in that sense. If the law were otherwise, it would defeat the legitimate commercial reason for

---

[133] Nevertheless, such a prohibition causes problems in receivables financing, see below.

[134] See para.7–70, below.

[135] A purported assignment could be a repudiatory breach, entitling the debtor to terminate the entire contract. This would depend on the wording of the contract. In some circumstances such a provision could fall foul of the doctrines or forfeiture or penalties, see Smith and Leslie, *The Law of Assignment* (2013), para.25.12. A distinction can be made between a clause drafted in terms of a "promise not to assign", breach of which does not invalidate the assignment, but which renders the purported assignor in breach of contract and a clause stating that the assignor "cannot assign" which renders the chose in action unassignable, but where a purported assignment would not necessarily constitute a breach of contract, see Tolhurst, *The Assignment of Contractual Rights* (2007), pp.265–270. Although this distinction appears to have been drawn in Australia *(Devefi Pty Ltd v Mateffy Pearl Nagy Pty Ltd* (1993) 113 A.L.R. 225), it does not appear to be part of English law.

[136] *Helstan Securites Ltd v Hertfordshire CC* [1978] 3 All E.R. 262. See also *Re Turcan* (1889) 40 Ch.D 5; *Shaw & Co v Moss Empires & Bastow* (1908) 25 T.L.R. 190; and *Spellman v Spellman* [1961] 2 All E.R. 498.

[137] See, for example, *Helstan Securities Ltd v Hertfordshire CC* [1978] 3 All E.R. 262, per Croom-Johnson J. at 265; *Linden Gardens Trust Ltd v Lenesta Sludge Disposals Ltd* [1994] 1 A.C. 85, per Lord Browne-Wilkinson at 109.

inserting the contractual prohibition, viz., to ensure that the original parties to the contract are not brought into direct contractual relations with third parties."[138]

However, the debtor is not concerned with the proprietary effects of an assignment as between the parties themselves, whether in relation to the application of the collected proceeds of the debt or in relation to the contract under which it arises. The former is taken first because it is the most straightforward. The position in relation to the benefit of the contract is more complex.

(1) Proceeds of the debt

3–39 The purpose of a no-assignment clause is to protect the debtor from having to deal with a different creditor. Therefore, as Professor Goode has suggested elsewhere,[139] the debtor can have no legitimate interest in controlling the application of his payment after it has reached the hands of the assignor, and reason rebels against the proposition that the assignor, having received from the assignee the price of sale of the debt, is then entitled to keep the debtor's payment for himself. A no-assignment clause will not be interpreted to invalidate the contract between assignor and the assignee, in the absence of the clearest words, nor will it normally invalidate the assignor's liability to account to the assignee for the debtor's payment when received,[140] so that the assignor holds those proceeds on trust for the assignee.[141] This view is supported by the decision in *Re Turcan*[142] and is treated as orthodoxy by many writers.[143] A no-assignment clause will also not prevent the creditor declaring himself a trustee of the proceeds in favour of a third party.[144]

If, however, clear words are used which attempt to prohibit assignment of the collected proceeds, it is thought that this would be contrary to public policy as an

---

[138] *Linden Gardens Trust v Lenesta Sludge Disposals Ltd* [1994] 1 A.C. 85, 108.

[139] R. Goode, "Inalienable Rights?" (1979) 42 M.L.R. 553, to which extensive references will be found in Lord Browne-Wilkinson's speech in *Linden Gardens Trust v Lenesta Sludge Disposals Ltd* [1994] 1 A.C. 85.

[140] *Linden Gardens Trust Ltd v Lenesta Sludge Disposals Ltd* [1994] 1 A.C. 85, per Lord Browne-Wilkinson at 108. See also *Don King Productions Inc v Warren* [2000] Ch. 291, 320.

[141] This is, of course, the position where there is no anti-assignment clause, see para.3–34, above.

[142] *Re Turcan* (1888) 40 Ch.D. 5, 10–11, and this interpretation is supported by Lord Browne-Wilkinson in *Linden Gardens Trust Ltd v Lenesta Sludge Disposals Ltd* [1994] 1 A.C. 85 at 106.

[143] B. Allcock, "Restrictions on the Assignment of Contractual Rights" [1983] C.L.J. 328, 335–336; Tolhurst, "Prohibitions on Assignment and Declaration of Trust" [2007] L.M.C.L.Q. 278; G. McMeel, "The modern law of assignment: public policy and contractual restrictions on transferability" [2004] L.M.C.L.Q. 483, 507–508; P. Zonneveld, "The Effectiveness of Contractual Restrictions on the Assignment of Contractual Debts" (2007) 22 J.I.B.F.L. 313 (relying on two New Zealand cases: *Hodder & Tolley Ltd v Cornes* [1923] N.Z.L.R. 876; and *Atwood & Reid Ltd v Stephens* [1932] N.Z.L.R. 1332); see Smith and Leslie, *The Law of Assignment* (2013), para.25.19.

[144] *Don King Productions Inc v Warren* [2000] Ch. 291, 321; Smith and Leslie, *The Law of Assignment* (2013), paras 25.33–25.36. Declaration of such a trust is very common in the invoice discounting type of receivables financing, where the assignor collects in the receivables and holds the proceeds on trust for the financier. This is one reason why the presence of anti-assignment clauses in supplier contracts is of less concern to those financing through invoice discounting as opposed to factoring and other more innovative forms of finance, see para.3–43, below.

unacceptable restraint on alienation.[145] Lord Browne-Wilkinson in the *Lenesta Sludge* case said that he expressed no view on this particular argument of Professor Goode, but he did indirectly support it by saying that a provision which sought to invalidate the contract between the assignor and the assignee may be ineffective on the grounds of public policy.[146] The extent to which a prohibition clause in the contract between the debtor and the purported assignor can affect the position between the assignor and the assignee is now considered in the context of a declaration of trust of the benefit of the contract.

(2) Benefit of contract

While the assignee of a non-assignable debt or other contract right looks primarily to the proceeds, he may also have a legitimate interest as beneficiary of the contract right before any proceeds have been received, and the court will give effect to this so long as it does not affect the right of the debtor to continue to deal exclusively with the assignor. This may be because the creditor has expressly declared a trust of the contractual rights (as opposed to just the collected proceeds) in favour of a third party, or because the court will imply such a trust as the only way of giving effect to the arrangement between the parties.[147] Whether such a trust is prevented by an anti-assignment clause is a matter of interpretation of the relevant clause.[148] In both the case of *Don King Productions Inc v Warren*[149] and the more recent Court of Appeal decision in *Barbados Trust Co Ltd v Bank of Zambia*[150] it was held that a clause which expressly prohibited assignment did not prevent a valid declaration of trust of the benefit of the contract.[151] Here, although the debtor can still obtain a good discharge by paying the creditor, which achieves one purpose of including a no-assignment clause in the contract, it may lose other benefits. The existence of the trust, once the debtor has notice of it, is likely to break the mutuality required for independent set-offs to continue to arise between the debtor and the creditor.[152] Further, as explained below, the assignee can bring an action against the debtor under the *Vandepitte* procedure.

3–40

The *Vandepitte* procedure[153] enables a beneficiary under a trust to sue in its own name, joining the trustee as a defendant, where the trustee refuses to sue to enforce a debt which is trust property. The procedure has the effect that the trustee's cause of action is enforced, so that judgment is given for the trustee, who

3–41

---

[145] Goode, "Inalienable Rights?" (1979) 42 M.L.R. 553.

[146] *Linden Gardens Trust Ltd v Lenesta Sludge Disposals Ltd* [1994] 1 A.C. 85, per Lord Browne-Wilkinson at 108.

[147] *Re Turcan* (1888) 40 Ch. D 5; *Don King Productions Inc v Warren* [2000] Ch. 291, 335; *Explora Group Plc v Hesco Bastion Ltd* [2005] EWCA Civ 646 at [104].

[148] *Don King Productions Inc v Warren* [2000] Ch. 291, 319.

[149] *Don King Productions Inc v Warren* [2000] Ch. 291.

[150] *Barbados Trust Co Ltd v Bank of Zambia* [2007] EWCA Civ 148.

[151] *Don King Productions Inc v Warren* [2000] Ch. 291 at 321; *Barbados Trust Co Ltd v Bank of Zambia* [2007] EWCA Civ 148 at [43], per Waller L.J., [80]–[89] per Rix L.J. This is based on the view that a declaration of trust is different from an equitable assignment, a view that has been subject to some criticism; see Smith and Leslie, *The Law of Assignment* (2013), para.25.32. See further fn.65, above.

[152] Goode, "Contractual Prohibitions against Assignment" [2009] L.M.C.L.Q. 300, 311.

[153] Named after *Vandepitte v Preferred Accident Insurance Corp of New York* [1933] A.C. 70.

then holds the proceeds on trust for the beneficiary. Here, therefore the debtor would be ordered to pay the assignor, which is still consistent with the no-assignment clause. In the *Barbados Trust* case the Court of Appeal, by a majority, held that the *Vandepitte* procedure could be used to enforce the debt, since it was merely a procedural short-cut to enable the trust to be enforced, and to disallow it would be to enable the debtor to raise a defence which he would not have had had the beneficiary forced the trustee to sue using a more tortuous procedure.[154] It is clear, however, that the result of this decision is that the debtor is put, de facto even though not de jure, into the same position as if the debt had been assigned in equity, namely that he is being sued by the "assignee", with the "assignor" joined as a defendant to the action. It was on this basis that Hooper L.J. dissented.[155] The debtor loses the third benefit of the no-assignment clause, namely the prevention of exposure to an assignee who may take a more rigorous approach to enforcement than his direct creditor. However, such exposure could arise for other reasons unconnected with assignment; for example, the creditor might be taken over by another, more aggressive, company.[156]

3–42   It is not entirely clear whether it is possible to draft a prohibition which prevents such a trust arising even when declared expressly. In the *Barbados Trust* case Waller L.J. took the view[157] that even if the prohibition clause had completely prohibited alienability, it could not have stopped the creditor declaring a trust of the contractual rights in favour of the third party, or the enforcement of such trust.[158] Hooper L.J. appeared to take the view that a more widely drawn clause would be effective to prohibit a declaration of trust, but that this was unnecessary since, on his view, the *Vandepitte* procedure could not be used to enforce a trust the declaration of it was whether or not prohibited by a no-assignment clause.[159] It is implicit from the judgment of Rix L.J. that he took the view that a clause could prohibit a declaration of trust, but that the clause in the case did not do so.[160] As a matter of principle, a person cannot be prevented by a contractual term from declaring a valid trust over his own property, except to the extent that the contractual counterparty is directly affected by that trust. Thus, in the same way that a clause prohibiting assignment means that any notice of assignment is ineffective vis-à-vis the debtor, where a clause prohibits a declaration of trust, any notice of that trust cannot affect the position of the debtor. Therefore he can obtain a good discharge by paying the creditor, and receipt of the notice will not prevent set-offs arising between the debtor and creditor.[161] However, the clause should not prevent the trust arising as between

---

[154] *Barbados Trust Co Ltd v Bank of Zambia* [2007] EWCA Civ 148 at [47], per Waller L.J. It should be noted that the Court of Appeal did not rule out that the *Vandepitte* procedure might be inappropriate in some commercial contexts, e.g. where the contracts were of a personal nature, ibid at [107].

[155] *Barbados Trust Co Ltd v Bank of Zambia* [2007] EWCA Civ 148 at [139].

[156] Goode, "Contractual Prohibitions against Assignment" [2009] L.M.C.L.Q. 300, 315.

[157] *Barbados Trust Co Ltd v Bank of Zambia* [2007] EWCA Civ 148 at [44]–[47].

[158] This includes enforcement by the *Vandepitte* procedure, see below.

[159] *Barbados Trust Co Ltd v Bank of Zambia* [2007] EWCA Civ 148 at [129]–[139].

[160] *Barbados Trust Co Ltd v Bank of Zambia* [2007] EWCA Civ 148, per Rix L.J. at [88].

[161] J. Marshall, "Declaring a Trust over Rights to an 'Unassignable' Contract" (1999) 12 Insolv. Intelligence 1. However, the creditor would not be able to rely on set-off vis-à-vis the debtor in this situation, as it would thereby be in breach of its obligations owed to the assignee under the declaration of trust. Goode, "Contractual Prohibitions against Assignment" [2009] L.M.C.L.Q. 300, 315 and fn.34.

the assignor and the assignee. This leaves open the question of whether the beneficiary could use the *Vandepitte* procedure to enforce the debt. There seems no reason why it could not do so. The use of the procedure is merely a short cut, to avoid the circuity of action whereby the assignee sues the assignor to force him to enforce the trust; further, the outcome of the use of the procedure is that the debtor is ordered to pay the assignor. The fact that this payment is then held on trust for the assignee is not a matter which affects the debtor. The only effect on the debtor is that the assignee decides when and how to bring the action, but, as previously mentioned, a debtor cannot entirely insulate himself from persons other than his creditor influencing enforcement.

The analysis above, whereby contractual clauses have effect to protect the debtor to a large extent but cannot prevent proprietary rights arising between the assignor and the assignee, reflects a balance between competing policy considerations of freedom of contract, on the one hand, and the prevention of inalienability of valuable property, particularly receivables, on the other.[162] However, the widespread use of clauses prohibiting assignment does cause some difficulties in relation to receivables financing. Receivables financiers who operate on a notification basis ("factors") usually refuse to finance receivables which include such clauses, as the debtor will refuse to pay the financier. Further, such receivables cannot be the subject of innovative forms of finance such as online auctions.[163] Invoice discounters have less of a problem, since they operate on a non-notification basis, and so difficulties usually only arise on the borrower's insolvency. They have developed various ways of working around the problem, such as checking for anti-assignment clauses before financing invoices, and obtaining waivers if necessary, taking fixed and floating charges over all the assets of the financed company to give them the right to appoint an administrator to enforce the receivables,[164] or taking a power of attorney to enable them to enforce.[165] These techniques, however, increase the cost of financing. Prohibitions of assignment of receivables are ineffective in many jurisdictions,[166] and there is considerable merit in the Law Commission's proposal for a similar provision in English law,[167] at least in a limited sphere.

3–43

(3)   Security Interests

So far we have considered contractual prohibitions on assignment in the context of absolute assignments of receivables. It is also important to consider the effect

3–44

---

[162] See *Barbados Trust Co Ltd v Bank of Zambia* [2007] EWCA Civ 148 at [112], per Rix L.J.

[163] See *http://marketinvoice.com/* [accessed September 24, 2013]. Such forms of finance are seen as critical for the revival of financing of small and medium-sized enterprises.

[164] This technique might not be effective were the clause to prohibit the granting of security as well as assignments.

[165] It would be necessary for the financier to have some sort of effective proprietary right in the receivables for the power of attorney to be irrevocable on the borrower's insolvency, Powers of Attorney Act 1971 s.4.

[166] See §9–406(d) of the American Uniform Commercial Code; art.6(1) of the UNIDROIT Convention on International Factoring (1988); art.9 of the 2001 United Nations Convention on the Assignment of Receivables in International Trade (2004); s.354(a) of the German Commercial Code (HGB); Security Interests (Jersey) Law 2012, art.39. See also O. Akseli, "Contractual prohibitions on assignment of receivables: an English and UN perspective" [2009] J.B.L 650.

[167] Law Commission, *Company Security Interests*, Law Com. No.296 (2005), para.4.40.

of such clauses on security interests. Since a mortgage of receivables is usually created by assignment, a clause prohibiting assignment would have the same effect on the creation of such a mortgage as it does on an absolute assignment. Similarly, the reasoning in the last few paragraphs also applies to a mortgage created by declaration of trust. A more interesting point is the extent to which a clause prohibiting assignment prohibits the grant of a charge over the relevant debt. It is, of course, possible that the clause would also prohibit the grant of a charge, or of security more generally; without such express words, whether it covered the grant of a charge would be a matter of construction (both of the agreement and of the charge in question). A "mere" charge does not involve the transfer or assignment of the charged asset, but many charges are drafted in such a way that they are likely to be construed as equitable mortgages, which do.[168] While it is possible, as a matter of strict law, to say that a "mere" charge is not an assignment, in many contexts a fixed charge (or a crystallised floating charge) is treated as one.[169] In the case of *Foamcrete* considered below, the Court of Appeal appears to have assumed that the clause (which prohibited only assignment and did not mention "charge") would cover the grant of a floating charge. For all these reasons, it seems likely that many clauses prohibiting assignment would be interpreted also to prohibit the grant of a charge, and that this would have the effect discussed above.[170]

3–45   The last case to be considered on this topic is the decision of the Court of Appeal in *Foamcrete (UK) Ltd v Thrust Engineering Ltd*,[171] which concerned a charge.

PTE, a company, granted its bank a debenture containing (inter alia) a floating charge over its undertaking and property, present and future. Later it entered into two agreements with Thrust Engineering, a joint venture agreement ("the principal agreement") and a supplementary "purchase of stock agreement" under which Thrust became liable to make payments for stock and work in progress. The principal agreement provided that rights and obligations under it could not be assigned by either party without the consent of the other. Subsequently PTE went into liquidation, and thereafter the bank transferred the debenture to Foamcrete, who gave notice of assignment to Thrust and, payment not having been made, instituted proceedings. Thrust contended that the assignment of the debenture was ineffective, being in breach of the no-assignment clause.

The Court of Appeal rejected the defence, holding, first, that the no-assignment clause was contained not in the principal agreement but in the purchase of stock agreement, but, secondly, if it was contained in the principal agreement then the bank's rights derived not from the assignment but from the floating charge, by which it "acquired an immediate beneficial interest in all the property, present and future, subject to the equitable charge prior to the creation of the debt due to PTE from Thrust Engineering"[172] and that the grant of the debenture could not possibly infringe the prohibition against assignment, which did not then exist.

---

[168] See para.3–21, above and fn.36.
[169] *Biggerstaff v Rowatt's Wharf Ltd* [1896] 2 Ch. 93; *NW Robbie & Co v Witney Warehouse Co* [1963] 1 W.L.R. 1324 CA.
[170] See also Goode, "Contractual Prohibitions against Assignment" [2009] L.M.C.L.Q. 300, 310.
[171] *Foamcrete (UK) Ltd v Thrust Engineering Ltd* [2002] B.C.C. 221.
[172] *Foamcrete (UK) Ltd v Thrust Engineering Ltd* [2002] B.C.C. 221, per Mummery L.J. at 225.

The decision is puzzling. Quite apart from the fact that a floating charge confers no interest in any specific asset prior to crystallisation,[173] it is well established that even in the case of a fixed charge of after-acquired property the chargee takes the property as he finds it, warts and all, so that if, for example, the property is acquired with the aid of an advance secured by a mortgage or charge agreed prior to the purchase the after-acquired property clause catches the property in its incumbered form, and therefore attaches only to the chargor's equity of redemption.[174] By the same token, where the after-acquired property clause picks up the benefit of a future contract, it can do so only on the contract terms, including any prohibition against assignment. Accordingly the debtor, Thrust, was not obliged to recognise either the fixed security interest produced by crystallisation of the floating charge or the title of the bank's assignee, and its defence should, it is submitted, have succeeded.

---

[173] See paras 4–03 et seq., below.
[174] See para.5–63, below.

CHAPTER 4

The Floating Charge

The floating charge is one of the most subtle creations of equity, and despite the **4–01** volume of case law and literature devoted to its analysis it remains conceptually elusive.[1] This is because a floating charge is an interest not in specific assets but in a constantly changing fund of assets and English law has always found it difficult to grapple with the concept of a fund.[2] To Maitland, one of the most brilliant legal minds in the history of English law, all equitable rights, including the rights of a beneficiary under an active trust, were rights in personam[3]; to the modern equity lawyer the beneficiary has something more, a proprietary interest in a trust fund which, though not attaching to specific assets while the trust continues in force nevertheless attracts proprietary remedies for the preservation of the fund, including the equitable right to claim traced assets improperly disposed of by the trustees. It can now be taken as settled that the floating charge creates an immediate interest in rem; what continues to be the subject of debate are the nature and incidents of that interest. It is these that it is proposed to explore in the present chapter. The general characteristics of a floating charge are described in Section 1 below. A detailed analysis of the distinction between fixed and floating charges and the degree of control necessary to ensure that a charge is characterised as a fixed charge is provided in Section 2. Priority issues, including the priority effect of a negative pledge clause in a floating charge, will be examined in Ch.5, below.

The present chapter focuses on floating charges by companies. In general, it is not possible for an unincorporated trader to grant a floating charge over goods, for under the Bills of Sale Act (1878) Amendment Act 1882 a security bill of sale is void, except as against the grantor, in respect of any personal chattels not specifically described in the schedule to the bill[4] or in respect of personal chattels so described of which the grantor was not the true owner at the time of execution of the bill.[5] Other classes of asset are outside the Bills of Sale Acts, but a general assignment of book debts by an unincorporated trader must be registered as if it

---

[1] The most comprehensive and penetrating treatment is to be found in W.J. Gough, *Company Charges*, 2nd edn (London: Butterworths Law, 1996), Chs 5–16. See also H. Beale, M. Bridge, L. Gullifer and E. Lomnicka, *The Law of Security and Title-Based Financing*, 2nd edn (Oxford: Oxford University Press, 2012), paras 6.68–6.139; and R. Calnan, *Taking Security: Law and Practice*, 2nd edn (London: Jordan Publishing, 2011), Ch.4.

[2] See also R. Nolan, "Property in a Fund" (2004) 120 L.Q.R. 108.

[3] Equity (2nd.), Lecture IX.

[4] Bills of Sale Act (1878) Amendment Act 1882 s.4.

[5] Bills of Sale Act (1878) Amendment Act 1882 s.5.

were a bill of sale.[6] Moreover, there are various exemptions from the Bills of Sale Acts. In particular, they do not apply to agricultural charges by a farmer, whether fixed or floating.[7]

1.   THE CONCEPTION OF THE FLOATING CHARGE

The genesis of the floating charge[8]

4–02 In *Holroyd v Marshall*[9] the House of Lords settled once and for all the efficacy of a charge over future property. It has been assumed for many years that the charge in *Holroyd v Marshall* was fixed. However, the ability of the chargor to substitute assets raises the issue whether such a charge would be categorised as fixed or floating in the light of *Re Spectrum Plus*.[10] The concept of a charge over future property was not new; indeed, in *Holroyd v Marshall* itself it was considered established. Such a device was most beneficial to the creditor, for it gave him a hold over all after-acquired property of the debtor falling within the classes of asset specified in the charge and precluded the debtor from disposing of such property free from the charge without the debtor's consent. From the debtor's viewpoint, the arrangement was quite acceptable as regards fixed assets but it was another matter in the case of stock in trade. To require a trading company borrowing money on the security of its stock to obtain the consent of the creditor every time it wished to dispose of an item of stock would create an intolerable administrative burden for both parties; and since the debtor could repay the advance only from the proceeds of sales, it was necessary to allow the company freedom to dispose of its trading stock in the ordinary course of business free from the charge. Could a charge instrument allow this to be done without vitiating the security effect of the agreement? It is interesting to contrast the answers to this question in American and English jurisprudence. Courts in the US roundly declared that to allow such freedom to the debtor was incompatible with the creation of a genuine security interest and was a fraud on creditors. If the creditor did not exercise reasonable dominium over the asset covered by the security agreement, his security was illusory and void.[11] At best, the security agreement conferred contractual rights on the creditor.

---

[6] Insolvency Act 1986 s.344(1). See also para.3–29, above.

[7] Agricultural Credits Act 1928 s.8(1). Section 7 of the Act has special provisions as to crystallisation of agricultural floating charges. See para.4–55, below.

[8] See R.R. Pennington, "The Genesis of the Floating Charge" (1960) 23 M.L.R. 630; and the historical account given by Lord Millett in *Agnew v Commissioners of Inland Revenue* (also known as *Re Brumark*) [2001] UKPC 28; [2001] 2 A.C. 710 at 717, giving the decision of the Privy Council on appeal from the New Zealand Court of Appeal. See also R. Gregory and P. Walton, "Fixed and Floating Charges- a revelation" [2001] L.M.C.L.Q. 123; and J. Getzler, "'The Role of Security over Future and Circulating Capital': Evidence from the British Economy *circa* 1850 – 1920" in J. Getzler and J. Payne (eds), *Company Charges: Spectrum and Beyond* (Oxford: OUP, 2006), Ch.10.

[9] *Holroyd v Marshall* (1862) 10 H.L. Cas. 191.

[10] *Re Spectrum Plus* [2005] UKHL 41; [2005] 2 A.C. 680. See paras 4–12 and 4–21, below.

[11] *Geilfuss v Corrigan*, 95 Wis. 651; 70 N.W. 306 (1897); *Benedict v Ratner*, 268 U.S. 354; 45 S.Ct. 566; 69 L.Ed. 991 (1925). There was, at that time, no provision for registration of security interests in the US, see P. Wood, "A Review of Brumark and Spectrum in an International Setting" in *Company*

The approach of the English courts was more accommodating to the needs of the inventory financier. The effect of the provision allowing the debtor company freedom to deal with the charged assets in the ordinary course of business was not to negate the security interest but merely to postpone its attachment so long as the debtor's powers of management continued.[12] In conformity with the principle previously stated, that a security interest does not attach until fulfilment of the conditions for attachment specified in the agreement, the charge floated over all assets of the company, present and future, within the description in the charge instrument, until the debtor company's power to manage the assets was brought to an end by the creditor's intervention in accordance with the terms of the charge instrument or by the debtor going into receivership or liquidation or upon the occurrence of some other event specified in the charge instrument. The charge then crystallised, fastening in specie on property within the description in the charge instrument in which the debtor company then had or subsequently acquired an interest. Thus in contrast to American law, English law permitted a form of security in which attachment was contractually postponed. It was not a specific security with a licence to the debtor company to deal with the assets in the ordinary course of business, but an ambulatory security dependent for its attachment on the fulfilment of a condition precedent, namely the occurrence of a crystallising event. The new device was first ruled effective by the Court of Appeal in *Re Panama, New Zealand and Australia Royal Mail Co*,[13] a decision upheld and applied in *Re Yorkshire Woolcombers Association Ltd*.[14]

The nature and characteristics of a floating charge

Despite *Re Panama*, some judges found it difficult to see how any security   4–03
interest could be said to exist prior to crystallisation. Surely until this time there was merely a contract between creditor and debtor for the provision of security? Certainly a floating charge does not do much for the creditor prior to crystallisation. He cannot exercise proprietary or possessory rights over the assets

---

Charges: Spectrum and Beyond (2006), p.149. For a detailed description of the American position prior to the Uniform Commercial Code, see G. Gilmore, *Security Interests in Personal Property* (Boston: Little, Brown, 1965), Chs 6 and 8.

[12] Indeed, for several centuries equity appears to have recognised the concept of a fixed mortgage by individual traders and partnerships covering both present and future property, the mortgagor being left in possession with power to deal with the mortgaged assets in the course of carrying on business, a process brought to an abrupt halt by the controversial decision of Jarvis C.J. in *Graham v Chapman* (1852) 12 C.B. 85. See the illuminating historical analysis by Gregory and Walton, "Fixed and floating charges—a revelation" [2001] L.M.C.L.Q. 123, which notes the influence of bankruptcy law in the development of constraints on non-possessory charges over future property. This article also points out the roots of the floating charge in the mortgage sanctioned in by the Companies Clauses Consolidation Act 1845, which enabled a public utility company to give a mortgage over its entire undertaking which could not be enforced piecemeal, but only once the company had ceased to be a going concern. Companies incorporated under the Companies Act began to grant such a mortgage, which was held to be valid by the courts on the grounds that the company's business would not be paralysed by the width of the charge, as the company could carry on its business until either winding up or the appointment of a receiver (see *Re Florence Land and Public Works Co* (1878) 10 Ch.D. 530, 546–547).

[13] *Re Panama, New Zealand and Australia Royal Mail Co* (1870) 5 Ch. App. 318.

[14] *Re Yorkshire Woolcombers Association Ltd* [1903] 2 Ch. 284; affirmed sub nom. *Illingworth v Houldsworth* [1904] A.C. 355.

either as against the company or as against third parties, nor does he have a locus standi to obtain an injunction against the company to restrain dealings with its assets in the ordinary course of business where the dealings are not in breach of the debenture or subject to the creditor's veto and his security is not in jeopardy.[15] Nevertheless, it is now established that a floating charge creates an immediate, albeit unattached, security interest. This idea is most clearly expressed by Buckley L.J. in *Evans v Rival Granite Quarries Ltd*[16]:

> "A floating charge is not a future security; it is a present security which presently affects all the assets of the company expressed to be included in it ... A floating security is not a specific mortgage of the assets, plus a licence to the mortgagor to dispose of them in the course of his business, but is a floating mortgage applying to every item comprised in the security, but not specifically affecting any item until some act or event occurs or some act on the part of the mortgagee is done which causes it to crystallise into a fixed security."[17]

How, then, do we identify a floating charge? What are the hallmarks of such a security? Valuable guidance is offered by the much-quoted judgment of Romer L.J. in *Re Yorkshire Woolcombers Association Ltd*[18]:

> "I certainly do not intend to attempt to given an exact definition of the term 'floating charge,' nor am I prepared to say that there will not be a floating charge within the meaning of the Act, which does not contain all the three characteristics that I am about to mention, but I certainly think that if a charge has the three characteristics that I am about to mention it is a floating charge. (1.) If it is a charge on a class of assets of a company present and future. (2.) If that class is one which in the ordinary course of the business of the company would be changing from time to time; and (3.) If you find that by the charge it is contemplated that, until some future step is taken by or on behalf of those interested in the charge, the company may carry on its business in the ordinary way so far as concerns the particular class of assets I am dealing with."

When read with the extract from the judgment of Buckley L.J., previously quoted, this passage (if modified to take account of automatic crystallisation) shows the two ingredients of a typical floating charge, namely that it is a present security in a fund of assets which the debtor company is left free to manage in the ordinary course of its business,[19] though not necessarily completely free.[20] Though on a literal reading of the judgment by Romer L.J. the type of charge he is describing is a charge on a changing fund of assets, it seems clear that what he

---

[15] *Re Borax Co* [1901] 1 Ch. 326; *Lawrence v West Somerset Mineral Railway Co* [1918] 2 Ch. 250. For a discussion of when an injunction can be obtained when the security is in jeopardy, see para.4–51, below.

[16] *Evans v Rival Granite Quarries Ltd* [1910] 2 K.B. 979.

[17] *Evans v Rival Granite Quarries Ltd* [1910] 2 K.B. at 999.

[18] *Re Yorkshire Woolcombers Association Ltd* [1903] 2 Ch. 284, at 295. See also [1904] A.C. 355, per Lord Macnaghten at 358.

[19] The concept of a floating charge as an interest in a fund has recently been endorsed in the decision by the Privy Council in *Agnew v Commissioners of Inland Revenue* [2001] UKPC 28; [2001] 2 A.C. 710, per Lord Millett at 719. For the meaning of "ordinary course of business" in the context of priorities see para.5–40, below.

[20] See para.4–23, below. See below for an analysis of the present status of Romer L.J.'s "essential ingredients".

was actually referring to was not a change in the nature of the fund (i.e. a shift from one class of asset to another) but rather a change from time to time in the composition of the fund, as where the fund consists of stock in trade where items of stock will move out of the fund on sale while others will move into the fund on production or acquisition. The status of the floating charge as a present security distinguishes it from a mere contract to give security at a future date on the occurrence of a designated uncertain event.[21] Its characteristic of an interest in a changeable fund of assets distinguishes it from an agreement for the provision of security over a particular asset where attachment is postponed.

In English law, a fund is considered to have an existence distinct from that of **4–04** its components. The contents of the fund are constantly changing as assets are removed from the fund and new assets come into it, but the identity of the fund itself remains unchanged, in much the same way as the river Thames remains the river Thames despite the fact that the water in it is never the same from one minute to the next. Indeed, an open-ended fund (i.e. one which by the terms of its establishment is capable of increase with the addition of new assets) has a notional existence even at times when there are no assets comprised in it. To carry the river simile a stage further, we should continue to speak of the river Thames even if, through a drought, it had temporarily dried up.[22]

An analogy is not hard to find. The interest of a beneficiary in a trust fund is exactly in point. So long as the trustee's power of management continues, the beneficiary has no rights in any specific asset within the fund. His interest is a floating interest of the same kind as that of the chargee under a floating charge.[23] The analysis of a floating charge as an interest in a fund appears to have been approved by Lord Walker in the *Spectrum* case.[24]

Hence the peculiarity of the floating charge is that, like an interest in a trust fund, it has immediate existence even prior to attachment. But is it of the essence of a floating charge that the fund should be open-ended? Recent cases have shown that Romer L.J.'s judgment offers a description, not a definition, and that while the first two characteristics (charge on a class of present and future assets, the class changing[25] from time to time in the ordinary course of business) are typical of a floating charge they are not distinctive of it, and it was the third

---

[21] cf. the view of Lord Scott in *Smith v Bridgend* [2001] UKHL 58; [2002] 1 A.C. 336 at [61]–[63] where he says "In my opinion, a charge expressed to come into existence on the occurrence of an uncertain future event and then to apply to a class of assets that cannot be identified until the event has happened would, if otherwise valid, qualify for registration as a floating charge". See para.2–15, above.

[22] As with the river Todd in Alice Springs, Australia, which is dry for most of the year. The annual boat race, designated Henley on Todd, is run by the two teams carrying their respective boats on their shoulders.

[23] For an analysis of property in a trust fund which does not rely on the concept of "floating interes'" see Nolan, "Property in a Fund" (2004) 120 L.Q.R. 108. Mr Nolan's view is that the beneficiary has a limited interest in the assets presently in the fund, subject to the rights of the trustees to overreach that interest and to substitute assets.

[24] *Re Spectrum Plus* [2005] UKHL 41; [2005] 2 A.C. 680 at [139]. Lord Walker, however, immediately afterwards cites with apparent approval the analysis by Professor Worthington in S. Worthington, *Proprietary Interests in Commercial Transactions* (Oxford: Clarendon Press, 1996), pp.74–77, which suggests that a floating charge is a defeasible fixed charge, see para.4–06, below.

[25] More accurately, the individual components of the class changing.

characteristic (freedom to deal) which was the hallmark of a floating charge.[26] Hence a closed fund, which is restricted to existing assets and cannot increase but can only reduce, because the debtor is obliged to pay over to the chargee the proceeds of assets sold instead of being able to use these to acquire new assets, nevertheless suffices for a floating charge.[27] Further, it is now clear from the opinion of Lord Scott in *Re Spectrum Plus* that it is possible, though unusual, to have a floating charge over a single identified asset.[28] So long as the debtor's powers of management continue, the fund remains in being until the last unit comprised in it is disposed of. In short, while a fund usually consists of a class or collection of present and future assets, the test of a fund is not whether it encompasses future assets or even the number of present assets comprised in it but the power given to the manager to deal with them free from interference by the beneficial owner or chargee so long as the power continues.

The relevance of intention to characterisation

4–05   It is necessary to distinguish the intention of the parties, as shown from the label used in the charge document, from the legal effect of what they have intended. When characterising a charge as fixed or floating, the first stage is to interpret the charge agreement to ascertain what rights and obligations the parties intended to create. At this stage the label used by the parties may be relevant, but only where the rights and obligations are not spelled out by the agreement.[29] The second stage is for the court to characterise the charge in accordance with the rights and obligations created, and at this stage the label used by the parties is ignored.[30]

Significance of the floating charge as a present security

4–06   At this point, one might well ask why the courts have found it necessary to describe the floating charge as a present security. This has led some commentators to advance the theory that a floating charge is a defeasible security interest which confers on the chargee the same quality of proprietary interest as that of a fixed charge except that it is defeasible,[31] or overreachable.[32] However,

---

[26] *Agnew v Commissioner for Inland Revenue* [2001] UKPC 28; [2001] 2 A.C. 710 at [13]; *Re Spectrum Plus* [2005] UKHL 41; [2005] 2 A.C. 680 at [111].

[27] *Re Bond Worth* [1980] Ch. 228, 267–268. This was the point overlooked in *Re Atlantic Computers Systems Plc* [1992] Ch. 505. See para.4–15, below.

[28] The example given by Lord Scott in *Spectrum* is that of an express assignment of a single debt by way of security at [107].

[29] *Re ASRS Establishment Ltd* [2000] 2 B.C.L.C. 631; *Ashborder BV v Green Gas Power Ltd* [2004] EWHC 1517 (Ch); [2005] B.C.C. 634. See para.4–21, below.

[30] *Agnew v Commissioners of Inland Revenue* [2001] UKPC 28; [2001] 2 A.C. 710, per Lord Millett at [32]. This is true even if the label is that the charge is floating, but the rights and obligations created by the parties are those of a fixed charge: the court will then characterise the charge as fixed, see The *Russell-Cooke Trust Co v Elliott* [2007] EWHC 1443 (Ch); [2007] 2 B.C.L.C. 637.

[31] See, for example, Worthington, *Proprietary Interests in Commercial Transactions* (1996), pp.79–86.

[32] Nolan, "Property in a Fund" (2004) 120 L.Q.R. 108. The differences between Mr Nolan's theory and that of Professor Worthingon are discussed in his article at 129. Mr Nolan's view of the chargee's pre-crystallisation interest is that it is, in any event, very limited since it is overreachable and cannot be enforced until crystallisation. In these circumstances there may be very little in substance between Mr Nolan's view and the view put forward in this book.

there are fundamental objections to this approach. In the first place, it is impossible to distinguish such a floating charge from a fixed charge with a licence to deal, a characterisation which the authorities have rejected.[33] Secondly, it is clear from the cases referred to above and many others in which they have been cited[34] that until crystallisation the charge does not attach to any asset in specie, so that it is quite different in nature from a fixed charge; if that were not the case, there would be no need for a concept of crystallisation. Thirdly, it is equally clear that crystallisation is not retrospective.

What, then, does this presently existing security interest give the floating chargee which he would not have under a mere contract to assign assets in the future? First, the occurrence of the crystallising event causes the charge to attach without the need for any new act on the part of the debtor.[35] Secondly, the debenture holder has the right, on crystallisation, to follow the assets into the hands of a purchaser or incumbrancer who prior to crystallisation took them from the company otherwise than in the ordinary course of the company's business.[36] Thirdly, restrictions in the floating charge on dealings in the assets by the company bind a subsequent party taking with notice of such restrictions, so that upon the floating charge crystallising it will have priority.[37] Fourthly, the procedural security which an execution creditor obtains by delivery of a writ of execution to the enforcement officer[38] takes effect subject to the prior equity of the debenture holder under the floating charge, so that if the charge crystallises before the execution is completed, the debenture holder obtains priority over the execution creditor, even though crystallisation does not occur until after the goods have become bound by the writ or even, indeed, until after their seizure by the enforcement officer.[39] Finally, by virtue of the fact that he has an existing security interest, albeit floating in character, the debenture holder has the right to apply to the court for the appointment of a receiver where his security is in jeopardy, even if the charge has not crystallised[40] and even if there has been no default.[41] Though the holding of a property interest by the applicant is not an

---

[33] *Evans v Rival Granite Quarries Ltd* [1910] 2 K.B. 979, 999. The difference is said to be that the fixed charge with a licence to deal is not defeasible (Worthington, *Proprietary Interests in Commercial Transactions* (1996), p.81), but the licence to deal plainly has the effect that it is defeasible.

[34] See, for example, *Re Benjamin Cope & Sons Ltd* [1914] 1 Ch. 800, per Sargant J. at 806; *Agnew v Inland Revenue Commissioners* [2001] UKPC 28; [2001] 2 A.C. 710; *Re Cosslett Contractors Ltd* [1998] Ch. 495, per Millett L.J. at 509–510; *Re JD Brian Ltd* [2011] IEHC 113; [2011] 3 I.R. 244 at [17]–[20].

[35] *Re JD Brian Ltd* [2011] IEHC 113; [2011] 3 I.R. 244 at [17]–[20].

[36] See para.5–42, below.

[37] See para.5–41, below; and as to notice paras 2–26 et seq., above.

[38] Courts Act 2003 Sch.7 para.8, to be replaced by Pt 3 of Sch.12 to the Tribunals, Courts and Enforcement Act 2007 from a day to be appointed.

[39] *Re Standard Manufacturing Co* [1891] 1 Ch. 627; *Re Opera Ltd* [1891] 3 Ch. 260; *Evans v Rival Granite Quarries Ltd* [1910] 2 K.B. 979, per Fletcher Moulton L.J. at 996; *Taunton v Sheriff of Warwickshire* [1895] 2 Ch. 319. See para.5–44, below.

[40] *Hubbuck v Helms* (1887) 56 L.T. 232; *Edwards v Standard Rollins Stock Syndicate* [1893] 1 Ch.574; *Re London Pressed Hinge Co Ltd* [1905] 1 Ch. 576; *Re Victoria Steamboats Ltd* [1897] 1 Ch. 158, where Kekewich J. held that the court could also appoint a manager. See also *Wily v St George Partnership Banking Ltd* (1999) 161 A.L.R. 1 at [45]–[47], per Finkelstein J.

[41] *Re London Pressed Hinge Co Ltd* [1905] 1 Ch. 576.

essential condition of the appointment of a receiver by the court[42] it greatly strengthens the case for such appointment, which has the effect of crystallising the charge.[43] Similar considerations apply to the grant of an injunction at the behest of the holder of a floating charge to restrain the company from disposing of its assets otherwise than as permitted by the charge.[44]

Attachment of the floating charge

4–07   When the debtor company's powers of management come to an end, the charge is said to crystallise, that is, it ceases to be an interest in a fund of assets and becomes attached to the specific assets then comprised in the fund and any further assets acquired by the company. Like a fixed charge, a floating charge takes effect as a security from the date of the security agreement. It is often said that once a floating charge has crystallised so as to become fixed it is treated in the same way as if it had been fixed from the outset. This, however, is not entirely the case. In the first place, crystallisation is not retrospective. Secondly, the fact that the charge started life as a floating charge means that even after crystallisation the company may have ostensible authority to deal with the charged assets, and this may affect priorities in the event of subsequent dealings.[45] Thirdly, for the purpose of certain provisions of the Insolvency Act 1986 the rule is: once a floating charge, always a floating charge. More accurately, a floating charge is defined as a charge which, as created, was a floating charge.[46] It follows that crystallisation of a charge before a winding-up or other event attracting the rights of preferential creditors does not prevent the charge from being subordinated to preferential debts and the prescribed part.[47] Conversely, a charge created as a fixed charge retains its status as such for the purposes of the Insolvency Act even though it has subsequently been converted into a floating charge pursuant to an agreement to that effect.[48] The result is that the chargee is not postponed to preferential creditors; on the other hand, he cannot appoint an administrative receiver,[49] nor can he appoint an administrator out of court, unless his fixed charge is part of a package of security interests which are over the whole or substantially the whole of the company's property, one of which is a floating charge.[50]

---

[42] See Lightman and Moss, *The Law of Receivers and Administrators of Companies*, 5th edn (London: Sweet & Maxwell/Thomson Reuters, 2011), para.29–003.

[43] See para.4–46, below.

[44] See para.4–51, below. Whether the court would grant a mandatory injunction to undo a disposition which to the knowledge of the disponee was in breach of the restriction in the floating charge is another matter. The court might well take the view that such an injunction is unnecessary, since on crystallisation the floating charge would anyway have priority, so that there is nothing to undo. See para.5–42, below.

[45] See paras 4–32 and 5–51, below.

[46] Insolvency Act 1986 s.251; and see ibid., s.40(1); Companies Act 2006 s.754(1); and para.5–68, below.

[47] See para.5–68, below.

[48] See paras 4–62 et seq., below. In these circumstances it may be that a new floating charge is created.

[49] As to the abolition of administrative receivership except in specified cases, see para.1–01, above, paras 4–09 and 4–65, below.

[50] Insolvency Act 1986 Sch.B1 para.14.

2.   FIXED CHARGE VERSUS FLOATING CHARGE

The nature of a floating charge has now been examined, together with the
characteristics which distinguish it from a fixed (or specific) charge. Though the
distinction is relatively easy to state, it has been found much harder to apply in
practice. Particular difficulty has been occasioned by charges over book debts and
the relationship between book debts and their proceeds. Everything turns on the
extent to which the chargee has contractual control, an issue we shall examine in
detail a little later.[51] At this stage it is just worth emphasising that the distinction
is not, as is frequently supposed, between a charge over existing assets and a
charge over future assets, nor between a charge over fixed assets and a charge
over current assets, but between a charge which leaves control with the chargee
and one which does not.

4–08

Significance of the distinction

Meanwhile we must address a preliminary question: what is the significance of
the distinction between a fixed and a floating charge? Is one preferable to the
other? Here it is necessary to distinguish legal from commercial considerations.
Assuming that the debtor company has a sound business, it is not in the interests
of either party unduly to fetter the company's ability to run its business, for it is
from the income generated by the company's trading activities that the creditor
will ultimately be paid. For the creditor to tie up the debtor with covenants so
stringent that the creditor will have to turn a blind eye to breaches in order to
avoid paralysing the business or impairing its efficiency is not good sense. This is
a point which lawyers can be inclined to overlook. Just as the old-style wills
draftsman used to provide a life interest for the testator's widow, rather than an
absolute interest, in order to defer estate duty, with the result that duty was
deferred but the widow was left destitute, so also the modern draftsman of
debentures can be inclined to go for overkill, driven by a desire to obtain the most
effective security for his client's advance. This will be considered later.[52]

4–09

A further advantage of the floating charge used to be that if this, with other
security, covers the whole or substantially the whole of the debtor company's
property, the chargee can take power to appoint an administrative receiver to
manage the entire business of the company, continue trading and hive down or
sell off the business as a whole in the event of default instead of merely having to
sell specific assets. Only the holder of a charge which (as created) was a floating
charge could do this.[53] Further, the floating chargee could block the appointment

---

[51] See paras 4–21 et seq., below.

[52] See paras 4–57 et seq., below.

[53] See Insolvency Act 1986 s.29(2). So long as there was a floating charge it is irrelevant that most of
the company's property was subject to fixed charges in favour of the same chargee.

of an administrator.[54] However, with certain exceptions administrative receivership is now abolished,[55] reflecting a concern that it undermined the prospects of reorganisation of a company through administration.[56] The floating chargee, that is, the chargee who has security interests over the whole or substantially the whole of the company's property at least one of which is a floating charge, is given the power to appoint an administrator out of court under a "fast-track" procedure not available to other creditors,[57] and thus has the ability to choose who is appointed.

4–10   Despite the virtues of a floating charge there is no question that a fixed charge has several advantages over a floating charge when it comes to protection of the creditor. In the first place, the creditor acquires immediate real rights over the asset which can only be cut off by a disposition to a bona fide purchaser of the legal estate or title for value without notice. Since most charges are registrable, most categories of third party will be fixed with notice of the charge,[58] and will accordingly be bound by it. By contrast, the disposition of an asset which is the subject of a floating charge will as a general rule take effect free from the charge, whether the disposition be outright or by way of charge or mortgage and whether or not the charge has been registered or the disponee knows of it.[59] Secondly, a floating charge is postponed to the rights of preferential creditors if the debenture holder takes possession of any of the charged assets[60] or if the company goes into receivership[61] or liquidation,[62] whereas a fixed charge[63] has priority over all unsecured claims, preferential or otherwise. The class of preferential creditors has

---

[54] This is because s.9(3) of the Insolvency Act 1986 generally required the court to dismiss an application for an administration order where there is an administrative receiver unless he consented. This remains the case in relation to those situations where an administrative receiver can continue to be appointed by a floating chargee, Insolvency Act 1986 Sch.B1 para.39.

[55] Insolvency Act 1986 s.72A(1), inserted by the Enterprise Act 2002 s.250(1). The exceptions relate chiefly to capital and financial market arrangements, public-private partnerships and other project finance arrangements, see Insolvency Act 1986 ss.72B–G. Floating charges created before September 15, 2003 are also excepted. See further para.4–65, below.

[56] It can be argued that the perceived mischief to which the insolvency provisions of the Enterprise Act are directed could have been dealt with by simply repealing s.9(3), so that an administration order could be made despite the appointment of an administrative receiver, who upon the making of the order would have to vacate office (Insolvency Act 1986 s.11(2)). Another possible route would have been to reform the duties of an administrative receiver, so that such duties were owed to creditors more generally, see R. Goode, *Principles of Corporate Insolvency Law*, 4th edn (London: Sweet & Maxwell/Thomson Reuters, 2011), para.10–49; and R. Stevens, "Security after the Enterprise Act" in *Company Charges: Spectrum and Beyond* (2006), p.158.

[57] Insolvency Act 1986 Sch.B1 para.14. Directors of the company and the company itself also have this power (Insolvency Act 1986 Sch.B1 para.22) but this is subject to the power of the floating chargee to veto such appointment and appoint its own choice of administrator (Insolvency Act 1986 Sch.B1 para.36).

[58] See para.2–31, above. Purchasers in the ordinary course of business of the legal interest are unlikely to have notice.

[59] See paras 5–40 et seq., below.

[60] Companies Act 2006 s.754.

[61] Insolvency Act 1986 s.40.

[62] Insolvency Act 1986 s.175. See further para.5–68, below, as to the effect of this provision and those referred to above, fnn.60 and 61.

[63] i.e. a charge which starts life as a fixed charge. See para.4–07, above.

been reduced by the abolition of Crown preference,[64] but the Enterprise Act 2002 has inserted s.176A into the Insolvency Act 1986,[65] which provides that a "prescribed part" is to be taken out of the assets subject to any floating charge and made available to the unsecured creditors. The relevant percentage is 50 per cent of the first £10,000 and 20 per cent of any assets above that figure, with a ceiling of £600,000 for the prescribed part.[66] Thirdly, a floating charge given by an insolvent company within the 12 months[67] prior to the onset of insolvency[68] is invalid except as to new value.[69] Fourthly, an administrator may dispose of assets subject to a floating charge without the leave of the court,[70] but leave is required for the disposal of assets subject to a fixed charge.[71] This distinction has become more significant now that the administration has replaced administrative receivership as the most usual method of enforcement of the floating charge. Since the 2013 reforms to the registration of company charges all charges are registrable, whether fixed or floating, unless they fall within one of the exceptions. Security financial collateral arrangements are exempted from registration under the FCARs[72]: while there is no necessary connection between the test for whether a charge is fixed, and whether it is a security financial collateral arrangement,[73] it is likely that most fixed charges over financial collateral[74] will fall under the FCARs, while many floating charges will not.[75]

These advantages of a fixed charge have led draftsmen to attempt to create fixed charges over many different types of assets, as discussed in the next paragraph. The next few sections of this book will discuss the current law on the difference between fixed and floating charges. The cases in which the courts have had to consider where the line should be drawn have largely arisen in the context of insolvency and the decisions to some extent reflect the policy of postponing priority of floating chargees to other creditors. The law, though clearer than it used to be, still contains some areas of uncertainty. It should be remembered that, despite the context of the cases, it is just as critical for a lender to know whether a charge is fixed or floating ex ante, that is, when it is granted, as at the point of insolvency of the chargor. In structured financing transactions, for example, this issue may have a considerable effect on the rating of the issued notes. Similarly, the issue is very important in the structuring of project finance transactions. It is therefore critical that the law in this area is as certain as possible, while also reflecting the balance of interests between floating chargees and other

---

[64] The only preferential creditors now are employees of the company, and the Secretary of State for Work and Pensions, who is subrogated to the claims of employees against the company to the extent that employees have claimed under ss.182–186 of the Employment Rights Act 1996.

[65] Enterprise Act 2002 s.252.

[66] The Insolvency Act 1986 (Prescribed Part) Order 2003. This has the effect that no deduction is made from floating charge assets over £2,985,000.

[67] Or two years in the case of a charge in favour of a person connected with the company.

[68] As defined by the Insolvency Act 1986 s.245(5).

[69] Insolvency Act 1986 s.245(2). See further para.5–72, below.

[70] See *Halsbury's Laws*, 4th edn (London: Butterworths Law, 1991) Vol.4(1), paras 665 et seq.; Insolvency Act 1986 Sch.B1 para.70.

[71] Insolvency Act 1986 Sch.B1 para.71.

[72] Financial Collateral Arrangements (No.2) Regulations 2003 (SI 2003/3226) reg.4.

[73] See para.6–32, below.

[74] Cash, securities and credit claims: see Ch.6, below for further discussion of what is included as financial collateral.

[75] See paras 6–33 et seq., below.

(unsecured) creditors. It might be said that these concerns have been allayed in relation to financial collateral by the disapplication of the insolvency conse-quences from the enforcement of security financial collateral arrangements.[76] However, since in order for a charge to be such an arrangement, the chargee must have "possession or control" of the collateral,[77] the uncertainty has just been moved to a slightly different test. In terms of English law, it might be better if the two tests were aligned, and that steps were taken to make the distinction as clear and easily ascertained as possible. However, the difficulties of achieving this, given that the FCARs enact an EU Directive,[78] should not be underestimated.

Over what classes of asset may a fixed charge be taken?

4–11   Until 1978 it was widely assumed that, because a floating charge is customarily taken over assets of a shifting character, any charge is a floating charge as regards such assets. In other words, it was thought that a fixed charge could not be taken over current (or circulating) assets, only over fixed assets. The latter have been statutorily defined for the purposes of a company's accounts as assets which are intended for use on a continuing basis in the company's activities, all other assets being current assets.[79] Thus fixed assets will normally include land and buildings,[80] fixtures, plant, equipment used for office purposes or in the manufacture of goods for sale or rental, and intellectual property rights, while the most common current assets are cash, trade and other debts, and inventory, including raw material and finished stock in trade held for sale or lease.

The reason why it had been assumed that current assets were not susceptible to a fixed charge was that by their nature they are either spent (e.g. cash) or consumed in the course of manufacture (e.g. raw materials) or held only temporarily as stock in trade prior to being sold or let on lease in the ordinary course of business, for which purpose it was essential for them to be transferred free from any security interest. But the decision in *Siebe Gorman & Co Ltd v Barclays Bank Ltd*[81] exposed the fallacy of this approach and showed that the material factor was not whether the charged assets were fixed or current but whether the debtor company was left with the right to deal with the assets in the ordinary course of business free from the security interest, a freedom incompatible with the concept of a fixed security but perfectly consistent with a floating charge, from which assets escape when disposed of in the ordinary course of business and which thus provides the creditor with security without paralysing the business. This led to the realisation that it is possible, if in most

---

[76] See para.6–26, below.

[77] See paras 6–33 et seq., below.

[78] Directive 2002/47/EC (on Financial Collateral Arrangements).

[79] Companies Act 2006 s.853(6).

[80] But land held by a developer may well constitute the developer's trading stock. See, for example, the decision of the New South Wales Court of Appeal in *Boambee Bay Resort Pty Ltd v Equus Financial Services Ltd* (1991) 26 N.S.W.L.R. 284.

[81] *Siebe Gorman & Co Ltd v Barclays Bank Ltd* [1979] 2 Lloyd's Rep. 142. *Siebe Gorman* was not overruled by the *Spectrum* case on this point. See also *Re Yorkshire Woolcombers Association Ltd* [1903] 2 Ch.D. 284, 294, per Vaughan Williams L.J. See paras 4–13 et seq., below.

cases very inconvenient, to have a fixed charge over current assets, and conversely (but with less inconvenience) to have a floating charge over fixed assets, such as land.

Again, the mere fact that assets subject to a charge are fixed assets and therefore likely to be held on a more permanent basis and not disposed of until they need replacement does not conclusively establish that the charge itself is a fixed charge, particularly where the assets are items of plant, furniture or equipment which are likely to need replacement from time to time. When read as a whole the charge instrument may be open to the construction that such assets were intended to be left outside the control of the chargee in the same way as current assets covered by the charge, as where the charge instrument is expressed to cover not only stock in trade and book debts but also plant, equipment and furniture of a kind likely to need replacement from time to time, and these assets are grouped with the stock in trade and book debts without differentiation.[82] The moral for the draftsman, in expressing a charge over such fixed assets as a fixed charge, is to make it very clear that the fixed assets are not to be disposed of free from the charge. In the light of the *Spectrum* case discussed below, it is hard to say whether even a power to make item-by-item substitutions, as opposed to a general power of disposition, is consistent with a charge being fixed.[83] But subject to any contrary inferences to be drawn from the charge instrument itself it is generally true to say that there is a presumption that a charge over current assets is a floating charge[84] and one over fixed assets is a fixed charge. Thus a charge on land will usually be considered a fixed charge even if it does not contain any express provision restricting disposition of the land by the chargor free from the charge. Such a restriction is taken for granted as inherent in the nature of the charge. The position might be otherwise where the chargor is a developer holding the charged land as part of its stock.

4–12

---

[82] See, for example, *National Provincial Bank of England Ltd v United Electric Theatres Ltd* [1916] 1 Ch. 132; *Re GE Tunbridge Ltd* [1995] 1 B.C.L.C. 34; *Re ASRS Establishment Ltd* [2000] 2 B.C.L.C. 631 (although note that Robert Walker L.J. at 640 expressed doubts as to whether this was a universal rule of construction); *Smith v Bridgend County BC* [2001] UKHL 58; [2002] 1 A.C. 336 at [44]; *Fanshaw v Amav Industries Ltd* [2006] EWHC 486 (Ch) at [33].

[83] Before *Spectrum* it was generally thought that where the chargor could only dispose of charged assets on terms that they are replaced on a unit-by-unit basis, replacements then becoming subject to the charge, the charge could be classified as fixed. The cases relied on were *Holroyd v Marshall* (1862) 10 H.L. Cas. 191, in which a charge over existing machinery and all machinery subsequently placed in the chargor's mill in addition to or in substitution for the original machinery was upheld as a fixed charge; and *Cimex Tissues Ltd* [1995] 1 B.C.L.C. 409, in which Mr Stanley Burnton Q.C. pointed out in his judgment (para.32) that, by way of exception to the general rule that a person can only grant a security bill of sale over goods of which he is the true owner at the time of granting the bill (Bills of Sale Act 1878 (Amendment) Act 1882 s.5), s.6 of the Act permits the inclusion of fixtures, plant and trade machinery brought on to land or premises in substitution for fixtures, plant and machinery specifically described in the Bill. However, the actual charge in Cimex Tissues did not include a power to substitute, and it is very dubious whether the decision survives *Agnew* and *Spectrum*. There are a number of Singaporean decisions about charges over shares where there was a power to substitute where such charges were held to be floating, see *Re Lin Securities (Pte)* [1988] 1 S.L.R. 340; *Dresdner Bank Aktiengesellschaft v Ho Mun-Tuke Don* [1993] 1 S.L.R. 114 Singapore CA; *Re EG Tan & Co (Pte)* [1990] 1 S.L.R. 1030 Singapore HC; cf. *Re TXU Europe Group Plc* [2004] 1 B.C.L.C. 519, where a contrary view was expressed obiter. The express exception for a power to substitute in the FCARs probably means that such cases are not now of great practical relevance, see paras 6–32 et seq., below.

[84] See para.4–21, below.

With these preliminary observations the application of the principles stated above to different classes of current asset will now be considered.

Receivables[85]

4–13   The principal area of dispute in relation to the characterisation of a charge as fixed or floating has concerned charges over receivables. Banks in particular have been concerned to show that restrictions in their debentures have established their charges as fixed, while liquidators (and preferential creditors) have been equally astute to seek to strike such charges down as unregistered floating charges. The result has been a substantial volume of litigation, in which we may distinguish four phases. In the first it was established in *Siebe Gorman*[86] that it is possible to take a fixed charge over receivables. In the second it was decided in *Re Brightlife*[87] that this required not only restrictions on the sale of the receivables themselves but control over their proceeds, resulting from their collection by the chargor. This control could be exercised either by the chargee collecting the receivables itself or by the chargor collecting them for the account of the chargee and without liberty to use them for its own purposes except with the post-collection consent of the chargee. The third phase showed a weakening of this approach and a trend towards accepting the label attached to the transaction by the parties, as well as some unorthodoxy in delineating the characteristics of a floating charge. Cases illustrative of this phase are *Re Atlantic Computer Systems Plc*,[88] *Re Atlantic Medical Ltd*,[89] and *Re New Bullas Trading Ltd*.[90] The fourth and final phase has seen a return to orthodoxy with the decisions of the Privy Council in *Agnew v Commissioners of Inland Revenue*,[91] and of the House of Lords in *Re Spectrum Plus*[92] emphasising that while the court looks to the agreement of the parties to determine their intention, the effect of what they have agreed is a matter of law. There have been relatively few cases since *Spectrum*[93] although some areas of uncertainty still remain.

In the analysis which follows it is assumed that the receivables are collected by the chargor, not by the chargee, so that the crucial issue is whether the chargor collected for its own account or for that of the chargee.[94] Although, to some extent, the cases analysed have been superceded by *Spectrum* it is still instructive

---

[85] The term "receivables" is used throughout, even though many of the older cases use the term "book debts". For discussion of receivables financing using outright assignments and fixed charges, see Ch.3, above. Although most of the cases have been in the context of debenture financing, characterisation of charges over receivables is also important in the contexts of structured finance and project finance, among others.

[86] *Siebe Gorman* [1979] 2 Lloyd's Rep. 142.

[87] *Re Brightlife* [1987] Ch. 200.

[88] *Re Atlantic Computer Systems Plc* [1992] Ch. 505.

[89] *Re Atlantic Medical Ltd* [1992] B.C.C. 653.

[90] *Re New Bullas Trading Ltd* [1994] B.C.C. 36.

[91] *Agnew v Commissioners of Inland Revenue* [2001] UKPC 28; [2001] 2 A.C. 710.

[92] *Re Spectrum Plus* [2005] UKHL 41; [2005] 2 A.C. 680.

[93] This may reflect the fact that, with the abolition of Crown preference, the category of preferential creditors is quite small, and there is no "repeat player" with the incentive to take a case to court.

[94] Lord Hope in *Spectrum* set out four ways for a chargee to achieve the necessary control for a charge to be fixed, which included collection by the chargee (at para.54). However, he also pointed out that "this method. . .is likely to be unacceptable to a company which wishes to carry on its business as normally as possible by maintaining its cash flow and its working capital". It should be

to consider the history as this can throw light on where the line is to be drawn in the areas of uncertainty which still remain.

(1) From Siebe Gorman to Brightlife

In the early 1970s, Barclays Bank began to use a form of fixed charge over   **4–14**
receivables. There was much discussion in legal circles as to whether such a
charge was possible, and in *Siebe Gorman & Co Ltd v Barclays Bank Ltd*[95] the
plaintiffs threw down the gauntlet. In that case, the debenture provided that the
company charged its receivables to the bank "by way of first fixed charge". The
company undertook to pay all monies received in respect of the receivables into
its account with the bank and not to charge or assign the receivables without the
consent of the bank. Some receivables (in the form of bills of exchange) were
assigned outright by the company to the claimant: when these were claimed by
the bank, the claimant argued that the bank's charge was floating and therefore
overridden by the assignment to it.

Slade J., applying the Canadian decision in *Evans Coleman & Evans Ltd v R.
A. Nelson Construction Ltd*[96] held that there was no reason why receivables could
not be the subject of a fixed charge if that was the intention of the parties. He held
that the vital element distinguishing a mere floating charge from a fixed charge,
namely the debtor's freedom to manage its assets in the ordinary course of
business, was lacking. The debenture gave the chargee control over the
receivables by prohibiting the debtor company from disposing of the charged
receivables without the plaintiffs' consent; it also imposed some control on
receipts by requiring these to be paid into an account with the chargee. There
were, however, no explicit restrictions on withdrawals from this account by the
chargor. Having held that the charge was, as intended, a fixed charge, Slade J.
concluded that this gave the chargee the right to assert its lien on the proceeds in
the account at any time, even when the account was in credit. As will be
discussed later, this reasoning was criticised in *Re Spectrum Plus*, although the
principle that a fixed charge over book debs was possible to achieve was not
dissented from.

A similar decision was reached by the Irish Supreme Court in *Re Keenan Bros
Ltd*,[97] where the chargee's control was even more explicit in that the proceeds had
to be paid into a special blocked account, not into the company's ordinary
account. The vital element of control of the proceeds was omitted from the
debenture given in *Re Brightlife Ltd*,[98] where the debtor company, though
prohibited from selling, factoring or discounting the charged receivables without
the consent of the debenture holder, was left free to collect them in, pay the
proceeds into the bank account and use them as its own moneys. It was held by
Hoffmann J. that the charge, though described as a fixed charge, was in truth a

---

noted that it is common for the "borrower" to collect in the receivables even when the financing is by
invoice discounting, that is, using outright assignment.
[95] *Siebe Gorman & Co Ltd v Barclays Bank Ltd* [1979] 2 Lloyd's Rep. 142.
[96] *Evans Coleman & Evans Ltd v R. A. Nelson Construction Ltd* (1958) 16 D.L.R. (2d) 123.
[97] *Re Keenan Bros Ltd* [1985] I.R. 401; [1986] B.C.L.C. 242.
[98] *Re Brightlife Ltd* [1987] Ch. 200.

floating charge,[99] for the company's ability to deal with receipts as its own was inconsistent with a fixed security. This was plainly correct.[100] It should be noted that the chargee in *Brightlife* was not a clearing bank, and so could not use the form of debenture used in *Siebe Gorman*, where the proceeds were required to be paid into a bank account held with the chargee.[101] This discrepancy between the position of clearing bank and non-bank lenders caused significant difficulties and eventually led to the drafting of the debenture in *Re New Bullas*.

(2) From Brightlife to Re New Bullas

4–15 There followed a curious interlude in which two lines of authority appeared to develop in opposite directions, each evolving independently of and without reference to the other.[102] On one side were *Re Brightlife*,[103] *Re Keenan Bros*[104] and *William Gaskell Group Ltd v Highley*[105]; on the other, *Re Atlantic Computers*,[106] *Re Atlantic Medical*[107] and *Re New Bullas*.[108] The first line of cases followed orthodox principles, and have now been approved by the House of Lords. The second line requires more attention. In the first of this second line of cases the Court of Appeal held that a charge on sub-leases and rentals was a fixed charge because it was not ambulatory in character but related to rights under specifically identified sub-leases in existence at the time of the charge, and was thus to be contrasted with the type of charge described by Romer L.J. and covering a class of present and future assets. This reasoning appears to have reflected two distinct ideas. The first was that the distinction between a fixed and a floating charge is largely correlated with the distinction between security over existing property[109] and security over future property. But *Holroyd v Marshall*[110] and *Tailby v Official Receiver*,[111] both decisions of the House of Lords, clearly establish the efficacy of a fixed charge over after-acquired property. Conversely, it is not a prerequisite of a floating charge that it extends to future assets as well as existing assets.[112]

---

[99] See also the decision of the High Court of Northern Ireland in *Re Armagh Shoes Ltd* [1982] N.I. 59; [1984] B.C.L.C. 405, in which the Court held that the mere designation of a charge on book debts as a fixed charge did not make it so, and that if the charge contemplated that the debtor would have freedom to manage the assets comprising the security it was a floating charge, even though that freedom was not expressly stated in the charge instrument.

[100] See para.4–13, above. The reasoning and decision in *Brightlife* was approved in *Spectrum* at [107].

[101] This distinction was recognised by Hoffmann J. in *Brightlife* at [210] and commented on in *Spectrum* at [87] by Lord Scott.

[102] See R. Goode, "Charges over Book Debts: A Missed Opportunity" (1994) 110 L.Q.R. 592.

[103] *Re Brightlife* [1987] Ch. 200.

[104] *Re Keenan Bros* [1986] B.C.L.C. 242.

[105] *William Gaskell Group Ltd v Highley* [1993] B.C.C. 200.

[106] *Re Atlantic Computers* [1992] Ch. 505.

[107] *Re Atlantic Medical* [1993] B.C.L.C. 386.

[108] *Re New Bullas* [1994] 1 B.C.L.C. 485.

[109] The court quite correctly classified sums payable in the future under existing contracts as present property.

[110] *Holroyd v Marshall* (1862) 10 H.L. Cas. 191. See para.4–12 fn.83, above for discussion as to whether the charge in *Holroyd v Marshall* was fixed.

[111] *Tailby v Official Receiver* (1888) 13 App. Cas. 523.

[112] This was confirmed by Lord Scott in *Spectrum* at [107] where he describes a floating charge over a specific debt.

The second idea underlying *Re Atlantic Computers* was that as the charge related to rentals due and to become due under existing and identified sub-leases it was not over a changing fund of assets. However, we have seen that the fund may be a closed fund, and its character as such is determined not by whether the assets are described as a class or are specifically identified (though the latter may be an indication that the charge is intended to be fixed) but whether the chargor is given continued power of management in the ordinary course of business free from interference by the chargee so long as that power continues. It is not necessary that the fund be a changing fund in the sense of picking up new assets.[113] Under the terms of the charge in that case the debtor was to be free to receive and utilise the sub-rentals it received until the chargee chose to intervene. Accordingly it could not be said that the sub-rentals had been unconditionally appropriated to the secured obligation. *Re Atlantic Computers* also drew a false analogy between the income from an asset and the proceeds of that asset.[114]

Next came *Re Atlantic Medical*,[115] where, however, the charge covered both present and future hire-purchase agreements, sub-leases and rentals. Vinelott J., having rather surprisingly concluded that the fact that the security covered future assets was not a ground for distinguishing *Re Atlantic Computers*, left unclear the precise reason for the characterisation. Finally came *Re New Bullas Trading*,[116] which involved a secured loan by a financier who was not a bank. Since for this reason the *Siebe Gorman* form of debenture could not be used, the parties used an agreement which created two distinct charges, a fixed charge over the receivables and a floating charge over the proceeds, so that the company still had access to the proceeds to use in the course of its business. The Court of Appeal succumbed to the beguiling argument that since the two assets were different the fact that the charge over the proceeds was expressed to be floating could not affect the fixed nature of the charge over the receivables themselves,[117] and it was entirely open to the parties themselves to agree that the charge on the receivables should be fixed and on the proceeds, floating.

In *Commissioners of Inland Revenue v Agnew*,[118] the New Zealand Court of Appeal concluded that *Re Atlantic Computers Ltd* was not in accordance with established authority. In upholding the substantive decision[119] the Privy Council made no comment on *Re Atlantic Computers*. Nor was the case mentioned in the judgments in *Re Spectrum*, although it was cited in argument. It is, however, submitted that neither that decision nor the decision in *Re Atlantic Medical* can stand.

---

[113] This follows both from the decision in *Siebe Gorman* and from the observation of Lord Millett in *Re Agnew* that of the three characteristics of a floating charge described by Romer L.J. in *Re Yorkshire Woolcombers Association Ltd* only the last one was truly determinative. It was also pointed out by Slade J. in *Re Bond Worth* [1980] Ch. 228, 267.

[114] See Goode, "Charges over Book Debts: A Missed Opportunity" (1994) 110 L.Q.R. 592, 599; and Beale, Bridge, Gullifer and Lomnicka, *The Law of Security and Title-Based* (2012), para.6.133.

[115] *Re Atlantic Medical* [1993] B.C.L.C. 386.

[116] *Re New Bullas Trading* [1994] 1 B.C.L.C. 485.

[117] The debenture included restrictions on the disposal of the debts themselves.

[118] *Commissioners of Inland Revenue v Agnew* [2000] 1 N.Z.L.R. 223.

[119] See below.

(3)   From Re New Bullas to Spectrum

4–16   Though the decision in *Re New Bullas* had its supporters,[120] it was not viewed with enthusiasm by lower courts and it was the views of its critics[121] that finally prevailed in the decision of the Privy Council in *Agnew v Commissioner of Inland Revenue*.[122] That case concerned a debenture which was expressed to confer a fixed charge on the company's receivables and their proceeds, excluding those proceeds which were received by the company before the charge crystallised or which the bank required to be paid into an account with itself (which it never did). Proceeds received by the company while the charge remained uncrystallised therefore fell within the floating charge which the debenture imposed on the company's other assets. The debenture was in very similar terms to that of *Re New Bullas*, despite the fact that the lender in *Agnew* was a bank. The effect of the debenture, therefore, was that while the bank reserved the power to intervene and take control of the proceeds, that power was never exercised.[123] The Privy Council had no hesitation in concluding, in agreement with the Court of Appeal of New Zealand, that the charge was a floating charge and that *Re New Bullas* had been wrongly decided.[124] The proposition that a charge over book debts could be characterised independently of the contractual provisions governing the application of the proceeds was robustly rejected.[125]

The decision restored the orthodoxy of *Re Brightlife*, and effected a symmetry with cases going back to the 19th century which established that the mere existence of a power of intervention is not sufficient to give a floating charge priority over the claims of execution creditors; it is necessary that the debenture holder shall actually have intervened to crystallise the charge by taking control of the charged assets.[126] Though only of persuasive authority, *Agnew* was regarded by the whole financial community as determinative in relation to the *New Bullas* form debenture, and throwing considerable doubt on whether the *Siebe Gorman*

---

[120] See, for example, A. Berg, "Charges over Book Debts: A Reply" [1995] J.B.L. 433; D.W. McLauchlan, "Fixed Charges over Book Debts—New Bullas in New Zealand" (1999) 115 L.Q.R. 365; and "New Bullas in New Zealand: Round Two" (2000) 116 L.Q.R. 211; P. Watts, "Fixed Charges over Book Debts" [1999] N.Z.L.R 46; Varen and Rubenstein, "Separation of Book Debts and their Proceeds" [1994] C.L.J. 225.

[121] See, for example, Goode, "Charges over Book Debts: A Missed Opportunity" (1994) 110 L.Q.R. 592; in the third edition of Lightman and Moss, *The Law of Receivers and Administrators of Companies*, 3rd edn (London: Sweet & Maxwell, 2000), paras 3–030 et seq.; S. Worthington, "Fixed Charges over Book Debts and other Receivables" (1997) 113 L.Q.R. 562; and, sub silentio, Millett L.J. in *Royal Trust Bank v National Westminster Bank Plc* [1996] 2 B.C.L.C. 682.

[122] *Agnew v Commissioner of Inland Revenue* [2001] UKPC 28; [2001] 2 A.C. 710.

[123] In *In the matter of Harmony Care Homes Ltd* [2009] EWHC 1961 (Ch) a power to control was exercised in respect of some proceeds, and as a result the charge over the receivables generating those proceeds was held to be fixed. See further para.4–22, below.

[124] It is ironic that just over a year after the decision in *Agnew* the floating charge in New Zealand, though not abolished, ceased to exist as a distinct form of security upon the coming into force of the *Personal Property Securities Act 1999*, which converted it into a fixed security interest. See See L. Widdup, *Personal Property Securities Act: a conceptual approach*, 3rd edn (Wellington: LexisNexis New Zealand, 2012), Ch.22, entitled "The Demise of the Floating Charge".

[125] *Agnew v Commissioner of Inland Revenue* [2001] UKPC 28; [2001] 2 A.C. 710, per Lord Millett at 729.

[126] See paras 4–37 et seq., below.

debenture would be classified by a court as a fixed charge.[127] The *Siebe Gorman* debenture was challenged in the case of *Re Spectrum Plus*,[128] when the House of Lords decided that such a debenture did not provide sufficient control on the part of the chargee for the charge to be fixed. The decision in *Spectrum* confirmed that the only criterion for deciding whether a charge was fixed or floating was the degree of control exercised by the chargee over "the charged assets", and that the presence or absence of the other two characteristics of a floating charge pointed out by Romer L.J. in *Re Yorkshire Woolcombers Association Ltd*[129] were not definitive.[130] The clearest exposition of the test is that of Lord Millett in *Agnew*, when he said:

> "the only intention which is relevant is the intention that the company should be free to deal with the charged assets and withdraw them from the security without the consent of the holder of the charge; or, to put the question another way, whether the charged assets were intended to be under the control of the company or of the charge holder."[131]

However, the decision in *Spectrum* has not answered all the questions concerning the characterisation of fixed and floating charges. Two main areas of uncertainty concern what degree of control is necessary for a charge to be fixed (this is discussed below)[132] and what is meant by "the charged assets" which have to be the subject of control. Where a charge covers receivables, it is clear that "the charged assets" include the proceeds so that to be fixed, the chargee must control the proceeds.[133] Thus it is not possible for there to be a fixed charge over receivables and a floating charge over the proceeds.[134] However, the position is less clear where the charge is over an income-generating asset. Where the asset is clearly separate from the income generated, for example, a chattel which could be hired out, control of the income is not required for a fixed charge over the asset itself. It is a matter of construction of the fixed charge as to whether it is over the asset itself, or over the lease by which the asset is hired out. If it is over the former alone, there is no need for the chargee to control any rental income.[135]

4–17

---

[127] That *Agnew* was a turning point can be seen, inter alia, from the fact that HMRC issued a statement in March 2006 to R3, the Association of Business Recovery Professionals (after the *Spectrum* decision) requiring funds distributed to chargeholders since the date of the *Agnew* decision on the basis of a *Siebe Gorman* type debenture to be repaid by chargeholders and distributed to creditors in the relevant order.

[128] *Re Spectrum Plus* [2005] UKHL 41; [2005] 2 A.C. 680.

[129] *Re Yorkshire Woolcombers Association Ltd* [1903] 2 Ch.D. 284, 295.

[130] *Re Spectrum Plus* [2005] UKHL 41; [2005] 2 A.C. 680 at [111].

[131] *Agnew v Commissioner of Inland Revenue* [2001] UKPC 28; [2001] A.C. 710 at [32].

[132] See paras 4–21 et seq., below.

[133] While it is not possible to have a fixed charge on receivables if the chargor is left free to collect the receivables for its own account, the converse is not true. There is nothing to preclude the grant of a floating charge on receivables, giving the chargor freedom to dispose of them in the ordinary course of business, and a fixed charge on the collected proceeds through a requirement that these are to be under the control of or held for the account of the chargee.

[134] For further discussion, see para.4–28, below.

[135] This is reasonably uncontentious as a matter of principle, however, the cases are not unproblematic. Where land is mortgaged, the mortgagor is entitled to the rentals until the mortgagee takes possession, at which point the mortgagee became entitled to the rentals by virtue of its legal or equitable ownership of the leasehold interest in the land. The fact that the mortgagor is entitled to the rentals does not prevent the charge over the land being fixed (*Rhodes v Allied Dunbar Pension*

However, in a less clear case, such as a charge over a chattel lease or a long-term contract, it is submitted that there are three main relevant factors: first, how directly the assets generates the income; secondly, how close the generation of income comes to being the sole value of the asset; and thirdly, whether the asset is destroyed by the generation of income. In the case of a chattel lease, the lease generates the income directly; there is nothing that needs to be done by the chargor except to collect in the income. This is directly comparable to receivables, and different from, for example, assets which generate income by being sold. Further, to the lessor of chattels, the whole value of the lease is in the rentals generated. The value of the charge is in the right to receive the rentals, or the sale of the lease on the basis of the future rentals: exactly the same method of calculating and receiving value as with receivables.[136] It is true that the payment of rentals does not immediately destroy the lease; this does not happen until the last rental is paid and the term expires, and if this factor were definitive, then this would destroy the argument. However, this would mean that all contracts under which payment was due in instalments would fall within this category, even where the chargor had total freedom to use the sums paid. This would give an odd distinction between receivables payable on one occasion and on a number of future occasions.[137] It is therefore suggested that for a charge over a chattel lease to be fixed, it is necessary for the chargee to control the rental payments.

The position in relation to long-term contracts is even more difficult. Here, although the asset generates the income directly, and the value of the asset derives solely from the generation of monetary income, and although it will, in the end, be destroyed by payment,[138] it could be argued that, in the case of a very long term contract,[139] the length of time that the asset exists before it is destroyed means that it has an independent existence from the income it generates. After all, all assets (except perhaps land) will eventually be destroyed by use or effluxion of time. Whether a long term contract has a separate existence from their proceeds (and so can be the subject of a fixed charge even though the chargor can dispose of the proceeds) is a matter of degree, depending on the length of time of the rights to payment and the extent to which the asset is treated as separate on capital or other markets. The problem with an analysis which depends on a matter

---

Services Ltd [1989] 1 W.L.R. 800, 807) although some commentators see the right of a mortgagor of land to receive rentals until the mortgagee goes into possession as a sui generis right which developed before, and without regard to, the distinction between fixed and floating charges, see Berg, "Charges over Book Debts: a Reply" [1995] J.B.L. 431, 464–5; F. Oditah, "Fixed charge over book debts after Brumark" (2001) 14 Insolv. Int. 49, 54. A charge over shares owned by a company who was free to use dividend payments and redemption moneys in the ordinary course of business was held to be fixed in *Arthur D Little Ltd (in administration) v Ableco Finance LLC* [2002] EWHC 701 (Ch); [2003] Ch. 217.

[136] G. Moss, "Fixed Charges over Book Debts: Puzzles and Perils" (1995) 8 Insolv. Int. 25, 26–27.

[137] See Worthington, "Floating Charges: the use and abuse of doctrinal analysis" in *Company Charges: Spectrum and Beyond* (2006), p.34; Oditah, "Fixed charge over book debts after Brumark" (2001) 14 Insolv. Int. 49, 54; and F. Oditah, "Recurrent Issues in Receivables Financing" in J. Armour and J. Payne (eds) *Rationality in Company Law: Essays in Honour of DD Prentice* (Oxford: Hart Publishing, 2009), pp.339–340.

[138] These are the three factors set out above as relevant to the question of whether the asset is separate from the income.

[139] One example of such a contract is a long-term loan, which will usually involve periodic payments and often one or more balloon payments. Another example of a long-term contract is a revenue-generating contract in a project finance transaction.

of degree is that it involves some uncertainty, which is undesirable for the reasons discussed above,[140] but the contrary view (that the entirety of the proceeds of any asset consisting of contractual rights to payment must be controlled by the chargee for a charge over that contract to be fixed) is also unpalatable.[141]

Stock in trade

The fact that a valid fixed charge can, at least in theory, be taken over receivables leads to the question whether a fixed charge is also possible over stock in trade. Plainly the theoretical answer is, yes. Now that the issue is seen to be the presence or absence of the debtor's freedom to manage its assets in the ordinary course of business, there is no reason to distinguish one class of changing asset from another. Where the instrument of charge over stock in trade precludes the debtor from disposing of its stock without the prior consent of the creditor then if the parties operate the agreement on the basis of this restriction a valid fixed charge is created.

4–18

That is the theory. In practice, in relation to both receivables and stock in trade, creating a fixed charge over them is likely to commercially impracticable. While there is in general no commercial necessity for a company to be given liberty to sell or charge its receivables in the course of business, a company does usually need to use the proceeds of the receivables in order to run its business, and therefore is unlikely merely to want to pay them into a blocked account from which it can only withdraw with the consent of the chargee, which is the level of control that *Spectrum* appears to require.[142] Stock is held for sale, not for use in the business, and a company cannot operate at all unless it can dispose of its stock in such a way as to give purchasers unencumbered title. So restrictions on the sale of stock in trade would be commercially impracticable.

It would be open to the creditor to stipulate that no item of stock was to be disposed of without the creditor's prior written consent, but in most cases the debtor company would find it impossible to live with such a restriction. A blanket consent in advance would not do, for this would be incompatible with the existence of a fixed security interest and would make the charge a floating charge.[143] So whilst the imposition of appropriate restrictions on dealings in stock

---

[140] See para.4–10, above.

[141] Long-term contracts often include a "waterfall" clause providing for the destination of payments. For discussion of such a clause as a control technique, see para.4–29, below.

[142] See below for discussion of possible ways to reconcile the necessary amount of control with the ability of the chargor to carry on its business. It is likely, however, that rather than pursue these ideas, lenders will adopt other forms of financing, such as invoice discounting. Indeed, this has been happening already. Figures from the Asset Based Finance Association show that there has been a steady growth in invoice discounting from 1995, with a significant increase in the rate of growth from 2003 onwards (although note the caveat in fn.5 of Ch.3, above that the increase is unlikely to explained totally by difficulties caused by the *Spectrum* decision). This accords with research by S. Frisby, "Report in Insolvency Outcomes", prepared for the Insolvency Service, June 2006.

[143] See Gough, *Company Charges* (1996), pp.630–63. Advance consent given in the charge agreement itself would mean that the document was internally inconsistent and that the charge was likely to be characterised as floating. This cannot be avoided by giving advance consent in another side agreement. Such an agreement will be taken into account in characterising the charge (*Re Spectrum Plus* [2005] 2 A.C. 680 at [158], per Lord Walker; *Hart v Barnes* [1982] 7 A.C.L.R. 310).

in trade would preserve the efficacy of the charge as a fixed charge, in practice it is rare that the parties will find such an arrangement workable.

An alternative is to utilise some form of pledge through constructive delivery to the creditor. One way of doing this is by field warehousing.[144] Another, less elaborate, method requires the debtor to acknowledge that any stock in trade of which it is in possession is held to the order of the chargee and that while the chargor is permitted to sell the goods in the ordinary course of business it does so as agent of the chargee and is to hold the proceeds of sale on trust for the chargee. This is not different in principle from the trust receipt mechanism.[145] It does, however, suffer from the defect (from the chargor's point of view) that it is not free to use the proceeds of sale as it wishes.

As with book debts, there is nothing in theory to prevent the chargor from granting a floating charge over the stock in trade and a fixed charge over the proceeds,[146] although, again, since the proceeds are likely to be receivables and the company will want to use the proceeds of the collected receivables in its business, this structure is unlikely to be commercially practicable.

Raw materials and goods in process

4-19 Similar considerations apply to security over raw materials and goods in process of manufacture. It is theoretically possible to have a fixed charge over these classes of asset, but generally impracticable to require the debtor company to obtain the creditor's consent to the processing of each batch of raw materials or to the making up of each item of goods in process.

Documents of title to stock in trade

4-20 What applies to stock in trade must at first sight be equally applicable to documents of title to trading stock. There is, however, the important difference that documents, unlike goods, can conveniently be possessed by the creditor. This allows a pledge of the goods by deposit of the documents, a common procedure for banks advancing the price of imported goods. The business purpose of the transaction can be achieved without significant loss of security by releasing the documents to the pledgor against a trust receipt, thus preserving the pledge.[147] For further security the bank may require the goods to be stored in an independent warehouse, the bank's consent being required before any goods are released from the warehouse.

---

[144] See para.4–25, below.

[145] See para.2–10, above; paras 4–20 and 4–25, below.

[146] *Re CCG International Enterprises Ltd* [1993] B.C.L.C. 1428.

[147] *Re David Allester Ltd* [1922] 2 Ch. 211. In that case, the court refused to recharacterise a trust receipt as a charge. However, at least as regards the proceeds of sale of the goods, it is arguable that the interest of a pledgee under a trust receipt is truly that of a chargee. See para.1–71, fn.327, above. This in itself would not be a problem if the chargee had sufficient control over the proceeds for the charge to be characterised as fixed, for example, if the purpose of the sale was merely to repay the pledgee/chargee, although the charge would be registrable.

3. SHIFTING ASSETS: CONTROL TECHNIQUES

Current assets distinguished from fixed assets

As described earlier,[148] when performing the exercise of deciding whether a **4–21** charge is fixed or floating, the court will adopt a two-stage approach.[149] In carrying out the first, interpretative, stage, the distinction between fixed and current assets becomes of some importance. Where the question of whether the chargor can dispose of the charged assets or not is expressly dealt with in the charge agreement, this will be interpreted according to the natural meaning of the words, and the nature of the assets charged will merely be part of the background against which this interpretation takes place,[150] and is usually irrelevant if a power to dispose is clearly set out in the agreement.[151] If a fixed charge is taken over the defendant company's factory or its business equipment without an express stipulation that the company shall not dispose of or incumber the asset without the chargee's consent, it is presumed that any disposal, whether absolute or by way of security, requires the consent of the chargee, for assets of this kind are held by the company for use in its business, not for resale. Of course, if the chargee habitually stands by and allows the company to sell or charge its fixed assets free from security without prior consent the court will consider this inconsistent with the charge being fixed, for one cannot on the one hand assert a fixed charge and on the other allow the company to deal with the charged assets as its own.[152] By contrast it is in the nature of circulating assets that they are turned over by manufacture (in the case of raw materials), sale (in the case of stock in trade) and collection (in the case of receivables), and the continuance of the debtor company's management powers over such assets is thus assumed unless negated by the agreement of the parties.[153] Hence the need for control techniques to prevent the debtor company from dealing with the charged assets as its own.

Legal and practical control

The distinction between the concepts of legal control and practical control is **4–22** discussed in Ch.6, below.[154] Broadly, legal control refers to the contractual position between the parties, whilst practical control refers to the actual ability of the chargee to prevent the chargor from disposing of the charged assets. It is clear that practical control alone is not sufficient for a charge to be fixed: it is critical

---

[148] See para.4–05, above.

[149] This is the process described by Lord Millett in *Agnew* [2001] UKPC 28; [2001] 1 A.C. 710 at [32].

[150] *Ashborder BV v Green Gas Power Ltd* [2004] EWHC 1517 (Ch) at [183].

[151] *Ashborder BV v Green Gas Power Ltd* [2004] EWHC 1517 (Ch) at [183].

[152] *Re Bond Worth Ltd* [1980] Ch. 228, per Slade J. at 261. See para.4–30, below.

[153] In *Re Armagh Shoes Ltd* [1982] N.I. 59; *In the matter of Lakeglen Construction Ltd* [1980] I.R. 347; *Hart v Barnes* (1982) 7 A.C.L.R. 310; *Re GE Tunbridge Ltd* [1995] 1 B.C.L.C. 34; [1994] B.C.C. 563.

[154] See paras 6–32 et seq., below. It should be remembered that the relevance of legal and practical control to whether a charge is fixed or floating is not the same as the test of whether a charge falls within the FCARs.

that the charge agreement establishes the necessary legal control, although other matters may be relevant to its interpretation. In the recent case of *Gray v G-T-P Group Ltd*[155] the subject of the relevant charge was money held by the chargee in its bank account on trust for the chargor. Until an event of default occurred, the chargee was obliged to transfer all or any of the funds in the account to the chargor on request: refusal to do so would have been in breach of trust and contract. The charge was held to be floating, on the grounds that although the factual cooperation of the chargee was required in order for the chargor to withdraw the funds from the account, this was merely an "administrative step" and did not amount to a requirement of consent.

Can the necessary control be purely legal or is practical control also required? Legal control is certainly sufficient in many situations. Take, for example, a fixed charge over fixed tangible assets. There is no need for the chargee to take practical steps to prevent the chargor from selling its machinery: it is sufficient if the charge agreement (on its proper construction) prohibits the chargor from doing so. Similarly, a party with a fixed charge over receivables does not need to take steps to prevent the receivables being sold (such as notifying the debtors): the contractual agreement that this is not permitted is sufficient. It would therefore be odd if practical control were required for any particular type of asset as a matter of law. In some cases, however, the presence or absence of practical control has been said to be relevant to the characterisation of a charge as fixed or floating.

First we should consider provisions in the charge agreement itself which relate to practical control. Characterisation of the charge, for which the relevant date is the date of creation of the charge,[156] is a matter of construction and interpretation of the charge agreement by using the two-stage process described in the *Agnew* case.[157] If the agreement provides that the chargor is permitted to withdraw the proceeds of charged receivables from a bank account, this is inconsistent with the label of the charge over the receivables as fixed, and the charge will be characterised as floating. Similarly, if the agreement provides that the proceeds are to be paid into a blocked bank account, this reinforces the legal prohibition on disposal of the proceeds, and makes it more likely that such a prohibition will be seen as genuinely intended by the parties. Similarly, provisions in other agreements entered into between the parties at the same time as (or before) the charge agreement may be relevant, so that if the charge agreement prohibits the chargor from disposing of the proceeds of receivables, and requires it to pay them into an account with the chargee, but the account agreement between the chargee and the chargor permits free withdrawal from that account, the contractual position between the parties is internally inconsistent, and the prohibition on disposal may well be held not to be genuinely intended.

The parties' actions may also be relevant to the interpretation of the charge agreement, although there is a well established rule that post-contractual conduct is not relevant to the interpretation of a contract[158] except to establish that it is a

---

[155] *Gray v G-T-P Group Ltd* [2010] EWHC 1772 (Ch).

[156] See para.4–07, above.

[157] See para.1–36, above.

[158] *James Miller & Partners Ltd v Whitworth Street Estates (Manchester) Ltd* [1970] A.C. 583 HL at 603, 611, 614; *L Schuler AG v Wickman Machine Tool Sales Ltd* [1974] A.C. 235 HL at 252, 260, 261, 265–268, 272–273. Despite the general move away from strict rules of interpretation of contracts

sham.[159] This issue has been considered in the context of a charge over receivables. Lord Millett in *Agnew* said that a stipulation that the account into which the proceeds are to be paid is to be a blocked account will not establish the charge as a fixed charge if the account is not operated as a blocked account in fact.[160] The precise meaning of this statement was not made clear, and the matter, though mentioned, was not fully clarified in *Spectrum*.[161] It would seem that if restrictions in the charge agreement are not adhered to in practice,[162] then either the agreement will be held to be a sham, and characterised as a floating charge,[163] or it is likely to be held to have been varied, which has the effect either of creating a new charge or decrystallising the old one.[164]

Two recent cases have further considered the interrelation between the terms of the charge agreement and the parties' conduct. Both concerned clauses modelled on that in *Re New Bullas* which provided for the release of the fixed charge on payment of proceeds of charged receivables into a specified bank account, unless certain events had occurred. In *Fanshaw v Amav Industries Ltd*[165] the clause provided for automatic release from the fixed charge unless the security had become enforceable or a declared default had occurred and the chargee had issued instructions to the chargor. In the absence of these events occurring, the proceeds were to be subject to the floating charge created by the agreement. The court held that the charge was floating as created,[166] and that this could not be changed into a fixed charge (as created) by the parties' conduct (four months after creation) in setting up a blocked account and paying all proceeds into that account. However, in *Re Harmony Care Homes Ltd*[167] the clause provided that the fixed charge was to be released when the proceeds were paid into a particular bank account unless the chargee gave directions. The chargee directed (at the outset) that the proceeds should be paid into a blocked account. It was held that the charge was fixed, since the debts and the proceeds had never been outside the control of the chargee. There thus seem to be a thin line between a fixed charge which is automatically released, but which includes a right on the part of the chargee to control the proceeds (this charge is floating and cannot be

---

(*Investors Compensation Scheme Ltd v West Bromwich Building Society* [1997] UKHL 28; [1998] 1 W.L.R. 896, 912–913), this particular rule is still observed and considered valid: *Dunlop Tyres Ltd v Blows* [2001] EWCA Civ 1032 at [21]–[22].

[159] *A G Securities v Vaughan* [1990] 1 A.C. 417 HL at 466 per Lord Oliver, 475 per Lord Jauncey.

[160] *Agnew v Commissioners of Inland Revenue* [2001] UKPC 28; [2001] 2 A.C. 710, per Lord Millett at [48].

[161] *Re Spectrum Plus* [2005] UKHL 41; [2005] 2 A.C. 680 at [160].

[162] Analysis of the relevance of post-contractual conduct has been considered by a number of academics, see S. Atherton and R. Mokal, "Charges over chattels: issues in the fixed/floating jurisprudence" (2005) 26 Company Lawyer 10; and A. Berg, "The cuckoo in the nest of corporate insolvency: some aspects of the Spectrum case" [2006] J.B.L. 22, 33–44; Beale, Bridge, Gullifer and Lomnicka, *The Law of Security and Title-Based Financing* (2012), paras 6.115–6.118.

[163] Where the document, by design, does not represent the true intention of the parties. Since a finding of a sham requires dishonesty, it is thought unlikely that a court would find that a standard form document was a sham.

[164] See paras 4–62 et seq., below.

[165] *Re Fanshaw v Amav Industries Ltd; Beam Tube Products Ltd* [2006] EWHC 486 (Ch). The point in issue was whether the chargee had priority over preferential creditors, and so the charge had to be fixed as created. The question of whether payment into the blocked account had the effect of crystallising the charge was not considered.

[166] Thus falling within s.40 of the Insolvency Act 1986.

[167] *Re Harmony Care Homes Ltd* [2009] EWHC 1961 (Ch).

saved by the exercise of the right) and a fixed charge where the release is not automatic but conditional on the non-exercise of a right on the part of the chargee to control the proceeds (this charge is fixed unless the release actually occurs, in which case the charge is floating). Hopefully, clauses such as these which provide for the release of the fixed charge on payment of the proceeds will become a thing of the past, but the point still remains that the parties' conduct can be of relevance where the charge agreement provides for different legal states of affairs depending on what is actually done. However, since the statutory insolvency consequences apply to a charge which is floating as created, it must be remembered that what the court has to do is to characterise the charge based on the position at the time of creation, and where there is a gap between that point and the conduct, the latter will only be relevant either as evidence of a sham or a variation.

Degree of control necessary

4-23   How much freedom can the debtor company be given to deal with charged assets if the charge is to retain its status as a fixed charge? Or to put the question another way, how far must the debtor's power to manage the charged assets be restricted? It is not possible to give a completely exhaustive reply to this question, although some guidance is given by the *Spectrum* case. At one end of the spectrum[168] is total freedom of management. This is plainly incompatible with a fixed security interest. A creditor cannot claim a fixed security in an asset in one breath and then in the next allow the debtor to dispose of the asset as if it were the debtor's own. At the other end of the spectrum is a total prohibition on dealings of any kind in the asset or its proceeds. Clearly in this case the charge is a fixed charge. Between the two ends of the spectrum lies an infinite range of possibilities. However, it now looks as though virtually all those possibilities will result in the charge being characterised as floating. The House of Lords made it clear in *Spectrum* that where the chargor is able to remove the assets from the scope of the charge the charge must be floating.[169] Thus only total prohibition of all dealings and withdrawals without permission is enough to create a fixed charge.[170] Taken literally, this would mean that even a power to make item by item substitutions would prevent a charge from being fixed, since a power to substitute includes a power to dispose. Although this particular point is still uncertain, it is clear that, if any power to substitute at all is to be held to be consistent with a fixed charge, it would have to be very specific in only permitting disposal of an item if a substitute item was immediately acquired, so that the security is in no way

---

[168] No pun intended.

[169] *Re Spectrum Plus* [2005] UKHL 41; [2005] 2 A.C. 680 at [107] per Lord Scott, [138], [139] per Lord Walker. It was on this basis that a concession was made that the relevant charge was floating in *In The Matter Of Lehman Brothers International (Europe) (In Administration)* [2012] EWHC 2997 (Ch) at [70].

[170] See Worthington, "Floating Charges: Use and Abuse of Doctrinal Analysis" in *Company Charges: Spectrum and Beyond* (2006), pp.29–30.

reduced.[171] It is clear that merely to label the charge "fixed" is not enough.[172] The instrument must restrict the debtor's dealing powers; and the restrictions must be meaningful, not a mere sham.

Let us now consider some of the more important control techniques. These divide into two groups; control through the charge instrument; and active policing of the control provisions. Many of them relate in some part to practical control: the relevance of this to the characterisation of a charge has already been discussed.

Control through the charge instrument

Controlling provisions in the charge instrument will vary according to the type of property given as security, and in particular, whether it is tangible (goods or documents) or intangible (debts, contract rights).

4–24

(1)   Provision for direct control of goods

In the case of goods, the creditor may stipulate for direct control by himself or his agents. There are various ways of achieving this, most of them being equally applicable to a pledge, which is the more common security device where the auditor assumes direct control of the goods. The fullest control is exercised by a requirement that the goods be stored in the creditor's own warehouse and released only with the approval of the creditor's warehouseman. This is a costly procedure and one which most debtors would view with the utmost disfavour. An alternative is to stipulate that the goods shall be stored in the creditor's name in an independent warehouse, the debtor being responsible for warehousing charges, or that, if stored by the debtor itself, the debtor will on each occasion procure the warehouse to attorn to the creditor, so that legal possession passes to the creditor. Warehousing in an independent warehouse is not uncommon and gives the chargee a considerable measure of security, but again involves the debtor in warehousing charges which it may find burdensome. Yet another variant is the "field warehousing" type of security, where the goods are warehoused on the debtor's own premises, the charge instrument providing that they are to be segregated from the debtor's other goods and kept in a distinct room or fenced off area under the supervision of an employee of the debtor who is for this purpose to be the agent of the creditor and to act in accordance with the creditor's instructions. Such a provision can sometimes be reinforced by a requirement that the segregated part of the premises in question be leased to the creditor at a nominal rent.

4–25

These different forms of warehousing arrangement provide a relatively high measure of control. But English law, in contrast to American law, also recognises

---

[171] For discussion of the authorities, see fn.83, above. See also Beale, Bridge, Gullifer and Lomnicka, *The Law of Security and Title-Based Financing* (2012), paras 6.120–6.128.

[172] *Re Armagh Shoes Ltd* [1982] N.I. 59; [1984] B.C.L.C. 405; *Re Brightlife Ltd* [1986] 3 All E.R. 673. The label could in some circumstances provide some evidence of the parties' intention when the courts are carrying out the first, interpretative, stage of characterisation, *Arthur D Little Ltd v Ableco Finance LLC* [2002] EWHC 701 (Ch); [2003] Ch. 217 at [31]. See para.4–21, above.

a pledge or charge in which the debtor simply acknowledges that he holds the goods to the order of the creditor until sale and holds the proceeds of sale on trust for the creditor.[173]

In the case of goods covered by documents of title—e.g. imported goods shipped under a bill of lading—the security agreement could provide for the shipping documents to be deposited with the creditor. Usually, this would be by way of pledge, rather than charge. The goods should not be consigned to the creditor—who might incur liability for unpaid freight—but the agreement should provide for them to be consigned to the debtor and indorsed to the creditor in blank. The shipping documents can later be released to the debtor under a trust receipt.[174]

(2) Provisions for segregation and preservation of charged property

4–26 To emphasise the point that the creditor regards himself as having an interest in specie in the charged assets, the instrument of charge could usefully contain provisions requiring the assets to be segregated from the debtor's other property, even if it is not possible to impose a requirement that the premises shall be under the actual control of a third party. This should be reinforced by undertakings as to insurance, safe custody and repair.

(3) Restrictions on dealings

4–27 Typically, these take the form of a prohibition against a dealing with or transfer of possession of any of the charged assets without the creditor's prior written consent, "dealing" here covering both outright transfer and the grant of a mortgage, charge or lease. Such a prohibition is effective to establish the charge as a fixed charge on goods even though there is no duty to account for the proceeds. This is because, in contrast to book debts, which can be realised either by sale or by collection, goods have to be sold to produce proceeds, and if the chargor of goods cannot dispose of the goods themselves without the chargee's consent it is not in a position to collect the proceeds.[175] As an alternative, the debenture can empower the debtor company to deal with the charged assets as the debenture holder's fiduciary agent, holding the proceeds separately for the debenture holder's account.[176] The debenture should make it clear that the agency is confined to the relations between the debenture holder and the company and that the latter is to deal as principal in relation to third parties and is not to

---

[173] See paras 1–71, 2–10 and 4–20, above.

[174] For a more detailed description of the position where bills of lading are pledged as part of the operation of a documentary credit, see Beale, Bridge, Gullifer and Lomnicka, *The Law of Security and Title-Based Financing* (2012), paras 5.35–5.38.

[175] The chargor is, however, in a position to give good title to buyers if the goods are sold in the ordinary course of business of the chargor, since the purchasers will not have constructive notice of the charge (see para.2–31, above). If the chargee habitually allows such sale the position would be the same as discussed in para.4–19, above.

[176] See (4), below.

commit the debenture holder to any contractual relationship with or liability to any third party.[177] It is also desirable to require dealings to be on commercially reasonable terms.

(4) Consent to disposition

It is clearly critical to the characterisation of a charge as fixed that the chargee must consent to any disposition of the charged assets by the chargor. It has already been mentioned that consent in advance, or a blanket consent, will not suffice.[178] However, how much freedom must the chargee have to withhold consent? Must it be total freedom or can its choice be contractually fettered? As mentioned above,[179] the charge in *Gray v G-T-P Group Ltd* was held to be floating where the charged assets were held by the chargee, but the chargee was obliged to transfer any of them to the chargor on request: it had no (legal) freedom to choose not to consent.[180] However, what would be the position if the right of the chargor to require release is restricted to what it reasonable, or (the other side of the same coin) the chargee's consent is limited by the charge agreement, for example a provision that consent is not to be unreasonably withheld? Here the chargee still has a choice whether or not to consent, so that its will is independent; it just must not behave in a way that no reasonable chargee would. Even where a charge is fixed, it could be argued that there would be an implied term that the chargee would not act wholly unreasonably, thus protecting the chargor against a wholly arbitrary and unreasonable refusal to allow withdrawal of an asset from the scope of the charge.[181]

4–28

(5) Accounting for proceeds

Where the debtor company is left free to dispose of the charged assets or, in the case of receivables, to collect them in, it is essential that the company be required to account for proceeds. There are various ways in which the required control can be effected: by providing for the chargee rather than the chargor collect the proceeds; by requiring the chargor to collect as agent for the chargee and pay the proceeds into a separate account opened by the chargor with its own bank but capable of being drawn on only with the chargee's consent, or into an account over which the chargee takes a fixed charge; or, where the chargee is itself a bank, by requiring the chargor to pay the proceeds into a blocked account opened

4–29

---

[177] This is the so-called "commission agency" which English law tends not to regard as an agency at all. See See S. Mills, *Goode on proprietary rights and insolvency in sales transactions*, 3rd edn (London: Sweet &Maxwell/Thomson Reuters, 2010), para.3.08 and, in relation to a comparable problem with reservation of title, para.5.77.

[178] See para.4–18, above.

[179] See para.4–22, above.

[180] The decision in *Queen's Moat Houses Plc v Capita* [2004] EWHC 868 (Ch), where a charge in similar terms was held to be fixed, is inconsistent with both *Gray* and *Spectrum* and cannot now be good law.

[181] For the distinction between a duty to act reasonably and a duty not to act unreasonably, see *Socimer International Bank Ltd v Standard Bank London Ltd* [2008] EWCA Civ 116; [2008] 1 Lloyd's Rep. 558 at [66]. See also *Yam Seng Pte Ltd v International Trade Corp Ltd* [2013] EWHC 111 (QB) on the implication of a duty of good faith into a contract in proper circumstances.

with the chargee.[182] But frequently debtor companies are reluctant to submit to such a restriction on their ability to handle incoming moneys representing trading income, and without it the court is likely to rule that the charge is not fixed but floating.[183] There is usually less difficulty in stipulating for control of proceeds of a fixed asset, such as an insurance policy.[184]

One technique that is being considered as a way of exercising control is the so–called "two account structure". Here the charge agreement provides that the proceeds are to be paid into a bank account with the chargee, or controlled by the chargee, and not to be withdrawn without the consent of the chargee. However, another agreement provides that the chargee will consent to withdrawals from that account into another account from which the chargor can withdraw freely. This structure was held by the Irish Supreme Court in *Re Keenan*[185] to be a fixed charge, although only one judge expressly considered the agreement relating to the second account, which was entered into at a later date than the charge agreement.[186] If such a structure is to stand a chance of being characterised as a fixed charge, the consent of the chargee to transfers to the second account would have to constitute independent acts of will: a blanket consent will not suffice. This might be achieved by providing that the chargee was under no obligation to consent to transfers, although it might be difficult to argue that such a provision represented the true intention of the parties if the chargee did habitually consent and such consent was relied upon by the chargor. Further, the agreement should provide for the amount left in the first account not to be reduced below a certain level.[187]

A refinement of this structure could be a fixed charge covering the receivables and proceeds up to a certain amount, the rest being subject to a floating charge. When the proceeds in the account exceeded that amount, the surplus could be withdrawn and placed in another account. There are, however, two problems with this structure. First, a chargee will usually want a fixed charge over *all* the chargor's receivables, and would therefore need to exert control over all the receivables and all the proceeds. Secondly, there is the problem of identifying the receivables which are subject to the charge,[188] and (lesser) problems of identifying part of a bank account.[189]Another control technique is where the charge agreement, or another agreement, provides that the proceeds of the debts should be disposed of in a particular way, including but not limited to the repayment of the secured loan, sometimes called a "payment waterfall".

---

[182] *Re Spectrum Plus* [2005] UKHL 41; [2005] 2 A.C. 680 at [54], per Lord Hope.

[183] *Re Brightlife Ltd* [1987] Ch. 200.

[184] *Re CCG International Enterprises Ltd* [1993] B.C.L.C. 1428, where the chargee bank took a charge over (inter alia) policies of fire insurance and could elect to apply any proceeds either to reinstatement of the property damaged by fire or to reduction of the chargor's indebtedness.

[185] *Re Keenan* [1986] B.C.L.C. 242.

[186] *Re Keenan* [1986] B.C.L.C. 242, 250.

[187] In *Re Keenan* this level was 5 per cent of the funds currently standing the blocked account, but it is thought that a better provision would relate the amount remaining in the blocked account to the amount outstanding on the secured debt.

[188] This might not always be the case, for example, where the chargor had one very large client over whose debts the chargee could take a charge. Alternatively, it could be the book debts resulting from a particular activity. It would, however, be necessary to provide that the proceeds of these debts would have to be paid into a separate bank account from the rest of the chargor's receivables.

[189] See paras 6–14 and 6–15, below.

Although, given the seemingly absolute nature of the judgments in *Spectrum* discussed above, there is a danger that this would amount to "consent in advance" to dispositions, and therefore to the charge being characterised as floating, it is submitted that the better view is that it is possible, if the clause is prescriptive enough as to the destination of the dispositions, for such a clause to give the chargee sufficient control over the proceeds for the charge to be characterised as fixed.[190]

In relation to both these techniques it should be noted that, when characterising a charge, the courts will look at all relevant agreements and not merely the charge agreement itself.[191]

Policing of the control provisions

As stated earlier, it is not sufficient to specify controls in the charge instrument. These must be shown to be more than a mere paper exercise. In particular, if the debtor is regularly allowed to dispose of the charged assets without regard to the restrictions imposed on it, the court is likely to take the view either that the contractual provisions were mere camouflage or that they have been waived by the creditor, in either case resulting in the security becoming characterised as a floating charge.[192] If substantial amounts are at stake, regular inspections of physical assets comprising the security, and of the debtor company's accounts, are advisable. A final cautionary word— though control is important, there is a line beyond which the activity of the secured creditor will cease to be mere control over the disposition of specific classes of asset and will constitute an exercise of management of the company's business with the concomitant statutory duties and liabilities imposed on officers, directors, and shadow directors.[193] **4–30**

4. CRYSTALLISATION OF A FLOATING CHARGE[194]

As we have seen, the essence of a floating charge is the liberty given to the debtor company to manage and deal with the assets comprising the security in the ordinary course of business. In taking a floating charge, the creditor binds himself not to intervene in the handling of the assets so long as the company runs under its own steam as a going concern. When the company goes into liquidation or receivership its management powers are brought to an end under the provisions **4–31**

---

[190] See N. Frome and K. Gibbons, "Spectrum— an End to the Conflict or the Signal for a New Campaign?" in *Company Charges: Spectrum and Beyond* (2006).
[191] *Re Spectrum Plus* [2005] UKHL 41; [2005] 2 A.C. 680 HL, [56]–[61] per Lord Hope, [116]–[119] per Lord Scott, [153] and [156]–[161] per Lord Walker.
[192] *Re Bond Worth Ltd* [1922] 2 Ch. 211; *Waters v Widdows* [1984] V.R. 503. See para.4–21, above.
[193] See Insolvency Act 1986 ss.206–219 and 251 (definition of "shadow directors"); Company Directors Disqualification Act 1986.
[194] Priority issues in relation to the crystallisation of a floating charge, including the effect of negative pledge clauses, are discussed in the next chapter.

of the charge instrument.[195] When this occurs, the charge is said to crystallise; and it is with crystallisation and its effects that much of the rest of the present chapter is concerned.

The general effect of crystallisation

4–32 Crystallisation puts an end to the authority conferred on the debtor company to manage the assets comprising the security. In consequence, the charge becomes converted into a fixed charge, fastening on all assets in which the company then has or subsequently acquires[196] an interest.[197] Though crystallisation does not per se put an end to the company's ability to continue its business,[198] it ceases to be able to dispose of the charged assets free from the charge without the consent of the chargee, who cannot give a blanket permission without refloating the charge.[199]

Crystallisation does not involve re-registration in the Companies Registry nor does it avoid the effects of non-registration, for no new security interest is created. All that happens is that the security interest brought into being by the floating charge ceases to float over a fund of assets and attaches in specie.

The effect of crystallisation is customarily analysed in purely property terms. This can be unfortunate, for it conceals the fact that by authorising the company to trade in its circulating assets free from the charge the debenture holder has held the company out as having wide powers of disposition, so that we are concerned as much with principles of agency law as those of property law.

If, then, we look at the effect of crystallisation in agency terms, it immediately becomes clear that we must distinguish the relationship between the chargee and the company from the relationships between the chargee and rival claimants to the security. Termination of the company's actual authority to manage its assets is purely a matter between the company and the debenture holder. No outsider is entitled to dictate the terms on which the company's management powers are to be brought to an end, or to complain if the company has accepted as a crystallising event acts or omissions which to the outsider may seem entirely trivial or capricious. But whether the ending of the company's actual authority binds third parties dealing with assets is an entirely separate question. In

---

[195] Receivership has become rare with the abolition under the Enterprise Act 2002 of the ability of most floating chargees to appoint an administrative receiver. For a discussion of whether the appointment of an administrator crystallises a floating charge, see para.4–45, below.

[196] *N W Robbie & Co Ltd v Witney Warehouse Ltd* [1963] 3 All E.R. 613; *Ferrier v Bottomer* (1972)126 C.L.R. 597; *Leichardt Emporium Pty Ltd v AGC (Household Finance) Ltd* [1979] 1 N.S.W.L.R. 701. In other words, crystallisation of the floating charge does not affect the continued operation of the after-acquired property clause. The scope of that clause is, of course, a matter of construction of the charge instrument. In *Re Rex Developments Pty Ltd* (1994) 13 A.C.S.R. 485, the Supreme Court of the Australian Capital Territory held by a majority (Higgins J. dissenting) that the security was confined to after-acquired property covered by a floating charge, so that once the charge crystallised no future property could fall within it. This construction is rather surprising, for a natural reading of the instrument, and the only one making commercial sense, would seem to indicate that all after-acquired property was intended to be covered, whether acquired before or after crystallisation of the charge.

[197] For a recent statement, see *Re JD Brian Ltd* [2011] IEHC 113; [2011] 3 I.R. 244 at [18].

[198] Assuming, of course, that the crystallising event is not an act which itself denotes cessation of trading. See para.4–36, below.

[199] See para.4–62, below.

answering this, it is not necessarily sufficient to say that the company is no longer authorised to sell or charge its assets, for it may still have apparent authority to do so. This is a matter which will be considered in the following chapter.[200]

Categories of crystallising event

Crystallising events fall broadly into four groups. First, there are events denoting the cessation of trading by the company as a going concern. Secondly, there is intervention by the debenture holder to enforce his security which deprives the company of de jure control of the charged assets and thus terminates its authority to deal with them free from the security interest. Thirdly, there are other acts or events specified in the debenture as causing the charge to crystallise. Fourthly, in the case of agricultural charges granted by a farmer the Agricultural Credits Act 1928 contains specific provisions for crystallisation. Crystallisation cannot occur during a moratorium in relation to an eligible company where directors of a company propose a voluntary arrangment.[201] Crystallisation occurs simultaneously with the relevant event; the law does not treat this as a conceptual impossibility by predicating that the crystallising event and crystallisation itself occur in sequence and not at the same time.[202]

4-33

Group 1: events denoting cessation of trading as a going concern

A floating charge crystallises on the occurrence of an event which is incompatible with the continuance of trading by the company as a going concern. Crystallisation is, in such cases, said to occur as a matter of law,[203] but this does not mean that there is any mandatory rule of law which precludes a charge from continuing to float where the company ceases trading, merely that the intention by the debenture holder to allow this to happen is so unlikely, and the result in most cases would be so nonsensical, that an express provision for crystallisation on cessation of trading or the ability to trade is unnecessary since the law will imply a term to that effect.[204] On the other hand, an event would not appear to be a crystallising event within this first category merely because its effect is to remove the management of the company's assets from its directors and transfer them to an administrative receiver[205] or an administrator.[206] Such an event may constitute a crystallising event within the second category but it is not inconsistent with continued trading by the company or even with the ultimate return of the company's management to the directors.

4-34

There are at least two types of event falling within the first category, namely liquidation of the company and de facto cessation of trading.

---

[200] See para.5–51, below.
[201] Insolvency Act 1986 s.1A, and Sch.A1 para.13.
[202] *Fire Nymph Products Ltd v The Heating Centre Pty Ltd* (1992) 10 A.C.L.C. 629, per Gleeson C.J. at 636; adopted by Chadwick J. in *Re Real Meat Co Ltd* [1996] B.C.C. 254.
[203] *Re Crompton & Co Ltd* [1914] Ch. 954 at 964, 965.
[204] *Re Brightlife Ltd* [1987] Ch. 200, per Hoffman J. at 212; referring to the judgment of Warrington J. in *Re Crompton & Co Ltd* [1914] Ch. 954 at 964–965; *Re Real Meat Co Ltd* [1996] B.C.C. 254, 261.
[205] See below.
[206] See below.

(1)   Liquidation

4–35   The winding up of a company, whether by resolution of the members or by order of the court, causes a floating charge to crystallise,[207] for upon liquidation a company must cease to carry on its business, except so far as may be required for its beneficial winding up.[208] This is so whether or not the liquidation is an insolvent liquidation. Hence the fact that the company is prosperous and goes into winding up purely for the purpose of reconstruction does not prevent the charge from crystallising.[209] In the case of a compulsory winding up, the winding up is deemed, by statute, to have commenced at the date of the presentation of the petition for winding up.[210] This relation back is to prevent dispositions of the company's assets in the run-up to insolvency, and chiefly relevant to the operation of s.127 of the Insolvency Act 1986 and other sections dealing with avoidance of pre-insolvency transactions.[211] There is no particular policy reason why the time of crystallisation should be similarly back-dated, and there is some Australian authority in support of the proposition that it is not.[212] The rule that a floating charge crystallises on winding up is not a creature of statute, but is a term implied into a charge agreement by a general rule of law.[213] Thus, it would seem more logical that in most cases crystallisation would not occur until the company had stopped trading, which would normally be at the time of the winding up order, rather than the presentation of the petition, which does not disable the company from trading and which in any event be dismissed.[214] For the same reason the appointment of a provisional liquidator does not crystallise the charge.[215] A fortiori the mere fact that the company has become insolvent is not a crystallising event unless so designated by the charge instrument,[216] in which event the case falls within Group 3 below.[217]

---

[207] *Re Panama, New Zealand and Australian Royal Mail Co* (1870) 5 Ch. App. 318; *Re Colonial Trusts Corp* (1879) 15 Ch.D. 465; *Wallace v Universal Automatic Machines Co* [1894] 2 Ch. 547; *Re Crompton & Co Ltd* [1914] Ch. 954; *Evans v Rival Granite Quarries Ltd* [1910] 2 K.B. 979.

[208] Insolvency Act 1986 ss.87(1), 167(1) and Sch.4 para.5.

[209] *Re Crompton & Co Ltd* [1914] Ch. 954 at 964. The position might be otherwise if there is an clause in the charge agreement providing that the charge will not crystallise on reorganisation, even if the company goes into liquidation for that purpose, although it is difficult to see how the charge can continue to float once the company whose assets are charged is no more. See discussion in *Encyclopoedia of Forms and Precedents Vol.11* (Companies) para.321; and *Sneath v Valley Gold* [1893] 1 Ch. 477.

[210] Insolvency Act 1986 s.129(2). However, if the company has previously gone into voluntary winding up, the date of commencement of winding up is the date of passing of the resolution (ibid., s.129(1)).

[211] Insolvency Act 1986 s.127 provides that dispositions of the company's property made after the commencement of the winding up is void. For criticism, see Goode, *Principles of Corporate Insolvency Law* (2011), para.13–127.

[212] *Stein v Saywell* (1969) 121 C.L.R. 529.

[213] See para.4–34, above; and see especially *Re Brightlife Ltd* [1987] 1 Ch. 200, per Hoffmann J. at 212.

[214] *Re Victoria Steamboats Co* [1897] 1 Ch. 158.

[215] *Re Obie Pty Ltd (No.2)* (1983) 8 A.C.L.R. 574.

[216] *Covacich v Riordan* [1994] 2 N.Z.L.R. 502.

[217] See paras 4–52 et seq., below.

(2) Cessation of trading

Where a company ceases trading, the law implies a term in the debenture that the floating charge will thereupon crystallise, whether or not the company is in winding up.[218] The practical problem is to determine at what point trading has ceased. Until the enactment of the Insolvency Act 1985 this could have been important, since as the law then stood a floating charge which crystallised otherwise than by appointment of a receiver, winding up or the taking of possession of the charged property had priority over subsequent preferential debts, for it had ceased to be a floating charge at the time such debts came into existence.[219] The possibility of such priority was, however, extinguished by the change in the definition of a floating charge so as to cover a charge which, as created, was a floating charge.[220]

4–36

Events not denoting cessation of trading

It is inherent in a floating charge that the debtor company retains the ability to function as a going concern. Once it ceases trading or is disabled from continuing to trade as a going concern the rationale for the freedom given to the company by the floating charge to dispose of its assets in the ordinary course of business disappears. But trading as a going concern does not necessarily require that the powers of management of the charged assets remain with the directors of the company. Those powers may have passed to an administrative receiver or an administrator or may have ceased to be exercisable through some other crystallising event but this does not of itself indicate that the company is no longer able to continue trading. Indeed, it is one of the functions of receivers and administrators to carry on the business of the company. The effect of the appointment of a receiver by the debenture holder himself or by the court on his application will now be examined, together with the impact of crystallisation of a prior or subsequent floating charge, and the effect of an administration order and the appointment of an administrator. It must be borne in mind that the following discussion addresses whether these events crystallise the floating charge only on the grounds of cessation of trading: many of them may trigger crystallisation on other grounds, such as the intervention by the debenture holder or as the occurrence of an event specified in the debenture as causing crystallisation.

4–37

(1) Appointment of an administrative receiver or receiver by or at the instance of the debenture holder[221]

The appointment of an administrative receiver by the debenture holder does not by itself result in a cessation of trading. On the contrary, the administrative

4–38

---

[218] *Re Woodroffes (Musical Instruments) Ltd* [1986] Ch.366, per Nourse J. at 378; *Re Real Meat Co Ltd* [1996] B.C.C. 254, per Chadwick J. at 261; *Re Sperrin Textiles Ltd* [1992] N.I. 323.

[219] *Re Woodroffes (Musical Instruments) Ltd* [1986] Ch.366, where, however, the debenture holder was unable to show that the company had in fact ceased trading prior to the appointment of the receiver.

[220] Insolvency Act 1986 ss.251 and 40(1).

[221] Due to s.72A of the Insolvency Act 1986, added by the Enterprise Act 2002, the part of this discussion relating to an administrative receiver now only applies to floating charges created before

receiver will usually carry on the business for a significant period in order to get it into shape before a "hive down" by transfer of the assets to a new company which can then be sold off to a purchaser with assets but no liabilities. The same applies to a receiver appointed by the court on the application of the debenture holder and authorised by the court to carry on the company's business.[222] The fact that a company can continue as a going concern even though under receivership is of little significance to the question of crystallisation where the receiver is appointed by the debenture holder himself, for it is settled that this falls within a distinct category of crystallising event, namely withdrawal of the company's authority from the debenture holder to deal with its assets in the ordinary course of business.[223] But the point becomes of considerable importance where the receiver is appointed by a prior or subsequent debenture holder.

(2) Crystallisation of another floating charge

4–39   If one chargee crystallises its charge by appointing a receiver, this has the effect of crystallising another charge over the same assets,[224] but otherwise crystallisation of one charge does not automatically have this effect,[225] in the absence of an express term in the second charge.[226]

(3) Appointment of administrator

4–40   An administrator can be appointed out of court, by the holder of a qualifying floating charge,[227] or by the company or the directors,[228] or by the court.[229] There is a hierarchy of objectives for the administrator, the first of which is the rescue of the company as a going concern.[230] Only if that is not possible is the

---

September 15, 2003, or falling within the exceptions listed in s.72B–72GA of the Insolvency Act 1986. It is still possible for a receiver to be appointed in relation to part of the company's assets under an express power in the charge agreement, or under s.101 of the Law of Property Act 1925 or by the court.

[222] Of course, the appointment of a receiver, whether by the debenture holder or by the court may lead to the cessation of trading, where the receiver, pursuant to a power conferred on him by the debenture deed or the court, decides to close the business. This will have no crystallising effect in relation to the debenture under which he was appointed (since this will previously have crystallised by virtue of his appointment—see below), but will have the effect of crystallising floating charges created under other debentures.

[223] See para.4–44, below.

[224] See Beale, Bridge, Gullifer and Lomnicka, *The Law of Security and Title-Based Financing* (2012), para.6.82; and the Canadian cases of *Federal Business Development Bank v Prince Albert Fashion Bin Ltd* [1993] 3 W.W.R. 464 at [17] (crystallisation of subsequent floating charge); and *Ontario Development Corp v FP Bourgault Industries Cultivator Division Ltd* [1995] 9 W.W.R. 342 at [23] (crystallisation of prior floating charge) though it is arguable that this conclusion is limited to where the appointment of the receiver has the effect of causing the company to cease to carry on business; see *Deputy Commissioner of Taxation v Lai Corp Property Ltd* (1986) 85 F.L.R. 220, 260–261 (dissenting judgment of Kennedy J.); *Re Sperrin Textiles Ltd* [1992] N.I. 323, 331.

[225] *Re Woodroffes (Musical Instruments) Ltd* [1986] Ch. 366.

[226] As in *Stein v Saywell* (1969) 121 C.L.R. 529.

[227] Insolvency Act 1986 para.14 Sch.B1.

[228] Insolvency Act 1986 para.14 Sch.B1.

[229] On the application by one or more of the persons listed in para.12 Sch.B1 to the Insolvency Act 1986.

[230] Insolvency Act 1986 para.3(1) Sch.B1.

administrator's objective to achieve a better result for the company's creditors than would be possible in a winding up, and only if that is not possible is the administrator to realise property to distribute to secured or preferential creditors. Pending the hearing of an application for an administration order, or in the period between the filing of a notice of intention to appoint an administrator and the actual appointment the company cannot be put into winding up, nor can security be enforced against the company or proceedings be commenced or continued against it without leave of the court.[231] Once an administration order is made these restrictions continue during the currency of the order unless the administrator otherwise agrees. An administrator appointed by the court may do anything necessary or expedient for the management of the affairs, business and property of the company and may in particular exercise all the powers conferred by Sch.1 to the Insolvency Act 1986.[232] That schedule expressly empowers the administrator (inter alia) to carry on the business of the company.[233] Hence the making of an administration order is in no way incompatible with the continuance of the company's business as a going concern and does not, it is thought, result in crystallisation of a floating charge in the absence of any express term to that effect in the debenture,[234] unless the administrator is appointed by the debenture holder.[235]

Group 2: intervention by debenture holder to take control of the assets

By taking a floating charge the debenture holder binds himself to allow the debtor company freedom to manage and deal with the charged assets in the ordinary course of business until such time as its authority from him to do so is withdrawn pursuant to the express or implied terms of the debenture. We have seen that there is an implied withdrawal of authority when the company goes into liquidation or ceases trading. The debenture holder can also signify the termination of the company's management powers by intervening to take control of the charged assets. But what types of intervention are to be considered sufficient for this purpose? An analysis of the authorities indicates that to be effective in crystallising a floating charge the debenture holder's act of intervention must satisfy a threefold test. First, it must be done with the intention of converting the charge into a fixed charge.[236] Secondly, it must be authorised by the express or implied terms of the debenture. Thirdly, it must divest the company of de jure control of the assets.[237] With the application of these tests it becomes relatively easy to determine whether the debenture holder's intervention has been effective to crystallise the charge.

4–41

---

[231] Insolvency Act 1986 para.44 Sch.B1.
[232] Insolvency Act 1986 paras 59(1), 60 Sch.B1.
[233] Insolvency Act 1986 para.14 Sch.B1.
[234] This view is supported by Lightman and Moss, *The Law of Receivers and Administrators of Companies* (2011), para.3–62.
[235] As to this, see para.4–45, below.
[236] *Evans v Rival Granite Quarries Ltd* [1910] 2 K.B. 979, per Fletcher Moulton L.J. at 997.
[237] See the Irish case of *Re JD Brian Ltd (In Liquidation)* [2011] IEHC 283 especially at [10], [17]–[19].

(1)   Intervention which is effective to crystallise the charge

4–42   **Taking of possession**   If the debenture holder lawfully takes possession of the charged assets this crystallises the charge,[238] for it ends the company's control. It is not necessary that he should seize all the assets at once, which in most cases would be impracticable. The debenture holder may take possession of part in the name of the whole,[239] whether the assets consist of land or of goods.[240]

4–43   **Order for possession or sale**   Though there appears no decision directly on the point, it seems clear that an order requiring the company to deliver up to the debenture holder possession of land or goods crystallises the charge, for the effect of such an order is to terminate the company's right to hold and deal with the land or goods in question. The same applies to an order for sale. But the mere institution of proceedings would not appear to suffice, for this does not divest the company of de jure control.[241]

4–44   **Appointment of receiver out of court**   The appointment of an administrative receiver by the debenture holder out of court has long been the most common method of crystallising a floating charge and is well established as effective for that purpose.[242] However, a floating chargee is no longer able to appoint an administrative receiver,[243] unless the charge is created before September 2003, or falls within one of the statutory exceptions.[244] Crystallisation does not depend on the receiver taking possession of the assets; the commencement of the receiver's appointment is all that is required,[245] for by executing a debenture which authorises the debenture holder to appoint a receiver in stated events the company implicitly recognises that its right to continue managing its business is terminated upon such appointment.

---

[238] *Mercantile Bank of India Ltd v Chartered Bank of India, Australia and China* [1937] 1 All E.R. 231.

[239] i.e. with the intention of asserting rights over the whole. The position is otherwise where the debenture holder seizes a particular asset with a view to leaving the company free to continue business with the remaining assets. Such a seizure, unless authorised by the debenture, is a breach of its terms and as such is ineffective to crystallise the charge. *Evans v Rival Granite Quarries Ltd* [1910] 2 K.B. 979, per Fletcher Moulton L.J. at 998. See para.4–49, 4–61, below.

[240] See F. Pollock and R. Wright, *Possession in the Common Law* (Oxford: Clarendon Press, 1888), pp.60–61, 70, 78–79.

[241] Moreover, the application might not succeed.

[242] *Evans v Rival Granite Quarries Ltd* [1910] 2 K.B. 979, and cases there cited.

[243] Insolvency Act 1986 s.72A, added by the Enterprise Act 2002.

[244] Insolvency Act 1986 ss.72B–72GA.

[245] Gough, *Company Charges* (1996), pp.165–166 considers it at least arguable that the mere appointment of a receiver does not by itself cause the charge to crystallise and that it is necessary for the receiver to take possession, for it is that that deprives the company of management powers and constitutes an appropriation to the security on behalf of the debenture holder. But the requirement of possession is not only unsupported by any authority, apart from a few fleeting and speculative judicial utterances, it runs counter to numerous cases in which the courts have held it to be settled law that appointment of a receiver by the debenture holder suffices to crystallise the charge. The fact that possession is unnecessary is put beyond doubt by cases which establish that an execution creditor on whose behalf the enforcement officer levies execution against goods the subject of a floating charge is postponed to the debenture holder if the latter appoints a receiver before sale by the enforcement officer (*Re Standard Manufacturing Co Ltd* [1891] 1 Ch. 627; *Re Opera Ltd* [1891] 3 Ch. 260).

Appointment of administrator out of court by qualifying chargeholder   The   **4–45**
power of a qualifying floating chargeholder to appoint an administrator[246]
replaces the power to appoint an administrative receiver. In one sense this does
amount to intervention by the chargeholder, but the chargeholder does not take
control of the assets. The administrator does not owe duties only to the
chargeholder, and, while pursuing his objectives,[247] is able to dispose of floating
charge assets without the leave of the court.[248] Therefore, contrary to what was
said in the last edition of this book, it is now thought that in the absence of a
provision in the charge agreement crystallising the charge on the appointment of
an administrator, that appointment, whether by the floating chargee or by anyone
else entitled to appoint, does not crystallise a floating charge.[249]

Appointment of receiver by the court   Where at the instance of the debenture   **4–46**
holder a receiver is appointed by the court,[250] the floating charge crystallises
when such appointment takes effect.[251]

(2)   Intervention which is ineffective to crystallise the charge

Default by the company   It is well established that unless otherwise provided   **4–47**
by the debenture[252] the mere fact that the company has defaulted and the
debenture holder has become entitled to enforce his security does not by itself
crystallise the charge; the debenture holder must actively intervene to terminate
the company's right to continue trading with the charged assets.[253]

Demand for payment   Similarly, a demand for payment does not by itself   **4–48**
crystallise the charge,[254] for it does not indicate an intention to make the security
a fixed security.

---

[246] Insolvency Act 1986 Sch.B1 para.14. This only applied to floating charges created after the date
this part of the Act came into force, namely September 15, 2003.

[247] These are set out in Insolvency Act 1986 Sch.B1 para.3. See para 4–40, above.

[248] Insolvency Act 1986 Sch.B1, para.70. The administrator has extensive powers of management of
the affairs of the company, see ibid. para.59.

[249] Goode, *Principles of Corporate Insolvency* (2011), para.11–30; L. Gullifer & J. Payne, *Corporate
Finance Law: Principles and Policy* (Oxford: Hart Publishing, 2011), pp.248–249.

[250] This is unusual, since from the viewpoint of the debenture holder an appointment by the court has
many disadvantages—delay, expense, restrictions on the receiver's freedom of action, etc.—which are
avoided by an appointment out of court. One of the few advantages of having a court-appointed
receiver is that foreign courts are more likely to recognise his status. It would still seem possible for a
floating charge holder to apply to the court for the appointment of a receiver, despite s.72A of the
Insolvency Act, since this section only abolishes the right of a floating charge holder to appoint an
administrative receiver, which is by definition an appointment out of court. However, the only
receiver a court is now likely to appoint is a receiver over specific assets.

[251] This will be at the time the order is made unless the receiver is ordered to give security and is not
given liberty to act until such security is given, in which case his appointment takes effect when he
furnishes the security. If the receiver, though ordered to furnish security, is given liberty to act
immediately, his appointment takes effect at once but lapses if the security is not duly furnished. This
presumably results in a refloating of the charge.

[252] See paras 4–52 et seq., below.

[253] *Evans v Rival Granite Quarries Ltd* [1910] 2 K.B. 979, per Fletcher Moulton L.J. at 993.

[254] *Re Hubbard & Co Ltd* (1898) 68 L.J. Ch.54, above.

4–49   **Assertion of rights over part of security**   In the absence of a provision in the debenture empowering him to do so, the debenture holder is not entitled to crystallise his security as to part only of the assets while leaving the charge to float as to the remaining assets.[255] The assets comprised in the floating charge constitute an indivisible fund and the debenture holder must assert his security interest in relation to the fund as a whole or not at all. If he purports to pounce down on a particular asset only, leaving the debtor company free to continue trading with the remaining assets, this constitutes a breach of his contract with the company and is accordingly ineffective as an act of intervention, so that the charge will continue to float as to all the charged assets.[256] So a debenture holder whose security covered the entire undertaking and assets of the company was held not to be entitled to give notice to the company's bank contesting the attachment of the company's credit balance by a judgment creditor in garnishee proceedings while leaving the company free to continue dealing with the rest of its assets, so that the judgment creditor was entitled to have the garnishee order made absolute.[257] Similarly, where a debenture provided for crystallisation by notice, a notice to the company purporting to terminate its dealing powers as to part only of the assets was held ineffective to crystallise the charge even as to such part.[258] However, it seems to be possible to crystallise in relation to part of the charged assets where the relevant part of the assets is very distinct, where the assertion of rights results in the appointment of a receiver[259] and where it is clearly possible for the company to cease trading in relation to one part of the assets but not the other. In *Re Griffin Hotel Co Ltd*,[260] the debenture holders had a floating charge over all the companies' assets, which were two hotels. The court appointed a receiver over one hotel but not over the other (which was subject to a prior mortgage): which was later held to have had the effect of crystallising the charge in relation to the one hotel but not the other.[261] Where partial crystallisation is permitted by the terms of the debenture, there seems to be no objection to it.[262]

4–50   **Institution of proceedings to enforce security**   As stated earlier, the institution of proceedings by a debenture holder to enforce his security by an order for possession, sale or the appointment of a receiver appears insufficient to crystallise the charge, as it does not itself put an end to the company's management powers.

---

[255] *Robson v Smith* [1895] 2 Ch. 118, 126; *Evans v Rival Granite Quarries Ltd* [1910] 2 K.B. 979, per Fletcher Moulton L.J. at 998 and per Buckley L.J. at 1000; *Re Caroma Enterprises Ltd* (1979) 108 D.L.R. (3d) 412, 419.

[256] *Evans v Rival Granite Quarries Ltd* [1910] 2 K.B. 979; *R v Consolidated Churchill Corp* [1978] 5 W.W.R. 625.

[257] *Evans v Rival Granite Quarries Ltd* [1910] 2 K.B. 979.

[258] *R v Consolidated Churchill Corp* [1978] 5 W.W.R. 625. See also *Re City Securities Pte* [1990] 1 S.L.R. 468, 489–490; overturned on appeal on different reasoning sub nom. *Dresdner Bank Aktiengesellschaft v Ho Mun-Tuke Don* [1993] 1 S.L.R. 114.

[259] This would be a receiver appointed by the court, or under s.101 of the Law of Property Act 1925, or under an express power in the charge agreement, and would not be an administrative receiver.

[260] *Re Griffin Hotel Co Ltd* [1941] Ch. 129.

[261] *Re Griffin Hotel Co Ltd* [1941] Ch. 129 at 135. See discussion in Gough, *Company Charges* (1996), p.171.

[262] See para.4–61, below.

The grant of injunctive relief   It has been suggested that the grant of an   **4–51**
injunction to restrain the debtor company from dealing with the assets in breach
of a restriction in the floating charge necessarily causes the charge to crystallise,
on the ground that until crystallisation the chargee cannot treat the charged assets
as specifically appropriated so as to ground an injunction.[263] This would not,
however, seem to be correct. In the first place, it is predicated on the assumption
that an injunction lies only where the subject matter of the application is specific
or ascertained property, that is, where the charge has crystallised. But as we have
noted earlier,[264] an injunction can be granted to restrain any threatened breach of
contract, even if it involves no property rights at all. Moreover, the proposition
confronts the logical difficulty that if it is only the injunction itself which
produces crystallisation the holder of a floating charge has no locus standi to
obtain it, for the charge has not yet attached to any specific assets. Secondly, an
injunction to restrain a threatened dealing in breach of the terms of the charge
instrument is not in itself inconsistent with the debtor company's continuing
authority to manage its business using the charged assets; all it does is to prohibit
the company from dealings in excess of its authority. If an injunction to restrain
the trustee of an active trust from dealing with the trust fund in breach of trust
does not of itself convert the active trust into a bare trust,[265] it is hard to see why
an injunction which seeks to do no more than keep the chargor to the terms of the
floating charge should be treated as ending its dealing powers altogether. The
position is, of course, otherwise where the breach complained of denotes the
cessation of the company's business, as in *Hubbuck v Helms*,[266] where the debtor
company decided to discontinue its business and implemented that decision by
contracting to sell all its major assets. The cessation of business is itself a
crystallising event preceding, and independent of, the grant of injunctive relief.

Group 3: other acts or events specified in the debenture as causing crystallisation

As we have seen, the mere fact that the debenture holder has become entitled to   **4–52**
enforce his security under the terms of the debenture does not by itself crystallise
the charge; he must actually exercise the right of enforcement. However, since the
acts or events which terminate the company's authority from the debenture holder
to manage its assets are a matter of contract between them, it is open to the
debenture holder to specify any method of crystallisation he chooses.[267] Two
distinct types of provision for crystallisation have been used. In the first, the
debenture holder is empowered to crystallise the charge by notice; in the second,
crystallisation is made to occur automatically on the occurrence of a designated
event.

---

[263] Gough, *Company Charges* (1996), p.231.
[264] See para.4–06, above.
[265] Which would normally be incompatible with the terms of the settlement or trust instrument. The
trustee might be replaced but that would not affect its continuance as an active trust.
[266] *Hubbuck v Helms* (1887) 56 L.J. Ch. 536.
[267] *Re Brightlife Ltd* [1987] Ch. 200; *Governments Stock and Other Securities Investment Co Ltd v
Manila Ry Co Ltd* [1897] A.C. 81, where the speeches in the House of Lords showed that they
regarded the matter as one of construction of the debenture.

(1)   Crystallisation by notice

4–53   This mode of crystallisation is sometimes termed "semi-automatic". The debenture holder is given the right to make the floating charge specific by notice, either at will or after the occurrence of a specified event. In *Re Woodroffes (Musical Instruments) Ltd*[268] it was conceded that this method of crystallisation was effective. In *Re Brightlife Ltd*[269] it was contended that the events of crystallisation were fixed by law and were three in number, namely winding up, the appointment of a receiver and cessation of the company's business, and that both as a matter of authority and in terms of public policy it was not open to the parties to stipulate other events as crystallising events. This contention was rejected by Hoffmann J., who held that the question was purely one of contract, and that Parliament having intervened on various occasions to regulate floating charges—as by requiring their registration and by subordinating them to preferential debts—it was not for the courts to impose additional restrictions on the parties' freedom of contract on grounds of public policy.[270] The Agricultural Credits Act 1928 provides expressly for crystallisation of a floating charge by notice, where so authorised by the charge instrument, where it is an agricultural charge given to a bank by a farmer.[271] A chargee cannot crystallise by notice during the moratorium that applies during a company voluntary arrangement.[272]

(2)   Automatic (express) crystallisation

4–54   Under an automatic crystallisation clause, no action on the part of the debenture holder is needed to crystallise the charge; crystallisation occurs automatically on the occurrence of a specified event. The use of automatic crystallisation clauses became fashionable in the 1970s, during which period there was a tendency to expand the range of crystallising events. Winding up and receivership were also invariably specified, though as mentioned earlier this was not strictly necessary, for it is a term implied by law that these events cause a charge to crystallise. Other events sometimes specified as crystallising events were the grant of security to the secured creditor or to another creditor; the levy of distress or execution against the debtor's assets; default by the debtor in its obligations to other creditors; the failure to maintain a given ratio of assets to liabilities or to keep the debtor's external borrowings to a given level. In recent years there has been a growing awareness of the disadvantages of automatic crystallisation, as described below, and insofar as automatic crystallisation clauses are used at all, their scope tends to be more narrowly confined.

---

[268] *Re Woodroffes (Musical Instruments) Ltd* [1985] 2 All E.R. 908.
[269] *Re Brightlife Ltd* [1987] Ch. 200.
[270] *Re Brightlife Ltd* [1987] Ch. 200 at 680–681. For a recent Irish decision to the same effect see *Re JD Brian Ltd* [2011] IEHC 113; [2011] 3 I.R. 244 at [56].
[271] Agricultural Credits Act 1928 s.7. See para.4–55, below.
[272] Insolvency Act 1986 para.13 Sch.A1.

Group 4: agricultural charges

Section 7 of the Agricultural Credits Act 1928 lists four categories of event causing a floating charge which is an agricultural charge given by a farmer to become fixed, though only as regards property comprised in the charge as existing at the time of crystallisation. These are:

(i) the making of a bankruptcy order against the farmer;
(ii) the death of the farmer;
(iii) the dissolution of the partnership where the property charged is partnership property; and
(iv) notice in writing to that effect by the bank on the happening of any event which by virtue of the charge confers on the bank a right to give such a notice.

4–55

The "validity" of automatic crystallisation clauses[273]

A question much canvassed is whether an automatic crystallisation clause is "valid". The word "valid" is in quotation marks because it conceals the real issue, which is not whether chargor and chargee are free to agree upon the circumstances in which the charger's management powers are to come to an end (clearly they can reach any agreement they like on this point) but what is the effect of crystallisation on third parties who are not aware of its having occurred. In other words, it is for the parties to the charge, and for them alone, to decide in what circumstances the security interest created by the charge is to attach so as to be enforceable against the debtor company in regard to specific assets; but whether the attached security interest prevails over a third party is a question not of validity but of priority, a point forcefully made by Dr W. J. Gough in his excellent book on company charges.[274] Unfortunately some of the argument directed against the validity of the automatic crystallisation clause fails to separate the issues of attachment and priority. It is assumed that to give effect to the wishes of the parties as to the events that are to cause the security interest to attach will as a necessary consequence result in the crystallised charge having priority over a subsequent fixed charge. But this is to confuse relations between chargor and chargee with relations between the chargee and third parties. More specifically, it confuses the debtor company's actual authority to dispose of its assets, which may be terminated at any time in accordance with the agreement between the parties, with the debtor's apparent authority to deal with its assets, which may continue notwithstanding that its actual authority has come to an end and the charge has thus crystallised. This has the effect that subsequent purchasers and chargees in the ordinary course of business without notice of the crystallisation take free of the crystallised charge.[275] However, this does not apply

4–56

---

[273] See T.C. Han, "Automatic Crystallisation, De-Crystallisation and Convertibility of Charges" [1998] C.F.I.L.R. 41; A Boyle, "The Validity of Automatic Crystallization Clauses" [1979] J.B.L. 231; Gough, *Company Charges* (1996), Ch.11.

[274] Gough, *Company Charges* (1996), pp.409 et seq.

[275] See para.5–51, below.

to execution creditors,[276] and so gaining priority over such creditors is the chief reason for inclusion of automatic crystallisation clauses into floating charges.

There is, as mentioned above,[277] limited English authority supporting the validity of semi-automatic and automatic crystallisation clauses. The most significant is *Re Brightlife Ltd*,[278] where Hoffmann J. had no difficulty in holding that the events upon which a floating charge is to crystallise are purely a matter of contract. Though that case involved crystallisation by notice rather than automatic crystallisation, the reasoning is equally applicable to automatic crystallisation clauses; indeed, Hoffmann J. several times referred to, and rejected, the submission by counsel that automatic crystallisation could occur only by reason of winding up, the appointment of a receiver or the cessation of business by the debtor company.[279] Automatic crystallisation upon the occurrence of a contractually designated event has also been endorsed by courts in Australia and New Zealand.[280]

Hence termination of the debtor company's actual authority to manage the charged assets by reason of such an event can be taken as established, subject to the question of interpretation discussed below.[281] The impact of crystallisation on priorities is discussed in the next chapter.[282]

The problem of overkill in automatic crystallisation clauses

4–57   The temptation to use the automatic crystallisation clause as a device to protect the charge from subordination to preferential creditors on a receivership or winding up has now been removed so far as English law is concerned.[283] There remains, however, the inducement of protecting the assets from execution creditors mentioned above.[284]

Nevertheless, the draftsman of the debenture should discipline himself against the adoption of a long catalogue of crystallising events. The draftsman has always to keep in mind the commercial objectives of the parties. It is all too easy, when acting for a lender, to set up safeguards which, if fully operated, would prevent the debtor from doing any business at all. Crystallisation is not something to be brought about lightly. Its effect is to paralyse the business, an event likely to cause as much damage to the debenture holder as to the debtor if it is made to occur needlessly. Suppose, for example, that the debenture were to provide for

---

[276] See para.5–51, below.

[277] See para.4–52, below.

[278] *Re Brightlife Ltd* [1987] Ch. 200.

[279] *Re Brightlife* [1987] Ch. 200 at 212 et seq.

[280] *Re Manurewa Transport Ltd* [1971] N.Z.L.R. 909; *Deputy Commissioner of Taxation v Horsburgh* [1984] V.R. 773; 2 N.Z.L.R. 513; *DFC Financial Services Ltd v Coffey* [1991] 2 N.Z.L.R. 513; *Fire Nymph Products Ltd v Heating Centre Pty Ltd* (1992) 7 A.C.S.R. 365; *Covacich v Riordan* [1994] N.Z.L.R. 502, where the designated triggering event was insolvency, i.e. the advent of a state of insolvency as opposed to a subsequent formal insolvency proceeding such as liquidation. Note that these lines of authority are inapplicable in Australia and New Zealand themselves following the New Zealand Personal Property Securities Act 1999 and the Australian Personal Property Securities Act 2009.

[281] See paras 4–59 et seq., below.

[282] See paras 5–51 et seq., below. See also para.4–32, above.

[283] See para.5–68, below.

[284] Para.4–56, above. See also paras 5–44 et seq., below.

the charge to attach if the debtor committed a breach of any of its covenants to the debenture holder or to any other secured creditor. The length and detail of present-day covenants are such that it is quite easy for the debtor to commit a purely technical breach without either party being aware of the fact. Some trivial default, such as the delay of a day in furnishing information or documents required to be furnished by a given date, may bring down the pack of cards by causing the charge to crystallise, despite the fact that the company is a profitable, soundly managed enterprise. The debenture holder, having discovered the occurrence of the crystallising event, then has the choice of actively reversing the crystallisation or of tacitly ignoring it by allowing normal trading to continue. In either event, the charge would become de-crystallised, by agreement or estoppel.[285]

If this were all, the debenture holder's advisers might still feel that no harm had been done. On the contrary, their client is surely getting the best of both worlds. He relies on the crystallisation clause where it suits him and ignores it where it does not. If only life were so simple! But the legal battlefield is strewn with the corpses of those who wanted the facility of saying one thing and doing another, of blowing hot one minute and cold the next. One of the most important concerns of the legal draftsman should be to see that his documents correspond to what the parties intend to do. It is bad drafting and dangerous practice to provide for automatic crystallisation on the assumption that if it proves inconvenient it can be ignored on the day. The tacit waiver of an automatic crystallisation clause may well have a much more profound effect than to de-crystallise the charge; it may lead the court to conclude that the whole clause should be ignored as not truly reflecting the intention of the parties. Put another way, no amount of legal language to the effect that waiver on one occasion is not to constitute waiver on other occasions will prevent the court from ruling, in a proper case, that if one crystallising event is simply disregarded the parties ought not to be taken too seriously in their specification of other crystallising events.

4–58

Interpretation of automatic and semi-automatic crystallisation clauses

One way of limiting the operation of such clauses is for them to be strictly interpreted, so that they will only operate to crystallise a charge when the legal effect of this is clearly intended by the parties. The courts in a number of jurisdictions have approved this approach.[286] This section will consider how such strict interpretation could operate in practice, and the extent to which this can ameliorate the problem of overkill discussed in the last section.

4–59

There are various consequences of the approach that crystallisation clauses should be strictly interpreted. One is that the occurrence of the designated event must be designated with sufficient certainty to be capable of being given legal

---

[285] See further para.4–62, below.
[286] *Government Stock Investment Co v Manila Railway Co* [1895] 2 Ch. 551, 561; *Re Brightlife Ltd* [1987] Ch. 200, 213; *Fire Nymph Products Ltd v Heating Centre Pty Ltd* (1992) 7 A.C.S.R. 365, 371; *Re Sperrin Textiles* [1992] NI 323, 331; *Covacich v Riordan* [1995] 2 N.Z.L.R. 502, 507; cf. *Deputy Commissioner of Taxation v Horsburgh* [1984] V.R. 773.

effect.[287] Another is that the clause providing for crystallisation must actually have that effect, in the context of the entire charge agreement, properly interpreted. The two English cases in which a notice pursuant to a clause providing for crystallisation by notice has been held to be effective are *Re Woodroffes (Musical Instruments) Ltd*[288] and in *Re Brightlife Ltd*.[289] In the former, it was conceded that the notice had the effect of crystallising the charge. In the latter, the charge agreement provided that the chargee could serve a notice crystallising the charge (cl.3(B)), and also a notice requiring a legal assignment of debts subject to the charge (cl.13): the chargee did both. Hoffmann J. appears to have held, without any consideration of the actual contractual effect of that notice, that the service of the crystallisation notice was enough to crystallise the charge. He then considered the effect of the service of the notice under cl.13 separately,[290] holding that this did also have the same effect since "[t]he company's obligation to execute an assignment removed that freedom to deal with the debts which made the charge float". Thus, to this limited extent, the English courts have held that, if the parties agree that the service of a notice will crystallise the charge, this agreement should be effective without examination of the provisions in the contract (if any) as to the actual effect of that notice.

4–60   A very different approach has recently been taken by the Irish High Court.[291] Here, the judge took the view that the provisions in the charge agreement as to the rights and obligations of the parties after the service of the notice (properly construed) must be consistent with the existence of the fixed charge, that is, the chargor must not have the right to deal with the charged assets.[292] The court used the same technique as that used to characterise a charge "as created": the "two stage" test articulated in *Agnew v Commissioners of Inland Revenue*.[293] Thus, first, the rights and obligations of the parties after the service of the notice were analysed, without regard to the label of "conversion into a first fixed charge" stated in the charge agreement.[294] The High Court held that, since there were no express restrictions on the chargor's dealing powers over the charge assets after the service of the notice, and since the express obligation to "carry on and conduct its business in a proper and efficient manner" continued to apply, there was no intention that the company should be held to be restricted in its use of or

---

[287] *Covacich v Riordan* [1994] 2 N.Z.L.R. 502.

[288] *Re Woodroffes (Musical Instruments) Ltd* [1985] 2 All E.R. 908.

[289] *Re Brightlife Ltd* [1987] Ch. 200.

[290] He said (at 215) "Although my decision that the notice under cl.3(B) crystallised the charge makes it unnecessary for me to decide whether the notice under cl.13 did so in respect of the book debts, I will add for the sake of completeness that in my judgment it did".

[291] *Re JD Brian Ltd (In Liquidation)* [2011] IEHC 283. This was a supplementary judgment to that in [2011] IEHC 113. The first judgment decided that preferential creditors had priority under the relevant statutory provision if the charge was floating as created and therefore the effect of the clause was irrelevant. Since the decision was to be appealed to the Supreme Court of Ireland, the judge gave a supplementary judgment on the question of whether the clause did crystallise the charge, so that all issues could be decided by the Supreme Court together. No appeal to the Supreme Court has yet been heard.

[292] See above in relation to the characterisation of a charge as fixed or floating.

[293] *Agnew v Commissioners of Inland Revenue* [2001] 2 A.C. 710, per Lord Millett at [32]. See para.4–05, above.

[294] *Re JD Brian Ltd (In Liquidation)* [2011] IEHC 283 at [13]–[16]. As in *Spectrum (Re Spectrum Plus Ltd* [2005] UKHL 41 [119]) the argument that the court could imply restrictions on the chargor's management powers from the label "fixed charge" was rejected.

powers over the charged property. Therefore, applying the second part of the test, the proper legal analysis was that the charge did not become fixed but remained floating, notwithstanding the semi-automatic crystallisation clause.[295] This case is not binding on the English courts, and it is important to consider whether the same approach would be followed here.

Although such limited direct authority as there is in English law does not necessarily support the Irish approach, more generally the approach to construction of charge agreements in the *Agnew* and *Spectrum* decisions is very similar. Further, if it were necessary to spell out the consequences of crystallisation expressly in a charge agreement, draftsmen would have every incentive not to draw the triggering net too widely, and to restrict automatic crystallisation to those events which are of such significance that, if one of them occurs, the creditor will almost inevitably want the company's powers of management to end, and to specify other less important events as entitling the debenture holder to intervene—by taking possession or by appointing a receiver—or to crystallise by notice if he so chooses. Further flexibility can be achieved by a suitably drafted clause providing for partial crystallisation of the charge. Thus, the Irish approach is to be preferred.

Partial crystallisation

It is open to the parties to a debenture to stipulate that the charge shall attach only to part of the assets comprising the security. There is no case bearing on the efficacy of automatic partial crystallisation, but in principle there can be no objection to it, for as previously stated, attachment of the security interest is purely the concern of chargor and chargee. Dr Gough has ingeniously suggested the use of partial crystallisation as a method of avoiding undesirable overkill. The charge would provide that if any particular asset was placed in jeopardy, e.g. through attempted mortgage or execution, the charge would crystallise as regards that asset but continue to float over the other assets of the debtor company.[296] Alternatively, though less effectively, the debenture could simple empower the debenture holder to intervene in relation to the asset in question, i.e. the partial crystallisation would not be automatic but would require some active step by the debenture such as the taking of possession, or the appointment of a receiver of the asset.

If the debenture makes no provision for partial crystallisation, the debenture holder is not entitled to appoint a receiver of part only of the assets comprised in the floating charge.[297]

4–61

---

[295] *Re JD Brian Ltd (In Liquidation)* [2011] IEHC 283 at [19].
[296] Gough, *Company Charges* (1996), pp.168 et seq., 401 et seq. The advice has clearly been heeded by draftsmen: the semi-automatic crystallisation clause in the *JD Brian* case provided for a notice in relation to "all the property, assets and rights for the time being subject to the said floating charge or over so much of the same as is specified in the notice".
[297] See para.4–49, above.

5. DE-CRYSTALLISATION AND RE-CRYSTALLISATION

De-crystallisation (refloatation)

4–62   Can crystallisation be reversed so as to cause the charge to float again over the assets? There is no authority on the point, and it is in principle possible for the debenture holder to agree that the charge should "refloat", that is, to restore the company's management powers. This is different from merely allowing the company to dispose of specific assets free from the charge, which, of course, a debenture holder can do whether the charge is a fixed charge or a crystallised floating charge.

There are a number of situations in which "decrystallisation" may occur. If the charge agreement is drafted in such a way that automatic crystallisation is triggered by a relatively minor event,[298] the debtor company may continue to dispose of the charged assets in the ordinary course of business. If the debenture holder stands by and allows the debtor to do this, it may be treated as waiving the effect of crystallisation and refloating the charge. There is very little authority on this point. The cases sometimes cited in support of waivers are hardly definitive. In *Campbell v Mount*[299] Master Burley of the Supreme Court of South Australia took the view that despite a default in payment which, under the terms of the charge, would have rendered it "enforceable", the breach was waived as the creditor allowed the company to carry on in business. It is not clear whether this meant that the charge never crystallised (because action by the debenture holder and not just mere default was required to crystallise the charge) or whether the crystallisation rather than just the breach was waived. The former explanation seems more likely in the light of the decision, on appeal, of the Supreme Court of South Australia[300] where it was assumed that despite the fact that the creditor permitted the company to trade after default, the charge did not crystallise until the company was wound up (or, per Debelle J.) on the appointment of the provisional liquidator, pursuant to the terms of the charge. The New Zealand case of *Covacich v Riordan*[301] is in fact authority for a much more surprising proposition: that after crystallisation a debenture holder can "allow constant dispositions of charged trading assets" without this having any effect on the fixed nature of the crystallised charge. It is very unlikely, in the light of the decision in *Spectrum*, that an English court would take this view.

The discussion so far presupposes that the chargee is aware of the crystallising event. A party cannot be held to have waived the effect of an event of which it had no knowledge. It is possible for crystallisation to occur without the knowledge of the chargee or, indeed, of either party, as where the relevant crystallising event is the advent of insolvency, the chargee is unaware of this and the chargor honestly believes that it is still solvent. In such a case the crystallisation remains effective as between the parties but the chargee may be estopped from asserting its rights against third parties acquiring an interest in the

---

[298] See para.4–57, above on the dangers of overkill in automatic crystallisation clauses.
[299] *Campbell v Mount* (1995) 123 F.L.R. 403, 407.
[300] Sub nom. *Re Fresjac Property Ltd* (1995) 95 S.A.S.R. 334.
[301] *Covacich v Riordan* [1994] 2 N.Z.L.R. 502.

charged assets in good faith and without notice of the crystallisation.[302] To avoid the results of such crystallisation, the parties may include a "decrystallisation" clause in the charge agreement, whereby the charge can be decrystallised by notice[303] or automatically on the occurrence of specified events.

The effect of decrystallisation is unclear. On one view, the decrystallised charge is exactly the same charge as the crystallised charge, on the basis that the incidents of the charge are for the parties to determine, and that the nature of the charge is matter of agreement.[304] On this view, no new charge is created and so no fresh registration under s.859A of the Companies Act 2006 is required. On another view, decrystallisation can only take effect by releasing the assets from the crystallised charge and the creation of a new floating charge.[305] This result has the drawback that the new charge might require fresh registration[306] and that the date of creation of the charge is brought forward.[307] It is difficult to know what view a court would adopt. It has been made clear by the courts[308] that the incidents of a fixed or floating charge are not just a matter of freedom of contract between the parties. Further, while the view that decrystallisation is just a matter of restoring powers of management to the chargor is consistent with the view that a floating charge is the same as a fixed charge, only defeasible, or overreachable, or with a license to deal, it is less easy to reconcile it with a view that on crystallisation the nature of the charge changes, so that it becomes a fixed charge on specific assets rather than an interest in a fund, or not a proprietary interest at all.[309]

4–63

If a crystallised charge can decrystallise, in theory the same could happen in relation to a charge which was created a fixed charge, for example, by the chargee allowing blanket withdrawals from a blocked bank account[310] or otherwise ignoring breach of agreed restrictions.[311] If the effect of this was that the resulting charge was the same charge as the original charge, it would severely undermine the statutory provisions for the priority of preferential creditors and the prescribed part, since such a charge would have all the advantages of a floating charge, and yet would not be a floating charge "as created" within the meaning of s.251 of the Insolvency Act 1986. In this situation, at least, the "decrysallisation" is likely to have the effect of creating a new floating charge.

---

[302] See para.5–51, below.

[303] See *Encyclopaedia of Forms and Precedents*, Vol.4 (1) Banking 576.

[304] This was the view expressed in the first three editions of this book, and also in Gough, *Company Charges* (1996), pp.404–406.

[305] R. Grantham, "Refloating a floating charge" [1997] C.F.I.L.R. 53; Tan, "Crystallisation, De-crystallisation and the Convertability of charges" [1998] C.F.I.L.R. 41. See also Beale, Bridge, Gullifer and Lomnicka, *The Law of Security and Title-Based Financing* (2012), paras 6.89–6.91.

[306] Although it is hard to see why this is required as a matter of policy.

[307] This might have adverse affects on priority, see Ch.5, below and it might mean that the charge ceases to be a charge created before September 15, 2003, so that the provisions of the Enterprise Act 2002 in relation to the "prescribed part" and the abolition of the right to appoint an administrative receiver apply.

[308] Both the Privy Council in *Agnew* and the House of Lords in *Spectrum*.

[309] Grantham, "Refloating a floating charge" [1997] C.F.I.L.R. 53, 63; Beale, Bridge, Gullifer and Lomnicka, *The Law of Security and Title-Based Financing* (2012), para.6.89. For discussion of the theories of the floating charge see paras 4–03 and 4–06, above.

[310] See para.4–21, above.

[311] See para.4–23, above.

4–64   Whatever the effect of decrystallisation, there is, of course, no objection to the resulting floating charge crystallising in due course, which will be necessary for its enforcement.

6.   ENFORCEMENT OF THE SECURITY

4–65   On the debtor company's default, the holder of a floating charge has all the remedies conferred by the terms of the debenture creating the floating charge. These will typically include the power to take possession of the charged assets, to sell them and to appoint a receiver,[312] or, in recent charges, an administrator.[313] Where a debenture is made by deed and the charge has crystallised the chargee has a statutory power to sell or to appoint a receiver,[314] and even in the case of a debenture not made by deed he can apply to the court for an order for sale or for the appointment of a receiver. But unless the debenture creates a mortgage or entitles the chargee to reinforce his charge by calling for a mortgage the holder has no power, even after crystallisation, to take possession unless so provided by the debenture, nor may he apply for foreclosure, this being a remedy limited to mortgagees, by virtue of their security ownership.[315] The few cases[316] in which the debenture holder under a debenture creating a floating charge has been held entitled to a foreclosure order are probably explained by a failure in those cases to address the issue of the distinction between a charge and a mortgage, which can be very fine and which is rarely addressed by the courts.

7.   THE FUTURE OF THE FLOATING CHARGE

4–66   From its early days the floating charge has generated intense hostility because of its potentially all-embracing scope and its perceived unfairness to ordinary trade creditors.[317] Legislation has sought to address this in various ways, for example, by making the floating charge a distinct registrable category[318] (the categories have now been abolished under the 2013 reforms[319]) by granting priority to

---

[312] Although this will be ineffective in relation to the appointment of an administrative receiver if the charge is created after September 15, 2003 and does not fall within the exceptions in ss.72B–72GA of the Insolvency Act 1986. However, such a power would mean that the charge would be a qualifying floating charge so that the chargeholder could appoint an administrator out of court, para.14(2)(c) Sch.B1 to the Insolvency Act 1986, provided that the holder has security over the whole or substantially the whole of the debtor's property.

[313] Such a power would also make the charge a qualifying floating charge so that the holder could appoint an administrator out of court, para.14(2)(b) Sch.B1 to the Insolvency Act 1986, provided that the holder has security over the whole or substantially the whole of the debtor's property. An alternative formulation would be to state that para.14 applied to the floating charge.

[314] Law of Property Act 1925 ss.101(1), 205(1)(xvi). But a statutory receiver has limited powers, which do not include the management of the company.

[315] See para.1–55, fn.238, above.

[316] *Sadler v Worley* [1894] 2 Ch. 170; *Re Continental Oxygen Co* [1897] 1 Ch. 511; *Re Carshalton Park Ltd* [1908] 2 Ch. 62, 67; *Re Gregory Love & Co* [1916] 1 Ch. 203, 209. See also Gough, *Company Charges* (1996), pp.129–130.

[317] See, for example, *Re London Pressed Hinge Co Ltd* [1905] 1 Ch. 576, per Buckley J. at 583.

[318] Companies Act 2006 s.860(7)(g).

[319] See para.2–19, above.

preferential creditors[320] and making the prescribed part available for unsecured creditors,[321] by defining a floating charge as one which as created is a floating charge,[322] and by providing a special ground of avoidance of floating charges in winding-up which is stricter than for fixed charges.[323] Recently there has been a further assault in that one of the advantages of a floating charge, namely the ability of the holder to appoint an administrative receiver,[324] has been substantially reduced,[325] although the floating chargee is given the right to appoint an administrator out of court.[326] Where an administrator is appointed, he can dispose of floating charge assets without the leave of the court,[327] and payment of an administrator's (or liquidator's) expenses is top-sliced out of assets which fall within a floating charge.[328] The floating charge also has a weak priority position vis-à-vis other secured creditors, since the devices of a negative pledge clause and automatic crystallisation are only of limited effect in the protection of the chargeholder's priority. The decisions in *Agnew* and *Spectrum*, which mean that it is very hard to create an effective fixed charge over debts, have not lead to a growth in floating charge lending, but to a growth in receivables financing.[329]

Hand-in-hand with the policy objections to some aspects of the floating charge has come the growing realisation that, however brilliant the conception and however useful the floating charge as a financing tool, it has become so overladen with case law and doctrine that it is now a subject of excessive complexity—as will have become apparent even from the relatively brief treatment in the present chapter—and that the desired results can be achieved much more simply by treating all charges, even if expressed as floating charges, as fixed security interests and laying down a priority rule to protect those to whom the company sells or charges assets in the ordinary course of business.[330] The floating charge owes nothing to statute; it is the pure creation of equity judges of the nineteenth century. Its success has been remarkable, but judge-made law, which is necessarily a patchwork of large numbers of individual cases each influenced by its own particular facts, can no longer serve as a substitute for structured personal property security legislation of the kind enacted throughout the US and Canada,

---

[320] Insolvency Act 1986 ss.40 and 175; Companies Act 2006 s.754.

[321] Insolvency Act 1986 s.176A.

[322] Insolvency Act s.251. This has the effect of negating the priority of a crystallised floating charge over post-crystallisation preferential debts.

[323] Insolvency Act 1986 s.245. See Goode, *Principles of Corporate Insolvency Law* (2011), paras 13–112 et seq.

[324] See para.4–45, above.

[325] See para.1–01, above.

[326] Insolvency Act 1986 para.14 Sch.B1. The company and the directors also have this right (para.22 Sch.B1) and there is some evidence that this procedure is increasingly being used, although often at the instigation of the floating charge holder, see Frisby, "Report in Insolvency Outcomes" prepared for the Insolvency Service, June 2006.

[327] Insolvency Act 1986 para.70 Sch.B1.

[328] Insolvency Act 1986 para.99 Sch.B1, Insolvency Act 1986 s.176ZA.

[329] Armour, "Shall we redistribute in insolvency?" in *Company Charges: Spectrum and Beyond* (2006), p.204; Frisby, "Report in Insolvency Outcomes" prepared for the Insolvency Service, June 2006.

[330] See R. Goode, "The Exodus of the Floating Charge" in D. Feldman and F. Meisel (eds), *Corporate and Commercial Law: Modern Developments* (London: Informa UK Ltd, 1996), Ch.10.

and more recently in New Zealand, and in Australia.[331] However, the project of the Law Commission of England and Wales on registration of company charges[332] looks unlikely to lead to legislative reform in the near future.[333]

---

[331] New Zealand Personal Property Securities Act 1999 and the Australian Personal Property Securities Act 2009.

[332] Law Commission, *Company Security Interests*, Law Com No.296 (2005).

[333] See para.2–33, above.

CHAPTER 5

Fixed and Floating Charges: Some Problems of Priority

1. INTRODUCTION

The holder of a security interest may well find himself in competition with others claiming rights in the collateral. The competitor may be an outright buyer, another secured creditor, an execution creditor, a landlord or other person claiming a right to distrain on the collateral, a liquidator seeking to invalidate the security interest and thereby claim the collateral for the benefit of the general body of creditors, or some other contender for superior rights. The considerations which lead to the taking of security in the first place[1] also apply to the priority of the interest taken. The primary concern, as before, is to provide the secured creditor with safeguards against the debtor's insolvency. If it were not for insolvency, the creditor would, sooner or later, recover his money with or without security and regardless of the ranking of any security taken. It is the risk of the debtor's insolvency that is the prime factor in the decision to take security, but the value of the security interest depends upon its priority. This does not, of course, mean that second, or even third, mortgages or charges have no value, merely that each successive mortgagee or chargee must be satisfied that after giving the prior security interests the debtor retains sufficient equity in the asset to provide the assurance each junior incumbrancer requires. However, a first mortgage is obviously superior to a second, not only because the first mortgagee has the primary claim on the asset but also because priority gives him control in the event that the debtor gets into financial difficulties. This control used to be at its most visible when a creditor holding a floating charge covering, with any fixed charges, the whole or substantially the whole of a debtor company's property appointed an administrative receiver to run the business, where possible sell it as a going concern either directly or through a hive-down[2] and pay off his debenture holders.[3] The creditor in a similar position now has the ability to appoint an

5–01

---

[1] See para.1–01, above.

[2] A procedure by which some or all of the assets of the company are sold, without transfer of the liabilities, to a specially formed subsidiary which is controlled by the receiver and which as a clean company free of debt may be able to trade profitably with a view to its sale, the proceeds flowing back to the company in payment of the price for the transferred assets. See generally Lightman and Moss, *The Law of Receivers and Administrators of Companies*, 5th edn (London: Sweet & Maxwell/ Thomson Reuters, 2011), paras 11–081 et seq.

[3] The receiver also has a duty to discharge preferential debts from the proceeds of assets subject to a floating charge to the extent that the company's free assets are not sufficient for the purpose. See para.5–68, below. For the near-demise of administrative receivership, see para.4–09, above.

administrator out of court, which gives less but still significant control.[4] Further, the holder of a first fixed charge or mortgage over a particular asset can still appoint a receiver[5] or enforce its security interest by sale or other means.[6] It is in the priority stakes that perfection of a security interest[7] acquires significance. Perfection does not guarantee priority, but an unperfected security interest will almost always be subordinated to or displaced by competing interests and by unsecured creditors in the debtor's bankruptcy or winding up.

The subject of priorities is of great complexity because English law has never developed a coherent legal structure for the ordering of competing interests. The common law adopted a straightforward first-in-time principle. The development of equitable ownership and security interests brought in its train a number of refinements, such as the relationship between an equitable interest and a subsequent legal title, priority as between competing equitable interests, including interests in debts and other intangibles, and the concepts of inferred and constructive notice of an interest. The introduction of a variety of statutory registration systems, each with its own priority rules and its own sanctions for failure to register, added to the complexity, and this has been exacerbated by the dual perfection requirements imposed by s.859A of the Companies Act 2006 and statutory provisions regulating the various specialist registers.[8] The courts have also had to consider the extent to which registration of a charge constitutes constructive notice of the existence of the charge and of its provisions. The result is an amalgam of common law rules and statutory provisions many of which lack any rational policy or responsiveness to modern commercial and financial requirements and by their complexity add significantly to transaction costs.

5–02   That this state of affairs continues to be tolerated in the 21st century, when the US and Canada have for many years had highly developed, market-responsive legislation which has worked[9] and when successive government reports have recommended the adoption of similar legislation in this country,[10] is a shocking indictment of the indifference of successive governments to the modernisation of our commercial law. It is, furthermore, very unfortunate that the work of the Law Commission on registration of company charges,[11] which the Law Commission rightly concluded could not be considered in isolation from general issues of perfection and priorities, led to no legislative response in the Companies Act 2006, and that the reforms introduced in April 2013[12] were very limited in scope, and did not address issues of priority. It is therefore necessary to examine the

---

[4] See para.4–40, above.

[5] Pursuant to a power in the security agreement, or, if the agreement is by deed, under the power in Law of Property Act 1925 s.101.

[6] Either pursuant to an express power in the agreement or, again if the agreement is by deed, under the power in Law of Property Act s.101. Once the underlying obligation has become due, a mortgagee also has a power of sale implied by law, *Re Morritt* (1886) L.R. 18 QBD 222, 233; *Deverges v Sandeman, Clark & Co* [1902] 1 Ch. 579, 588–589.

[7] See paras 2–16 et seq., above.

[8] See paras 2–21 and 2–32 et seq., above.

[9] And which has now been adopted in New Zealand and Australia, as well as in Jersey. See para.1–04, above.

[10] See para.1–04, fn.19, above.

[11] Law Commission, *Company Security Interests (a consultative report)*, Law Com. CP/176/2004; Law Commission, *Company Security Interests*, Law Com. No.296 (2005).

[12] See Ch.2, above.

current rules critically, and for work to continue on consideration of further reform.[13] At the outset we need to be aware of the fundamental difference between a fixed mortgage or charge and a floating charge. In relation to the subject of a fixed charge, the priority of the charge as against competing interests is governed primarily by rules of property law and equity.[14] But in the case of assets the subject of a floating charge, the power of disposition given to the company attracts rules of commercial law as well, for the company is trading in the assets comprising the security with the consent of the debenture holder, so that under the principle of authority akin to that which underlies agency law the debenture holder's security interest may be overreached by a disposition which is within the company's actual or ostensible powers of management. This does not mean that the company is the agent of the debenture holder; on the contrary, the company deals with the charged assets on its own behalf. But in so doing it is held out by the debenture holder as authorised to deal with the assets in the ordinary course of business free from the floating charge, and a third party taking without notice of any restriction of such authority is thus entitled to the act in reliance on the company's apparent powers of disposition even if the transfer to the third party is in breach of the terms of the debenture. In general, those apparent powers are limited only by the requirement that the dealing be in the ordinary course of the company's business, a requirement liberally interpreted by the courts.[15] Accordingly priority issues arising in relation to floating charges will be examined separately.

2.   PRINCIPLES OF PRIORITY AT COMMON LAW[16]

The following are the principal priority rules established at common law to regulate the priority of competing fixed interests generally.[17] The impact of legislative registration requirements on competition between fixed security interests is discussed in Section 3; and between a fixed security interest and other types of interest in Section 4; while the ranking of the floating charge is examined in Section 5.

5–03

Rule 1: nemo dat quod non habet

A person cannot in general transfer a better title than he himself possesses.

5–04

   Another formulation of the rule is that as between competing interests the first-in-time prevails. The first formulation is usually used in relation to competing legal interest in goods, the second to competing equitable interests and interests in land. The rule applies where the competing interests are both legal

---

[13] See para.2–33, above for discussion of the various reform projects that are currently in train.

[14] See below.

[15] See para.5–40, below.

[16] "Common law", as opposed to statute, is here used in its broad sense of judge-made law, including equity.

[17] For a very clear description of the principal rules, see the judgment of Millett J. in *Macmillan Inc v Bishopsgate Investment Trust Plc (No.3)* [1995] 1 W.L.R. 978 at 999 et seq.

interests and also where they are both equitable interests.[18] However, in a competition between an equitable interest and a subsequent legal interest, this rule may be overridden by r.2, below. It follows that as between competing equitable interests, the conversion of one of these into a legal interest may move the case from r.1 to r.2.

Rule 1 is subject to a number of exceptions at common law.[19]

Common law exceptions to the nemo dat rule

(1) Actual or apparent (ostensible) authority

5–05   A non-owner can sell or charge an asset if he has either actual or apparent (ostensible) authority from the owner to do so. Even if not in fact authorised to make the disposition, he will have apparent authority to do so if he has been held out by the owner as authorised to dispose; and where there is such a holding out, an innocent third party will not be bound by limitations on the power of disposal which were not known to him.[20] This principle is of particular importance in the case of the floating charge. The chargee confers on the chargor power to deal with its assets in the ordinary course of business free from the charge, but may seek to impose restrictions on the exercise of such power. The question then is what steps are necessary and sufficient to give notice of those restrictions to third parties, a matter discussed earlier.[21]

(2) Apparent ownership

5–06   Distinct from apparent authority is the concept of apparent ownership, where the owner of an asset holds out another as being the owner. This is significantly wider in its effect in that while an unauthorised disposition by an agent binds his principal only if the agent acts within the scope of his apparent authority, no such limitation applies to a disposition by a person invested with apparent ownership, for an owner needs no authority, so that the fact that the disposition is on unusual terms or not in the ordinary course of business is irrelevant except so far as it bears on the transferee's good faith and the reasonableness of his belief that the transferor was the owner.[22]

(3) Postponement of equitable interest to subsequent legal interest

5–07   An equitable interest is in certain circumstances postponed to a subsequent legal interest. See r.2, below.

---

[18] The first in time rule applies to equitable interests even when the second is taken for value and without notice of the first (*Phillips v Phillips* (1861) 4 De. G. F. & J. 208).

[19] For the statutory exceptions, see paras 5–13 et seq., below.

[20] For a detailed treatment, see *Bowstead & Reynolds on Agency*, P.G. Watts (ed.), 19th edn (London: Sweet & Maxwell/Thomson Reuters, 2010), paras 8–013 et seq. In the context of security interests, see also H. Beale, M. Bridge, L. Gullifer and E. Lomnicka, *The Law of Security and Title-Based Financing*, 2nd edn (Oxford: Oxford University Press, 2012), Ch.15.

[21] See paras 2–25 et seq., above.

[22] *Lloyds and Scottish Finance Ltd v Williamson* [1965] 1 W.L.R. 404, 410. See also *Bowstead & Reynolds on Agency* (2010), para.8–127 fn.755.

(4)   Successive assignments of choses in action

The priority of successive assignments of a debt or other chose in action is **5–08** governed by the rule in *Dearle v Hall*[23] under which an assignee who takes without notice of an earlier assignment and is the first to give notice of assignment to the debtor obtains priority over the earlier assignee.[24] The rule applies also to a contest between the holder of an equitable right to claim a debt as proceeds of his property and a subsequent purchaser or mortgagee of the same debt.[25] The statutory provisions for registration of security interest considerably reduce the impact of the rule in *Dearle v Hall* in receivables financing, for the second assignee will usually have notice of a prior security interest by virtue of its registration.[26] The rule is wholly unsuited to modern receivables financing. Over a century ago Lord Macnaghten commented: "I am inclined to think that the rule in *Dearle v Hall* has on the whole produced at least as much injustice as it has prevented".[27] The proposals of the Law Commission for registration of all assignments of receivables,[28] would have replaced the rule in *Dearle v Hall* with a much more rational system of priority based on date of registration, in relation to receivables financing.

The rule does not apply at all in relation to the assignment of registered shares in a company, since the company can neither enter a notice of assignment in its register of members[29] nor validly accept such a notice,[30] and the same applies to an assignment of dematerialised ("uncertificated") securities registered electronically in the CREST system[31]; nor does the rule apply to a contest between the

---

[23] *Dearle v Hall* (1828) 3 Russ. 1.

[24] The requirement that the later assignee be without notice of the earlier assignment, which is the so-called second limb of the rule in *Dearle v Hall*, was not in fact part of the decision in that case and was a refinement added by later cases. For a good historical account of the development of the rule see J. de Lacy, "Reflections on the Ambit of the Rule in *Dearle v Hall* and the Priority of Personal Property Assignments" (1999) 28 Anglo-Am. L.R. 87, 197.

[25] See para.5–37, below.

[26] See discussion in paras 2–25 et seq., above on what amounts to constructive notice.

[27] *Ward v Duncombe* [1893] A.C. 369 at 393. See also F. Oditah, *Legal Aspects of Receivables Financing* (London: Sweet & Maxwell, 1990), pp.140 et seq.; G. McCormack, *Secured Credit under English and American Law* (Cambridge: CUP, 2004), pp.244–245; Beale, Bridge, Gullifer and Lomnicka, *The Law of Security and Title-Based Financing* (2012), para.14.10.

[28] Law Commission, *Company Security Interests*, Law Com. No.296 (2005), Ch.4. The proposals were limited to assignments in the course of financing of trade receivables. For comment, see J. L. Yap, "Reconsidering Receivables" (2011) 32 Comp. Law. 297.

[29] Companies Act 2006 s.126, which provides that no notice of any trust, express, implied or constructive, shall be entered on the register. The assignment of shares constitutes the assignor a trustee for the assignee (*Hardoon v Belilios* [1901] 1 A.C. 118). Hence the method by which a mortgagee perfects his title is by entry on the register in place of the mortgagor, a process which is a novation, not an assignment. See para.3–14, above; para.6–38, below.

[30] *Société Générale de Paris v Walker* (1885) 11 App. Cas. 20, per Earl of Selbourne at 30–31, confirming that the rule in *Dearle v Hall* does not apply to registered shares. See also *Macmillan Inc v Bishopsgate Investment Trust Plc (No.3)* [1995] 1 W.L.R. 978, 993.

[31] Uncertificated Securities Regulations 2001 reg.23(3), which prohibits an Operator of a system from entering on its register notice of any trust, express, implied or constructive. Before he has been entered on the register a mortgagee or other transferee has a mere equitable interest, and this continues to be the case during the period between the time the transferor has been removed from the register and the time the transferee is entered on it, during which time the transferor is a trustee for the transferee (Uncertificated Securities Regulations 2001 regs 31(2) (b), 31(4)).

holder of a floating charge and a subsequent fixed chargee or assignee[32] or to the assignment of debt which by the terms of the contract creating it is non-assignable, for the debtor is then under no obligation to recognise a notice of assignment.[33] Further, the rule does not apply to a negotiable instrument, so if the holder of a bill of exchange assigns the underlying debt to A and then negotiates the bill to B, B has priority notwithstanding that A has given notice of assignment to the acceptor, for the latter is required to pay the current holder who presents the bill for payment, and no one else.[34]

Rule 2: a legal interest acquired for value and without notice overrides prior equitable interest

5–09   An equitable interest is overreached by a disposition of the legal title to a bona fide purchaser for value without notice. The principle remains unaffected by the 1925 property legislation, but the registrability of most categories of security interest in one register or another makes it difficult for a subsequent legal purchaser to claim that he took without notice. However, the concept of notice continues to give rise to difficulties, as is discussed above.[35]

The time when the subsequent purchaser is required to be without notice is not when he takes the legal title but when he makes his advance. This rule enables the holder of a later equitable interest who makes his advance without notice of the prior equitable interest to effect a *tabula in naufragio* by getting in the legal title,[36] thereby securing priority even if by the time he takes the legal title he has acquired notice of the prior equitable right.[37] But it would seem that only a fixed equitable interest can be promoted in this way, and that the interest of the holder of a floating charge is too nebulous to enable him to jump ahead of a prior fixed charge by getting in the legal title after notice of the fixed charge. The *tabula in naufragio* is not available in the case of competing assignments of a debt. A statutory assignee, despite having the legal title, is postponed to a prior equitable assignee who gave notice first, for s.136 of the Law of Property Act 1925 expressly provides that the statutory assignee is to take subject to equities, and

---

[32] See para.5–40, below.

[33] See para.3–38, above.

[34] Indeed, even if the holder of the bill assigns it while retaining the instrument, the debtor can ignore the notice of assignment, for his duty remains to the holder who presents the bill, whether the holder is the assignor or anyone else (*Bence v Shearman* [1898] 2 Ch. 582).

[35] Paras 2–25 et seq., above.

[36] Or having the best right to the legal title, as where he procures the mortgaged property to be conveyed to trustees on his behalf, *Macmillan Inc v Bishopsgate Trust Plc (No.3)* [1995] 1 .L.R. 978, 1001.

[37] *Taylor v Russell* [1892] A.C. 244; *Bailey v Barnes* [1894] 1 Ch. 25. The rule applies also to a mortgage of shares, where a creditor who takes a share certificate and executed transfer by way of equitable mortgage and makes his advance without notice of a prior equitable interest can obtain priority by registering the transfer (*Dodds v Hills* (1865) 2 H. & M. 424; which Millett J. in *Macmillan Inc v Bishopsgate Investment Trust Plc (No.3)* [1995] 1 W.L.R. 978 considered (at 1004) to be still good law despite attacks made upon it).

this includes a prior equitable interest of which the debtor has been given notice.[38] However, a statutory assignee who collects payment without notice may be able to rely on his legal title.[39]

Rule 3: a mortgagee may in certain conditions tack further advances for which he will rank in priority to a subsequent mortgagee

The common law attached great importance to the legal estate, so much so that it provided two situations in which a legal mortgagee or a person having the best right to under a mortgage could tack such advances to his initial advance and rank in priority to a subsequent mortgagee even if the mortgage was not expressed to cover further advances and even if these were not made until after the execution of the second mortgage. The first situation was where the further advances were made without notice of the second mortgage. Under the rule in *Hopkinson v Rolt*,[40] notice of the second mortgage terminated the right to tack further advances, a rule considered necessary to avoid the first mortgagee having a monopoly over the debtor's financing. The rule was applied even if the prior legal mortgagee was under an obligation to make the further advances[41]; this seems to undermine the rationale of *Hopkinson*, which was that the first mortgagee could decline to make further advances once it had notice of the second mortgage. However, if the first mortgage, as is common, includes a negative pledge clause[42] then the mortgagor will be in breach by granting a second mortgage without the consent of the first mortgagee, and this is likely to have the effect of giving the first mortgagee the right to refuse to make further advances even where it would otherwise be obliged to do so.[43] The second situation was the *tabula in naufragio*, where if a legal mortgage was granted to A followed by a mortgage to B and then a third mortgage to C, who made his advance without notice of B's mortgage, C could purchase A's interest and use the legal estate he had thereby acquired to tack his own advance in priority to B, who was thus squeezed out. In addition to these cases, any mortgagee, legal or equitable, could tack further advances if the mortgage expressly covered such advances and the mortgagee, at the time of making them, had no notice of the subsequent mortgage. As will be seen, the

5–10

---

[38] *E Pfeiffer Weinkellerei-Weineinkauf GmbH & Co v Arbuthnot Factors Ltd* [1988] 1 W.L.R. 150; *Compaq Computers Ltd v Abercorn Group Ltd* [1991] B.C.C. 484. See also *Harding Corp Ltd v Royal Bank of Canada* [1980] W.W.R. 149. This view is strongly criticised by Oditah, *Legal Aspects of Receivables Financing* (1990), para.6.15; and see also G. Tolhurst, *The Assignment of Contractual Rights* (Oxford: Hart Publishing, 2006), Ch.5, who disagrees with the premise underlying these decisions that the difference between a statutory and an equitable assignment is procedural and not substantive.

[39] A point left open by Phillips J. in *E Pfeiffer Weinkellerei-Weineinkauf GmbH & Co v Arbuthnot Factors Ltd* [1988] 1 W.L.R. 150 at 163 but conceded in *Compaq Computers Ltd v Abercorn Group Ltd* [1991] B.C.C. 484 at 500.

[40] *Hopkinson v Rolt* (1861) 9 Cas. 514.

[41] *West v Williams* [1899] 1 Ch. 132.

[42] See J. Porteous and L. Shackleton, "A question of great importance to bankers, and to the mercantile interests of the country" (2012) 7 J.I.B.F.L. 403.

[43] R. Calnan, *Taking Security, Law and Practice*, 2nd edn (London: Jordan Publishing, 2011), para.7–229.

tabula in naufragio in this context has in some contexts been abolished by statute but the other form of tacking remains, albeit modified by statute; the position, however, is unfortunately unclear.[44]

Rule 4: priority rules may be varied by agreement

5–11   The rights of a secured creditor may be subordinated or waived altogether by agreement with the party in whose favour the subordination or waiver is to be given. The priority effect of waivers and subordinations is discussed later in the present chapter.[45]

3.   THE IMPACT OF LEGISLATION

5–12   The priority rules laid down at common law have been significantly affected by legislation, which either changed the rules or, through the operation of registration systems, provided a new system of perfection and greatly reduced the number of cases in which a person could claim to be without notice of a competing interest, as well as making notice irrelevant in some cases.

Statutory exceptions to the nemo dat rule

5–13   The principle *nemo dat quod non habet*, to which, as we have seen, there were several exceptions at common law, has been further qualified by legislation designed to protect innocent transferees for value and thereby facilitate the free movement of goods in the stream of trade. Principal among these are dispositions by a mercantile agent,[46] a seller or buyer in possession[47] and a hirer or buyer holding a motor vehicle under a hire-purchase or conditional sale agreement.[48]

The effect of registration provisions on priority rules

5–14   As has been previously described, registration systems fall into two broad groups: registration of company charges under s.859A of the Companies Act 2006 and registration in specialist registers provided by special statutes, e.g. in relation to land, ships, aircraft, and intellectual property.

---

[44] See paras 5–17 et seq., below.

[45] See paras 5–59 et seq., below. As to whether a subordination agreement creates a security interest, see paras 1–84 et seq., above.

[46] Factors Act 1889 s.2.

[47] Factors Act 1889 ss.8, 9; Sale of Goods Act 1979 ss.24, 25. A disposition by a buyer holding under a conditional sale agreement falling within the Consumer Credit Act 1974 is excluded from the operation of s.8 of the Factors Act and s.25 of the Sale of Goods Act.

[48] Hire-Purchase Act 1964 ss.27–30. For detailed analyses of the common law and statutory exceptions to the *nemo dat* rule, particularly in the context of sale transactions, see *Goode on Commercial Law*, E. McKendrick (ed.), 4th edn (London: Penguin, 2010), Ch.16; *Benjamin's Sale of Goods*, M. Bridge (ed.), 8th edn (London: Sweet & Maxwell, 2010), Ch.7; M. Bridge, L. Gullifer, G.McMeel, S. Worthington, *The Law of Personal Property* (London: Sweet & Maxwell, 2013), Ch.13.

(1) Registration as notice

The effect of registration of a charge as notice of its existence varies from one **5–15** statutory system to another. Registration under s.859A of the Companies Act 1985 constitutes notice to all those who could reasonably be expected to search the register,[49] and thus reduces the ability of a subsequent incumbrancer to plead want of notice and thereby take advantage of the legal purchaser principle or the rule in *Dearle v Hall*, though it probably has little, if any, impact on the doctrine of tacking.[50] Registration of a charge of unregistered land under the Land Charges Act 1925 is deemed to constitute actual notice to all persons and for all purposes connected with the land affected.[51] The question of notice does not arise in relation to competing legal charges over registered land, where priority is determined by the order of registration irrespective of notice.[52] Equitable charges are protected by notice in the register under the Land Registration Act 2002.[53]

(2) When registration is a priority point

Registration under the Companies Act is merely a perfection requirement, not a **5–16** priority point, so that the order of registration is irrelevant, and the primary, first-in-time common law rule prevails so long as the registration is effected within the statutory 21-day period. In relation to other registers, the priority of interests registrable in other specialist registers is usually determined by the order of registration,[54] not by the order of creation. This is true, for example, of mortgages of registered land,[55] ship mortgages,[56] aircraft mortgages,[57] agricultural charges[58] and bills of sale.[59] It seems also to be true for successive charges over unregistered land, though the position remains a little less clear. Under s.97 of the Law of Property Act 1925 the priority of puisne mortgages[60] is determined by the order of registration, whereas s.4(5) of the Land Charges Act 1972 renders such a puisne mortgage void against a subsequent purchaser (including a subsequent mortgagee) unless this is registered before completion of the purchase. The combined effect of these two sections appears to be that a registered puisne mortgage takes priority over an earlier unregistered interest, and

---

[49] See para.2–31, above.

[50] See para.5–22, below.

[51] Law of Property Act 1925 s.198.

[52] Land Registration Act 2002 s.48(1).

[53] Land Registration Act 2002 s.32. This gives protection under s.29(2)(a)(i).

[54] Subject to certain rules designed to give protection for a limited period to a party who registers a priority notice or makes a re-completion search prior to registration of the security interest. See paras 5–30 et seq., below.

[55] Land Registration Act 2002 s.48. This is subject to the qualification that an equitable charge may be protected by notice in the register (s.32(3)).

[56] Merchant Shipping Act 1995 s.16(1) and Sch.1 para.8(1).

[57] Mortgaging of Aircraft Order 1972 (SI 1972/1268) art.14. Article 5 allows for the registration of a priority notice, but the intended mortgage must be completed and registered within the ensuing 14 days. In all these cases notice of the prior interest is irrelevant.

[58] Agricultural Charges Act 1928 s.8(2).

[59] Bills of Sale Act 1878 s.10.

[60] i.e. mortgages not protected by deposit of the title deeds.

also over later (registered) ones.[61] However, the position in relation to an earlier mortgage which is registered after the creation of, but not the registration of, a second mortgage is unclear. On the better view, the second mortgage has priority over the first: the registration of the first is irrelevant as it is already void vis-à-vis the second. This means that s.97 takes effect subject to s.4(5),[62] and that registration is a perfection requirement, not a priority point. To this extent registration under the Land Charges Act possesses the same characteristic as registration under the Companies Act. However, the requirements of the two systems for the preservation of priority are different. Under s.859A of the Companies Act all that the first chargee has to do is to register within the 21 days allowed[63]; under s.4(5) of the Land Charges Act he has to register before completion of the subsequent mortgage. Registration of a mortgage of a patent is largely but not entirely determinative of priority, in that a registered mortgagee will have priority over an earlier unregistered mortgage, but only if he does not have notice of it.[64] The same is true of mortgages of trade marks,[65] and probably mortgages of registered designs.[66]

Statutory changes to the rules on tacking

5–17   Section 94 of the Law of Property Act modified the existing rules for tacking of further advances, and, except in this regard, the right to tack was abolished by s.94(3). The exact scope of s.94(3) is a matter of some debate. There are two areas of uncertainty. First, the term "tack" is not defined in s.94: it clearly includes the tacking of further advances by a mortgagee,[67] but whether it includes the *tabula in naufragio* rule[68] is less clear.[69] The context of s.94 appears to indicate that the abolition only relates to the tacking of future advance (an alternative scheme for which is established by s.94(1)); however, Millett J. in

---

[61] *Megarry and Wade: Law of Real Property*, C. Harpum, S. Bridge and M. Dixon (eds), 8th edn (London: Sweet & Maxwell, 2012), paras 26–028 et seq.

[62] *Megarry and Wade: Law of Real Property* (2012), paras 26–033 et seq.

[63] The effect is that the subsequent chargee who makes a search before expiry of the 21 days allowed to the first chargee for registration and who finds nothing on the register will be postponed to the first chargee if the first chargee registers within the 21-day period, even if by then the second chargee has registered.

[64] Patents Act 1977 s.33(1). It appears from the wording of the statute that this rule applies even where the second mortgage is also not registered, cf. Beale, Bridge, Gullifer and Lomnicka, *The Law of Security and Title-Based Financing* (2012), para.14.66. A preferable rule would be that priority was by date of registration, and there are judicial comments to the effect that this is the position under the current law, see *Fraser v Oystertec Plc* [2003] EWHC 2787; [2004] F.S.R. 22 at [70], which seems to envisage registration of T2 as necessary to assert priority; and *Finecard International Ltd v Urquhart Dyke & Lord* [2005] EWHC 2481 (Ch); [2006] F.S.R. 27 where Peter Smith J. said at [15] "The purpose of that paragraph is to provide that priority as between persons who claim to have acquired the property in a patent shall be regulated by the priority according to registration".

[65] Trade Marks Act 1994 s.25(3).

[66] See Registered Designs Act 1949 s.19(4) and the discussion in Beale, Bridge, Gullifer and Lomnicka, *The Law of Security and Title-Based Financing* (2012), paras 14.72–14.76.

[67] See para.5–10, above. Note that in the Law of Property Act 1925 "mortgage" includes a charge (s.205(1)(xvi)).

[68] Para.5–09, above.

[69] See Beale, Bridge, Gullifer and Lomnicka, *The Law of Security and Title-Based Financing* (2012), para.14.90; and R. Calnan, "Reforming Priority Law" (2006) 1 J.I.B.F.L. 4.

Macmillan Inc v Bishopsgate Trust (No.3)[70] stated that the *tabula in naufragio* doctrine had been abolished "in relation to mortgages": this statement was made in the context of a discussion of mortgages of land, and he later made it clear that the doctrine still operates in relation to mortgages of shares.[71] Further, in an earlier first instance case, it was held that the doctrine had only been abolished as regards priority between mortgagees and that it still applied where one of the equitable interests was not a mortgage, but arose from rights under a specifically enforceable contract.[72] Secondly, while it is clear that s.94(3) does not apply to registered land[73] and that it covers mortgages of unregistered land,[74] opinion is divided as to whether it covers mortgages of personalty.[75] Subssections 94(2) and (4) indicate that the section only relates to mortgages of land; there are, however, good policy reasons for s.94 to cover mortgages of personalty as well, and, since this is a possible interpretation on the wording of s.94(3), it is submitted that this is the better view.[76]

(1) Mortgages of unregistered land

Where a mortgage[77] of unregistered land is taken to secure further advances— **5–18** the typical case is a mortgage to secure a bank current account—s.94(1) of the Law of Property Act 1925 gives the mortgagee the right to make further advances ranking in priority to subsequent mortgages, legal or equitable, in three cases:

(a) where an arrangement has been made to that effect with the subsequent mortgagees;
(b) where the prior mortgagee had no notice of such subsequent mortgage at the time he made the further advance; and
(c) where the mortgage imposes on him an obligation to make such further advances.

---

[70] *Macmillan Inc v Bishopsgate Trust (No.3)* [1995] 1 W.L.R. 978, 1002.

[71] Since mortgages of shares were not at that time required to be registered, it is possible for a second equitable mortgagee to acquire his mortgage without constructive notice of the first equitable mortgage. The present position is that a mortgage over shares would be registrable unless it was a security financial collateral arrangement under the FCARs, which is reasonably likely unless it was a floating charge, see para.6–38, below.

[72] *McCarthy & Stone Ltd v Julian S Hodge & Co Ltd* [1971] 2 All E.R. 973, 981. See also M. Hapgood (ed.), *Paget's Law of Banking*, 13th edn (London: Butterworths Law, 2007), para.32.36.

[73] Law of Property Act 1925 s.94(4). Tacking in relation to mortgages of registered land is governed by s.49 of the Land Registration Act 2002, which introduces significant changes.

[74] Calnan, *Taking Security, Law and Practice* (2011), paras 7–68 to 7–70 is of the view that is does not; G. McCormack, "Priority of Charges and Registration" (1994) J.B.L. 587 assumes that it does, and this assumption also seems to be made by David Richards J. in *Re Rayford Homes Ltd* [2011] EWHC 1948 (Ch) at [31].

[75] Calnan, *Taking Security, Law and Practice* (2011), paras 7–68 to 7–70 is of the view that is does not; G. McCormack, "Priority of Charges and Registration" (1994) J.B.L. 587 assumes that it does, and this assumption also seems to be made by David Richards J. in *Re Rayford Homes Ltd* [2011] EWHC 1948 (Ch) at [31].

[76] See Beale, Bridge, Gullifer and Lomnicka, *The Law of Security and Title-Based Financing* (2012) para.14.90; and Porteous and Shackleton, "A question of great importance to bankers, and to the mercantile interests of the country" (2012) 7 J.I.B.F.L. 403.

[77] This includes a charge (Law of Property Act 1925 s.205(1)(xvi)).

Hence a mortgagee who makes a further advance without notice of the subsequent mortgage is now given priority even if he is only an equitable mortgagee and the mortgage is not expressed to secure further advances. But unless the prior mortgagee makes the further advance pursuant to an arrangement with the subsequent mortgagee or alternatively is committed by the terms of the prior mortgage to make the further advance, the prior mortgagee will be postponed to the subsequent mortgagee if he makes the further advance after notice of the second mortgage. If the legislation had stopped at this point, banks operating current accounts would have been in considerable difficulty, for registration of the second mortgage constitutes actual notice,[78] and it is obviously impracticable for the bank to make a search every time the mortgagor draws on his account and before honouring such drawing. To deal with this, s.94(2) of the Law of Property Act provides that a mortgagee is not deemed to have notice of a mortgage merely by reason that it was registered as a land charge if it was not so registered at the time when the original mortgage was created or when the last search (if any) by the prior mortgagee was made, whichever last happened. The correct sequence for the prior mortgagee to adopt is: take mortgage, search, make initial advance. To make a search and then take the mortgage and make the initial advance is not safe, for the second mortgagee might register between the time of the search and the time of the first mortgage.

5–19   It should be borne in mind that s.94 only gives protection in relation to further advances. Thus if the mortgagor grants a mortgage to M1 to secure a current account and before drawing on the account mortgages the same property to M2, who registers his mortgage, and M1 then makes his initial advance, then under the rule in *Hopkinson v Rolt*[79] he will be postponed to M2 as regards that advance even if not having actual notice of the second mortgage and even if committed to make the advance,[80] though as to any further advances he would enjoy the protection of s.94. The moral for M1 is to search before making his initial advance.

The first mortgagee should be careful to ensure that he reserves in his mortgage instrument the right to exclude the rule in *Clayton's Case*,[81] e.g. by ruling off the debtor's account upon receiving notice of a subsequent mortgage and crediting later payments to a new account. If the creditor fails to do this, such payments will, under the rule in *Clayton's Case*, be applied in reduction of the earlier indebtedness first, thus reducing that part of the debt as regards which the mortgagee has priority over the later mortgage. For example, M1 takes a charge to secure a current account and has advanced £1,000 when he receives notice of a second charge in favour of M2. Subsequently the debtor pays £800 into his account, and later draws £800 out of it. The debit balance is £1,000, the figure at which it stood when M1 received notice of M2's charge, but the effect of *Clayton's Case* is to reduce the pre-notice indebtedness to M1 to £200, leaving the post-notice advance of £800 postponed to M2's charge. A line across the account is all that is necessary to prevent this unfortunate occurrence. It was the failure of Barclays Bank to draw that line which led to their having to meet

---

[78] Law of Property Act 1925 s.198. For the effect of registration under s.859A of the Companies Act 2006, see para.5–22, below.

[79] *Hopkinson v Rolt* (1861) 9 H.L.C. 514. See para.5–10, above.

[80] On which point the rule surely deserves reconsideration by the House of Lords.

[81] *Devaynes v Noble, Clayton's Case* (1816) 1 Mer. 572.

almost the whole of the plaintiff's claim in the *Siebe Gorman* case,[82] despite having won the argument on the legal issues raised in that case.

(2) Mortgages of registered land

Section 94 of the Law of Property Act 1925 does not apply to mortgages of registered land,[83] and the position is governed by s.49 of the Land Registration Act 2002,[84] which provides that the proprietor of a registered charge may only make a further advance ranking in priority to a subsequent charge if:

5–20

(a)   he has not received from the subsequent chargee notice of the creation of the subsequent charge;

(b)   the further advance is made pursuant to an obligation which was entered in the register at the time of creation of the subsequent charge;

(c)   the parties to the prior charge have agreed a maximum amount for which the charge is security and such agreement was entered in the register at the time of creation of the subsequent charge; or

(d)   there is agreement with the subsequent chargee.

Limb (c) represents a marked departure from the rule in *Hopkinson v Rolt* in that it applies even if the further advance is made after notice of the subsequent charge and is entirely voluntary. Effectively this enables the first chargee to obtain a monopoly of the debtor's non-purchase-money financing[85] by the simple device of specifying a maximum sum well beyond any amount that the chargee is likely to lend or the asset given in security is likely to be worth. This seems a retrograde step.[86]

(3) Mortgages of personalty

Where the mortgage relates to pure personalty, such as goods or receivables, the mortgagee's right to tack further advances is probably governed by s.94(1) of the Law of Property Act 1925,[87] but the provisions of s.94(2) as to the effect of registration as a land charge do not, of course, apply, and notice of the subsequent mortgage, whether actual of constructive,[88] puts an end to the right to tack except

5–21

---

[82] *Siebe Gorman & Co Ltd v Barclays Bank Ltd* [1979] 2 Lloyd's Rep. 142.

[83] Law of Property Act 1925 s.94(4).

[84] Land Registration Act 2002 Sch.13.

[85] A purchase-money security interest may enjoy favoured treatment. See paras 5–63 et seq., below.

[86] It has received criticism from other quarters. See, for example, *Emmet and Farrand on Title, Bulletin No. 21*, July 2002 (Conv.), p.6; and *Paget's Law of Banking* (2007), para.32.33. The Law Commission acknowledged these reservations in its paper which led to the 2002 Act, but stressed that this method was only one option, which might be useful in some circumstances, such as where a development was to be financed by a series of agreed advances. The method is used in some other countries, including Sweden (see Law Commission, *Land Registration for the Twenty-First Century*, Law Com. No.271 (2001) para.7.35).

[87] See para.5–18, above. If it is not governed by that section, then the rule in *Hopkinson v Rolt* applies, as discussed in para.5–10, above.

[88] For the effect of registration under s.859A of the Companies Act 2006, see paras 2–23 et seq., above.

where the further advance is made by arrangement with the subsequent mortgagee or the first mortgagee is obliged to make it by the terms of the mortgage.

(4) Registration under the Companies Act 2006

5–22   Whilst s.94 of the Law of Property Act 1925 prevents registration of a land charge from constituting notice for the purpose of tacking, no such provision has been enacted in relation to the effect of registration in the Companies Registry of a charge (whether on land or on other assets) of a charge given by a company, pursuant to s.859A of the Companies Act 1985. If such registration were to constitute notice to a prior mortgagee under a mortgage securing a current account it would destroy the efficacy of s.94(1), a conclusion any court would be reluctant to reach. There is in fact nothing in the Companies Act itself which makes registration equivalent to notice; such an effect, where it occurs at all, results from the equitable doctrine of constructive notice which (inter alia) fixes a party with notice of facts which he would have discovered if he had made usual and proper enquiries. Registration in a public register may constitute constructive notice of matters recorded in the register,[89] but as has been submitted earlier[90] this is the case only where the circumstances are such that the party in question could reasonably have been expected to search. Having regard to the impracticability of searches by banks prior to each drawing by the mortgagor, and to the express provisions of s.94 of the Law of Property Act designed specifically to deal with the problem, it seems clear that registration under s.859A of the Companies Act does not constitute notice sufficient to put an end to the prior mortgagee's right to tack.[91]

(5) The restrictions on tacking considered

5–23   The uncertainty about the scope of s.94(3)[92] is very unfortunate, and could usefully be clarified. It would, though, be worth considering the whole area. The *tabula in naufragio* rule is inconsistent with the general principle that a person taking an interest in an asset, who has notice of an earlier interest in the same asset, cannot have priority over that earlier interest,[93] and should be abolished completely so that the holder of a legal interest only has priority over an equitable interest if he had no notice of it at the time he took his legal interest.[94] The doctrine of tacking future advances has also been criticised,[95] with good reason, as it unduly favours the second mortgagee (particularly when combined with *Clayton's case*) and (in a situation where the rule in *Hopkinson v Rolt* applies rather than s.94) may leave the first mortgagee with the choice of breaching an

---

[89] See, for example, *Re De Leeuw* [1922] 3 Ch. 540.

[90] See para.2–31, above.

[91] See Beale, Bridge, Gullifer and Lomnicka, *The Law of Security and Title-Based Financing* (2012), para.14.87.

[92] Discussed at para.5–17, above.

[93] This principle is consistent with both the bona fide purchaser rule and the rule in *Dearle v Hall*.

[94] Calnan, "Reforming Priority Law" (2006) 1 J.I.B.F.L. 4.

[95] Calnan, "Reforming Priority Law" (2006) 1 J.I.B.F.L. 4; Calnan, *Taking Security; Law and Practice* (2011) paras 7.206 et seq.

obligation to make future advances or losing priority to a second mortgagee of whom it has notice.[96] While the doctrine might be more understandable in the context of term loans which are made in one payment (for example, for the purchase of land) it makes less sense when applied to facilities which are drawn down when required, or revolving facilities, and such lenders are obliged to take complicated steps to protect themselves.[97] The personal property security legislation introduced in the US, Canada, Australia and New Zealand abolishes tacking completely, so that a lender has priority from the date of registration in relation to all advances made, so long as the registered security agreement covers such advances.[98] One possible disadvantage to this approach is that one lender potentially has a monopoly on lending to the borrower: this is overcome by a statutory priority for purchase money security interests[99] and also, of course, by the possibility of priority agreements with later lenders.

4.   PRIORITY OF COMPETING SECURITY INTERESTS

I now turn to examine the particular case of competition among fixed security interests. This would be much easier if, as under art.9 of the Uniform Commercial Code,[100] it was possible to take the requisite steps for perfection in any order, with priority going back to the time of filing of a financing statement covering an existing or intended security interest, and filing was always a priority point, not merely a perfection requirement. Unhappily the lack of a coherent system of perfection and priority means that the outcome of a priority dispute concerning registrable interests depends very largely on the particular type of registration system that is applicable, coupled, if the charge is unregistered, with the overriding effect of s.859H of the Companies Act 2006 (where the charge is given by a company and is registrable under that Act)[101] and the company later goes into liquidation or administration. The rules discussed in Section 2, above also come into play. The number of variables thus involved makes it difficult to set out a simple set of rules. The right to tack further advances ranking in priority has already been discussed[102] and we do not need to return to it.

We should note as a preliminary that ss.859A and 859H trump all other perfection requirements in the sense that where a security interest registrable

5–24

---

[96] Porteous and Shackleton, "A question of great importance to bankers, and to the mercantile interests of the country" (2012) 7 J.I.B.F.L. 403.

[97] See Porteous and Shackleton, "A question of great importance to bankers, and to the mercantile interests of the country" (2012) 7 J.I.B.F.L. 403; Calnan, *Taking Security; Law and Practice* (2011), paras 7.221 et seq.

[98] This was for the purpose of facilitating the use of secured credit and reducing the cost of lending, see T. Jackson and A Kronman, "Secured Financing and Priorities Among Creditors" (1979) 88 Yale L.J. 1143, 1180; A. Duggan and D. Brown, *Australian Personal Property Securities Law* (Chatswood (Aust.): LexisNexis Australia, 2012), p.154; UNCITRAL, *Legislative Guide to Secured Transactions* V.A. 6(d) para.138. See also Security Interests (Jersey) Law 2013 s.33 (as amended by the Security Interests (Amendment of Law) (Jersey) Regulations 2013).

[99] See para.5–67, below.

[100] See also the various Personal Property Securities Acts in Canada, Australia and New Zealand, and the Security Interests (Jersey) Law 2012 s.29 (as amended by the Security Interests (Amendment of Law) (Jersey) Regulations 2013).

[101] See paras 2–18 et seq., above.

[102] See paras 5–10 and 5–17, above.

under s.859A is also registrable in a specialist register, any priority given by registration in the latter will be displaced if the security interest is not also registered under s.859A within the time allowed. A charge registrable under that section and not registered within 21 days or such later time as is permitted by the court is void against a liquidator or administrator and creditors.[103] For this purpose "creditors" means secured creditors,[104] execution creditors and lienees and creditors in the winding-up or administration[105]; it does not include unsecured creditors of a company that is not in winding-up or administration. A charge not registered within the 21-day period may be registered later with leave of the court,[106] which is almost invariably given unless the company is already in liquidation or administration or the process for putting it into liquidation or administration has been initiated.[107] But the order granting leave is invariably expressed to be subject to a proviso that it is without prejudice to the rights of intervening secured creditors, so that the penalty for late registration is subordination to a security interest created after the creation of the first charge.[108] The proviso does not, however, protect intervening unsecured creditors.[109] There are five main priority rules.

First rule: where there are no additional perfection requirements,[110] priority is determined by the order of creation, subject to any applicable exceptions to the nemo dat rule[111]

5–25   There are various cases in which a security interest which has attached is valid against third parties without more.[112] In such case priority is determined by the rules set out in Section 2, above.

Second rule: first unregistered charge is void against a second charge whether registered or not

5–26   Where there are statutory provisions which require registration as perfection, the question arises whether an unperfected security interest is void or valid as against the holder of another unperfected security interest. There are three possible views: either the first interest is void as against the second, but the second is valid against the first, so that in terms of priority the second wins. This view is based on the argument that, since s.859H,[113] which renders an unregistered charge void

---

[103] Companies Act 2006 s.859H.

[104] *Re Monolithic Building Co* [1915] 1 Ch. 643.

[105] *Re Ashpurton Estates Ltd* [1983] Ch. 110, 123.

[106] Companies Act 2006 s.859F(3). The order does not itself perfect the unregistered security interest, which must be registered in conformity with the order.

[107] *Re Ashpurton Estates Ltd* [1983] Ch. 110.

[108] earlier drafting of the proviso has been changed following the case of *Watson v Duff, Morgan & Vermont (Holdings) Ltd* [1974] 1 W.L.R. 450.

[109] *Re MIG Trust Ltd* [1933] Ch. 542, per Romer L.J. at 570.

[110] Here "perfection" is used in the wide sense to include the giving of public notice in order to gain priority even when it is not required by statute in order for the security interest to be enforceable in the debtor's insolvency. See para.2–16, above.

[111] See paras 5–04 et seq., above.

[112] See para.2–19, above.

[113] Formerly s.874.

against creditors does not state that their charges must have been registered, this must mean that it is not so limited and includes chargees with unregistered charges: if this is taken to its logical conclusion, though, this would mean that each charge would be void against each other, so that neither has priority until an application is made to the court to register out of time.[114] The practical consequences of this are complicated and unattractive. Another view is that each charge is valid against the other, so that the normal priority rules apply (which would normally be that the first in time wins). The current position is uncertain: and while there is a judicial dictum that it is against a *registered* charge that an unregistered charge is void,[115] this misquotes the then statute, which did not in fact contain the word "registered", and there seems to be no real reason to limit the statute's wording in this way, in that the registration (or lack of it) of the second charge has no effect on a prior chargee,[116] and that if the first charge applied to register out of time, leave would normally be given subject to the interest of the second chargee[117] (although it would seem that the first chargee could just take a fresh charge and register it, thus obtaining priority over the second unregistered chargee).

Where it is possible to give public notice other than by statutorily required registration, the rule also applies. For example, if there are successive assignments of a debt but neither assignee gives notice to the debtor and the equities are otherwise equal, the assignments rank in order of creation.[118] Similarly, two unregistered mortgages of registered land rank in order of creation, even if protected by a notice or caution.[119] However, once electronic conveyancing becomes compulsory, it will not be possible to create a disposition of registered land, including a mortgage, without registration.[120]

5–27

Third rule: a perfected security interest[121] normally has priority over an unperfected security interest

This rule, in contrast with the preceding two rules, deals with a contest between a perfected security interest and an unperfected security interest. In general, the perfected security interest wins.[122] There are two qualifications. First, the perfection requirement embodied in s.859A of the Companies Act 2006 allows a

5–28

---

[114] R. R. Pennington, *Company Law*, 8th edn (London: Lexis Nexis UK, 2001), p.635.

[115] *Re Monolithic Building Co* [1915] 1 Ch. 643, 662: "I confess my inability to see that it means anything else than exactly what it says, namely, that it is void against any creditor who has a registered charge on the company's property".

[116] This argument has some support from the old American case of *United States v New Orleans Railroad* (1870) 79 U.S. 362, 365.

[117] See para.5–24, above. The proviso applies to interests "acquired" after the creation of the first unregistered interest.

[118] See *Rice v Rice* (1854) 2 Drew 73, per Sir R.T. Kindersley V.C. at 77–78.

[119] *Mortgage Corp Ltd v Nationwide Credit Corp Ltd* [1994] Ch. 49.

[120] Land Registration Act 2002 s.93. Plans to introduce e-conveyancing are "on hold for the immediate future" following very negative responses to the 2010 consultation paper, see *http://www.landregistry.gov.uk/__data/assets/pdf_file/0006/3102/econveyancing_cons.pdf* [accessed September 27, 2013].

[121] Again, "perfection" is used in the wide sense mentioned at fn.110 and para.2–16, above.

[122] For discussion of the practical effects of this, see Beale, Bridge, Gullifer and Lomnicka, *The Law of Security and Title-Based Financing* (2012), para.13.19.

21-day period of protection for the unregistered charge.[123] Secondly, in a registration system which allows for the registration of priority notices an unperfected interest registered before expiry of the priority notice has priority as from the time of registration of the notice or, under the rules of some registration systems, before the time of creation.[124]

It has also been argued[125] that if the unregistered security interest is second in time, it will have priority over an earlier registered interest if this would be the case under the general law, for example, if the second interest were a purchase money security interest.[126] The position here is uncertain, as there is no indication that the legislation is to be limited in this way.[127]

Fourth rule: in some circumstances, the giving of public notice is a priority point

5–29   The most obvious method of giving public notice, that of registration under s.859A of the Companies Act 2006, is not a priority point, although it renders the registered interest enforceable against other secured creditors and against unsecured creditors in the debtor's insolvency. However, in other registration systems priority is determined by the order of registration.[128] Further, other means of giving public notice can operate as a priority point. Thus under the rule in *Dearle v Hall* the priority of successive assignments of a chose in action is governed by the order in which notice of assignment is given to the debtor.[129] Where a security interest involves possession by the security holder, for example, a pledge, one might say that the giving of public notice was a priority point. However, in fact, priority between a pledge and an interest perfected by registration in the Companies Register is determined by the normal priority rules. If the other interest is legal, the *nemo dat* rule applies. If the other interest is equitable, either the pledge predates the other interest, in which case the *nemo dat* rule applies, or if the registered interest predates the pledge, the pledgee, who has a legal interest, takes free of the equitable interest as a legal purchaser for value without notice,[130] or, if the pledgee has actual or constructive notice of the registered interest,[131] it will take subject to that interest.

5–30   Some specialist register systems give an intending secured creditor temporary protection for his prospective security interest by one or both of two protective devices, the priority notice and the pre-completion search.

---

[123] However, this will not help the unregistered chargee if the charge is of a kind which is also registrable in a specialist register the rules of which give a registered charge priority over an unregistered charge and the subsequent chargee effects registration first.

[124] See paras 5–31 et seq., below.

[125] *Goode on Commercial Law* (2010), and in the first three editions of this book.

[126] See paras 5–63 et seq., below.

[127] See Beale, Bridge, Gullifer and Lomnicka, *The Law of Security and Title-Based Financing* (2012), para.13.18.

[128] See para.5–16, above.

[129] Subject to the qualification that the second assignee had no notice of the prior assignment. There are various exceptions to the rule in *Dearle v Hall*, see para.5–08, above.

[130] Para.5–09, above.

[131] Constructive notice would depend on whether he would be expected to search the register, which is a matter of some dispute, see para.2–31, above; and Beale, Bridge, Gullifer and Lomnicka, *The Law of Security and Title-Based Financing* (2012), para.14.06.

(1)   Priority notice

The priority notice procedure allows the intending secured creditor to obtain   **5–31**
priority for his prospective security interest by registering a priority notice and
then taking and perfecting his security interest within a specified period
(renewable for successive periods before each period has expired), priority then
dating back, under some rules, to the time of registration of the (latest) priority
notice[132] and, under others, to the time of creation of the security interest.[133]

(2)   Pre-completion search

An intending mortgagee of unregistered land who makes a search for registrable   **5–32**
charges is not affected by any entry in the register before the expiration of the
15th day after the date of the search certificate and before completion of his
mortgage if such entry is not made pursuant to a priority notice and the mortgage
is completed before the expiration of 30 days from the date of the certificate.[134]
Similarly, an intending mortgagee of registered land can, by making a search with
priority, secure protection against a subsequent incumbrancer if he completes and
registers his mortgage within 30 days.[135]

Fifth rule: priorities may be varied by agreement

Nothing in either the common law or the statutory priority rules precludes   **5–33**
competing secured creditors from making an agreement to vary the priority that
would otherwise apply, and most of the statutory registration rules make express
provision for this. As has previously been pointed out,[136] a subordination
agreement does not result in an exchange of security interests between the two
secured creditors, it merely gives the beneficiary of the subordination priority
over the grantor of the subordination, not over an intermediate secured creditor.
Subordination agreements are extremely common in domestic and international
finance and do not require the consent of the debtor[137]: particular issues in
relation to them are discussed later in this chapter.[138] They remain effective in the
debtor's winding up as they do not affect the position of other creditors so as to
contravene the principle of pari passu distribution.[139]

---

[132] As in the case of ship mortgages (Merchant Shipping Act 1995 Sch.1 para.8; Merchant Shipping (Registration of Ships) Regulations 1993 (SI 1993/3138) reg.59) and aircraft mortgages (Mortgaging of Aircraft Order 1972 (SI 1972/971) art.14(2)(iii)). For aircraft mortgages the priority is lost unless the mortgage is made and registered within 14 days. There is no time limit for ship mortgages, although the priority notice will lapse after thirty days if not renewed. Merchant Shipping (Registration of Ships) Regulations 1993 (SI 1993/3138) reg.59(6) and (7).

[133] As in the case of land charge over unregistered land (Land Charges Act 1972 s.11). But the charge must be taken and registered within 30 days.

[134] Land Charges Act 1972 s.11(5),(6).

[135] Land Registration Rules (SI 2003/1417) reg.151.

[136] See para.1–85, above.

[137] *Cheah Theam Swee v Equiticorp Finance Group Ltd* [1992] 1 A.C. 472.

[138] See paras 5–59 et seq., below.

[139] See para.5–60, below, and, for a discussion of the nature of subordination, paras 1–84 et seq., above.

Marshalling of securities

5–34   It may happen that the junior secured creditor, SC2, has security in one item of property, asset A, while the senior secured creditor, SC1, has security both over asset A and over asset B. Without the doctrine of marshalling, SC2 could be adversely affected by SC1's decision to look to asset A in the first instance to obtain payment of the amount due to him, which would reduce S2's security or even extinguish it altogether. The doctrine of marshalling does not affect SC1's right to look to asset A,[140] either on its own or at the same time as resorting to asset B, but it protects SC2 by allowing him to resort to asset B to the extent to which he has been deprived of his own security by reason of SC1's recourse to asset A.[141]

Effect of priorities on enforcement by a secured creditor

5–35   If mortgages are granted in succession to SP1 and SP2 and there are no factors to displace SP1's priority, he may realise his security, take what is due to him and then account for any surplus to SP2, who will in turn deduct what is due to him and hand over any remaining surplus to the mortgagor. Where there are three or more incumbrancers it would seem that SP1's duty is to hand over the whole of any surplus to SP2, leaving it to him to take what is due to him and pass any balance to SP3, rather than SP1 being responsible for distribution among all interested parties in order of priority.[142]

However, it is not only the senior mortgagee who can enforce. SP2 may realise his security, but if he is selling free from SP1's mortgage he must obtain SP1's consent and must apply the proceeds in discharge of that mortgage before taking what is due to him. If, however, SP2 is selling subject to SP1's mortgage SP1 is not affected by the sale and his consent is not required. His mortgage continues to attach to the property and SP2 is not accountable to him for any part of the proceeds, but must take what is due to him and then pass any surplus to the next mortgagee, if any, or, if none, to the debtor. Where SP1 has himself become entitled to enforce his mortgage and chooses to do so after SP2 has initiated steps to enforce his own mortgage, SP1 is entitled to take control in priority to SP2.

---

[140] *Manks v Whiteley* [1911] 2 Ch. 448, per Parker J. at 466; *Chase Corp (Australia) Pty Ltd v North Sydney Brick and Tile Co Ltd* (1994) A.C.S.R. 586, per Cohen J. at 1008–1009. For a detailed discussion of the topic see the monograph by P. Ali, *Marshalling of Securities* (Oxford: Oxford University Press, 1999); and also Beale, Bridge, Gullifer and Lomnicka, *The Law of Security and Title-Based Financing* (2012), paras 18.05–18.09.

[141] *Szepietowski v The Serious Organised Crime Agency* [2011] EWCA Civ 856 at [2].

[142] *Re Thomson's Mortgage Trusts* [1920] 1 Ch. 508; W. Clark (ed.), *Fisher & Lightwood's Law of Mortgage*, 13th edn (London: LexisNexis, 2010), para.30.47. See also s.105 of the Law of Property Act 1925, which obliges a mortgagee or receiver appointed by him to account to "the person entitled to the mortgaged property" on sale or other realisation of the mortgaged assets.

5. COMPETITION BETWEEN A FIXED CONSENSUAL SECURITY INTEREST AND OTHER TYPES OF INTEREST

Secured creditor versus outright buyer

A legal mortgagee has priority over a subsequent buyer to whom the mortgagor wrongfully sells the charged asset.[143] An equitable mortgagee or chargee is postponed to a subsequent buyer who acquires the legal title in good faith and without notice of the prior equitable mortgage or charge. The extent to which registration constitutes notice has been discussed earlier.[144]

5–36

There is one oddity. While a charge not duly registered under s.859A of the Companies Act is void as against a subsequent chargee, the section says nothing about a subsequent buyer. Accordingly failure to register does not invalidate the unregistered charge against the buyer, and priorities will be determined by the common law rules. A legal mortgagee will retain its priority under the first-in-time rule; an equitable mortgagee or chargee will be postponed to a buyer who takes the legal title for value and without notice but prevails against any other kind of buyer, for example, the purchaser of charged debts who has not given notice to the debtor, if the unregistered chargee has given notice.[145]

Secured creditor versus holder of non-consensual right or interest

A consensual security interest may come into conflict with a right or interest created by law. If the non-consensual right is purely personal, or is ad rem rather than in rem,[146] the security interest usually prevails. There are, however, statutory exceptions. A landlord is entitled to distrain for rent on any goods on the demised premises, whether or not the property of the tenant, though if distress is levied on goods the subject of a fixed charge the chargee may perhaps be able to procure their release by service of a notice under s.1 of the Law of Distress Amendment Act 1908.[147] A statutory right to arrest an aircraft for non-payment of airport dues has priority over a security interest in the aircraft.[148]

5–37

Where the consensual security interest comes into conflict with a non-consensual right in rem, such as an equitable tracing right, the principles governing priority between competing consensual interests apply. Suppose, for

---

[143] There are certain exceptions, such as estoppel, which are not discussed here. Section 24 of the Sale of Goods Act 1979 does not apply here, because s.62(4) of that Act prevents the provisions of the Act applying to a mortgage or other security. However, there are good policy reasons why this is unsatisfactory, see M. Bridge, *The Sale of Goods*, 2nd edn (Oxford: Oxford University Press, 2009), paras 2.84–2.85; *The Diamond Report*, para.13.2.9.

[144] See paras 2–25 et seq., above.

[145] For discussion of possible reform dealing with this point, see para.2–23, above.

[146] See para.1–18, above.

[147] See para.5–48, below. The common law right to distrain for unpaid rent has been replaced by a commercial rent arrears recovery right by ss.71 and 72 of the Tribunals Court and Enforcement Act 2007. These sections are not yet in force, but the Government has announced its intention to bring the regime into force in 2014, see T. Pilgrim, "Commercial rent arrears recovery gets the go ahead" (2013) 17 L. & T. Review 56.

[148] See *Channel Airways Ltd v City of Manchester* [1974] 2 Lloyd's Rep. 456, per Forbes J. at 461.

example, that B, in the possession of O's goods, wrongfully sells them on credit, and assigns the proceeds, in the shape of the debt due from the purchaser for the price, to M by way of mortgage under a statutory assignment in conformity with s.136 of the Law of Property Act 1925. O asserts an equitable tracing claim to the debt as proceeds of its asset,[149] while M claims as mortgagee. In this situation M cannot simply rely on his legal title, even if he took without notice of O's equitable interest, because even a statutory assignee takes subject to equities, which for this purpose includes O's equitable interest in the proceeds,[150] and this overrides the general rule giving priority to a bona fide purchaser of the legal title for value and without notice. So the starting position is that O has the superior interest by virtue of being first-in-time. What is not clear is whether this can be displaced in favour of M if he is the first to give notice to the debtor[151] and thereby obtain priority under the rule in *Dearle v Hall*.[152]

Various kinds of lien have priority even over a consensual security interest created before the events giving rise to the lien. These include the possessory lien of carriers and the various kinds of maritime lien. Whether a consensual security interest has priority over statutory charges depends on the particular statute.[153]

6. RANKING OF THE FLOATING CHARGE

5–38   So far, the discussion has been confined to priority issues relating to fixed security interests. The floating charge attracts entirely different principles because of the right given to the debtor, and much depends on whether the competing interest arose before or after crystallisation. The position of the holder of a floating charge in relation to preferential creditors and the prescribed part raises distinct considerations and will be dealt with separately later in the present chapter.[154]

---

[149] See para.1–64, above.

[150] *Compaq Computers Ltd v Abercorn Group Ltd* [1992] B.C.C. 484; following the decision of Phillips J. in *E Pfeiffer Weinkellerei-Weineinkauf GmbH v Arbuthnot Factors Ltd* (1987) 3 B.C.C. 608. However, in both cases the "owner's" interest arose by way of equitable assignment and not tracing right. This situation is likely to arise in the context of a conflict between a title-retention seller claiming the proceeds of resale under the title reservation clause and a subsequent factor or invoice discounter buying the receivable resulting from the resale, an issue generating much academic debate (see the 2nd edition of this book at pp.120–122, and R. Goode, *Commercial Law*, 2nd edn (London: Butterworths Law, 1998), pp.818–819). Usually the issue has been rendered moot by a finding that the contractual proceeds provision created a charge void for want of registration. But where this is not so the question arises as to the correct principles which apply to a contest between the holder of an equitable tracing right and a mortgagee of the proceeds.

[151] As he almost always will, since it is likely to be some time before O discovers the wrongful resale and the identity of the purchaser.

[152] This point was argued but not decided in *Compaq Computers Ltd v Abercorn Group Ltd* [1992] B.C.C. 484, since it was held that the seller's interest in the debt arose by way of assignment and not by operation of law. The authorities are inconclusive. For further discussion see D. MacLauchlan, "Priorities—Equitable tracing rights and assignments of debts" (1980) 96 L.Q.R. 90, 95–98; Oditah, *Legal Aspects of Receivables Financing* (1990), pp.137–139; M. Smith and N. Leslie, *The Law of Assignment*, 2nd edn (Oxford: Oxford University Press, 2013), para.27.105.

[153] An example of a statutory charge having priority over a mortgage is provided by s.87(6) the Agricultural Holdings Act 1986 in relation to tenants' charges created under s.85(2) of the Act.

[154] See para.5–68, below.

As against interests arising prior to crystallisation

The ranking of a floating charge in relation to subsequent interests arising prior to **5–39** the crystallisation of the charge depends partly on the type of interest in question and partly on whether the floating charge contains restrictions on dealings of which the subsequent claimant has notice. The peculiar nature of the floating charge creates difficulties of analysis in the context of priorities, for whilst the charge is a present security it is non-specific and in principle does not affect third parties at all while it continues to float. Since crystallisation of the charge, which converts it from a floating security to a fixed security, is not retrospective, the subordination of intervening interests which occurs in certain conditions described below is not always easy to explain and, indeed, has never been fully analysed by the courts.[155] It is clear that there are certain situations in which a floating charge retains its priority over subsequent interests, but it would seem that such priority is inchoate so long as the charge continues to float and can only be asserted upon crystallisation.

(1)   Buyer or incumbrancer in ordinary course of business

It is the essence of a floating charge that the company has an implied authority to **5–40** dispose of its assets in the ordinary course of business. For this purpose "ordinary course of business" is widely interpreted, embracing dispositions by way of sale,[156] hire-purchase,[157] specific mortgage or charge,[158] and, indeed, any other form of bona fide disposition which is intra vires the company and is designed to promote rather than to terminate or destroy its business.[159] Even a sale of its goodwill, assets and undertaking will be considered in the ordinary course of business if intended in furtherance of the business,[160] and not with a view to ceasing trading.[161] In *Ashborder BV v Green Gas Power Ltd*, a recent decision in which the authorities were analysed at length,[162] Etherton J. summarised the position as follows[163]:

> "It may be helpful to summarise briefly the following conclusions that I have reached
> from the decided cases that I have reviewed: (1) The question whether a particular
> transaction is within the ordinary course of a company's business in the context of a
> floating charge is a mixed question of fact and law; (2) it is convenient to approach

---

[155] A point well made by Mahoney J.A. in *Reynolds Bros (Motors) Pty Ltd v Esanda Ltd* (1983) 8 A.C.L.R. 422, 427.

[156] *Hamer v London, City & Midland Bank Ltd* (1918) 87 L.J.K.B. 973; *Reynolds Bros (Motor) Pty Ltd v Esanda Ltd* (1983) 8 A.C.L.R. 422.

[157] *Dempsey and National Bank of New Zealand v Traders' Finance Corp Ltd* [1933] N.Z.L.R. 1258.

[158] *Cox Moore v Peruvian Corp Ltd* [1908] 1 Ch. 604; *Re Hamilton's Windsor Ironworks* (1879) 12 Ch.D. 707.

[159] See *Ashborder BV v Green Gas Power Ltd* [2004] EWHC 1517 at [227]; and W.J. Gough, *Company Charges*, 2nd edn (London: Butterworths Law, 1996), p.198.

[160] e.g. by way of amalgamation (*Re Borax Co* [1901] 1 Ch. 326) or disposal of a loss-making part of the business to enable the remainder of the business to be continued profitably (*Re HH Vivian & Co Ltd* [1900] 2 Ch. 654).

[161] *Hubbuck v Helms* (1887) 56 L.J. Ch. 536; *Hamilton v Hunter* (1982) 7 A.C.L.R. 295; *Torzillu Pty Ltd v Brynac Pty Ltd* (1983) 8 A.C.L.R. 52.

[162] *Ashborder BV v Green Gas Power Ltd*, especially at [2004] EWHC 1517 [202]–[216] and [227].

[163] *Ashborder BV v Green Gas Power Ltd* [2004] EWHC 1517 at [227].

the matter in a two stage process; (3) first, to ascertain, as a matter of fact, whether an objective observer, with knowledge of the company, its memorandum of association and its business, would view the transaction as having taken place in the ordinary course of its business, and, if so (4) second, to consider whether, on the proper interpretation of the document creating the floating charge, applying standard techniques of interpretation, the parties nonetheless did not intend that the transaction should be regarded as being in the ordinary course of the company's business for the purpose of the charge; (5) subject to any such special considerations resulting from the proper interpretation of the charge document, there is no reason why an unprecedented or exceptional transaction cannot, in appropriate circumstances, be regarded as in the ordinary course of the company's business; (6) subject to any such special considerations, the mere fact that a transaction would, in a liquidation, be liable to be avoided as a fraudulent or otherwise wrongful preference of one creditor over others, does not, of itself, necessarily preclude the transaction from being in the ordinary course of the company's business; (7) nor does the mere fact that a transaction was made in breach of fiduciary duty by one or more directors of the company; (8) such matters in (6) and (7) may, however, where appropriate and in all the circumstances, be among the factors leading to the conclusion that the transaction was not in the ordinary course of the company's business; (9) transactions which are intended to bring to an end, or have the effect of bringing to an end, the company's business are not transactions in the ordinary course of its business."

Given the implied authority of the debtor company to continue to deal with its assets in the ordinary course of business, it follows that the buyer, incumbrancer or other party acquiring an interest in the charged assets in the ordinary course of business has priority over the holder of the floating charge, even if he takes with knowledge of its existence.[164] Where, in this situation, the charge covers book debts or other receivables, the rule in *Dearle v Hall* does not apply, for the floating chargee, having impliedly authorised the subsequent fixed charge, cannot jump ahead by being the first to give notice to the debtor after the charge has crystallised.[165]

5–41   If the debenture imposes restrictions on sales or subsequent incumbrances and the particular sale or charge, though in the ordinary course of business, is in breach of such restrictions, the floating charge will, on crystallisation, retain its priority if the buyer or incumbrancer took with notice of the restrictions, whether his interest is legal or equitable.[166] This stems from the fact that the floating charge, though ambulatory, is a present security,[167] not a mere contract right, so that restrictions contained in it will constitute an equity binding those who have notice of them. It is true that in *Griffiths v Yorkshire Bank Plc*[168] Morritt J., disapproving of a dictum by Chadwick J. in *Re Portbase Clothing Ltd*,[169] expressed the view that a restriction on the grant of subsequent charges is purely

---

[164] *Re Castell & Brown Ltd* [1898] 1 Ch. 315; *English & Scottish Mercantile Investment Co v Brunton* [1892] 2 Q.B. 700.

[165] *Ward v Royal Exchange Shipping Co Ltd* (1887) 58 L.T. 174; *Re Ind Coope & Co Ltd* [1911] 3 Ch. 223.

[166] *English & Scottish Mercantile Investment Co Ltd v Brunton* [1892] 2 Q.B. 700, per Lord Esher M.R. at 707; *Cox v Dublin City Distillery Co* [1906] I.R. 446; *Wilson v Kelland* [1910] 2 Ch. 306. As to whether registration constitutes notice, and whether this has changed in the light of the 2013 reforms, see paras 2–25 et seq., above.

[167] See para.4–06, above.

[168] *Griffiths v Yorkshire Bank Plc* [1994] 1 W.L.R. 1427.

[169] *Re Portbase Clothing Ltd* [1993] Ch. 388 at 401.

contractual and has no proprietary or priority effects.[170] But the learned judge's attention does not appear to have been drawn to the earlier authorities clearly supporting the position taken by Chadwick J. to the effect that a negative pledge clause creates an equity in favour of the holder of the floating charge[171] or to the authorities stating that the grant of a subsequent floating charge ranking in priority to the first floating charge is prima facie outside the chargor's dealing powers.[172] The position is otherwise, however, where the subsequent purchaser or incumbrancer takes without notice of the restrictions contained in the floating charge,[173] for the third party is entitled to assume that the company retains the power to deal with its assets in the ordinary course of business and in the absence of notice of the restriction he will obtain priority.[174]

Where the subsequent purchaser or incumbrancer takes with notice of the fact that the disposition to him is in breach of the debenture creating the floating charge, the debenture holder's right to assert his security interest would appear to be exercisable only on crystallisation and until then would, it is thought, be merely inchoate. Unless otherwise provided by the debenture, the wrongful dealing by the company does not of itself cause the charge to crystallise,[175] and until crystallisation the debenture holder has no right to any specific asset capable of being asserted against the third party. The exact effect of a buyer or an incumbrancer taking subject to an uncrystallised floating charge is complex and relatively unexplored. This is because, in all reported cases, the relevant floating charge crystallised by the time the matter is considered by the court and so all statements on this issue are obiter. Further, sensible chargeholders will attempt to protect themselves by including a provision for automatic crystallisation triggered by the grant of an interest in breach of the restriction.[176] Lord Phillips in the Court of Appeal decision in the *Spectrum Plus* litigation,[177] called for the effect of restrictions on disposal to be more fully explored.

The following is an attempt to take up the challenge laid down by Lord Phillips and to explore the effect of a restriction on disposal.[178] The problem is the same whether the disposition was in breach of a restriction of which the disponee has notice, or was outside the ordinary course of business.[179] A distinction should be made between a disposition to a buyer and one to an

---

[170] *Griffiths v Yorkshire Bank Plc* [1994] 1 W.L.R. 1427 at 1435–1436.

[171] *Re Portbase Clothing Ltd* [1993] Ch. 388 at 401.

[172] *Re Benjamin Cope & Sons Ltd* [1914] 1 Ch. 800; *Re Household Products Co Ltd* (1981) 124 D.L.R. (3d) 325.

[173] As to when registration constitutes notice, see paras 2–25 et seq., above.

[174] *English & Scottish Mercantile Investment Co v Brunton* [1892] 2 Q.B. 700; *Welch v Bowmaker (Ireland) Ltd* [1980] I.R. 251.

[175] *Reynolds Bros (Motors) Pty Ltd v Esanda Ltd* (1983) 8 A.C.L.R. 422, per Mahoney J.A. at 427. However, many agreements will make such a disposition a crystallising event, see, for example, *Re Manurewa Transport Ltd* [1971] N.Z.L.R. 909; *Fire Nymph Products Ltd v The Heating Centre Property Ltd* (1992) 7 A.C.S.R. 365; *ABN Amro Bank NV v Chiyu Banking Corp Ltd* [2001] 2 H.K.L.R.D. 175.

[176] For discussion of the effect of such clauses, see paras 4–56 et seq., above: unless carefully drafted to specify the assets over which crystallisation is to take place, the consequences of crystallisation may be interpreted as too far-reaching to be realistically intended by the parties.

[177] *Re Spectrum Plus* [2004] EWCA Civ 670; [2004] Ch. 337 at [30].

[178] See also Beale, Bridge, Gullifer and Lomnicka, *The Law of Security and Title-Based Financing* (2012), paras 15.08–15.09, 15.12, 15.25.

[179] See para.5–42, below.

incumbrancer. A buyer is bound by the charge once the charge has crystallised.[180] Before that point, what remedy does the chargeholder have? A mandatory injunction requiring the buyer to restore the assets to the company, even if theoretically available, would not normally be appropriate, for ex hypothesi the debenture holder will have priority on crystallisation of the charge, so that the improper dealing causes him no loss and the only relief he could expect is a declaration that his charge enjoys priority.[181] If he discovers the debtor company's intentions in time he can no doubt obtain a quia timet injunction to restrain a threatened disposition in breach of the debenture,[182] but it seems unlikely that the court would go further than ordering that any disposition should be on terms preserving the priority of the floating charge, for in most cases a disposition on such terms would be permitted by the debenture.

What if the buyer disposes of the assets subject to the floating charge before crystallisation? Can the floating chargeholder follow the assets, or trace into the proceeds? The authorities are very limited, but appear to lead to the rather strange conclusion that there is an inchoate right to the assets, which can be enforced on crystallisation, but that the buyer can dispose of the assets "in the ordinary course of business carried on by the chargor company".[183] This is obviously unlikely to happen, so if the buyer still has the assets or their traceable proceeds at the time of crystallisation, it would appear that the floating chargeholder can claim them at that point.

In relation to a subsequent incumbrancer, who takes with notice of a restriction in a floating charge, it is again clear that once the floating charge has crystallised, the subsequent fixed chargee cannot enforce his charge without accounting to the floating chargeholder as a prior incumbrancer.[184] Before the floating charge crystallises, the company still has the right to dispose of the assets vis-à-vis the floating chargeholder, but not vis-à-vis the fixed chargeholder. This appears to lead to the conclusion that the company can dispose of the assets free from the floating charge, but not the fixed charge unless the holder of the fixed charge

---

[180] This has been the result in three Australian cases, where in each case, there was a disposition outside the ordinary course of business before the charge crystallised by the appointment of a receiver and in each case, the disponee was held to hold the assets subject to the charge. However, in *Hamilton v Hunter* (1982) 7 A.C.L.R. 295 the significance of the later crystallisation was not discussed in the judgment. In *Torzillu Pty Ltd v Brynac Pty Ltd* (1983) 8 A.C.L.R. 52 it was conceded that if the disposition was outside the ordinary course of business, the charge bound the purchaser. In *Re Bartlett Estates Pty Ltd* (Sup. Ct. Qnd.) (1988) 14 A.C.L.R. 512, again there was little discussion of the significance of crystallisation.

[181] This view may be said to have some support from the analysis of Dowsett J. in *Re Bartlett Estates Pty Ltd* (Sup. Ct. Qnd.) (1988) 14 A.C.L.R. 512, 516–517, where he refers to the right of the floating chargee to intervene before the disposition (see fn.153, above), and then says: "It follows that he may also intervene to recover property so mishandled, at least where the rights of third parties do not intervene". In that case, the charge had crystallised before the action was commenced, and so the result of the intervention was that the funds disposed of were subject to the crystallised charge. However, if the intervention had been before crystallisation, the likely result would be a declaration as described in the text.

[182] Nourse J. in *Re Woodroffes Ltd* [1986] Ch. 366, 378 envisages that such injunctive relief is available when the threatened disposition is outside the ordinary course of business. See also *Atkins v Mercantile Credits Ltd* (1985) 10 A.C.L.R. 153, 157.

[183] *Hubbuck v Helms* (1887) 56 L.J. Ch. 536.

[184] *Re Portbase Clothing Ltd* [1993] Ch. 388, 401.

consents[185]: if he does not consent, then the disposition is unauthorised and the proceeds are subject to the fixed charge, if he does consent then any right to the proceeds depends upon the terms of the authorisation.[186] This leads to the further conclusion that if the fixed chargeholder chooses to enforce his security before the floating charge crystallises, and by means which do not lead to the crystallisation of the floating charge, the fixed chargeholder does not have to account to the floating chargeholder as a prior chargeholder[187] (and any surplus would only fall within the floating charge if it was an asset covered by that charge). If, however, the floating charge crystallised before or during enforcement, there will be such a duty to account.

(2) Buyer or incumbrancer outside ordinary course of business

Where assets are disposed of by the debtor company to a buyer or incumbrancer outside the ordinary course of business, the transaction is ex hypothesi outside both the actual authority of the company. Thus the exception to the *nemo dat* rule of an authorised disposition does not apply. This means, therefore, that the buyer or incumbrancer will take subject to the floating charge unless one of the other exceptions apply. It is possible that a buyer might fall within the exception of a bona fide purchaser without notice.[188] Where, however, the second disposition is equitable, or where the second buyer or incumbrancer has notice that the disposition is outside the ordinary course of business (which is reasonably likely to be the case)[189] then the effect of such a disposition is similar to that of a disposition in breach of a restriction contained in the debenture discussed above. The buyer or incumbrancer takes subject to the floating charge,[190] but the priority of the debenture holder as floating chargee is inchoate and can only be asserted once the charge has crystallised. The mere fact that the disposition is outside the ordinary course of business does not in itself cause crystallisation, though it may trigger automatic crystallisation or entitle the debenture holder to intervene to assert his security interest and thereby crystallise the charge, either pursuant to

5-42

---

[185] *Re Camden Brewery Ltd* (1911) 106 L.T. 598n; *Re Robert Stephenson & Co* (1912) 106 L.T. 595, 597. These cases concerned a fixed charge that was made subject to a prior floating charge by agreement, but this does not seem a valid point of distinction in this context. The relevant passage from *Re Camden Brewery* was quoted by Chadwick J. in *Re Portbase Ltd* [1993] 3 Ch. 388, 398–399, apparently with approval. See also Gough, *Company Charges* (1996), pp.274–275.

[186] See para.1–63, above.

[187] *Re Robert Stephenson & Co Ltd (No.1)* [1913] 2 Ch. 201, 205. For the duty to account, see para.5–35, above.

[188] See para.5–09, above. This view is supported by a dictum in *Re Bartlett Estates Pty Ltd* (Sup. Ct. Qnd.) (1988) 14 A.C.L.R. 512, 516; and see also *Reynolds Bros (Motors) Ply Ltd v Esanda Ltd* (1983) 8 A.C.L.R. 422, per Mahoney J.A. at 427. This exception would not, however, apply where the first interest was itself a legal interest, and thus in the cases of *Taylor v M'Keand* (1880) 5 C.P.D. 358; *Payne v Fern* (1881) 6 Q.B.D. 620, where goods were subject to bills of sale which only permitted dispositions in the ordinary course of business, purchasers were held to take subject to the interests of the holders of the bills of sale, despite having bought the goods in good faith and without notice.

[189] Presumably the buyer or incumbrancer would also need to have notice of the existence of the floating charge, but if the charge is registered, both incumbrancers and buyers outside the ordinary course of business would normally be expected to search the register (see para.2–31, above) and so would have constructive notice of the charge.

[190] *Hamilton v Hunter* (1982) 7 A.C.L.R. 295; *Torzillu Pty Ltd v Brynac Pty Ltd* (1983) A.C.L.R. 52; *Re Bartlett Estates Pty Ltd* (Sup. Ct. Qnd.) (1988) 14 A.C.L.R. 512.

the terms of the debenture or by obtaining an order for appointment of a receiver on the ground of jeopardy to the security.

(3) Later floating charge

5–43   The courts have held, in *Re Benjamin Cope Ltd*,[191] that the dealing power implied in a floating charge does not extend to the grant of a subsequent floating charge over the same assets, since the grant of such a charge would have the effect of totally undermining the first charge.[192] However, in the absence of express restrictions, it remains permissible for the company to grant a subsequent floating charge over part of those assets ranking in priority to or pari passu with the earlier floating charge.[193] This proposition is supported by the case of *Re Automatic Bottle Makers Ltd*[194] concerning a debenture in which there was a blanket express restriction on the creation of subsequent charges (cl.6), qualified by a clause permitting the grant of charges over certain classes of assets (cl.7). The Court of Appeal held that this permission extended to floating charges over such assets as well as fixed charges, and rejected an argument, based on *Re Benjamin Cope Ltd*, that cl.7 could not be construed in this way as it would grant the chargor a greater power than it would have had were cll.6 and 7 not in the agreement. The ratio of *Re Benjamin Cope Ltd* was limited to the situation where the subsequent charge was over all the assets comprised in the first charge.

Where the first floating charge is only over part of the assets there is, of course, no objection to the grant of a subsequent floating charge over different assets.

(4) Execution creditor

5–44   An execution creditor takes free from a floating charge if, but only if, the execution is completed,[195] or payment is made to avoid execution,[196] prior to crystallisation of the charge.[197] There remain some unresolved questions as to when execution is to be considered completed for this purpose.

---

[191] *Re Benjamin Cope Ltd* [1914] 1 Ch. 800.
[192] Hence the first floating charge has priority even though the later charge is the first to crystallise (*Re Household Products Co Ltd* (1981) 124 D.L.R. (3d) 325).
[193] *Re Automatic Bottle Makers Ltd* [1926] Ch. 412.
[194] *Re Automatic Bottle Makers Ltd* [1926] Ch. 412.
[195] *Re Opera Ltd* [1891] 3 Ch. 260; *Robson v Smith* [1895] 2 Ch. 118; *Evans v Rival Granite Quarries Ltd* [1910] 2 K.B. 979. The rule is well established but has attracted much critical discussion. See, for example R. Calnan, "Priorities Between Execution Creditors and Floating Charges" [1982] 10 N.Z.U.L.R. 111; D.M. Hare and D. Milman, "Debenture holders and creditors—problems of priority" [1982] L.M.C.L.Q. 57; Gough, *Company Charges* (1996), pp.319 et seq. The Law Commission's proposals in their report; Law Commission, *Company Security Interests* Law Com. No.296 (2005), included reversal of this rule, except as regards further advances made after the chargeholder knows that the execution creditor has acquired an interest unless the chargeholder was obliged to make the advance (Report paras 3.201–3.204).
[196] *Robinson v Burnell's Vienna Bakery Co* [1904] 2 K.B. 624; *Heaton & Dugard Ltd v Cutting Bros Ltd* [1925] 1 K.B. 655.
[197] It is to avoid this result that most floating charges include a provision for automatic crystallisation on the taking by any creditor of any step to levy execution, see para.4–54, above.

Execution against goods   Mere seizure by the enforcement officer[198] does not   **5–45**
suffice; there must at least have been a sale.[199] The question is whether sale alone
defeats the debenture holder if the floating charge crystallises after sale and
before receipt of the proceeds by the enforcement officer or their transfer to the
execution creditor. For the purpose of insolvency law, seizure and sale are all that
are necessary to complete the execution,[200] subject to the execution creditor being
divested of his rights if within 14 days of receipt of the proceeds by the
enforcement officer the judgment creditor becomes bankrupt or goes into
liquidation or the enforcement officer receives notice of a pending bankruptcy or
winding up petition or of a meeting having been called to pass a resolution for
voluntary winding up.[201] There seems no reason why seizure and sale should not
equally perfect the execution creditor's right to the proceeds vis-à-vis the holder
of a floating charge even before these have been paid to the enforcement
officer,[202] subject to divestment as stated above. If the execution creditor is
divested of his rights under the above statutory provisions and the floating charge
has crystallised after sale but before divestment, do the statutory provisions enure
for the benefit of the debenture holder or the general body of creditors? Under
such provisions the title of the trustee or liquidator is expressed to be good only
as against the execution creditor, not against third parties such as a chargee under
a crystallised charge. However, we have predicated that the execution creditor
obtains priority over the debenture holder as a result of a sale prior to
crystallisation of the charge. Accordingly, since the trustee or liquidator displaces
the execution creditor he necessarily displaces the debenture holder and is thus to
be entitled to the proceeds of the execution up to the amount covered by the writ
of execution, any surplus being caught by the crystallised charge.

Execution against debts   An attachment of debts by third party debt   **5–46**
proceedings[203] does not result in completed execution until their receipt by the
execution creditor.[204] Even a payment into court by the third party pursuant to the
third party order is insufficient, for this does not of itself vest title to the moneys
in the execution creditor.[205]

---

[198] This word has been substituted for "sheriff" in the relevant legislation by Courts Act 2003 Sch.8 para.295(2).

[199] See cases cited fn.195, above. There is a curious provision in s.183(3)(a) and s.346(5)(a) of the Insolvency Act 1986 to the effect that for the purposes of those sections an execution against goods is completed by seizure and sale "or by the making of a charging order under section 1 of the Charging Orders Act 1979". The quoted words are clearly a drafting error since the 1979 Act makes no provision for a charging order against goods.

[200] Insolvency Act 1986 ss.346(5)(a), 183(3)(a); *Roberts Petroleum Ltd v Bernard Kenny Ltd* [1983] 2 A.C. 192, per Lord Brightman at 213.

[201] Insolvency Act 1986 ss.183(3) and (4); 346(3), (4); *Re Greer* [1895] 2 Ch. 217, per Chitty J. at 221. These statutory provisions displace the vesting of the right to the proceeds in the execution creditors which would otherwise arise when the enforcement officer received the proceeds. See also *Bluston & Bramley v Leigh* [1950] 2 K.B. 548.

[202] A view supported by a dictum in the judgment of Kneller J.A. in *Lochab Bros v Kenya Furfural* [1985] L.R.C. (Comm.) 737, 747.

[203] These are in substance the same as the former garnishee proceedings, CPR Pt 72.

[204] *Cairney v Back* [1906] 2 K.B. 746. The case is distinguishable from the earlier decision in *Robson v Smith* [1895] 2 Ch. 118 in that the charge had not crystallised in that case, the debenture holder's attempt to collect in the garnisheed debt being held ineffective in the absence of the appointment of a receiver or other crystallising event. In *Cairney v Back* Walton J. expressed the view that the absence

5-47 **Execution against land, securities and funds in court** By virtue of statute a special rule applies to attachment of land, securities and funds in court by way of a charging order. Under s.3(4) of the Charging Orders Act 1979 a charge imposed by a charging order has the like effect and is enforceable in the same courts and in the same manner as an equitable charge created by the debtor under his hand. This applies even to a charging order nisi,[206] which will thus have priority over an uncrystallised floating charge unless the effect of the order is negated by the court exercising its discretion to refuse to make it absolute.[207] Execution against land may be completed not only by a charging order but by seizure or the appointment of a receiver.[208]

(5) Landlord or local authority levying distress

5-48 A landlord levying distress for rent on the goods of the company on the demised premises is not subject to the floating charge. In this particular case, as will be seen,[209] it is irrelevant whether the distress is levied before or after crystallisation. A local authority may distrain for unpaid business rates before crystallisation of the floating charge but not after.[210]

(6) Debtor asserting right of set-off

5-49 The trading power implicit in a floating charge encompasses the ability of the company to engage in mutual dealings with a customer as the result of which the customer acquires a right of set-off. Since on crystallisation the debenture holder cannot acquire rights over the company's assets greater than those the company has itself, it follows that the debenture holder's rights over book debts and other contract sums due to the company are subject to the debtor's rights of set-off in respect of cross-claims arising prior to notice of crystallisation.[211] The fact that the debtor was aware of the existence of the floating charge at the time he concluded the transaction generating the right of set-off is irrelevant, for ex hypothesi the company had authority to enter into such a transaction free from the ambit of the floating charge. A good illustration is *Biggerstaff v Rowatt's Wharf Ltd*.[212]

---

of the appointment of a receiver in *Robson v Smith* was irrelevant to the decision in that case, but this dictum is plainly incorrect. It may be noted that for the purpose of insolvency law also it is the time of receipt of the debt which constitutes completion of the execution (Insolvency Act 1986 ss.346(5)(c), 183(3) (b); *Roberts Petroleum Ltd v Bernard Kenny Ltd* [1983] 2 A.C. 192, per Lord Brightman at 213). See to the same effect the Insolvency Act 1986 s.346(5)(c).

[205] *Coopers & Lybrand Ltd v National Caterers Ltd* (1982) 47 C.B.R.(N.S.) 57.

[206] *Roberts Petroleum Ltd v Bernard Kenny Ltd* [1983] 2 A.C. 192, per Lord Brightman at 205.

[207] *Roberts Petroleum Ltd v Bernard Kenny Ltd* [1983] 2 A.C. 192.

[208] Insolvency Act 1986 ss.183(3)(c) and 346(5)(b).

[209] See para.5–53, below.

[210] *Re ELS Ltd* [1995] Ch.11, rightly declining to follow *Re Marriage, Neave & Co* [1896] 2 Ch. 663. The latter case was distinguished on the basis that it concerned a "mere charge" rather than, as in *ELS Ltd*, a charge which took effect as a mortgage. Where a charge took effect as a mortgage, on crystallisation the goods were assigned to the chargeholder and no longer were the "goods of the debtor". For further discussion see see Beale, Bridge, Gullifer and Lomnicka, *The Law of Security and Title-Based Financing* (2012), paras 16.27–16.29.

[211] *Biggerstaff v Rowatt's Wharf Ltd* [1896] 2 Ch. 93. See para.7–70, below.

[212] *Biggerstaff v Rowatt's Wharf Ltd* [1896] 2 Ch. 93.

The defendant company, having executed a debenture creating a floating charge over its assets, contracted to sell 7,000 barrels of oil to a firm of oil merchants, who paid the price in advance. The company failed to deliver the majority of the barrels. The oil merchants themselves owed the company a substantial sum for wharfage rent, but when, on the appointment of a receiver for the debenture holders, he sought to recover the rent, the oil merchants claimed a right to set off their cross-claim for recovery of the price of the undelivered barrels.

The Court of Appeal held that they were entitled to exercise the right of set-off against the receiver, despite the fact that at all relevant times they were aware of the floating charge.

As against interests arising subsequent to crystallisation

Once a floating charge crystallises, so as to become fixed, the general rule is that except for preferential insolvency creditors and the prescribed part for unsecured creditors it has priority over subsequent interests,[213] including rights of set-off,[214] in just the same way as if it had been fixed at the outset. To this principle there are at least three exceptions:

5–50

(1) Subsequent purchaser or chargee without notice of crystallisation

Though there appears to be no authority directly on the point, it is submitted that, in accordance with the principle of apparent authority referred to earlier,[215] a purchaser or incumbrancer under a transaction concluded after crystallisation but before the purchaser or incumbrancer had notice of crystallisation, takes free from the floating charge (in the case of purchase)[216] or has priority over it (where he is an incumbrancer) if he had had dealings with the company prior to crystallisation or was aware of the existence of the floating charge at the time he paid out his money. In such a case, the subsequent party is entitled to say that he was unaware of the termination of the company's authority to manage its assets and is thus not bound by the termination of that authority. This, of course, is on the assumption that the transaction was in the apparent course of the company's business. As previously stated, there is no reported case exactly on the point,[217]

5–51

---

[213] See *Re Real Meat Co Ltd* [1996] B.C.C. 254. For insolvency, see para.5–68, below.

[214] But only rights of set-off arising after the account debtor (the debtor company's debtor) received notice that the charge had crystallised. See para.7–70, below.

[215] See paras 4–32, 5–02, above.

[216] A purchaser might also take free as a bona fide purchaser of the legal interest without notice of the charge, *ABN Amro Bank NV v Chiyu Banking Corp Ltd* [2001] 2 H.K.L.R.D. 175,190; cf. *Fire Nymph Products Ltd v Heating Centre Property Ltd* (1992) 7 A.C.S.R. 365, 374 where a legal purchaser was held to take subject to a crystallised charge where it was held to have notice of the charge and its contents by failing to discharge the onus of proof.

[217] However, support for the views expressed in the text can be found in *ABN Amro Bank NV v Chiyu Banking Corp Ltd* [2001] 2 H.K.L.R.D. 175. In that case, the question of priority arose between a floating charge which crystallised on the grant of the subsequent (fixed) charges. The fixed chargeholders had constructive notice of the floating charge by reason of its registration, but not of the negative pledge or automatic crystallisation clauses. The Hong Kong Court of First Instance decided the case on the basis of *Dearle v Hall*, and the subsequent chargeholders, who had given notice first, had priority. However, it can be argued that it was only because the first chargeholder had apparent

but the result suggested is in accordance with principle, and this view is shared by Dr Gough in his monograph on company charges.[218]

This situation does not apply to unsecured creditors, for they have no interest in the assets of the company and are therefore not concerned with the company's actual or ostensible dealing powers. So an execution creditor who fails to complete his execution before crystallisation of the floating charge is postponed to the charge even if he proceeds to complete the execution without notice of the fact that there is a charge which has crystallised.[219]

(2) Subsequent purchaser or chargee of debts and the rule in Dearle v Hall

5–52   In a contest between the holder of a crystallised charge over debts and a subsequent purchaser or fixed chargee, the fact that crystallisation comes first is not by itself enough to guarantee priority, for if the purchaser or later chargee took without notice of the crystallisation then even if it does not qualify for priority on the principle described in (1) he will still gain priority under the rule in Dearle v Hall if he is the first to give notice to the debtor.[220]

(3) Landlord levying distress[221]

5–53   Crystallisation does not put an end to a landlord's right to distrain on the goods of the company for rent. This is because at common law the landlord is entitled to distrain on any goods on the demised premises, whether or not belonging to the tenant,[222] and a mortgagee (or chargee, whether fixed or floating) does not have the required interest to serve a notice under s.1 of the Law of Distress Amendment Act 1908.[223]

7.   WAIVER OF A SECURITY INTEREST[224]

5–54   It is not uncommon for the holder of a security interest to agree to waive or subordinate it in favour of a third party proposing to finance the debtor by purchase of or loan against assets comprising the security. It does not usually pay the first financier to try to preserve a monopoly of the debtor company's financing. The debtor's access to other funding will expand his business base and

---

authority to grant the subsequent charges that the first limb of *Dearle v Hall* was relevant at all: without such apparent authority the subsequent chargeholders would have had notice of a fixed charge and the second limb of *Dearle v Hall* would have applied.

[218] Gough, *Company Charges* (1996), p.255 when dealing with the effect of express crystallisation clauses.

[219] *Robson v Smith* [1891] 3 Ch. 260. See paras 5–44 et seq., above.

[220] *ABN Amro Bank v Chiyu Banking Corp Ltd* [2001] 2 H.K.L.R.D. 175, see fn.217, above.

[221] For a detailed discussion see Beale, Bridge, Gullifer and Lomnicka, *The Law of Security and Title-Based Financing* (2012) paras 16.17–16.26.

[222] *Re Coal Consumers Association* (1876) L.R. 4 Ch. D. 625. Note that this is soon to be reformed, see fn.147, above.

[223] *Cunliffe Engineering Ltd v English Industrial Estates Corp* [1994] B.C.C. 972.

[224] This section relates to waiver in relation to consensual security and not to the body of law dealing with waiver of non-consensual security, for example possessory or equitable liens, by the taking of additional or substitute security.

thus enhance the value of the first financier's security. It may therefore be of advantage to the secured creditor, or at least of no disadvantage to him, to grant a waiver to a subsequent financier or to subordinate his security interest to that of the later financier. Subordination is dealt with a little later. For the moment we will discuss waiver of a security interest, or of covenants contained in the security agreement, by a promise not to invoke them against the later financier. Waiver is to be distinguished from contractual subordination in that it is voluntary rather than contractual[225] and it may deal with matters other than subordination, for example, waiver in favour of a purchaser (which operates as a release and not merely subordinates but destroys the security) and waiver of a negative pledge clause in a floating charge.

Waivers take a variety of forms.[226] They may be formal or informal; often no more than an exchange of letters is involved. They may be given without reference to any limit of indebtedness or they may be a waiver as to a given slice of the obligations owed to the first financier, on the basis that as regards indebtedness above the stated figure, the security will continue to bind the assets. It is not usually necessary to get a waiver from a creditor who holds a floating charge imposing no restrictions on the debtor's dealing powers; but even in such a case, now unusual, a waiver may be desirable in certain situations to avoid a possible argument that the later transaction was not within the company's ordinary course of business. Waiver of a negative pledge clause in a floating charge is designed to preclude the chargee from invoking the clause against the subsequent secured creditor in whose favour it was waived.

The effect of waiver

In what circumstances is a waiver enforceable by the party in whose favour it is given? Though the question appears not to have been decided in this specific context, the general principle of promissory (or equitable) estoppel applies to preclude the secured creditor giving the waiver, either temporarily or permanently, from asserting his security interest or restrictive clause against the subsequent secured creditor[227] where the latter alters his position in reliance upon it (as by advancing the secured loan) so as to render it inequitable for the first creditor to resile from his promise.[228] Two questions arise in relation to waivers. First, is the effect of a waiver temporary or permanent? Secondly, does it bind the secured creditor's assignee if taking for value and without notice of it?

5–55

(1) Temporary or permanent?

An operative waiver cannot, of course, be withdrawn as to purchases already contracted or value already given by the beneficiary of the waiver in reliance on it, but it may be withdrawn, on reasonable notice, as to value given after expiry of

5–56

---

[225] This is the legal characterisation (see H. Beale (ed.), *Chitty on Contracts*, 31st edn (London: Sweet & Maxwell/Thomson Reuters, 2012), paras 22–040 et seq.), but in the world of commerce and finance the term "waiver" is not infrequently used to denote a contractual release or subordination.

[226] See S. Wilken, *The Law of Waiver, Variation and Estoppel*, 3rd edn (Oxford: Oxford University Press, 2012), Ch.5.

[227] A waiver may also be given to an unsecured creditor or to the debtor himself.

[228] See generally *Chitty on Contracts*, (2012), para 3–085 et seq.

the notice, except where there is a contractual commitment to provide such value.[229] For example, a bank holding a floating charge that contains registered restrictions on factoring of the company's debts waives that provision in favour of a factoring company which is considering entering into a factoring agreement with the debtor. If the agreement is a facultative agreement, under which the factor is not obliged to purchase receivables offered to it, the bank can give reasonable notice withdrawing its waiver as to purchases by the factor after expiry of the notice. By contrast a whole turnover agreement, under which all receivables not already in being are to be sold to and to vest in the factor upon their coming into existence, commits the factor to future purchases and creates a present assignment of future receivables taking effect as from the time of the agreement.[230]

(2) Is a transferee bound?

5–57 A lender takes a fixed charge over a company's assets and then agrees to waive his security over part of those assets in favour of a third party. The lender then assigns its charge to a new financier, but inadvertently omits to inform that financier of the waiver. Is the latter bound? There appears to be no authority on the point but in the first two editions of this book[231] the view was expressed that the new financier is bound even if without notice of the waiver, an analogy being drawn with the disposition of goods by one having apparent authority or apparent ownership. However, in the third and subsequent editions it is submitted that this view is wrong and that the analogy is false. Waiver of a security interest in favour of a subsequent incumbrancer does not constitute a disposition; it is a mere equity, binding the subordinated creditor and a transferee from him taking with notice of the waiver or by way of gift but having no effect on a purchaser for value (whether at law or in equity) taking without notice. The beneficiary of the subordination can readily protect himself against this result by requiring the charge in favour of the subordinated creditor to be indorsed with a note of the subordination. Similarly, waiver in favour of a purchaser, though operating as a release of the security as between the parties, does not affect a bona fide transferee for value without notice.

Waiver of a floating charge compared with certificate of non-crystallisation

5–58 It is not uncommon for those advising the purchaser or mortgagee of property comprised in a floating charge (particularly land) to ask the chargee for a certificate that the floating charge has not crystallised. The presumed object of this procedure is to estop the debenture holder from subsequently claiming that at the time of the sale or mortgage the debtor company's powers of management had already been brought to an end. Now it may well be that a debenture holder is

---

[229] The position is thus closely analogous to that arising on the termination of a continuing guarantee. See paras 8–05, 8–06, below.

[230] See para.2–13, above. For an instructive discussion, see F.R. Salinger, *Salinger on Factoring*, N. Ruddy, S. Mills and N. Davidson (eds), 4th edn (London: Sweet & Maxwell, 2006), paras 7–10 et seq., and, for a form of priority agreement, App.9 to that work.

[231] And in the third edition of R. Goode, *Commercial Law* (London: Butterworths, 2004), p.666.

unwilling to give a waiver but prepared to give a certificate of non-crystallisation. In such a case, that is the best the purchaser or mortgagee can get and he must take his chance. He ought, however, to be left in no doubt that compared with a waiver a certificate of non-crystallisation is very much second best. The reason is that the debenture holder himself will not necessarily be aware of events that have caused his charge to crystallise; he is therefore unlikely to be willing to give a certificate that goes beyond a statement that he is unaware of the occurrence of any crystallising event. This will not protect the party to whom it is given if it transpires that, unbeknown to the debenture holder, his charge had in fact crystallised. Certainly no one should accept a certificate of non-crystallisation unless he is satisfied that he is unable to get a waiver, for if he can get the latter, which solves his problems, why go for the oblique approach of a certificate of non-crystallisation, when what he really wants is an assurance that the debenture holder will not assert his security over the assets in question?

8.   SUBORDINATION OF A SECURITY INTEREST

The nature of secured and unsecured subordination has been discussed earlier[232] **5–59** and reference has been made to the fact that it is open to two creditors holding security over the same asset to reverse by agreement the order of priority that would otherwise apply.[233] The effect is the same as that of waiver; the subordination constitutes an equity binding the party giving it and an assignee from him who is a volunteer or takes with notice of the subordination but not affecting a bona fide purchaser for value (whether acquiring a legal or an equitable interest) without notice of the subordination. There are two aspects of subordination which will now be developed in the context of the impact of the debtor's insolvency. The first is whether a subordination agreement relating to unsecured debt is likely to be held unenforceable in bankruptcy or winding up as contravening the statutory requirement of pari passu distribution. The second is the resolution of a circularity problem which arises where the debtor has granted a floating charge to one creditor and a fixed charge to another over the same asset and because of a subordination agreement between the two creditors the floating charge has priority over the fixed charge.

Does contractual subordination contravene the pari passu principle?

Secured creditors are not affected by the pari passu principle, so that an **5–60** agreement for the subordination of secured debt is not open to objection on that ground where the debtor becomes insolvent. There has in the past however, been a concern that a liquidator or trustee is precluded by statute from giving effect to that form of subordination agreement by which the junior creditor whose debt is unsecured undertakes not to prove in the bankruptcy or winding up until the senior creditor has received 100 pence in the pound. The reason advanced was that under the Insolvency Act 1986 (re-enacting previous insolvency legislation) the company's property remaining after the satisfaction of preferential debts is

---

[232] See paras 1–84 et seq., above.
[233] See para.1–85, above.

required to be applied in discharge of its liabilities pari passu,[234] that this requirement forms part of a mandatory set of statutory rules governing the administration of estates in bankruptcy and liquidation which cannot be excluded by contract,[235] and that the exclusion of the subordinated creditor from proving in the bankruptcy or winding up before the senior creditor has been paid in full contravenes the rule of pari passu distribution.

One issue is whether the statutory rules for administration of assets in insolvency embody private rights in favour of creditors which any creditor is free to waive or subordinate so long as he does not thereby prejudice the others, or whether they are rules of public policy designed to ensure that in the public interest insolvent estates are to be administered in a proper and orderly way. The latter view was adopted in one House of Lords decision, in which a creditor attempted to exclude its right of insolvency set-off.[236] The general principle that parties cannot contract out of the statutory pari passu distribution of assets on insolvency, except by the creation of proprietary interests, has been affirmed in a number of important cases.[237]

Despite these decisions, it has been made clear in a number of cases that none of the forms of contractual subordination commonly used contravene the principle. The more straightforward situation from this point of view is that of a turnover subordination, where the subordinated creditor agrees to hold the dividends and distributions it receives on trust for the senior creditor.[238] It is clear that this does not infringe the pari passu rule since the subordinated creditor proves in the insolvency in the normal way.[239] This form is the most advantageous for the senior creditor, since it results in him obtaining a double dividend, and the subordination benefits only him and not all the other creditors as well, as is the case in other forms of subordination.[240] Another reasonably straightforward form is where the subordinated debt is expressed as a contingent obligation, so that it is only payable if the senior creditor is paid in full, or if the debtor has sufficient assets to pay the senior creditor in full. This does not infringe the pari passu rule, since if the contingency is not satisfied, the subordinated debt is valued at nil by the liquidator, and if the contingency is

---

[234] Insolvency Act 1986 ss.107, 328(3). For a recent clear statement of the pari passu principle, see *Revenue and Customs Commissioners v Football League Ltd* [2012] EWHC 1372 (Ch) at [63]–[65]; and also *Belmont Park Investments Pty Ltd v BNY Corporate Trustee Services Ltd and Lehman Brothers Special Financing Inc* [2011] UKSC 38 at [6]. The same rules apply in an administration where the administrator distributes assets to unsecured creditors, Insolvency Rules 1986 r.2.69.

[235] *National Westminster Bank Ltd v Halesowen Presswork & Assemblies Ltd* [1972] A.C. 785.

[236] *National Westminster Bank Ltd v Halesowen Presswork & Assemblies Ltd* [1972] A.C. 785.

[237] *British Eagle International Airlines Ltd v Compagnie Nationale Air France* [1975] 1 W.L.R. 758; *Belmont Park Investments Pty Ltd v BNY Corporate Trustee Services Ltd and Lehman Brothers Special Financing Inc* [2011] UKSC 38 at [6]. See also *Revenue and Customs Commissioners v Football League Ltd* [2012] EWHC 1372 (Ch) at [63]–[65].

[238] It is also possible, though less likely, that no trust is involved and the subordinated creditor is merely contractually obliged to hand over dividends and distributions received.

[239] This is confirmed, though not directly, by the decision in *Re British and Commonwealth Holdings Plc (No. 3)* [1992] 1 W.L.R. 672; and also by Lloyd J. in *Re SSSL Realisations (2002) Ltd, Manning v AIG Europe (UK) Ltd* [2004] EWHC 1760 (Ch) at [25]. There is, however, a possible issue as to whether the turnover trust is a registrable charge, see para.1–86, above and para.8–24, below.

[240] This point is confirmed by Lloyd J. *Re SSSL Realisations (2002) Ltd; Manning v AIG Europe (UK) Ltd* [2004] EWHC 1760 (Ch) at [27] and illustrated by the facts of that case. See further para.8–24, below.

satisfied the subordinated creditor is paid pari passu with the other creditors.[241] The most controversial formulation is a plain contractual subordination, where the subordinated creditor agrees not to claim or prove until the senior creditor has been fully paid, without creating a contingent debt. It could possibly be argued that this infringes the pari passu rule, since the senior creditor is better off in the distribution than he otherwise would be, as are the rest of the other creditors. However, this is looking at the situation the wrong way round. If anything, the result of the agreement is that the subordinated creditor is worse off, rather than the senior creditor being better off, and the subordinated creditor is free to bargain for this position, for which he will usually receive an enhanced return. This form of subordination has, accordingly, been held to be valid in a number of cases.[242] The recent case of *SSSL Realisations* also confirmed that, where both the debtor and the subordinated creditor were insolvent, the question of the validity of the subordination agreement vis-à-vis the pari passu rule has to be looked at separately in relation to each insolvency, despite the deleterious effect of the subordination agreement on the creditors of the subordinated creditor.[243]

This judicial confirmation of the validity of subordination agreements is very much to be welcomed. Such agreements are widely used in corporate finance: for example, as a means of increasing available credit, as a way for banks to increase their capital base and in bond issues as a means for some bondholders to receive a higher return. Subordination agreements are enforceable in most developed countries,[244] and it would be most unfortunate if English law took a different view.[245]

Subordination of a fixed charge to a floating charge: a circularity problem[246]

A fixed chargee, C, who would ordinarily have priority over an earlier floating **5–61** chargee, F, in the absence of restrictions of which he has notice, may agree with F that his charge shall be subordinated to the floating charge. If the company then goes into liquidation having preferential creditors (P), a neat circularity problem arises. The liquidator indicates that as there are insufficient free assets for the purpose, he proposes to pay P out of the assets comprised in the floating charge,

---

[241] G. Fuller, *Corporate Borrowing: Law and Practice*, 4th edn (Bristol: Jordans Ltd, 2009), p.153.

[242] *Horne v Chester & Fein Property Developments Pty Ltd* (1987) 11 A.C.L.R. 485; *Re Maxwell Communications Corp Plc (No.2)* [1994] 1 B.C.L.C. 1; *SSSL Realisations (2002) Ltd*; sub nom. *Manning v AIG Europe UK Ltd* [2004] EWHC 1760 (Ch); confirmed on appeal sub nom. *Squires v AIG Europe (UK) Ltd* [2006] EWCA Civ 7; [2006] 2 W.L.R. 1369.

[243] *SSSL Realisations (2002) Ltd, Manning v AIG Europe (UK) Ltd* [2004] EWHC 1760 (Ch) at [45].

[244] See P. Wood, *Project Finance, Securitisations and Subordinated Debt*, 2nd edn (London: Sweet & Maxwell, 2007), pp.204–207.

[245] It should be noted, though, that the turnover trust and contingent debt structures are generally used, rather than a straight contractual subordination.

[246] Following the *Spectrum* case, it is now difficult to create a fixed charge over receivables (see paras 4–13 to 4–17, above), which were the subject matter of the charges in the *Portbase* case. This is likely to mean that the circularity problems described in this section are less likely to arise, although the same issue would arise were the recipient of an outright transfer under, for example, an invoice discounting arrangement, to agree to subordinate his interest to that of a floating chargee.

pursuant to s.175(2)(b) of the Insolvency Act 1986.[247] On the other hand, he must allow C first bite out of the assets comprised in the fixed charge (which are also within the floating charge), as a fixed charge has priority over preferential claims. F protests that this cannot be right, since he has priority over C by virtue of the agreement between them. We thus have a scenario which is not unfamiliar to property lawyers:

- P has priority over F under s.175(2)(b)[248];
- C has priority over P as a matter of general law; and
- F has priority over C by virtue of their agreement.

How should the liquidator distribute the estate? As it happens, this particular circularity problem is a lot easier to solve than those posed by our property textbooks and arising from conflicting statutory provisions. Indeed, Professor Gilmore, who devotes an entire chapter to the mysteries of circularity which makes one wonder how we ever managed before computers, dismisses the circularity through contractual subordination as not a true circularity at all.[249] At all events, the problem is readily soluble through the principle of subrogation. Since F has priority over C by virtue of their agreement, so that C would be accountable to F for moneys received in the liquidation to the extent of C's subordination, all the interests are satisfied by treating F as subrogated to C to the extent necessary to give effect to the subordination agreement. That is to say, F will collect from the liquidator in right of C the amount due to C, or such part of that amount as is necessary to satisfy F's claim. As regards any balance due to F, this is postponed to the claims of P under s.175(2)(b). That this is the correct solution was conceded in *Re Woodroffe's (Musical Instruments) Ltd*.[250] However, in *Re Portbase Clothing Ltd*,[251] Chadwick J. felt unable to adopt this approach and preferred to follow the Victorian decision in *Waters v Widdows*,[252] where Nicholson J. held that the fixed chargee, in subordinating its claims to those of the floating chargee, also subordinated them to the preferential debts. In that case the result was said to be dictated by the statutory policy of protecting preferential creditors. It is hard to see why. The purpose of the legislation is to give preferential debts priority over those secured by a floating charge, not over debts secured by a fixed charge. The result is that the preferential creditors gain a windfall from an agreement to which they were not party, which was not intended to benefit them and which can do so only at the expense of the fixed chargee.

---

[247] See further para.5–68, below as to the subordination of a floating charge to the claims of preferential creditors in various insolvency-related events.

[248] The same point would now apply to the prescribed part under s.176A Insolvency Act 1986, if the floating charge was created after September 15, 2003.

[249] G. Gilmore, *Security Interests in Personal Property* (Boston: Little,Brown, 1965), para.39.1.

[250] *Re Woodroffe's (Musical Instruments) Ltd* [1986] Ch. 366, 368, 375. Similarly Gilmore, *Security Interests in Personal Property* (1965), fn.79. This solution was also the one recommended by the Law Commission to deal with the situation which was likely (in the absence of contrary agreement) to arise under a "first to file" scheme whereby a floating charge had priority over a subsequent fixed charge, see Law Commission, *Company Security Interests*, Law Com. No.296 (2005), paras 3.181–3.187.

[251] *Re Portbase Clothing Ltd* [1993] Ch. 388.

[252] *Waters v Widdows* [1984] V.R. 503. See also *Deputy Commissioner of Taxation v Horsburgh* [1984] V.R. 773.

It is, however, necessary to address the technical arguments on which **5–62** Chadwick J. reached his conclusions in his carefully reasoned judgment. First, whereas in the ordinary way the property the subject of the floating charge, and thus available for preferential creditors, was only the equity of redemption remaining in the chargor after the grant of the fixed charge, the effect of the priority agreement was that the whole of the debtor's interest in the property, not merely the equity of redemption, fell within the floating charge. So by subordinating itself to the holder of the floating charge the fixed chargee was in effect swelling the assets that are subject to the floating charge and thereby increasing the amount available to preferential creditors. Secondly, recourse to the doctrine of subrogation would have put the floating chargee in the same position as if the fixed chargee had assigned his charge to the floating chargee or declared a trust of the proceeds in favour of the floating charge, when in fact there has been no such assignment or declaration of trust, merely a subordination. It would have been open to the two chargees to exchange their security interests but they had not done so. The answer to the first point is that the statutory provisions are designed to provide for payment to preferential creditors from assets which would be free assets of the company but for the floating charge. However, the additional assets that become available to the floating chargee as the result of the subordination do not come from the company and would not form part of its free assets if there were no floating charge; they come from the fixed chargee and are released on the basis that it is the holder of the floating charge, and no one else, who will benefit from them. As to the second point, it is in the nature of subrogation to a security interest that it places the subrogee in much the same position as if the security interest had been assigned to him. Thus a surety who pays off the debt is subrogated to the rights of the secured creditor, including any security interest, and it has never been an objection that the surety could have taken an assignment instead of paying off the debt.

If the fixed chargee, despite the subordination agreement, had collected the debt due to it when there was still an amount due to the holder of the floating charge, it is clear that the sum collected would have been held on trust for the floating chargee.[253] Applying the principle of subrogation does no more than short-circuit this procedure and allow the floating chargee to enforce the chargee's priority directly and for its own benefit, so achieving the result intended by the subordination agreement but without disturbing the position of the preferential creditors, who are neither prejudiced nor enriched by a purely inter-creditor agreement.

9. THE AFTER-ACQUIRED PROPERTY CLAUSE AND THE SUBSEQUENT PURCHASE-MONEY SECURITY INTEREST

We now turn to a priority question which has caused difficulty in a number of **5–63** countries and which has been answered in a highly unsatisfactory manner by English case law. This is the case where A makes an advance to the debtor on the

---

[253] This at least is the position once the floating charge has crystallised, see para.5–40, above.

security of its future property and the debtor subsequently acquires an asset with funds provided by B on the security of that asset. Whose interest has priority, A's or B's? There are good policy reasons to give priority to B. First, it provides a good counterweight against what would otherwise be A's monopoly on the financing of the debtor.[254] Secondly, since it is B's money that has furnished the new asset, why should this accrue as a windfall to A's security?[255] Thirdly, it is possible to achieve the same effect under English law in relation to some assets by B using a retention of title device.[256] It is unfortunate if the same does not apply in relation to assets for which this is not possible, for example, intellectual property. Unfortunately, English law has never recognised the priority of the purchase-money security interest as such except where it attaches at the very moment of the debtor's acquisition of the asset by virtue of a pre-acquisition agreement for security. Indeed, the courts have examined the sequence of operations with meticulous detail to find out whether the debtor's interest in the asset was encumbered at the outset by the purchase-money mortgage (in which case A's after-acquired property clause can attach to the asset only in its encumbered form, so that B wins, even if taking with notice of A's security interest) or whether on the other hand there was a moment of time (*scintilla temporis*) in which B was the unincumbered owner of the asset before granting the purchase-money security interest, in which event A's after-acquired property clause flashes in to catch the asset seconds before the purchase-money security interest takes effect.

All the leading cases concern competing claims to an interest in land.[257] In three cases supporting the first analysis,[258] A had a charge over after-acquired property of C, including land. C purchased land, financed by a loan from B secured with a mortgage, the agreement for which preceded the purchase. In each case, the court held that B, even if not taking a complete transfer by way of mortgage until after acquisition of the asset, had an equitable interest in it by virtue of agreement from the outset, so that there was no gap into which A's after-acquired property clause could insert itself. However, in *Church of England*

---

[254] See para.5–23, above where it was argued that the rules against tacking should be abolished to encourage secured lending, but this needs to be balanced by the possibility of granting a purchase money security interest.

[255] For further discussion of the relevant policy considerations, see C. Walsh, "The Floating Charges is Dead: Long Live the Floating Charge" in A. Mugasha (ed.), *Perspectives in Commercial Law* (London: Prospect Publishing, 2000), pp.129, 134.

[256] Where the purchase-money interest is not a security interest but reservation of title under a conditional sale or hire-purchase agreement the problem does not arise, because it is clear that the after-acquired property clause in a mortgage can only attach to goods in the form in which they are acquired by the debtor, so that if they are acquired under a conditional sale or hire-purchase agreement the conditional seller or owner has priority, the debtor's interest being limited to its rights under the agreement.

[257] The principle does, however, appear to apply to personal property as well. This was the assumption made in *State Securities Plc v Liquidity* [2006] EWHC 2644 (Ch), which concerned a contest between a floating chargee and a receivable financier, although the decision was inconclusive since it concerned an application for an interlocutory injunction.

[258] *Wilson v Kelland* [1910] 2 Ch. 306; *Re Connolly Bros Ltd (No.2)* [1912] 2 Ch. 25; *Security Trust Co v The Royal Bank of Canada* [1976] A.C. 503. In the first two cases, A's charge was floating, and although it contained a negative pledge clause there was no notice of the clause to B, and so B would have had priority on ordinary principles, see para.5–41, above. This argument could not have been made in the third case, since B had notice of the crystallisation of A's charge by the time it took the mortgage.

Building Society v Piskor,[259] the competing interest was not a prior charge, but sub-tenancies granted by the purchaser before completion with the consent of the vendor. B advanced the money on completion of C's purchase, without any prior binding agreement to do so. The court declined to accede to the argument that the purchase and mortgage should be treated as one transaction. Execution of the conveyance vested the title in the purchaser, and fed the titles of the sub-tenants, an instant (*scintilla temporis*) before the purchase-money mortgage took effect. Therefore the sub-tenancies were binding on the mortgagee.

The decision in *Piskor* was overruled by the House of Lords in *Abbey National Building Society v Cann*,[260] where the priority battle was between A, who claimed an equitable interest in the property by virtue of a constructive or resulting trust and B, to whom C had agreed to grant a mortgage to secure the purchase money lent. The House of Lords made it clear that in this situation the property is acquired subject to the mortgage, since the property would not have been acquired unless the funds had been lent, and the funds would not have been lent were it not for the grant of a mortgage to secure them.[261] The basis of the decision, and the rejection of the approach in *Piskor*, was that the finding that there was no evidence in that case to support the existence of such a prior agreement flew in the face of reality, which was that in the vast majority of cases the two transactions are indissolubly bound together in that there will almost invariably be a pre-completion agreement for a charge.[262] Both Lord Jauncey and Lord Oliver seemed to be in no doubt that the priority of the purchase-money charge resulted from the pre-completion agreement for a charge, which fettered the property at the moment of its acquisition.[263] It is submitted that *Cann* addressed one factual reality, the near-inevitability of a pre-completion agreement for a charge, but failed to focus on the much more significant reality, that even without such an agreement the conveyance and simultaneously executed charge constitute a single, indivisible transaction. Such an approach would give substance to the priority of the purchase-money security interest, reflecting what the House of Lords appears to have intended but failed to state.

An unresolved question is whether, for the purpose of securing his priority, it suffices if B secures an agreement for a charge before completion of the purchase or whether he must go further and get it before exchange of contracts. The latter is probably the only safe course. On exchange of contracts, the prior charge, by virtue of the after-acquired property clause, fastens on the debtor's equitable interest arising on exchange of contracts. If the agreement for the purchase-money mortgage is not concluded before that exchange, the equitable mortgage created by that agreement will be second in time and therefore rank after the prior charge. It is true that B may be able to jump ahead by getting a legal mortgage or charge on completion, but this *tabula in naufragio* is available to him only if he was without notice of the prior charge (or in the case of the floating charge, of restrictions on subsequent charges) before making his advance.

5–64

---

[259] *Church of England Building Society v Piskor* [1954] 1 Ch. 553.

[260] *Abbey National Building Society v Cann* [1991] 1 A.C. 56.

[261] *Abbey National Building Society v Cann* [1991] 1 A.C. 56 at 92 and 101–102.

[262] *Abbey National Building Society v Cann* [1991] 1 A.C. 56, per Lord Oliver at 92–93; per Lord Jauncey at 101.

[263] *Abbey National Building Society v Cann* [1991] 1 A.C. 56, per Lord Jauncey at 102; per Lord Oliver at 92.

5–65   Since the *Cann* decision there have been a number of cases purporting to follow it, which appear to extract two rather different principles from the case. The first principle is that a court is required to look at substance over form, so that when two transactions are very closely bound together they cannot be separated into the grant of a greater interest and then the grant-back of a lesser, but must be seen as a grant of a limited interest.[264] The second is that the *Cann* analysis is limited to where a purchase is funded by a mortgage which is granted at the same time as the purchase and subject to a preceding agreement and does not apply to other types of transaction. In *Cook v The Mortgage Business*,[265] A was the vendor of property to C on terms that A would continue to live in the property for the rest of her life. C borrowed the purchase price from B who was secured by a mortgage. The *Cann* analysis was applied to the B/C transaction (so that B took its mortgage free of A's interest) but not to the sale and lease-back between A and C, which could have been analysed as the grant of a limited interest to C.[266]

5–66   In fact, this line of cases has moved away from the central issue discussed here. It is argued that the presence or lack of a *scintilla temporis* should not be the determining factor. The argument that the prior charge attaches to the after-acquired property only in its incumbered state would apply equally to a non-purchase-money security interest taken by the second chargee before the debtor acquired the asset. But such an interest should not qualify for protection against an after-acquired property clause in a prior charge. What should establish the priority for the purchase-money security interest is not merely its attachment to the new asset ab initio but the inequity that would result in allowing the prior chargee a windfall increase in his security brought about not with the debtor's money or new funds injected by the prior chargee but with financing provided by the later incumbrancer. Conversely, the reason why a later non-purchase-money security interest should be postponed even where there is no *scintilla temporis* is that to accord it priority would enable the debtor to commit a fraud on the first incumbrancer by whittling down the value of his security in future property acquired by the debtor with his own money. Such a consideration cannot apply where the debtor's acquisition of the asset results not from the use of his own money but from funds provided by the second financier, who would not have advanced them at all without the protection of a purchase-money security interest.

The rigid insistence on the absence of a *scintilla temporis* between the acquisition of the new asset by the debtor and the attachment of the later security interest does, of course, avoid factual disputes as to whether the second incumbrancer's advance was or was not a purchase-money advance, that is, an advance intended to be used and in fact used by the debtor to acquire the new

---

[264] See R. Calnan, "A question of priority: substance or form?" (2012) 4 J.I.B.F.L. 225; relying on the approach in *Whale v Viasystems Technograph Ltd* [2002] EWCA Civ 480; and *Redstone Mortgages Plc v Welch* [2009] 3 E.G.L.R. 71; and rejecting the Court of Appeal's approach in *Cook v The Mortgage Business* [2012] EWCA Civ 17.

[265] *Cook v The Mortgage Business* [2012] EWCA Civ 17.

[266] Calnan, "A question of priority: substance or form?" (2012) 4 J.I.B.F.L. 225. A similar line of reasoning was adopted in *Redstone Mortgages Plc v Welch* [2009] 3 E.G.L.R. 71.

asset.[267] However, it has been possible to deal with such factual disputes in other jurisdictions which recognise the priority of the purchase money security interest.[268] Where only part of the advance is required or used for the purchase, the financier's priority should be limited to that part.

The *scintilla temporis* doctrine is highly unsatisfactory, in this context at least,[269] and it is high time English law got round to upholding the priority of the purchase-money security interest without insisting on the need for a binding agreement for security before exchange of contracts or completion. This would have been the result of implementation of the Law Commmission's proposals for reform of the law on company security interests put forward in the Consultative Report of 2004.[270] However, this proposal was abandoned, even in relation to "true" security interests, when quasi-security interests were taken out of the proposed scheme in the final report.[271] This is unfortunate, since, as mentioned above, there are good policy reasons for it where it is not possible for the purchase money financier to use retention of title to protect its interests.

5–67

10. IMPACT OF INSOLVENCY ON A SECURITY INTEREST

Priority of certain creditors over the floating charge

(1) The nature of the priority of preferential debts

In an earlier chapter, attention was drawn to one of the major weaknesses of a floating charge, namely that it is subordinated to the claims of preferential creditors if, when the company is not in course of being wound up, the debenture holder takes possession of any property comprised in the charge[272] or appoints a receiver[273] or if the debtor company goes into winding up or a distribution is made when the company is in administration.[274] A similar priority is now

5–68

---

[267] cf. §1(1) of the Ontario Personal Property Security Act: "purchase-money security interest means ... (b) a security interest taken by a person who gives value for the purpose of enabling the debtor to acquire rights in or to the collateral to the extent that the value is applied in acquiring the rights".

[268] Such as the UCC and PPSA jurisdictions: the US, Canada, New Zealand and now also Australia and Jersey (Security Interests (Jersey) Law 2012 art.34.

[269] It may well be that the "substance over form" reasoning is appropriate in the context of cases which do not involve a priority battle between two financiers.

[270] Law Commission, *Consultation Paper on Company Security Interests*, Law Com. CP/176/2004 3.204.

[271] Law Commission, *Company Security Interests*, Law Com No.296 (2005), para.3.146.

[272] Companies Act 2006 s.754.

[273] Insolvency Act 1986 s.40. This section applies whether or not the receiver is an administrative receiver.

[274] Insolvency Act 1986 s.175(2)(b), which applies whether the company goes into compulsory or voluntary liquidation, and para.65(2) Sch.B1 which applies s.175 to a distribution by an administrator. Section 175(2)(b) differs from s.40 and from s.196 of the Companies Act 1985 in the way that it gives effect to the priority, providing that the preferential debts are to be paid out of the floating charge assets only to the extent that the assets available to general creditors are insufficient for the purpose, whereas the latter statutory provisions provide for payment to preferential creditors in the first instance out of assets subject to the floating charge, the chargee having a right to recoupment from the assets available for payment to general creditors.

accorded to the prescribed part of assets comprise in the charge, which is ringfenced for unsecured creditors.[275] A charge is a floating charge within the legislation if it is a floating charge as created,[276] so the priority of preferential creditors and the prescribed part cannot be avoided by the use of an automatic crystallisation clause.[277] So preferential debts and the prescribed part have priority over a floating charge[278] whether they arise before or after crystallisation. Moreover assets which come in under the charge after it has crystallised (e.g. through a receiver's or an administrator's trading activity) are within the preferential net even though there was never a moment when they were subject to a floating charge, for the statutory provisions catch all assets potentially within the scope of the floating charge, including those acquired by the company after crystallisation.[279] The range of preferential debts is now severely reduced, since Crown preference has been abolished from September 2003.[280] However, the deduction of the prescribed part for unsecured creditors from floating charge assets will mean that in most cases approximately the same amount will be deducted as when the Crown was a preferential creditor.[281]

A receiver appointed under a floating charge is under a statutory duty to pay preferential creditors out of the assets coming into his hands in priority to the claims of the debenture holder.[282] However, this duty applies only in relation to assets the subject of the floating charge, not those comprised in a fixed charge. Hence if a receiver is appointed under a debenture containing both a fixed and a floating charge, the mere fact that he is appointed under a floating charge does not attract the operation of the statutory provisions to the assets coming into his hands under the fixed charge.[283] Further, if the receiver, on selling the assets the subject of the fixed charge, realises a surplus, that surplus cannot be said to be caught by the floating charge, even if the proceeds are in a form covered by the charge, for ex hypothesi the sum realised has been sufficient to discharge the debt due to the debenture holder, so that there is no longer any obligation left to be secured. It follows that the receiver's duty is to hand the surplus back to the company if it is not in liquidation or to the liquidator if it is.[284] In relation to an administrative receiver, these circumstances are likely now only to arise in relation to floating charges created before September 2003, to which the

---

[275] Insolvency Act 1986 s.176A. See para.4–10, above and para.5–70, below.

[276] Insolvency Act 1986 ss.40(1), 251; Companies Act 2006 s.754(1).

[277] Interestingly, a court in Ireland held that this was the result even on the previous wording of the Insolvency Act (that is, before s.251 was introduced) which is still the position in Ireland, see *Re JD Brian Ltd* [2011] IEHC 113; [2011] 3 I.R. 244.

[278] Insolvency Act 1986 ss.40, 175(2).

[279] *Inland Revenue Commissioners v Goldblatt* [1972] 1 Ch. 498.

[280] Enterprise Act 2002 s.251.

[281] The prescribed part, however, is only deducted from assets subject to a floating charge created after September 15, 2003. Further, the provisions do not apply to a financial collateral arrangement, see para.6–26, below and Financial Collateral Arrangements (No.2) Regulations 2003 reg.10(3).

[282] Insolvency Act 1986 s.40(2). See further R. Goode, *Principles of Corporate Insolvency Law*, 4th edn (London: Sweet & Maxwell/Thomson Reuters, 2011), p.367.

[283] *Re Lewis Merthyr Consolidated Collieries Ltd* [1929] 1 Ch. 498; *Re G.L. Saunders Ltd* [1986] 1 W.L.R. 215.

[284] *Re G.L. Saunders Ltd* [1986] 1 W.L.R. 215.

provisions about the prescribed part do not apply. However, if the receiver is not an administrative receiver, the same reasoning applies to the receiver's obligation in relation to the prescribed part.[285]

If payment is made to preferential creditors when a receiver is appointed under a floating charge, or possession is taken of the floating charge assets, this can be recouped out of unencumbered assets available for payment of general creditors,[286] although given that floating charges are usually taken over all the assets of the company, this is a rare occurrence.

(2) Events triggering the priority of preferential debts

As stated above, any one of four distinct events can trigger the priority of preferential debts over a floating charge and thus establish a priority point at which the preferential debts have to be determined, namely the taking of possession of the security by or on behalf of the chargee,[287] the appointment of a receiver[288] and the winding-up of the debtor company[289] and the making of a distribution by an administrator.[290] On the appointment of a receiver by the holder of a floating charge the claims of all floating chargees (not just the appointing floating chargee) are subordinated to those of the preferential creditors.[291]

5–69

(3) The prescribed part

If the company goes into liquidation or administration, or there is a receiver appointed over the company's property, the office holder in each case must make the prescribed part[292] of the company's net property available for unsecured creditors, and must not distribute that part of the property to the floating chargeholder except insofar as it exceeds the amount required for the satisfaction of unsecured debts. The net property is defined as property which but for this section would be available for the satisfaction of the claims of holders of

5–70

---

[285] This only applies to the company's net property, which is property which would be available for the satisfaction of claims of floating charge holders (s.176A(6) of the Insolvency Act 1986).

[286] Insolvency Act 1986 s.40(3) and s.754(4) of the Companies Act 2006.

[287] In this context, the taking of possession includes the realisation of intangible assets, *Re Oval 1742 Ltd* [2007] EWCA Civ 1262; [2008] 1 B.C.L.C. 204. However, since the concept of realisation is not as clear cut as the taking of possession, the facts of each case have to be examined in order to determine whether the debenture holder is actually realising the charged assets, or whether the indebtedness is merely being discharged by the company out of the proceeds of those assets.

[288] A receiver acts independently of the debenture holder who appointed him and therefore in taking possession does not act "on behalf of" the debenture holder so as to bring s.754 of the Companies Act 2006 into play concurrently with s.40 of the Insolvency Act 1986 (*Re H & K Medway Ltd* [1997] 1 W.L.R. 1422).

[289] Insolvency Act 1986 s.387. If the winding-up immediately follows an administration, the relevant date for the calculation of preferential debts is the date on which the company entered administration.

[290] Insolvency Act 1986 s.387. If the winding-up immediately follows an administration, the relevant date for the calculation of preferential debts is the date on which the company entered administration.

[291] *Re H & K Medway Ltd* [1997] 1 W.L.R. 1422. This is also the position in relation to the prescribed part, see Insolvency Act s.176A(6) which specifically refers to "any floating charge created by the company".

[292] This is 50 per cent of the first £10,000 and 20 per cent of the excess, with a maximum of £600,000, see Insolvency Act 1986 (Prescribed Part) Order 2003 (SI 2003/2097).

debentures secured by, or holders of, any floating charge created by the company. This has the effect that the prescribed part is calculated on the basis of the amount of floating charge assets after deducting the payment of preferential claims. Further, it appears that the expenses of an administrator or a liquidator would be deducted from the amount of floating charge assets before the calculation of the prescribed part.[293]

Where the assets secured by the floating charge, after the deductions referred to above are insufficient to pay the debts secured by the floating charge, the floating chargeholder in theory becomes an unsecured creditor in relation to the shortfall. However, a recent decision has confirmed that he cannot participate in the prescribed part, since the term "unsecured creditors" in s.176A of the Insolvency Act 1986 refers only to those creditors whose debts were initially unsecured, rather than those whose security has proved to be insufficient.[294] This is clearly right as a matter of policy, since s.176A was designed to protect the ordinary unsecured creditors at the expense of floating chargeholders, and not to give the latter two bites at the cherry. If a floating chargeholder chose not to enforce his security and proving as an unsecured creditor, the position is different and he can participate in the prescribed part.[295]

(4) Expenses of winding up and administration

5–71   The expenses of administration are payable out of floating charge assets in priority to the claims of any floating chargeholder.[296] It would also seem that they are payable in priority to the claims of preferential creditors, and before calculation of the prescribed part, although this is not clear from the statutory provisions.[297] The statutory provisions in relation to liquidation expenses were somewhat opaque and the position has now been clarified by s.176ZA of the Insolvency Act 1986,[298] so that it is now clear beyond argument that the expenses of winding up are payable out of floating charge assets in priority to the claims of preferential creditors and floating chargeholders. Further, although the expenses of the winding up are to be paid out of the assets available for general creditors, if any are available, rather than out of floating charge assets, they are not to be paid out of the prescribed part.[299]

---

[293] See below. This is not expressly provided in the Insolvency Act. However, both the liquidator's costs are payable out of floating charge assets in priority to the claims of preferential creditors (s.176ZA(2)(b)), and so it would seem that both should be deducted in calculating the prescribed part, which is only calculated on floating charge assets available for the claims of floating chargeholders. It would therefore seem strange if the position differed in relation to the costs of an administration.

[294] *Re Airbase (UK) Ltd: Thorniley v Revenue and Customs Commissoners* [2008] EWHC 124 (Ch); [2008] 1 B.C.L.C. 437.

[295] *Re PAL SC Realisations 2007 Ltd* [2010] EWHC 2850 (Ch); *Re JT Frith Ltd* [2012] EWHC 196 (Ch).

[296] Insolvency Act 1986 para.99(3) Sch.B1.

[297] There is no mention of the preferential creditors in para.99. However, s.176ZA of the Insolvency Act (see below) expressly provides that the liquidator's expenses have priority over these two entitlements, and the reasoning behind that section was to put the liquidator in the same position as an administrator (*Hansard*, November 3, 2005). In relation to the prescribed part see para.5–70, above.

[298] Rules relating to the operation of this section and providing, inter alia, for consent of a floating chargeholder to be required in order for the liquidator to incur certain litigation expenses, have now been enacted Insolvency (Amendment) Rules 2008.

[299] Insolvency Act 1986 s.176ZA, inserted by s.1282 of the Companies Act 2006.

Avoidance of a security interest in insolvency proceedings[300]

Apart from avoidance at common law or in equity (e.g. for misrepresentation or undue influence), there are various statutory grounds on which a validly created security interest may be rendered void or liable to be set aside. In every case except one the grounds for avoidance are dependent upon the company being in an insolvency proceeding of some kind. Some of the statutory provisions apply to all forms of security, others are confined to floating charges. Avoidance of the security has no effect on the secured creditor to the extent that he has realised his security or otherwise obtained payment before the commencement of the insolvency proceeding which renders the security vulnerable,[301] because to that extent the security has already been satisfied, there is nothing for the secured creditor to enforce and the invalidation of the security interest is not retrospective. There are eight statutory grounds on which a security interest given by a company can be attacked, namely that it:

5–72

(1)   contravenes the principle of pari passu distribution,[302] as where it is expressed to come into existence only on the advent of winding-up;

(2)   was not registered as required by statute[303];

(3)   is a transaction at undervalue[304];

(4)   is a preference of a creditor or surety[305];

(5)   secures an extortionate credit bargain[306];

(6)   is a floating charge given by an insolvent company otherwise than for new value and the company goes into winding up or administration within the statutory period[307];

(7)   was given after the commencement of a winding up by the court and has not been sanctioned by the court[308]; and

(8)   is a transaction made to defraud creditors.[309]

---

[300] For more detailed discussion, see Goode, *Principles of Corporate Insolvency Law* (2011), Ch.13; R. Parry, J. Ayliffe, S. Shivli, H. Anderson and W. Trower, *Transaction Avoidance in Insolvencies*, 2nd edn (Oxford: Oxford University Press, 2011).

[301] *Re Row Dal Construction Pty Ltd* [1966] V.R. 249; *Mace Builders (Glasgow) Ltd v Lunn* [1987] Ch. 191. The commencement of winding up dates from the presentation of the petition for winding up, s.129 of the Insolvency Act 1986 (applied, in the context of a charge invalid under s.245 of the Insolvency Act 1986, in *Re Shoe Lane Ltd; Power v Sharp Investments Ltd* [1994] 1 B.C.L.C. 111).

[302] Now embodied in the Insolvency Act 1986 s.107 (voluntary winding-up), and the Insolvency Rules 1986 r.4.181(1) (compulsory winding-up). See further, *Revenue and Customs Commissioners v Football League Ltd* [2012] EWHC 1372 (Ch) at [63]–[65]; and also *Belmont Park Investments Pty Ltd v BNY Corporate Trustee Services Ltd and Lehman Brothers Special Financing Inc* [2011] UKSC 38 at [6].

[303] Companies Act 2006 ss.859H. See paras 2–18, 3–24 and 3–29, above.

[304] Insolvency Act 1986 ss.238, 240, 241.

[305] Insolvency Act 1986 ss.239–241.

[306] Insolvency Act 1986 s.244.

[307] Insolvency Act 1986 s.245.

[308] Insolvency Act 1986 s.127. But see para.6–26, below as to the Financial Collateral Arrangements (No.2) Regulations 2003.

[309] Insolvency Act 1986 s.423.

Ground (1) applies only in winding-up, voluntary or compulsory, or if an administrator give notice[310] that he intends to make a distribution[311]; grounds (2)–(6) apply only if the debtor company is in administration or winding up; ground (7) is confined to companies in compulsory winding up; and ground (8) may be invoked whether or not the company is the subject of an insolvency proceeding. Provisions similar to those applicable in relation to grounds (2)–(5) and (7) apply to security given by an individual,[312] and there is an additional provision, not applicable to security given by a company, which renders a general assignment of trade debts void against the debtor's trustee in bankruptcy unless this has been registered as if it were a bill of sale.[313] These are dealt with in detail elsewhere.[314]

Market charges[315]

5–73　Part VII of the Companies Act 1989 introduced special rules for market charges designed to immunise charges in favour of an investment exchange, the Stock Exchange, and clearing houses, from many of the effects of general insolvency law and the Insolvency Act 1986.[316] To these were added money market charges[317] and system charges in favour of settlement banks.[318] The statutory provisions relating to market charges have been buttressed by subordinate legislation[319] and by regulations[320] implementing the 1998 EC Settlement Finality Directive.[321] They are considered further in Ch.6, below.

11.　SOME TYPICAL PRIORITY PROBLEMS OUTSIDE INSOLVENCY

5–74　It may be helpful to conclude with a series of twelve short but typical priority problems arising from competing interests outside insolvency[322] and the manner in which each problem is resolved by the priority rules described earlier. In each case the security is given by a company, it is assumed that any registration requirements have been duly complied with, and unless otherwise stated there is no waiver or subordination agreement.

---

[310] Under Insolvency Rules 1986 r.2.95 pursuant to Insolvency Act 1986 Sch.B1 para.65.

[311] *Revenue and Customs Commissioners v Football League Ltd* [2012] EWHC 1372 (Ch) at [89].

[312] Bills of Sale Act (1878) Amendment Act 1882 s.8; Insolvency Act 1986 ss.284, 339–343.

[313] Insolvency Act 1986 s.344.

[314] Goode, *Principles of Corporate Insolvency Law* (2011), Ch.13.

[315] See Ch.6, below.

[316] Companies Act 1989 ss.173–181.

[317] Financial Markets and Insolvency (Money Markets) Regulations 1995 (SI 1995/2049).

[318] Financial Markets and Insolvency Regulations 1996 (SI 1996/1469).

[319] Financial Markets and Insolvency Regulations 1991 (SI 1991/880); Financial Markets and Insolvency Regulations 1996 (SI 1996/1469).

[320] Financial Markets and Insolvency (Settlement Finality) Regulations 1999 (SI 1999/2979), as amended.

[321] Directive on settlement finality in payment and securities settlement systems, EC 98/26. See para.6–23, below.

[322] Of course, in reality the priority position usually only matters when the debtor is insolvent.

Problem 1

Debtor gives a first fixed charge on an existing tangible asset to A, followed by a second fixed charge to B.

Assuming that the charge to A is not securing further advances on land,[323] A wins provided that his charge is duly registered. Since registration is purely a perfection requirement, not a priority point,[324] it makes no difference that B is the first to register or that A's charge was not registered at the time B made his search.

5–75

Problem 2

Debtor gives a fixed charge over future property to A, then acquires equipment from B under reservation of title.

B wins, since A cannot acquire greater rights than the debtor company, and the latter becomes the owner only on payment of the purchase price to B.

5–76

Problem 3

Debtor gives a fixed charge over future property to A, then acquires a new asset with money advanced by B, to whom debtor gives a purchase-money mortgage.

Assuming that the mortgage, or an agreement for the mortgage, was made prior to the debtor's acquisition of the asset, so that there was no *scintilla temporis* during which the asset was held by the debtor unincumbered,[325] B wins, for A's after-acquired property clause can attach to B's future property only in the form in which it is acquired, that is, mortgaged to B, and thus bites only on B's equity of redemption.

5–77

Problem 4

Debtor gives a fixed charge over existing and future book debts to A,[326] then factors its existing and future book debts to B.

If, when the debts became vested in B under the factoring agreement, B had notice of A's charge (whether by reason of registration or otherwise),[327] A wins; in any other case (including purchase by B before registration of A's charge and without other notice of it) A has an initial priority but this is displaced under the rule in *Dearle v Hall*[328] if B is the first to give notice of his interest to the relevant debtor.[329]

5–78

---

[323] As to which see Problem 6.

[324] See paras 2–23, 5–16, above.

[325] See paras 5–63 et seq., above.

[326] It should be borne in mind that, following the *Spectrum* decision, there is much less likely to be an effective fixed charge over book debts. See para.4–16, above.

[327] As to the effect of registration as notice, see paras 2–25 et seq., above.

[328] See paras 5–08, 5–09, above.

[329] See para.5–08, above.

Problem 5

5-79   Debtor factors its existing and future book debts to A, then gives a fixed charge over existing and future book debts to B.

A has an initial priority but this is displaced under the rule in *Dearle v Hall* if B makes his advance without notice of A's rights and is the first to give notice to the relevant debtor. In this case notice cannot be derived from registration since A's rights are acquired by purchase, not by way of security, and are therefore not registrable.

Problem 6

5-80   Debtor charges an existing asset to A to secure present and future advances. After A has advanced £10,000, debtor charges the asset to B to secure a contemporaneous advance. Later, A advances a further £5,000. A has priority as to his initial advance of £10,000, and also has priority as to the further advance of £5,000 if at the time he made this he had no notice of the charge to B.[330] If the asset consists of unregistered land, registration of B's charge does not constitute notice for this purpose.[331]

Problem 7

5-81   Debtor gives a floating charge over book debts to A, then sells or grants a fixed charge over the debts to B.

B wins, unless the charge in favour of A precludes the debtor from granting a subsequent fixed charge ranking in priority to or pari passu with A's floating charge and B takes his charge with notice of the restriction on subsequent charges: it is likely that B will search the register and therefore have actual notice of the restriction, but he is also very likely to have constructive notice following the reforms brought into force in 2013.[332]

Problem 8

5-82   Debtor gives a fixed charge over its equipment to A, who fails to register the charge. Subsequently debtor sells the equipment to B.

A's failure to register does not of itself invalidate the charge against B,[333] but B obtains priority by virtue of his legal title if he bought without notice of A's charge.

---

[330] See paras 5–18 to 5–21, above. If the asset is unregistered land or personalty, the position is probably governed by s.94(b) of the Law of Property Act 1925, if the asset is registered land, the position is governed by s.49 of the Land Registration Act 2002.

[331] See para.5–18, above.

[332] See paras 2–24 to 2–30, above.

[333] Since s.859H of the Companies Act 2006 renders an unregistered charge void only against the liquidator or a creditor, not against a purchaser.

Problem 9

Debtor charges its receivables to A under an agreement which provides that the   **5–83**
charge is to be by way of fixed charge and debtor is not to dispose of the
receivables but is to collect them in and pay them into a special account
controlled by A.[334] Debtor receives payment by cheque from various customers
but pays the cheques into its overdrawn account with B.

B wins if collecting the cheques without negligence[335] and without notice of
A's claim, since B's acquisition of the legal title to the proceeds of the cheques for
value and without notice overrides A's equitable charge.

Problem 10

Debtor charges its receivables to A under an agreement which provides that the   **5–84**
charge is to be by way of fixed charge and debtor is not to dispose of the
receivables. Debtor is left free to collect them in and use them as its own moneys.
Debtor subsequently grants a fixed charge of the receivables to B, with a duty to
pay collections into an account controlled by B.

B wins. A's charge, though expressed to be fixed, is no more than a floating
charge,[336] and this is subordinate to a subsequent fixed charge, in the absence of
restrictions on subsequent charges of which the later fixed chargee has notice.[337]

Problem 11

Debtor gives a floating charge over its stock in trade to A. The charge provides   **5–85**
that A may at any time convert it into a fixed charge by service of a crystallisation
notice. Subsequently A gives notice crystallising the charge. A week later, debtor
gives a fixed charge over the stock in trade to B.

B wins if he had dealings with the debtor prior to crystallisation or if he dealt
with the debtor after crystallisation and with knowledge of the floating charge,
provided that in either case he had no notice that the charge had crystallised.[338]

---

[334] This would appear, in its face, to create a fixed charge, even after the *Spectrum* decision.
However, if A did not object to the payment of the proceeds by debtor into the account with B, the
fixed charge could be held to have decrystallised by waiver, which could have the effect of creating a
new floating charge, or the original characterisation could be held to be a sham. See para.4–30, above.
[335] Since A's agreement with debtor gives A not merely equitable ownership of the cheques but also a
right to their immediate possession, A has a claim against B for conversion in collecting the cheque
(this being a strict liability tort) unless B can rely on s.4 of the Cheques Act 1957, which requires that
B collect the cheque in good faith and without negligence. But s.4 operates solely to protect B against
a claim for conversion; it does not in itself give B an overriding title (see R. Goode, "The Right to
Trace and Its Impact in Commercial Transactions" (1976) 92 L.Q.R. 360, 528, at 558); for this, B
must rely on the common law priority in favour of the bona fide legal purchaser for value.
[336] See paras 4–13 et seq., above.
[337] See paras 5–39, 5–40, above.
[338] See para.5–51, above.

Problem 12

5–86   Debtor gives a floating charge over all its present and future assets and undertaking to A, the charge providing that debtor is not to dispose of its book debts or other receivables. Subsequently A gives B a waiver of its charge over debtor's receivables in consideration of B entering into a factoring agreement with debtor for sale of debtor's existing and future receivables. B purchases receivables under the factoring agreement. A then assigns its loan portfolio and security for payment to C, who buys without notice of the waiver.

Though the waiver operates as a release as between A and B it does not affect C as a purchaser for value without notice of the waiver, so that C has priority over B.[339]

---

[339] See para.5–57, above.

CHAPTER 6

Interests in Financial Collateral

1. INTRODUCTION

This chapter was originally concerned with security interests in corporate **6–01** investment securities, that is securities issued by a company and traded on a market,[1] but has been extended to cover other forms of financial collateral. The scope and application of the Financial Collateral Directive ("FCD")[2] and the implementing Financial Collateral Arrangements (No.2) Regulations ("FCARs")[3] are so important to the capital markets that this subject warrants a more comprehensive discussion here than previously. Financial collateral comprises cash, credit claims and securities. Each asset class has a rather restrictive definition in the FCD and the FCARs: this will be considered below.

These asset classes can, of course, be used as security for any kind of loan or in any kind of financing transaction. However, the FCD is specifically concerned with their use as collateral in transactions on the capital markets, where collateral is required as credit protection by counterparties, brokers, clearing houses and

---

[1] There is a considerable body of literature concerning the ways in which securities are now held. Early studies include J. Benjamin, *Interests in Securities* (Oxford: Oxford University Press, 2000); J. Benjamin and M. Yates, *The Law of Global Custody*, 2nd edn (London: Butterworths, 2002); A.O. Austen-Peters, *Custody of Investments: Law and Practice* (Oxford: Oxford University Press, 2000); P. R. Wood, *Comparative Law of Securities and Guarantees* (London: Sweet & Maxwell, 1995), Ch.VI; and, for a comparative treatment of the conflict of laws issues, R. Potok, *Cross-Border Collateral: Legal Risk and the Conflict of Laws* (Haywards Heath: Tottel Publishing Ltd, 2002). See also Law Commission, *The UNIDROIT Convention on Substantive Rules regarding Intermediated Securities: Updated Advice to the Treasury* (May 2008), Ch.2. More recent literature includes M. Evans (ed.) *Tolley's Company Law Service (Charges over Shares)* (London: Butterworths, 2009); L Gullifer & J Payne (eds) *Intermediated Securities: Legal Problems and Practical Issues* (Oxford: Hart Publishing, 2010); H. Beale, M. Bridge, L. Gullifer and E. Lomnicka, *The Law of Security and Title-based Financing*, 2nd edn (Oxford: OUP, 2012), especially Chs 3 and 6; J. Benjamin, *Financial Law* (Oxford: OUP, 2007), Ch.19; M. Bridge, L. Gullifer, G. McMeel, S. Worthington, *The Law of Personal Property* (London: Sweet & Maxwell, 2013), Chs 23 and 32. Once again the reader is reminded that "securities" should not be confused with security interests but denote issues on the market, and debt issues may be either secured or unsecured. Similarly, the grant of a security interest, though forming an element in a typical securitisation, is to be distinguished from it. Securitisation denotes the total process by which non-tradable debt assets are converted into tradable debt assets by transferring them from the original creditor (the originator) to a special-purpose vehicle which raises money from the market by issuing bonds or notes, using the transferred assets as security. Where the transferred debts are secured by a security interest in other assets, the grant of a security interest in them operates as a sub-charge.
[2] Directive 2002/47/EC (on Financial Collateral Arrangements) as amended by Directive 2009/44/EC of May 6, 2009 [2009] O.J. L146/37.
[3] SI 2003/3226, amended by SI 2009/2462 and SI 2010/2993.

central counterparties, and settlement banks. It should be noted that securities, in particular, can move through the system acting as collateral for several different transactions. Thus securities owned by A may be lent to B under a securities lending arrangement, B then uses them as collateral for a loan from C (under a repo arrangement), C then posts collateral to D for a loan or for exposure on a derivatives transaction under a security arrangement with a right of use, D is then able to re-use the securities in a repo and so on. To some extent, the same is true of credit claims, and even cash collateral, although where the purpose of the transaction is financing, the resulting cash is often used for an operational purpose rather than reinvestment. One very important use of collateral is as margin posted to a central counterparty or clearing house,[4] as security for the members' obligations to it. With the increased use of central counterparties in relation to derivatives transactions,[5] the use of collateral in this regard will become very critical, although, so long as effective close-out netting is used, margin only needs to be posted for the net amount. Another very important use is as security for banks which provide payment for settlement of securities transactions, such as dealings through CREST.

The European Community has long been concerned to limit systemic risk[6] to ensure both the efficiency and the stability of dealings among participants in recognised clearing and settlement systems. To that end two Directives were issued, the 1998 Settlement Finality Directive[7] and, as already mentioned, the Financial Collateral Directive. Both override rules of national law that were thought to impair the legal efficacy of financial collateral arrangements and enforcement within or outside insolvency. The Financial Collateral Directive, in particular, also had other aims, namely, to achieve a degree of uniformity across jurisdictions in rules relating to perfection and enforcement, and also uniformity between rules applicable to title transfer collateral arrangements and security collateral arrangements,[8] and to remove legal uncertainty in relation to certain market practices such as the right of use and close-out netting.[9] Both Directives also attempted to deal with existing uncertainty as to the choice of the law governing intermediated securities.[10]

Title transfer and security collateral arrangements

6–02   Financial collateral arrangements are divided into two categories, title transfer financial collateral arrangements and security financial collateral arrangements. This distinction, which is explored below,[11] reflects the industry usage whereby collateral is either provided by transferring legal title to the collateral taker, who

---

[4] See para.7–09, below.

[5] This will be required from 2014 under EMIR, the European Market Infrastructure Regulation, Regulation 648/2012 on OTC derivatives, central counterparties and trade repositories. See *http://www.fca.org.uk/firms/markets/international-markets/emir#* [accessed September 30, 2013].

[6] The risk that the failure of one major participant will have a domino effect on the system as a whole.

[7] Directive on Settlement Finality in Payment and Securities Systems (98/26 dated May 19, 1998), 1998), implemented in the UK by the Financial Markets and Insolvency (Settlement Finality) Regulations 1999 (SI 1999/2979).

[8] See paras 6–02 and 6–27 et seq., below.

[9] See paras 6–46 and 7–90, below.

[10] Discussed at paras 6–53 et seq., below.

[11] Paras 6–27 et seq., below.

then owes a personal obligation to the collateral provider to return equivalent assets, or it is provided by the grant of a security interest over the collateral. The attraction of title transfer arrangements, at least under English law, is that usually no difficulties then arise about the re-use of the collateral, or whether the arrangement needs to be registered, or as to whether the arrangement can be enforced by close-out netting or appropriation of the collateral, since such restrictions as exist in this regard only apply to security interests (except, perhaps, in the consumer sphere). In any event, these advantages are available in relation to title transfer collateral arrangements under the FCD and FCARs, while they are only available in respect of a security collateral arrangement if it falls within the criteria laid down in the FCARs, most notably whether the collateral is in the "possession or control" of the collateral taker. Title transfer arrangements include repos and securities lending, but also include the provision of collateral under the ISDA Credit Support Annexe (English law) in relation to derivatives transactions and provision of margin to a central counterparty.

Margin requirements and haircuts

Unless the collateral used is cash, questions of valuation arise. There are two potential uncertainties of valuation: one is the valuation of the exposure which is being collateralised, and the other is the value of the collateral itself. In relation to the latter, the collateral taker needs to be sure that it has sufficient collateral to cover its exposure in the event of a default, taking account of the fact that the collateral itself may fluctuate in value, and that it may not be perfectly liquid, that is, it may not be able to be realised easily at its market value. There are two ways of dealing with these uncertainties. First, non-cash collateral is usually subject to a "haircut" (or initial margin), that is, it is valued at a certain percentage less than its market value (or more collateral than its market value is required to be posted). Secondly, the (net) exposure and the collateral are "marked to market" at frequent intervals, and if the value of the collateral (including any haircut) falls below the exposure, top-up collateral may be required. The valuation may go either way, and, so that assets are not uselessly tied up as collateral, a collateral provider will usually have the right to withdraw "excess collateral".[12]

6–03

2.   TYPES OF FINANCIAL COLLATERAL

Cash

Cash is defined in the FCARs as "Money in any currency, credited to an account, or a similar claim for repayment of money and includes money market deposits and sums due or payable to, or received between the parties in connection with the operation of a financial collateral arrangement or a close-out netting arrangement".[13] The last part, referring to sums due, payable or received in connection with the operation of a financial collateral arrangement or a close-out

6–04

---

[12] This is the reason that there is this exception to the "possession or control" requirement under the FCARs, see para.6–36, below.
[13] FCARs reg.3(1).

netting arrangement, was added by the United Kingdom Government and does not appear in the FCD. The rationale for the addition was that it would be odd if a security interest created over the "proceeds" of a collateral arrangement would not be protected under the FCARs.[14] It has been pointed out that it does not necessarily follow that such a security interest should be protected, since it could be independent of the main collateral arrangement.[15] While this could be true, depending on the details of the transaction, it is also likely in many longer term arrangements, net balances could be included in the collateral given in relation to the whole transaction, and it would be odd if protection depended on whether those net balances were actually paid, so that they became "money credited to an account" or not. The certainty this gives could be welcome, given the uncertainty of the phrase "a similar claim for repayment of money" which is taken from the FCD itself.[16]

Cash is seen, in many ways, as the "best" collateral since it is liquid and does not require valuation. It is therefore very important that it is included within the protection of the FCARs. However, the wide scope of the FCARs[17] means that any security interest granted by a company over its bank account potentially comes within their scope.[18] This gives the bank particular protection in insolvency, to the possible detriment of other creditors of the company, in a situation where there is no question of systemic risk.[19]

Credit claims

6–05   Credit claims, that is, claims for the repayment of a loan made by a bank or credit institution,[20] were added to the definition of financial collateral in the FCD in 2009[21] and to the definition in the FCARs in 2010.[22] The purpose of the extension was to include bank loans which could be used for collateralisation of central bank operations, as well as providing an alternative to securitisation.[23] In fact, the impact is even wider, since any use of such a loan in a collateral arrangement is potentially covered, although the fact that the definition relies on

---

[14] HM Treasury, *A Consultation on the implementation of the Directive on Financial Collateral Arrangements* (July 2003) (Treasury Condoc) 2.7.

[15] L Ho, "The Financial Collateral Directive's practice in England" (2011) 26 J.I.B.L.R. 151, 155.

[16] The extended wording may also cover an arrangement which operates as a substitute for multilateral set-off in relation to transactions involving a group of companies, see Ho, "The Financial Collateral Directive's practice in England" (2011) 26 J.I.B.L.R. 151, 155.

[17] See para.6–25, below.

[18] See, for example, the facts of *Gray v G-T-P Group Ltd; Re F2G Realisations Ltd (In Liquidation)* [2010] EWHC 1772 (Ch).

[19] See L. Gullifer, "What Should we do about Financial Collateral?" (2012) 65 C.L.P. 377.

[20] Defined in art.4(1) of Directive 2000/48.

[21] Directive 2009/44 EC of May 6, 2009 amending Directive 98/26/EC on settlement finality in payment and securities systems and Directive 2002/47/EC on financial collateral arrangements as regards linked systems and credit claims.

[22] By SI 2010/2993 reg.1.

[23] European Commission, *Proposal for a Directive amending Directive 98/26/EC on settlement finality in payment and securities systems and Directive 2002/47/EC on financial collateral arrangements as regards linked systems and credit claims* (March 17, 2003) COM (08) 213, para.1.2.

the original source of the loan means that where loans which have been assigned to the collateral provider are used as collateral, the collateral taker needs to check the identity of the original lender.[24]

Financial instruments

The definition of these in the FCARs includes most types of securities. Thus it includes shares, tradeable bonds and other types of debt securities, and "any other securities which are normally dealt in and which give the right to acquire any such shares, bonds, instruments or other securities by subscription, purchase or exchange or which give rise to a cash settlement (excluding instruments of payment)".[25] Share warrants[26] are therefore included as are shares in private companies,[27] and all kinds of debt issues such as bonds, notes, debentures and loan stock.

6–06

In their traditional form securities were paper-based and held by the investor directly from the issuer, and the law relating to security interests in them was, and remains, tolerably well settled. However, paper-based securities are now rare, and although direct holdings (through CREST) of dematerialised securities are common in the United Kingdom,[28] indirect holding through intermediaries is extremely widespread throughout the developed world. The European Commission has proposed that all securities traded on recognised markets should be issued in "book-entry" form, that is, either as an immobilised global note[29] or in dematerialised form.[30] The move from direct to indirect holdings, from segregated (or non-fungible) securities accounts to pooled (or fungible) securities accounts and from paper-based to paperless (dematerialised) securities, though greatly increasing efficiency and reducing cost and risk, has nevertheless presented new challenges for the domestic and international legal community. These challenges are identified and discussed in this chapter, both from the point of view of English law and from a wider EU and global perspective. But first it is necessary to give a brief description of these changes in practice and their implications.

---

[24] R. Parsons and M. Dening, "Financial collateral – an opportunity missed" (2011) F.M.L.R. 164, 165.

[25] The following are also included in the definition: "units of a collective investment scheme within the meaning of the Financial Services and Markets Act 2000, eligible debt securities within the meaning of the Uncertificated Securities Regulations 2001, money market instruments, claims relating to or rights in or in respect of any of the financial instruments included in this definition, and any rights, privileges or benefits attached to or arising from any such financial instruments". See FCARs reg.3(1).

[26] Warrants are instruments which entitle the holder to convert them into shares. They enable an investor to make a highly geared investment.

[27] This point appears to have been agreed between the learned experts who gave evidence to the British Virgin Islands Court of Appeal in *Alfa Telecom Turkey Ltd v Cukurova Finance International Limited* HCVAP2007/027.

[28] For an account of holding through CREST see paras 6–09 et seq., below.

[29] See para.6–07, below.

[30] See European Commission, *Proposal for a Regulation improving securities settlement in the European Union and on CSDs and amending Directive 98/26/EC* (March 7 2012) COM (12) 73 final available at *http://eur-lex.europa.eu/LexUriServ/LexUriServ.do?uri=CELEX:52012PC0073:EN:PDF* [accessed September 30, 2013]. See especially art.3 and para.3.3.2.

3. METHODS OF HOLDING SECURITIES

The move from direct to indirect (book-entry) holdings

6–07   Over the past few decades there has been a strong move from direct holdings of securities to indirect (book-entry) holdings. In the case of a direct holding of registered securities the investor's legal entitlement is recorded in, and derived from, registration in the issuer's books and is evidenced by a certificate, and the securities are transferred by execution of a transfer instrument and registration of the transfer.[31] In the case of bearer securities title is not recorded on the issuer's register but is vested in the holder of the certificate for the time being and is transferred by delivery.[32]

By contrast, in the case of an indirect holding of securities the investor's rights are derived from a credit to its securities account with a nominee, custodian or other intermediary which itself holds direct from the issuer or from a higher-tier intermediary. Transfers are made through the account in much the same way as a bank funds transfer. The first-tier intermediary, whose nominee holds direct from the issuer, is usually a national central securities depositary (CSD) for domestic issues[33] or an international central securities depositary (ICSD) for international issues. The world's largest depository is The Depository Trust Company of New York (DTC). The two leading ICSDs in Europe are Euroclear Bank and Clearstream.

To reduce administration and the cost of security printing of individual certificates for investors, international securities, especially debt securities, are commonly issued in the form of a single global note representing the entire issue and deposited with a common depository for Euroclear and Clearstream.[34] This describes the "Classic Global Note" system, but in addition, there is now a system known as the "New Global Note" system, which is for international debt securities and is mandatory if such securities are to be eligible collateral provided to the European Central Bank for Eurosystem money operations.[35] Here the securities are held by a "common safekeeper", while other services are provided by a "common service provider". Although not necessary for the structure, in

---

[31] In the UK registered securities are usually shares. The operation of the companies' share register (the register of members) is governed by Companies Act 2006 Pt 8 Ch.2. Though registration is necessary to confer or transfer the legal title, it is only prima facie evidence of ownership, Companies Act 2006 s.127. A person with a superior right to the securities may apply to the court for an order directing that he be placed on the register in place of the existing registrant, Companies Act 2006 s.125.

[32] In the past, most debt securities issued in the UK were bearer securities.

[33] There is no CSD in the UK for UK securities in the sense described above. CREST (now called Euroclear UK & Ireland Ltd) which is discussed below is a settlement system, through which dematerialised UK securities can be held but it does not hold securities since its members hold direct from the issuer, not from CREST. However, CREST members can themselves be intermediaries holding securities for others. See further paras 6–09 et seq., below.

[34] A similar system applies for national securities, which are held by a CSD. In the UK, eligible debt securities can be issued in dematerialised form and held through the CREST system.

[35] The system was introduced on June 30, 2006 for global bearer notes, and on June 30, 2010 for global registered notes.

order for the securities to be eligible collateral for the European Central Bank operations, the safekeeping function must be carried out by the ICSD.[36]

Participants of Euroclear and Clearstream are the first-tier beneficiaries and they will in turn hold for customers of their own, and so on, down the chain. Interests in the global note may be exchangeable for definitive certificates, so that an investor exercising the right to obtain definitive certificates acquires a direct relationship with the issuer, either through delivery in the case of bearer securities or through registration, in the case of registered securities. But not infrequently the global note is intended to be permanently immobilised and not to be exchangeable for definitives except in extreme situations, such as the issuer's default and failure of the trustee of the issue to take the requisite default measures when requested to do so by a given percentage of investors and on being furnished an indemnity.

This tiering of relationships, illustrated in Figures 1 and 2, has several advantages. It creates a pyramid structure in which the issuer can deal with a relatively small number of large players, who in turn will hold accounts for a greater number of smaller participants, and so on down through the pyramid to the ultimate investor. The effect is substantially to reduce both the volume and the movement of paper involved in the issue and transfer of securities and the risk of loss or theft of negotiable securities. Moreover, the aggregation of holdings in undesignated pools of intangibles held by a securities intermediary in an omnibus account[37] facilitates book-entry transfers of those securities from one customer of the intermediary to another, thus enabling a substantial volume of transfers to be effected in-house,[38] as well as providing "pools" of collateral which can be lent to shadow banks and other financial institutions to use as collateral for funding purposes.[39] A transfer need be executed and registered only if and when a customer exercises his right to require delivery or redelivery of the securities credited to his account.

The movement of securities is not necessarily from issuer to first-tier intermediary and down the custody chain, but may start from the other end. Securities originally held by an investor direct may be deposited with its securities intermediary, who will either transfer them into its own name or deposit them with its intermediary into whose name they will be transferred.[40]

The nature of the interest of the account holder whose securities are held with an intermediary has been a matter of some debate and is discussed in more detail below. There has also been considerable discrepancy as to nomenclature. The Financial Collateral Directive refers to "book-entry securities", while the

---

[36] See press release of European Central Bank, June 13 2006, at *https://www.ecb.int/press/pr/date/2006/html/pr060613.en.html* [accessed September 30, 2013].

[37] See para.6–08, below.

[38] Where the transferee holds its account with a different intermediary, it is necessary to effect the transfer through the books of a higher-tier intermediary common to the intermediaries of transferor and transferee, if there is one, or if not, to go up the chain until a common intermediary is reached.

[39] See J. Benjamin, G. Morton and M. Raffan, "The future of securities financing" (2013) 7 L.F.M.R. 4.

[40] This has become less common now that most securities are either issued in dematerialised form or in the form of global notes.

Principles recently drawn up by the European Commission[41] refer to "account-held securities". Other terms that have been used are "securities entitlement",[42] "interests in securities"[43] and "intermediated securities".[44] The last term will be used in this chapter.

Figure 1: Classic Global Note structure: Specimen Chain

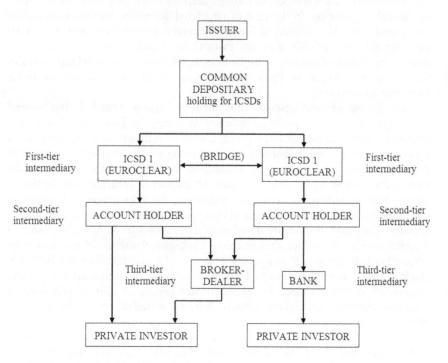

The length of the holding chain varies according to many factors, including the jurisdiction(s) involved.[45]

1.   This diagram gives an example of a Classic Global Note structure where a global note is issued to a common depository. For registered securities the common depository's nominee is shown as the registered holder, and the note itself is held in the vaults of the common depository.
2.   A global note is sometimes deposited with a single ICSD, in which case it is lodged with a specialised depository, usually a sub-custodian of the ICSD in the country of issue.
3.   The issuer has to negotiate with the ICSD to secure eligibility of the issue for deposit with the ICSD.

---

[41] See para 6–12, below.
[42] UCC art.8.
[43] Benjamin, *Interests in Securities* (2007), Ch.2.
[44] Geneva Securities Convention, see para.6–12, below.
[45] See P. Paesch, "Market Needs as Paradigm" in P-H. Conac, U. Segna, L. Thevenoz (eds), *Intermediated securities: the impact of the Geneva Securities Convention and the future European legislation*(Cambridge: CUP, 2013), p.29.

4.   Below the level of the ICSDs, chains can take a number of different forms, depending on the players involved and on whether a participant holds directly from another party or through an intermediary or has part of its holding direct and the rest through an intermediary. Account holders with an ICSD may be custodians, broker-dealers, central banks, CSDs or other financial intermediaries.

5.   The diagram illustrates why a "look-through" legal regime may be difficult, if not impossible, to operate. The broker-dealer from whom the investor on the left-hand side acquired its holding may have procured these by acquisition from the CSD or custodian participant of Euroclear, the CSD or custodian participant of Clearstream, transfer from its own house account or a mixture of the three. There may be no way of identifying the source of the private investor's entitlement, particularly when account is taken of netting through a clearing system.

Figure 2: New Global Note structure: Specimen Chain

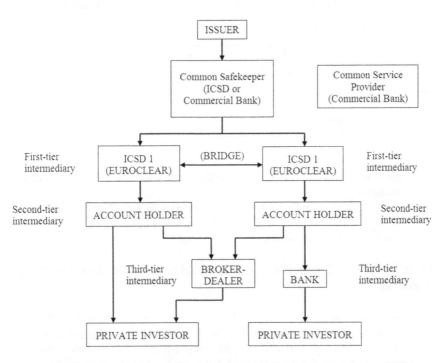

1.   This diagram illustrates the New Global Note structure. The securities are held by the Common Safekeeper. This will either be an ICSD (Clearstream or Euroclear) where the securities are to be potentially eligible for European Central Bank operations, or a commercial bank if this eligibility is not required. The Common Service Provider, who provides all other services except safekeeping, will be a commercial bank.

2.   The issuer has a direct relationship with the ICSD in all cases.

3.   Fig.2, like fig.1, shows how the private investor's holding may be derived through different routes.

Figure 3: Dematerialised securities held through CREST: Specimen Chain

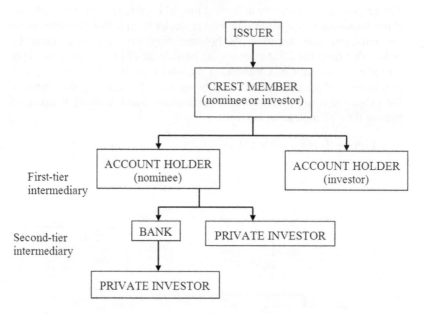

1.   The CREST member holds direct from the issuer, but (unlike with a global note) there can be many direct holders, some of which may be ultimate investors.
2.   If the CREST member is a nominee, it can hold for other investors or for other nominees. As with the other two structures, the chain can take a number of different forms.

Omnibus (pooled, fungible) accounts and segregated (non-fungible) accounts

6–08   The most common holding pattern for a securities intermediary is to hold all securities of a particular issue which it holds for clients in an omnibus account with the issuer or a higher-tier intermediary without designation of the individual customers for whom the securities are held. Such accounts are also known as pooled, or fungible, accounts.[46] An intermediary in an EU Member State is obliged to keep any securities held for its own account in a separate account.[47]

---

[46] For a discussion of "fungible" in this context see para.6–14, below.
[47] See arts 13(7) and (8) of the Markets in Financial Instruments Directive 2004/39/EC as implemented by Directive 2006/73/EC ("MiFID") and CASS Rules 6.2.1 implementing art.13(7). See also art.35 of the *Proposed Regulation improving securities settlement in the European Union and on CSDs and amending Directive 98/26/EC*. There are also strict rules of segregation in relation to client money, see CASS r.7.4, also even if these are not complied with, client money is still held on statutory

The advantage of pooling is that it reduces administration and enables transfers of the securities from one customer to another to be effected solely through the books of the intermediary itself without the involvement of its own intermediary, who though aware that the omnibus account is held for the customers of its own customer, the lower-tier intermediary, and not for that intermediary for its own account, will have no knowledge of the interest of any particular customer of the lower-tier intermediary and thus no knowledge of transfers between its customers. A less common and convenient holding pattern is for the intermediary to hold a customer's securities entitlement in an account with the issuer or a higher-tier intermediary, the account being in the name of the customer's intermediary but carrying a designation showing that the account is held for a particular customer, segregated from the pooled securities held for other customers in an omnibus account. Such segregated accounts are also termed non-fungible accounts. Because each such account has to be separately recorded in the books of the higher-tier intermediary, transfers must be effected through that intermediary instead of being purely book-entry transfers within the books of the customer's intermediary. Necessarily, therefore, the higher-tier intermediary is on notice of the particular customer's interest,[48] although not necessarily of the identity of that client.[49]

Uncertificated (dematerialised) securities

(1) The CREST system

A further major step in the reduction of the issue and movement of paper has been the shift from certificated (i.e. paper-based) to uncertificated (i.e. dematerialised, or paperless) issues and transfers. In the United Kingdom these are now effected through the CREST computer system operated by Euroclear UK & Ireland Ltd (formerly CRESTCo), which is given statutory underpinning by the Uncertificated Securities Regulations 2001,[50] supplemented by the CREST rules and conditions. Participants in the CREST system, that is, those who have a business relationship with it, may communicate with CREST only through the gateway computer of a user, that is, a person who has a computer link to CREST and inputs instructions to CREST either for others or on its own account. A participant may also be a user. Accounts are maintained only for CREST members. They may be full members, who have direct computer access to CREST as users, or sponsored members, who connect with CREST through the

6–09

---

trust and, whether segregated or not segregated, should be pooled on the insolvency of the financial institution holding the money and distributed to the clients, see *Re Lehman Brothers International (Europe) (In Administration)* [2012] UKSC 6.

[48] For the possible significance of this, see para.6–22, below.

[49] See para.6–10, below for where the intermediary holds through CREST.

[50] Uncertificated Securities Regulations 2001 (SI 2001/3755), as amended. The Uncertificated Securities (Amendment) (Eligible Debt Securities) Regulations 2003 (SI 2003/1633), extended the operation of CREST to debt securities issued by companies and by public authorities. Though the regulations do not refer specifically to Euroclear UK & Ireland Ltd, it is the organisation approved as Operator by the Treasury. For a good general description of dematerialisation and the CREST system, see M. Yates and G. Montagu, *The Law of Global Custody*, 4th edn (London: Bloomsbury Professional Ltd, 2013), Ch.9; and Benjamin, *Interests in Securities* (2000), paras 9.46 et seq. For fuller detail, see the CREST Reference Manual (November 2007).

services of a user. Any individual or company may apply to become a CREST member.[51] Dematerialisation does not by itself affect the direct relationship between investor and issuer; it simply records holdings and transfers in electronic form. Accounts are opened for members in their own name, whether they are full members or sponsored members. Issuers have dealings with the CREST system, usually through their registrars, for the purpose of dematerialising and rematerialising their securities, recording transfers, and the like.

(2)   Dematerialisation

6–10   New securities may be issued in dematerialised form where permitted by the Operator and authorised by the issuer's articles of association or a directors' resolution.[52] Existing paper-based securities, including bearer securities, may be dematerialised, on a request to the issuer by or through a member, by lodgment with the issuer of the relevant certificates and an executed transfer in favour of a member, followed by a dematerialisation notice from the issuer to the Operator.[53] The former bearer thereafter holds its securities entitlement through its account with CREST if it is a member or otherwise through its account with a securities intermediary. Both the Operator and the issuer of registered equity securities are required to maintain a share register, but it is the Operator register, not the issuer register, that now constitutes the primary and definitive record of entitlement to uncertificated shares.[54] In relation to debt securities, the only register is the Operator register, though in some cases the issuer is obliged to keep a record of entries that have been entered on that register.[55] Despite this structure, Euroclear UK & Ireland Ltd itself is neither the holder nor the custodian of UK securities and is therefore not a securities intermediary standing between its members and the issuer but is more akin to a registrar who holds the primary records. It is therefore not a CSD,[56] nor does it act as a nominee. It is, though, a recognised clearing house and provides an electronic transfer and settlement system.

---

[51] Individual investors, who will be sponsored members, are called personal members and pay a very low tariff of £10 a year, see the Euroclear 10 point guide to becoming a member at *https://www.euroclear.com/dam/Brochures/MA1563_Becoming_a_client_10_point_guide.pdf* [accessed September 30, 2013].

[52] Uncertificated Securities Regulations 2001 regs 14–18, in respect of shares, and reg.19 in respect of securities other then shares. Shares cannot have premium listing (see Listing Rules 1.5) unless they are eligible for electronic settlement, which is realistically only the case if they are dematerialised, see Listing Rules 6.1.

[53] Uncertificated Securities Regulations 2001 reg.33. Securities admitted to CREST are termed participating securities.

[54] This is because, if there is a conflict between the issuer and the operator register, the latter prevails. See Uncertified Securities Regulations 2001 regs 20(5) and 24(2),(3). The issuer is also obliged to keep a record of all the entries on the CREST register, Uncertified Securities Regulations 2001 reg.20(6) and Sch.4 para.5. The Operator maintains separate registers for each class of uncertificated securities, and the register for any one class consists of all the securities held by the system-members in their stock accounts. References in statute and other instruments to the company's register of members are to be construed as referring to both the issuer register and operator register unless the context otherwise required or they are inconsistent (Uncertified Securities Regulations 2001 reg.20(4)).

[55] Uncertified Securities Regulations 2001 regs 21 and 22.

[56] It does, however, describe itself as such, despite not performing all the functions of a CSD, notably holding securities as custodian (see, for example, the brochure "Streamlined Real Time Settlement" available at *https://www.euroclear.com/dam/PDFs/Settlement/EUI/MA2740-CREST-settlement.pdf*

Dematerialised securities can be held by an investor directly (as a CREST member) or through an intermediary who is a CREST member.[57] Each CREST member having a stock account with CREST for a particular issue of securities remains in a direct relationship with the issuer, though it can only effect registered transfers[58] through CREST. Each member will have a separate stock account for each class of securities he holds and a cash memorandum to record payments made and received in respect of securities. As mentioned earlier, the accounts of securities intermediaries are required to distinguish between securities held for customers and those held for themselves. Securities held by intermediaries for customers are usually in an omnibus account which does not differentiate between one customer and another, though an account may be individually designated to show that the account in the name of the intermediary is held for a particular customer segregated from the holdings for other customers.[59] Securities belonging to the intermediary itself are held in a house account.

Transfers can only be made on the instructions of a member and from one member's account to that of another.[60] A person other than a member wishing to initiate a transfer must do so through a member.[61] If the transferee holds an account with the same member the transfer is effected by in-house book entry, in other cases by transfer to the transferee's member for the account of the transferee. Legal title is prima facie conferred or transferred when the issue or transfer of securities to a member is recorded in the Operator register.[62]

(3)   Rematerialisation

A person holding uncertificated securities may have them reconverted into certificated securities by arranging for its member to issue an instruction to the Operator to that effect, the Operator in turn issuing a rematerialisation notice to the issuer.[63] The Operator must thereupon delete the entry in its register recording the member as holder of the units in question and the issuer must enter the

6–11

[accessed September 30, 2013]. It is also a member of the European Central Depositories Association and may well fall within the definition of "CSD" in the *Proposed Regulation improving securities settlement in the European Union and on CSDs and amending Directive 98/26/EC* art.2 since it operates a securities settlement system and (arguably) provides initial recording of securities in a book entry system (see Annex A). It is, however, not at all clear that it is, or should be, a CSD within the terms of the Principles set out in the EU Consultation Document "*Legislation on Legal Certainty of Securities Holding and Dispositions*" (DG MArkt G2 MET/OT/acgD (2010) 768690 ("the EU Principles")); see H. Motani, "The Proposed EU Legislation" in Conac, Segna, Thevenoz (eds), *Intermediated securities: the impact of the Geneva Securities Convention and the future European legislation* (2013), p.72.

[57] In that case, the analysis below in relation to intermediated securities will apply.

[58] Off-register dealings take effect in equity only.

[59] The description of the account should not give any indication of the identity of the beneficial owner, see CREST Manual (revised August 30 2013), p.43. See para.6–08, above.

[60] The system is thus closely analogous to the bank clearing systems, which are confined to the clearing banks, which make transfers to each other through their respective accounts with the Bank of England. Transfers made by or to a sponsored member are made by users on the instructions of the sponsored member.

[61] Who is then termed the sponsoring system-participant.

[62] Uncertificated Securities Regulations 2001 reg.24. Entry in the issuer register is also prima facie evidence of title but not if inconsistent with an entry in the Operator register (reg.24(2)).

[63] Uncertificated Securities Regulations 2001 reg.32(2)(b),(3)(b).

member as holder in the issuer register.[64] Until that has been done the member retains title to the transferred units,[65] an important provision which avoids conversion of a legal title into an equitable interest during the interval. The issuer must then issue a certificate to the relevant person where the terms of the issue of the security so require.[66]

Legal developments in relation to the holding of investment securities

6–12   Investment securities, whether held directly or indirectly and whether in paper-based or dematerialised form, represent an immensely valuable form of collateral. It is therefore essential to the stability of financial systems and the avoidance of systemic risk that the legal regime in place should, wherever possible, remove grounds for uncertainty as to the validity of security interests in financial collateral and as to the law applicable to them. As mentioned earlier, settlement finality, and the use of securities as financial collateral, has been the subject of Directives.[67] Considerable work has also been done to harmonise the identification of the law applicable to securities, especially intermediated securities. Both the Settlement Finality Directive[68] and the Financial Collateral Directive[69] include limited choice of law rules in relation to intermediated securities, and a conflict of laws Convention[70] was concluded at a Diplomatic Conference at the Hague in December 2002, although it is not yet in force. Each of these will be considered later.

As a result of concerns about the possible level of systemic risk, various investigations have, over the years, been instigated in Europe and in the United Kingdom.[71] Work on the harmonisation of substantive law has been carried out by UNIDROIT, culminating in the adoption of the Convention on Substantive Rules for Intermediated Securities (the "Geneva Securities Convention") in 2009.[72] The European Commission is also working on harmonisation, and has published two consultations. A summary of responses was published in

---

[64] Uncertificated Securities Regulations 2001 reg.32(4) and (5).

[65] Uncertificated Securities Regulations 2001 reg.32(6).

[66] Uncertificated Securities Regulations 2001 reg.32(7).

[67] See para.6–01, above and further paras 6–23 et seq., below.

[68] Settlement Finality Directive art.9(2).

[69] Financial Collateral Directive art.9, enacted as reg.19 of the FCARs.

[70] Convention on the law applicable to certain rights in respect of securities held with an intermediary.

[71] In the UK, FMLC report. Issue 3: *Property Interests in Investment Securities* (July 2004) and advice provided to the Treasury by the Law Commission regarding the UNIDROIT Convention on Substantive Rules regarding Intermediated Securities (May 2007 and May 2008). In Europe, the Legal Certainty Group reported on the treatment of interests in securities held with an intermediary (August 11, 2006).

[72] So far, this has one signatory and no ratifications. See H. Kanda, C. Mooney, L. Thevenoz, S. Beraud and T. Keijser, *Official Commentary on the UNIDROIT Convention on Substantive Rules for Intermediated Securities* (Oxford: OUP, 2012); and L. Thevenoz, "The Geneva Securities Convention" in Conac, Segna, Thevenoz (eds), *Intermediated securities: the impact of the Geneva Securities Convention and the future European legislation* (2013).

September 2011, but no draft legislation has been forthcoming yet.[73] A draft regulation on securities settlement and the authorisation and supervision of CSDs has been published[74]; this, however, does not address some of the more substantive issues that arise in relation to the holding of securities. A very high proportion of holdings of intermediated securities involve some cross-border element somewhere in the chain,[75] and the significant differences in approach of various legal systems to such issues as the conceptual basis of the holding of intermediated securities, the validity of transfers, protection of a good faith purchaser, priority rules and the protection of client assets could potentially cause severe problems. Given that the cross-border issues do not arise just between EU states, though, there is a strong argument for adoption of the Geneva Securities Convention rather than a separate European harmonisation exercise.

4. THE NATURE OF THE ACCOUNT HOLDER'S INTEREST IN INTERMEDIATED SECURITIES

While there is very considerable difference between the analyses in various jurisdictions as to what an account holder actually has when he holds securities with an intermediary,[76] the position under English law is reasonably clear. An account holder has a beneficial interest under a trust or sub-trust; the intermediary being the trustee or sub-trustee.[77]   **6–13**

The following discussion will focus on one of the main points of contention in this area, namely whether the subject matter of the account holder's interest is sufficiently identified for his proprietary interest to be valid, especially when securities are held in an omnibus account.

Shares directly held

It is necessary for the subject matter of a transfer of assets to be sufficiently identified so that it is clear what assets are being transferred. This requirement applies whether the transfer takes place at law or in equity, and whether it is an   **6–14**

---

[73] The latest publicly available minutes for the working group on Securities Law Legislation are dated November 19, 2012, and, while adoption of the Geneva Securities Convention was discussed, the only decision made was that a further meeting was desirable.

[74] *Proposal for a Regulation improving securities settlement in the European Union and on CSDs and amending Directive 98/26/EC.*

[75] Paesch estimates that roughly 40 per cent of all holding, trading and collateral operations by EU market participants involve some cross-border element, see Paesch, "Market Needs as Paradigm" in *Intermediated securities : the impact of the Geneva Securities Convention and the future European legislation* (2013), p.35.

[76] For an analysis of the main approaches, see Paesch, "Market Needs as Paradigm" in *Intermediated securities: the impact of the Geneva Securities Convention and the future European legislation* (2013), pp.31–34.

[77] This is considered in more detail below, but has been confirmed by the English courts in a number of cases: see *Re Lehman Brothers International (Europe) (In Administration)* [2009] EWHC 2545 (Ch) at [49]–[72]; *Re Lehman Brothers International (Europe) (In Administration)* [2010] EWHC 2914 (Ch) at [226]; *Mills v Sportsdirect.com Retail Ltd* [2010] EWHC 1072 (Ch) at [4] and [70]; *Re Lehman Brothers International (Europe) (In Administration)* [2012] EWHC 2997 (Ch) at [163].

absolute transfer or by way of security.[78] With fungible tangible property, such as grains of wheat, identification can take place either by separation of the wheat to be transferred from any other wheat, or by the transfer of a fractional share of a bulk. The problem with shares is that physical separation is impossible. When A is registered as the legal owner of 50 directly held registered shares there is no way of identifying these shares as different from any other shares of the same issue, except as "the shareholding of which A is registered as owner". It is indisputable that, when issued, shares of a single issue are identical and, now that registered shares are in practice unnumbered,[79] there is no way to distinguish one share from another at the time of issue, or the time of transfer. If identification in the sense of separation was required in relation to transfers of shares, no transfer of shares at law would ever be valid. The "problem" of identification is thus the same in relation to the interests of legal owners of shares as it is in relation to the equitable interest of a beneficiary under a trust of shares, although it is the latter issue which has attracted the most attention by the courts and by commentators. If one cannot identify the subject matter of a declaration of trust of 40 shares out of a shareholding of 100, one cannot identify 40 shares which are transferred at law by registration of 40 shares in the name of the transferee.

If the problem is the same, the solution also has to be the same. One reason why there appears to be concern over identification of shares held on trust, but not in relation to identification of a shareholding at law, is that is said that the shareholding at law is identified by registration.[80] This is true, but not in the sense that registration separates 50 shares from all the other shares of that issue, but in the sense that registration identifies the legal owner's interest as a shareholder of 50 shares, i.e. his shareholding. That shareholding then acquires a history which could be said to distinguish it from other people's interests in shares of the same issue (shareholdings). So long as it is possible to trace the history of that interest (which is evidentially made easier by the fact of registration) that interest becomes a separate "thing" from other people's interests. The same reasoning applies to transfers in equity (i.e. off the register). The documentation may be less clear, or easy to obtain, but at least in theory the history of the beneficiary's shareholding can be traced. Conceptually the process is the same.[81]

---

[78] See paras 2–05 et seq., above.

[79] If shares are fully paid up they do not need to be numbered (Companies Act 2006 s.543). This restates s.182(2) of the 1985 Act and in practice dispenses with numbers, see comment in *Palmer's Company Law Annotated Guide to the Companies Act 2006*, 2nd edn (London: Sweet & Maxwell, 2009). Even numbered shares are identical and interchangeable, *Ind's case* (1872) 7 Ch. App. 485, 487 (though note that in this case, where A had transferred certain numbered shares to B in circumstances when A did not have shares of those numbers, B was trying to argue that the transfer was void and he was not a contributory. The Court of Appeal held that since A did have shares (though not of those numbers) to transfer to B, B was rightly registered as a shareholder, but it was clear that they were influenced by the fact that creditors would have relied on the fact that B's name had been on the register and B could not now avoid this).

[80] E. Micheler, *Property in Securities, A Comparative Study* (Cambridge: CUP, 2007), p.130. This is the case whether the shares are certificated or dematerialised.

[81] The process, of course, can become very complicated, in that A's holding of 50 shares may be split up and sold to different people or may be combined with other people's shareholdings in a single ownership. But because there is no way to identify the particular shares, the chain of title has to be traced through the history of the transfers of the shareholdings: there is no other way of doing it.

The decision of the Court of Appeal in *Hunter v Moss*,[82] where it was held that it was possible to declare a trust of 50 of the trustee's 950 shares, rests on this kind of reasoning, as do the cases following it.[83] The argument running through the cases is that if there is a clear intention to declare a trust, there is no reason not to permit such a trust[84] since whenever identification becomes relevant, it is possible to identify the relevant interest.[85] The interchangeability of the shares means that the trustee's obligations can always be fulfilled, without it being necessary to identify separate shares while they are held on trust.[86]

However, what this reasoning does not really explain is what the "interest" of the shareholder (legal or equitable) actually relates to: what is it that he owns? If it is said to relate to separate shares, then the identification problems mentioned above become insuperable. Therefore, in relation to the interest of a beneficiary under a trust, it is usually said that what he owns is a co-ownership right in the "parcel" of shares owned by the legal owner.[87] Thus when A is the legal owner of 100 shares in X, and declares himself trustee of 50 shares for B and 50 shares for C, B and C are tenants in common in equity of A's shareholding.[88] If this analysis is necessary, and effective, to explain the nature of B's interest (as beneficiary), it must also be necessary to explain the nature of A's interest (as legal owner), since there is no more identification by separation of A's shares than there is of B's. It is this process of reasoning which led Professor Goode, in the previous edition of this book, to the conclusion that what a shareholder owns is an interest in the company's share capital, which, for the sake of convenience, is measured in units but which is in fact a fractional interest.[89] There is thus no problem of identification in relation to the transfer of shares either at law or in equity.

The view of shares as a fractional interest in the share capital of the company does not in any way challenge the accepted view of the position of shareholders vis-à-vis the company. It is clear that shareholders do not have co-ownership or

---

[82] *Hunter v Moss* (1994) 1 W.L.R. 452, upholding decision at first instance (1993) 1 W.L.R. 934.

[83] *Re Harvard Securities* [1997] 2 B.C.L.C. 369; *Re C A Pacific Finance Ltd* [2000] 1 B.C.L.C. 494; *White v Shortall* [2006] N.S.W.S.C. 1379. S. Worthington, "Sorting out ownership interests in a bulk: gifts, sales and trusts" (1999) J.B.L. 1. In relation to a trust of part of a debt, see *Associated Alloys v ACN 001 452 106* (2000) 202 C.L.R. 588; and *SSSL Realisations*; sub nom. *Squires v AIG Europe UK Ltd* [2004] EWHC 1760 (Ch) at [54], approved by the Court of Appeal at [122].

[84] *Brady v Stapleton* (1952) 88 C.L.R. 322.

[85] For example, where shares are disposed of by the trustee in breach of trust, or where the question of liability to Capital Gains Tax arises. For a discussion of the position in these situations, see Worthington, "Sorting out ownership interests in a bulk: gifts, sales and trusts" (1999) J.B.L. 1; and *White v Shortall* [2006] N.S.W.S.C. 1379 at [248]–[268]. However, if there is a disposition which is not a breach of trust, it is not clear that on the current law the same rules apply, although they could be extended to cover this situation.

[86] *Re C A Pacific Finance Ltd* [2000] 1 B.C.L.C. 494, 508.

[87] Underhill and Hayton, *Law relating to Trusts and Trustees*, 18th edn, D. Hayton, P. Matthews and C. Mitchell (eds) (London: LexisNexis Butterworths, 2010) arts 8.14–8.22; G. Morton, "Commentary on 'The Dematerialisation of Money Market Instruments'" in S. Worthingon (ed.), *Commercial Law and Commercial Practice* (Oxford: OUP, 2003), p.295; Yates and Montagu, *The Law of Global Custody* (2013), para.3.42; Benjamin, *Interests in Securities* (2000), paras 2.77–2.91. See also *Re Lehman Brothers International (Europe) (In Administration)* [2010] EWHC 2914 (Ch) at [232].

[88] This co-ownership is often provided for expressly in an agreement with an intermediary.

[89] R. Goode, "Are Intangible Assets Fungible?" [2003] L.M.C.L.Q. 379; J. Benjamin, "Demateriali-sation of Money Market Instruments", in S. Worthingon (ed.), *Commercial Law and Commercial Practice* (Oxford: Hart Publishing, 2003), pp.262–264; M. Ooi, *Shares and other Securities in the Conflict of Laws* (Oxford: OUP, 2003), para.3.14.

any other proprietary rights in the assets of the company,[90] but that being a shareholder confers on that person a mixture of contractual and statutory rights against the issuer. On one view this means that a share is merely a bundle of personal rights against the issuer. The shareholder, however, is in a different position from those to whom debts are owed by the company, e.g. debenture holders. This is sometimes described as saying that the shareholder has an interest "in the company measured by a sum of money".[91] The shareholder is seen as a member of the company, but since shares also have a value that is independent from, though related to, the value of the company, which is realised by the transfer of shares by sale or as security, shares are treated as property.[92] The entire share capital is therefore an asset of value which can be owned by any number of people. The view discussed means that rather than each individual share giving the shareholder a different interest or a different piece of property, the entirety of his shareholding measures the extent of his interest in the share capital, so that a shareholding of 100 shares out of an issued share capital of 1000 shares is, conceptually, a tenth interest in the share capital, even though it is called 100 shares for convenience.[93]

As explained above, once the legal owner's fractional interest (say one tenth) is identified by registration, it becomes in some sense different from that of another legal owner who might own similar fractional interest (one tenth). This is because each fractional interest acquires a history, and can be seen as a different "thing" from another fractional interest.[94] It may be that these "things" are separate enough for it to be possible to speak of them being equivalent rather than exactly the same, and this may explain the various judicial, statutory and other references to "equivalent securities".[95] It may also mean that what is returnable on the second leg of a repo or other title transfer collateral arrangement is not

---

[90] *Short v Treasury Commissioners* [1948] 1 K.B. 122.

[91] *Borland's Trustee v Steel Brothers & Co* [1901] 1 Ch. 279, 288, where Farwell J. said that "A share is the interest of a shareholder in the company measured by a sum of money, for the purpose of liability in the first place, and of interest in the second, but also consisting of a series of mutual covenants entered into by all the shareholders inter se". The idea that shareholders have an interest in the company explains why shareholders have a voice in the running of the company, in a way, for example, that debenture-holders do not (R. Grantham, "The Doctrinal Basis of the Rights of Company Shareholders" (1998) 57 C.L.J. 554, 582–584; Gower and Davies, *Principles of Modern Company Law*, 9th edn (London: Sweet & Maxwell, 2012), paras 23-1 to 23-3; M. Bridge, L. Gullifer, G. McMeel, S. Worthington, *The Law of Personal Property* (London: Sweet & Maxwell, 2013), paras 23-015 et seq.).

[92] S. Worthington, "Shares and shareholders: Property, Power and entitlement" (2001) 22 Comp. Law. 258, 260.

[93] The fact that shares are easily and frequently traded means that it is far more convenient to refer to parts of the share capital as units, since fractional interests are frequently split or combined when transferred in such a way that to express what is traded as a fractional share would involve complex arithmetic. See also, from *Lindley on Companies*, 6th edn (London: Sweet & Maxwell, 1902) quoted in *Gore-Browne on Companies*, 45th edn, A. Alcock (ed.) (Bristol: Jordans, 2004), "The proportion of capital to which each member is entitled is his share".

[94] Although, in practice, a fractional interest, at least in publicly traded shares, is likely to be split up or combined with other interests in the course of trading.

[95] *Crerar v Bank of Scotland* [1921] S.C. 736; affirmed [1922] S.C. (HL) 137; *Ellis & Co's Trustee v Dixon-Johnson* [1924] 2 Ch. 451, 470–471, 473; affirmed [1925] A.C. 489: *Solloway v McLaughlin* [1938] 1 A.C. 247, 256; Financial Collateral Directive art.2 (1)(i) (definition) and art.5 (right of use); FCARs reg.3 (definition) and reg.16 (right of use); Global Master Repurchase Agreement (2000 version) cll.2(s) and (t) (definition) and cl.1(a) (primary obligation to deliver equivalent securities).

necessarily exactly the same asset[96] in that it may have a different history (although, of course, it is still just a fractional interest in the company's share capital).

If we see A's (the legal owner's) shareholding as a fractional interest in the share capital of one tenth (measured as 100 shares) then, if he declares a trust of 50 of them for B and 50 of them for C, what do B and C have? In one sense, B has an equitable interest in one twentieth of the share capital, as does C. However, in order to meet the question of identification in relation to the trust, it also must be the case that B and C are tenants in common in equity of A's shareholding. B's equitable interest is entirely dependent upon A remaining legal owner of a sufficiently large shareholding to enable A to hold one twentieth of the share capital on trust for B. This analysis becomes critical where there is a situation of shortfall. If A disposed of some of his shareholding, so that he no longer held one tenth (100 shares) but one twentieth (50 shares), then he could not, obviously, hold one twentieth (50 shares) on trust for B and one twentieth on trust for C. However, because B and C are equitable tenants in common of A's shareholding, their half interests would reduce to one fourtieth (25 shares) each. If the reduction takes place because of the breach of trust of the trustee, the trustee owes a duty to each co-owner to replace the missing property, and, if it could be traced into the hands of someone who does not have a defence, the property could be recovered.[97]

It should be seen that there are, then, two analyses involving co-ownership that are being suggested here. The first, which has not been the subject of much discussion in the literature or the cases, is that a shareholder is a co-owner of the issued share capital of the company so that all he has is a fractional interest in that share capital. When a fractional interest is split into two (smaller) fractional interests, there can be no problem of identification in relation to the subject matter of the split, even if the split is effected by a declaration of trust. This is the argument made here in relation to the facts of *Hunter v Moss*. On the other hand, where fractional interests previously belonging to two different people are combined in one legal ownership[98] but the two people continue to be beneficial owners, a further conceptual step is required. This is because each person's fractional interest has acquired a history, and so if one is mixed with another, there has to be some explanation of why those separate histories are ignored. This is that there is express or implied agreement that the two fractional interests should be combined into one larger fractional interest co-owned (in equity) by the two people. It is this co-ownership analysis which has been accepted, especially recently, by commentators and judges as explaining how securities are held in an omnibus account by an intermediary.[99] It is this (second) co-ownership analysis

---

[96] Morton, "Commentary on 'The Dematerialisation of Money Market Instruments'" in *Commercial Law and Commercial Practice* (2003), pp.299–300.

[97] This rather bald statement needs some explanation and qualification in practice. The issue of shortfall, tracing and protection of bona fide purchasers is dealt with at para.6–20, below.

[98] Legal ownership is used here for the sake of exposition, but it is likely that the person holding the combined interests will itself be a beneficial owner, that is, an intermediary who has an account with another intermediary or a CSD, see above.

[99] In addition to the commentators mentioned in fn.87, above; see *Re Lehman Brothers International (Europe) (In Administration)* [2009] EWHC 2545 (Ch) at [56]; *Re Lehman Brothers International (Europe) (In Administration)* [2010] EWCA Civ 917 at [171]; *Re Lehman Brothers International (Europe) (In Administration)* [2010] EWHC 2914 (Ch) [232]–[239]; *Mr Peter Eckerle, Mr Willem*

which leads to the potential shortfall discussed above. If the two persons holding fractional interests wish to be protected against shortfall, they must make it clear that they do not agree to the (second) co-ownership taking place. Thus they must insist that the person holding for them (the intermediary) differentiates their individual fractional interests by means of book entries. If the intermediary is the legal owner (e.g. a CSD) then it is sufficient if this is in its own books, so that there are two separate trusts. If the intermediary is itself an account holder with a higher tier intermediary or a CSD, then the book entry segregation must take place in the books of that higher tier intermediary.[100]

It is therefore clear that the result in *Hunter v Moss* is correct, and there should be no danger that an English court would hold that a trust of part of a shareholding failed for lack of identification. However, in relation to the holding of securities with an intermediary in an omnibus account, any possible uncertainty is unwelcome. There is also the possible problem of shortfall referred to above. A specially tailored statutory approach in relation to intermediated securities, such as is proposed in the Geneva Securities Convention, could lay any such uncertainty to rest once and for all.[101]

Debt securities[102]

6–15   At law, each debt is distinct and can only be co-owned as a joint tenant.[103] Debt securities used to be individual choses in action owed to each holder (either as a bearer of bearer securities, or as a registered holder) or were issued as loan or debenture stock constituted under a trust deed or deed poll.[104] In the case of stock constituted under a trust deed, the obligation is owed to the trustee, who holds it on trust for the stockholders, who are not themselves creditors of the company.[105] The stockholders are therefore co-owners (tenants in common) of the obligation in equity. In the case of a deed poll, although there is only one single debt it is for the benefit of all stockholders, who can enforce it, so that the stockholders hold the legal right to the debt as tenants in common.[106] Nowadays, Eurobonds

---

Bertheux, Mr Stephan Hallensleben v Wickeder Westfalenstahl GmbH, Dnick Holding Plc [2013] EWHC 68 (Ch) at [14(g)]; A. Dilnot and L. Harris, "Ownership of a fund" (2012) 5 J.I.B.F.L. 272; C. Cooke, "Lehman Brothers: certainty of trusts and the RASCALS litigation" (2011) 3 J.I.B.F.L. 136. Underhill and Hayton (18th edn, 2010) also seem to accept this analysis in relation to shares, see art.8.21 fn.5.

[100] Ideally, for ultimate protection, there would be segregation all the way up to the CSD level: if not, there is danger from shortfall combined with insolvency at any level. See para.6–20, below.

[101] See para.6–12, above.

[102] For a detailed discussion of the nature of debt instruments, see *Tolley's Company Law Service*, B5028 et seq., J. Richards and A Gregson (eds) (London: LexisNexis Butterworths, 2011) and C4001 et seq., M. Evans (ed.) (London: LexisNexis Butterworths, 2009). See also L. Gullifer and J. Payne, *Corporate Finance Law: Principles and Policy* (Oxford: Hart Publishing, 2011) pp.327–339.

[103] Normally, intangible property cannot be held at law as tenants in common, but only as joint tenants. *In Re McKerrell* [1912] 2 Ch. 648, 653; R. Smith, *Plural Ownership* (Oxford: OUP, 2004), p.209; *Crossley Vaines' Personal Property*, 5th edn, E. Tyler and N. Palmer (eds) (London: Butterworths, 1973), p.57.

[104] Gullifer and Payne, *Corporate Finance Law: Principles and Policy* (2011), pp.329–330. Note that stock is now usually held through CREST.

[105] *Re Dunderland Ore Ltd* [1909] 1 Ch. 446; *Tolley's Company Law Service*, C4002 (2009).

[106] This is the only workable solution, despite the usual rule that debts cannot be held as tenants in common.

(including domestic issues issued in the form of Eurobonds) are issued as global notes held by a depositary or common safekeeper, who will either be a CSD (or ICSD) or acting on its behalf.[107] The CSD or ICSD will be the legal owner of the single obligation represented by the note, which will be held on trust for its account holders as beneficial co-owners, so each owns (in equity) a fractional interest in the debt obligation.[108] Again, this would be the case whether each account holder has a separate account (this is the "first" co-ownership analysis) or in a pooled or omnibus account (the "first" *and* "second" co-ownership analyses).

Intermediated securities

In the light of the above analysis, we should now consider in more detail the nature of rights to intemediated securities. One thing is obvious under English law,[109] namely that where securities are held through an intermediary there is no relationship between the investor and the issuer, only between the investor and its intermediary. The nature of that relationship is governed by the agreement between the parties. It would be possible for the investor to have no more than a personal right to the transfer of securities. This will depend on the agreement between the parties and the status of the "intermediary", and can conceivably change throughout the relationship. In some circumstances, the parties may intend full ownership to pass even though the arrangement leaves the economic benefits of the securities with the "investor".[110] But, since such an arrangement would leave the investor exposed to the risk of his intermediary's insolvency, under English law the normal agreement, express or implied, is that the intermediary's holding is as trustee for the investor to the extent of the latter's entitlement. Whether the intermediary at each level has a proprietary interest in the underlying securities will, of course, depend on the applicable law.

6–16

What, however, is the precise nature of that entitlement? Holdings through an omnibus account and holdings through a segregated account will be treated separately. It needs to be remembered that, apart from the CSD or ICSD at the top of the chain, all participants in the chain are both account providers and account holders, except for the "ultimate holder" at the bottom of the chain. The terms "account provider" and "account holder" are used here with this proviso.

(1)   Holdings through an omnibus account

An account holder in an omnibus account typically has a combination of personal and proprietary rights: a personal right to the transfer of the intermediated securities, either to it as account holder or to direct the transfer to be made to

6–17

---

[107] See para.6–07, above.

[108] This is the analysis under English law, however, it should be remembered that the CSD or ICSD is likely to be in another jurisdiction, for example, Euroclear is in Belgium and Clearstream in Luxembourg.

[109] The position varies in other jurisdictions.

[110] One such example was the process put in place between Lehman Brothers International Europe (LBIE) and its affiliates. When LBIE first acquired the securities for the affliliates it held those securities on trust for them, but as soon as the RASCALS process of continuous repos commenced, full beneficial title passed to LBIE and remained there. See *Re Lehman Brothers International (Europe) (In Administration)* [2011] EWCA Civ 1544 especially at [78].

another party, with various ancillary personal rights[111]; and a proprietary right in the form of co-ownership of the pool of securities held by the intermediary from the issuer direct or through its account with a higher-tier intermediary.[112] The characteristic of an intermediated holding is that the investor's title derives neither from registration in the issuer's register or in CREST nor from possession but from his account with his intermediary. It is therefore not inaccurate to describe the account as the root of title. The effect of the co-ownership is that if the intermediary becomes insolvent the securities held for its customers belong in equity to them and do not form part of the intermediary's estate available to its creditors. The intermediary is thus a trustee for its customers, who are beneficial co-owners of the pool of securities held on their behalf, if the intermediary is a first-tier intermediary (usually a CSD or ICSD) holding direct from the issuer it has legal title to the securities. A second-tier intermediary, however, will itself be merely an equitable co-owner of the pool of securities held by its own, first-tier intermediary for the latter's customers; and to the extent that the lower-tier intermediary is holding for its customers and not for itself it is a sub-trustee, while any such customer holding for customers of its own is a sub-sub-trustee, and so on.[113]

An intermediary owes a duty to its customers to hold sufficient quantities of each issue of securities to meet their entitlements. If there is any shortfall, as where the intermediary misappropriates part of the pool, the co-ownership interests of its customers abate proportionately.[114]

6–18   So far, the position is reasonably clear. But we still have to address the question: what exactly is it that the customers co-own? Do they, as conventional trust law might suggest, have beneficial co-ownership of the underlying securities themselves? Or do they, as under art.8 of the Uniform Commercial Code, have something based on a different concept, which is co-ownership not of a specific thing (the shares themselves) but of a package of rights vis-à-vis the intermediary which art.8 describes as "a securities entitlement"?[115] The Geneva Secuties Convention defines the package of rights conferred by a credit to a securities

---

[111] e.g. to require the intermediary to collect and transfer to the investor dividends and other distributions it receives, and to vote in accordance with the investor's instructions. It is not always the case that the ultimate holder will have these rights, see J. Payne, "Intermediated Securities and the Right to Vote in the UK" in L. Gullifer and J. Payne (eds), *Intermediated Securities: Legal Problems and Practical Issues* (Oxford: Hart Publishing, 2010).

[112] See above, and Geneva Securities Convention art.9. See also EU Principles (fn.56, above) art.3.

[113] This analysis now has judicial approval, see *Re Lehman Brothers International (Europe) (In Administration)* [2010] EWHC 2914 (Ch) at [226]; *Re Lehman Brothers International (Europe) (In Administration)* [2012] EWHC 2997 (Ch) at [163].

[114] See para.6–14, above. This is also the position under art.26 of the Geneva Securities Convention. The issue of shortfall is discussed further at para.6–20, below.

[115] For early analysis of the elements of the security entitlement package, see James Steven Rogers, "Policy Perspectives on Revised U.C.C. Article 8" (1996) 43 U.C.L.A. L. Rev. 1431, 1450; S. L. Schwarcz, "Intermediary Risk in a Global Economy" (2001) 50 Duke L.J. 1541. The concept of the securities entitlement had its genesis in a pioneering article by C. W. Mooney, "Beyond Negotiability: A New Model for Transfer and Pledge of Interests in Securities Controlled by Intermediaries" (1990) 12 Cardozo L. Rev. 305.

account in art.9, supplemented by art.24[116]; the functional approach of the Convention means that the rights are described, but the package of rights is not given a legal label.

The content of the securities entitlement under art.8 and the investor's rights under the Geneva Securities Convention largely match the entitlement of the holder of a securities account under the English law trusts analysis, which consists of a combination of personal rights (including rights to delivery or transfer of the underlying security) and co-ownership of whatever is held by the intermediary for its customers, whether it holds direct from the issuer or from a higher-tier intermediary.[117] There are several reasons why this right of co-ownership and other rights embodied in the securities entitlement should be treated as a separate bundle of rights exercisable only through and against the investor's own intermediary. As mentioned earlier, this separate bundle of rights is identified in this book as "intermediated securities".

One crucial point is that, to make the system of indirect holdings and pooled funds work, it is essential that each investor should be considered to have a relationship exclusively with its own intermediary and that neither he nor his secured or execution creditors should be able to assert rights against higher-tier intermediaries or the issuer.[118] That is already the position in most cases under English trust law, where it is only in exceptional cases that the beneficiary under a sub-trust can have recourse to the head trustee; in general he must look exclusively to his own trustee.[119] If that is the rule even where the head trustee knows of the existence and ultimate entitlement of the beneficiary, it is even more necessary to adhere to it where, as in the case of tiered holdings of securities, the intermediary at each level knows only of, and deals only with, its own customers, not customers of lower-tier intermediaries. Indeed, even if an intermediary did know of a lower-tier customer it could not be expected either to reveal information about its own customer in breach of its duty of confidentiality or to concern itself with the lower-tier customer's rights so as to inhibit its obedience to transfer instructions given by its own customer. The concept of the securities entitlement under UCC art.8 and the bundle of rights defined in art.9 of the Geneva Securities Convention identify the securities intermediary as the exclusive source of the customer's rights and remove the temptation to think of him as having rights which are traceable up the chain of intermediaries. Under an "indirect" holding system this would be difficult, if not impossible, in practice,

6–19

---

[116] Art.9 rights are: the right, enforceable against the intermediary, to receive and exercise the rights attached to the securities, the right to effect a disposition by instructions to the relevant intermediary and the right by instructions to the intermediary, to cause the securities to be held other than through a securities account. Art.24 provides that an intermediary must hold or have available securities equivalent to the number credited to the securities accounts it maintains for account holders. See also Principle 3.1 and 4.1 of the Principles set out in the *EU Consultation Document "Legislation on Legal Certainty of Securities Holding and Dispositions"*, and see para.6–19, below.

[117] For an analysis of how the Convention creates rights which can be seen as proprietary rights under English law see L. Gullifer, "The Intermediated Proprietary Protection of Investors", in "Contractual Prohibitions Against Assignment" Ch.11 in J. Armour and J. Payne (eds), *Rationality in Company Law: Essays in Honour of DD Prentice* (Oxford: Hart Publishing, 2008).

[118] Some systems, such as the German, French and Spanish systems, are "direct holding" systems where investors can enforce rights directly against the issuer as well as against their immediate intermediary.

[119] For an example in relation to a house, see the decision of the Privy Council in *Hayim v Citibank NA* [1987] A.C. 730.

not merely because an intermediary will not have knowledge of any customers other than its own but also because, with netting arrangements and sourcing of the same securities from different intermediaries, there is no reliable way of establishing the links in the chain.[120] Also the applicable law could differ from tier to tier.

Thus any interest the investor may ultimately have in the underlying security is derived only from his own intermediary, not from the issuer or a higher-tier intermediary. If, therefore, the investor's intermediary never acquired a valid title from its own intermediary or if, though it did, it has dissipated its security holdings, the investor is left with a purely personal remedy, while in the case of a shortfall the interests of all investors holding accounts with that intermediary abate proportionately.[121] Again, the investor's entitlement against its own intermediary may become subject to contractual set-off. To allow the investor to bypass his own intermediary by recourse direct to the issuer or to a higher-tier intermediary would be to risk treating him as having rights in the underlying security which he had never acquired and promoting him above those having a better right and would also interfere with the ability of the issuer and higher-tier intermediaries to honour their own contractual obligations. Moreover, it would be wholly impracticable, with a large and rapid turnover of transactions, for anyone other than the investor's own intermediary to be able to verify within the limited time available that the investor did indeed have an interest in the securities.

6–20   It is convenient at this point to examine the issue of shortfall in a little more detail. First, it is necessary to understand the possible contexts in which shortfall may arise.[122] As we have seen, the account holder (AH) is credited by the account provider (AP) with the number of securities he holds. Thus, if AH acquires 100 shares in Z Ltd, AP will make a credit entry in its books.[123] However, unless AH has acquired those securities from another account holder with AP, in which case AP will just make the relevant credit and debit entries, in order to credit AH with those securities, AP needs to have a credit entry for that amount of securities in Z Ltd in its own account with a higher tier intermediary in which it holds all the Z Ltd securities which it holds for its account holders. Thus one possibility is that such an entry never happens through mistake or fraud. Another possibility is that, although AP did have such a credit, it mistakenly or fraudulently causes its account to be debited with 100 Z Ltd securities. However, another possibility is that AP is permitted to cause such a debit entry to be made because it has a "right of use" over AH's intermediated securities because it has a security interest over them in relation to sums due or potentially due to it by AH.[124] Where the securities are held in a pooled account, AP may well have a right of use over all

---

[120] J.S. Rogers, "Of Normalcy and Anomaly: Thoughts on Choice of Law for the Indirect Holding System", *The Oxford Colloquium on the Conflict of Laws, A Special Supplement to Butterworths Journal of International Banking and Financial Law* (September 1998), p.47; Rogers, "Policy Perspectives on Revised U.C.C. Article 8" (1996) 43 UCLA L. Rev. 1431. See also Schwarcz, "Intermediary Risk in a Global Economy" (2001) 50 Duke L.J. 1541.

[121] See para.6–20, below.

[122] For details and worked examples, in the US context, see C. Mooney, "The truth about shortfall in intermediated securities" in *Intermediated securities: the impact of the Geneva Securities Convention and the future European legislation* (2013), Ch.7.

[123] See Geneva Securities Convention art.11 where the term "credit entry" is used for the source of title.

[124] See paras 6–46 et seq., below for discussion of the right of use.

or a high proportion of the securities in the account, and these can be of value to AP either to raise cash using a repo,[125] or to earn income by "lending" them under a securities lending transaction.

If not sufficient Z Ltd securities are credited to AP's account with its intermediary to meet all the credits that AH and its fellow account holders have with AP, there is a shortfall. This does not matter to the account holders providing AP is solvent, since AP is obliged to acquire sufficient securities to satisfy any claim by them to "their" securities and, if this is not possible, to compensate them for breach of trust in cash. It is significant if AP becomes insolvent, however, this requires further examination. First, if the shortfall is due to the exercise of the right of use, this means that the account holders probably owe sums to AP secured by a security interest in the securities.[126] Thus, because of the operation of close-out netting, AP's obligation to deliver securities only relates to securities of the value left once the amounts due are deducted. Secondly, if the securities have been transferred from AP's account under a repo or stock lending agreement, the counterparty will be contractually obliged to return equivalent securities at some stage. So long as the counterparty is not insolvent as well, equivalent securities should be returned to AP's account with its intermediary, thus reducing or extinguishing the shortfall. Alternatively, if there is close-out netting in the repo or securities lending agreement which is triggered by AP's insolvency, AP may be entitled to retain the cash collateral it has received from the counterparty. Whether that cash collateral is held on trust for these particular account holders depends, probably, on the terms of the agreement between AP and AH, but it is certainly possible that AP's rights against its counterparty (including the right to retain the cash collateral) could be held on trust for the account holders.[127] Even if it is held on trust, there may be an issue of identification unless the cash is placed in a segregated account pending return of equivalent securities.

It can be seen that, perhaps, the eventuality of a shortfall as a result of exercise of a right of use may not be quite as dramatic as might be envisaged, but it does potentially leave the account holders exposed to risk in relation to any surplus value over and above what they owe to AP, and to the insolvency risk of AP's counterparty. It now seems reasonably clear that any such loss would be borne pari passu among all account holders, although this is by no means the only possible solution under English law.[128] It is by far the most practical solution, since any other would complicate tracing exercises with resulting delay and expense.[129] However, under English law, it would probably be necessary to imply

---

[125] See para.6–01, above.

[126] Of course, at any particular time, a particular account holder may not owe anything, although, depending on the terms of the agreement with the intermediary, the intermediary may have a right of use of the securities.

[127] See *Re Lehman Brothers International (Europe) (In Administration)* [2010] EWHC 2914 (Ch) at [240]; *Lift Capital Partners Pty Ltd v Merrill Lynch International* (2009) 253 A.L.R. 482 [89]–[91].

[128] For discussion of the possible tracing solutions, see B. McFarlane and R. Stevens, "Interests in Securities: Practical Problems and Conceptual Solutions" in *Intermediated Securities: Legal Problems and Practical Issues* (2010), pp.40–44.

[129] See G. Moss, "Issues arising from insolvency", in *Intermediated Securities: Legal Problems and Practical Issues* (2010), p.67.

a term in the agreement between the account provider and the account holders providing for pro rata apportionment of shortfall.[130]

There is also the risk of mistaken or fraudulent transfers. In theory, if a beneficiary's assets are transferred to a third party by a trustee in breach of trust, that beneficiary could trace its assets and claim them from a third party who does not have a defence to that claim, for example, that he was a bona fide purchaser. In relation to intermediated securities this issue is much more complex. First, given that transfers are made at the level of a higher tier intermediary and are settled by netting, it would be very hard to trace a transfer of a particular parcel of securities to a specific recipient. However, if tracing were possible, the question arises as to when a recipient would have the defence of being a bona fide purchaser. Under English law this is problematic, since the interest acquired by an account holder is equitable, and there is no, or limited, operation of the bona fide purchaser defence available to the acquirer of a legal interest.[131] This issue has been directly dealt with under the Geneva Securities Convention, which gives quite extensive protection to a good faith purchaser without knowledge of a conflicting claim.[132]

6–21   Detachment of the securities entitlement from the underlying security also enables us to see that the customer is the legal holder of the contractual rights conferred on him by the account agreement and that, in contrast to the position as regards any proprietary interest he may have, he may make a statutory assignment of his contractual rights.[133] Again, the priority of successive assignments of a securities account will be governed by the rule in *Dearle v Hall* if such assignments are not prohibited by the terms of the custody agreement.[134] Finally, the concept establishes the source and location of the entitlement for conflict of laws purposes, whereas if this is conceived as a direct entitlement to the securities themselves there is a danger that the entitlement will be treated as derived from the issuer and will therefore be governed by the issuer's law. The

---

[130] This is also the effect of art.26 of the Geneva Convention. If the intermediary does acquire or originally holds securities of the same type as the dissipated holdings it will be seen as having complied with its duty to hold sufficient securities under art.24 and those securities will be appropriated to the rights of the account holders under art.25. The Principles set out in the *EU Consultation Document "Legislation on Legal Certainty of Securities Holding and Dispositions"* provide for an obligation to hold sufficient securities (Principle 4.1) but do not provide for what is to happen on a shortfall. In theory, if Principle 4.1 were to be complied with there would never be a shortfall, but it is not clear how this is compatible with a right of use. The Geneva Securities Convention provides specifically for a right of use, see art.34.

[131] G. Davies, "Using Intermediated Securities As Collateral: equitable interests with inequitable results" (2007) 2 J.I.B.F.L. 70. For a slightly different view, see B. McFarlane and R. Stevens, "Interests in Securities: Practical Problems and Conceptual Solutions" in *Intermediated Securities: Legal Problems and Practical Issues* (2010), pp.52–54.

[132] Geneva Securities Convention art.18. cf. Principle 8 of the EU Principles (fn.56 above which is in slightly different terms, see Thevenoz, "Transfer of Intermediated Securities" in *Intermediated securities: the Impact of the Geneva Securities Convention and the future European legislation* (2013)).

[133] Transfer of legal title to registered shares themselves may be effected only by a novation through entry of the transfer on the register of the issuer or, in the case of dematerialised securities, the CREST register, and not by assignment. See para.6–10, above.

[134] In practice securities intermediaries usually prohibit assignment and decline to accept notice of assignment, so that the giving of a notice has no perfection effect and the rule in *Dearle v Hall* does not apply. Equitable claims or assignments cannot be registered on the CREST register (Uncertificated Securities Regulations 1999 reg.23(3)).

better view, and that which reflects the realities of the market place, is that embodied in the place of relevant intermediary approach (PRIMA), i.e. that the relevant law is that of the place of the relevant intermediary.[135] This is fully in accordance with general conflict of laws principles, which looks to the place of the root of title.[136] In the case of directly held registered shares, the root of title is the register maintained by the company,[137] so that the law of the company's place of incorporation applies; in the case of bearer securities, the root of title is the certificate and the applicable law is the lex situs of the securities at the time of the relevant dealing; in the case of indirectly held registered securities, the root of title is the securities account with the intermediary, hence the PRIMA law.

Since English commercial law is anything if not practical, we can reasonably conclude that subject to the terms of the agreement between him and the securities intermediary, the credit of securities to a customer's securities account entitles him to a co-ownership interest in the bundle of rights held by the intermediary itself (from its own intermediary or, if none, from the issuer direct), coupled with a personal right to the delivery or transfer, or re-delivery or re-transfer, of the deposited securities, and consequent restoration of the customer's direct link with the issuer, but no rights against any other intermediaries. The position in English law, at present, relies on a trusts analysis, which seems to lead to the right general conclusion, but could lead to difficulties if classic trusts law were rigidly applied, without regard to the particular commercial context. These difficulties would be exacerbated in a cross-border context. There is a great deal to be said for a functional approach in relation to intermediated securities: this is what has been done in the Geneva Securities Convention, and is what is proposed in the EU Principles.[138]

(2) Holdings in a segregated (non-fungible) account

Suppose now that the customer's holding is in a segregated, or non-fungible, account, so that the holding does not form part of the pool of securities which its intermediary holds with its own intermediary but is reflected in a separate account showing that the lower-tier intermediary's holding is for the customer, not for itself or for customers generally. Does this affect the previous analysis? There is clearly no problem in relation to identification here.[139] However, this particular customer is in a different position from others, in that he will not be subject to the danger of a shortfall that arises in relation to a pooled account.

6–22

---

[135] The unsuitability of the application of art.14 of Regulation (EC) No.593/2008 of the European Parliament and of the Council of June 17, 2008 on the law applicable to contractual obligations (Rome I), is pointed out in Dicey, Morris & Collins, *The Conflict of Laws*, 15th edn (London: Sweet & Maxwell, 2012) paras 24–071 et seq. PRIMA is also the underlying approach adopted in the 2002 Hague Convention on the law applicable to certain rights in respect of securities held with an intermediary (but the parties can designate the applicable law) and Principle 14 of the EU Principles (above fn.56). Art.9 of the FCARs also follows a PRIMA approach for arrangements within its scope. See para.6–53, below.

[136] i.e. the best evidence of title, though not necessarily conclusive. The principle that the securities account is the root of title was applied by Stein J. in the US District Court for the Southern District of New York in *Fidelity Partners Inc v First Trust Co of New York*, 58 F.Supp 2d 52 (1997).

[137] Or in the case of CREST securities, by Euroclear UK & Ireland Ltd.

[138] See para.6–12, above.

[139] See para.6–14, above.

Where, for example, the intermediary wrongfully disposes of part of the pooled funds, the disposition will not affect the holder of the non-fungible account.[140] However, an account holder is still at risk if the securities are held in a pooled account by its account provider's intermediary: there could still be a shortfall affecting it if both the account provider and its intermediary became insolvent.[141]

5. THE SETTLEMENT FINALITY DIRECTIVE AND THE FINANCIAL COLLATERAL DIRECTIVE

The Settlement Finality Directive[142]

6–23   The effect of this Directive and implementing regulations is largely to remove from attack under general insolvency law the rules of a designated settlement system, and transactions (including the realisation of collateral security) effected in connection with participation in such a system. Thus system rules governing default arrangements, in particular, arrangements for netting and the closing out of open positions,[143] and the application or transfer of collateral security,[144] are to be respected notwithstanding rules of insolvency law which might otherwise invalidate them.[145] Thus, the proceedings of the designated market are not to be invalidated on the grounds of inconsistency with insolvency law,[146] and various insolvency provisions are expressly disapplied or modified.[147] Of some importance also is the conflict of laws rule embodied in art.9(2) of the Directive[148] which provides that where securities are provided as collateral to a (system) participant and/or central bank of a Member State and their right with

---

[140]   This is also the position under the Geneva Securities Convention, see art.26(2)(a).

[141]   See para.6–20, above.

[142]   Directive on Settlement Finality in Payment and Securities Systems (98/26 dated May 19, 1998), implemented in the UK by the Financial Markets and Insolvency (Settlement Finality) Regulations 1999 (SI 1999/2979).

[143]   See Ch.7, below.

[144]   Including security provided under a charge or repurchase or similar agreement for the purpose of securing rights and obligations potentially arising in connection with the system.

[145]   Note too that Pt VII of the Companies Act disapplies the moratorium regime applied in administration in para.43 Sch.B1 to the Insolvency Act 1986, to market charges and system charges, see Financial Markets and Insolvency (Money Market) Regulations 1995 (SI 1995/2049) and Financial Markets and Insolvency Regulations 1996 (SI 1996/1469).

[146]   Financial Markets and Insolvency (Settlement Finality) Regulations 1999 (SI 1999/2979) reg.14.

[147]   Financial Markets and Insolvency (Settlement Finality) Regulations 1999 (SI 1999/2979) reg.15: modification of the rules of insolvency set-off (see para.7–90, below), reg.16 disapplies the rules on disclaimer of property and rescission of contracts, reg.17 disapplies the rules on avoidance of past transactions, and reg.19 disapplies, in relation to a collateral security charge, the restrictions imposed by paras 43(2), 70, 71 and 72 of Sch.B1 to the Insolvency Act 1986 on the enforcement of security while a petition for an administration order is pending or the order is in force do not apply. Note that if there is a charge ranking in priority to the collateral security charge the court may order steps to protect the position of that chargee, reg.19(2). Insolvency Act s.127 (which invalidates dispositions made after the commencement of a winding up unless approved by the court) does not apply to a disposition of property as the result of which it becomes subject to a collateral security charge (reg.19(3)).

[148]   Implemented in the UK by reg.23 of the Financial Markets and Insolvency (Settlement Finality) Regulations 1999. It is likely that art.9(2) will be modified in the light of the Hague Convention on the law applicable to certain rights held with an intermediary.

respect to the securities is legally recorded in a register, account or centralised deposit system located in a Member State the rights of holders of the collateral are to be determined by the law of that Member State. One effect of this is that concerning rights in relation to securities held through an account with a securities intermediary in a Member State, it is the PRIMA law that applies. There is some possible discrepancy between this approach and that adopted by the 2002 Hague Convention on indirectly held securities,[149] although the differences are not likely to be particularly significant in practice.[150]

The Directive on Financial Collateral Arrangements

The Financial Collateral Directive is altogether broader and more ambitious in scope. Its purpose is to facilitate the provision of financial collateral under bilateral transactions, and thereby promote not only the stability of the market but also its efficiency, by requiring Member States to disapply rules of law and statutory provisions that would otherwise invalidate financial collateral arrangements and provision, whether before insolvency (as by rendering void transactions not carried out or perfected in conformity with prescribed formalities) or on insolvency. The Directive covers both directly held and intermediated securities, as well as cash and credit claims.[151] The Directive is implemented in the United Kingdom by the Financial Collateral Arrangements (No.2) Regulations 2003 (referred to in this chapter as the FCARs)[152] and it is these regulations which will be considered below. The Geneva Securities Convention also has a number of provisions relating to collateral transactions, which to a large extent replicate the provisions of the Financial Collateral Directive.

6–24

(1)   Scope of the FCARs

The FCARs have a very wide scope of application, since they apply to any collateral arrangement between non-natural persons.[153] This is much wider than that required by the FCD, which only applies to arrangements between regulated or public financial institutions, or between such institutions and "non-natural persons", that is, not individuals.[154] The Treasury explains the extension on the grounds of simplicity, since there was then no need to include the complicated definitions and jurisdictional limits that are found in the FCD, and also on the basis that it achieved the policy objectives, that is, to reduce systemic risk and to

6–25

---

[149] See para.6–54, below.

[150] L. Thevenoz, "The Geneva Securities Convention" in *Intermediated securities: the impact of the Geneva Securities Convention and the future European legislation* (2013), pp.11–12.

[151] See paras 6–04 et seq., above.

[152] Financial Collateral Arrangements (No.2) Regulations 2003 (2003/3226) amended by SI 2009/2462 and SI 2010/2993.

[153] FCARs reg.3.

[154] FCD art.1(2). The FCD contained an option in art.1(3) for Member States to restrict the operation of the implementing legislation to financial institutions, but few exercised this option, see K. Lober and E. Klima, "The Implementation of Directive 2002/47 on Financial Collateral Arrangements" (2006) 21 J.I.B.L.R. (2006) 203.

increase the efficiency of the markets.[155] It must be borne in mind, however, that by disapplication of so many provisions, particularly those applying on insolvency, protection which would otherwise be available to other creditors (especially unsecured creditors) is eroded. The scope of the disapplication has to be a question of balancing interests of creditors in addition to ease of identifying which transactions fall within it. The question of whether the "gold-plating" of the FCARs fell within the power conferred on HM Treasury under s.2(2)(b) of the European Communities Act was raised in the course of the *Cukurova* litigation.[156] The actual decision was as to whether the claimants were entitled to an extension of time within which to make their challenge to the vires of the FCARs. The judge's review of the merits of the challenge was for the sole purpose of deciding whether the merits were so strong that they would outweigh what otherwise would be undue delay.[157] He decided that they were not. After a full discussion of whether the "gold-plating" of the FCARs was sufficiently closely connected to the purpose being achieved[158] by the FCD not to be ultra vires. The judge made the point that the wider scope of the FCARs enabled major players on the financial markets, such as hedge funds, who were not included (or not necessarily included) in the definitions in the FCD to be protected.[159] He also made the more general point that the wider the scope of the FCARs the better the protection against systemic risk.[160]

Of course, the judge was only considering the vires of the FCARs and not considering in abstract where the line should be drawn. On this basis the very broad scope of the FCARs seems undesirable. First, it means that totally straightforward business financing arrangements, such as a loan made to a company secured by a charge over its bank account, are included. An example of this is the arrangement in the case of *Gray v G-T-P Group Ltd; Re F2G Realisations Ltd (In Liquidation)*,[161] which was where a provider of store card debit services had a right of retention of money in a bank account (held in its name) if its customer, a supplied or laminate floors, defaulted in payment of certain charges. Not only is such a transaction not systemically important, but there are good reasons to apply the normal insolvency regime to such arrangements.[162]

As discussed above, the FCARs cover financial collateral in the form of cash, credit claims or financial instruments.[163] They apply to "financial collateral

[155] HM Treasury, *Consultation Paper, on the implementation of the Directive on Financial Collateral Arrangements* (2003) para.2.3.

[156] *R (on the application of Cukurova Finance International Ltd) v HM Treasury* [2008] EWHC 2567 (Admin).

[157] *R (on the application of Cukurova Finance International Ltd) v HM Treasury* [2008] EWHC 2567 (Admin) at [52].

[158] The test laid down in *Oakley Inc v Animal Ltd* [2005] EWCA Civ 1191.

[159] *R (on the application of Cukurova Finance International Ltd) v HM Treasury* [2008] EWHC 2567 (Admin) at [95].

[160] *R (on the application of Cukurova Finance International Ltd) v HM Treasury* [2008] EWHC 2567 (Admin) at [96].

[161] *Gray v G-T-P Group Ltd; Re F2G Realisations Ltd (In Liquidation)* [2010] EWHC 1772 (Ch).

[162] See Gullifer, "What Should we do about Financial Collateral?" (2012) 65 C.L.P. 377. The arrangement was held not to fall within the FCARs in that particular case as there was not possession or control on the part of the collateral taker, see para.6–34, below.

[163] FCARs reg.3. "Financial instruments" are defined in reg.3 and cover virtually all forms of instrument issued on a market. It also appears that shares in private companies are included: this point

arrangements", which includes both title transfer financial collateral arrangements and security financial collateral arrangements, whether or not these are covered by a master agreement. Both sorts of arrangements are required to be evidenced in writing. The distinction made in the Directive between arrangements for the provision of financial collateral and its actual provision does not appear in the FCARs. The precise scope of the definitions of title transfer financial collateral arrangements and security financial collateral arrangements is discussed below in the context of an examination of each type of arrangement.[164]

(2) Disapplication of rules

So long as (a) an arrangements falls within the definition of one or the other category of financial collateral arrangements; (b) the collateral is cash, credit claims or financial instruments; and (c) the parties are non-natural persons, various statutory provisions rules are disapplied. One of the main purposes of the Directive (and therefore the FCARs) is to reduce to a minimum the requirements for attachment and perfection of a security interest, or, where relevant, a title transfer arrangement.[165]

6–26

The FCARs therefore provide that various statutory formalities do not apply to any financial collateral arrangements. Thus, the requirements of writing and signature for a guarantee,[166] for the disposition of an equitable interest,[167] and for a statutory assignment of a chose in action[168] are disapplied.[169] The registration requirements under s.859A of the Companies Act 2006[170] are also disapplied. In the past the effect of this was not dramatic, as there were no formal requirements under English law for the attachment of a security interest in registered securities, and formal perfection requirements in the shape of registration in the Companies Registry apply only to floating charges, charges on book debts and charges to secure any issue of debentures. Under the new regime applicable from April 6, 2013[171] all charges are registrable except (among others) a charge statutorily excluded from s.859A,[172] which therefore includes all security financial collateral arrangements. The risk of recharacterisation of a sale and repurchase as a registrable security transaction has been eliminated, but the need to register floating charges still remains because of the uncertainty as to the scope of "possession or control".[173]

---

appears to have been agreed between the learned experts who gave evidence to the British Virgin Islands Court of Appeal in *Alfa Telecom Turkey Ltd v Cukurova Finance International Limited* HCVAP2007/027.

[164] See paras 6–27 et seq., below.

[165] There are, of course, no registration requirements for a title transfer arrangement, but it is possible that the requirements of writing under s.53(1)(c) or s.136 of the Law of Property Act 1925 might apply.

[166] Statute of Frauds 1677 s.4. It is unclear when this provision would apply to financial collateral arrangement anyway.

[167] Law of Property Act 1925 s.53(1)(c).

[168] Law of Property Act 1925 s.136.

[169] FCARs reg.4.

[170] And also under s.4 of the Industrial and Provident Societies Act 1967.

[171] See Ch.2, above.

[172] Companies Act 2006 s.859A(6)(c).

[173] See paras 6–33 et seq, below.

In order to make enforcement of financial collateral arrangements quick and easy, various insolvency provisions are also disapplied.[174] Thus, if the collateral provider goes into administration, the usual moratoria[175] do not apply, nor has the administrator power to deal with charged assets.[176] Further, the preferential status given to certain creditors over floating charge assets[177] does not apply. Similar provisions applying on winding up[178] and on the appointment of a receiver[179] are also disapplied, as are the liquidator's power to disclaim onerous property,[180] and provisions invalidating dispositions after the commencement of the winding up[181] and floating charges in the run-up to insolvency.[182] It should be noted that these insolvency provisions are also disapplied in relation to designated settlement systems and collateral security charges,[183] enforcement of systems charges[184] and market charges,[185] and operations on recognised markets, clearing systems and involving central counterparties.[186] However, unless the security or title transfer arrangements which benefit from this disapplication of insolvency provisions fall within the FCARs, they do not attract the other disapplications and benefits available under those Regulations,[187] except for provisions upholding the validity of close-out netting.[188]

Another, related, purpose of the Financial Collateral Directive was to remove legal uncertainty in relation to common practices which had developed in the markets, particularly in relation to title transfer collateral arrangements. The FCARs reflect this to the extent necessary in English law by providing that close-out netting provisions take effect in accordance with their terms,[189] and for enforceable rights of use and appropriation (if provided for in the agreement) in relation to security financial collateral arrangements.[190]

---

[174] Reg.8 covers provisions restricting the enforcement of security on insolvency, and reg.10 covers provisions avoiding contracts and floating charges.

[175] Insolvency Act 1986 Sch.B1 paras 42 and 43.

[176] Insolvency Act 1986 Sch.B1 paras 70 and 71.

[177] Insolvency Act 1986 Sch.B para.65(2) (applying s.175 to a distribution made by an administrator) and paras 99(3) and (4) (relating to the administrator's expenses) as well as s.176A of the Insolvency Act 1986 (prescribed part).

[178] Insolvency Act 1986 ss.175, 176ZA.

[179] Insolvency Act 1986 s.40.

[180] Insolvency Act 1986 s.178.

[181] Insolvency Act 1986 s.127.

[182] Insolvency Act 1986 s.245.

[183] Financial Markets and Insolvency (Settlement Finality) Regulations 1999 (SI 1999/2979).

[184] Financial Markets and Insolvency Regulations 1996 (SI 1996/1496).

[185] Companies Act 1989 s.174.

[186] Companies Act 1989 Pt VII.

[187] See the "Gap Analysis" annexed to the reply of the Financial Law Committee of the City of London Law Society of October 22, 2010 to the Treasury consultation on the Implementation of the amending EU Directive 2009/44/EC.

[188] See para.7–94, below.

[189] FCARs reg.12. For discussion, see para.7–94, below.

[190] FCARs regs 16–18. For further discussion see paras 6–46 et seq., below.

6. INTERESTS IN FINANCIAL COLLATERAL CREATED BY TITLE TRANSFER

Types of title transfer arrangements

Repos and stock lending

In the securities industry it is common for securities to be transferred upon terms of re-transfer at a later date. Two important types of arrangement are sale and repurchase ("repo"), and stock lending. The flow of dealings in international securities between parties regularly engaged in such transactions is usually governed by one of the forms of standard-term master agreement, with relevant annexes, issued by a global trade association. For repos parties typically use the IBMA/ISMA Global Market Repurchase Agreement (GMRA),[191] while for stock lending the standard form is the Global Master Securities Lending Agreement (GMSLA) issued by the International Securities Lenders Association (ISLA).[192]

6–27

Title transfer collateral arrangements, such as repos and securities lending, are techniques which can be used for a number of functions in the capital markets.[193] Basically, repos are used to borrow money using securities as collateral, while securities lending is used to borrow securities (for a fee) against collateral of cash or other securities, default being dealt with by close-out netting.[194] However, the motivation of parties to these transactions are more various[195]: some are seeking a return on their assets (cash or securities), others are looking for a cheap form of financing, others are seeking to transform one type of asset into another, so that it can offer better collateral for a transaction while others wish to cover short selling.[196] The effect of repos and securities lending being used in the market is that securities, which otherwise would sit in accounts earning no money, are used to support short term financing, to increase liquidity in the markets and to manage portfolios of securities.

The classic repo is a sale of securities under an agreement by which equivalent securities are to be repurchased at a later date at a repurchase price equal to the original sale price but with a separate additional payment.[197] The repo may be for a fixed term, which can range from overnight to a year or more, or it may be an open-term repo in which the buyer can renew its retention of the securities from

---

[191] The current version is GMRA 2011.

[192] The current version is the GMSLA 2010.

[193] For a detailed account, see Financial Stability Board (FSB), *Interim report on securities lending and repos* (April 2012); and the very helpful information on the website of the International Capital Markets Association, ICMA at *http://www.icmagroup.org/Regulatory-Policy-and-Market-Practice/short-term-markets/Repo-Markets/* [accessed September 30, 2013].

[194] See para.7–21, below.

[195] See the analysis of the market in the FSB Interim report at pp.1–8.

[196] This is the selling of borrowed securities: eventually the seller will have to buy securities in the market to return them to the lender: if this can be done at a lower price than the short sale, the seller makes a profit. Uncovered short selling (where the seller does not hold borrowed securities covering the sale) is illegal under the EU Short Selling Regulation (Regulation (EU) 236/2012 of the European Parliament and of the Council of March 14 2012 on short selling and certain aspects of credit default swaps [2012] O.J. L86/1.

[197] For an account of a typical repo, see *Re Lehman Brothers International (Europe) (In Administration)* [2010] EWHC 2914 (Ch) at [78]–[79].

day-to-day. The sell/buy-back form of repo is where the repurchase price, instead of being the same as the original sale price, is a forward price which consists of the aggregate of the original sale price and an interest equivalent. So the interest element is not a separate add-on, as in the case of the classic repo, but forms an element of the calculation of the repurchase price. However, the commercial objectives of the two types of transaction are broadly the same, namely, on the part of the seller to raise funds and, on the part of the buyer, to earn money through the finance charge.

Stock lending differs from the repo both in its commercial purposes and in its legal characterisation. Whereas a repo is driven by a need for cash, the purpose of the stock loan is, from the perspective of the borrower, to cover a short position in the securities in question and, from the perspective of the lender, to put securities for which it has no immediate need to profitable use through a charge for the loan. A stock loan does not involve a sale for a money price and a repurchase for a money price.[198] It is simply a transfer of ownership of securities[199] against an undertaking by the transferee to retransfer equivalent securities at a later date and to pay a fixed fee for the loan.[200] Apart from the fee no money consideration is involved in either leg of the transaction.

Title transfer credit support arrangements

6–28   Another type of title transfer arrangement is used for the provision of cash or securities as collateral for obligations under derivative or other transactions. The collateral could be provided to an individual counterparty or to a central counterparty. A typical arrangement is that found in the Credit Support Annex to the ISDA Master Agreement, which provides for outright transfer of collateral depending on the net exposure of the transferee to the credit risk of the transferor, with provision for the return of collateral if the exposure reduces.[201] The agreement states specifically that it does not create a security interest.

Methods of transfer

6–29   Thus, title transfer arrangements are those, including, but not limited to, repos and securities lending agreements, under which full ownership of collateral is transferred to the collateral taker.[202] This reflects the securities industry's usage in treating title transfer as a form of collateral even though in English law an

---

[198] See *Re Lehman Brothers International (Europe) (In Administration)* [2010] EWHC 2914 (Ch) at [80]–[81].

[199] It is sometimes said that because of the transfer of ownership the label "stock lending" is a misnomer. This is a misconception. A loan is not the same as a bailment. It involves the transfer of ownership followed by retransfer at a later date (the typical case is the loan of money), whereas under a bailment the bailee acquires a purely possessory interest and ownership remains with the bailor. The loan is similar to the Roman law contract of *mutuum*.

[200] It is also usual for the borrower to provide collateral as security for its re-transfer obligation, typically either other securities or cash.

[201] Credit Support Annex 1995 para.2.

[202] Some countries do not recognise the grant of security by title transfer. Art.6 of the Financial Collateral Directive requires Member States to ensure that a title transfer financial collateral arrangement can take effect in accordance with its terms.

outright transfer does not constitute a security interest.[203] If the collateral is cash, it must be transferred into an account in the name of the collateral taker; in the case of credit claims, these would be novated or assigned[204] to the collateral taker. In the case of direct holdings of securities, outright title transfer is by entry on the company register (if certificated) or the CREST register[205] (if uncertificated). In the case of intermediated securities title transfer would normally take place by transfer to the collateral taker's account, that is, novation. In theory it might be possible also to transfer title to intermediated securities by assignment of the account holder's rights against the account provider. However, this raises a number of problems. First, while it might be reasonably straightforward if the account was a segregated account and all the securities held in the account were being transferred, the analysis is more difficult if the account is a pooled one and/or if only part of the account holder's holding is being transferred. What is then being assigned? It would be an assignment of part of the account holder's rights against the account provider, and it would be difficult to identify these. Secondly, most intermediaries contractually prohibit assignment. Thirdly, it is hard to see how such an assignment could fall within the definition of title transfer financial collateral arrangement in the FCARs which is considered below. Title transfer arrangements do not include mortgages, which transfer only security ownership, not full ownership, but do include outright sale and repurchase agreements which are intended to fulfil a security function even if not, under English law, constituting security agreements.[206]

Comparison of title transfer arrangements and security arrangements

In the financial markets, both title transfer arrangements, as described above, and security arrangements, described below, are used. The latter arrangement is often called a "pledge" although it is not a possessory security and is not technically a pledge under English law, but a mortgage or charge.[207] A similar confusion of nomenclature arises in relation to "lien" which is also used to denote what English law would term a charge.[208]

6–30

Although the securities industry treats title transfer arrangements as secured transactions in terms of commercial purpose and economic effect, in law the outright transfer of ownership, if that is what is genuinely intended by the parties, is not converted into a security interest merely because the transfer agreement incorporates a repurchase obligation.[209] To reinforce this, the documentation

---

[203] See para.1–40, above. Title transfer collateral arrangements are also recognised by the Geneva Securities Convention at art.31.

[204] Presumably, under English law, the assignment could be statutory or equitable, although it is doubtful if the latter would fall within the FCARs, see para.6–31, below.

[205] Uncertificated Securities Regulations reg.27(1). Depending on the type of securities, this may also need to be entered on the issuer's register, see para.6–10, above.

[206] See para.1–40, above.

[207] See para.1–51, above.

[208] *Re Lehman Brothers International (Europe) (In Administration)* [2012] EWHC 2997 (Ch) at [34] et seq.

[209] See para.1–40, above. The repurchase obligation relates to equivalent securities: if this means that different securities from those sold can be the subject of the repurchase, then the transaction cannot be a security transaction as there is no right to redeem. See para.6–14, above for a discussion of the

usually includes an express provision that no security interest is intended.[210] The reason why title transfer arrangements are regarded commercially as secured transactions is that the parties safeguard themselves against the effect of a default—by the buyer in failing to resell or by the seller in failing to pay the repurchase price—by a close-out provision by which the resale/repurchase obligation is converted into a money obligation and the two money obligations are netted or set off against each other and reduced to a net balance payable by one party to the other.[211]

From the viewpoint of the transferee title transfer has certain advantages over a security interest. First, as absolute owner the buyer can do what it likes with the purchased securities without having to stipulate for rights of sale or "use".[212] Secondly, possible registration requirements are avoided. Thirdly, there is no problem with enforcement by appropriation (or retention) of the collateral. Fourthly, there are no issues which arise from the right to withdraw "excess" collateral (or to substitute equivalent collateral). However, from the perspective of the transferor, they are exposed to the credit risk of the transferee to the extent that the securities or cash transferred exceed their credit exposure, that is, the net balance that would be produced by close-out netting, since the transferee's obligation to return equivalent securities or cash is merely personal, and the securities or cash transferred is likely to have been used in a title transfer arrangement with another counterparty.

Title transfer financial collateral arrangements within the FCARs

6–31   Many of the provisions of the FCARs have no application to title transfer arrangements, such as the disapplication of formalities.[213] There is no need for the protection of the FCARs to protect the right of use, or appropriation, and although the protection of close-out netting might be helpful in the interests of legal certainty, this may well be achieved under another statutory provision if the arrangement relates to transactions on a capital market.[214] The same is true of the disapplied insolvency provisions: many of them do not apply to title transfer arrangements (such as those relating to the floating charge) and those which would otherwise apply may well be disapplied elsewhere.[215] Despite this, it is

---

nature of a shareholder's interest. If what is transferred and retransferred is a co-ownership interest in the issued share or loan capital, then it is arguable that it is the same asset and that accordingly the immunity of title transfer from attack as a security interest rests solely on the fact that it is intended as an outright transfer of ownership, not on any argument that the seller does not have a right to repurchase the same asset as that which it transferred. However, it could be argued that once the shareholder's fractional interest has acquired an identity by its history, then what is returned on the second leg of a repo is an interest with a different history and therefore an equivalent but not identical thing. On this view a repo (or other title transfer arrangement) cannot be a security interest.

[210] See, for example, the ISDA Credit Support Annex.

[211] See para.7–21, below.

[212] See further para.6–46, below.

[213] See para.6–26 and fn.165, above for possible provisions which might need to be disapplied.

[214] See para.7–94, below.

[215] Note, though, that the definitions in the Companies Act 1989 and the other relevant regulations are not comprehensive, and there may be "gaps": see the "Gap Analysis" annexed to the reply of the Financial Law Committee of the City of London Law Society of October 22, 2010 to the Treasury consultation on the Implementation of the amending EU Directive 2009/44/EC.

worth considering what title transfer arrangements fall within the FCARs, since this may be significant in particular fact situations.

Reg.3 of the FCARs defines a title transfer financial collateral arrangement as:

> "an agreement or arrangement, including a repurchase agreement, evidenced in writing, where—
>
> (a)   the purpose of the agreement or arrangement is to secure or otherwise cover the relevant financial obligations owed to the collateral-taker;
>
> (b)   the collateral-provider transfers legal and beneficial ownership in financial collateral to a collateral-taker on terms that when the relevant financial obligations are discharged the collateral-taker must transfer legal and beneficial ownership of equivalent financial collateral to the collateral-provider; and
>
> (c)   the collateral-provider and the collateral-taker are both non-natural persons."

It will be seen that the definition is limited to where the purpose of the arrangement is to secure or cover relevant obligations. Thus, if a repo or a securities lending arrangement could be said not to have such a purpose, it does not fall within the FCARs.[216] However, the wording of the Financial Collateral Directive makes it clear that it is the provision of the collateral which must have a security purpose, rather than the entire arrangement[217]: this is likely to be the case in most repos where the securities are provided to "secure" the obligation to repay the cash, and in many securities lending arrangements, in that cash or other securities are provided to secure the obligation to return equivalent securities.

It will be seen that it is necessary that the collateral provider transfers full legal and beneficial ownership in the collateral to the collateral taker. This requirement is reasonably straightforward to analyse in relation to cash and credit claims. It means that cash must be transferred to the collateral taker's account and the collateral taker must not then hold it on trust for the collateral provider. In relation to credit claims, it means that the transfer must be by novation or statutory assignment: an equitable assignment would not be sufficient. In relation to directly held securities, the same applies: legal title must be transferred by the appropriate registration. However, since intermediated securities are, on the accepted analysis under English law,[218] equitable interests under a trust or sub-trust, it is difficult to see how legal ownership (as opposed to beneficial ownership) can be transferred.[219] This is not the only place where the phrase "legal and beneficial ownership" causes difficulty in the FCARs.[220] The phrase has been used in the FCARs as a synonym for the phrase "full ownership", used in the Financial Collateral Directive. The intention is clearly to signify full ownership, as opposed to a lesser interest by way of security: under English law such an absolute interest can be full legal ownership (ownership where there is no equitable interest at all) or absolute beneficial ownership, for example, the

---

[216] *Re Lehman Brothers International (Europe) (In Administration)* [2012] EWHC 2997 (Ch) at [93].

[217] Financial Collateral Directive art.2(1)(b). See also *Re Lehman Brothers International (Europe) (In Administration)* [2012] EWHC 2997 (Ch) at [98] in relation to a security arrangement.

[218] See para.6–17, above.

[219] G. Davies, "Using Intermediated Securities As Collateral: equitable interests with inequitable results" (2007) 2 J.I.B.F.L. 70.

[220] See the discussion below in relation to appropriation para.6–50, below.

beneficiary's interest under a non-discretionary trust. Ideally, this phrase in the FCARs would be amended, perhaps to "full ownership or full beneficial ownership". Pending that, it is suggested that, despite the wording, it might be necessary to interpret it in this way. However, the transferee's ownership of the intermediated securities would have to be absolute, even if equitable. Thus it could not be by way of a mortgage, or in a situation where the transferee holds the securities on trust for the transferor (for example, as an intermediary).

7. SECURITY INTERESTS IN FINANCIAL COLLATERAL

Security interests which fall within the FCARs

6–32   Before considering how security interests can be created in financial collateral, it is worth considering the criteria for a security interest to fall within the FCARs. This is very significant, given the protection given to such interests by the disapplication of rules, as discussed above.[221] Security financial collateral arrangements are defined in the FCARs as arrangements "where the collateral-provider creates or there arises a security interest in financial collateral to secure those obligations".[222] A security interest is defined as "any legal or equitable interest or any right in security, other than a title transfer financial collateral arrangement, created or otherwise arising by way of security" and expressly includes all four types of security interest: pledge, lien, mortgage[223] and charge. However, security financial collateral arrangements only include arrangements whereby "the financial collateral is delivered, transferred, held, registered or otherwise designated so as to be in the possession or under the control of the collateral-taker or a person acting on its behalf".[224] The meaning of "possession or control" has been the subject of two first instance decisions[225] and very considerable debate among commentators.[226]

---

[221] See para.6–26, above.

[222] FCARs reg.3.

[223] On the wording of the Directive there was an argument that a mortgage, which involves transfer of ownership to the mortgagee, was not included but this problem has been expressly rectified by the drafting of the Regulations.

[224] FCARs 2003 reg.3. The requirement of possession or control appears in the Preamble to the Directive (para.9) as the only possible perfection requirement which a Member State can impose.

[225] *Gray v G-T-P Group Ltd; Re F2G Realisations Ltd (In Liquidation)* [2010] EWHC 1772; *Re Lehman Brothers International (Europe) (In Administration)* [2012] EWHC 2997 (Ch).

[226] "Replies of a working group of the City of London Law Society Financial Law Committee to the Questionnaire of February 2006 to the Private Sector from the European Commission for the Drafting of the Evaluation Report in relation to the Financial Collateral Directive" [2006] 6 J.I.B.F.L. 263; M. Hughes, "The Financial Collateral Regulations" [2006] 2 J.I.B.F.L. 64; D. Turing, "New Growth in the Financial Collateral Garden" (2005) 1 J.I.B.F.L. 4; A Zacaroli, "Taking Security over Intermediated Securities: Chapter V of the UNIDROIT (Geneva) Convention on Intermediated Securities" in *Intermediated Securities: Legal Problems and Practical Issues* (2010); Beale, Bridge, Gullifer and Lomnicka, *Law of Security and Title-based Financing* (2012), paras 3.33–3.59; Ho, "The Financial Collateral Directive's practice in England" (2011) 26 J.I.B.L.R. 151, 158–163; CLLS response to the consultation paper issued in August 2010 by HM Treasury on the implementation of EU Directive 2009/44/EC, summarised in R. Parsons, "HM Treasury's consultation paper on financial collateral: extracts from the CLLS Financial Law Committee's response" [2011] 1 J.I.B.F.L. 6; K. Zander and J. Fox, "A tentative step forward — amendments to the Financial Collateral Arrangements

It is first worth describing briefly the history of the concept of possession or control. When the Financial Collateral Directive was in its drafting stages, the first mention of "possession or control" was in the report in November 2001 by the Committee on Economic and Monetary Affairs of the European Parliament,[227] where it was suggested as a compromise between the view of the Commission that a collateral agreement should be in writing[228] and signed, and the fact that some Member States had abolished such a requirement some years previously.[229] The suggestion was that the collateral had to be "provided" and the provision evidenced in writing. "Provision" was defined as "delivered, transferred, held, registered or otherwise designated so as to be in the possession or under the control of the collateral taker".

6–33

The policy basis of the "possession or control" requirement in the FCD is made clear in recitals 9 and 10. Recital 9 states that there is a single perfection requirement in order to limit the administrative burden on parties using financial collateral. Interestingly, that perfection requirement is defined in the 2002 version as delivery, transfer, holding or registration, etc. so as to be in the possession or under the control of the collateral taker, while in the 2009 version it is just that the collateral be "under the control" of the collateral taker.[230] Recital 10 says that provision is limited to dispossession, in order to "provide a balance between market efficiency and the safety of the parties to the arrangement and third parties, thereby avoiding inter alia the risk of fraud". It is worth considering a little against what risks dispossession is meant to provide safety: this can then inform our later discussion of what "dispossession" actually means. In relation to third parties, the risk would seem to be that of invisibility of security interests; in relation to the parties to the arrangement, the risk seems to be that the collateral taker will assert that there is a security interest when none was in fact granted, or maybe that a collateral provider will deny the existence of a security interest that was granted. It is these risks which cause some jurisdictions to impose strict formalities on the creation of security interests, such as notarisation, although they have never been thought particularly significant in English law.

The "possession or control" requirement in the Financial Collateral Directive was subject to two exceptions: any right of substitution or withdrawal of excess collateral (both standard industry practices) was not to prevent the collateral

---

Regulations" (2011) 3 C.R.I. 77; R. Parsons and M. Dening, "Financial collateral — an opportunity missed" (2011) 5 L.F.M.R. 164; Gullifer, "What Should we do about Financial Collateral?" (2012) 65 C.L.P. 377; S. Goldsworthy, "Taking possession and control to excess: issues with financial collateral arrangements under English law" [2013] J.I.B.F.L. 71. See also the analysis in the Law Commission, *Company Security Interests*, Law Com. No.296 (2005), Ch.5.

[227] Document A5-04172001 p.22.

[228] Article 2 in European Commission, *Proposal for Directive of European Parliament and the Council on financial collateral arrangements*, March 27 2001, COM (2001) 168 final.

[229] The fact that the requirements were a compromise, reached as a result of "long and complex negotiations" is clear from the *Communication from the Commission to the European Parliament concerning the Common Position of the Council on the adoption of a Directive of the European Parliament and of the Council on financial collateral arrangements* COD 2001/0086 para.3.2.2.2., which also stresses the link between the requirement of "dispossession" and the fact that the collateral must be "provided" to the collateral taker.

[230] The change was presumably made to accommodate credit claims, but it is not entirely clear why the "possession" part was omitted.

being in the possession or under the control of the collateral taker. The requirement was duly included in the FCARs, when they were made in 2003.[231]

6–34 The case of *Gray v G-T-P Group Ltd; Re F2G Realisations Ltd (In Liquidation)*[232] was decided before the FCARs were amended in 2010. It concerned a charge over a bank account in the name of the chargee, who was a supplier of debit card services to the chargor, a manufacturer of laminate flooring. The account was held on trust by the chargee for the chargor, so that the chargee was obliged to pay sums from the account to the chargor on demand until one of certain specified events occurred, such as default or insolvency. The court held, unsurprisingly, that the charge was floating, but also had to decide whether it fell within the FCARs, since it was unregistered. The cash was held not to be in the "possession or control" of the chargee since, although the bank account was in its name, it had no legal control over the cash. This was because it was obliged to transfer cash to the chargor and could not prevent the chargor from disposing of the cash. The judge's decision focused largely on the requirement of control, since he decided that "possession" could have no application to intangibles.[233]

This last point provoked concern and calls for a statutory definition of "possession".[234] Such a definition was provided in the 2010 amendments to the FCARs, although the drafting of the provision causes, arguably, more difficulties than it solves.[235] Possession is defined as including the case where collateral is transferred into an account in the name of the collateral taker, but only where the collateral provider's rights are limited to the right of substitution or withdrawal or excess collateral. After the amendments, but actually concerned with the interpretation of the pre-amendment Regulations, came the decision of Briggs J. in the course of the Lehman administration.[236] In that case, the collateral taker held securities as intermediary for the collateral provider; the collateral provider granted the collateral taker a charge, which would have been over its beneficial interest under the trust of which the collateral taker was the trustee. Thus the case was very similar to the *Gray* case[237] (although much more fully argued), and, perhaps unsurprisingly, the judge followed the *Gray* decision, holding that the fact that the collateral provider's right to withdraw was greater than a "right to withdraw excess collateral" since it could withdraw securities which would have been required to cover exposure of secured parties other than the collateral taker.[238]

6–35 The concepts of possession and control will now be analysed in the light of this history. There now seems little doubt that "possession", in this context, can

---

[231] FCARs reg.3.

[232] *Gray v G-T-P Group Ltd; Re F2G Realisations Ltd (In Liquidation)* [2010] EWHC 1772.

[233] *Gray v G-T-P Group Ltd; Re F2G Realisations Ltd (In Liquidation)* [2010] EWHC 1772 at [54].

[234] CLLS reponse to the consultation paper issued in August 2010 by HM Treasury on the implementation of EU Directive 2009/44/EC, 5.9–5.13.

[235] See below.

[236] *Re Lehman Brothers International (Europe) (In Administration)* [2012] EWHC 2997 (Ch).

[237] Although the differences between a securities account and a bank account perhaps need to be borne in mind. What the chargee in *Lehman* held on trust for the chargor was its beneficial interest in the securities held by its intermediary (or a CSD), whereas what the chargee in *Gray* held on trust was its contractual right against the bank.

[238] See para.1–16, above.

apply to intangibles.[239] While the disjuncture in the Regulations "in the possession *or* under the control" would seem to indicate that either is enough to satisfy the requirement, the (partial) definition of possession in the amended FCARs seems to indicate that at least some element of control is required for possession, in that the collateral provider must have no, or very limited, ability (in law or in practice) to call for or dispose of the collateral.[240] The cases also support this view. If mere "possession", that is, that the collateral was in the name of the collateral taker, was enough, then the charges in *Gray* and *Lehman* would have fallen within the FCARs.[241]

Control can be either negative (prevention of dealings with the collateral by the collateral provider) or positive (where the collateral taker can take or dispose of the collateral without any further involvement of the collateral provider).[242] It can also be practical (the actual ability of the collateral taker to dispose of the collateral or to prevent the collateral provider from disposing of the collateral) or legal (the control (or lack of it) established by the rights and prohibitions in the security agreement). It is clear that negative control is required and that positive control is not enough to fulfil the requirement,[243] and also that positive control is not required.[244] Of course, in many situations there will be positive as well as negative control.

It is also reasonably clear from the cases and from the amendment to the FCARs that practical control is not enough, and that legal control is required. There was practical control in *Gray* in that the collateral taker could have refused to transfer the cash to the collateral provider (although it would then have been in breach of trust, so there was no legal control). There was also practical control in

---

[239] FCARs as amended, reg.3(2); *Re Lehman Brothers International (Europe) (In Administration)* [2012] EWHC 2997 (Ch) at [131].

[240] Having said this, Briggs J. seemed to envisage that there would be situations in which "the collateral is sufficiently clearly in the possession of the collateral taker that no further investigation of its rights of control is necessary": *Re Lehman Brothers International (Europe) (In Administration)* [2012] EWHC 2997 (Ch) at [136]. It is hard to imagine what situations could fall within this description, in that it is always possible for the collateral taker and collateral provider to agree that the collateral provider must, in certain circumstances, transfer some or all of the collateral to the collateral provider: this would be true even if the collateral were tangible and were kept by the collateral taker on their premises under lock and key. Maybe the judge's statement is just about the burden of proof: in that situation it would be up to the collateral taker to adduce evidence of an ancillary agreement.

[241] See, in particular, *Re Lehman Brothers International (Europe) (In Administration)* [2012] EWHC 2997 (Ch) at [131]. Of course, the decisions in both cases are entirely consistent with the definition of "possession" that has been added to the FCARs: the difficulty with this is whether the line drawn is certain enough and whether it accords sufficiently with market practice.

[242] Positive control is sufficient to comply with the "control" requirement under UCC art.8.

[243] In both the *Gray* and *Lehman* cases the focus was on the rights of the collateral provider rather than the collateral taker. This was also the view of the Law Commission, *Company Security Interests*, Law Com. No.296 (2005) 5.53–5.54. This is because of the wording of para.10 in the Preamble to the Directive which makes it clear that the Directive covers only "those financial collateral arrangements which provide for some form of dispossession". If the debtor has the right to deal, it is not dispossessed, and also because the exceptions for substitution and withdrawal of excess collateral would not be necessary if negative control were not required. See also Beale, Bridge, Gullifer and Lomnicka, *Law of Security and Title-based Financing* (2012), para.3.47.

[244] Law Commission, *Company Security Interests*, Law Com. No.296 (2005) 5.53–5.54. The main reason for this is that appropriation without a court order (art.4 of the Directive, reg.17 of the Regulations) is only possible if such a power is given in the financial collateral agreement: the situation where the agreement provides that there is no power or only a limited power to appropriate is therefore envisaged, but this would be inconsistent with positive control.

Lehman in that the securities were held by the collateral taker in its account with its own intermediary or with a CSD and it could have refused to transfer securities to the collateral provider, although it would have been in breach of its intermediary agreement.[245] There is a strong argument that practical control alone should be sufficient. If the concern is with invisibility, then outward signs are more important than the contractual position between the parties. Of course, the identity of an account holder is still a private matter between the collateral taker and the account provider, but at least the account provider is a third party who could be asked for information by an interested party.[246] This view is reflected in the Geneva Securities Convention, where practical control is sufficient for the creation of a security interest enforceable in insolvency.[247]

6–36   It is less clear whether, under English law, legal control but not practical control is sufficient. For example, would a clause in a security agreement that the collateral provider is not permitted to dispose of any of the collateral without the leave of the collateral taker (a typical fixed charge) be sufficient if the collateral were cash held in a bank account in the name of the collateral provider, or securities held by the collateral provider with a third party intermediary? Such an arrangement gives no publicity of the interest (and so does not protect against "invisibility risk") nor could it really be said to amount to "dispossession". Thus it might seem that both legal and practical control are required for a security arrangement to fall within the FCARs. However, Briggs J. appeared to envisage a situation, presumably sufficient to fall within the FCARs, where "the collateral remains wholly in the possession of the collateral provider, but on terms which give a legal right to the taker to ensure that it is dealt with in accordance with its directions".[248] This would seem to be a straightforward fixed charge: the issue of whether this (legal) control would be enough is particularly significant in relation to credit claims.[249]

The level of negative legal control required at first sight is reasonably clear. The collateral provider must have no rights to call for or dispose of the collateral except the right to substitute financial collateral of the same of greater value, or to withdraw excess collateral.[250] However, it is not clear what other rights the collateral provider may have consistent with the arrangement falling within the FCARs. Briggs J. was of the opinion that there could be such rights, but was

---

[245] The Master Custody Agreement, known in the case as "MCA".

[246] This view is supported by the submission made in the letter of Financial Markets Law Committee dated November 3, 2010 to HM Treasury replying to the consultation on the Treasury consultation on the Implementation of the amending EU Directive 2009/44/EC. See also Parsons and Dening, "Financial collateral – an opportunity missed" (2011) F.M.L.R. 164.

[247] Non-Convention law may not require any further step (art.12(2) for effectiveness on insolvency). The requirements of the Convention, which amount to practical control, are that the collateral taker is an intermediary (art.12(3)(a)), where the collateral is in the name of the collateral taker (art.11), where there is a control agreement (art.12(3)(c)) and where there is a designating entry (art.12(3)(b)). At least the first two of these could also be seen as amounting to "possession".

[248] *Re Lehman Brothers International (Europe) (In Administration)* [2012] EWHC 2997 (Ch) at [136].

[249] See para.6–45, below.

[250] *Re Lehman Brothers International (Europe) (In Administration)* [2012] EWHC 2997 (Ch) at [134], where Briggs J. says that "dispossession" is meaningless if the collateral provider has more rights than these.

non-committal about what they are.[251] It is therefore uncertain whether rights such as the right to dividends or income, voting rights, the right to require a third party custodian to transfer collateral if the collateral taker is insolvent and the secured obligations are paid and the right to have a role in the day to day valuation of the collateral (all common features of collateral arrangements) would be fatal to consistency.[252] The drafting of reg.3(2) of the FCARs[253] makes it clear that *any* rights other than substitution or withdrawal of excess collateral prevent collateral being in the possession of the collateral taker. The implication is that any such rights are also fatal to control, in that possession (being an outward sign of the security interest) might be thought to require less, not more, control than "control" itself. However, such a conclusion would cut across many arrangements used in practice, and would be very unfortunate.[254]

As Briggs J. points out, the extent (and usefulness) of the rights of substitution and withdrawal which are consistent with an arrangement falling within the FCARs should not be underestimated.[255] They mean that what the collateral taker has is possession or control of a pool of collateral rather than to specific assets.[256] However, what is actually meant by "excess" collateral is not clear, either in law or in practice. Briggs J. defined excess collateral as "property in the Custody Account in excess of the property which the custodian believes will be sufficient to cover any exposure that the custodian has to the client".[257] However, this begs a number of questions, depending on the context. First, does it matter who has the power to value the exposure and the collateral (the value of both of which can change daily). Can it be the collateral provider or must it be the collateral taker? Secondly, does the method of valuation matter: could the parties agree that it be done by a method which, objectively speaking, does not always accord with market value? Thirdly, can the parties agree that more collateral than the value of the exposure must remain in the account (presumably so) or that only, say, 60 per cent of the outstanding obligations need remain (presumably not, though it is not clear why this should necessarily be fatal). Fourthly, is "exposure" a technical requirement or one that can be a matter of agreement? For example, are contingent liabilities included? And if the parties agree that they are not included, is that fatal? The uncertainty of the scope of this, very significant, exception to the absolute nature of possession or control is unfortunate in a regime which purports to create legal certainty.

The following sections consider the methods of creation of security interests in financial collateral, and discuss in context whether the requirement of possession or control is likely to be fulfilled. However, one general point is worth

6–37

---

[251] *Re Lehman Brothers International (Europe) (In Administration)* [2012] EWHC 2997 (Ch) at [132].
[252] See Goldsworthy, "Taking possession and control to excess: issues with financial collateral arrangements under English law" [2013] J.I.B.F.L. 71.
[253] Added by the 2010 amendments.
[254] Goldsworthy, "Taking possession and control to excess: issues with financial collateral arrangements under English law" [2013] J.I.B.F.L. 71.
[255] *Re Lehman Brothers International (Europe) (In Administration)* [2012] EWHC 2997 (Ch) at [133].
[256] This is, of course, a separate point from the fact that the collateral may be securities held in a pooled account.
[257] *Re Lehman Brothers International (Europe) (In Administration)* [2012] EWHC 2997 (Ch) at [139].

mentioning. It is clear from the foregoing discussion that not all floating charges will fall within the FCARs, but that some (where the only rights of the chargor are of substitution or withdrawal of excess collateral) will be. There are, moreover, indications that the regulations were intended to apply to at least some floating charges. The list of security interests covered includes "a charge created as a floating charge where the financial collateral charged is delivered, transferred, held, registered or otherwise designated so as to be in the possession or under the control of the collateral-taker or a person acting on its behalf".[258] Further, some of the disapplied provisions are those only applicable to floating charges.[259] Further, if a floating charge which does not otherwise fall within the FCARs crystallises so that the chargee obtains not only legal but also practical control, it could be argued that it then falls within the FCARs.[260] The result of this is also not entirely clear. Logically, it would mean that the insolvency provisions are disapplied, that enforcement could take place by appropriation, and that any close-out netting provisions are preserved, that is, it has prospective effect. It is less clear that lack of registration could be overcome, at least in relation to other secured creditors. If the crystallisation precedes liquidation or administration, then presumably the charge will not be invalid for non-registration against the liquidator or administrator.

Security interests in directly held securities[261]

Certificated registered securities

6–38   A security interest in certificated registered securities directly held by the debtor may be created either on or off the issuer's register. A legal mortgage is created by entry of the name of the mortgagee on the register as holder of the securities. An equitable mortgage or charge may be effected by a transfer of ownership to the mortgagee by way of security or by an agreement for transfer or for a charge. An off-register mortgage of registered securities takes effect in equity only, while a charge is necessarily equitable.[262] Almost invariably, in the case of shares, the secured creditor will protect himself by taking a deposit of the share certificate and procuring the debtor's execution of a blank transfer form, which in case of need the creditor can complete by designating himself or a third party as transferee and lodge with the issuer for registration. Execution of the transfer is not an ingredient in the creation of the mortgage or charge, solely a means by which the creditor can get himself or a third party (e.g. the creditor's nominee or securities intermediary) on the register and thereby obtain legal title. Registration converts the equitable mortgagee or chargee into a legal mortgagee by

---

[258] FCARs reg.3.

[259] See para.6–26, above.

[260] Beale, Bridge, Gullifer and Lomnicka, *Law of Security and Title-based Financing* (2012), para.3.79. HM Treasury *Consultation Paper on the implementation of the Directive on Financial Collateral Arrangement* (2003), para.2.10; cf. Ho, "The Financial Collateral Directive's practice in England" (2011) 26 J.I.B.L.R. 151, 162.

[261] For a detailed and practical discussion, see *Tolley's Company Law Service*, C4001 et seq., (2009).

[262] Neither an equitable mortgage nor a charge, being equitable interests, can be entered on the company's register, s.126 of the Companies Act 2006.

novation.[263] However, no notice of assignment or trust can be entered onto the company register[264]: this includes the trust of the equity of redemption and so the mortgagee will be registered as a new member of the company and holder of the shares, not as a mortgagee.

A mortgage by an off-register assignment is also possible but is a vulnerable form of security in that the company is neither obliged nor entitled to register a notice of assignment, so that the rule in *Dearle v Hall* does not apply[265] and the mortgagee, as an equitable mortgagee, will be subordinate to a prior equitable mortgage or charge. Where the creditor has the transfer registered in the name of its nominee or intermediary, the latter will hold the legal title and the creditor will be the beneficial owner, in each case in common with others holding an interest in securities of the same issue. A legal mortgagee should have possession or control under the FCARs, since the mortgagor's rights are necessarily limited. Similarly, where the equitable mortgagee or chargee takes a deposit of the share certificate, it will have negative (practical) control as the mortgagor or chargor cannot dispose of the shares, although it is possible (though unlikely) that it might have rights in the security agreement which would prevent the necessary negative legal control.

Can certificated registered shares be mortgaged or charged back to the issuer to secure a loan by the issuer? As we have seen,[266] there is now considered to be no conceptual problem in doing this, but there are statutory restrictions. The general rule is that a company cannot acquire its own shares and any purported acquisition, whether by purchase, subscription or otherwise,[267] is void.[268] Moreover, the prohibition cannot be bypassed by taking the shares in the name of a nominee, for if this is done the shares are to be treated as held by the nominee on his own account and the company is to be regarded as having no beneficial interest in them.[269] However, a private company may provide in its articles for a lien or charge on shares to secure payments due to it, whether in respect of the

---

[263] Since what is registered is a transfer, the security interest is necessarily a legal mortgage, not a charge. A mortgagee is trustee of the mortgagor's equity of redemption and is therefore not entitled, in the absence of agreement, to look to any surplus resulting from realisation of the security to satisfy by way of set-off other, unsecured obligations of the debtor, since set-off is available only against money claims, not against property claims. See paras 1–40 and 1–73, above. The creditor should therefore obtain a general set-off agreement or alternatively, if there are mutual redelivery obligations, an agreement that for the purpose of settling accounts these are to be converted into obligations to pay current market value, thus allowing of set-off. If the creditor has included a power to appropriate the collateral, this will enable him to enforce the mortgage by taking the collateral in satisfaction of the underlying secured obligation. However, the mortgagee must value the collateral (in accordance with the terms of the agreement or in a commercially reasonable manner) and account to the mortgagor for any surplus (regs 17 and 18 of the FCARs). Since this obligation to account is a money obligation, it should be possible to set-off other obligations of the debtor against it, but it is still safer to provide expressly for such a set-off.

[264] Companies Act 2006 s.126.

[265] See para.5–08, above.

[266] See paras 1–44, 3–12, above.

[267] These words would seem to preclude a mortgage of shares to the company, as opposed to a charge or lien. See below.

[268] Companies Act 2006 s.658(1) and (2). Under s.659(2)(c) a company may forfeit or accept the surrender of shares, if so permitted by the articles, but only for failure to pay sums in respect of the shares.

[269] Companies Act 2006 s.660.

shares or otherwise,[270] and while a lien or charge to a public company on its own shares is usually void,[271] a charge on the shares is permitted (inter alia) where the ordinary business of the company includes the lending of money or the provision of credit or hire-purchase if the charge arises in connection with a transaction entered into by the company in the ordinary course of its business.[272] In this context, "charge" would seem to bear its technical meaning of an incumbrance, as opposed to a mortgage, the grant of which would offend against the rule that a company cannot acquire its own shares. The charge may be enforced by sale of the shares.[273]

6–39   The normal priority rules apply. While the security interest is merely equitable it is subordinate to a prior equitable interest under the first-in-time rule,[274] although the holder of the subsequent interest could obtain priority if he has procured the deposit of the share certificate and a blank transfer form and registers himself as holder.[275] This is the case even if he knows of the prior equitable interest at the time of the registered transfer.[276] A subsequent equitable security interest is also liable to be displaced by a subsequent mortgage or sale to a third party who acquires the securities in good faith, for value and without notice and becomes registered as the holder. This could occur where the debtor fraudulently procures a fresh share certificate by misrepresenting that he has lost the original. A mortgagee with notice of prior equitable interests takes subject to them. However, if in the latter case the mortgagee grants a sub-mortgage and the sub-mortgagee is registered as transferee and takes without notice of the equitable interests he will have priority even though the mortgagee himself was subordinated.

Bearer securities

6–40   Bearer securities may be pledged or mortgaged by delivery. The pledgee or mortgagee acquires in the case of pledge a limited legal interest and in the case of mortgage legal title by way of security.[277] Alternatively bearer securities may be charged by an agreement for charge, with or without delivery, though delivery is necessary if the charge is to be converted into a pledge or legal mortgage. It is also possible to assign bearer securities without delivery, but such an assignment takes effect only in equity and is displaced by a subsequent legal mortgage created by delivery.[278]

---

[270] See *Gore-Browne on Companies* (2004), para.21.

[271] Companies Act 2006 s.670(1).

[272] Companies Act 2006 s.670(3). It is necessary in addition for the charge to be authorised by the articles.

[273] In theory they may also be forfeited and cancelled, but this involves a reduction of capital and requires confirmation by the court.

[274] The rule in *Dearle v Hall* does not apply. See para.5–08, above.

[275] See para.6–38, above.

[276] *Dodds v Hill* (1865) 2 H. & M. 424; *Macmillan Inc v Bishopsgate Investment Trust Plc* [1995] 1 W.L.R. 978, 1003–1004. See para.5–09, above.

[277] Whether the transaction is a mortgage or pledge will be characterised by the intention of the parties, see *Sewell v Burdick* (1884) 10 App. Cas. 74, 78 and, for a discussion of the consequences of this distinction, see *Tolley's Company Law Service*, C4015 (2009).

[278] In that delivery passes the legal title to the mortgagee (by way of security) and the subsequent mortgagee will take free of any equitable interest of which he has no notice.

Bearer debt securities[279] may be pledged or mortgaged back to the issuer by delivery. On default they may be sold to a third party.

Uncertificated securities

A legal mortgage of uncertificated securities can be created by transfer from the **6–41** mortgagor's stock account with CREST to the mortgagee's stock account or, if the mortgagee is not a CREST member or sponsored member, to the stock account of his nominee.[280] This will normally meet the requirement of possession or control under the FCARs.[281] Depending on the type of securities, the transfer will be recorded on the CREST register, and maybe also on the issuer register.[282] However, such an entry will not record that the transfer is by way of security, since no entry of a trust (which here would include the equity of redemption of the mortgagor) can be made on the CREST register.[283] An equitable security interest in uncertificated securities directly held by the debtor may be created by an off-register mortgage or an equitable charge. This means, however, that there is no public notice of the charge, and the chargee could lose priority to a subsequent purchaser or incumbrancer taking a legal mortgage. Since charges over securities are not required to be registered in the Company Charges register if they fall within the FCARs[284] there are only two possible methods for the chargee to give public notice and to prevent effectively any other purchaser or incumbrancer obtaining legal title. The first is by obtaining transfer of the charged securities to a sub-account as an escrow balance, the sub-account being in the name of the chargor but under the control of another CREST member who is the chargee's escrow agent.[285] CREST (Euroclear UK & Ireland Ltd) itself has no involvement in the escrow balance. On default the escrow agent can transfer the securities into the creditor's name if he is a CREST member. If the debt is discharged without recourse to the escrow balance this is transferred back to the chargor's main account. Since the collateral provider has no ability to deal with the shares, there is likely to be sufficient possession or control for the arrangement to fall within the FCARs, unless the collateral provider has the right to require a withdrawal under the security agreement over and above "excess

---

[279] Bearer shares are rarely issued in the UK because of their exposure to stamp duty, and in any event a purported mortgage of them to the issuer would be void under s.658 of the Companies Act 2006. The prohibition does not apply to debt securities.

[280] Security agreements may provide for collateral transferred to the creditor or its nominee to be held in a segregated account, separate from the creditor's beneficially owned holdings, to avoid problems arising from commingling of the creditor's assets and the assets subject to the debtor's equity of redemption in the event of the creditor's insolvency.

[281] This is so long as the mortgagor has no rights to withdraw more than excess collateral, but such rights are likely to turn the legal mortgage into a floating charge.

[282] See para.6–10, above. The issuer register is reconciled to the CREST register.

[283] Uncertificated Securities Regulations 2001 reg.23(3).

[284] See paras 2–19 and 6–26, above.

[285] This can be seen as the electronic equivalent of the creation of an equitable mortgage by deposit of certificates (see para.6–38, above and *Tolley's Company Law Service* C4013 (2009)). The effect of control is to give limited public notice of the interest, and also is to enable the chargee to enforce the charge without recourse to the mortgagor. It has the effect that only the chargee or its escrow agent can give the relevant instruction (TFE meaning Transfer from Escrow) to release the holding from the account, see Beale, Bridge, Gullifer and Lomnicka, *The Law of Security and Title-based Financing* (2012), para.3.55 and fn.171.

collateral". An alternative is for the chargee to be appointed sponsor of a chargor who is a CREST member. This method is used by settlement banks to take a floating "system charge" over the securities held by a CREST member: the bank has an irrevocable power of attorney to appoint itself sponsor in the chargor's name if the pre-agreed "debit cap" is exceeded, at which point only the bank can give instructions to the CREST system in relation to the securities.[286] Until the time that the power is exercised the collateral-giver has the power to deal with the securities, and so the charge does not fall within the FCARs (and would require registration).[287] However, on exercise of the power the collateral-taker obtains both negative and positive control.

CREST does not accept notices of assignment, so although the debtor can effect a mortgage by assignment rather than by transfer to the account of the creditor or his nominee there is no way of giving notice of the assignment, and so the priority of successive assignments is governed not by the rule in *Dearle v Hall* but by the first-in-time rule.

The rules governing a charge-back of certificated securities to the issuer[288] apply equally to a charge-back of uncertificated securities, and the priority rules are the same as for certificated securities.

Security interests in indirectly held securities

6–42 Where securities are intermediated, the top of the chain can be either a CSD or ICSD holding an immobilised global security or a CREST member holding an account with CREST. Either way, as discussed above, the interest of any person in the chain other than the first tier holder will be equitable. Thus intermediated securities can be mortgaged by transfer to the mortgagee's account,[289] which effects an equitable mortgage: a legal mortgage of intermediated securities is not possible as the interest of the mortgagor is equitable.[290] Intermediated securities can also be charged by agreement, the chargee gaining control, if desired, by the agreement of the intermediary to allow the account to be operated only on the instructions of the chargee[291] alternatively by transfer of part of the securities to a separate account in the name of the chargor but under the chargee's control. There are a number of advantages for the chargee in taking such control, which would appear in most cases to amount to both positive and negative control, and thus the charge will fall within the FCARs, subject to the extent of the chargor's withdrawal rights.[292] One advantage, therefore, is the protection given by the FCARs. Another is equivalent to publicity, in that the intermediary would not

---

[286] For details, see Beale, Bridge, Gullifer and Lomnicka, *The Law of Security and Title-based Financing* (2012), para.3.64.

[287] The system charge is likely to fall within the provisions in Pt VII of the Companies Act 1989 disapplying insolvency provisions (see para.6–26, above) because of the application of the Financial Markets and Insolvency Regulations 1996 (SI 1996/1469). However, the other advantages of the FCARs would not apply to it until the bank obtained the necessary control.

[288] See para.6–38, above.

[289] An in-house transfer if the mortgagee has an account with the same intermediary, or if not, a transfer to the mortgagee's intermediary through a common higher-tier intermediary.

[290] See para.1–12, above for reasons why a mortgage is equitable rather than legal.

[291] i.e. an attornment. See para.3–32, above.

[292] See para.6–36, above.

permit any dealings with the asset without the chargee's consent (this probably also has the effect that the charge is a fixed one) and so notice of the chargee's interest is given to the outside world.

The securities could also be mortgaged by an assignment of the account, and notice of assignment to the intermediary, if given, would obtain for the mortgagee the advantages set out in Ch.3, above in relation to giving notice of assignment to an account debtor,[293] although if the account holder was still permitted to give instructions to the intermediary, there would probably not be sufficient control on the part of the security holder for the transaction to be a security financial collateral arrangement, and so the charge would probably be registrable. A mortgage by assignment has the disadvantage that the mortgagee takes subject to equities, including any rights of set-off the intermediary may have for cross-claims in respect of dealings prior to receipt of the notice of assignment.

Under the Geneva Securities Convention, a security interest can be created by transfer by credit to the mortgagee's securities account,[294] but also by a combination of a security agreement and one of the following: either that the mortgagee is the intermediary of the account in which the securities are held or that a designating entry in favour of the mortgagee has been made in the account or a control agreement in favour of the mortgagee applies.[295] Both a designating entry and a control agreement are defined as methods whereby the mortgagee can obtain positive or negative control.[296]

Priorities are governed by the normal rules, bearing in mind that the interests of account holders are equitable. The rule in *Dearle v Hall* will apply both to security interests created by transfers and by assignment. However, where there is a transfer the trustee (the intermediary) will have notice of the transfer as soon as it takes place, and so a mortgage created by transfer will have priority over subsequent interests, as well as prior interests created by assignment of which no notice is given to the intermediary. Priority as between successive assignees is governed by the rule in *Dearle v Hall* in the normal way.

6–43

Security interest over cash

It is possible to create a legal mortgage over cash by transferring it into an account (with a third party bank) in the name of the collateral taker, although if the collateral provider has the right to demand withdrawals from the account (as in the *Gray* case)[297] this will only amount to a floating charge and, depending on the scope of the rights of the collateral provider, will not fall within the FCARs. If the account remains in the name of the collateral provider but is held with a bank who is not the collateral taker, then a security interest is likely to be a charge. In order for it to fall within the FCARs, it would be necessary for the collateral

6–44

---

[293] Para.3–30, above.

[294] Geneva Securities Convention art.11.

[295] Geneva Securities Convention art.12. These methods are only effective if the Contracting State has made a declaration to that effect (art.12(5)).

[296] Geneva Securities Convention arts 1(k) and (l). Which are applicable depends on the substance of the declaration of the relevant Contracting State, art.12(6)-(7). For a discussion of positive and negative control and whether the control envisaged by the Geneva Securities Convention is the same as that clarified in the FCARs, see para.6–35, above.

[297] See para.6–34, above.

provider to have no rights other than the right to withdraw excess collateral stipulated in the regulations (it is hard to see that the right of substitution has any meaning in relation to cash in a bank account): this would provide the necessary negative legal control. However, it may also be necessary for the chargee to have some level of practical control,[298] in which case it would have to give notice to the third party bank of the limited rights of withdrawal of the collateral provider. It is also not entirely clear whether there is the necessary control if the collateral taker permits the collateral provider to withdraw from the account in breach of the restrictions in the security agreement. The view of Briggs J. in the *Lehman* case was that future conduct was not relevant to the interpretation of an agreement where the matter was dealt with clearly and expressly in the absence of a sham.[299]

If the cash is in an account held with the collateral taker, it is possible for the collateral provider to grant the collateral taker a charge over that account: this would operate as a charge-back. For there to be the necessary amount of legal control, the charge agreement would have to prevent the collateral provider from withdrawing any cash other than excess collateral.[300] It would also be necessary for the banking agreement relating to the account to restrict withdrawals in a similar fashion, otherwise the legal rights and obligations between the parties would be inconsistent. Thus it is necessary for the account to be "blocked",[301] not just as a matter of practical control but also legal control, since the latter cannot solely be concerned with the rights of the parties in one (security) agreement but must include the totality of rights and obligations between the parties.

Security interest over credit claims[302]

6–45 The principles governing the requirement of possession or control under the FCARs, unclear as they are, become far more difficult to apply when applied to credit claims. This is because the concept of possession, in the sense of being held in an account, is not satisfactorily applied to this form of financial collateral, and the concept of control is particularly difficult to apply. One view is that, in order to have legal and practical negative control over the credit claims, the collateral taker must notify all the claim debtors (that is, those who are indebted to the collateral provider) of its interest, and must require proceeds of all claims to be paid into a blocked account, with only excess collateral being permitted to be withdrawn. It would be possible for the collateral provider to substitute other credit claims for those nominated, but the collateral taker would then have to give notice to those debtors and impose the same requirements as to the proceeds. Another view, based largely on the impracticability of the first view in the real world, is that the collateral taker does not need to give notice to debtors until

---

[298] See paras 6–35 et seq., above.
[299] *Re Lehman Brothers International (Europe) (In Administration)* [2012] EWHC 2997 (Ch) at [151].
[300] Again, it is hard to see that the right of substitution is relevant here.
[301] Beale, Bridge, Gullifer and Lomnicka, *The Law of Security and Title-based Financing* (2012), para.3.71.
[302] For detailed discussion see Beale, Bridge, Gullifer and Lomnicka, *The Law of Security and Title-based Financing* (2012), paras 3.81 et seq.

default of the collateral provider, and that the collateral provider can use the proceeds for its own purposes up to that time.

The second view has support from the fact that the preparatory documents for the amendments to the Financial Collateral Directive and the amended Directive itself appear to envisage that notification of the claim debtor is not, and should not, be necessary for the provision of credit claims as collateral, and that identification of the relevant claims should be sufficient.[303] Further, the FCARs themselves provide that the collateral provider should be able to collect in the credit claims itself until further notice[304]: it would be very odd if the collateral provider were then to have to pay the proceeds to the collateral taker or into a blocked account in order for the security agreement to fall within the FCARs. The position remains unfortunately unclear.

8. RIGHTS OF USE

Right of use/re-hypothecation

As discussed above,[305] the liquidity of the market is increased if a party taking an interest in securities as collateral is given a right to "use" or "re-hypothecate" the collateral, which is generally understood in a broad sense to include outright sale or the grant of a sub-mortgage or sub-charge. Such a right is inherent in a title transfer collateral arrangement, and security collateral agreements commonly provide for this. In the absence of agreement, whether express or implied from a course of dealing or from market usage, a secured party is not allowed to make an outright disposal of the collateral unless the power of sale has become exercisable on default.[306] However, it is open to the parties to agree that the mortgagee is to have a power of sale even without default, and such an agreement is not void as impairing the equity of redemption,[307] which simply attaches to the proceeds of sale.[308] The mortgagee ought normally to give notice before selling,[309] though presumably even this can be dispensed with by agreement where it is not

6–46

---

[303] *Proposal for a Directive amending Directive 98/26/EC on settlement finality in payment and securities systems and Directive 2002/47/EC on financial collateral arrangements as regards linked systems and credit claims*, para.3.1.1.2; Financial Collateral Directive arts 1(5) and 3(1).

[304] FCARs reg.3(1).

[305] Para.6–01, above.

[306] A right of sale on default is implied by law, *Re Morritt* (1886) L.R. 18 Q.B.D. 222, 223; *Deverges v Sandeman, Clark & Co* [1902] 1 Ch. 579, 588–589, 592–593; *Stubbs v Slater* [1910] 1 Ch. 632, 639, and, if the mortgage is by deed, exists under Law of Property Act 1925 s.101. These statutory rights are almost invariably displaced by an express power of sale.

[307] *The Maule* [1977] 1 W.L.R. 528. See also *Langton v Waite* (1868) L.R. 6 Eq. 165, where the court held that until the time came for redelivery a broker had no right to sell stock mortgaged to secure a margin loan "in the absence of express contract", which plainly implies that the broker could have contracted for a right of sale. There seems no good reason why the right of sale should be express; it suffices that it is a term of the contract, express or implied.

[308] With a right of use, it is a matter of interpretation of the agreement whether the collateral taker holds the "proceeds" of the use, that is the purchase price under a repo, or cash (or securities) given as collateral for the obligation to return equivalent securities given under a securities lending arrangement, subject to the collateral provider's equity of redemption, that is, on trust for the collateral provider subject to its own rights under the security collateral agreement.

[309] *Fletcher and Campbell v City Marine Finance Ltd* [1968] 2 Lloyd's Rep. 520.

oppressive but part of normal market practice. The secured party is always free to sub-mortgage or sub-charge the securities without the debtor's consent, for this constitutes simply a dealing with his own security interest and takes effect subject to the debtor's equity of redemption.

The FCARs provide that where a transaction is a security financial collateral arrangement, a provision in the agreement giving a right of use and/or disposition is valid according to its terms.[310] Irrespective of implementation of the Directive the very existence of art.5 should make it abundantly clear that conferment of a right of re-use is standard international practice and is not open to attack on public policy grounds. However, two issues have arisen in relation to the right of use.[311]

6–47   The first is where securities are held by an intermediary for an account holder, who grants the intermediary a security interest containing a right of use over those securities. Does the right of use, which permits the intermediary to transfer an absolute interest in those securities to a third party, prevent the normal analysis (that the intermediary holds the securities on trust for the account holder) applying? This issue was considered by Briggs J. in another Lehman case,[312] who concluded that, although the right of use, together with the other terms of the intermediary agreement, meant that the trust was a rather unusual one,[313] it did not prevent a trust arising, given the clear intention of the parties.[314] Clearly, once the securities are transferred to a third party, the subject matter of the trust is (temporarily) lost, but, depending on the terms of the agreement, the intermediary may well hold the obligation of the counterparty to return equivalent securities on trust for the account holder, and maybe also any collateral provided by that counterparty as security for performance of that obligation to return.[315]

6–48   The second issue is the effect of the exercise of the right of use on the collateral provider, who only has an unsecured claim against the collateral taker for any surplus collateral over and above the obligation which is secured.[316] After the Lehman collapse it was thought that collateral providers under prime brokerage agreements should have more information about rights of use, and the CASS rules were amended to provide that such agreements should have a disclosure annexe making the collateral provider's risks clear.[317]

---

[310] FCARs reg.16.

[311] See Beale, Bridge, Gullifer and Lomnicka, *The Law of Security and Title-based Financing* (2012), paras 6.49–6.53.

[312] *Re Lehman Brothers International (Europe) (In Administration)* [2009] EWHC 2545 (Ch).

[313] *Re Lehman Brothers International (Europe) (In Administration)* [2009] EWHC 2545 (Ch) at [52].

[314] *Re Lehman Brothers International (Europe) (In Administration)* [2009] EWHC 2545 (Ch) at [63]–[64].

[315] See *Re Lehman Brothers International (Europe) (In Administration)* [2010] EWHC 2914 (Ch) at [240]; *Lift Capital Partners Pty Ltd v Merrill Lynch International* (2009) 253 A.L.R. 482 at [89]–[91].

[316] This is subject to the point made in the last paragraph about an equivalent interest in a claim against a counterparty, or the collateral given for that claim.

[317] CASS r.9.3.1.

9.   ENFORCEMENT

The Financial Collateral Directive provided that Member States were required to ensure that on the occurrence of an enforcement event[318] the collateral taker has a range of enforcement measures available, subject to the parties' agreement. These measures have been implemented by the FCARs as follows:

6–49

Financial instruments   Enforcement can be by sale or appropriation, the value[319] being set-off in discharge of the relevant financial obligation. Restrictions on sale that would otherwise apply during an administration, or pending the appointment of an administrator, or during a moratorium under a company voluntary arrangement have been disapplied.[320] Regulations 17 and 18[321] permit the remedy of appropriation,[322] which means taking the collateral in satisfaction of the underlying obligation, while accounting to the collateral-giver for any surplus value,[323] but only where the security financial collateral includes a power of appropriation. In the case of an equitable mortgage, appropriation can be effected by the collateral-taker becoming absolute beneficial owner of the securities: there is no need to obtain legal title.[324] Rather unfortunately, when reg.17 of the FCARs was amended in 2010, the new draft provided that the effect of appropriation was that all "beneficial and legal interest of the collateral provider vests in the collateral taker". This is clearly a mistake, and what is surely meant is that absolute interest vests, whether legal or equitable.[325] The draft is particularly unfortunate in relation to intermediated securities, where the interest of the account holder is necessarily equitable. Where the collateral consists of securities, these need to be valued by the collateral-taker in order to calculate any surplus: the valuation must be done according to the terms of the arrangement, but in any event in a commercially reasonable manner. This obviously raises the question of what would be seen as commercially reasonable by the courts, but it is likely that a valuation process agreed in advance by the parties would be seen as such unless it was unconscionable. Relief against forfeiture can be given against an appropriation in a suitable case, although this will be very rare. Thus where tender had been made of the secured obligation but refused, where the purpose of the appropriation was to obtain shares in order to acquire control of

6–50

---

[318]   Defined by art.2(1)(l), and also reg.3 of the regulations, as an event of default or any event agreed between the parties on the occurrence of which, under the terms of a collateral financial arrangement or by operation of law, the collateral taker is entitled to realise or appropriate financial collateral or a close-out netting comes into force. Again, the drafting is a little strange, for read literally it does not cover a right of realisation given by law unless the relevant event is one agreed between the parties! This comes from the misplacing of the phrase "or by operation of law", which should have been inserted after "parties." It is thought that art.2(1)(l) and the regulations are to be interpreted as if drafted in this way.

[319]   The reference to "value" rather than "proceeds" as regards the remedy of sale is no doubt designed to protect the collateral provider against the risk of a sale at undervalue.

[320]   FCARs reg.8.

[321]   As amended by the 2010 amendments.

[322]   English law did not previously recognise appropriation, which is in effect a sale by the mortgagee to himself and therefore not permitted even if at full value, *Hodson v Deans* [1903] 2 Ch. 647; *Farrar v Farrars Ltd* (1888) 40 Ch. D. 395.

[323]   FCARs regs 17 and 18.

[324]   *Cukurova Finance International Ltd v Alfa Telecom Turkey Ltd* [2009] UKPC 19.

[325]   Ho, "The Financial Collateral Directive's practice in England" (2011) 26 J.I.B.L.R. 151, 172.

the issuer and where the valuation did not take into account the full control value of the shares, relief was given.[326] Enforcement of title transfer collateral arrangements by close-out netting and set-off is very common, and these are given protection by the regulations from invalidation in the event of winding up proceedings or reorganisation measures in relation to either party.[327]

6–51   **Cash**   Enforcement can be by set-off against, or application in discharge of, the relevant financial obligations. The remedy of appropriation also applies to cash, but there is no question of valuation since only enough cash to satisfy the underlying obligation need be appropriated.

6–52   **Credit claims**   The collateral taker would take an assignment of the claims if it does not already have one, and would probably seek to sell the claims to a third party. In theory at least, it could also appropriate them and sue the debtors.

10.   CROSS-BORDER SECURITIES AND THE CONFLICT OF LAWS

Introduction

6–53   Where dealings in securities involve a foreign element, so that it is necessary to make a choice between legal systems, the applicable law is to be determined by the conflict of laws rules of the forum state. In England the applicable law depends on whether the securities are registered or bearer securities and on whether the securities are held directly or indirectly.[328]

In all cases concerning certificated (as opposed to dematerialised) securities it is necessary to distinguish title to the certificate from title to the underlying securities. Where certificates relating to securities are transferred, it is for the lex situs of the certificates at the time of transfer to determine the effect of the transfer on title to the certificate, but it is for the law of the issuer's incorporation to determine the manner in which the underlying securities may be transferred and thus whether they are to be characterised as registered securities or bearer securities.[329] So if the holding of United Kingdom registered bonds is evidenced by a certificate which is later delivered to Creditor A by way of pledge in New York and the bonds are later mortgaged in London to Creditor B, who in good faith is told by the bondholder that the certificate has been lost, takes a transfer and registers it with the issuer of the bonds, then while the efficacy of the pledge will be determined by New York law, priority between A and B will be

---

[326] *Cukurova Finance International Ltd, Cukurova Holding AS v Alfa Telecom Turkey Ltd* [2013] UKPC 2. See also *Cukurova Finance International Ltd, Cukurova Holdings AS v Alfa Telecom Turkey Ltd* [2013] UKPC 20, where the terms of relief were decided.

[327] See reg.8(1) which disapplies s.127 of the Insolvency Act 1986 (avoidance of post-petition dispositions) and reg.12. Reg.12 does not apply if at the time of entering into the agreement or of the relevant financial obligation coming into existence, one party was aware or should have been aware of the commencement of insolvency proceedings, widely defined (reg.12(2)). See para.7–94, below.

[328] See generally Ooi, *Shares and Other Securities in the Conflict of Laws* (2003).

[329] See *Macmillan Inc v Bishopsgate Investment Trust (No.3)* [1996] 1 W.L.R. 387; Dicey, Morris & Collins, *The Conflict of Laws* (2012), paras 22–044 and 22–045.

determined by English law and normally be accorded to B as bona fide holder for value of the legal title through registration, A's interest in the bonds (as opposed to the certificate as a piece of paper) being purely equitable. Again, if the bonds are issued as bearer bonds in London and the certificates are taken to New York and there pledged, an English court, having characterised the bonds under English law as bearer bonds transferable by delivery, will apply New York law as the lex situs to determine the efficacy of the pledge. Neither the two EC Directives referred to above nor the Hague Convention discussed below deal with conflict of laws issues in relation to directly held securities.

As regards indirectly held securities the EC Financial Collateral Directive and the FCARs,[330] like the Settlement Finality Directive, applies PRIMA in determining the law applicable to dealings in securities involving a foreign element.[331] However, under the Hague Convention this is adopted in modified form to give effect to party choice.

The Hague Convention on the law applicable to indirectly held securities[332]

The 2002 Hague Convention on the law applicable to certain rights in respect of securities held with an intermediary embodies PRIMA as the underlying concept except that the focus is now on the law selected by the parties to govern the account agreement,[333] subject to satisfaction of a so-called "reality test" which in essence requires that the intermediary in question carries on the business of maintaining the securities account (though not necessarily the particular account in question) in the state whose law is selected.[334] The Convention determines the law applicable to the legal nature and effects against the intermediary and third parties of (a) the credit of securities to a securities account with an intermediary; and (b) a disposition of securities held with an intermediary, including charge-backs to the intermediary and perfection requirements and priority rules, as well as requirements for realisation of an interest in securities and whether a disposition of securities held with an intermediary extends to entitlements to dividends, income and other distributions. It also preserves the application of the PRIMA law to these issues notwithstanding the opening of an insolvency proceeding.

The Convention is limited to securities held with an intermediary and has no application to securities held directly from the issuer. It is confined to proprietary rights and does not extend to contractual or other personal rights. However, the

6–54

---

[330] FCARs reg.19.

[331] Settlement Finality Directive art.9. This is also thought to reflect the position at common law. See para.6–21, above.

[332] See the Explanatory Report: R. Goode, H. Kanda and K. Kreuzer, assisted by C. Bernasconi, *Hague Securities Convention: Explanatory Report* (Hague Conference on Private International Law, 2005). The Convention has only two ratifications and is not yet in force.

[333] 2002 Hague Convention art.4(1).

[334] 2002 Hague Convention art.5(1) provides an intermediate fallback rule if the parties fail to select a law or the selection is ineffective for want of compliance with the reality test, while art.5(2) provides the ultimate fallback rule (place of the intermediary's incorporation, etc.) if neither of the previous rules applies. It is recognised that this will in many cases have little or no connection with the parties or transaction; its one merit is certainty, and it is envisaged that it will be triggered only in a very small percentage of cases.

question whether the account holder's rights against its intermediary are proprietary or personal is determined by the PRIMA law. If under that law the rights are characterised as purely personal the Convention has no further application as regards relations between the account holder and the intermediary but it continues to govern the legal nature and effects of a disposition of those personal rights, since the disposition is a transfer of property.

The approach adopted in the Hague Convention, which was borrowed from art.8 of the Uniform Commercial Code, seems at first sight strange and counter-intuitive, since it is axiomatic in most legal systems that parties to a contract cannot select a law to govern the rights of third parties.

Nevertheless, the solution has a number of advantages. It subjects the determination of all proprietary rights to the same law and by focusing on the (deemed) place of the account it reflects the well-established lex situs principle in the conflict of laws. Third parties proposing to purchase a securities entitlement or to take such entitlement as collateral for a loan will certainly want to have sight of the account agreement and will thereby be able to see the full terms of the agreement, including designation of the deemed place of the account.

CHAPTER 7

Set-Off, Netting and Abatement

1. SET-OFF: NATURE, CLASSIFICATION AND DEVELOPMENT

(i) Nature of set-off and netting

Set-off

Set-off is the right of a debtor who is owed money by his creditor on another **7–01**
account or dealing to secure payment for what is owed to him by setting this off
in reduction of his own liability.[1] For example, A sells raw materials to B to be
made up into finished products which B then sells to A. If A owes B £1,000 for
products sold and delivered to him but is owed £400 by B for raw materials then
in any claim against him A is not obliged to pay B the £1,000 he owes and then
sue separately for recovery of the £400 (or if B is in liquidation, prove in the
liquidation in competition with other creditors) he is owed but may set-off the
latter sum against his indebtedness and discharge the debt by paying B (or B's
liquidator) the balance of £600.

Set-off is available both outside and within bankruptcy and liquidation. In both
cases it provides a speedy remedy to secure payment but the policy reason for
providing the remedy depends on the type of set-off involved. Contractual set-off
is recognised as an incident of party autonomy in the conclusion of contracts. The
banker's right of combination is similar except that it derives from implied rather
than express agreement. In the case of independent (or statutory) set-off the
remedy is given primarily to avoid circuity of action. By contrast, the policy
underlying transaction (or equitable) set-off is that it would be unjust to allow a
party to enforce his money claim without giving credit for the cross-claim if so
required. Similarly the provision of insolvency set-off reflects the view that

---

[1] See P. Wood, *English and International Set-off* (London: Sweet & Maxwell, 1989); and P. Wood,
Law and Practice of International Finance: Set-off and netting, derivatives and clearing systems
(London: Sweet & Maxwell, 2007); R. Derham, *Set-Off*, 4th edn (New York: Oxford University Press,
2010); S. McCracken, *The Banker's Remedy of Set-off*, 3rd edn (Hayward's Heath: Bloomsbury
Professional, 2010). The leading early works are R. Babington, *A Treatise on the Law of Set-Off*
(London: H. Butterworth, 1827); B. Montagu, *Summary of the Law of Set-Off*, 2nd edn (1828); and
two American publications, O. Barbour, *Treatise on the Law of Set-Off* (W. & A. Gould, 1841); and T.
W. Waterman, *Treatise on the Law of Set-Off*, 2nd edn (New York: Baker, Voorhis & Co, 1872). For
historical and comparative surveys, see W. H. Loyd, "The Development of Set-Off" 64 U.Pa.L.Rev.
541 (1916); and M. E. Tigar, "Automatic Extinction of Cross-Demands: Compensation from Rome to
California" 53 Cal.L.R. 224 (1965).

where parties have been giving credit to each other in reliance on their ability to secure payment by withholding what is due from them it would be unjust, on the advent of liquidation, to deprive the solvent party of his security by compelling him to pay what he owes in full and be left to prove for his own claim. This has traditionally been the policy justification for what is a clear exception to the pari passu principle,[2] in that it allows the solvent party to collect payment ahead of other creditors to the extent of the set-off and thus puts him in a position analogous to that of a secured creditor.[3]

Thus set-off is an essential tool in the hands of a debtor who has a cross-claim against his creditor and is particularly used in banking transactions and in mutual dealings in the financial markets. But in dealings on an organised market the legal protection of netting and set-off has in recent years been seen as fulfilling a much more fundamental need, namely the reduction of systemic risk, hence the issue of EU Directives and of implementing national legislation designed to ensure that rules of insolvency law do not imperil rights of set-off in market contracts.[4] This special treatment of market and related contracts should be constantly borne in mind as a major qualification of the general principles discussed in the present chapter.

Is set-off a substantive or procedural defence?

7–02   An important question is whether a right of set-off, either automatically or when asserted, operates: (a) so as to reduce or extinguish the claim immediately; (b) as a substantive defence which does not reduce or extinguish the claim immediately; or (c) as a mere procedural device. The last two possibilities have the result that the claim and cross-claim are not reduced or extinguished until judgment or agreement. Another way of putting the question is to ask whether the set-off is a defence (i.e. a substantive defence) or a mere cross-claim which can be set up in proceedings to avoid circuity of action, and also to ask when it enables the defendant to have any judgment against him reduced by the amount of the cross-claim. The distinction is significant in that if set-off operates as a substantive defence, failure to meet the claim cannot be regarded as a default so as to trigger self-help default remedies such as acceleration of payment, termination of an agreement, repossession of goods, the appointment of a receiver, and the like. By contrast, set-off as a procedural defence does not affect liability for the claim and can be asserted only in proceedings and for the purpose of reducing or extinguishing the amount for which the claimant is entitled to judgment or of showing why non-monetary equitable relief based on default in payment should not be given. It follows that failure to meet the claim is a default entitling the holder of the claim to pursue self-help default remedies, though if he later sues for recovery of, say, an accelerated balance of liability, the set-off can be asserted in reduction of the accelerated sum.

---

[2] An additional justification is that it simplifies the liquidation process.

[3] Set-off does not in law constitute a form of security, for the debtor who asserts it is not acquiring any rights over an asset of the creditor but simply seeking to reduce or extinguish the claim against him. See para.7–14, below and paras 1–20 et seq., above.

[4] See paras 6–36 et seq., above and para.7–94, below.

We shall return to this question later.[5] Suffice it to say at this point that the answer depends on the type of set-off. Independent set-off,[6] whether under the Statutes of Set-Off or as applied by analogy in equity, is procedural only and the claimant is entitled to treat the claim and cross-claim as entirely distinct and independent of each other, so that the latter does not operate to reduce or discharge the former or affect the remedies for its enforcement except in legal proceedings in which the set-off is asserted.[7] Other forms of set-off, including transaction (or equitable) set-off, are now recognised as substantive defences. It is now clear that this does not necessarily entail that the claim is extinguished or reduced by the cross-claim before judgment. However, extinguishment or reduction can take place as the result of agreement, either ex ante, that is, contractual set-off, or ex post, that is, after the claim and cross-claim have arisen.

Types of set-off

There are five main types of set-off. The labels traditionally used to describe these are decidedly uninformative, and the terminology coined by Professor Wood,[8] which is much more meaningful, has gained acceptance in the courts. Features common to all forms of set-off other than contractual set-off are that: (a) they are confined to situations in which both claim and cross-claim are for money[9] or one party's claim is to money and the other's is to property which the first party is authorised to dispose of and thus convert into money; and (b) they require mutuality of parties, that is, the claim and cross-claim must be due from the same parties in the same right.[10] The five types of set-off are the following.

(1)   Independent set-off

This embraces two distinct forms of set-off. The first is sometimes known as statutory set-off, by which is meant set-off under rules carried over from the former Statutes of Set-Off, and sometimes as legal set-off, by way of contradistinction with equitable transaction set-off. The second is that form of set-off which equity applied by analogy with the Statutes of Set-Off, where all the conditions for statutory set-off were present except that one of the liquidated

7–03

7–04

---

[5] Paras 7–36, 7–47 and 7–54, below.

[6] See Pt 4, below.

[7] If the claim is for money, the set-off operates to reduce the amount for which the claimant is entitled to judgment. If it is for non-monetary equitable relief, such as specific performance, the existence of the set-off is a factor which the court can take into account in exercising its discretion whether to grant relief (*BICC Plc v Burndy Corp* [1985] Ch. 232). See para.7–52, below.

[8] In his superb and massive work Wood, *English and International Set-Off* (1989); see fn.1, above.

[9] It is not clear what policy objection there can be to set-off in respect of non-money fungibles. If each party has a duty to deliver or transfer items of property that are mutually interchangeable, why should not the party with the larger obligation be entitled to deduct what is due to him and deliver or transfer the balance? This can be done by agreement but not, it seems, in the absence of agreement. Some civil law jurisdictions permit set-off of fungibles which are liquid and deliverable, see Wood, *Law and Practice of International Finance: Set-off and Netting, Derivatives, Clearing Systems* (2007), para.2–098. See also UNIDROIT Principles of International Commercial Contracts (PICC, 2010) art.8.1 (Comment, para.3).

[10] This point has been challenged in relation to transaction set-off, see para.7–53, below.

cross-claims was equitable.[11] The particular characteristics of independent set-off are (a) that it is a purely procedural defence which does not operate to reduce or extinguish the creditor's claim except at the point where judgment is given for the balance; (b) that both the claim and cross-claim must be liquidated; and (c) that, in contrast to transaction set-off, it is not necessary that the claim and cross-claim should be connected to each other. It is only in this latter feature that independent set-off has any utility in modern law[12]; in all other respects it is overshadowed by the much broader transaction set-off.

(2) Transaction set-off

7–05 This term, as used by Professor Wood and by Hoffmann L.J. in *Aectra Refining Inc v Exmar NV*,[13] includes both the common law right of abatement and the form of set-off, traditionally labelled equitable set-off, which arises where the claim and cross-claim, even if not arising from the same transaction, are so closely connected that it would be inequitable for one claim to be enforced without credit being given for the other. Though transaction set-off was historically seen as a purely procedural remedy,[14] in modern law it is now capable of operating as a substantive defence in those cases where this is not precluded by the nature or terms of a contract between the parties.[15] It is thus different in character from set-off given by way of analogy to the Statutes of Set-Off.[16] The precise manner in which it operates as a substantive defence, however, is not completely clear, and this will be discussed in detail later on.[17]

(3) Contractual set-off

7–06 Contractual set-off is that for which provision is made by express agreement of the parties. Outside insolvency it is free of several of the limitations governing other forms of set-off. It operates as a substantive defence, taking effect upon the occurrence of the act or event agreed between the parties, and, depending on the wording of the agreement, may have the effect of extinguishing or reducing the claim.

---

[11] See paras 7–10 and 7–41, below.

[12] See para.7–46, below. The relationship between independent and transaction (equitable) set-off is discussed in *Fuller v Happy Shopper Markets Ltd* [2001] EWHC 702 (Ch); [2001] 2 Lloyd's Rep. 49 at [26], where the argument that transaction set-off is only available when independent set-off does not apply is rejected.

[13] *Aectra Refining Inc v Exmar NV* [1994] 1 W.L.R. 1634, 1649. Subsequent cases have adopted this nomenclature, although in many cases the term is used synonymously with equitable set-off.

[14] See para.7–47, below.

[15] For further discussion see para.7–54, below.

[16] See *The Nanfri, Federal Commerce Navigation Ltd v Molena Alpha Inc* [1978] Q.B. 927, 974; *BICC Plc v Burndy Corp* [1985] 1 Ch. 232; *Pacific Rim Investments Pte Ltd v Lam Seng Tiong* [1995] 3 S.L.R. 1, where the Singapore Court of Appeal rightly rejected the contrary view expressed in the second edition of this work at pp.138 et seq. The view expressed in the text has been confirmed in a number of recent cases, *Fuller v Happy Shopper Markets Ltd* [2001] 2 Lloyd's Rep. 49 at [22]; *Benford Ltd v Lopecan SL* [2004] 2 Lloyd's Rep. 618 at [10]; [2001] EWHC 702 (Ch); *Safeway v Interserve* [2005] EWHC 3085 (TCC) at [52]; *Burton v Mellham* [2006] UKHL 6; *Fearns v Anglo-Dutch Paint and Chemical Co Ltd* [2010] EWHC 2366 (Ch) at [50(3)].

[17] See paras 7–54 et seq., below.

(4) Current account set-off

By this is meant the implied contractual right given to bankers operating different current accounts for the same customer to combine them and treat them as one, thus setting off a debit balance on one account against a credit balance on the other. Though current account set-off could be regarded as a form of contractual set-off,[18] the label "contractual set-off" is usually reserved for express contractual provisions by which mutual obligations may be netted out, i.e. set-off against each other. Current account set-off is a substantive right which, when exercised, consolidates the different accounts and reduces the customer's monetary position to a single net debit or credit balance. It is not clear what type of act constitutes exercise of the right. The traditional view was that the accounts were to be treated as notionally a single account from the beginning unless otherwise agreed.[19] But it seems more realistic to treat the accounts as distinct until actually combined by notice, book-entry or the initiation of a computer process transferring balances to one account from the other or others, and until then to treat the right of set-off as an unexercised equity.[20]

7–07

(5) Insolvency set-off

This is the right of set-off given by insolvency law, and as regards companies by r.2.85 and r.4.90 of the Insolvency Rules 1986. It is now clear that this too operates as a substantive rule of law and is not dependent on the taking of any procedural steps.[21]

7–08

Netting[22]

The terms "netting" and "set-off" are sometimes treated as interchangeable but in financial circles netting is used to denote contractual arrangements by which claims of different parties against each other are reduced to a single balance. The simple form of contractual set-off is a clause in a contract providing that one party is entitled to set-off against any sums it owes to the other all sums owed to it by the other. This basic form is typically used where it is known in advance that the mutual obligations will be monetary or the various contracts will be unilateral and thus executed from the beginning,[23] so that no special contractual arrangements are required to convert non-monetary obligations (e.g. to deliver commodities) into monetary obligations or to cancel executory contracts or close them out by offsetting or reverse transactions. But there are many contractual relationships which are not of this character and require a process that leads, automatically or by unilateral action by one party, to consolidation of the mutual

7–09

---

[18] This predicates that the accounts are to be treated as separate rather than evidencing a single indebtedness. See para.7–11, below.

[19] See, for example, *Bailey v Finch* (1871) L.R. 7 Q.B. 34, per Blackburn J. at 40.

[20] See para.7–31, below.

[21] *Stein v Blake* [1996] 1 A.C. 243.

[22] The current editor would like to thank Ed Murray, of Allen & Overy, for his considerable help and advice in relation to this section and later sections on netting in this chapter.

[23] Because a unilateral contract is by definition a contract in which only one party makes a promise and the other accepts by performance or commencement of performance.

claims into a single net balance. This contractually adopted process is what constitutes netting: the precise legal form of which will vary according to the contractual provisions and the context. There have been a number of statutory definitions of netting,[24] and, more specifically, close-out netting, which is defined in the context of the provision of financial collateral as where:

(a)   the obligations of the parties are accelerated to become immediately due and expressed as an obligation to pay an amount representing the original obligation's estimated current value or replacement cost, or are terminated and replaced by an obligation to pay such an amount; or

(b)   an account is taken of what is due from each party to the other in respect of such obligations and a net sum equal to the balance of the account is payable by the party from whom the larger amount is due to the other party.[25]

Some forms of netting can thus be viewed as both the procedure for, and the outcome of, a contractually completed set-off, although other forms of netting may take effect by the termination of obligations and their replacement with a new obligation to pay the net amount. Netting includes such arrangements as bilateral contract consolidation,[26] settlement netting,[27] the adoption of institutional rules governing bilateral and multilateral clearing and settlement or providing for novation of all relevant contracts to a clearing house or central counterparty,[28] and, the most important type, close-out netting. The main objective of netting is to limit exposure to the credit risk of the counterparty, by preventing cherry-picking by an insolvency officer, by reducing the uncertainty of the application of the rules of insolvency set-off and by preventing exposure to post-insolvency market fluctuations. Some forms of netting also reduce the number of settlements, thus saving costs, and minimise the risk resulting from time delays during settlement. From a market and regulatory perspective netting, particularly close-out netting, provides a measure of protection against systemic risk and, in so doing, influences capital adequacy requirements. Providing it is effective, since the use of close-out netting reduces the exposure of a party from a gross to net amount, it dramatically reduces amount of collateral that is required to be posted to counterparties and central counterparties, such as clearing houses, as well as reducing the amount of loss-absorbing capital that is required to be held by financial institutions.[29] The use of central counterparties will increase

---

[24] Financial Markets and Insolvency (Settlement Finality) Regulations 1999 (SI 1999/2979) reg.2(1); Banking Act 2009 s.48(1)(d).

[25] Financial Collateral Arrangements (No.2) Regulations 2003 (SI 2003/3226) reg.3. See also Banking Act 2009 s.48(1)(d): "'close-out' netting arrangements, under which actual or theoretical debts are calculated during the course of a contract for the purpose of enabling them to be set-off against each other or to be converted into a net debt".

[26] Otherwise known as netting by novation.

[27] Also termed payment netting.

[28] See paras 7–19 et seq., below.

[29] EU Capital Requirements Directive (Directive 2006/48/EC (especially Annex III Pt 7) and Directive 2006/49/EC (especially Annex 1, paras 1–3). For discussion of the importance of netting, particularly close-out netting, in reducing exposure see UNIDROIT, *Adoption of the Principles on the Operation of Close-out Netting Provisions*, CD (92) 6(a) 2013. In 2012, the Gross Market Value of outstanding over-the-counter (OTC) derivatives products was \$24.7trn whereas after netting it was

dramatically in relation to the derivatives market when the clearing obligations imposed by EMIR come into force, which will probably be in 2014.[30]

(ii)   A brief history of set-off[31]

Both the common law courts and courts of equity recognised set-off by contract and in bankruptcy as far back as the seventeenth century. Set-off in other cases was not recognised at common law, though equity appears to have been more liberal even before the Statutes of Set-Off. Bankruptcy legislation on set-off was later extended to companies but subsequently separate rules were devised for companies.[32] Running in parallel with bankruptcy statutes from 1729 onwards were the Statutes of Set-Off, which were designed to mitigate the rigour of the common law and avoid circuity of action by allowing set-off of mutual debts where claim and cross-claim were both for liquidated debts which had become due. In considering whether the requirement of mutuality was satisfied the courts looked at the legal title only, whereas courts of equity, applying the Statutes by analogy, were willing to look behind the legal title to the beneficial ownership. Though the Statutes of Set-Off were eventually repealed, the powers they conferred on courts were preserved and now exist by virtue of s.49(2) of the Senior Courts Act 1981. However, in many cases this statutory, or independent or legal, set-off has become unnecessary, being subsumed by the larger equitable doctrine which developed and which allows set-off both of liquidated and of unliquidated claims where claim and cross-claim were so inseparably connected that it would be inequitable to allow the claimant to enforce his claim without giving credit for the amount of the cross-claim.[33]

7–10

Until modern times this transaction (or equitable) set-off was almost invariably raised by way of defence to a money claim in proceedings, rather than as an answer to a prayer for non-monetary relief or to the exercise of self-help default remedies, so that its significance as a substantive defence was slow to emerge. It is only relatively recently that the courts have given consideration to the position where the claimant, instead of suing for money, has resorted to self-help or has sought non-monetary relief such as specific performance, in either case based on the defendant's default in payment, and have concluded that the defence is substantive, so that where the cross-claim equals or exceeds the

---

$3.6trn, 14.3 per cent of Gross Market Value of 0.6 per cent of Notional Value (source, ISDA OTC Derivatives Market Analysis end-year 2012, based on data from BIS semi-annual review and ISDA research (June 2013)).

[30] See *http://www.fca.org.uk/firms/markets/international-markets/emir#* [accessed October 2, 2013]. EMIR is the European Market Infrastructure Regulation, Regulation 648/2012 on OTC derivatives, central counterparties and trade repositories.

[31] For a more extended account, see the second edition of this book at pp.133 et seq.

[32] See paras 7–75 et seq., below.

[33] Independent set-off is still relied on where there are mutual but unconnected claims, such as in *BICC Plc v Burndy Corp* [1985] 1 Ch. 232; *Glencore Grain Ltd v Agros Trading Co* [1999] 2 Lloyd's Rep. 410; *Metal Distributors (UK) Ltd v ZCCM Investment Holdings Plc* [2005] 2 Lloyd's Rep. 37; *Newcastle Building Society v Mill* [2009] EWHC 740 (Ch) (although in that case independent set-off was held to be excluded by the rules of CREST).

claim the defendant is entitled to assert that he was never in default, so that the claimant was not entitled to resort to self-help or to obtain non-monetary judicial relief.[34]

(iii)   Set-off distinguished from cognate rights

Set-off distinguished from running-account balance

7–11   Set-off presupposes the existence of two distinct claims. It does not apply to individual debits and credits on a single current account, for these have no distinct identity but form part of a single blended fund under which only the balance is payable by or to a party.[35]

When set-off constitutes payment

7–12   Both statutory set-off and that form of equitable set-off applied by analogy of the statutes of set-off[36] are to be distinguished from payment in that they do not operate as a pro tanto satisfaction of the creditor's claim except at the point of judgment for the balance; payment discharges the obligation, whilst a plea of set-off admits the subsistence of the obligation but asserts the right to set a countervailing obligation against it.[37] However, the exercise of a contractual set-off in respect of an ascertained amount does constitute payment.[38] The exercise of a right of transaction set-off, though a substantive defence, does not extinguish or reduce the claim until judgment or agreement,[39] and so does not amount to payment, although it will prevent the claimant taking steps to which it otherwise would have become entitled on non-payment.[40] Where the debtor incurs expense in performing acts which should have been done by his creditor, such expenditure normally gives rise to a right of set-off rather than ipso facto constituting payment of his own indebtedness. However, there are exceptional cases in which such expenditure is itself deemed in law to represent a pro tanto payment of the debt. The most notable example is the right of the tenant who, after due notice to his landlord to carry out repairs for which the latter is

---

[34] See para.7–54, below.

[35] *Halesowen Presswork and Assemblies Ltd v Westminster Bank Ltd* [1970] 1 Q.B. 1, per Buckley L.J. at 46; *Re Charge Card Services Ltd* [1987] Ch. 150, per Millett J. at 174.

[36] See paras 7–04 and 7–10, above.

[37] See para.7–04, above. The distinction is well put in *Halsbury's Laws of England*, 5th edn (London: Butterworths, 2009), Vol 11, para.642: "Set-off [i.e. independent set-off] is entirely distinct from payment. Payment is satisfaction of a claim made by or on behalf of a person against whom the claim is brought . . . Set-off exempts a person entitled to it from making any satisfaction of the claim brought against him, or of so much of the claim as equals the amount which he is entitled to set off . . . Where there has been payment, the party against whom the claim is brought pleads accord and satisfaction, which in effect alleges that the claim no longer exists. On the other hand, a plea of set-off in effect admits the existence of the claim, and sets up a cross-claim as being ground on which the person against whom the claim is brought is excused from payment and entitled to judgment on the claimant's claim. Until judgment in favour of the defendant on the ground of set-off has been given, the claimant's claim is not extinguished".

[38] See paras 7–22 et seq., below.

[39] *Fearns v Anglo-Dutch Paint and Chemical Co Ltd* [2010] EWHC 2366 (Ch).

[40] See para.7–54, below.

responsible, executes the repairs at his own expense and is then entitled to treat that expenditure as pro tanto payment of rent under the lease.[41]

Set-off distinguished from condition of right to repayment

The claimant cannot, of course, claim payment under a contract unless the contractual conditions precedent, if any, to his right to payment have been fulfilled. This is not a matter of set-off but of contract. If I am to be paid £10,000 for performing acts A, B and C I am not entitled to payment until those acts have been performed.[42] Moreover—and this is another factor which distinguishes a substantive defence from a set-off—it is not necessary that I shall have undertaken to perform the acts in question; it suffices that their performance is a condition[43] of my right to payment. By contrast set-off involves a cross-claim and thus an assertion that the claimant has broken a duty owed to the defendant.   7–13

Set-off distinguished from security over a credit balance

The right to set-off one debt against another does not constitute an equitable security interest or, indeed, confer on the defendant any right in rem over the claim of the claimant; it is merely a right to set up one personal claim against another in reduction or discharge of the defendant's liability.[44] This distinction between a real right and a personal right is of particular significance in relation to contractual set-off, which will be examined later. It has, however, been blurred by judicial recognition of the charge-back, by which a debtor takes a security interest over his own obligation.[45] Since the mechanism for enforcing this is by book-entry, which is also the means for effecting a contractual set-off, the question whether a particular transaction gives rise to a charge or a contractual set-off appears to depend upon the label given to it by the parties.   7–14

---

[41] See para.7–59, below.

[42] The distinction between the situation described here (a "pure" defence) and the situation covered by abatement is not always clear, since abatement covers both situations where the goods or services are worth less because they were defective, and where they were not provided at all, see *Totsa Total Oil Trading SA v Bharat Petroleum Corp Ltd* [2005] EWHC 1641 (Comm) at [22]–[24]. This often will not matter, but may do if the interpretation of a contractual provision prohibiting "set-off" is in issue. In that case, a clause providing for payment "without discount, deduction, withholding, set-off or counterclaim" was wide enough to cover non-payment for short delivery, but in *Acsim (Southern) Ltd v Danish Contracting and Development Co Ltd* (1989) 47 B.L.R. 55 the Court of Appeal held that a clause merely prohibiting "set-off" did not cover either a pure defence or abatement.

[43] The term "condition" is, of course, used here not as a contrast with warranty but as denoting any act or event, whether promissory or otherwise and whether constituting a major or a minor term, the performance or occurrence of which is necessary to earn payment.

[44] See paras 1–20 et seq., above; and *Electro-Magnetic (S) Ltd v Development Bank of Singapore Ltd* [1994] 1 S.L.R. 734.

[45] See para.3–12, above.

Set-off distinguished from abatement

7–15   The common law doctrine of abatement, though similar in its effect to substantive transaction set-off, is nevertheless an independent doctrine limited by its own rules. It is discussed later.[46]

Set-off distinguished from counterclaim

7–16   Whilst both set-off and counterclaim are cross-claims and as such are deemed to be separate actions for the purpose of the Limitation Act 1980,[47] they are different in character. Set-off is a defence to a money claim or a claim for relief based on the non-payment of money, it can only be asserted in respect of a cross-claim for money, and it is purely defensive, so that the defendant is not entitled to any judgment in his favour for any surplus of his cross-claim over the claim. A counterclaim is not as such a defence at all, merely a separate claim.[48] It is thus not confined to money but may encompass any cause of action which can conveniently be tried as part of the action. Accordingly any cross-claim capable of being asserted as a set-off can be pleaded as a counterclaim, either in lieu of set-off or as to any surplus over the sum covered by the plea of set-off, whereas a cross-claim capable of being asserted as a counterclaim can be pleaded as a set-off only if it is for a money sum and satisfies any other conditions for a valid set-off.[49]

2.   CONTRACTUAL SET-OFF AND NETTING

7–17   While there is some overlap between contractual set-off and netting, there are some forms of netting which do not constitute contractual set-off and vice versa. Contractual set-off refers to an agreement that two or more distinct obligations are to be set-off against each other, while netting agreements may do this, but may involve the termination of obligations and the creation of a single net obligation. Netting arrangements may also involve other techniques, such as flawed asset arrangements. While there are some limits on the scope of contractual set-off and netting outside insolvency,[50] the chief potential limits are when one or both parties are insolvent.[51]

---

[46] See paras 7–62 et seq., below.

[47] Limitation Act 1980 s.35(1), by which the notional separate action is deemed to have been commenced on the same date as the original action. "Set-off" in that section probably does not include transaction set-off, *Henriskens Rederi A/S v THZ Rolimpex (The Brede)* [1974] 1 Q.B. 233, 245–246, per Lord Denning (although this conclusion was not endorsed by the other members of the Court of Appeal in that case, see Cairns L.J. at 254 and Roskill L.J. at 264); *Westdeutsche Landesbank Girozentrale v Islington London BC* [1994] 4 All E.R. 890, 945, where Hobhouse J. expressly agreed with the view of Lord Denning; *Filross Securities Ltd v Midgeley* (1999) 31 H.L.R. 465, 472 CA; *Philip Collins Ltd v Davis* [2000] 3 All E.R. 808, 831; *Cheltenham BC v Laird* [2009] EWHC 1253 (QB) at [459].

[48] Under the Civil Procedure Rules it is designated as a type of Pt 20 claim.

[49] See Civil Procedure Rules r.16.6. See also para.7–72, below.

[50] These are considered below in this section.

[51] These are considered in the section on insolvency set-off, see para.7–90, below.

(i) Types of netting arrangement

We have previously seen that netting includes a bilateral or multilateral arrangement for conversion of mutual claims into a single net claim. For this purpose a number of techniques are available which in normal circumstances can be expected to be effective. The techniques are often combined in a single agreement.[52] These include the following:

Netting by novation (contractual consolidation)

Netting by novation, or contractual consolidation, involves the amalgamation of two or more executory contracts into a single new contract to be performed at a future time. To the extent that contracts to be netted are executory, only those with the same settlement date can be amalgamated[53]; payment obligations which have accrued can, if wished, be netted into one debit or credit balance on a particular date.[54] The characteristic of this form of netting, which distinguishes it from settlement netting, is that the fusion of the claims on both sides into a new claim for a single balance or a single delivery obligation occurs immediately upon the occurrence of the event stipulated by the contract,[55] whereas in settlement netting the payment obligations remain separate until they have been netted out at the payment date and the net balance paid or delivery obligation discharged.[56] Netting by novation is most useful in multilateral netting arrangements, as it ensures that market participants are exposed only to the credit risk of the clearing house, rather than to the credit risk of each member. A clearing house using this system will insist on the posting of marked to market collateral by participants to cover its exposure to their credit risk.[57]

Contractual consolidation may be effected by provision for bilateral consolidation of contractual obligations or by clearing house rules providing for novation of notified contracts to the clearing house. In the former case a single master agreement may provide that in stated eventualities, which could include notice by one party to the other, all outstanding contracts between them shall be consolidated into and replaced by a single contract under which only the net balance is payable. Alternatively, a master agreement may provide for the automatic consolidation of each contract with subsequent contracts as and when these come into existence, so that no set-off situation ever arises. Where clearing house rules provide for this type of netting, the clearing house becomes substituted as a principal in relation to each of the parties.[58] For example, under

7–18

7–19

---

[52] S. Firth, *Derivatives: Law and Practice* (London: Sweet & Maxwell, 2012), para.5–023.

[53] See J. Benjamin, *Financial Law* (Oxford: OUP, 2007), para.12.09.

[54] See, for example, the netting of debits and credits at the end of each month described in *British Eagle International Air Lines Ltd v Compagnie Nationale Air France* [1975] 1 W.L.R. 758, 766.

[55] See below and *Goode on Commercial Law*, E. McKendrick (ed.), 4th edn (London: Penguin Books, 2010), pp.509–510.

[56] Note that settlement netting can be used for settlements occurring throughout the life of a transaction.

[57] Wood, *Law and Practice of International Finance: Set-off and Netting, Derivatives, Clearing Systems* (2007), para.4–012.

[58] See Wood, *Law and Practice of International Finance: Set-off and Netting, Derivatives, Clearing Systems* (2007), para.4–011. For an example of the effectiveness of this approach, see House of Lords European Union Committee, *The Future Regulation of Derivatives Markets; Is the EU on the Right*

the General Regulations of the London Clearing House (LCH), members who are parties to a sale transaction are required to register it with LCH, whereupon the transaction is automatically novated and replaced by two separate transactions in both of which LCH is substituted for one party as the principal, becoming seller to the original buyer and buyer from the original seller.[59] The effect of this system of automatic novation is that payment and delivery obligations become owed by and to LCH. In this way payment rights and obligations arising from all dealings entered into by a particular trader settling on a particular date are internalised and consolidated into a single credit or debit balance in the trader's current account with LCH due or to be paid on that date.

It is also possible to achieve a similar effect in relation to matured debits and credits without novation, but by using a "flawed asset" technique, specified in the rules of the clearing house, so that each debit or credit which would otherwise arise between members of a clearing house is only ever owed to or from the clearing house as part of a net balance.[60]

Netting by novation does, of course, depend upon the obligations on both sides having the same settlement date (if executory) and being of the same kind. It is not possible to net a payment obligation against a delivery obligation or vice versa. So where mutual dealings involve both delivery and payment obligations, or where executory contracts have different settlement dates it is necessary to devise some contractual procedure, such as rescission or close-out, by which the obligations are terminated and converted into a net balance.[61] Similarly, while the fact that the claim and cross-claim are in different currencies is no bar to a right of set-off,[62] completion of the set-off requires either that one currency is converted to the other or that both currencies are converted to a third currency at a given rate of exchange.

Settlement (or payment) netting

7–20   As mentioned above, whereas contractual consolidation involves the amalgamation of unmatured claims, settlement netting is the process by which matured claims[63] are netted out and paid. It is only the act of payment of the net balance which extinguishes the claims on both sides. The purpose of settlement netting is to avoid "settlement risk", where a party who has already paid is exposed to the insolvency risk of the other party until it has paid.[64] Again, settlement netting may be effected either by bilateral arrangements[65] or by multilateral arrangements through a clearing house. In the former case the parties simply agree that

---

Track? Report with Evidence, HL Paper No.93 (10th Report of Session 2009/10, March 31, 2010), para.69, which describes how LCH Clearnet avoided any loss from the insolvency of Lehman Bros by the use of collateral to liquidate its portfolio.

[59] General Regulations LCH Clearnet Ltd reg.3.

[60] This was the technique which was held in *International Air Transport Association v Ansett Australia Holdings Ltd* [2008] H.C.A. 3 to be effective in the insolvency of a market participant, see para.7–92, below.

[61] This is close-out netting. See para.7–21, below.

[62] See para.7–25, below.

[63] These could be claims arising in the course of a transaction, as and when the payment obligations accrue.

[64] See Firth, *Derivatives: Law and Practice* (2012), paras 5–024 to 5–025.

[65] See, for example, s.2(c) of the ISDA Master Agreement.

when claims on both sides mature those on one side shall be set-off against those on the other and the balance paid. In the case of netting through a clearing house the procedure is that at the end of each clearing (which may be daily or at such other intervals as the clearing house rules prescribe) the position of each clearing house member is netted out in relation to all other clearing house members to produce a "net net" series of balances in which members are either creditors or debtors in relation to the clearing as a whole. Payment is then made by in-house transfers from debtor members to creditor members in the books of the clearing house or of a bank (typically the central bank) where all the clearing house members hold an account. These multilateral netting arrangements have not always proved effective in the event of an insolvency of a clearing house member, but the problem has been considerably alleviated by changes to the systems (either by introducing novation netting, or using the "flawed asset" approach described above) and also legislation. The impact of insolvency on settlement netting is considered later.[66]

Close-out netting

It is hard to overstate the significance of close-out netting to the financial markets. Its main point is to reduce all present, future and contingent indebtedness to a single net balance between parties in the event of one party's insolvency, so that the exposure of the other party is limited irrespective of the provisions of national insolvency rules. In the United Kingdom, where insolvency set-off has a wide scope between mutual parties,[67] its main functions are to turn non-money obligations, such as obligations to deliver or transfer securities, into money obligations,[68] to avoid the uncertainty that comes from the valuation of future and contingent debts by an insolvency officer,[69] and to avoid exposure to market fluctuations between the time of insolvency and the time that the insolvency officer actually calculates the set-off, which might otherwise be taken into account under the hindsight principle.[70] If it is desired to have a net balance involving transactions with more than one party, it is necessary to combine novation netting with close-out netting. To a limited extent in the United Kingdom, and to a much greater extent in some other countries,[71] there is a danger that an insolvency officer would be able to disclaim some transactions and perform others, that is, to "cherry-pick". This leaves a counterparty having to pay in full sums owed to the insolvent party, while only receiving a small fraction of the amount it is owed. Protection against cherry-picking is the main benefit of close-out netting worldwide, and it is significant that many jurisdictions have enacted legislation expressly validating close-out netting provisions and disapplying insolvency rules which would otherwise interfere with their

7–21

---

[66] See paras 7–90 et seq., below.
[67] See paras 7–76 et seq., below.
[68] The limitation of insolvency set-off to money obligations is discussed at paras 7–86 et seq., below.
[69] This need for valuation is discussed at para.7–80, below.
[70] See para.7–80, below.
[71] For a brief surveys, see Wood, *Law and Practice of International Finance: Set-off and Netting, Derivatives, Clearing Systems* (2007), p.10.

operation.[72] Despite this, there is concern that the laws on close-out netting differ significantly between jurisdictions, and UNIDROIT has recently adopted a set of Principles on the Operation of Close-out Netting, with a view to providing an international legislative standard.[73]

The UNIDROIT Principles define a close-out netting provision as one on the basis of which:

> "upon the occurrence of an event predefined in the provision in relation to a party to the contract, the obligations owed by the parties to each other that are covered by the provision, whether or not they are at that time due or payable, are automatically or at the election of one of the parties reduced to or replaced by a single net obligation, whether by way of novation, termination or otherwise, representing the aggregate value of the combined obligations, which is thereupon due and payable by one party to the other".[74]

The specified events which trigger close-out netting usually relate to the insolvency of one party, including the commencement of insolvency proceedings for that party or a related party, but also including events which pose a serious risk to that party's credit, as well as breaches of the agreement.[75]

There are various techniques used for achieving this effect, which appear in many of the standard form agreements.[76] One is that parties enter into a single master agreement which governs all transactions between them: this is intended to prevent an insolvency officer "cherry picking", by disclaiming some contracts and performing others.[77] The actual close-out provisions operate by providing for acceleration or termination of all the contracts between the parties, the replacement of delivery obligations with value-payment obligations, and foreign currency claims with base currency claims, and netting of the resultant money claims.[78] Depending on how this is drafted this can be effected by a set-off of aggregated credits and debits,[79] or by all obligations being replaced by a single obligation to pay the net balance.[80]

The latter technique, when used in the ISDA Master agreement, is combined with flawed asset provisions making each party's performance obligations conditional upon there having been no default by the other party so that on default, the non-defaulting party is therefore entitled to withhold performance.[81]

---

[72] See Wood, *Law and Practice of International Finance: Set-off and Netting, Derivatives, Clearing Systems* (2007), Ch.7.

[73] UNIDROIT, *Adoption of the Principles on the Operation of Close-Out Netting Provisions.*

[74] UNIDROIT Principles principle 2.

[75] For example, s.5 of the ISDA Master Agreement (2002) sets out a wide variety of events of default and "termination events" (which are events outside the control of the parties which make it desirable to close-out particular transactions).

[76] Examples of these are the ISDA Master Agreement (2002), the GMSLA 2010 produced by ISLA (International Securities Lending Association), which relates to securities lending and the GMRA 2011 produced by ICMA (International Capital Markets Association), which relates to repos.

[77] ISDA Master Agreement (2002) cl.1(c), GMRA 2011 cl.1 and GMSLA 2010 cl.1.

[78] This type of close-out netting was described by Lightman J. in *Enron Europe Ltd v Revenue and Customs Commissioners* [2006] EWHC 824 (Ch) at [20], one of the few recent cases to consider a netting agreement.

[79] See GMLSA 2010 cl.11 and GMRA 2011 cl.10.

[80] See ISDA Master Agreement s.6(e)(i).

[81] ISDA Master Agreement 2002 s.2(a)(iii). The interpretation of this clause has been the subject of a number of recent decisions.

Thus a non-defaulting party who has, by the terms of the contract, a right to elect whether or not to trigger the close-out netting process, does not have to make payments to a counterparty who may not be able to make reciprocal payments,[82] while deciding whether and when to activate that trigger. The Court of Appeal has recently held that the effect of the ISDA flawed asset clause is to suspend the obligations to make payment until either the default is cured or close-out netting is triggered.[83] However, it does not eliminate the underlying debt obligations, so that the non-defaulting party can only prove in the insolvency proceedings of the defaulting party for the net amount due to it, taking into account the suspended obligations. This flawed asset provision has proved controversial, since it can result in a defaulting party being kept permanently out of money to which it would otherwise be entitled were close-out netting to take place,[84] and it enables the non-defaulting party to decide whether or when to close-out when the same choice is not available to the defaulting party, thus leading to moral hazard and uncertainty.[85] The ability of the non-defaulting party to suspend its obligations indefinitely, while a product of freedom of contract, could seem disproportionate to its need for protection: it is primarily protected by the ability to close-out, which is a fair protection since it takes into account the possibility that the defaulting party is in the money. The Court of Appeal rejected the argument that there should be an implied term bringing the suspension of obligations to an end either after a reasonable time (that is, a time within which the non-defaulting party "should" have exercised its right to terminate) or once the transactions between the parties had reached maturity.[86] However, a consultation paper of the United Kingdom Treasury[87] urged a market solution to the perceived problems with s.2(a)(iii), and ISDA has consulted on the possibility of inserting a time limit in the clause within which termination rights must be exercised, failing which the suspension will lift.[88] There was further uncertainty as to whether an unlimited suspension contravened the anti-deprivation principle: this was dispelled by the Court of Appeal's decision that it did not, at least where the non-defaulting party's right to prove was limited to the net amount due.[89]

As mentioned above, close-out netting performs an important function in converting non-money obligations to money obligations, which can then be

---

[82] Described by one commentator as "throwing good money after bad": C. Baker, "Rethinking the ISDA flawed asset" (2012) 27 J.I.B.L.R. 250.

[83] *Lomas v JFB Firth Rixson Inc* [2012] EWCA Civ 419 at [35], [62].

[84] This was the argument made by counsel for LBSF in the *Lomas* case who argued that this was a deprivation contravening the anti-deprivation principle, see [82] and paras 7–90 and 7–93, below. For further discussion, see HM Treasury, *Establishing Resolution Arrangements for Investment Banks* (December 2009) paras 7.5–7.14.

[85] Baker, "Rethinking the ISDA flawed asset" (2012) 27 J.I.B.L.R. 250.

[86] *Lomas v JFB Firth Rixson Inc* [2012] EWCA Civ 419 at [36]–[45].

[87] HM Treasury, *Establishing Resolution Arrangements for Investment Banks* (September 16, 2010) paras 7.5–7.14.

[88] ISDA, *Consultation with Members of the International Swaps and Derivatives Association, Inc. on proposed amendments to s.2(a)(iii) and related provisions of the ISDA Master Agreement* (April 8, 2011). ISDA are still considering what amendments to make, specifically what length the time limit should be and whether it should be limited to insolvency events of defaults. In formulating the Principles of Close-out Netting, UNIDROIT took the view that this issue was a matter of policy, and therefore the Principles take a neutral position (UNIDROIT, *Adoption of the Principles on the Operation of Close-out Netting Provisions*, para.43).

[89] *Lomas v JFB Firth Rixson Inc* [2012] EWCA Civ 419 at [91]–[94]. See para.7–93, below.

netted or set-off. This function is particularly important in relation to title transfer collateral arrangements,[90] including repos, securities lending and the provision of collateral to central counterparties. The provisions include various procedures for valuing the securities or other non-cash collateral at market rates.[91] There seems little doubt that close-out netting in this context is also valid in insolvency proceedings: this is considered below.[92]

(ii) Availability of contractual set-off

7–22   Barring the advent of insolvency, in which event contractual set-off is displaced by the rules governing insolvency set-off,[93] the limits on contractual set-off are for the most part practical rather than legal. The ordinary requirement of mutuality may be overridden by the agreement of the parties, so that, for example, a parent company may agree to allow debts due from its subsidiaries to be set-off against its own credit balance; the parties may agree to allow a claim that would not otherwise have become due to be accelerated for purposes of set-off; and set-off may be effected in any manner provided by the contract without need of legal proceedings. But since the object of set-off is to reduce a monetary liability to a net balance even a contractual set-off cannot be fully effected unless both claim and cross-claim have been reduced to money—in the case of an unliquidated claim, by having it crystallised into a liquidated claim[94]; in the case of property, by having it valued for set-off purposes; and in the case of a claim and cross-claim in different currencies, by converting one currency to the other, or both currencies to a third currency, at a specified or ascertainable rate of exchange. However, though it would not strictly be a case of set-off there is nothing to preclude the parties from agreeing to net out mutual claims relating to non-money fungibles, so that, for example, if A is due to deliver 100 tonnes of coffee to B under one contract and to receive 30 tonnes of coffee of the same description from B under another contract, A can perform his obligation by delivering 70 tonnes to B.[95]

Contractual set-off in respect of unliquidated and contingent claims

7–23   It is not uncommon for a party to stipulate for a right to set-off unliquidated, and even contingent, claims against moneys due to the other. Is such a stipulation valid? We cannot give a sensible answer to this question without first asking what the word "set-off" means in this context. It is important to bear in mind that exercise of contractual set-off results in the extinguishment pro tanto of the claim against which the right of set-off is exercised. Obviously it is not possible to do this unless and until the quantum of the two claims is ascertained. If, for example, a bank's customer has a credit balance of £10,000 and the bank seeks to exercise a contractual right to "set-off" an unliquidated claim for damages for fraud, the two claims cannot at that stage be combined, because one of them is unquantified

---

[90] See paras 6–27 et seq., above.
[91] GMRA cl.10(f); GMSLA cl.11.3.
[92] See para.7–93, below.
[93] See paras 7–90 et seq., below.
[94] See para.7–23, below.
[95] See fn.9, above.

so that we are unable to say to what extent, if at all, the credit balance is reduced. On the other hand, we must seek to give some meaning to the term of the agreement which enables the bank to "set-off" even an unliquidated claim. The answer seems clear enough; what the bank is really obtaining, when imposing such a stipulation, is a right to withhold payment of the credit balance pending quantification of its claim (whether by agreement or by judicial decision or arbitral award), coupled with the right to set-off that claim when it has been quantified. In other words, the so-called contractual set-off in relation to unliquidated claims is in effect two rights rolled up into one: in the first instance, a right to suspend payment, while leaving the customer's credit balance intact; and later, when the amount of the claim has become liquidated, a set-off which will result in pro tanto extinguishment of the credit balance.

The application of the set-off clause to a contingent claim is likely to produce a similar effect, though this depends on the circumstances and on the agreement between the parties. Where the contingent claim is of a known maximum amount—as in the case of a guarantee of a fixed indebtedness—it is a question of construction of the agreement whether the bank is intended to have a mere right to suspend payment until the liability matures and the actual amount becomes known, with an ensuing right of set-off, or whether on the other hand the bank is to have an immediate right to set-off the maximum liability, upon terms of re-crediting the customer with the appropriate amount if the actual liability proves to be less. In most cases, the former construction is likely to prevail.[96]

Cross-border set-off

Assuming that the right of set-off is governed by English law, the mere fact that the claim and cross-claim arise from accounts in different countries does not in itself affect a right of set-off given by contract.   7–24

Cross-currency set-off

Similarly, the parties are entitled to contract for a claim in one currency to be set-off against a claim in another,[97] though as stated above it is necessary to reduce the two claims to the same currency in order to give effect to the set-off.   7–25

(iii)   Legal limits of contractual set-off

In the relationship between them contracting parties are free to agree on almost any terms for contractual set-off they may choose and these will be effective so long as they are not cut off by insolvency.[98] It is, however, another matter where the rights of third parties may be affected. Three situations in particular require a   7–26

---

[96] It has been pointed out by Dr Derham, however, that where the contingent debt is a flawed asset, a right to suspend payment until the occurrence of the contingency would not add anything to the existing agreement, and so the second construction of the set-off agreement may reflect the parties' intentions more accurately, Derham, *The Law of Set-off* (2010), para.16.04.

[97] See further para.7–33, below as to the banker's right of combination in respect of accounts maintained in different currencies.

[98] See paras 7–90 et seq., below as to the impact of insolvency on contractual set-off.

brief comment, namely set-off against an assignee of the debt, set-off against a money claim in which a third party has an interest and the effect of a freezing injunction.

Contractual set-off against an assignee

7–27   In general an assignee of a debt takes subject to equities,[99] including the debtor's right of contractual set-off as regards cross-claims on another account for advances made to the creditor prior to the debtor's receipt of notice of assignment.[100] Where the terms of the set-off extend to contingent liabilities of the creditor to the debtor it would seem that the assignee takes subject to those contingent liabilities.[101] The question of whether the debtor can assert a contractual set-off in respect of claims arising from new dealings with the creditor after the debtor has received notice of assignment, when the set-off agreement predates the assignment, is a matter of some debate. The better view is that the assignee takes subject to the set-off agreement, which is an equity affecting the assigned debts, and therefore to any post-assignment cross-claims which fall within the set-off agreement.[102] Where the payment undertaking is embodied in a negotiable instrument which comes into the hands of a holder in due course he takes free from all equities, so that a set-off available against the original creditor cannot be pleaded in answer to a claim on the instrument.[103] Finally, if the debtor has agreed not to assert rights of set-off against an assignee he is bound by that agreement.[104] Similarly, if a debenture is issued on terms that it is to be transferable free from equities the issuer is not entitled to assert a right of set-off against a transferee of the debenture.[105]

Set-off against a money claim belonging to a third party

7–28   Though other forms of set-off require mutuality of parties, so that, for example, A cannot set-off against his indebtedness to B a debt due to B from C, it is usually

---

[99] For the effect of assignment on other forms of set-off, see paras 7–67 et seq., below.

[100] For support for this view, see Derham, *The Law of Set-off* (2010), para.17.52.

[101] See para.7–23, above for an analysis of how contractual set-off is likely to operate in relation to contingent debts.

[102] This is a different view from that previously expressed in this book, and is taken despite the fact that cross-claims arising after assignment are not susceptible to independent set-off and transaction set-off, see para.7–67, below. However, the forceful arguments in favour of the view now expressed in the text in Derham, *The Law of Set-off* (2010), paras 17.55–17.57; and P. Wood, *English and International Set-Off* (London: Sweet & Maxwell, 1989), review at (1990) 106 L.Q.R. 515, 518–519 are convincing. A contrary view is taken in Wood, *English and International Set-Off* (1989), but it is conceded that the position is unclear.

[103] In relation to bills of exchange this is specifically provided by s.38(2) of the Bills of Exchange Act 1882. A similar approach is achieved by the CREST Rules, which apply to all instruments transferred through CREST including many money market instruments, and which operate by agreement, see *Newcastle Building Society v Mill, Kaupthing Singer and Friedlander Ltd (Isle of Man) Ltd* [2009] EWHC 740 (Ch).

[104] *Re Agra & Masterman's Bank* (1866-67) L.R. 2 Ch. App. 391; *John Dee Group Ltd v WMH (21) Ltd* [1998] B.C.C. 972; *Newcastle Building Society v Mill, Kaupthing Singer and Friedlander Ltd (Isle of Man) Ltd* [2009] EWHC 740 (Ch). As to the exclusion of transaction and independent set-off by agreement, see para.7–73, below.

[105] *Hilger Analytical Ltd v Rank Precision Industries Ltd* [1984] B.C.L.C. 301.

open to a party to contract out of the requirement of mutuality and allow a claim vested in him to be made available as a set-off against another party's debt. A common example arises in relation to bank accounts maintained for a group of companies where each member of the group agrees that its credit balance may be the subject of set-off in respect of debit balances of other members of the group. But the requirement of mutuality can be abrogated only by consent of the party affected. So a money claim against a person in his personal capacity cannot be set-off against money due to him as trustee unless the beneficiaries consent or the person asserting the money claim gave value and was without notice of the trust.[106]

Contractual set-off and the freezing injunction

Where the claimant in an action obtains a freezing injunction[107] freezing the defendant's bank account, then it was held in *The Theotokos*[108] that unless otherwise provided by the injunction a bank having notice of it may not exercise any right of set-off against the defendant's credit balance except by obtaining a variation of the injunction.[109] Following this case, it has become standard practice to include in the injunction a clause: "This injunction does not prevent any bank from exercising any right of set-off it may have in respect of any facility which it gave to the respondent before it was notified of this order' which should obviate the need for the bank to apply to the court for a variation of the injunction".[110]

7–29

(iv) The impact of insolvency on contractual set-off and netting

This is considered in detail in the section on insolvency set-off below.[111]

7–30

---

[106] *Middleton v Pollock Ex p. Nugee* (1875) L.R. 20 Eq. 29; *Barclays Bank Ltd v Quistclose Investments Ltd* [1970] A.C. 597 HL. See Wood, *English and International Set-Off* (1989), pp.1050 et seq.; Derham, *The Law of Set-off* (2010), paras 17.122 et seq., which deals with types of set-off other than contractual. Dr Derham is of the view that the requirement of mutuality is not strict in relation to equitable set-off, where special circumstances justify the occurrence of set-off despite mutuality: Derham, *The Law of Set-off* (2010), paras 4.67 et seq.; and R. Derham, "Equitable set-off: a critique of Muscat v Smith" (2006) 122 L.Q.R. 469. See para.7–53, below.

[107] Formerly known as a Mareva injunction, this restrains the defendant from dealing with its assets, or removing them from the jurisdiction, pending trial of the action. The injunction is granted where there is reason to believe that the defendant may dissipate his assets or withdraw them from the claimant's reach so as to defeat any judgment the claimant may obtain.

[108] *Oceanica Castelana Armadora SA of Panama v Mineralimportexport (The Theotokos)* [1983] 1 W.L.R. 1294.

[109] See also *In Re K* [1990] 2 Q.B. 298, which related to a restraining order in drug trafficking proceedings.

[110] *Oceanica Castelana Armadora SA of Panama v Mineralimportexport (The Theotokos)* [1983] 1 W.L.R. 1294, 1302. See *Atkins Court Forms*, Vol.23 Form 17.

[111] Paras 7–90 et seq., below.

3.   CURRENT ACCOUNT SET-OFF

The nature of the right to combine accounts

7–31   Unless otherwise agreed between the parties, a banker has, by the custom of bankers, a right to combine two or more current accounts held for the same customer in his own right,[112] and this is so whether the accounts are held at the same branch[113] or at different branches.[114] So the bank can refuse to honour a cheque drawn on an account in credit if the credit balance[115] is insufficient to cover a debit balance on another current account with the customer of the bank.[116] Astonishingly it is still unclear whether the right of combination, which Professor Wood has conveniently termed "current account set-off", is a true set-off or merely an entitlement on the part of the bank to treat its relationship with its customer as a single relationship and the various accounts as a single account on which there is a single balance due from or to the bank. On the latter view, which enjoys considerable judicial[117] and academic[118] support, the accounting is automatic and, unlike set-off, requires no act on the part of the bank. Nevertheless there are strong arguments in favour of the view that the right of combination is not a matter of account but an implied contractual right to set-off a debit balance on one account against a credit balance on another.[119] In the first place, it is much more realistic. The notion that parties who establish and operate separate accounts are to be treated as dealing with each other only by a single account is contrary not only to appearances but also to intentions. Secondly, if the combination were automatic this would enure for the benefit of the customer as well as the bank, so that the customer could overdraw on one account so long as he had a sufficient balance on another. But it is well established that he cannot do this. The bank is entitled to refuse to honour a cheque if there are insufficient funds in the account on which it is drawn even if there is a separate account, current or otherwise, with a credit balance sufficient to cover the cheque.[120] If the customer wishes the accounts to be combined he must give an instruction to the bank to transfer the balance on the account in credit to the account in debit. Thirdly, there are several judgments which make it clear that the combination of accounts, far from being automatic, is a matter of

---

[112] *National Westminster Bank Ltd v Halesowen Presswork & Assemblies Ltd* [1972] A.C. 785; *Garnett v M'Kewan* (1872) L.R. 8 Ex. 10; *Cumming v Shand* (1860) 5 H. & N. 95.

[113] *National Westminster Bank Ltd v Halesowen Presswork & Assemblies* [1972] A.C. 785; *Direct Acceptance Corp v Bank of New South Wales* (1968) 88 W.N. (N.S.W.) (Pt 1) 498; *Cumming v Shand* (1860) 5 H. & N. 95.

[114] *Garnett v M'Kewan* (1872) L.R. 8 Ex. 10; *Prince v Oriental Bank* (1878) 3 App. Cas. 325.

[115] When added to any agreed overdraft facility.

[116] *Garnett v M'Kewan* (1872) L.R. 8 Ex. 10.

[117] See, for example, *Garnett v M'Kewan* (1872) L.R. 8 Ex. 10; *Halesowen Presswork and Assemblies Ltd v Westminster Bank Ltd* [1971] 1 Q.B. 1, per Buckley L.J. at 46, cited with approval by Millett J. in *Re Charge Card Services Ltd* [1987] 1 Ch. 150 at 173–174; and by Otton J. in *Re K* [1990] 2 Q.B. 298, 303.

[118] Derham, *The Law of Set-off* (2010), paras 15.03 et seq.

[119] For support for this view, see S. McCracken, *The Banker's Remedy of Set-Off*, 3rd edn (London: Bloomsbury Professional, 2010), p.29.

[120] *Garnett v M'Kewan* (1872) L.R. 8 Ex. 10; *Barclays Bank Ltd v Okenarhe* [1966] 2 Lloyd's Rep. 87, per Mocatta J. at 95. For criticism see E.P. Ellinger, *Ellinger's Modern Banking Law*, E Ellinger, E Lomnicka and C Hare (eds), 5th edn (Oxford: OUP, 2011), p.267.

choice for the bank. Thus in *Halesowen* Lord Denning stated that "the banker has a right to combine accounts whenever he pleases"[121]; while in *Re EJ Morel Ltd*[122] Buckley J. said that "where all the accounts are current the banker can combine these accounts in whatever way he chooses".[123] The fact that the banker has a right to combine accounts but not an obligation to do so indicates that combination is simply a form of contract consolidation, in which exercise of the contractual right of set-off and netting produces a single balance. The situation is thus quite different from that with which Millett J. had to deal in *Re Charge Card Services Ltd*,[124] where there was in fact a single current account, so that the question of set-off could not arise.

As in the case of non-contractual set-off, there must be mutuality of parties, in the absence of agreement to the contrary. If the accounts are either held by or kept with two distinct legal entities there is no right of combination. So the account of a company at a particular bank cannot be combined with that of its parent or subsidiary at the same bank without an authorisation from both companies[125]; and the account of a company with one bank cannot, in the absence of agreement, be combined with that held by the company with a parent, subsidiary or associated company of the first bank.

Cross-border combination

Does the right to combine accounts apply where the accounts are not merely held in different branches of a bank in the same country but at branches in different countries? Assuming the right of set-off to be governed by English law, the answer in principle would seem to be yes, though it may be that in such a case the court would more readily infer an agreement to keep the accounts separate.[126] Again, there must be mutuality of parties.   **7–32**

Cross-currency combination

The fact that the debit balance on one account is in a currency different from the credit balance on the other would not seem to preclude the bank from combining the two accounts, though again the difference in currencies will be a factor to take into account in determining whether there is an implied agreement to keep the accounts separate[127]: the lack of an express or a satisfactory implied mechanism for ascertaining the balance due at any given time could be a reason in favour of   **7–33**

---

[121] *Halesowen Presswork and Assemblies Ltd v Westminster Bank Ltd* [1971] 1 Q.B. 1 at 34.

[122] *Re EJ Morel Ltd* [1962] Ch. 21.

[123] *Re EJ Morel Ltd* [1962] Ch. 21 at 31.

[124] In *Re Charge Card Services Ltd* [1987] Ch. 150.

[125] The assent of the company whose account is in credit is not sufficient, for the company whose account is in debit can object to an officious reduction or discharge of its liability. There is, of course, no problem where there is only one operating account, as where the account is in joint names or where one company in a group effectively acts as banker to the others, holds the operating account with the bank, receives payments for other companies in the group and makes payments on their behalf, these being recorded for information only by memorandum accounts designed to show the state of account between the account holder and the other members of the group.

[126] See *Paget's Law of Banking*, 13th edn (London: Butterworths Law, 2006), para.29–20.

[127] See *Paget's Law of Banking* (2006), para.29–24.

such an implication.[128] There was at one time much debate as to whether claims arising in different currencies could be set-off against each other, for on one view foreign currency was not money but a commodity. The obligation to furnish it was thus a delivery obligation for the breach of which the remedy was unliquidated damages, not a payment obligation, for which the remedy was a claim in debt, and it is well established that a delivery obligation may not in general be set-off against a money claim.[129] In continental Europe there remains a diversity of views, the courts of some jurisdictions taking the view that obligations in different currencies are not of the same nature and are therefore not susceptible to set-off while others consider that set-off is available. In England it is now established that a claimant is entitled to judgment in a foreign currency,[130] that the judgment is for payment, not for delivery, and that the claim is thus for debt, not for damages. The commodity conception of foreign currency, so far as it ever existed, is now dead[131] and there seems no reason why a claim in one currency cannot be set-off against a claim in another, though at the point of enforcement of any balance it is necessary to convert the foreign currency claim into sterling.

Exclusion of the right of combination

7–34   Current account set-off, or the right to combine accounts, may be excluded by express or implied agreement. Where, for example, the customer has a fixed loan account and a current account, the court will usually infer an agreement that these accounts should be kept separate, as otherwise the customer could never safely draw cheques without having sufficient in the current account to cover the debit balance on the loan account, and this would frustrate the purpose of the arrangement.[132] But if the customer becomes bankrupt or goes into liquidation the agreement to keep the accounts separate comes to an end, not only as an implied term of the agreement but because the provisions of insolvency law as to set-off are mandatory.[133]

---

[128] Derham, *The Law of Set-off* (2010), paras 15.78–15.81.

[129] See para.7–21, above; para.7–83, below.

[130] See *Miliangos v George Frank (Textiles) Ltd* [1976] A.C. 443; *The Halcyon The Great* [1975] 1 W.L.R. 515; *Re Kaupthing Singer & Friedlander Ltd* [2009] EWHC 1633 (Ch) at [115].

[131] *Barclays Bank International Ltd v Levin Bros (Bradford) Ltd* [1977] 1 Lloyd's Rep. 51, per Mocatta J. at 59: "In my view, however, the decision in the Miliangos case has revolutionised the position and has disposed of the once common assumption that foreign currency must be treated by our Courts as if a commodity, e.g. a foreign cow ...". See also *Camdex International Ltd v Bank of Zambia (No.3)* [1997] 6 Bank. L.R. 43.

[132] *Bradford Old Bank v Sutcliffe* [1918] 2 K.B. 833. This inference can only be rebutted by clear words of agreement to the contrary, *Fraser v Oystertec Plc* [2006] 1 B.C.L.C. 491 at [18]. For an example of an express exclusion of set-off in a loan and guarantee transaction see *Continental Illinois National Bank & Trust Co of Chicago v Papanicolaou* [1986] 2 Lloyd's Rep. 441.

[133] *National Westminster Bank Ltd v Halesowen Pressork & Assemblies Ltd* [1972] A.C. 785. See para.7–78, below.

4.   INDEPENDENT (STATUTORY) SET-OFF

Independent set-off as a procedural shield

Independent, or statutory, set-off is a procedural defence designed to avoid   **7–35**
circuity of action where both claim and cross-claim are liquidated and due.[134] In
contrast to transaction set-off, it is not necessary that the claim and cross-claim
are closely connected; they may be wholly independent of each other. It will be
recalled that there are two forms of this: set-off provided under the Statutes of
Set-Off and set-off given in equity by analogy to the statute.

Both forms of independent set-off are procedural only. Though in modern
practice pleaded as a defence,[135] the defendant's cross-claim does not constitute a
denial of liability; on the contrary, it amounts to an admission that the defendant
is liable on the claim and a contention that he is entitled to set-off his cross-claim
in reduction or extinction of the amount for which the plaintiff is entitled to
judgment. Accordingly the cross-claim does not reduce the defendant's liability
on the claim,[136] and the set-off takes effect only on and from the date of
judgment.[137]

Significance of the procedural character of independent set-off

Several important consequences flow from the fact that independent set-off is a   **7–36**
procedural defence, not a substantive defence. First, neither the existence of the
cross-claim nor its assertion without or prior to proceedings provides justification
for withholding payment to the other party. Secondly, since the remedy can be
asserted only where the promisee has brought proceedings, it does not prevent
him from exercising extra-judicial rights and remedies for default, such as
forfeiture of a lease, distress,[138] contractual acceleration of the promisor's
monetary liability, invocation of a cross-default clause,[139] termination of the
contract and repossession of any goods of the promisee supplied, for example,
under a leasing agreement. In all such cases the existence of the cross-claim does
not in itself reduce the promisor's liability or affect the extra-judicial remedies

---

[134] *Aectra Refining and Manufacturing Inc v Exmar NV* [1994] 1 W.L.R. 1634 at 1650, per Hoffmann
L.J.
[135] CPR r.16.6.
[136] *Fuller v Happy Shopper Markets Ltd* [2001] EWHC 702 (Ch); [2001] 2 Lloyd's Rep. 49 at [25].
[137] *Stein v Blake* [1996] A.C. 243, per Lord Hoffmann at 251; Glencore *Glencore Grain Ltd v Agros
Trading* [1999] 2 Lloyd's Rep. 410 at [28]; *Henriksens Rederi A/S v THZ Rolimpex (The Brede)*
[1974] Q.B. 233, per Lord Denning M.R. at 245–246; *Fearns v Anglo-Dutch Paint and Chemical Co
Ltd* [2010] EWHC 2366 (Ch) at [15].
[138] *Townrow v Benson* (1818) 3 Madd. 203; *Fuller v Happy Shopper Markets Ltd* [2001] EWHC Ch
702; [2001] 2 Lloyd's Rep. 49.
[139] i.e. a clause in a contract entitling the promisee to exercise default remedies where the promisor
defaults in his obligations under a separate contract, whether with the promisee under the first contract
or with a third party. If proceedings are brought for the outstanding balance of the accelerated liability
the defendant will be able to assert his cross-claim in diminution of that liability if the conditions for
independent set-off are established, but that, of course, is quite different from the effect of the
substantive defence provided by transaction set-off which would enable the defendant to say that, to
the extent of his set-off, the promisee could not rely on failure to pay as entitling him to exercise his
remedies. See paras 7–37 and 7–47 et seq., below.

available to the promisee, and the promisor's only resort is to such other forms of equitable relief as may be available, e.g. relief against forfeiture. Thirdly, since set-off is a cross-claim it can be answered with a plea that it is time-barred under the Limitation Act 1980.[140] Fourthly, the debtor is not permitted to set-off against a claim by the creditor's assignee a cross-claim arising after the debtor received notice of the assignment,[141] whereas a substantive defence is an inherent qualification of the rights assigned and the fact that default by the assignor giving rise to the defence did not occur until after the debtor received the notice of assignment does not preclude him from pleading it against the assignee.[142]

The procedural character of set-off has no adverse effect on the defendant so long as the claimant does not exercise any self-help remedy but proceeds solely by action, for set-off then protects the defendant both as to the amount of the judgment and as to costs. But against self-help independent set-off gives no protection. Two simple illustrations will demonstrate the significance of the point. In each case it is assumed that the contract does not itself, either expressly or by implication, make the promise and the counter-promise mutually dependent or confer on the debtor a right to combine accounts.

7–37 *Example 1* C agrees to lend D £12,000, repayable by 12 half-yearly instalments of £1,000 each. The loan agreement provides that on default in payment of any one instalment the full outstanding balance shall immediately become due. D, who under a totally unconnected transaction has previously sold goods to C at a price of £600 which C has not paid, pays the first instalment due under the loan agreement but deducts the £600 from the second instalment and remits the balance of £400 to C. In making this deduction D commits a breach of the loan agreement which entitles C to invoke the acceleration clause and call up the outstanding balance of £10,600. C invokes the clause and then sues D for the £10,600. In those proceedings D can set-off his cross-claim for £600 by way of independent set-off. That cross-claim did not reduce D's liability under the loan agreement so as to entitle him to withhold payment of it; the cross-claim could be enforced only by set-off in C's action or by separate action, and was thus ineffective to prevent the triggering of the acceleration clause.

7–38 *Example 2* O supplies equipment to H under a hire-purchase agreement which empowers O Ltd to terminate the agreement and repossess the goods if H fails to pay an instalment of the total price within 14 days of the due date. Shortly afterwards O enters into a separate hire-purchase agreement with H pursuant to which O delivers different equipment to which he has no title. Upon discovering this, H demands repayment of the instalments paid under the second agreement and, when repayment is not forthcoming, deducts the amount from an instalment due under the first agreement. This he is not entitled to do, and if the amount due under the first agreement remains unpaid for more than 14 days O can terminate the agreement and repossess the equipment. If O brings proceedings to recover the arrears H can set-off his cross-claim as a pro tanto defence to the claim but cannot recover the equipment unless he obtains relief against forfeiture.

In the above cases, the creditor exercised self-help remedies—acceleration of liability in the one case, termination and repossession in the other—against which

---

[140] See para.7–72, below.
[141] See para.7–70, below.
[142] See para.7–70, below.

the debtor's right of set-off was no protection. But where the creditor exercises no self-help remedies and institutes proceedings for both the amount due and non-monetary relief consequent on default in payment, a set-off sufficient to extinguish the amount due (whether or not claimed by the plaintiff in addition to the non-monetary relief) would seem to entitle the defendant to have the claim dismissed.[143]

Independent set-off may be pleaded in addition to or in lieu of a substantive defence

A defendant who has a substantive defence to a claim for payment may nevertheless decide not to invoke it and rely simply on a right of independent set-off; or he may plead the substantive defence with an alternative plea of set-off in case the first plea is unsuccessful. In order for set-off to be available under the rules established by the Statutes of Set-Off, five conditions must be satisfied.

7–39

Conditions of entitlement to independent set-off

(1) Both claim and cross-claim must be for sums of money or for relief based on the non-payment of money

It is, of course, inherent in all forms of set-off that they concern the setting of one money claim against another. However, it is not essential that the claim should itself be for money; it suffices that it is a claim for relief based on the non-payment of money, e.g. specific performance[144] or forfeiture of a lease.

7–40

(2) Both claim and cross-claim must be for debts

Independent set-off is confined to debts, so that both claim and cross-claim must be liquidated or ascertained with certainty at the time of pleading.[145] However, it has been held that if the claim is by nature a liquidated claim, e.g. is for agreed hire charges, the fact that the amount is in dispute does not prevent it from being asserted by way of independent set-off.[146]

7–41

Equity regards beneficial ownership of a liquidated claim as sufficient for independent set-off even if the bare legal title was in another, and applies the Statutes of Set-Off by analogy.[147]

---

[143] See para.7–52, below.

[144] *BICC Plc v Burndy Corp* [1985] Ch. 232. While the presence of an independent set-off is clearly a factor to take into account in relation to the court's discretionary decision whether or not to award specific performance, it seems odd that it is a complete defence, since until judgment the set-off is not a substantive defence to the claim on which specific performance is based. The dissenting judgment of Kerr L.J. to this effect is to be preferred in relation to independent set-off. See para.7–52, below.

[145] *Hanak v Green* [1958] 2 Q.B. 9, per Morris L.J. at 17; *Stooke v Taylor* (1880) 5 Q.B.D. 569, per Cockburn J. at 575; and see para.7–10, above. Claims for restitution of a liquidated amount (*Lagos v Grunwaldt* [1910] 1 K.B. 41, 48; *Biggerstaff v Rowatt's Wharf Ltd* [1896] 2 Ch. 93) and for liquidated damages (*Axel Johnson Petroleum AB v MG Mineral Group AG* [1992] 1 W.L.R. 270, 272 (CA)) can also be the subject of independent set-off.

[146] *Aectra Refining and Manufacturing Inc v Exmar NV* [1994] 1 W.L.R. 1634.

[147] See paras 7–04 and 7–10, above.

(3)   Both debts must be due at the time of pleading and judgment

7–42   In contrast to transaction set-off or insolvency set-off, there is clear authority that independent set-off is available only where both claim and cross-claim are due at the commencement of the action.[148] Neither a future claim nor a contingent claim may be set-off against a present debt. Accordingly an unmatured note may not be set-off against a deposit that has become repayable to the maker of the note, still less may a contingent claim against the creditor as surety be set-off against the debt due to the creditor, except in bankruptcy or by contract. Moreover, the cross-claim must not only be due at the time of pleading but must still be outstanding at the time of judgment.[149]

(4)   The claim and cross-claim must be mutual

7–43   By this is meant that the two claims must be between the same parties in the same right. So a purely joint liability cannot be pleaded by way of set-off against a several debt.[150] Originally, statutory set-off required identity of legal ownership of the claim and cross-claim.[151] Thus, if a debtor is sued in respect of a debt owed by him personally, he cannot seek to set-off a debt owed to him as trustee for a beneficiary.[152] However, this is qualified in two ways. First, where a claim is held on trust or subject to an equitable assignment, the debtor cannot assert an independent set-off in relation to a cross-claim which arose after he had notice of the trust or assignment.[153] Secondly, as described above,[154] equity acts by analogy to the Statutes of Set-off and permits independent set-off between a debtor whose debt is held on trust and the beneficiary of that trust. Thus, where a trustee sues to enforce a debt held by him on trust for a beneficiary, the debtor can rely on independent set-off in respect of a debt owed by the beneficiary,[155] and, if a debtor is sued in respect of a debt owed by him personally he could rely on independent set-off in respect of a debt held on trust for him.[156] However, the existence of the trust must be clear for these propositions to apply. Where the trust is disputed and the assertion of the trust involves the taking of accounts to establish whether the alleged beneficiary does indeed have a cross-claim against the plaintiff, there will be no set-off.[157] Similar reasoning has been applied in various decisions concerning banks, so that a bank cannot refuse to pay a

---

[148] *Richards v James* (1848) 2 Exch. 471. For argument against this rule, see para.7–72, below.
[149] *Briscoe v Hill* (1842) 10 M. & W. 735, per Parke B. at 738.
[150] *Vulliamy v Noble* (1817) 3 Mer. 593, per Lord Eldon L.C. at 618.
[151] *Tucker v Tucker* (1833) 4 B. & Ad. 745, per Littledale J. at 751; *Forster v Wilson* (1843) 12 M.&W. 191, 203.
[152] *Phillips v Howell* [1901] 2 Ch. 773.
[153] For further discussion in the context of assignment, see paras 7–67 et seq., below. In relation to trust, see *Barclays Bank Ltd v Quistclose Investments Ltd* [1970] A.C. 597 HL.
[154] See para.7–41, above. *In Re Whitehouse & Co* (1878) 9 Ch. D. 595, 597.
[155] *Thornton v Maynard* (1874-75) L.R. 10 C.P. 695.
[156] *Cochrane v Greene* (1860) 9 C.B. N.S. 448.
[157] *Re Willis Percival & Co Ex p. Morier* (1879) 12 Ch.D. 491.

customer whose account is in credit merely because it is arguable, but not clear, that the account in credit is a nominee account for a person who is indebted to the bank.[158]

Mutuality is also required in relation to the capacity in which each party owes and is owed the claim and cross-claim. Thus a claim by a beneficiary to recover trust property from a trustee cannot be the subject of independent set-off in relation to a debt owed by the beneficiary to the trustee personally.[159]

(5)   Both claim and cross-claim must be subject to determination by the court

The independent set-off mechanism cannot operate if the claim is to be tried in court proceedings but the proceedings on the cross-claim have been stayed and referred to arbitration pursuant to an arbitration agreement.[160] The reverse also applies, so that where the claim is being considered by an arbitrator but the cross-claim does not fall within the arbitrator's jurisdiction, independent set-off cannot operate.[161] The question of jurisdiction is a matter of interpretation of the arbitration agreement.[162] **7–44**

Further, if the cross-claim is the subject of an exclusive jurisdiction clause conferring jurisdiction on another EU Member State, art.23 of the Brussels 1 Regulation[163] provides that the English court has no jurisdiction, and so such a cross-claim cannot form an independent set-off.[164] If the jurisdiction is not that of a Member State, so that the Brussels 1 Regulation does not apply, the court has discretion to stay the cross-claim, and so will not permit it to be raised as an independent set-off unless a stay would be refused.[165] However, in either case the

---

[158] *Bhogal v Punjab National Bank* [1988] 2 All E.R. 296; *Uttamchandani v Central Bank of India* (1989) 139 N.L.J. 222 CA; *Saudi Arabian Monetary Agency v Dresdner Bank AG* [2004] EWCA Civ 1074; [2005] 1 Lloyd's Rep. 12 at [23].

[159] *Whitaker v Rush* 27 E.R. 272, (1761) Amb 40; *Stumore v Campbell & Co* [1892] 1 Q.B. 314; *Talbot v Frere* (1878) 9 Ch. D. 568; *Lloyds Bank NZA Ltd v National Safety Council of Australia Victorian Division (in liq)* (1993) 10 A.C.S.R. 572.

[160] *Aectra Refining and Manufacturing Inc v Exmar NV* [1994] 1 W.L.R. 1634.

[161] *Metal Distributors (UK) Ltd v ZCCM Investment Holding Plc* [2005] EWHC 156 (Comm).

[162] *Metal Distributors (UK) Ltd v ZCCM Investment Holding Plc* at [18]; *Econet Satellite Services Ltd v Vee Networks Ltd* [2006] EWHC 1664 (Comm) at [17]. It is more likely that the cross-claim will fall within the arbitration clause if the set-off is a transaction set-off rather than an independent set-off, see *Norscot Rig Management PVT Ltd v Essar Oilfields Services Ltd* [2010] EWHC 195 (Comm) at [18 (iii)].

[163] Council Regulation (EC) 44/2001 of December 22, 2000 on jurisdiction and the recognition and enforcement of judgments in civil and commercial matters. Art.17 of the Convention on Jurisdiction and Enforcement of Judgments in Civil and Commercial Matters (Brussels, September 27 1968; EC 46 (1976); Cmd 7395)) and Art.17 of the Lugano Convention (the Convention on Jurisdiction and the Recognition and Enforcement of Judgments in Civil and Commercial Matters ([2009] O.J. L147/5) apply in similar terms to a choice of Danish court, and a choice of Icelandic, Norwegian and Swiss court respectively.

For a detailed discussion of the operation of this article, see Albert Venn Dicey and John Humphrey Carlile Morris in Lawrence Collins (ed.), *Dicey, Morris and Collins on the conflict of laws*, 15th edn (London: Sweet & Maxwell, 2012), Ch.12 s.2.

[164] *Aectra Refining and Manufacturing Inc v Exmar NV* [1994] 1 W.L.R. 1634, 1651. cf. Case 23/78 *Nikolaus Meeth v Glacetal Sarl* [1979] 1 C.M.L.R. 520.

[165] *Glencore Grain Ltd. v Agros Trading Co* [1999] 2 Lloyd's Rep. 410 CA at [21].

court can, if it considers it necessary to protect the cross-claimant, stay the proceedings on the claim or stay execution pending resolution of the cross-claim in the other jurisdiction.[166]

(6)   The circumstances must not be such as would make it inequitable for the defendant to plead set-off

7–45   Even where independent set-off would otherwise be available, it will be denied where there is an equity to prevent it, as where the rights, though legally mutual, are not equitably mutual[167] or where there is an express or implied agreement between the parties precluding set-off.[168]

Significance of independent set-off

7–46   Independent set-off has become of diminished importance with the expansion of transaction set-off. There is, however, one case in which recourse to the rules of independent set-off[169] is necessary, namely where the claim and cross-claim, whether arising under the same or separate transactions, are unconnected, so that the cross-claim does not satisfy the requirement of equity that it should be inseparably connected with the claim. So, for example, in an action for money due under a bill of exchange a liquidated sum payable to the defendant under a transaction unconnected with that for which the bill was given may, it is thought, be set-off at law under the rules established by the Statutes of Set-Off[170] though it cannot be set-off in equity.

5.   TRANSACTION (EQUITABLE) SET-OFF

(i)   General principles

Nature of transaction set-off

7–47   Transaction set-off is that form of equitable set-off which arises where the claim and cross-claim are closely connected. The term "transaction set-off" can also include abatement, which is discussed in more detail below,[171] and which is a common law doctrine with specific limitations. There is considerable overlap between equitable set-off and abatement, and in most cases the former will

---

[166] *Aectra Refining and Manufacturing Inc v Exmar NV* [1994] 1 W.L.R. 1634, 1652. For the principles on which a court will issue such a stay, see *AB Contractors Ltd v Flaherty Bros Ltd* (1978) 16 B.L.R. 8.

[167] *Re Whitehouse & Co* (1878) 9 Ch.D. 595, per Jessel M.R. at 597.

[168] See para.7–73, below.

[169] Embodying rules previously applied under the Statutes of Set-Off, which required that both claim and cross-claim be legal, and those applied by equity by analogy with the Statute, which looked to beneficial rather than legal title. See paras 7–04 and 7–10, above.

[170] See para.7–57, below.

[171] See paras 7–62 et seq., below.

include the latter, so that there is no need to plead abatement separately.[172] In this section, the discussion is focused on equitable set-off, which is to be contrasted with the right of independent set-off given by equity by analogy with the Statutes of Set-Off as previously described. Historically transaction, or equitable, set-off was perceived as procedural in character, so that it operated not as a substantive defence but, like independent set-off, as a means of reducing the amount for which the plaintiff was entitled to judgment. However, this perception changed in the light of the decision of the Court of Appeal in *Hanak v Green*,[173] and it is now clear that it provides a substantive defence, despite the fact that the claim is not actually extinguished before judgment (or earlier agreement).[174] What remains unclear is the manner of its exercise and the precise analysis of how it operates.[175]

The practical effects of transaction set-off operating as a substantive defence are numerous and arise in a number of different contexts. First, and very significantly, it can be relied upon as a defence to default, which would otherwise give rise to a self-help remedy on the part of the creditor. Secondly, it is no bar to the exercise of the set-off in proceedings that the cross-claim is subject to arbitration or a foreign jurisdiction.[176] The question of whether a transaction set-off based on a cross-claim under a separate contract is justiciable by an arbitrator depends on the scope of the arbitration agreement, [177] but the nature of the set-off and the consequent closeness of the cross-claim to the claim make it more likely that it will fall within the scope of that agreement unless excluded by clear words, than if only independent set-off were available.[178] Thirdly, transaction set-off can be asserted against an assignee of the claim at any time, even if it arises after the debtor has notice of the assignment.[179] Fourthly, the fact that a cross-claim is subject to a time bar which bar the remedy but does not extinguish the claim does not stop it being available as a transaction set-off, but would prevent it being relied upon as an independent set-off.[180] The position is different where there is a time bar which extinguishes the claim.[181] Fifthly, once transaction set-off has arisen in respect of a claim, interest will only run on any

---

[172] For situations where a claimant may prefer to rely on abatement rather than equitable set-off, see para.7–65, below.

[173] *Hanak v Green* [1958] 2 Q.B. 9.

[174] *Fearns v Anglo-Dutch Paint and Chemical Co Ltd* [2010] EWHC 2366 (Ch).

[175] See paras 7–54 et seq., below.

[176] *Aectra Refining and Manufacturing Inc v Exmar NV* [1994] 1 W.L.R. 1634, 1649–1650; *Ronly Holdings v JSC Zestafoni G Nikoladze Ferroalloy Plant* [2004] EWHC 1354 (Comm) at [33]; *Bim Kemi AB v Blackburn Chemicals Ltd* [2001] EWCA Civ 457 at [9]; *Prekons Insaat Sanayi AS v Rowlands Castle Contracting Group Ltd* [2006] EWHC 1367 (Comm).

[177] *Econet Satellite Services Ltd v Vee Networks Ltd* [2006] EWHC 1664 (Comm), where the governing UNCITRAL Arbitration Rules expressly excluded set-off arising from a different contract from that giving rise to the arbitration.

[178] *Norscot Rig Management PVT Ltd v Essar Oilfields Services Ltd* [2010] EWHC 195 (Comm) at [18 (iii)].

[179] See para.7–70, below.

[180] *Henriksens Rederi A/S v THZ Rolimpex (The Brede)* [1974] Q.B. 233 CA; *Westdeutsche Landesbank Girozentrale v Islington LBC* [1994] 4 All E.R. 890, 943–945; *Filross Securities Ltd v Midgeley* (1999) 31 H.L.R. 465, 472 CA; *Philip Collins Ltd v Davis* [2000] 3 All E.R. 808, 831; *Cheltenham BC v Laird* [2009] EWHC 1253 (QB) at [459]; *Miom 1 Ltd, The Isle of Man Steampacket Co Ltd v Sea Echo ENE (No.2)* [2011] EWHC 2715 (Admlty); [2012] 1 Lloyds Rep. 140.

[181] *Aries Tanker Corp v Total Transport Ltd* [1977] 1 W.L.R. 185 HL. See discussion at para.7–54, below.

balance once the set-off is taken into account.[182] Sixthly, where a counterclaim amounts to a transaction set-off, the court is unlikely to order the defendant to provide security for costs of that counterclaim,[183] while if the defendant is seeking security for the costs of the claim, the fact that the defence is a transaction set-off can be a reason in favour of awarding security for costs.[184]

It should also be remembered that transaction set-off can be relied upon as a procedural defence in the same way as independent set-off if the latter does not apply because one or both of the claims are unliquidated. Although this does not arise specifically from its nature as a substantive defence, a number of cases concerning the requirements for transaction set-off have arisen in this context.[185]

Prerequisites of equitable set-off

7–48   This section, and those following, deal specifically with equitable set-off as opposed to abatement, which is discussed below,[186] although "transaction set-off", strictly speaking, encompasses both concepts. Therefore, the term "equitable set-off" will be used. There are various general requirements for equitable set-off. Even where there would otherwise be a right of set-off it may be excluded by agreement.[187]

(1)   The requirement based on close connection between the claim and the cross-claim

7–49   The cross-claim must be so closely connected with the claim as to render it inequitable to allow the plaintiff to obtain judgment on his claim without giving credit for the cross-claim.[188] Earlier authorities referred to the requirement that the cross-claim "impeach" the claim[189] but more recently this label has been discarded as unhelpful and replaced by the "inseparable connection" test.[190] Even this test has been called "not all that helpful" by Rix L.J. in the most recent Court of Appeal authority on the point.[191] He stressed that there were two elements to the test of whether the relevant connection exists: the formal element of "close

---

[182] *Newman v Cook* [1963] V.R. 659, 676; *Kiteley v Allison* Unreported December 4, 1994 QBD; *Barnett v Peter Cox Group Ltd* (1995) 45 Con.L.R. 131 CA; *Connaught Restaurants Ltd v Indoor Leisure Ltd* [1994] 1 W.L.R. 501, 503.

[183] *Pimlott v Meregrove Holdings* [2003] EWHC 1766 (QB).

[184] *Autoweld Systems Ltd v Kito Enterprises LLC* [2010] EWCA Civ 1469. It should be borne in mind that any decision in relation to security for costs is always very fact specific.

[185] For example, *Hanak v Green* [1958] 2 Q.B. 9; *Geldof Metaalconstructie NV v Simon Carves Ltd* [2010] EWCA Civ 667.

[186] See paras 7–62 et seq., below.

[187] See para.7–73, below.

[188] *Rawson v Samuel* (1841) Cr. & Ph. 161; *Hanak v Green* [1958] 2 Q.B. 9; *The Teno* [1977] 2 Lloyd's Rep. 289; *British Anzani (Felixstowe) Ltd v International Maritime Management (UK) Ltd* [1980] Q.B. 137.

[189] *Rawson v Samuel* (1841) Cr. & Ph. 161, 179.

[190] *Bim Kemi v Blackburn Chemicals Ltd* [2001] 2 Lloyd's Rep. 92, 99–101, adopting the speech of Lord Brandon in *Bank of Boston Connecticut v European Grain and Shipping Ltd* [1989] A.C. 1056 at 1102–1103. See also *Benford Ltd v Lopecan* [2004] EWHC 1897 (Comm) at [14]; *National Westminster Bank Plc v Rabobank Nederland* [2005] EWHC 1368 (Comm) at [45]; *S & D Property Investments Ltd v Nisbet* [2009] EWHC 1726 (Ch).

[191] *Geldof Metaalconstructie NV v Simon Carves Ltd* [2010] EWCA Civ 667 at [43(iii)].

connection", which is governed by "principle and not discretion",[192] and the "functional" element, namely that it would be unjust to enforce the claim without taking the cross-claim into account, because the "ultimate rationale of the regime is equity".[193] Given that equitable set-off operates as a substantive defence, it is clearly important that the tests for its availability are as clear as possible, since this determination will often have to be made quickly, either by the parties (to decide whether a self-help remedy is available) or by a tribunal in an interlocutory situation.[194] Thus it is appropriate for the test to be one of principle, rather than discretion. It is certainly possible to extract principles governing both parts of the test from the authorities, although the weight given to these principles is very fact specific, leaving the position less certain than would be desirable. If parties wish to know for certain whether or not set-off would be available to prevent the exercise of a self-help remedy, the only fail-safe way is to specify its availability, or to exclude it, contractually.

The principles governing the "formal" element are clearest where the claim and cross-claim arise from the same contract. Although there is longstanding authority that the mere fact that the cross-claim arises out of the same transaction as the claim is not by itself sufficient to attract a right of equitable set-off[195]; there will usually be a set-off[196] unless the case falls within one of several specific classes of claim, or there are special circumstances.[197] The specific classes, which are considered below, concern freight, rent and negotiable instruments or other payment instructions. Relevant special circumstances are where the claim and the cross-claim relate to different aspects or parts of the transaction, and are temporally or geographically separate. An example of the former is where the debtor on a claim relating to the supply of goods or services receives payment from a sub-supply of those goods and services immediately, when the cross-claim was for an unrelated breach of the supply contract arising some time after the claim.[198] An example of the latter is *Sankey v The Helping Hands Group Plc*,[199] where a claim arising from breach of a promise to grant shares in a subsidiary set up to market a product in one part of the world, could not be set-off against sums due in respect of a license to market it in another part of the world, as well as relating to exploitation of the relevant invention in very different ways.[200]

It is not a barrier to set-off that the cross-claim arises out of a separate contract or other cause of action, but the formal part of the test operates in a rather different way. In this situation the close connection must be established positively; again, certain principles can be extracted from the case law. There is

7–50

---

[192] *Geldof Metaalconstructie NV v Simon Carves Ltd* [2010] EWCA Civ 667 at [43(v)].

[193] *Geldof Metaalconstructie NV v Simon Carves Ltd* [2010] EWCA Civ 667 at [43(v)].

[194] For example, in an application for an interim arbitral award, see *SL Sethia Liners Ltd v Naviagro Maritime Corp (The Kostas Melas)* [1981] 1 Lloyd's Rep. 18; *Modern Trading Co Ltd v Swale Building and Construction Ltd* (1990) 24 Con. L.R. 59.

[195] *Government of Newfoundland v Newfoundland Ry Co* (1888) 13 App. Cas. 199 at 212.

[196] Unless it is contractually excluded.

[197] *Geldof Metaalconstructie NV v Simon Carves Ltd* [2010] EWCA Civ 667.

[198] See the argument of Simon Brown L.J. in *Esso Petroleum Co Ltd v Milton* [1997] 1 W.L.R. 938, 951–952; *Nextcall Telecom Plc v British Telecommunications Plc* Unreported December 19, 2000 QBD.

[199] *Sankey v The Helping Hands Group Plc* Unreported October 5, 1999 CA.

[200] The weakness of the cross-claim seems also to have been a factor in the decision, see para.7–51, below.

likely to be a close enough connection when the claim and the cross-claim arise out of the same transaction,[201] even where one claim is for breach of contract and the other is for another cause of action such as misrepresentation[202] or restitution.[203] Similar reasoning applies where the "transaction" is actually the business relationship between the parties, so that where a cross-claim was for sums due by a former partner to the partnership, this was held to be sufficiently connected to a claim for damages for breach of the agreement made in the course of the partner leaving the partnership.[204] In a case which seems to illustrate the extreme boundary of the principle, a cross-claim for damages for breach of a tenancy agreement in relation to premises from which the claimant's son had operated a veterinary practice was held to be sufficiently closely connected to a claim for money due under a contract for the sale of the practice to the landlord.[205] On the other side of the line are a series of cases in which cross-claims for losses suffered from contracts being in breach of competition law have not been permitted to be set-off against claims for sums due under that contract.[206] Further, where the claim and cross-claim relate to separate transactions arising out of single trading relationship between the parties, this, without more, will not be a sufficiently close connection.[207] Thus, equitable set-off was not available where the claim and cross-claim arose out of insurance contracts negotiated separately by the parties, even though they were part of an "overall programme".[208] However, where there is an overarching supply or distribution agreement which is breached, the resulting cross-claim is likely to be sufficiently closely connected to a claim for breach of a contract entered into as a result of the overarching agreement.[209]

Other factors relevant to closeness of connection where the claim and cross-claim do not arise from the same contract are whether the contracts were negotiated together or separately,[210] the closeness, or otherwise, of the subject

---

[201] See, for example, *British Anzani (Felixstowe) Ltd v International Marine Management (UK) Ltd* [1980] Q.B. 137, where the claim was for rent due under a lease and the cross-claim was for breach of an agreement to enter into that lease. Similar reasoning was used in the Scottish case of *Inveresk Plc v Tullis Russell Papermakers Ltd* [2010] UKSC 19.

[202] *National Westminster Bank Plc v Rabobank Nederland* [2005] EWHC 1368 (Comm).

[203] *Hanak v Green* [1958] 2 Q.B. 9.

[204] *Simms v Conlon* [2004] EWHC 585 (Ch).

[205] *Bankes v Jarvis* [1903] 1 K.B. 509.

[206] *Nextcall Telecom Plc v British Telecommunications Plc* Unreported December 19, 2000 QBD at [68]; *3 Com Europe Ltd v Medea Vertriebs GmbH* [2004] UKCLR 356. See also *Scottish & Newcastle Plc v Bond* Unreported March 25, 1997 QBD; *Star Rider Ltd v Inntrepreneur Pub Co Ltd* [1998] 60 E.G. 140; *Gibbs Mew Plc v Graham Gemmell* [1999] E.C.C. 97 CA; *Courage Ltd v Crehan* [1999] E.C.C. 455 CA. In this line of cases, which relates to whether a claim that a "tie" to a particular brewery is contrary to competition law can be set-off against a claim for rent by the brewery landlord, the lack of close connection is reasonably apparent.

[207] *Esso Petroleum Co Ltd v Milton* [1997] 1 W.L.R. 938, 951; *Bim Kemi AB v Blackburn Chemicals Ltd* [2001] EWCA Civ 457 at [30].

[208] *Peninsular and Oriental Steam Navigation Co v Youell* [1997] 2 Lloyd's Rep. 136.

[209] *Dole Dried Fruit and Nut Co v Trustin Kerwood Ltd* [1990] 2 Lloyd's Rep. 309; *Benford Ltd v Lopecan* [2004] 2 Lloyd's Rep. 618.

[210] *Watson v Mid Wales Rly Co* (1866–67) L.R. 2 C.P. 593, 598; *Peninsular and Oriental Steam Navigation Co v Youell* [1997] 2 Lloyd's Rep. 136, 144; *Geldof Metaalconstructie NV v Simon Carves Ltd* [2010] EWCA Civ 667 at [10], [44].

matter of the contracts,[211] and the actions of the party opposing the set-off in treating the claim and cross-claim as linked.[212] The actions of the party relying on the set-off are, not surprisingly, irrelevant in this regard as a party should not be allowed to "manufacture" a connection ex post.

The "functional" element of the test, that is, whether it is manifestly unjust to **7–51** enforce the claim without taking into account the counterclaim, is even more fact dependent. Again, certain relevant factors can be deduced from the cases. One is the strength of the cross-claim, and, possibly, also the ease with which it can be calculated.[213] Another is the conduct of the cross-claimant, who will not be permitted to rely on his own wrongful conduct to create a set-off.[214]

The "close connection" test just discussed has its drawbacks, chiefly its uncertainty of application. The importance of uncertainty, however, varies according to the context. A party may seek to rely on transaction set-off in the course of litigation, maybe as a defence to an application for summary judgment. Here, whether equitable set-off is available largely affects the cash flow of the parties.[215] Where it is relied upon as a defence to a self-help remedy, however, the stakes are much higher. The party purporting to exercise the remedy has to make a decision as to whether there is a defence to default or not. If it makes the "wrong" decision, it is at risk of being in repudiatory breach itself or at least of losing the protection it clearly wanted when it negotiated the self-help remedy as part of the contract. There are various possible ways of dealing with this potentially significant uncertainty. As discussed later, the courts have dealt with uncertainty as to the quantum and even the merits of an unliquidated equitable set-off by permitting a party to rely on a self-help remedy exercised reasonably and in good faith, even if it turns out later not to have been justified.[216] This approach could be extended to uncertainty as to whether there is sufficient close connection between the claim and cross-claim. Secondly, the best way for parties to achieve certainty is to include provisions in their contracts specifying whether or not set-off is available. The general law is then just a default position against which parties contract. Viewed in this light, the best way forward for the general law is to proceed along the lines of firm principle, so that parties can predict as

---

[211] *Bim Kemi AB v Blackburn Chemicals Ltd* [2001] EWCA Civ 457 at [35]; *Geldof Metaalconstructie NV v Simon Carves Ltd* [2010] EWCA Civ 667 at [47].

[212] *Geldof Metaalconstructie NV v Simon Carves Ltd* [2010] EWCA Civ 667 at [46]; *Addax Bank BSC (c) v Wellesley Partners LLP* [2010] EWHC 1904 (QB) at [44]–[45].

[213] *Esso Petroleum Co Ltd v Milton* [1997] 1 W.L.R. 938, 952, per Thorpe L.J.; *Star Rider Ltd v Inntrepreneur Pub Co* [1998] 1 E.G.L.R. 53; *Antiquesportfolio.com.plc v Rodney Fitch & Co Ltd* [2001] E.C.D.R. 5 ChD.

[214] For a particularly blatant example, see *Bluestorm Ltd v Portvale Holdings Ltd* [2004] EWCA Civ 289. See also *Smith v Bridgend* [2001] UKHL 58; [2002] 1 A.C. 336 at [78] where a contractual right of set-off was void because it created an unregistered charge, it was held that it was no part of equity to provide, via equitable set-off, an alternative security. Mere unattractive or unexplained conduct will not necessarily prevent an equitable set-off, see *Mellham Ltd v Burton (Collector of Taxes)* [2006] UKHL 6 at [28].

[215] The purpose of the test here is to distinguish between situations where a creditor should be entitled to be paid its debt immediately, rather than have to wait for the determination of an unliquidated cross-claim, which may be far from certain to succeed, and situations where it is unfair for the cross-claimant to have to pay the whole of the claim upfront since the claimant will have to pay much of the money back when the cross-claim is eventually determined.

[216] See para.7–56, below.

far as possible ex ante whether they are in a "grey area" or not, so that it is clear whether the transaction costs required for negotiating contractual provisions are worth incurring.[217]

Of course, where the two contracts are not closely connected and transaction set-off is not available, the cross-claimant is not wholly devoid of protection, but will have to fall back on independent set-off or its equitable analogy, for which purpose it is necessary that both claims be liquidated, and which cannot be used as a substantive defence.

(2) Cross-claim must be based on non-payment of money

7–52   The second requirement is that the claim be for money or for relief based on the non-payment of money. It had at one time been thought that unless the claim was for money set-off, was not available at all, even if the relief claimed was based on the non-payment of money, e.g. forfeiture or specific performance. However, in *BICC Plc v Burndy Corp*[218] the Court of Appeal held, by a majority,[219] that it sufficed that the claim there made for specific performance was based on the non-payment of money, and that if this requirement were satisfied there was no reason why set-off should not be pleaded as a defence to a claim for specific performance, whether the set-off was legal or equitable. In relation to equitable (transaction) set-off the majority view seems correct, for as Dillon L.J. cogently observed:

> "I cannot see that it can make any difference in substance whether the claim for the other relief is joined in one action with the claim for payment to which the set-off is a valid defence, or whether only the other relief is claimed, leaving the claim to payment to be raised in a subsequent action or to be resolved by the application of the set-off."[220]

However, this cannot be true of legal (independent) set-off, which does not constitute a substantive defence. The set-off in question in *BICC v Burndy Corp* was independent set-off, as the claims were not sufficiently connected for transaction set-off to be available.[221] Accordingly, in relation to this form of set-off Kerr L.J. was surely right in concluding that the defendant was not entitled to relief as a matter of right and that if relief was to be given it could only be because the court was entitled to take the existence of the cross-claim into account in exercising its discretion to refuse the equitable remedy of specific performance.

---

[217] Of course, there are already many standard form contracts which exclude (or include) rights of set-off. Even in relation to commercial parties it is clear that these are, and should be, subject to the reasonableness test under the Unfair Contract Terms Act 1977, see below para.7–73.

[218] *BICC Plc v Burndy Corp* [1985] 1 Ch. 232.

[219] Kerr L.J. dissented, holding that set-off could be asserted only as a defence to a claim for money, and that if the claim was for non-monetary relief, such as specific performance, the existence of the cross-claim went only to the exercise of the court's discretion in equity.

[220] *BICC Plc v Burndy Corp* [1985] 1 Ch. 232 at 249. It is not necessary that the right to payment shall have accrued due at the date of commencement of proceedings. See para.7–72, below.

[221] *BICC Plc v Burndy Corp* [1985] 1 Ch. 232, 249.

In the case of equitable set-off the ability to set-off a money claim against non-monetary relief based on a default in payment is not confined to judicial relief but extends to set-off against a landlord's right of distress.[222]

(3) There must be mutuality

Thirdly, the claims must be mutual, that is, due from the same parties in the same right.[223] This view has had recent support from the decision of the Court of Appeal in *Smith v Muscat*.[224] In this case, a tenant had an equitable set-off for damages for disrepair against rent due to his landlord. The reversion was sold to a second landlord, and the question was whether the tenant could assert this set-off against the second landlord, who had the right to sue for the past rent under s.141 of the Law of Property Act 1925. Buxton L.J. stated clearly that equitable set-off of a cross-claim is only available when it is owed by the same party as that making the claim,[225] and the Court of Appeal decided the case on the basis that the second landlord took, as assignee, subject to the equitable set-off which was available against the first landlord.[226] This reasoning has been heavily criticised[227] on the basis that the second landlord was not an assignee in equity, nor under s.136 of the Law of Property Act, but instead sued as legal owner of the property, and therefore the principle of taking subject to equities did not apply.[228] On the basis of this criticism it has been argued that, although lack of mutuality is usually a good reason for equitable set-off not being available, there is no absolute bar and in appropriate cases equitable set-off could be available.[229] It certainly appears that lack of mutuality may not be an absolute bar in Australia.[230] However, the tenor of recent cases in England is against this. In *Edlington Properties Ltd v JH Fenner & Co Ltd*[231] the Court of Appeal held that the decision in *Smith v Muscat* was limited to set-off against rent accruing before the reversion was transferred, and thus confirmed that the set-off in that case only

7–53

---

[222] *Eller v Grovecrest Investments Ltd* [1995] Q.B. 272; *Fuller v Happy Shopper Markets Ltd* [2001] EWHC Ch 702; [2001] 2 Lloyd's Rep. 49.

[223] *Middleton v Pollock Ex p. Nugee* (1875) L.R. 20 Eq. 29.

[224] *Smith v Muscat* [2003] EWCA Civ 962. See also *R (on the application of Burkett) v Hammersmith and Fulham LBC* [2004] EWCA Civ 1317 at [58], per Brooke L.J.; *Edlington Properties Ltd v JH Fenner & Co Ltd* [2006] EWCA Civ 403 at [20].

[225] *Smith v Muscat* [2003] EWCA Civ 962 at [45]. It has to be said, however, that Buxton L.J.'s view of equitable set-off is much more restricted than that espoused in this book: he says that equitable set-off only operates as an incident of litigation at [44], and that the main purpose of equitable set-off (as opposed to independent set-off) is that it enables unliquidated claims to be set-off as well as liquidated claims at [39]. See para.7–54, below.

[226] See para.7–69, below.

[227] Derham, "Equitable set-off: a critique of Muscat v Smith" (2006) 122 L.Q.R. 469. See also Derham, *The Law of Set-off* (2010) paras 17.84–17.88.

[228] This is based on the decision of *Reeves v Pope* [1914] 2 K.B. 284 which was not cited in *Smith v Muscat*.

[229] Derham, "Equitable set-off: a critique of Muscat v Smith" (2006) 122 L.Q.R. 469, 477–478.

[230] *Murphy v Zamonex Pty Ltd* (1993) 31 N.S.W.L.R. 439 at 465; applied *Kendray v Hassall* [2001] N.T.S.C. 40; *Forsyth v Gibbs* [2008] Q.C.A. 103. See also Derham, *The Law of Set-off* (2010) paras 4.69–4.83.

[231] *Edlington Properties Ltd v JH Fenner & Co Ltd* [2006] EWCA Civ 403.

bound the second landlord by virtue of the assignment being subject to equities and not as a result of any relaxation of the requirement of mutuality.[232]

The mutuality required for equitable set-off is, not surprisingly, that of beneficial and not legal titles. Thus where a trustee sues to enforce a debt held by him on trust, the defendant may set-off a debt due from the beneficiary,[233] and where it is the beneficiary who is sued he may set-off a debt due from the claimant to the trustee and held on trust for him. As mentioned earlier,[234] the position is the same in relation to independent set-off, this being one example of where equity acts by analogy to the Statutes of Set-off. Of course, if the set-off relied upon is equitable set-off, in accordance with the usual rule, the debt must be so closely connected with the claim that the defendant beneficiary can show equitable grounds for being protected against the claim. Unlike independent set-off, however, equitable set-off operates as a substantive defence to a claim, so where a debt is held on trust, any equitable set-off arising in respect of it affects the beneficiary, even if it arises after the debtor has notice of the trust.[235]

It is submitted that where one of the claims is vested in a single creditor and the other in joint creditors, set-off is no more available in equity than at law,[236] and that the cases commonly relied on to support a right of set-off in such a case[237] did not concern set-off in the true sense at all but were decided on different grounds.[238]

The operation of equitable set-off as a substantive defence

7–54   As mentioned earlier,[239] there are a number of consequences which flow from the fact that equitable set-off is a substantive defence. These show that it takes effect as such at a time earlier than when judgment is given on the claim. However, the manner of its operation is still a matter for debate. There have been a number of dicta indicating that it operates by extinguishing or reducing the claim at the point at which it takes effect as a substantive defence[240]; if this were the case, the only amount due and owing after that point would be the balance and each separate

---

[232] See also *Lehman Brothers International (Europe) (in administration) v CRC Credit Fund Ltd* [2009] EWHC 3228 (Ch) at [331], where the reasoning seems to support the "lack of mutuality" analysis.

[233] *Bankes v Jarvis* [1903] 1 K.B. 549.

[234] Para.7–43, below.

[235] This is demonstrated by the cases involving an equitable assignment of a debt, see para.7–70 r.3.

[236] Except where the joint debt is also due severally (*Fletcher v Dyche* (1787) 2 Term Rep. 32).

[237] *Ex p. Stephens* (1805) 11 Ves. 24; *Vulliamy v Noble* (1817) 3 Mer. 593.

[238] *Middleton v Pollock Ex p. Knight* (1875) 20 L.R. Eq. 515, where Jessel M.R. pointed out (at 518–523) that *Ex p. Stephens* was decided not on set-off but on the ground that the right of set-off the defendant debtor would have enjoyed if she had asserted it in due time was concealed from her by the fraud of the creditors, and that *Vulliamy v Noble* was not a case of set-off as between a single debt on one side and a joint debt on the other but turned on an agreement between the parties by which the proceeds of securities giving rise to the single debt were to be applied in discharge of the joint obligation, leaving the single creditor entitled to payment of the balance. For criticism of this analysis, see Derham, *The Law of Set-off* (2010), paras 4.72–4.76.

[239] Para.7–47, below.

[240] See *Federal Commerce & Navigation Co Ltd v Molena Alpha Inc (The Nanfri)* [1978] 2 Q.B. 927, 974, per Lord Denning; *Eller v Grovecrest Investments Ltd* [1995] 1 Q.B. 272, 280–281 CA; *Fuller v Happy Shopper Markets Ltd* [2001] 2 Lloyd's Rep. 49 at [22]; *Safeway Stores Ltd v Interserve Project Services Ltd* [2005] EWHC 3085 (TCC) at [53]; *Mellham Ltd v Burton (Collector of Taxes)* [2006] UKHL 6 at [29]; *Altonwood Ltd v Crystal Palace FC (2000) Ltd* [2005] EWHC 292 (Ch) at [32];

claim would no longer exist. There is also some authority supporting the view that equitable set-off does not actually extinguish or reduce the claim at the point of operation, and that this can only take place at the point of judgment or agreement between the parties.[241]

In the last edition of this book, the view of Buxton L.J. in *Mellham v Burton*[242] and *Smith v Muscat*[243] was considered. He doubted that equitable set-off could be effective otherwise than as an "incident of litigation",[244] or that it could be used before litigation to justify paying less than is due,[245] and thus avoid triggering a "self-help" remedy on the part of the claimant. These views were challenged on the grounds that the predominant weight of authority was that equitable set-off was a substantive defence, which could be used as an answer to a self-help remedy,[246] and, in the light of the numerous dicta to this effect,[247] the conclusion was reached that equitable set-off could extinguish a claim before judgment, leaving the question open as to at what point this occurred.

More recently, the argument that equitable set-off extinguishes or reduces the claim before judgment has been heard and rejected by the court, although its operation as a substantive defence was confirmed and clarified. In the first instance decision of *Fearns v Anglo-Dutch Paint and Chemical Co Ltd*,[248] the issue concerned the precise timing at which the claim and cross-claim are converted into the same currency. Thus, unlike the other cases in which the dicta referred to above had taken place, this case was entirely on this specific point. Further, the arguments made in favour of the timing of the extinguishment or reduction of the claim are convincing both on grounds of principle and policy, and the conclusion on this point reached or assumed in previous editions of this book must now be rejected.

The main argument from authority relied upon in the *Fearns* case[249] was based on the House of Lords decision in *Aries Tanker Corp v Total Transport Ltd*.[250] That case concerned a time bar included in the Hague Rules, which had the unusual effect of extinguishing the liability as well as the remedy. The set-off[251]

Prekons Insaat Sanayi AS v Rowlands Castle Contracting Group Ltd [2006] EWHC 1367 (Comm) at [11], [28]. [30]. See also McCracken, *The Banker's Remedy of Set-Off* (2010), pp.140–142.

[241] *Aries Tanker Corp v Total Transport Ltd* [1977] 1 W.L.R. 185; *Fearns v Anglo Dutch Paint & Chemical Co* [2010] EWHC 2366 (Ch).

[242] *Mellham v Burton* [2003] EWCA Civ 173.

[243] *Smith v Muscat* [2003] EWCA Civ 962.

[244] *Smith v Muscat* [2003] EWCA Civ 962 at [44].

[245] *Mellham v Burton* [2003] EWCA Civ 173 at [10]–[12].

[246] *Federal Commerce & Navigation Co Ltd v Molena Alpha Inc (The Nanfri)* [1978] Q.B. 927, both per Lord Denning at 974 and per Goff L.J. at 982; *Aectra Refining and Manufacturing Inc v Exmar NV* [1994] 1 W.L.R. 1634, 1650; *Eller v Grovecrest Investments Ltd* [1995] 1 Q.B. 272; *Pacific Rim Investments Pte Ltd v Lam Seng Tiong* [1995] 3 S.L.R. 1; *Fuller v Happy Shopper Markets Ltd* [2001] EWHC Ch 702; [2001] 2 Lloyd's Rep. 49 at [22]; *Safeway v Interserve* [2005] EWHC 3085 (TCC) at [53]; *Burton v Mellham* [2006] UKHL 6 at [29]. See also Derham, "Equitable set-off: a critique of Muscat v Smith" (2006) 122 L.Q.R. 469.

[247] See fn.240, above.

[248] *Fearns v Anglo-Dutch Paint and Chemical Co Ltd* [2010] EWHC 2366 (Ch).

[249] *Fearns v Anglo-Dutch Paint and Chemical Co Ltd* [2010] EWHC 2366 (Ch) at [31]–[32].

[250] *Aries Tanker Corp v Total Transport Ltd* [1977] 1 W.L.R. 185. This decision had already been relied upon by some commentators in support of the conclusion that transaction set-off does not extinguish the claim, Derham, *The Law of Set-Off*, 3rd edn (Oxford: OUP, 2003), para.4–31.

[251] The actual defence relied upon by the defendants was that of abatement, but Lord Wilberforce's views were expressed in general terms, "I fail to understand how a claim which has ceased to exist can

arose (and was asserted) well before the time bar expired so if it had had the effect of extinguishing the claim (and cross-claim), the cross-claim could not have been affected by the time bar. The House of Lords, however, held that it was so affected, thus deciding that it had not been reduced or extinguished when the set-off took effect. The *Fearns* decision was also grounded on practical arguments. First, that the cross-claim could still be paid in full from another source after the assertion of the equitable set-off, and this would enable the claimant to enforce the claim in full.[252] No authority was relied upon for this proposition, except the definition of equitable set-off as arising from the injustice of enforcement because of the cross-claim, so that if this were removed there would be no more injustice. However, the *Fearns* analysis does give either party the option of satisfying their obligations without recourse to the set-off, which could sometimes be to their advantage, and it does appear that such an option is available in relation to abatement.[253]

The final argument relied upon in the *Fearns* case reflects the use of equitable set-off as a substantive defence. Since an unliquidated claim can give rise to an equitable set-off, its quantum may be uncertain at the time that the set-off is asserted. Thus the courts have held that so long as a set-off is asserted on reasonable grounds and in good faith, it will be a valid defence to a self-help remedy, even if later it is decided that the cross-claim is for a lower amount or even that it is not a valid claim at all.[254] It is pointed out in the *Fearns* case that this approach would not be possible were the existence or assertion of an equitable set-off to extinguish or reduce the claim.[255] Instead, the position would be similar to insolvency set-off, which operates automatically at the point when insolvency proceedings commence, but which is quantified later with the benefit of hindsight.[256] Thus, in exercising (or refusing to accept) a self-help remedy, both parties would act at their peril pending a final decision on the quantum and maybe the merits of the cross-claim.[257] In contrast, the good faith approach is a suitably practical way to approach the use of equitable set-off as a defence to a self-help remedy; otherwise the resulting uncertainty would considerably reduce its usefulness in this regard.

---

be introduced for any purpose into legal proceedings, whether by defence or (if this is different) as a means of reducing the respondents' claim, or as a set-off, or in any way whatsoever" (at 188).

[252] *Fearns v Anglo-Dutch Paint and Chemical Co Ltd* [2010] EWHC 2366 (Ch) at [26].

[253] *Davis v Hedges* (1870–71) L.R. 6 Q.B. 687.

[254] *SL Sethia Liners Ltd v Naviagro Maritime Corp (The Kostas Melas)* [1981] 1 Lloyd's Rep. 18, 26–27; *Modern Trading Co Ltd v Swale Building and Construction Ltd* (1990) 24 Con. L.R. 59.

[255] *Fearns v Anglo-Dutch Paint and Chemical Co Ltd* [2010] EWHC 2366 (Ch) at [30]. The judge also pointed out that it would be unfair if the claim were to be extinguished or reduced at the point at which the set-off arose, since this could be unknown to one or both parties and could allow a self-help remedy to be challenged ex post, but if the set-off only operated at the point at which it was asserted (see below) this would be contrary to the line of cases where mere tender, without accord and satisfaction, was not enough to extinguish a debt, *Fearns v Anglo-Dutch Paint and Chemical Co Ltd* [2010] EWHC 2366 (Ch) at [34]–[35].

[256] See paras 7–79 to 7–80, below.

[257] See the analysis of Goff L.J. in *The Nanfri, Federal Commerce Navigation Ltd v Molena Alpha Inc* [1978] Q.B. 927, 981, rejected in later cases in favour of Lord Denning's "good faith" approach: *Santiren Shipping Ltd v Unimarine SA (The Chrysovalandou Dyo)* [1981] 1 Lloyd's Rep. 159, 164. See also *SL Sethia Liners Ltd v Naviagro Maritime Corporation (The Kostas Melas)* [1981] 1 Lloyd's Rep. 18, 26–27.

On the basis of these arguments, the judge in the *Fearns* case decided that equitable set-off does not extinguish or reduce the claim or cross-claim until judgment or agreement,[258] and that, therefore, it was at this point that the claim and cross-claim were to be converted into a common currency. It is probably also the case that abatement has a similar effect.[259] However, the judge also confirmed that equitable set-off operated as a substantive defence:

> "In addition, where the two claims are (i) made reasonably and in good faith and (ii) so closely connected that it would be manifestly unjust to allow one party to enforce payment without taking into account the cross-claim, neither party may exercise any rights contingent on the validity of its claim except in so far as it exceeds the other party's claim (equitable set-off)."[260]

While not explicit, it does seem from this that the operation of the substantive defence comes from the unconscionability of the assertion by the claimant that he is entitled to the whole of his claim, and his consequent exercise of a self-help remedy.[261] While this may justify its operation, more is needed to explain how precisely it operates, particularly given the variety of consequences which flow from it being a substantive defence.[262] Derham suggests that it operates "in equity as a complete or partial defeasance of the plaintiff's claim", despite the fact that that claim continues to exist.[263] Thus, while the claimant is still owed the claim at law, in equity he is treated as only being entitled to the balance. This would explain not only why the claimant could then not rely on a default to trigger a self-help remedy, but also why interest only runs on the balance,[264] and why a court can take account of a cross-claim even though it is subject to an arbitration agreement, since, if it amounts to transaction set-off, it actually affects the claimant's entitlement to the claim.[265] There is, however, another argument to explain the arbitration cases, which is that when a transaction set-off is asserted, this does not amount to the bringing of legal proceedings and so is not within s.9 of the Arbitration Act 1996 (which section gives the court the power to order a stay).[266]

The analysis of defeasance in equity does not explain the substantive operation **7–55** of abatement, which is a common law defence. It would, however, be odd if abatement operated differently from equitable set-off, and indeed both are included in the classification of transaction set-off by Hoffmann L.J. in *Aectra Refining and Marketing Inc v Exmar NV*, described as operating "in law or in equity as a complete or partial defeasance of the plaintiff's claim".[267] Quite what is meant by defeasance in law is unclear, although it is very clear that abatement

---

[258] *Fearns v Anglo Dutch Paint & Chemical Co* [2010] EWHC 2366 (Ch) at [50(1)].

[259] See para.7–64, below.

[260] *Fearns v Anglo Dutch Paint & Chemical Co* [2010] EWHC 2366 (Ch) at [50(3)].

[261] Derham, *The Law of Set-off* (2010), para.4.30.

[262] See para.7–47, below.

[263] Derham, *The Law of Set-off* (2010), para.4.30.

[264] See para.7–47, above.

[265] *Aectra Refining and Manufacturing Inc v Exmar NV* [1994] 1 W.L.R. 1634, 1649–1650; *Bim Kemi AB v Blackburn Chemicals Ltd* [2001] EWCA Civ 457 at [9]; *Prekons Insaat Sanayi AS v Rowlands Castle Contracting Group Ltd* [2006] EWHC 1367 (Comm).

[266] *Prekons Insaat Sanayi AS v Rowlands Castle Contracting Group Ltd* [2006] EWHC 1367 (Comm) at [11].

[267] *Aectra Refining and Marketing Inc v Exmar NV* [1994] 1 W.L.R. 1634, 1649.

does operate as a substantive defence.[268] A clue to the meaning may come from the statutory embodiment of abatement in relation to sale of goods in s.53(1)(a) of the Sale of Goods Act 1979, which gives the buyer the choice whether to set up the breach in "diminution or extinction of the price" or to sue for damages separately.[269] Maybe, therefore, abatement acts as a power to extinguish the claim on judgment, which power binds the claimant to the extent that he cannot exercise any self-help remedies based on default.

7–56   Given the previous discussion, the precise moment from which transaction set-off operates as a substantive defence becomes reasonably clear: it must be (at the earliest) the moment it is asserted as such. If it operated before assertion, a claimant could be misled into believing that his claim was not in dispute and into exercising default remedies only to find later that he had no right to do so.[270] Further, both parties may wish to keep the claim and cross-claim separate, and there may be complications where a cross-claim is available against two or more claims, and the party having the cross-claim has an interest in deciding against which claim he wishes his cross-claim to be set-off.

Support for this view can be drawn from the description of transaction set-off as a self-help remedy by Lord Denning M.R. in *The Nanfri*[271]:

> "Again take the case where the contract gives a creditor a right to take the law into his own hands—to take a particular course of action if a sum is not paid—such as to forfeit a lease for non-payment of rent, or to withdraw a vessel for non-payment of hire. There the distinction between set-off and cross-claim is crucial. When the debtor has a true set-off it goes in reduction of the sums owing to the creditor. If the creditor does not allow it to be deducted, he is in peril. He will be liable in damages if he exercises his contractual right of withdrawal wrongly."[272]

The case postulated by Lord Denning is where the creditor "does not allow" the set-off to be deducted from his claim, which implies that the other party is asserting the right to deduct the amount of the set-off and is refused. That provides a sensible solution to the problem. If set-off is asserted before the creditor has resorted to self-help he should give credit for it before taking self-help measures and is precluded from taking such measures if the set-off exceeds his claim.[273] Where, on the other hand, the other party does not contest the claim on the ground that he has a right to deduct the amount of his cross-claim the creditor should be entitled to treat the other party as in default and to pursue his self-help remedies on the basis that the other party is electing to

---

[268] See para.7–64, below.

[269] The common law is to the same effect, see *Davis v Hedges* (1870–71) L.R. 6 Q.B. 687.

[270] See a similar point made by the judge in *Fearns v Anglo Dutch Paint & Chemical Co* [2010] EWHC 2366 (Ch) at [34], although there it related to the argument that equitable set-off extinguished the claim.

[271] *The Nanfri* [1978] Q.B. 927.

[272] *The Nanfri* [1978] Q.B. 927 at 974.

[273] This was the situation in *Santiren Shipping Ltd v Unimarine SA* [1981] 1 Lloyd's Rep. 159; *Pacific Rim Investments Pte Ltd v Lam Seng Tiong* [1995] 3 S.L.R. 1; *Eller v Grovecrest Investments Ltd* [1995] 1 Q.B. 272; and *Fuller v Happy Shopper Markets Ltd* [2001] EWHC Ch 702; [2001] 2 Lloyd's Rep. 49. In all of these cases the set-off was asserted before the self-help remedy was attempted. Although not a case of self-help, the same reasoning applied in *Safeway v Interserve* [2005] EWHC 3085 (TCC) since the cross-claim had been asserted well before the date the set-off took effect.

keep his cross-claim in existence and to utilise it in some other fashion, for example, in reduction of some other existing or future claim of the creditor. If the position were otherwise the creditor would have to suspend his self-help remedy indefinitely to await a possible future assertion of a right of set-off. Thus where the remedy for default in payment of an instalment is to make the entire balance of the debt become due and payable, an acceleration before the assertion of a right of set-off should be considered effective so as to make the full balance of the debt payable, though the debtor would remain entitled to set-off his cross-claim against that balance.

As mentioned earlier, the cross-claim may not be liquidated at the time the set-off is asserted, and Lord Denning in *The Nanfri* made it clear that it can operate as a defence to a self-help remedy provided that it is quantified "by a reasonable assessment made in good faith".[274] He went on to add that "[i]f it subsequently turns out that he has deducted too much, the [claimant] can of course recover the balance. But that is all". Thus the claimant would not, then, be able to claim that the over-deduction was a repudiatory breach of contract[275]; moreover, if the claimant had ignored the set-off and purported to exercise a self-help remedy, then he will be taken to have acted wrongfully even if the set-off turns out to have been for less than was asserted.[276]

(ii) Particular types of transaction

Set-off against liability on a negotiable instrument

A negotiable instrument, such as a bill of exchange, a promissory note or a negotiable certificate of deposit, generates an autonomous payment obligation, a contract entirely distinct from that of the underlying transaction in respect of which is was given. The courts are extremely reluctant to allow a breach of the underlying contract to be set up as a defence to a claim on a negotiable instrument, for fear that this will adversely affect its marketability as the equivalent of cash. Hitherto almost all the reported decisions have been concerned with bills of exchange. The typical case in which the question arises is where a seller of goods who receives a bill of exchange as conditional payment of the price applies for summary judgment on the bill after its dishonour and the defendant seeks leave to defend on the ground that the seller committed a breach of the contract of sale, e.g. by delivering defective goods. There does not appear

7–57

---

[274] *Federal Commerce & Navigation Co Ltd v Molena Alpha Inc (The Nanfri)* [1978] 2 Q.B. 927, 975, per Lord Denning; *Santiren Shipping Ltd v Unimarine SA (The Chrysovalandou Dyo)* [1981] 1 Lloyd's Rep. 159. Further, in the context of an application by a claimant to an arbitrator for an interim award in relation to the claim, it has been said that a cross-claimant can assert an equitable set-off as a defence to such an award, providing that it is made on reasonable grounds and in good faith, *SL Sethia Liners Ltd v Naviagro Maritime Corp (The Kostas Melas)* [1981] 1 Lloyd's Rep. 18, 26–27; *Modern Trading Co Ltd v Swale Building and Construction Ltd* (1990) 24 C.L.R. 59.

[275] This is contrary to the view of Goff L.J. In the same case, who said of the deducting party "Of course he acts at his peril and, if he is wrong, he will enable the owner to determine the charterparty if he is willing for his part to act at his peril the other way". However, Lord Denning's view was preferred by Mocatta J. in *Santiren Shipping Ltd v Unimarine SA (The Chrysovalandou Dyo)* [1981] 1 Lloyd's Rep. 159, 164.

[276] This analysis of the line of cases starting with *The Nanfri* is supported by the reasoning of the judge in the *Fearns* case at [2010] EWHC 2366 (Ch) [26]–[30].

to be a reported case in which a set-off in the strict sense has been upheld. The authorities clearly establish that an unliquidated cross-claim cannot be set-off against liability on a bill of exchange, so that where defective goods are accepted by the buyer, restricting his rights to a claim for damages for breach of warranty, these cannot be set-off against liability on the bill but must be claimed in a separate action.[277] Still less is the defendant entitled to set-off a claim for unliquidated damages arising under an entirely separate contract.[278] Refusal of set-off in these cases, though often described as a rule particularly applicable to bills of exchange, follows the general equitable rule that an unliquidated claim arising under one contract cannot be set-off against a liquidated claim made on a separate and unconnected contract. However, where the claimant is not a holder in due course[279] the defendant is entitled to plead total or partial failure of consideration as a defence to a claim on the bill where this gives him a right to recover a liquidated amount.[280] So if the buyer exercises a right to reject defective goods, with a consequent claim for recovery of the price as money paid on a total failure of consideration, he can set this up as a complete defence to a claim on a bill given for the price, whilst if he accepts some goods but exercises a right to reject the remainder he can defend an action on the bill as to that part of it which represents the price of the rejected goods.[281] In these cases, the buyer's cross-claim is not correctly described as a set-off; it is a substantive defence to a claim on the bill.

What remains unclear is whether there is a special rule in relation to negotiable instruments where the defendant's cross-claim does not arise out of the underlying transaction which represents the consideration for the bill but is a liquidated claim based on an unconnected contract, e.g. a claim for repayment of a loan made to the holder of the bill. Such a claim would not constitute a substantive defence, for it does not affect the consideration for which the instrument has been given, nor could it be asserted as a transaction set-off, the contract generated by the instrument being considered unconnected to the underlying contract.

However, in the ordinary way it would be available as an independent set-off.[282] Is the usual rule displaced where the claimant's claim is based on a negotiable instrument? There seems no reason why it should be. Where the defendant's claim is liquidated, so that it can be seen from the outset to what

---

[277] *James Lamont & Co v Hyland Ltd* [1950] 1 K.B. 585; *Brown Shipley & Co Ltd v Alicia Hosiery Ltd* [1966] 1 Lloyd's Rep. 668; *Cebora SNC v SIP (Industrial Products) Ltd* [1976] 1 Lloyd's Rep. 271; *Nova (Jersey) Knit Ltd v Kammgarn Spinnerei GmbH* [1977] 1 W.L.R. 713; *Montebianco Industrie Tessili SpA v Carlyle Mills (London) Ltd* [1981] 1 Lloyd's Rep. 509.

[278] *Nova (Jersey) Knit Ltd v Kammgarn Spinnerei GmbH* [1977] 1 W.L.R. 713 at 720, 732.

[279] Failure of consideration cannot be set up against a holder in due course. See Bills of Exchange Act 1882 s.38(2).

[280] *Forman & Co v Wright* (1851) 11 C.B. 481; *Thoni GmbH & Co KG v RTP Equipment Ltd* [1979] 2 Lloyd's Rep. 282.

[281] *Forman & Co v Wright* (1851) 11 C.B. 481.

[282] See paras 7–35 et seq., above.

extent it represents an offset to the claimant's claim, the defendant ought to be allowed to plead it by way of set-off even against a claim on a negotiable instrument.[283]

Set-off against liability under other payment instruments

The negotiable instrument is only one form of autonomous payment instrument. Others include the irrevocable commercial credit, the performance bond or guarantee and the standby credit.[284] These differ from the negotiable instrument in two respects. First, they are not negotiable, so that the question of holder in due course status does not arise. Secondly, they are considered enforceable by mercantile usage despite the fact that they are unsupported by consideration,[285] and accordingly they are not susceptible to challenge on the ground of failure of consideration. Like negotiable instruments, they would appear to be immune from transaction set-off arising from a claim under the underlying transaction, for they too are treated as autonomous contracts.[286] But the issuer of such a credit, bond or guarantee is entitled to plead a statutory set-off in the unusual case where there is an existing relationship between the issuer and the beneficiary and a liquidated sum is due to the issuer from the beneficiary under some separate account.[287]

7–58

In *Esso Petroleum Co Ltd v Milton*[288] the Court of Appeal held by a majority (Simon Brown L.J. dissenting) that an obligation to pay by direct debit was governed by similar considerations, so that where the debtor cancelled the direct debit the creditor was entitled to summary judgment for the amount due to him without set-off.

Defence and set-off against rent

For many years the view prevailed among practitioners that a landlord was entitled to be paid his rent without deduction and that rent was not subject to the

7–59

---

[283] For a detailed argument in support of this, see Derham, *The Law of Set-off* (2010), paras 5.35–5.41 criticising obiter dicta to the opposite effect in *Safa Ltd v Banque du Caire* [1990] 2 Q.B. 514, 524; and *Solo Industries UK Ltd v Canara Bank* [2001] 1 W.L.R. 1800 at [22].

[284] The commercial credit is a primary undertaking issued by a bank to a beneficiary such as the seller under a related trade transaction undertaking to accept, pay or negotiate a draft, or pay without a draft, on presentation of specified documents. The bank is the first port of call for payment and the buyer or other party at whose request the credit is opened (the account party) cannot be called upon to pay unless the bank fails to honour the credit. A performance bond or guarantee is a credit designed to support non-monetary performance of a contract, as opposed to payment, and is intended to be called upon only if the account party defaults under the underlying contract, though the bank's liability to pay is not dependent on proof of actual default, merely on presentation of a demand with such other document, e.g. a certificate of default, as may be specified in the credit. A standby credit fulfils broader business functions than the performance bond or guarantee but is legally indistinguishable from it.

[285] See *Goode on Commercial Law* (2010), pp.1078–1079.

[286] *Discount Records Ltd v Barclays Bank Ltd* [1975] 1 W.L.R. 315; *Edward Owen Engineering Ltd v Barclays Bank International Ltd* [1978] 1 Q.B. 159; *United City Merchants (Investments) Ltd v Royal Bank of Canada (The American Accord)* [1983] A.C. 168.

[287] *Hong Kong and Shanghai Banking Corp v Kloeckner AG* [1990] 2 Q.B. 514.

[288] *Esso Petroleum Co Ltd v Milton* [1997] 1 W.L.R. 938.

ordinary rules of abatement and set-off. It is now clear that this is not so, and that in principle no special treatment is accorded to a claim for rent.

Cross-claims by a tenant against his landlord which are available to be set up in answer to the landlord's claim for rent fall into one of two categories: those which constitute a substantive defence to the rent claim and those which can merely be pleaded by way of set-off. The distinction is of significance in that a defence which goes to the whole of the rent claim prevents the tenant from being in breach of his rent obligation under the lease, whereas a cross-claim by way of set-off is merely a countervailing claim, not a payment of rent as such, and its availability would not prevent the landlord from exercising a right of forfeiture for non-payment of rent, though in the ordinary way the court would obviously treat a set-off covering the whole of the arrears of rent as a ground for granting relief against forfeiture.[289]

There are at least three cases in which the tenant's cross-claim constitutes a substantive defence to the landlord's claim for rent:

(1) where the landlord has committed a breach of an obligation in the lease, or in another contract, and the performance of that obligation is expressly made a condition of the tenant's liability for rent;

(2) where the landlord has failed to carry out a repairing covenant after receiving notice of disrepair and the tenant has expended money in having the repairs carried out himself[290]; and

(3) where at the request of the landlord money has been paid by the tenant in discharge of some obligation of the landlord connected with the demised premises.[291]

In case (1), the defence derives from the express condition precedent to the tenant's liability for rent. Case (2), which at first sight appears to be an application of the common law principle of abatement enunciated in *Mondel v Steel*,[292] is in fact founded on a quite separate common law principle, namely that the tenant's expenditure in carrying out the landlord's repairing obligations is equivalent to pro tanto payment of the rent.[293] This being the case, the defence does not depend on the tenant showing a diminution in the value of the premises by reason of the disrepair.[294] On the other hand, the tenant must show that the landlord has broken his covenant, by failing to repair after having had notice of

---

[289] Under s.146 of the Law of Property Act 1925.

[290] *Taylor v Beal* (1591) Cro. Eliz. 222; *Lee-Parker v Izzet* [1971] 3 All E.R. 1099; *British Anzani (Felixstowe) Ltd v International Marine Management Ltd* [1980] Q.B. 137.

[291] *Taylor v Beal* (1591) Cro. Eliz. 222; *British Anzani (Felixstowe) Ltd v International Marine Management Ltd* [1980] Q.B. 137 at 148.

[292] *Mondel v Steel* (1841) 8 M. & W. 858. See para.7–62, below.

[293] *Lee-Parker v Izzet* [1971] 3 All E.R. 1099; *British Anzani (Felixstowe) Ltd v International Marine Management Ltd* [1980] Q.B. 137 at 148. See also *Edlington Properties Ltd v JH Fenner & Co Ltd* [2006] EWCA Civ 403 at [53].

[294] *Lee-Parker v Izzet* [1971] 3 All E.R. 1099; *British Anzani (Felixstowe) Ltd v International Marine Management Ltd* [1980] Q.B. 137 at 148. See also *Edlington Properties Ltd v JH Fenner & Co Ltd* [2006] EWCA Civ 403 at [53].

disrepair.[295] Moreover, it is not sufficient that the tenant has incurred a liability for the cost of repairs; he must have actually paid for them.[296] There appears to be a division of judicial opinion as to whether the tenant must go further and show that the quantum of the expenditure has either been accepted by the landlord or held by a judgment or award as proper and reasonable, so that damages are not at large. No such requirement is mentioned in the judgment of Goff J., in *Lee-Parker v Izzet*,[297] whereas in the latter case of *British Anzani (Felixstowe) Ltd v International Marine Management (UK) Ltd*[298] Forbes J. considered that until such acceptance or award the tenant's cross-claim remained a matter of assessment and was thus unliquidated and could not be treated as equivalent to payment of the rent. Even if this be so, it is clear that the tenant has at least a set-off as regards his expenditure, although the proper quantum remains to be established.[299] Case (3) is likewise treated as equivalent to payment of rent, constituting a substantive defence to the extent of the payment. Even where the tenant does not fall into one of the above categories, he is entitled to set-off a cross-claim against rent in accordance with the equitable rules previously discussed. In particular, he may set-off even an unliquidated claim for damages where this is based on the lease itself or on an agreement which is closely connected with it, e.g. the building agreement under which the lease was granted.[300]

Set-off against freight and hire[301]

There is a well-settled rule that there can be no set-off against a claim for freight, which is payable without deduction.[302] However, in more recent cases a distinction has been drawn between freight for the carriage of cargo and hire for the use of a vessel under a time charterparty. In the latter case, the charterer has been held entitled to make deductions for loss suffered through breakdown of machinery and speed reduction in the chartered vessel.[303] Indeed, the courts have

7–60

---

[295] *Lee-Parker v Izzet* [1971] 3 All E.R. 1099; *British Anzani (Felixstowe) Ltd v International Marine Management Ltd* [1980] Q.B. 137 at 148. See also *Edlington Properties Ltd v JH Fenner & Co Ltd* [2006] EWCA Civ 403 at [53].

[296] *Lee-Parker v Izzet* [1971] 3 All E.R. 1099; *British Anzani (Felixstowe) Ltd v International Marine Management Ltd* [1980] Q.B. 137 at 148. See also *Edlington Properties Ltd v JH Fenner & Co Ltd* [2006] EWCA Civ 403 at [53].

[297] *Lee-Parker v Izzet* [1971] 3 All E.R. 1099.

[298] *British Anzani (Felixstowe) Ltd v International Marine Management (UK) Ltd* [1980] Q.B. 137.

[299] *British Anzani (Felixstowe) Ltd v International Marine Management (UK) Ltd* [1980] Q.B. 137; *Melville v Grapelodge Developments Ltd* (1980) 39 P. & C.R. 179.

[300] *British Anzani (Felixstowe) Ltd v International Marine Management (UK) Ltd* [1980] Q.B. 137. Such a set-off is also a substantive defence which prevents the landlord from taking a self-help remedy on the grounds of non-payment of rent, see *Eller v Grovecrest Investments Ltd* [1995] 1 Q.B. 272; and *Fuller v Happy Shopper Markets Ltd* [2001] EWHC Ch 702; [2001] 2 Lloyd's Rep. 49.

[301] For a good analysis, see F. D. Rose, "Deductions from freight and hire under English law" [1982] L.M.C.L.Q. 33. See also J. Shepherd, "The rule against deduction from freight reconsidered" [2006] J.B.L. 1.

[302] *Aries Tanker Corp v Total Transport Ltd* [1977] 1 All E.R. 398.

[303] *Federal Commerce Navigation Ltd v Molena Alpha Inc (The Nanfri)* [1978] 1 Q.B. 927, 976; *Santiren Shipping Ltd v Unimarine SA* [1981] 1 Lloyd's Rep. 159. But there is no right of deduction in respect of a cross-claim not based on deprivation of or prejudice in the use of the vessel (*Leon Corp v Atlantic Lines & Navigation Co Inc (The Leon)* [1985] 2 Lloyd's Rep. 470; *Western Bulk Carriers K/S v LI Hai Maritime Inc* [2005] EWHC 735 (Comm)).

said that the deduction need not be a completely accurate assessment of the charterer's loss; it suffices that it was a reasonable assessment made in good faith.[304] The judgments refer to this right of deduction as an equitable set-off, but it could also be seen as an application of the common law doctrine of abatement enunciated in *Mondel v Steel*[305]; either way it falls under the heading of transaction set-off, which, as we have seen, is a substantive defence.

Set-off against secured debt

7–61   The fact that a debt is secured by a mortgage does not preclude it from being subject to transaction set-off, whether for liquidated or unliquidated damages, in proceedings for recovery of the debt.[306] The rule that there cannot be set-off against a property claim is irrelevant here, for the set-off is not against the asset given in security but against the sum secured.

6.   ABATEMENT

The common law doctrine of abatement

7–62   The old common law doctrine that promise and counter-promise were generally to be treated as independent, so that failure to perform the one did not excuse non-performance of the other, found its strongest expression in contracts of sale of goods. The buyer wishing to withhold payment because the goods were not up to warranty was met with the answer that the sole condition of his obligation to pay the price was the transfer of property to him, and that this having happened the contract was partially executed, with the result that the buyer could not unilaterally retransfer the property and treat the contract as discharged.[307] However, in due course the rigour of the rule was mitigated by allowing the defendant to set up his claim for damages for breach of warranty in diminution of the price, on the basis that by reason of the breach what was supplied to the defendant was reduced in value. The locus classicus for the description of this right of abatement is the judgment of Parke B. in *Mondel v Steel*[308]:

> "It must however be considered that in all these cases of goods sold and delivered with a warranty, and work and labour, as well as the case of goods agreed to be

---

[304] *Santiren Shipping Ltd v Unimarine SA* [1981] 1 Lloyd's Rep. 159, 164.

[305] *Mondel v Steel* (1841) 8 M. & W. 858. See para.7–62, below.

[306] *TSB Bank v Platts* [1998] 2 B.C.L.C. 1. The position is otherwise where the mortgagee's claim is for possession. While the normal rule is that set-off is available even against a claim for non-monetary relief where it is based on default in payment (see *BICC v Burndy Corp* [1985] Ch. 232), a mortgagee is in a special position because of his legal estate to take possession immediately the mortgage has been executed and despite the absence of default (*National Westminster Bank Plc v Skelton* [1993] 1 All E.R. 242; *Ashley Guarantee Plc v Zacaria* [1993] 1 All E.R. 254; *Lexi Holdings v Pooni* [2008] EWHC 1143 (Ch) at [27]; *Deutsche Bank (Suisse) SA v Gulzar Ahmed Khan* [2013] EWHC 482 (Comm) at [311]). See also para.7–82, below.

[307] *Street v Blay* (1831) 2 B. & Ad. 456.

[308] *Mondel v Steel* (1841) 8 M. & W. 858. *Mondel v Steel* was not in fact the root decision (see *Street v Blay* (1831) 2 B. & Ad. 456 and cases there cited) but provides the most detailed exposition of the doctrine of abatement.

supplied according to a contract . . . it is competent for the defendant, in all of those, not to set-off, by a proceeding in the nature of a cross action, the amount of damages which he has sustained by breach of the contract, but simply to defend himself by showing how much less the subject-matter of the action was worth, by reason of the breach of contract; and to the extent that he obtains, or is capable of obtaining, an abatement of the price on that account, he must be considered as having received satisfaction for the breach of contract, and is precluded from recovering in another action to that extent; but no more."[309]

In the case of contracts of sale of goods the doctrine of abatement was carried into what is now s.53(1)(a) of the Sale of Goods Act 1979.

Scope of the doctrine of abatement

The doctrine of abatement enunciated in *Mondel v Steel* does not extend to contracts generally. It is confined to a strictly limited group of contracts: sale of goods, other forms of supply of goods (e.g. by way of lease or hire-purchase) and contracts of work and labour.[310] Abatement for defective work may be pleaded even in answer to a claim by a builder for payment under an architect's interim certificate.[311] However, it is limited to reduction in value of the goods or work and cannot be pleaded to support other types of claim, such as damages for delay.[312]

7–63

Is abatement a substantive defence?

It is clear that abatement is a doctrine entirely distinct from set-off. In contrast to transaction set-off prior to 1873, it has always taken the form of a defence; it is limited to the amount by which the plaintiffs breach has diminished the value of his performance; and it is available to the defendant as a matter of right, not of judicial discretion. But is it a substantive defence or, like independent set-off, purely procedural? In *Gilbert-Ash (Northern) Ltd v Modern Engineering (Bristol) Ltd*,[313] Lord Diplock entertained no doubt that it was the former:

7–64

> "That it was no mere procedural rule designed to avoid circuity of action but a substantive defence at common law was the very point decided in *Mondel v Steel*."[314]

---

[309] *Mondel v Steel* (1841) 8 M. & W. 858 at 870–872.

[310] *Gilbert-Ash (Northern) Ltd v Modern Engineering (Bristol) Ltd* [1974] A.C. 689 at 717; *Aries Tanker Corp v Total Transport Ltd* [1977] 1 W.L.R. 185, per Lord Wilberforce at 190; *Multiplex Constructions (UK) Ltd v Cleveland Bridge UK Ltd* [2006] EWHC 1341 (TCC) [652]; *John Grimes Partnership Ltd v Gubbins* Unreported March 16, 2012 CC. Contracts of employment may possibly be within the doctrine as well. See *Sim v Rotherham Metropolitan BC* [1987] 1 Ch. 216, where Scott J. found it unnecessary to decide the point, holding that the right to deduct was in any event given as a matter of set-off.

[311] *Gilbert-Ash (Northern) Ltd v Modern Engineering (Bristol) Ltd* [1974] A.C. 689 at 717, overruling a line of prior authority to the contrary.

[312] *Davis v Hedges* (1871) L.R. 6 Q.B. 687; *Henrisken Rederi A/S v THZ Rolimpex (The Brede)* [1974] 1 Q.B. 233, per Lord Denning M.R. at 248; *Mellowes Archital Ltd v Bell Projects Ltd* (1997) 87 B.L.R. 26.

[313] *Gilbert-Ash (Northern) Ltd v Modern Engineering (Bristol) Ltd* [1974] A.C. 689.

[314] *Gilbert-Ash (Northern) Ltd v Modern Engineering (Bristol) Ltd* [1974] A.C. 689 at 717.

This statement,[315] at the time, probably was not correct; it runs counter to the express words of the judgment of Parke B. in *Mondel v Steel*, where, referring to the statement of Lord Tenterden in *Street v Blay*[316] that the right to set up the damages for breach of warranty in diminution of the price was given "on the principle, it should seem, of avoiding circuity of action". The High Court of Australia has held in a majority decision that abatement is purely procedural and that the breach of warranty does not by itself work a reduction or extinguishment of the buyer's liability for the price,[317] and a similar ruling has been given in another Australian case.[318]

However, so far as English law is concerned Lord Diplock's statement has since received support from the Court of Appeal in *The Brede*[319] and Hoffmann L.J. in *Aectra Refining and Marketing Inc v Exmar NV*,[320] so that, as with equitable set-off, it must today be seen as a substantive defence. In relation to contracts of sale of goods the principle of *Mondel v Steel* is now embodied in s.53(1)(a) of the Sale of Goods Act 1979, which allow the buyer to treat any breach of condition on the part of the seller as a breach of warranty and set it up in diminution of the price.[321] The term "transaction set-off" includes both equitable set-off and abatement.[322]

Present significance of abatement

7–65   It might be thought that there is little need to rely on abatement at the present day since the ground is largely covered by the substantive defence of equitable set-off. That, indeed, was the view of Scott J. as expressed in his instructive judgment in *Sim v Rotherham Metropolitan BC*.[323]

However, it may occasionally be preferable to rely on abatement rather than an equitable set-off. A contractual term may exclude all types of set-off, but not abatement,[324] and a different limitation period may apply to the two defences.[325]

---

[315] Which beguiled Professor Goode in the first edition of this book.

[316] *Street v Blay* (1831) 2 B. & Ad. 456 at 462.

[317] *Healing (Sales) Pty Ltd v Inglis Electrix Pty Ltd* [1969] A.L.R. 533. See in particular the judgments of Kitto J. at 541 and Windeyer J. at 547, 552.

[318] *Newman v Cook* [1963] V.R. 659.

[319] *Aectra Refining and Marketing Inc v Exmar NV* [1974] 1 Q.B. 233. An argument based on *Healing (Sales) Pty Ltd v Inglis Elecrix Pty Ltd* was put to the Court of Appeal in that case (see argument at 240 and judgment of Roskill L.J. at 259) but rejected.

[320] *Aectra Refining and Marketing Inc v Exmar NV* [1994] 1 W.L.R. 1634 at 1650. See also *Sim v Rotherham Metropolitan BC* [1987] 1 Ch. 216, 258; and *Totsa Total Oil Trading SA v Bharat Petroleum Corp Ltd* [2005] EWHC 1641 (Comm).

[321] For discussion of how abatement operates as a substantive defence, see para.7–55, above.

[322] *Aectra Refining and Marketing Inc v Exmar NV* [1994] 1 W.L.R. 1634 at 1649–1650, per Hoffmann L.J.

[323] *Sim v Rotherham Metropolitan BC* [1986] 3 All E.R. 387 at 412, 413. See also *Fuller v Happy Shopper Markets Ltd* [2001] EWHC Ch 702; [2001] 2 Lloyd's Rep. 49 at [26].

[324] *Mellowes Archital Ltd v Bell Products Ltd* (1997) 87 B.L.R. 26, 29 CA; *Acsim (Southern) Ltd v Danish Contracting and Development Co Ltd* (1989) 19 C.L.R. 1; (1989) 47 B.L.R. 55. A similar issue, on a differently worded clause, arose in *Multiplex Constructions (UK) Ltd v Cleveland Bridge UK Ltd, Cleveland Bridge Dorman Long Engineering* [2006] EWHC 1341 (TCC) at [97]. cf. *Totsa Total Oil Trading Sa v Bharat Petroleum Corp Ltd* [2005] EWHC 1641 (Comm).

[325] Limitation Act 1980 s.36(2), which preserves the court's right, in the exercise of its equitable jurisdiction, to refuse relief on the grounds of acquiescence or otherwise, would not apply to abatement, which is a common law defence.

Abatement may provide a defence where the cross-claimant has suffered no loss under orthodox principles of contractual damages,[326] and being a common law right, it is available as of right and is not dependent on the discretion of the court or on unconscionability.[327]

Although abatement is treated as a substantive defence, there is yet to be a definitive ruling as to whether abatement can be relied on to defeat the exercise of a self-help remedy. However, there seems no reason why this should not be the case, and the principles that apply to equitable set-off apply to abatement.

7. THE EFFECT OF ASSIGNMENT ON INDEPENDENT AND TRANSACTION SET-OFF

Set-off by assignee

The assignee[328] of a debt or other chose in action is entitled to plead it by way of set-off to the same extent as if it had been vested in him from the beginning.[329] He cannot, however, set-off against his creditor's assignee a debt purchased by him after notice of assignment,[330] unless this gives rise to a transaction set-off.[331] If the assignment is by way of mortgage, however, permitting the assignee to rely on the assigned debt by way of set-off would jeopardise the mortgagor's equity of redemption in two ways. First, since the assignment is by way of security, any surplus value over and above the value of the secured obligation is held on trust for the mortgagor, and therefore cannot be used by the mortgagee by way of set-off. Secondly, the mortgagor has a right to redeem the whole debt on payment of the secured obligation which would be destroyed were the mortgagee permitted to rely on set-off. Thus the mutuality between the assignee and the debtor is destroyed in relation to the entire debt.[332] However, if the mortgagor has already defaulted and the security interest is in the process of being enforced, set-off may be permissible to the extent of the secured obligation, if this is sufficiently ascertained.

7–66

---

[326] Derham, *The Law of Set-off* (2010), para.2.134.

[327] *Gilbert-Ash (Northern) Ltd v Modern Engineering (Bristol) Ltd* [1974] 1 A.C. 698, 717.

[328] The position is the same whether the assignment is statutory or equitable: *Clark v Cort* (1840) Cr. & Ph. 154; *Tony Lee Motors Ltd v M S Macdonald & Son* (1974) Ltd [1981] 2 N.Z.L.R. 281.

[329] *Bennett v White* [1910] 2 K.B. 643; *Daleri Ltd v Woolworths Plc* [2008] EWHC 2891 (Ch).

[330] *NW Robbie & Co Ltd v Witney Warehouses Ltd* [1963] 1 W.L.R. 1324 CA. This is merely a specific application of the wider rule that precludes an assignee from setting up new equities arising after notice of assignment. See para.7–69, below. For the purpose of this rule and others set out below a fixed charge and a floating charge which has crystallised are equated with an assignment.

[331] *The Government of Newfoundland v The Newfoundland Rly Co* (1888) L.R. 13 App. Cas. 199 PC; *Business Computers Ltd v Anglo-African Leasing Ltd* [1977] 1 W.L.R. 578, 585.

[332] See Derham, *The Law of Set-off* (2010), para.11.42; and Wood, *English and International Set-off* (1989), para.16–198. It is also thought that the same argument applies where the mortgage is created by novation, since the same jeopardy to the mortgagor's equity of redemption exists.

Defences and set-off against assignee[333]

7–67   There are four distinct rules governing the debtor's defensive rights against an assignee.

7–68   **First rule: assignee takes subject to defences**   Since the assignee cannot stand in any better position than his assignor, he takes subject to all substantive defences and rights of abatement open to the debtor against the assignor, whether or not existing at the time the debtor received notice of the assignment. This rule does not constitute any special protection for the debtor against an assignee; it is simply an application of the principle that *nemo dat quod non habet*: the assignor cannot transfer greater rights than he himself possesses.

7–69   **Second rule: assignee takes subject to equities**   It is a rule of equity that the assignee takes "subject to equities". This rule is often treated as synonymous with the first but it is in fact a distinct rule evolved by courts of equity[334] to protect the debtor against injustice that might result from an assignment. In the case of a statutory assignment this second rule is now embodied in s.136 of the Law of Property Act 1925, under which the assignment is effectual in law "subject to equities having priority over the right of the assignee".[335] Despite the fact that the statute refers to "equities" this includes independent set-off,[336] but not a mere counterclaim.[337] A debtor cannot set-off against an assignee a cross-claim against the assignor which is not eligible to be set-off against the latter.[338] However, there would seem to be no reason why the debtor should not set-off, against the assigned debt, a cross-claim against the assignee,[339] unless the assignment is by way of mortgage, in which case the argument made above concerning the jeopardy to the mortgagor's equity of redemption applies, with the qualification that the debtor must be on notice that the assignment is by way of mortgage.[340]

---

[333] For a thought-provoking reappraisal of the rules, see A. Tettenborn, "Assignees, equities and cross-claims: principle and confusion" [2002] L.M.C.L.Q. 485.

[334] Who prior to the introduction of statutory assignments in the Supreme Court of Judicature Act 1873 were the only courts prepared to recognise the assignability of choses in action, but were only prepared to allow the assignee to enforce the debt on the basis that the debtor could raise equitable defences that would have been available against the assignor, see *Edlington Properties Ltd v JH Fenner & Co Ltd* [2006] EWCA Civ 403 at [13]. For the position where the contract itself excludes equities see para.7–73, below.

[335] The rule also applies to where there is an "automatic assignment" of arrears under s.141 of the Law of Property Act 1925 (*Muscat v Smith* [2003] EWCA Civ 962) but this probably is not the case in relation to leases granted after January 1, 1996 to which s.3 applies: *Edlington Properties Ltd v JH Fenner & Co Ltd* [2006] EWCA Civ 403 at [48].

[336] *Glencore Grain Ltd v Agros Trading Co* [1999] 2 Lloyd's Rep. 410 at [31].

[337] *E Pellas & Co v The Neptune Marine Insurance Co* (1879–80) L.R. 5 C.P.D. 34.

[338] *Bank of Boston Connecticut v European Grain and Shipping* [1989] 1 A.C. 1056, 1110–1111, per Lord Brandon; rejecting an argument to the contrary based on dicta in *Government of Newfoundland v Newfoundland Railway Co* (1888) 13 App. Cas. 199. In that case the set-off, which would otherwise have been equitable, was unavailable because the claim was for freight. See also *Aboussafy v Abacus Cities Ltd* [1981] 4 W.W.R. 660 where independent set-off was unavailable since the claim sought to be set-off was unliquidated.

[339] *Banco Central SA & Trevelan Navigation Inc v Lingoss & Falce Ltd (The Raven)* [1980] 2 Lloyd's Rep. 266, 273 QB, Com.

[340] This also applies where the mortgage is by novation, see para.3–03 fn.17, above.

Third rule: receipt of notice of assignment fixes eligibility for set-off This is   **7–70**
that the debtor cannot set-off against the assignee cross-claims arising after he has
received notice of assignment.[341] The reason for this rule is obvious: to allow the
debtor, by further voluntary dealings with the assignor after receipt of notice of
assignment, to bring into existence further cross-claims and set them off against
the debt assigned would enable him to cut down at will the value of the assigned
debt to the detriment of the assignee. When he receives the notice of assignment
the debtor knows that the debt is no longer held by the assignor; if despite this he
goes on dealing with the assignor the risk is on him and he cannot put it upon the
assignee. The following points should be noted in connection with this third rule:

(1)   It is not sufficient that the cross-claim arises under a contract concluded
      between the assignor and the debtor before notice of assignment was given;
      it is necessary that a debt should actually have arisen in favour of the debtor
      under the contract before he received notice of the assignment of his
      creditor's claim.[342] On the other hand, it is immaterial that the debt has not
      yet fallen due for payment; it suffices that the obligation has become a
      present debt but payable in the future[343] as opposed, for example, to a
      purely contingent liability. Further, as long as the contract under which the
      claim (as opposed to the cross-claim) arose is in existence at the date of the
      notice of assignment, then it does not matter that the actual claim arises and
      is payable after the date of that notice.[344]

(2)   The relevant date is not the assignment but the date on which the debtor
      receives notice of it. For this purpose notice of the existence of a floating
      charge does not affect the debtor's right to set up fresh equities, for a
      floating charge gives no rights over any particular asset until crystallisa-
      tion,[345] and is thus not equated with an assignment. So a debtor who
      continues to deal with a company after notice that it has granted a floating
      charge is nevertheless entitled to set-off a cross-claim arising before
      crystallisation of the charge,[346] or after crystallisation and before he has
      received notice of it.[347] But he cannot set-off claims arising after he has
      received notice of crystallisation.[348]

(3)   The rule does not apply at all where the cross-claim is not a mere set-off but
      a substantive defence to the claim or a right of abatement; nor does it apply

---

[341] *Roxburghe v Cox* (1881) 17 Ch.D. 520; *Re Pinto Leite & Nephews* [1929] 1 Ch. 221; *Business Computers Ltd v Anglo-African Leasing Ltd* [1977] 2 All E.R. 741; *S v S, Lloyd Platt & Co* [2010] EWHC 1415 (Fam). For criticism, see Derham, *The Law of Set-off* (2010), para.17.15; and Tettenborn, "Assignees, equities and cross-claims: principle and confusion" [2002] L.M.C.L.Q. 485, 496.

[342] *Roxburghe v Cox* (1881) 17 Ch.D. 520.

[343] *Roxburghe v Cox* (1881) 17 Ch.D. 520; *Christie v Taunton, Delmard, Lane & Co* [1893] 2 Ch. 175.

[344] *Rother Iron Works Ltd v Canterbury Precision Engineers Ltd* [1974] Q.B. 1; *Marathon Electrical Manufacturing Corp v Mashreqbank PSC* [1997] 2 B.C.L.C. 460.

[345] See paras 4–03 et seq., above.

[346] *Biggerstaff v Rowatt's Wharf Ltd* [1896] 2 Ch. 93.

[347] *Business Computers Ltd v Anglo-African Leasing Ltd* [1977] 2 All E.R. 741.

[348] *Business Computers Ltd v Anglo-African Leasing Ltd* [1977] 2 All E.R. 741; *NW Robbie & Co Ltd v Witney Warehouse Co Ltd* [1963] 1 W.L.R. 1324 CA.

even to a pure set-off where this is closely or inseparably connected with the claim, whether arising under the same contract or under different contracts.[349]

7–71   **Fourth rule: no set-off for cross-claims against intermediate assignees**   The fourth rule, which has been criticised,[350] is that the assignee takes subject only to equities available against his assignor, not to cross-claims of the debtor against an intermediate assignee,[351] because what the second assignee is asserting is not the rights of the first assignee but those of the original creditor.[352] On the other hand, in the relations between the second assignee and the original creditor, the second assignee cannot acquire a better title to the debt than his predecessor, so that if the first assignment is void or voidable at the suit of the original creditor, the second will be similarly affected.[353]

Fifth rule: non-assignable debts   If the debt is unassignable,[354] then the debtor can ignore any notice of assignment, and can assert set-offs arising at any point.[355] However, the creditor may be able to circumvent a non-assignment clause, by declaring itself trustee of the debt for the "assignee".[356] Unless the clause also prevents a declaration of trust,[357] the trust would break the mutuality between the debtor and the creditor, so that the debtor cannot rely on independent set-offs arising after notice of the declaration of trust.[358]

---

[349] *Smith v Parkes* (1852) 16 Beav. 115; *Government of Newfoundland v Newfoundland Rly Co* (1888)13 App. Cas. 199; *Business Computers Ltd v Anglo-African Leasing Ltd* [1977] 2 All E.R. 741, per Templeman J. at 748.

[350] Tettenborn, "Assignees, equities and cross-claims: principle and confusion" [2002] L.M.C.L.Q. 485 at 491.

[351] *Banco Central SA & Trevelan Navigation Co v Lingoss & Falce Ltd (The Raven)* [1980] 2 Lloyd's Rep. 266; *Re Milan Tramways Co* (1884) 25 Ch.D. 587.

[352] *Re Milan Tramways Co* (1884) 25 Ch.D. 587, per Cotton L.J. at 593. For an argument to the contrary in relation to statutory assignment, see Derham, *The Law of Set-off* (2010), para.17.63; G. Tolhurst, *The Assignment of Contractual Rights* (Oxford: Hart Publishing, 2006), para.8.96.

[353] *Barnard v Hunter* (1856) 2 Jur. N.S. 1213; *Southern British National Trust Ltd v Pither* (1937) 57 C.L.R. 89. The principle that a contract cannot be avoided after an innocent third party has acquired an interest in the subject matter does not apply where what are transferred are the contract rights themselves, as opposed to the goods or other property the subject of the contract.

[354] See para.3–38, above.

[355] *Don King Productions Inc v Warren (No.1)* [2000] Ch. 291, 319.

[356] Para.3–40, above.

[357] In which case, the debtor will not be affected by a notice of the trust, although the creditor would then not be able to rely on set-off arising after this time as it would then be in breach of its obligations to the beneficiary of the trust, see R. Goode, "Contractual Prohibitions against Assignment" [2009] L.M.C.L.Q. 300, 315 and para.3–42, above.

[358] Goode, "Contractual Prohibitions against Assignment" [2009] L.M.C.L.Q. 300, 311.

8.   OTHER ASPECTS OF INDEPENDENT AND TRANSACTION SET-OFF

Pleading set-off

Set-off is pleaded by way of defence to the claimant's claim.[359] In the case of independent set-off the sum to be set-off had to have accrued due to the defendant by at the time of commencement of the action,[360] but this requirement was later considered[361] to have been dispensed with by rules of court in relation to transaction set-off.[362] In addition, a party can amend his statement of case to include a cause of action accruing after the commencement of proceedings with the permission of the court.[363] It would thus seem odd for there to be a blanket ban on pleading set-off arising after the commencement of proceedings, although leave would be required to do so. Neither independent set-off nor transaction set-off extinguishes the claim until judgment, so if there is no rule against pleading a set-off arising after commencement of proceedings, there is no substantive law reason to prevent a party relying on it,[364] and it is submitted that this should be the position in relation to both transaction and independent set-off.[365]

7–72

If the defendant sets up a cross-claim which was statute-barred at the date of commencement of the action,[366] the plaintiff may rely on the Limitation Act 1980 in his reply, thus negating the set-off. This is one of the factors distinguishing independent set-off from a substantive defence (including transaction set-off), which is not subject to the Limitation Act.[367]

---

[359] CPR r.16.6. This may be done even if the defendant is also filing a Pt 20 claim, e.g. a counterclaim. So if the amount of the cross-claim exceeds the claim the defendant should plead set-off to the extent necessary to extinguish the claim and counterclaim any balance.

[360] *Richards v James* (1848) 2 Ex. 471.

[361] In *Wood v Goodwin* [1884] W.N. 17.

[362] RSC Ord.18, r.9, which provided that "a party may in any pleading plead any matter which has arisen at any time, whether before or since the issue of the writ". This provision is not included in the Civil Procedure Rules, but has not been repealed.

[363] CPR r.17; *Vax Appliances Ltd v Hoover Plc* [1990] R.P.C. 656, 661; *Hendry v Chartsearch Ltd* [1998] C.L.C. 1382, 1388–1389 CA; *Maridive and Oil Services (SAE) v CNA Insurance Co (Europe) Ltd* [2002] EWCA Civ 369 at [20]–[24]; *John Michael Finlan v Eyton Morris Winfield* [2007] EWHC 914 (Ch). For a discussion of the principles applied by the court in giving leave, see *The White Book*, 17.3.5.

[364] There are statements in recent cases suggesting that the position in *Richards v James* has not changed (*Stein v Blake* [1996] A.C. 243, 251 HL; *Edmunds v Lloyds Italico & l'Ancora Compagnia di Assicurazione e Riassicurazione SpA* [1986] 1 W.L.R. 492, 495 CA; *Redwin v Lynch* Unreported February 23, 1998 CA. But in none of these cases was the argument in the text expressly made. Further, the *Edmunds* case concerned transaction set-off, yet *Richards v James* (a case of independent set-off) was relied upon, which reduces the force of this authority.

[365] See also Derham, *The Law of Set-off* (2010), paras 2.08–2.12.

[366] A claim by way of set-off is deemed to be a separate action commenced on issue of the plaintiff's writ (Limitation Act 1980 s.35).

[367] *Henriksens Rederi A/S v THZ Rolimpex (The Brede)* [1974] Q.B. 233; *Westdeutsche Landesbank Girozentrale v Islington London BC* [1994] 4 All E.R. 890, 943–945; *Filross Securities Ltd v Midgeley* (1999) 31 H.L.R. 465, 472 CA; *Philip Collins Ltd v Davis* [2000] 3 All E.R. 808, 831; *Cheltenham BC v Laird* [2009] EWHC 1253 (QB) at [459]; *National Westminster Bank v June Frankham* [2013] EWHC 1199 (QB) at [51].

Exclusion of set-off by agreement

7–73 It is open to the parties to contract out of the right of independent or transaction set-off,[368] whether by issuing securities that are expressed to be free from equities,[369] or by providing that payment is to be made without deduction or set-off,[370] or by specifying deductions that a party can make from the other party's entitlement so as to exclude by implication other deductions, including set-off.[371] To be effective, the exclusion must use clear words, to rebut the presumption that neither party intends to abandon any remedies it has for breach.[372] A contractual waiver or exclusion of a right of set-off is not against public policy[373] and is binding on the debtor except where it is rendered void under the Unfair Contract Terms Act 1977,[374] which is rare where the contract is between commercial parties.[375]

Set-off by and against the Crown

7–74 In general, set-off may be pleaded both by and against the Crown by virtue of the Crown Proceedings Act 1947. However, in proceedings by the Crown, the defendant cannot plead set-off against a claim for taxes, duties or penalties or rely

---

[368] *Gilbert-Ash (Northern) Ltd v Modern Engineering (Bristol) Ltd* [1974] A.C. 689. But not set-off in insolvency. See para.7–78, below.

[369] *Re Blakely Ordnance Co* (1867) L.R. 3 Ch. 154; *Re Agra and Masterman's Bank* (1866-67) L.R. 2 Ch. App. 391; *Hilger Analytical Ltd v Rank Precision Industries Ltd* [1984] B.C.L.C. 301. This would automatically be the case if the debt were embodied in a negotiable instrument. In relation to debt securities which are held and traded through CREST, the rules provide that they must be "transferable free from any equity, set-off or counter-claim between the issuer and the original or any intermediate holder of the security" (r.7.3.2); see also *Newcastle Building Society v Mill; Re Kaupthing Singer and Friedlander Ltd (Isle of Man) Ltd* [2009] EWHC 740 (Ch); [2009] 2 Lloyd's Rep. 154.

[370] *John Dee Group Ltd v WMH (21) Ltd* [1998] B.C.C. 972; *Coca-Cola Finance Corp v Finsat International Ltd* [1996] 3 W.L.R. 849.

[371] *Mottram Consultants Ltd v Bernard Sunley & Sons Ltd* [1975] 2 Lloyd's Rep. 197 (Lord Morris of Borth-y-Gest and Lord Salmon dissenting).

[372] *Gilbert-Ash (Northern) Ltd v Modern Engineering (Bristol) Ltd* [1974] A.C. 689, 717; *BOC Group Plc v Centeon LLC* [1999] EWCA Civ 1293. This rule applies equally to transaction set-off, see *Connaught Restaurants Ltd v Indoor Leisure Ltd* [1994] 1 W.L.R. 501, 509–510; *Federal Commerce & Navigation Co Ltd v Molena Alpha Inc (The Nanfri)* [1978] 2 Q.B. 927; and independent set-off, *BICC Plc v Burndy Corp* [1985] Ch.232, 248 CA; *Newcastle Building Society v Mill; Re Kaupthing Singer and Friedlander Ltd (Isle of Man) Ltd* [2009] EWHC 740 (Ch); [2009] 2 Lloyd's Rep. 154 at [19]; cf. *Anselm v Anselm* Unreported June 29, 1999 Ch WL 1865275.

[373] *Coca-Cola Finance Corp v Finset* [1996] 3 W.L.R. 849; *Newcastle Building Society v Mill; Re Kaupthing Singer and Friedlander Ltd (Isle of Man) Ltd* [2009] EWHC 740 (Ch); [2009] 2 Lloyd's Rep. 154 at [16].

[374] *Stewart Gill Ltd v Horatio Myers & Co Ltd* [1992] 1 Q.B. 600.

[375] *Schenkers Ltd v Overland Shoes Ltd* [1998] 1 Lloyd's Rep. 498; *RÖHLIG (UK) Ltd v Rock Unique Ltd* [2011] EWCA Civ 18; *Governor & Co of the Bank of Scotland v Reuben Singh* Unreported June 17, 2005 QBD; *FG Wilson (Engineering) Ltd v John Holt & Co (Liverpool) Ltd* [2012] EWHC 2477 (Comm); *Deutsche Bank (Suisse) SA v Gulzar Ahmed Khan* [2013] EWHC 482 (Comm).

by way of set-off on a claim for repayment of taxes, duties or penalties.[376] Further, without leave of the court no set-off can be pleaded by or against the Crown where:

(1)   the Crown is sued or sues in the name of a government department and the subject matter of the set-off does not relate to that department[377]; or
(2)   the Crown is sued or sues in the name of the Attorney-General.[378]

The effect of these restrictions is to displace the principle that the Crown is indivisible and to preclude set-off against taxes completely or, as between two claims involving two different Government departments, except where leave is given by the court.

9.   INSOLVENCY SET-OFF: GENERAL PRINCIPLES

The focus in the passages which follow is on the rules of set-off applicable in the winding-up of companies, but similar considerations apply to the bankruptcy of individuals,[379] and important differences will be highlighted. The rules governing insolvency set-off apply in liquidation, and also in administration once the administrator has issued a notice of proposed distribution under r.2.95 of the Insolvency Rules 1986.[380]

7–75

The right of set-off in insolvency

The right of set-off in administration is to be found in r.2.85 and in company liquidations in r.4.90 of the Insolvency Rules 1986.[381]
    The rules provide that, at the relevant point,[382] an account shall be taken of what is due from each party to the other in respect of mutual credits, mutual debts and mutual dealings, and the sums due from one party shall be set-off against the sums due from the other,[383] and only any balance owed by the company is provable in the administration or liquidation.[384] Present, future, liquidated, unliquidated, certain and contingent liabilities owed by or to the company are all

7–76

---

[376] CPR r.66.4(1) and (2).

[377] CPR r.66.4(4).

[378] CPR r.66.4(3).

[379] Insolvency Act 1986 s.323.

[380] Insolvency Rules 1986 (SI 1986/1925). This regime was introduced in 2003 by the Insolvency (Amendment) Rules 2003 (SI 2003/1730). For discussion of the implications of the change see para.7–85, below.

[381] Insolvency Rules 1986 (SI 1986/1925).

[382] This is different in respect of liquidation and administration and will be discussed at para.7–85, below.

[383] Insolvency Rules 1986 rr.2.85(3) and 4.90(3).

[384] Insolvency Rules 1986 rr.2.85(8) and 4.90(8). Any balance payable to the company is payable to the administrator or liquidator as part of the assets if it is due and payable, but if it is contingent or prospective, the balance is to be paid when it has become due and payable.

included.[385] The solvent party must be "any creditor of the company proving or claiming to prove for a debt" in the administration or liquidation, as the case may be.[386]

Principles underlying insolvency set-off

7–77   The basic principles in relation to liquidation were elucidated in two masterly analyses, by Hoffmann L.J. at first instance in *MS Fashions Ltd v Bank of Credit and Commerce International SA (No.2)*[387] and Lord Hoffmann (as he had now become) in *Stein v Blake*[388]:

> "Certain principles as to the application of these provisions have been established by the cases. First, the rule is mandatory ('the mandatory principle'). If there have been mutual dealings before the winding-up order which have given rise to cross-claims, neither party can prove or sue for his full claim. An account must be taken and he must prove or sue (as the case may be) for the balance. Secondly, the account is taken as at the date of the winding-up order ('the retroactivity principle'). This is only one manifestation of a wider principle of insolvency law, namely, that the liquidation and distribution of the assets of the insolvent company are treated as notionally taking place simultaneously on the date of the winding up order: see *In re Dynamics Corp of America* [1976] 1 W.L.R. 757, 762, per Oliver J. Thirdly, in taking the account the court has regard to events which have occurred since the date of the winding up ('the hindsight principle'). The hindsight principle is pervasive in the valuation of claims and the taking of accounts in bankruptcy and winding up."[389]

While, as regards insolvency set-off in liquidation, the date at which the account is notionally taken is the date of the winding-up order, in relation to administration it is the date of the notice of proposed distribution.[390] In what follows, these dates will be referred to as "the date of account".

The mandatory principle

7–78   Insolvency set-off is mandatory and cannot be excluded by agreement of the parties. This was so held by a majority decision of the House of Lords in *National Westminster Bank Ltd v Halesowen Presswork and Assemblies Ltd*.[391] The reason given is that the statutory provisions are considered to regulate matters of public interest in the orderly administration of the estate and are not purely a source of

---

[385] Insolvency Rules 1986 rr.2.85(4) and 4.90(4). Any balance of a future or contingent debt owed to the insolvent party is not payable until it falls due, see rr.2.85(8) and 4.90(8). There are no equivalent provisions in relation to future and contingent debts owed to a bankrupt individual and such debts, it would seem, cannot be the subject of insolvency set-off in bankruptcy.

[386] Insolvency Rules 1986 rr.2.85(2) and 4.90(1).

[387] *MS Fashions Ltd v Bank of Credit and Commerce International SA (No.2)* [1993] Ch. 425; affirmed [1993] Ch. 439.

[388] *Stein v Blake* [1996] A.C. 243. This case concerned s.323 of the Insolvency Act 1986, which is the equivalent provision in relation to personal bankruptcy.

[389] *MS Fashions Ltd v Bank of Credit and Commerce International SA (No. 2)* [1993] Ch. 425, at 432–433, relating to liquidation.

[390] Given pursuant to r.2.95. That this is the relevant date is made clear by r.2.85(3).

[391] *National Westminster Bank Ltd v Halesowen Presswork and Assemblies Ltd* [1972] A.C. 785, Lord Cross dissenting.

private rights enacted for the benefit of individual debtors of the estate having cross-claims against it. This majority ruling in *Halesowen*, though consistent with the imperative language of the set-off provision, constitutes an impediment to the reorganisation of companies in financial difficulty, a fact recognised in *Halesowen* but in the majority view requiring legislation to deal with it. The Insolvency Law Review Committee gave much thought to the matter, pointing out that it was a common practice for a company in difficulty, when negotiating a moratorium with its creditors, to agree to open a new bank account with its existing bankers and keep this in credit, the bank for its part undertaking not to set-off existing indebtedness, so that the fund would be preserved intact for any liquidator and the bank would not receive a preference. The present law makes it necessary for the company to open another account with a different bank.[392] The Committee concluded that there was no sound policy for maintaining the prohibition against contracting-out of insolvency set-off and good commercial reasons for reversing it, and they recommended legislation to that effect.[393] No steps have yet been taken to implement this recommendation.

It is also possible to take steps which have the same effect as contracting out of insolvency set-off: this fact makes the rule against contracting out all the more strange. A creditor can agree not to prove in the debtor's insolvency,[394] which prevents set-off since the debt is not a provable debt. Alternatively, the creditor could declare himself trustee of the debt owed to him. This would break the mutuality required for insolvency set-off, though it would be necessary for the declaration to relate to the debt itself and not just to the proceeds.[395]

The retroactivity principle

The effect of this principle is that the account between the company and the creditor asserting a right of set-off is considered to be taken as at the date of account even though it is not taken, and in practice cannot be taken, until a later date. In other words, insolvency set-off is self-executing and, once the facts are known, operates automatically from the date of account without the need for any procedural step.[396] It follows that it is not open to the creditor to assign his claim against the company after that date but before the actual taking of the account, for the claim must be treated as ipso jure ceasing to exist as a separate claim at the date of account, the claim and cross-claim being then automatically combined by force of law to produce a single net debit balance due to or from the creditor. This net balance, if in favour of the company, is capable of assignment by the liquidator or, if in favour of the solvent party, by that party, at any time after the date of the account, without the need to wait for the taking of accounts.[397] This

7–79

---

[392] Insolvency Law and Practice (Cmnd. 8558, 1982) para.1341.

[393] Insolvency Law and Practice (Cmnd. 8558, 1982) para.1342.

[394] *Re SSSL Realisations (2002) Ltd* [2004] EWHC 1760 (Ch) at [39]; upheld on appeal [2006] EWCA Civ 7.

[395] Derham, *The Law of Set-off* (2010), para.6.144 fn.424. There are indications, though, that the court would be wary of allowing the parties to contract out of insolvency set-off by a declaration of trust, see *Re ILG Travel Ltd (In Administration)* [1995] 2 B.C.L.C. 128, 161.

[396] *Stein v Blake* [1996] A.C. 243, per Lord Hoffmann at 254, 255, 258.

[397] *Stein v Blake* [1996] A.C. 243, per Lord Hoffmann at 258. See also *Farley v Housing and Commercial Developments Ltd* (1984) 1 B.C.C. 99150, 99157.

follows from the fact that the ultimate quantification of claim and cross-claim and the striking of a balance take effect from the date of account. Further, neither the claim nor the cross-claim can be separately enforced after that date, whether in court or arbitral proceedings.[398]

The hindsight principle

7–80   This is closely linked to the principle of retroactivity. In order to determine the state of accounts as at the date of account, the court or insolvency officer looks at events which have occurred between that date and the date when the account is actually taken. The hindsight principle applies in particular to the valuation of claims, whether these are made by way of set-off or otherwise.[399] Contingent claims which crystallise into debts after the date of liquidation are brought into account as debts and may be revalued accordingly[400] with retrospective effect.[401] Future debts are discounted in accordance with the statutory formula,[402] although this does not apply to a balance owed to the company, which is only payable when it falls due.[403] Similarly, amounts put in for existing but unliquidated claims may be adjusted if the claims become liquidated or are able to be more accurately valued in the light of post-liquidation events. It follows from the hindsight principle, as well as from the retroactivity principle, that an assignment of the net balance can be made at any time after the date of account whether or not the net balance has then been struck.

An area of difficulty is the treatment of debts which exist at the date of account, but which are paid by third parties by the date on which the account is actually taken. In theory, the self-executing nature of insolvency set-off means that the debt is extinguished or reduced at the date of account, so that the subsequent payment is superfluous and has no extinguishing effect.[404] Despite this, in one case the court held the payments should be taken into account as extinguishing or reducing the claim, applying the hindsight principle.[405] However, there are both pragmatic and policy reasons for taking account of such payments, even if the conceptual purity of self-executing insolvency set-off is

---

[398] *Bouygues (UK) Ltd v Dahl-Jensen (UK) Ltd* [2000] B.L.R. 522; *Enterprise Managed Services Ltd v Tony McFadden Utilities Ltd* [2009] EWHC 3222 (TCC) [66]–[68].

[399] This principle is clear in relation to all provable debts, see *Re Northern Counties of England Fire Insurance Co* (1880) 17 Ch. D. 337; *Wight v Eckhardt Marine GmbH* [2003] UKPC 37; [2004] 1 A.C. 147; Insolvency Rules rr.2.81 and 4.86(1). Rules 2.85(5) and 4.90(5) apply rr.2.81 and 4.86(1) expressly to claims which are the subject of set-off.

[400] See Insolvency Rules 1986 rr.2.81 and 4.86(1).

[401] Subject only to the qualification that revaluation does not disturb distributions of dividend already made (*Ellis and Company's Trustee v Dixon-Johnson* [1924] 1 Ch. 342, 357), though any additional sum payable as the result of it will have priority in any future distribution.

[402] Insolvency Rules 1986 rr.2.105 and 11.13.

[403] *Re Kaupthing Singer and Friedlander Ltd (In Administration)* [2010] EWCA Civ 518 at [35]. The portion of the debt due to the company which, discounted, is required to effect the set-off is calculated, and the balance is payable without discount on the due date.

[404] The third party might have an unjust enrichment claim against the creditor on the grounds of mistake.

[405] *Bank of Credit and Commerce International (Overseas) Ltd v Habib Bank Ltd* [1999] 1 W.L.R. 42, 50–52, criticised by Derham, *The Law of Set-off* (2010) at paras 6.139–6.141. The creditor's failure to follow the proper appeal procedure in relation to the liquidator's rejection of its proof (which was rejected as the debt had already been paid) was another reason for the decision.

threatened. If a creditor chooses to accept a payment in relation to a debt which may have been extinguished or reduced by set-off,[406] it should not then be able to go back on that decision and rely on an insolvency set-off. Further, the third party's intention to benefit the insolvent party would otherwise be thwarted. While it is possible to restore the parties to the position at the time of the date of account using the law of unjust enrichment, this seems a complicated and costly solution to a problem which does not arise if matters occurring after the date of account are taken into account.

Conditions of application of insolvency set-off

In order for rr.2.85 or 4.90 to apply six conditions must be satisfied[407]:   **7–81**

(1)   the claim by the solvent party must be one which would be admissible for proof at the date of account;
(2)   there must have been mutual credits, mutual debts or other mutual dealings between the parties;
(3)   the company's claim must not have been based on the creditor's wrongdoing[408];
(4)   the mutual dealings must have taken place before the cut-off date;
(5)   the claims on both sides must be such as will in their nature terminate in debts; and
(6)   the debt which the creditor seeks to set-off must not be a debt of the category excluded by r.2.85(2)(e) or r.4.90(2)(d).

We shall examine each of these conditions in turn.

(1)   The claim by the solvent party must be one which would be admissible for proof at the date of taking of the account

The claim by the solvent party must be provable[409] in the insolvency proceedings,   **7–82**
so, for example, it cannot be statute-barred[410] or debarred by the rule against double proof.[411] This follows from the words of r.2.85(2) and r.4.90(1) "any

---

[406] Another possible situation is where the creditor accepts, or even solicits, a payment from a guarantor on the grounds that the guarantee provides sufficiently clearly for his liability to remain despite the operation of insolvency set-off, see *Rayden v Edwardo Ltd* [2008] EWHC 2689 (Comm); criticised by Derham, *The Law of Set-Off* (2010), paras 18.38–18.39.

[407] R. Goode, *Principles of Corporate Insolvency Law*, 4th edn (London: Sweet & Maxwell, 2011), para.9–22.

[408] This relates to a claim for misfeasance or proceedings for other similar wrongdoing, see para.7–84, below.

[409] *In Re Fenton Ex p. Fenton Textile Association Ltd* [1931] 1 Ch. 85; affirmed *Secretary of State for Trade v Frid* [2004] UKHL 24 at [13].

[410] *Pott v Clegg* (1847) 16 M. & W. 321.

[411] *In Re Fenton Ex p. Fenton Textile Association Ltd* [1931] 1 Ch. 85. See para.8–23, below. Where the rule against double proof precludes insolvency set-off, it also precludes the operation of the rule in *Cherry v Boultbee*, see *Mills v HSBC Trustee (CI) Ltd* [2011] UKSC 48.

creditor of the company proving or claiming to prove for a debt".[412] According to the relevant rules,[413] a provable debt, while it can be future or contingent, must accrue, or arise out of an obligation incurred, before the date of entry into insolvency proceedings.[414] The meaning of "obligation incurred" in this context was a matter of some uncertainty,[415] but the position has now been greatly clarified by the recent decision of the Supreme Court in *Re Nortel Companies*[416] (*Nortel*). This confirmed that a contingent debt arising out of a pre-existing contractual obligation is included, and suggested three criteria governing whether an obligation falls within the definition in the more difficult case of where it arises out of a non-contractual source, such as statute or tort.[417] The first criterion is that the insolvent party must have "taken, or be subjected to, some step or combination of steps which had some legal effect (such as putting it under some legal duty or into some legal relationship)". The second is that this step, or these combination of steps "resulted in it being vulnerable to the specific liability in question, such that there would be a real prospect of that liability being incurred", and the third is "whether it would be consistent with the regime under which the liability is imposed to conclude that the step or combination of steps gave rise to an obligation under Rule 13.12(1)(b)". The Supreme Court made it clear that, as a matter of principle, it was desirable if "every debt or liability capable of being expressed in money terms should be eligible for proof",[418] and commented that "[t]he notion that all possible liabilities within reason should be provable helps achieve equal justice to all creditors and potential creditors in any insolvency".[419] The *Nortel* decision, which has the effect of not only clarifying the law but also extending the scope of provable contingent debts, also thereby extends the scope of debts available for insolvency set-off.[420]

Although the requirement of provability does not apply to a claim owed *to* the company by a creditor, similar considerations apply, since such a claim must arise out of an obligation incurred before the cut-off date.[421] It is important to

---

[412] A possible problem in relation to administration is that, in relation to certain claims, the date of the account is very different from that on which eligibility for proof is determined (the "cut-off" date (r.2.85(2)), see D. Turing, "Setting off down a new road" (2004) 9 J.I.B.F.L. 349; and para.7–85, below.

[413] Insolvency Rules 1986 rr.12.3 and 13.12, see also s.382 of the Insolvency Act 1986 in relation to bankruptcy.

[414] That is, the date on which the company goes into liquidation or enters administration, or the commencement of the bankruptcy. In relation to market contracts on recognised exchanges or through recognised clearing houses, and in relation to securities settlement systems, a net sum which is payable as a result of default proceedings is statutorily provided to be a provable debt, s.163 of the Companies Act 1989, Financial Markets and Insolvency (Settlement Finality) Regulations 1999 (SI 1999/2979) reg.15.

[415] The cases which had caused this uncertainty, particularly *R (on the application of Steele) v Birmingham City Council* [2005] EWCA Civ 1824; and *Glenister v Rowe* [2000] Ch. 76 were overruled by the Supreme Court in *Nortel*.

[416] *Re Nortel Companies* [2013] UKSC 52.

[417] *Nortel* [2013] UKSC 52 at [76]–[77].

[418] This was a quotation from the report of the Review Committee on Insolvency Law and Practice (the Cork Report) 1982 Cmnd 8558 para.1289. See *Nortel* [2013] UKSC 52 at [92].

[419] *Nortel* [2013] UKSC 52 at [93].

[420] The co-extensiveness of the test for provable debts, and for debts which can be set-off, was made clear in the case of *HMRC v Millichap* [2011] B.P.I.R. 145.

[421] *HMRC v Millichap* [2011] B.P.I.R. 145. See para.7–85, below for discussion of the cut-off date.

remember that not all claims eligible for proof are also eligible for set-off. The requirement of mutuality must also be satisfied,[422] as well as the other criteria discussed below.

The requirement of provability also affects whether insolvency set-off applies to secured claims. Where the insolvent party is owed a debt for which it has security, the existence of the security will not prevent insolvency set-off arising, since the non-insolvent party is clearly a creditor of the company proving or claiming to prove for a debt.[423] However, where the debt owed by the insolvent party is secured, the position is less clear. On one view, insolvency set-off operates automatically to any mutual debts: this takes place (notionally) at the date of account and it should not matter whether either debt is secured, or whether the secured party later choose to enforce his security, since by that time the debt is already extinguished or reduced by set-off.[424] This view, though, overlooks the requirement that the solvent party be a "creditor of the company proving or claiming to prove for a debt". If a creditor chooses not to prove in the liquidation or the distribution by the administrator, then it does fall within this requirement.[425] A secured creditor has the option of surrendering its security and proving for the whole debt,[426] but the default position, if it does not exercise this choice, is that it enforces or values its security and only proves for the balance due to it, if any.[427] Thus the debt, to the extent that it is secured, is not a provable debt, unless the election to surrender is made.[428] The choice whether to surrender or to enforce its security will often be taken by the solvent party after the date of account. Providing that the choice is made before the date the account is taken, the insolvency officer can take account of this choice by the operation of the hindsight principle. Unless the solvent party chooses to prove for the whole debt, insolvency set-off only applies to the unsecured balance, if any.[429]

---

[422] *Bank of Credit and Commerce International SA v Prince Fahd Bin Salman Abdul Aziz Al-Saud* [1997] B.C.C. 63. See para.7–83, below.

[423] *Hiley v Peoples Prudential Assurance Co Ltd (in liq)* (1938) 60 C.L.R. 468. This was also the situation in *Re ILG Travel Ltd* [1995] 2 B.C.L.C. 128.

[424] *MS Fashions Ltd v Bank of Credit and Commerce International SA (No.2)* [1993] Ch. 425, 446, per Dillon L.J.; *Re ILG Travel Ltd* [1995] 2 B.C.L.C. 128,159. These two general statements that insolvency set-off applies to debts whether secured or unsecured both rely on the cases cited in fn.423 which dealt with the situation where the insolvent party held security for the debt owed to it by the non-insolvent party. See also Goode, *Principles of Corporate Insolvency Law* (2011), para.9–23.

[425] *Kitchen's Trustee v Madders* [1950] Ch. 134; *Re Bank of Credit and Commerce International SA (No.8)* [1996] Ch. 245.

[426] Insolvency Rules 1986 rr.4.88(2) and 2.83(2).

[427] Insolvency Rules 1986 rr.4.88(1) and 2.83(1) (realising security) and 4.75(1)(e) and 2.72(3)(vii) (valuing security).

[428] See McCracken, *The Banker's Remedy of Set-off* (2010). This argument that meets the criticism that the relevant time to test provability is at the date of account, and it is irrelevant whether the creditor actually proves or not (*Stein v Blake* [1996] A.C. 243, 253, per Lord Hoffmann, relying on *Re Daintrey Ex p. Mant* [1900] 1 Q.B. 546, 568). In any event, Lord Hoffmann's dictum was in the context of an account not being linked to any step in the insolvency proceedings, rather than in relation to the application of r.4.90 to secured claims.

[429] *Re Norman Holding Co Ltd* [1991] B.C.L.C. 1; *Stewart v Scottish Widows and Life Assurance Society Plc* [2005] EWHC 1831 (QB). The latter case makes clear (at [185]) that Lord Hoffmann's opinion in *Stein v Blake* [1996] A.C. 243, 253 cannot be said to have overruled *Re Norman Holdings*, which was cited in the printed case in *Stein v Blake* but not in argument. See also *BCCI (No.8)* [1996] Ch. 245, 256: "Set-off ought not to prejudice the right of a secured creditor to enforce his security in any order he chooses and at a time of his choice", per Dillon L.J.

(2)   Mutual credits, mutual debts and other mutual dealings

7–83   The inclusion of the phrase "and other mutual dealings" in the rule by s.39 of the Bankruptcy Act 1869 might be thought to narrow the scope of insolvency set-off to contractual claims. However, the purpose of s.39 was to widen the scope of the right of set-off, and in *Re West End Networks Ltd; Secretary of State for Trade and Industry v Frid* the House of Lords decided that the phrase did not have this limiting effect but extended to cross-claims such as that arising from the imposition of a statutory obligation or the commission of a tort.[430] The *Frid* case concerned the Secretary of State's statutory liability to employees on the insolvency of the company. Despite the width of Lord Hoffmann's dicta, it is not clear that all tort claims are included. The tort claim given as an example by Lord Hoffmann to arise from "dealings", that in *Gye v McIntyre*,[431] was for a fraudulent misrepresentation, which, although inducing the insolvent person to enter into a contract with a third party, arose from business dealings since the creditor was the tenant of the third party company. Can a claim in negligence or conversion against the company be said to arise from "mutual dealings"? This is an important question, as it is now clear that such tort claims, even contingent ones, are "debts" for the purposes of proof in a winding up or administration,[432] and one interpretation of Lord Hoffmann's dicta in *Frid* is that all such debts now fall within r.2.85 and r.4.90. However, it is not necessarily the case that all provable debts can be set-off and the requirement of "mutual dealings" could be said to be an additional limiting factor.[433] For example, a misappropriation of a company's property has been held not to be a "dealing",[434] as has a claim in conversion.[435]

The requirement of mutuality has two facets. First, the respective characters of the claim and the cross-claim must be commensurate. This means that claim and cross-claim must both be monetary claims or claims which a party is entitled to have reduced to money.[436] So a person holding property as bailee or trustee for another cannot set-off against his delivery or accounting obligation a money claim against the bailor or beneficiary. This rule is so strictly applied that even if the property held by the trustee is itself a money fund, the trustee is not permitted to set-off his personal claim against the beneficiary, and if the beneficiary goes into insolvency proceedings the trustee must transfer the fund to the insolvency officer intact and is left to prove in the insolvency proceedings for his cross-claim.[437] The same rule applies where it is the insolvent party who is the

---

[430] *Re West End Networks Ltd; Secretary of State for Trade and Industry v Frid* [2004] UKHL 24 at [24]. In relation to statutory obligations, see also *Re Curtis (Builders) Ltd* [1978] Ch. 162.

[431] *Gye v McIntyre* (1991) 171 C.L.R. 609.

[432] Insolvency Rules rr.12.3 and 13.10 as interpreted in *Re T & N Ltd* [2005] EWHC 2870 (Ch) which concerned contingent negligence claims for exposure to asbestos.

[433] See Derham, *The Law of Set-Off* (2010), paras 7.24–7.26 and 8.53–8.54.

[434] *Manson v Smith* [1997] 2 B.C.L.C. 161, 164; followed in *Re A company (No.1641 of 2003)* [2004] 1 B.C.L.C. 210 at [25].

[435] *Smith (Administrator of Cosslett (Contractors) Ltd) v Bridgend County BC* [2002] 1 A.C. 336 at [35]. For criticism, see A Berg, "Cosslett – Section 395 and set-off in the House of Lords : part 2" (2002) Insolvency Intelligence 20.

[436] See para.7–86, below.

[437] This conclusion arises in a number of contexts in which money is held on trust. One is where money is held for a particular purpose and cannot be applied for a different purpose, namely towards

trustee.[438] Secondly, there must be mutuality of parties, that is, the claim and cross-claim must be between the same parties in the same right. So it is not possible to set-off against a claim by the insolvent party a cross-claim against a third party, even if prior to liquidation there had been a valid contractual set-off along these lines, for on winding-up any contractual set-off, so far as not already exercised, disappears.[439] Again, a claim against the insolvent party cannot be set-off against a claim vested in that party as trustee for a third party,[440] nor can a claim by the insolvent party against a debtor be set-off against a claim (against the insolvent party) held on trust by that debtor.[441] In determining mutuality the court will look at the beneficial ownership of claim and cross-claim rather than the legal title, so that a claim held on trust for a beneficiary can be set-off against a debt owed by that beneficiary to the person owing the claim.[442] Clear evidence, however, is required that the beneficial interest is vested in someone other than the party holding the legal title.[443] The same applies where a debt has been assigned. However, this is only the case where the set-off arose after the debtor had notice of the trust or the assignment: if it arose before that time the beneficiary or assignee takes the debt subject to the set-off.[444] Further, a transaction set-off arising after notice may still bind the beneficiary or assignee.[445]

(3)   The company's claim must not have been based on the creditor's wrongdoing

There are several reasons for this condition. First, a claim in respect of wrongdoing does not arise out of "mutual dealings". This has been held to be the case in relation to misfeasance by a director of the insolvent company[446] and in   **7–84**

---

discharge of a cross-claim, without the consent of the person for whom it is held (*National Westminster Bank Plc v Halesowen Presswork and Assemblies Ltd* [1972] A.C. 785, per Lord Kilbrandon at 821; *In Re Mid-Kent Fruit Factory* [1896] 1 Ch. 567). Another is where a secured creditor holds the surplus after enforcing a security interest: this cannot be set-off against another debt owed by the insolvent party to the creditor (*Talbot v Frere* (1878) 9 Ch. D. 568; *Re Gedney* [1908] 1 Ch. 804). The same principle would, of course, apply if the trust were express, constructive or resulting. Another way of reaching the same result is to say that a contract claim and a trust claim do not constitute mutual dealings *Elgood v Harris* [1896] 2 Q.B. 491, 494).

[438] *Lehman Brothers International (Europe) (In Administration) v CRC Credit Fund Ltd* [2009] EWHC 3228 (Ch) at [331]; *Re Lehman Brothers International (Europe) (In Administration)* [2012] EWHC 2997 (Ch) at [55].

[439] See para.7–90, below.

[440] *Re Arthur Saunders Ltd* (1981) 17 B.L.R. 125, 133; *Barclays Bank Ltd v Quistclose Investments Ltd* [1970] A.C. 597 HL; *Newcastle Building Society v Mill* [2009] EWHC 740 (Ch) at [9].

[441] *Forster v Wilson* (1843) 12 M. & W.91; 152 E.R. 1165.

[442] *Bailey v Finch* (1871) L.R. 7 Q.B. 34; *Bailey v Johnson* (1872) L.R. 7 Ex. 263.

[443] *Bank of Credit and Commerce International SA v Prince Fahd Bin Salman Abdul Aziz Al-Saud* [1997] B.C.C. 63.

[444] See para.7–70, above.

[445] See para.7–70, above. It is not entirely clear whether this applies after the insolvency of the debtor, but the nature of transaction set-off as a substantive defence would seem to indicate that it should, see Derham, *The Law of Set-off* (2010), paras 6.25–6.32.

[446] *Manson v Smith* [1997] 2 B.C.L.C. 161, 164; followed in *Re A company (No.1641 of 2003)* [2004] 1 B.C.L.C. 210 at [25]; *Bracken Partners Ltd v Gutteridge* [2003] EWHC 1064 (Ch) at [56].

relation to a claim for conversion of the company's property,[447] although fraudulent misrepresentation claims based on negotiations of a transaction with the insolvent party do appear to come within the scope of "mutual dealings".[448] It does not appear to be the heinous nature of the wrongdoing which is determinative, but the closeness of the claim to a contractual claim: conversion is a tort of strict liability, while many breaches of contract can involve a considerable amount of wrongdoing.[449] Another reason for this condition is said to be that a creditor, otherwise unsecured, should not be able to build up a set-off by his own wrongdoing.[450] However, if this is the case, it is difficult to see why a claim based on intentional contractual wrongdoing can be set-off. Further, this argument would lead to the conclusion that a claim founded on the wrongdoing of the creditor cannot be set-off, while a claim founded on the wrongdoing of the company can, whereas this would not seem to be the case if wrongdoing is not included in "mutual dealings".

(4)   The mutual dealings must have preceded the cut-off date

7-85   The "cut-off date" is the date after which claims incurred by either the company or the creditor cannot be included in the account. It is not necessary that the dealings should have given rise to mutual debts prior to the cut-off date, it suffices that the mutual dealings have created obligations which give rise to claims that can be set against each other at the time when it becomes necessary to ascertain the state of account between the parties.[451] Under r.4.90, in relation to liquidations,[452] the cut-off date is the earliest of the following:

(a)   the date of the winding-up order;
(b)   the date when the creditor had notice that:
    (i)   a meeting of creditors had been summoned under s.98; or
    (ii)   a petition for the winding up of the company was pending[453];
(c)   where the liquidation is immediately preceded by an administration:
    (i)   the date when the creditor had notice that an application for an administration order was pending or a person had given notice of intention to appoint an administrator; or
    (ii)   the commencement of that administration.[454]

---

[447] *Smith (Administrator of Cosslett (Contractors) Ltd) v Bridgend County BC* [2002] 1 A.C. 336 at [35].

[448] *Gye v McIntyre* (1991) 171 C.L.R. 609. See also *Jack v Kipping* (1882) 9 Q.B.D. 113; *Tilley v Bowman Ltd* [1910] 1 K.B. 745; *Kitchen's Trustee v Madders* [1950] Ch. 134.

[449] S. Frisby, "The flawed site saga: Cosslett in the House of Lords" (2002) Insolvency Lawyer 137.

[450] *Manson v Smith* [1997] 2 B.C.L.C. 161, 165.

[451] *Stein v Blake* [1996] 1 A.C. 243.

[452] The position in relation to bankruptcy is governed by s.323 of the Insolvency Act 1986. The cut-off date is the earliest of either the date of the bankruptcy order or the date on which the creditor had notice that a bankruptcy petition relating to the bankrupt was pending.

[453] The purpose of this is to prevent the creation of claims after the creditor has notice that liquidation is imminent: the creditor then extends credit to the company at its own risk, see Financial Markets Law Committee (FMLC), *Report on Issue 108: Administration set-off and expenses* (November 2007) para.2.3.

[454] Insolvency Rules 1986 r.4.90(2).

In most cases (at least where the liquidation is not preceded by an administration) the cut-off date will be shortly before the date of the account (the date of the winding-up order).

However, the position is different in relation to administrations. There, the cut-off date is the earliest of the following:

(a)   the commencement of the administration;
(b)   the date when the creditor had notice that:
    (i)   an application for an administration order was pending; or
    (ii)   any person had given notice of intention to appoint an administrator;
(c)   where the adminstration is immediately preceded by a winding-up:
    (i)   the creditor had notice that a meeting of creditors had been summoned under s.98 or a petition for the winding up of the company was pending; or
    (ii)   the date of the winding-up order.[455]

Leaving aside the unusual case where the administration is preceded by a liquidation, this still means that the cut-off date is likely to be considerably earlier than the date of the account (the date of the distribution notice), unlike the position in liquidation.[456] The policy behind the cut-off date in liquidation (that once a creditor knew liquidation was pending, they extended credit at their own risk) backfires when the purpose of the insolvency proceedings is corporate rescue, which would normally involve creditors extending further credit to the company. The effect of the rule is that there is little incentive for creditors to extend credit once the company is in administration, or if they do, they would want to exercise any non-insolvency set-off right (which continues until a distribution notice is served) as soon as possible.[457] Also, unlike liquidation, it is often not clear whether an administration will result in a distribution at all: if corporate rescue is achieved this will not happen, but even if the administrator initially pursues corporate rescue, he may end up making a distribution, because the corporate rescue fails, or, if the business is sold as a going concern, he decides to distribute to creditors rather than to put the company into liquidation or use a scheme of arrangement or CVA.[458] This uncertainty is unfortunate.[459]

---

[455] Insolvency Rules 1986 r.2.85(2).

[456] For a full discussion of the ramifications of this, see the FMLC, *Report on Issue 108: Administration set-off and expenses* and *Addendum* (March 2011) which propose either that administration expenses should be treated as mutual dealings, or that the cut-off date for debts incurred by the company should be the date of the distribution notice and not the date of the onset of administration. See also Turing, "Setting off down a new road" (2004) 19 J.I.B.F.L. 349.

[457] While it is reasonably clear that independent and transaction set-off will apply during this period (although the effect of the moratorium in para.43(6) Sch.B1 to the Insolvency Act 1986 is that no proceedings can be brought in relation to any claims against the insolvent company), it is less clear that a contractual set-off which does not fall within the mutuality requirements of r.2.85 will apply. (FMLC, *Report on Issue 108: Administration Set-off and Expenses: Addendum* (March 2011), paras 5.1–5.3). It is possible that credit extended to the company after the onset of administration would be recoverable pursuant to the "super-priority" over floating charge assets under the Insolvency Act 1986 Sch.B1 para.99, but even this does not give as much protection as insolvency set-off.

[458] FMLC, *Report on Issue 108: Administration set-off and expenses* (November 2007), fn.348 paras 3.3–3.5.

[459] Other potential problems with r.2.85 are set out in the FMLC letter to the Insolvency Service dated January 6, 2012.

(5)   The claims on both sides much be such as will in their nature terminate in debt

7–86   Set-off is in principle confined to mutual money obligations. The solvent party cannot rely on set-off to withhold property of the company in his possession or control, whether as bailee or as bare trustee, and in the latter case this applies as much to a money fund held by the solvent party as bare trustee for the company as it does to tangible property so held.[460] Accordingly if B, a bailee of goods owned by A Co, wrongfully sells the goods he cannot set-off a debt due to him from the company against his obligation to account for the proceeds, for the company's claim to the proceeds is not a mere money claim in debt but a claim to ownership of the money fund which is enforceable as a proprietary claim in equity. An additional ground for refusing a set-off is that a person cannot take advantage of his own wrong by converting another's property into money and that this is not a dealing.[461] It should be stressed, however, that a set-off is only not available where the claim (by either party) is for the return of property belonging to it held by the other, either as bailee (if the property is tangible) or on trust. Where the claim is a contractual claim for the delivery or transfer of property, this, if breached or disclaimed, would give rise to a claim for damages. Thus such a claim is, at the relevant time, a contingent debt, and can therefore be the subject of insolvency set-off.[462]

However, there are at least two apparent exceptions to the rule precluding set-off against property and trust moneys. First, if the property of the company in liquidation is subject to a lien or other security interest in favour of the solvent party and the security carries through to the proceeds of sale, it may be enforced by retention of the proceeds to the extent of the amount owing to the secured creditor.[463] This is not a true set-off, merely a method of enforcing the security interest. Second, if property of the company is held by another with instructions or authority to convert it into money, then so long as that authority remains unrevoked at the time of liquidation the other party, on selling the property, can set-off against his liability to account for the proceeds a debt owed to him by the company in liquidation, even if the sale does not take place until after winding up, provided that the proceeds are received by the claimant by the time it becomes necessary to ascertain the state of accounts between him and the company.

The basis of this second exception is the principle established in *Rose v Hart*,[464] which has been said to constitute an anomalous exception to the rule that a money claim may not be set-off against a proprietary claim and to the separate mutuality rule that trust funds are not susceptible to set-off.[465] But this is doubtful. The essence of the rule in *Rose v Hart* is the provision of mutual credits,

---

[460] See para.7–83, above.

[461] *Smith v Bridgend County BC* [2002] 1 A.C. 336 at [35].

[462] If the obligation to deliver or transfer had been carried out by the time that the account is taken, then the contingency has not and will not occur, and so the "contingent debt" will be valued at zero on the application of the hindsight principle.

[463] Any surplus will be held on trust for the insolvent party and cannot be the subject of insolvency set-off, see *Talbot v Frere* (1878) 9 Ch. D. 568; *Re Gedney* [1908] 1 Ch. 804 and fn.437, above.

[464] *Rose v Hart* (1818) 8 Taunt. 499.

[465] Derham, *The Law of Set-off* (2010), para.10.18.

the solvent party extending credit to the company in reliance on his prospective receipt of the proceeds of the company's property for which the company gives credit to him, and that the credits are such "as must in their nature terminate in debts".[466] Hence the true basis of the decision in *Rose v Hart* would seem to be that the person holding the company's property with instructions to convert it into money has implied authority, by virtue of their mutual dealings, to regard himself as a mere debtor for a sum equal to the proceeds, not as a trustee of the proceeds themselves, which he is free to treat as his own moneys.[467]

The significance of the distinction is well-established in decisions on reservation of title to goods under contracts of sale which authorise resale by the buyer but impose no express requirement that he is to account for the proceeds of sale. In such cases the court is likely to infer that the buyer is merely to be a debtor for the amount of the proceeds (or of such part of them as is necessary to discharge his price obligation), not a trustee.[468] A similar principle applies where the terms of the agreement between the parties impose on the solvent party a duty to hold the proceeds on trust for the company but entitle him to deduct sums due to him from the company. Such an agreement will be construed as creating a charge on the proceeds, so that the solvent party is not a bare trustee but one whose trust obligation applies only to the balance remaining in his hands after he has deducted from the proceeds the amount due to him.[469] The absence of a duty to keep the proceeds segregated from the solvent party's own moneys is not inconsistent with such a trust.[470] The position is otherwise where the solvent party is a bare trustee of the proceeds and thus has a duty to make them over to the company in liquidation without deduction.[471]   **7–87**

All this presupposes that the disposition of the company's property was authorised, for if it was not the person making it can hardly contend that he had authority to treat the proceeds as his own. Moreover, as previously mentioned, a person cannot rely on his own wrongdoing to create a set-off or to serve as a mutual dealing. So if he never had authority to sell in the first place or his authority was revoked prior to the sale he will be a trustee of the entire proceeds and will have no right to set-off his cross-claim against his duty to account.[472]

In the light of these considerations the decision of the Court of Appeal in the controversial decision in *Rolls Razor Ltd v Cox*[473] is hard to justify. In that case the authority of the solvent party, an employee of the insolvent company, to sell the company's goods in his possession had been revoked by the company before the goods were sold. The principles discussed above lead to the conclusion that the employee held the proceeds on trust for the company and therefore there was no mutuality, and therefore no set-off, in relation to debts owed to him by the   **7–88**

---

[466] *Rose v Hart* (1818) 8 Taunt. 499, per Gibbs C.J. at 506.

[467] For further discussion see Derham, *The Law of Set-off* (2010), paras 10.19–10.20.

[468] *Re Andrabell Ltd* [1984] 3 All E.R. 407; *Hendy Lennox Ltd v Grahame Puttick Ltd* [1984] 2 All E.R. 152.

[469] *Re ILG Travel Ltd* [1995] 2 B.C.L.C. 128, 158; *Re Greenport Ltd (In Liquidation) Obaray v Gateway (London) Ltd* [2004] 1 B.C.L.C. 555, 565.

[470] *Re ILG Travel Ltd* [1995] 2 B.C.L.C. 128. See also *Re SSSL Realisations (2002) Ltd* [2004] EWHC 1760 (Ch) [49]–[54].

[471] *Re ILG Travel Ltd* [1995] 2 B.C.L.C. 128; *Henry v Hammond* [1913] 2 K.B. 515.

[472] *Rose v Hart* (1818) 8 Taunt. 499; *Eberle's Hotels & Restaurant Co Ltd v Jonas* (1887) 18 Q.B.D. 459.

[473] *Rolls Razor Ltd v Cox* [1967] 1 All E.R. 397.

company. However, the Court of Appeal held that there was a set-off, although they rejected the argument that the employee had a lien over the goods on the grounds that this was excluded by the employment contract which required him to deliver up the goods on the termination of the agreement. Surely it was equally inconsistent with the agreement that he should be allowed to sell the goods after termination of his authority and then deduct what was due to him from the proceeds. The decision in *Rose v Hart*[474] was specifically predicated on the assumption that the agent's authority to sell remained unrevoked up to the time of sale, and the same was true of the decision in *Palmer v Day*.[475] Nor could it be said that the defendant's authority to sell was irrevocable because it was coupled with an interest,[476] namely the right to look to the proceeds for payment of his commission, for this, too, was prohibited by the agreement. Accordingly it could not be said that there were mutual credits, and that being so the defendant's authority to sell had been effectively brought to an end by the company and would in any event have come to an end on the winding-up.[477] The defendant was thus not a mere debtor but a trustee, who ought not to have been allowed to profit from his own act of conversion.[478] It is true that the set-off provisions are mandatory—a point relied on by Lord Denning M.R. to overcome the contract point—but they do not apply at all unless the test of mutuality is satisfied, and this is not the case where the claim on one side is to payment of money and on the other to delivery of property held on trust or to the proceeds of property wrongfully converted. The present position has rightly been described as anomalous.[479]

(6) Solvent party's debt must not be excluded by rule 2.85(2)(e) or rule 4.90(2)(d)

7–89   Generally a person owing the company money is entitled to set-off against his liability a claim vested in him as assignee, so a debtor to a company can purchase a claim against the company and set this off against the company's claim on him.[480] However, there is a general principle of insolvency law preventing a debtor to the company from improving his position vis-à-vis other creditors by buying in claims against the company after notice of a formal act indicative of the company's inability to pay its debts,[481] and this principle is reflected in r.4.90(2)(d), so that a debt cannot be set-off if it was acquired by a creditor, by assignment or otherwise, pursuant to an agreement between the creditor and any

---

[474] *Rose v Hart* (1818) 8 Taunt. 499.

[475] *Plamer v Day* [1895] 2 Q.B. 618.

[476] See *Bowstead and Reynolds on Agency*, 19th edn (London: Sweet & Maxwell, 2010), paras 10–006 and 10–007.

[477] *In Gromal (UK) Ltd v WT Shipping Ltd* Unreported July 13, 1984 CA, the Court of Appeal held that where a freight forwarder's authority to sell goods had come to an end, there could be no set-off between a monetary debt owed to the insolvent company and a claim for goods belonging to the company.

[478] See para.7–84, above.

[479] P. Wood, *English and International Set-off* (London: Sweet & Maxwell, 1989), para.9–304.

[480] Goode, *Principles of Corporate Insolvency Law* (2011), para.9–34.

[481] See *Re Eros Films Ltd* [1963] Ch. 565. See *Lightman & Moss: The Law of Administrators and Receivers of Companies*, 4th edn (London: Sweet & Maxwell, 2007), at paras 20–029 et seq.

other party where that agreement was entered into after the cut-off date.[482] These provisions have been mirrored in r.2.85(2)(e), except that, as discussed above, the cut-off date for administration is much earlier.[483] However, unlike the situation in relation to the incurring of debts, there are sound policy reasons for prohibiting trafficking in debts after the date of administration (or notice of intention to appoint an administrator).[484]

The effect of insolvency on contractual set-off and netting

As discussed above,[485] the rules of insolvency set-off are mandatory, and displace all other forms of set-off not exercised prior to the date of account. This is of no great significance in relation to independent set-off, transaction set-off and current-account set-off, for in virtually every situation in which these forms of set-off are available there would be an automatic set-off under the rules of insolvency set-off. Indeed, the latter are broader, not only because they are self-executing but also because insolvency set-off extends to future and contingent claims, which would be outside the scope of the three other forms of set-off just mentioned. But contractual set-off is in a different category, for outside insolvency the parties are free to agree on almost any kind of netting and set-off arrangement they choose.[486]

7–90

The most significant situation in which contractual set-off goes beyond insolvency set-off is where the debts to be set-off are not mutual, that is, where there is an agreement that (where A is the insolvent company) a debt owed by A to B can be set-off against a debt owed to A by C. The significant question is whether the liquidator is bound by this agreement, or whether he can choose to ignore it, sue C and let B prove in the liquidation (or, if the contracts are executory, require performance of the profitable contract while disclaiming or declining to perform the unprofitable contract and leaving the other party to prove in the winding-up).[487] If the liquidator were bound by the agreement, he would not be able to sue C nor would B be able to prove in the liquidation.

There are two principles which render contractual arrangements, entered into before a party becomes insolvent, unenforceable on the insolvency of that party.[488] These principles have been discussed in some detail in recent cases.[489] The first is the anti-deprivation principle, which applies where there is a

---

[482] For the cut-off date in liquidation, see para.7–85, above.

[483] Para.7–85, above.

[484] See the FMLC, *Report on Issue 108: Administration set-off and expenses* (November 2007), which does not propose any change to the rules in this regard.

[485] See para.7–78, above.

[486] See para.7–22, above.

[487] This is because of the rule that sums earned by the company by post-liquidation activity are not part of its general assets and are thus not susceptible to set-off of pre-liquidation claims. See para.7–101, below.

[488] The principles only apply when and if the insolvent party enters into insolvency proceedings. However, the precise timing depends on which principle is involved and which insolvency proceedings are involved, see below.

[489] *Belmont Park Investments Pty Ltd v BNY Corporate Trustee Services Ltd and Lehman Brothers Special Financing Inc* [2011] UKSC 38; *Revenue and Customs Commissioners v Football League Ltd* [2012] EWHC 1372 (Ch); in *LBSF v Carlton Communications* [2011] EWHC 718 (Ch); *Lomas v JFB Firth Rixson Inc* [2010] EWHC 3372 (Ch) (first instance) and *Lomas v JFB Firth Rixson Inc* [2012] EWCA Civ 419 (on appeal).

deliberate intention to evade the insolvency laws by contractually providing for the insolvent party to be deprived, on insolvency, of assets it otherwise would have for distribution to creditors.[490] This principle operates in both liquidation and administration.[491] The second is the pari passu principle. This principle provides that the distribution of the assets of the insolvent party should be distributed to unsecured creditors on a pari passu basis,[492] and also renders void any contractual or other provision which has the effect of distributing assets belonging to the insolvent estate on a basis which is not pari passu.[493] This principle operates regardless of the intention of either the insolvent party or the contractual counterparties, and there is no requirement that the contractual provision is triggered by the insolvency.[494] Its purpose, which is fundamental to insolvency law, is to preserve equality of distributive treatment among creditors although, because of the many true and false exceptions to it, it is sometimes said to preserve equality only among creditors of the same class.[495] Since the principle relates to the distribution made to creditors, it applies when distribution is the overriding purpose of insolvency proceedings, that is, to liquidation, bankruptcy and to administration once a notice of distribution has been issued. Thus, any contractual arrangements which have their effect before the company enters liquidation, or an individual is declared bankrupt, or a notice of distribution is issued by an administrator (collectively, "the relevant date") will not be rendered void by the principle.[496]

Since the pari passu principle operates regardless of intention to evade the insolvency laws, and regardless of whether a provision is triggered by insolvency or not, it would, absent statutory provisions, render unenforceable any set-off, even where the debts are mutual, on the basis that the creditor who can rely on set-off is "paid" in full, leaving fewer assets for distribution to the other creditors, who will only be paid a proportion of what is owed to them. Further, set-off pursuant to an agreement has the effect of enabling the creditor to opt out of the collective insolvency procedure, and have his debt paid by other means (these means involving a detriment to A's assets).[497] However, under English law insolvency set-off of mutual debs is permitted and statutorily provided for, for the policy reasons set out earlier.[498] Thus the effect of the pari passu principle is only to invalidate contractual arrangements providing for set-off which falls outside

---

[490] *Belmont Park Investments Pty Ltd v BNY Corporate Trustee Services Ltd and Lehman Brothers Special Financing Inc* [2011] UKSC 38 at [78]–[79]; *Revenue and Customs Commissioners v Football League Ltd* [2012] EWHC 1372 (Ch) at [69].

[491] *Revenue and Customs Commissioners v Football League Ltd* [2012] EWHC 1372 (Ch) at [100].

[492] Insolvency Act 1986 ss.107 and 306(1) (voluntary winding-up and personal bankruptcy), r.4.181 of the Insolvency Rules 1986 (winding-up by the court) and r.2.69 (administration).

[493] *Revenue and Customs Commissioners v Football League Ltd* [2012] EWHC 1372 (Ch) at [64].

[494] *Revenue and Customs Commissioners v Football League Ltd* [2012] EWHC 1372 (Ch) at [65].

[495] R. Mokal, "Priority as pathology: the pari passu myth" (2001) 60 C.L.J. 581.

[496] *Revenue and Customs Commissioners v Football League Ltd* [2012] EWHC 1372 (Ch) at [76]–[90].

[497] *British Eagle International Air Lines Ltd v Compagnie Nationale Air France* [1975] 1 W.L.R. 758, 780, where Lord Cross says: The question is, in essence, whether what was called in argument the "mini liquidation" flowing from the clearing house arrangements is to yield to or to prevail over the general liquidation; see Mokal, "Priority as pathology: the pari passu myth" (2001) 60 C.L.J. 581, 599–600.

[498] See para.7–01, above.

the scope of insolvency set-off. This is likely to be the case in relation to multilateral netting agreements,[499] since the mutuality requirements are not met.

Netting through a clearing house works perfectly well as regards transactions   **7–91**
settled before winding-up or administration of a member, but may be unenforceable in relation to unsettled transactions after that date. For this reason, netting arrangements are designed to ensure as far as possible either that all netting and all set-offs are completed before the relevant date,[500] so that there is no need to resort to insolvency set-off, or that the contractual rights on both sides will have undergone such conversion (if any) as may be necessary to satisfy the requirements of the Insolvency Rules as to mutuality of claims and parties.[501] For this purpose a number of techniques are available which in normal circumstances can be expected to be effective. These have been described earlier.[502]

We consider, first, the impact of general insolvency law on uncompleted multilateral netting arrangements and close-out netting arrangements, and, secondly, the ameliorating effect of statutory provisions relating to market contracts and financial collateral.

Effect under the general insolvency law

Multilateral netting   The decision of the House of Lords in *British Eagle*   **7–92**
International Air Lines Ltd v Compagnie Nationale Air France[503] concerned a multilateral netting arrangement. The International Air Transport Association (IATA) set up a clearing house system by which sums due from member airlines to each other would be netted out each month, remittances being sent by IATA to airlines having a net credit balance and collected from airlines with a net debit balance. British Eagle went into liquidation owing money to a number of airlines but with a claim against Air France which the liquidator sought to recover. Air France pleaded that the liquidator was bound by the IATA system and could collect only from IATA and then only such sum (if any) as was due it after netting out the claims of airlines who were creditors of British Eagle. The liquidator's contention that this contravened the pari passu rule, in that it removed from British Eagle's estate for the benefit of other member airlines a sum due from Air France which would otherwise have been an asset available to the general body of creditors of British Eagle, was upheld by the House of Lords by a majority of three to two. It was not suggested that the arrangements were in themselves in any way improper, but in the view of the majority their effect was to give other members of IATA to whom British Eagle owed money a preference over its general creditors. This decision is now seen as a clear application of the pari passu principle rather than the anti-deprivation principle.[504] It is clear that the crucial question in *British Eagle* was whether its claim to payment was against Air France directly, with IATA acting simply as agent in providing a clearing

---

[499] See para.7–92, above.

[500] See para.7–85, above for definition of the relevant date.

[501] See para.7–83, above.

[502] See paras 7–19 et seq., above.

[503] *British Eagle International Air Lines Ltd v Compagnie Nationale Air France* [1975] 1 W.L.R. 758.

[504] *Belmont Park Investments Pty Ltd v BNY Corporate Trustee Services Ltd and Lehman Brothers Special Financing Inc* [2011] UKSC 38.

mechanism, or whether on the other hand the claim was simply an item in the computation of British Eagle's net debit or credit balance with IATA, the latter acting as principal. If, as the majority held, British Eagle's contractual entitlement lay directly against Air France then clearly its subjection to the claims of other clearing house members was an infringement both of the pari passu principle[505] and of the requirement of mutuality in insolvency set-off. But if, as was the view of the minority, the effect of the clearing house arrangements was that British Eagle's claim was only to such sum as after netting out in the clearing fell to be credited or debited to its account with IATA, then its counterparty for the purpose of computing its claim was IATA, which would clearly be entitled to set-off cross-claims vested in it in respect of services supplied to British Eagle by other airlines, by the normal operation of insolvency set-off. It is reasonably clear that if the transaction between the member airlines had been novated and replaced by contracts with IATA,[506] this would have been the inescapable conclusion, and thus any clearing house system which adopts this structure, such as the London Clearing House, will not fall foul of the principle in *British Eagle*. However, the question still arose whether the effect described above could be achieved merely by contractual terms without novation.

This question has been answered in the affirmative by the High Court of Australia in the recent case of *International Air Transport Association v Ansett Australia Holdings Ltd*.[507] The IATA agreement considered there was the same as that in *British Eagle*, except for the addition of reg.9(a), which provided that:

> "With respect to transactions between members of the Clearing House which are subject to clearance through the Clearing House as provided in Regulations 10 and 11 and subject to the provisions of the Regulations regarding protested and disputed items, no liability for payment and no right of action to recover payment shall accrue between members of the Clearing House. In lieu thereof members shall have liabilities to the Clearing House for balances due by them resulting from a clearance or rights of action against the Clearing House for balances in their favour resulting from a clearance and collected by the Clearing House from debtor members in such clearance."

A majority of the High Court took the view that this achieved the object set out above, so that the only claim or liability of each member airline was against IATA, and was for the final balance of all the claims of member airlines entered for the clearance.[508] This meant that there was no debt owed to Ansett, the insolvent airline, by any other other airline, and thus no property of Ansett which could be said to removed from the company's assets before the execution of the Deed of Company Arrangement.[509] Thus there was no contravention of the anti-deprivation principle discussed above, based on *Ex p. Mackay*. The majority rejected an argument that the agreement was nonetheless unenforceable as contrary to public policy in that it amounted to contracting out of the collective

---

[505] As discussed above.

[506] See para.7–19, above.

[507] *International Air Transport Association v Ansett Australia Holdings Ltd* [2008] H.C.A. 3.

[508] *International Air Transport Association v Ansett Australia Holdings Ltd* [2008] H.C.A. 3 at [60].

[509] Under Australian insolvency law, a company may execute a Deed of Company Arrangement as an alternative to proceeding from voluntary administration into liquidation, see R. Bollen, "British Eagle revisited: airlines 'jumping the queue' in insolvency" (2008) 23 J.I.B.L.R. 354.

procedure. This argument focused on the fact that airlines in relation to which Ansett had no mutuality might have their claims against Ansett fully satisfied by the operation of the netting system whereas other creditors' claims might not be so satisfied.[510] This appears to be a version of the second principle discussed above: however, the majority held that this argument had no merit when, by operation of the agreement, those airlines never had claims against Ansett: they only had claims against IATA. Kirby J. dissented, on the grounds that, despite the addition of reg.9(a) and in the absence of novation,[511] the claims of each airline against another remained,[512] and thus the agreement was unenforceable as an attempt to contract out of the statutory collective procedure.[513]

It thus appears that in relation to multilateral netting arrangements, any danger of unenforceability from the principle in *British Eagle* is relatively easily overcome by drafting. However, if the efficacy of an arrangement depends on contractual interpretation, there is always a danger that a court dealing with different contractual wording will give a different interpretation from the one desired, so that the safest path to immunity from the *British Eagle* principle is legislation.[514]

Close-out netting   There are three techniques used in close-out netting which are potentially vulnerable on insolvency. The first is the use of a Master Agreement, governing all transactions between the parties with the purpose that an insolvency officer cannot cherry pick between contracts. This could be said not to accord with reality, since in fact the transactions between the parties are separate and the link between them is thus "artificial".[515] This could lead to recharacterisation, which would have the effect of separating the contracts and, at least in theory, enabling an insolvency officer to "cherry pick".[516] However, the courts are slow to recharacterise commercial agreements, and in the one case in which this provision has been considered (admittedly, not an insolvency case, but one where the court was considering whether the termination and close-out provisions were penal), the Master Agreement clause was said to be permissible on the grounds of freedom of contract.[517] A solvent party will rarely rely solely on a Master Agreement clause to avoid cherry-picking, however, since it will also be protected by close-out netting provisions and often a flawed asset clause as well.

The "flawed asset" clause[518] discussed earlier,[519] which makes the absence of default on the part of one party a condition precedent to the obligations of the

7–93

---

[510] *International Air Transport Association v Ansett Australia Holdings Ltd* [2008] H.C.A. 3 at [92].

[511] *International Air Transport Association v Ansett Australia Holdings Ltd* [2008] H.C.A. 3 at [137].

[512] *International Air Transport Association v Ansett Australia Holdings Ltd* [2008] H.C.A. 3 at [145].

[513] *International Air Transport Association v Ansett Australia Holdings Ltd* [2008] H.C.A. 3 at [172].

[514] M. Bridge, "Clearing houses and insolvency in Australia" (2008) 124 L.Q.R. 379, 384. See para.7–94, below for discussion of the relevant legislation.

[515] Derham, *The Law of Set-off* (2010), para.16.44. The artificiality is less where the Master Agreement includes flawed assert and close-out netting provisions as in the ISDA Master Agreement, see below.

[516] Firth, *Derivatives: Law and Practice* (2012), paras 5–045 to 5–046.

[517] *BNP Paribas v Wockhardt EU Operations (Swiss) AG* [2009] EWHC 3116 (Comm) at [49].

[518] ISDA Master Agreement s.2(a)(iii).

[519] Para.7–21, above.

other party, has been challenged as contrary to the anti-deprivation principle,[520] since if the non-defaulting party does not exercise its right to terminate, its payment obligations in relation to debts becoming due after the default remain suspended and the defaulting party is "deprived" of any benefit to which it would otherwise be entitled. Such an entitlement would only arise if the defaulting party was "in the money"; however, it is in precisely this situation that a non-defaulting party might choose not to close out, since this would crystallise its loss. So far the courts have held that the flawed asset clause does not fall foul of the anti-deprivation principle, for two main reasons. First, it is designed to protect the non-defaulting party in a situation where its obligations are a "quid pro quo" for the continuing provision of services (such as an interest rate hedge or credit protection) by the defaulting party after default, as opposed to a "quid pro quo" for services provided before that date. Thus where a contract is potentially wholly or partly executory after default, the non-defaulting party has a commercially justifiable reason for protecting itself against having to make payments for services which are unlikely to be rendered. The presence of a commercially justifiable reason for a clause is usually sufficient to show that it is not a deliberate attempt to evade the insolvency laws.[521] The clause will not offend the principle even where, on the actual facts of the case, the default occurred after the defaulting party had no more services to perform, if it potentially covered other situations falling within the "quid pro quo" analysis.[522] Secondly, on the interpretation of the relevant terms by the Court of Appeal, the defaulting party, if out of the money, is only obliged to pay the non-defaulting party on a net basis.[523] Thus if the non-defaulting party proves in the defaulting party's insolvency, it must give credit for its debt obligations, even though the obligation to pay them is otherwise suspended. This means that the insolvent defaulting party is not deprived of the whole of the benefit of the obligations owed to it by the non-defaulting party, but only to the benefit to the extent that it exceeds the amount it itself owes. This "deprivation" is commercially justifiable on the grounds mentioned earlier.[524] The commercial reasonableness, and therefore enforceability, of the flawed asset clause thus seems well established, but there is one caveat. The courts have stressed that the application of the anti-deprivation principle depends on the particular facts of each case,[525] and a variation in the terms, or maybe the context, of the agreement could lead to a different result. It is clear that a provision which had the effect that the defaulting party's obligations

---

[520] A challenge on the basis of the pari passu principle has also been made, but dismissed on the grounds that the effect of the clause is to prevent the payment obligation arising, so there is never any property which is prevented from being distributed: this is in contrast to the *British Eagle* case where the existence of the debt owed to British Eagle by Air France was a critical factor in the decision, see para.7–92, above.

[521] *Belmont Park Investments Pty Ltd v BNY Corporate Trustee Services Ltd and Lehman Brothers Special Financing Inc* [2011] UKSC 38 at [100], [177]; *Lomas v JFB Firth Rixson Inc* [2010] EWHC 3372 (Ch) at [115]; *Lomas v JFB Firth Rixson Inc* [2012] EWCA Civ 419 [86]–[92].

[522] *Lehman Brothers Special Financing Inc v Carlton Communications Ltd* [2011] EWHC 718 (Ch) at [38].

[523] This is, of course, on a settlement netting basis, since close-out netting has, ex hypothesi, not occurred.

[524] *Lomas v JFB Firth Rixson* Inc [2010] EWHC 3372 (Ch) at [115]; *Lomas v JFB Firth Rixson Inc* [2012] EWCA Civ 419 at [92].

[525] *Lomas v JFB Firth Rixson Inc* [2012] EWCA Civ 419 at [91].

were payable on a gross basis would be very vulnerable to being struck down as contrary to the anti-deprivation principle.[526]

The third potentially vulnerable technique is the close-out netting provision itself. Although the details vary, the critical ingredients are the termination of all outstanding contracts between the parties or the acceleration of the parties' obligations to each other, the valuation of the obligations (which has the effect of turning delivery obligations to money obligations) and the aggregation of values to form one net amount.[527] Generally these provisions are invulnerable as they have the same effect as the operation of insolvency set-off,[528] which applies to future and contingent debts as well as present debts. However, obligations to do something other than pay money (such as delivery obligations) cannot be set-off in insolvency against money obligations,[529] and so to the extent that a close-out netting provision has this effect, it could be said not to be protected by being within insolvency set-off,[530] thus if it falls foul of the pari passu principle or the anti-deprivation principle, it will be unenforceable. If there were no close-out netting provision, unless property in the items to be delivered has already passed, the obligation to deliver is merely contractual. If it is the insolvent party who is obliged to deliver, a liquidator could choose to breach or disclaim the contract[531] or to perform it. Breach or disclaimer would turn the obligation into a money claim, which could be the subject of set-off, but performance would mean that the solvent counterparty was obliged to pay its money obligation in full. A close-out netting provision effectively takes from the insolvency officer the choice of performance, and imposes a solution similar to that on breach or disclaimer. While this could be, theoretically, a deprivation,[532] it is unlikely to fall foul of the anti-deprivation principle for two reasons. First, the "deprivation" is for full value, which is a well-recognised exception to the anti-deprivation principle[533]; this is also a good reason why the provision does not offend the pari passu principle. Secondly, there are good commercial reasons for the provision, namely increase in certainty and reduction in credit and systemic risk: the anti-deprivation principle therefore does not apply.[534]

The statutory preservation of netting arrangements   In order to promote   **7–94** certainty and reduce systemic risk, there are special statutory provisions preserving netting arrangements in relation to settlement systems, market contracts, clearing houses and the provision of financial collateral. As a result, if

---

[526] *Lomas v JFB Firth Rixson Inc* [2010] EWHC 3372 (Ch) at [115].

[527] UNIDROIT, *Adoption of the Principles on the Operation of Close-Out Netting Provisions* at [32].

[528] Although they do not necessarily take effect by set-off, but may do by consolidation of all outstanding contracts into a single net balance, such as, broadly speaking, under the ISDA Master Agreement s.6(e)(i).

[529] See para.7–86, above.

[530] R. Derham, "Set-off and netting of foreign exchange contracts in the liquidation of a counterparty: Part 2. Netting" [1991] J.B.L. 536, 40.

[531] An administrator has no power to disclaim.

[532] Derham, *The Law of Set-off* (2010), para.16.38. Derham points out that this would not be objectionable if there was only one contract (relying on *Shipton, Anderson & Co (1927) Ltd v Micks, Lambert & Co* [1936] 2 All E.R. 1032) but might be objectionable where the close-out netting provisions related to a number of contracts. This issue may not arise where there is a Master Agreement clause.

[533] *Borland's Trustee v Steel Bros & Co Ltd* [1901] 1 Ch. 279.

[534] See above.

an arrangement falls within these provisions, it cannot be impugned as contrary to insolvency law, including the pari passu principle or the anti-deprivation principle. Part VII of the Companies Act 1989[535] preserves the validity of market contracts, and the default rules and the non-default settlement rules of recognised investment exchanges and recognised clearing houses.[536] Settlement rules including multilateral netting provisions are thereby protected, as are any close-out netting provisions which fall within the default rules or are contained within market contracts, which are contracts entered into on, or subject to the rules of, an exchange or through a recognised clearing house.[537] Similar protection is extended to default arrangements on "designated systems", that is, systems used for settlement and payment of transfers of securities, by the Financial Markets and Insolvency (Settlement Finality) Regulations 1999,[538] which enact the Settlement Finality Directive 1998.[539] These protected default arrangements expressly include netting,[540] which is defined as "the conversion into one net claim or obligation of different claims or obligation between participants resulting from the issue and receipt of transfer orders between them, whether on a bilateral or multilateral basis and whether through the interposition of a clearing house, central counterparty or settlement agent or otherwise". Close-out netting in relation to the provision of collateral is also protected. Regulation 12 of the Financial Collateral Arrangements (No.2) Regulations 2003[541] provides that a close-out netting provision[542] in a financial collateral arrangement[543] takes effect in accordance with its terms despite the fact that one of the parties is in insolvency proceedings, unless, when the arrangement was entered into or the relevant obligations incurred, one party was aware or should have been aware that insolvency proceedings had commenced or were pending.[544] While the wording of the Regulations is not entirely clear, it seems probable that only bilateral close-out netting is included within the protection.[545] The recitals to the Directive enacted by the Regulations specifically provide that

---

[535] As amended by Financial Markets and Insolvency Regulations 1991/880, Financial Markets and Insolvency Regulations 1998/1748, Financial Markets and Insolvency Regulations 2009/853, Financial Services and Markets Act 2000 (Over the Counter Derivatives, Central Counterparties and Trade Repositories) Regulations 2013/504.

[536] Companies Act 1989 s.159. The terms "recognised investment exchange" and "recognised clearing house" have the same meaning as in the Financial Services and Markets Act 2000, see s.190 of the Companies Act 1989.

[537] The details of the definition of "market contract" are somewhat complex and are contained in s.155 of the Companies Act 1989, as amended by the Financial Services and Markets Act 2000 (Over the Counter Derivatives, Central Counterparties and Trade Repositories) Regulations 2013/504 to include transactions cleared through a central counterparty pursuant to EMIR (the European Market Infrastructure Regulation, Regulation EU No 648/2012 on OTC derivatives, central counterparties and trade repositories).

[538] Financial Markets and Insolvency (Settlement Finality) Regulations 1999 (SI 1999/2979) reg.14.

[539] EC Directive 98/26 art.3(2).

[540] Financial Markets and Insolvency (Settlement Finality) Regulations 1999 (SI 1999/2979) reg.2.

[541] Financial Collateral Arrangements (No.2) Regulations 2003 (SI 2003/3226), enacting the Financial Collateral Directive 2002, EC Directive 2002/47.

[542] For the definition of close-out netting, see para.7–09, above.

[543] See paras 6–24 et seq., above.

[544] Financial Collateral Arrangements (No.2) Regulations 2003 (SI 2003/3226) reg.12 (1) and (2).

[545] See A. Fawcett, "The Financial Collateral Directive: an Examination of some Practical Problems Following its Implementation in the UK" (2005) 20 J.I.B.L.R. 2005 295, 296; Ho, "The Financial Collateral Directive's practice in England" (2011) 26 J.I.B.L.R. 151, 169.

only bilateral financial collateral arrangements, and bilateral close-out netting arrangements are within the scope of the Directive,[546] and the definition of "close-out netting" in the Regulations refers to obligations of the "parties", that is, the parties to the financial collateral arrangement.

One question which is not entirely clear in relation to any of these statutory protective measures is whether their effect is that the contractual close-out or settlement netting provisions completely displace insolvency set-off, or whether insolvency set-off continues to apply where it would normally do so, with only the contractual provisions which would otherwise be unenforceable remaining valid. The answer to this question could, potentially, be of great significance in relation to the timing of the netting (which in turn could affect the exchange rate used in a currency conversion) or where there is a prohibition on assignment of the net amount which would not be valid in relation to the product of insolvency set-off. Both of these issues would lead to very unwelcome uncertainty. One argument, which would depend on the wording of the close-out netting provision, is that it does not operate by way of set-off at all, but that the contracts are terminated and replaced with a new obligation to pay the net amount.[547] Thus, although the economic effect is the same as under insolvency set-off, the legal effect is not, and so insolvency set-off cannot displace the contractual terms. Where the contract includes a provision for set-off of obligations arising under different agreements, however, the question raised above seems to be a real issue.

Where default proceedings relate to market contracts, and designated settlement systems, it seems reasonably clear that the effect of the statute is that the default proceedings, including any netting, displace insolvency set-off until a net sum is produced: that net sum is then a provable debt and can be the subject of insolvency set-off.[548] In relation to financial collateral arrangements, the position is far from clear. The argument that insolvency set-off displaces the contractual provisions where possible is supported by the fact that reg.14 disapplies Insolvency Rules rr.2.86 and 4.91 (which provide conversion rates for provable debts that are not in sterling and which apply to insolvency set-off by virtue of rr.2.85(6) and 4.90(6)) where a financial collateral arrangement provides for a conversion rate of non-sterling obligations, provided that that rate is not unreasonable or the contractual mechanism is used to impose an unreasonable rate. This disapplication would not be necessary if insolvency set-off were displaced totally by the contractual close-out netting provisions.[549] However, the terms of reg.12 of the Financial Collateral Arrangements (No.2) Regulations 2003 support the view that insolvency set-off is displaced by the contractual scheme, and this also has the benefits of consistency with the other carve-outs discussed above, as well as not requiring an analysis to take place of whether the

7–95

---

[546] Directive 2002/47 recitals 3, 5 and 14. It has been made repeatedly clear that the Regulations are to be interpreted in accordance with the Directive, see, for example, *Re Lehman Brothers International (Europe) (In Administration)* [2012] EWHC 2997 (Ch) at [76].

[547] This is the way that the ISDA Master agreement is drafted.

[548] This is the combined effect of ss.159 and 163 of the Companies Act 1989 (in relation to market contracts) and regs 14 and 15 of the Financial Markets and Insolvency (Settlement Finality) Regulations 1999 (in relation to securities settlement systems).

[549] See Ho, "The Financial Collateral Directive's practice in England" (2011) 26 J.I.B.L.R. 151, 167–168; Parsons and Dening, "Financial collateral — an opportunity missed" (2011) 5 L.F.M.R. 164, 172; and also HM Treasury, *Consultation Document on the Implementation of the Directive on Financial Collateral Arrangements* (July 2003), para.5.9.

close-out netting provisions actually provide for set-off, or for a netting arrangement which does not involve the setting off of obligations under different contracts.

The new bank resolution procedure enacted in the Banking Act 2009 provides for stabilisation techniques involving the transfer of some of a bank's assets and liabilities to a private sector purchaser, a bridge bank or public sector ownership.[550] Since this might potentially disrupt set-off or netting arrangements, these are protected by the Banking Act 2009 (Restriction of Partial Property Transfers) Order,[551] which provides that a partial property transfer shall not apply to such arrangements.

10.   INSOLVENCY SET-OFF: PARTICULAR SITUATIONS

(i)   Set-off in relation to deposits taken by a bank

7–96   The operation of insolvency set-off in relation to loans made by a bank and deposits taken by the same bank raises a number of interesting issues. There are various possible situations which will be considered. The first, and simplest, is where a customer, whose deposit account is in credit, has also borrowed money from the bank. Without more, insolvency set-off operates whether the customer or the bank becomes insolvent, so that only the balance can be the subject of action or proof. The second situation is where the customer with the deposit account in credit is not the same entity as the borrower. The depositor may give a personal guarantee which contains a principal debtor clause, so that his liability is not merely contingent, or he may give a personal guarantee which does not contain a principal debtor clause and provides for payment on demand, so that his liability is contingent on demand being made. It is also possible that he gives no personal guarantee at all but merely deposits funds with the creditor as security for the loan to the borrower. In any of these situations, the debtor may be insolvent, the depositor may be insolvent or the bank may be insolvent.[552]

---

[550] Banking Act 2009 ss.11–13.

[551] SI 2009/322 reg.3.

[552] The Banking Act 2009 introduces a new resolution and insolvency regime for banks, which can be instigated by the Bank of England, the Financial Conduct Authority or the Secretary of State. A bank may be put into the Special Resolution Regime, which seeks to stabilise its position without formal insolvency proceedings by transfer of some or all of its assets and liabilities to other entities. Despite the fact that partial property transfers are possible, there is a saving for set-off and netting arrangements (Banking Act 2009 (Restriction of Partial Property Transfers) Order 2009/322 reg.3). If the bank is put into insolvency proceedings, these are governed by the Banking Act and the regulations made under it. Rule 72 of the Bank Insolvency (England and Wales) Rules 2009/356 is largely the same as Insolvency Rule r.4.90, but insolvency set-off is disapplied in relation to eligible depositors, that is, those retail depositors who are eligible for compensation under the Financial Services Compensation Scheme, see r.73, Bank Insolvency (England and Wales) Rules 2009/356 and s.93(3) of the Banking Act 2009.

(1)   Deposit reinforced by personal guarantee containing a principal debtor clause

If the debtor is insolvent, the bank will be able to recover from the depositor   **7–97**
under the guarantee. If the depositor is insolvent, the bank will be able to recover
from the debtor. If both are insolvent, the bank can recover in both insolvencies,
providing it does not recover more than 100p in the pound.[553] However, if the
bank becomes insolvent, the question arises whether the depositor can set-off his
liability to pay the debt against the bank's liability to him to return the deposit or
whether the bank can claim the whole debt from the depositor, and leave him to
prove for his deposit in the liquidation.[554]

On the facts assumed here, Hoffmann L.J. held that as a matter of construction
the effect of the principal debtor clause was that the director was not merely
making a deposit by way of security but was assuming a personal liability for
repayment jointly and severally with the borrower company, or alternatively
severally, that such liability was not merely contingent and that accordingly the
liquidation of the bank resulted in an automatic set-off of the deposit against the
liability, thus pro tanto extinguishing the indebtedness of the borrower company.
It was therefore not open to the liquidator, as it would have been if there had been
no principal debtor clause, to recover from the borrower without giving credit for
the deposit, leaving the director to prove as an unsecured creditor for the amount
of his deposit released from the charge as the result of the borrower's repayment.

On the finding of a personal guarantee as a matter of construction the result
reached was inevitable. However, it has to be said that the evidence for a personal
guarantee was decidedly tenuous; and the conclusion that the charge itself could
be analysed as the creation of a personal liability not exceeding the amount of the
deposit[555] is not sustainable, for it imports a personal liability where none is
needed except, of course, for the purpose of arriving at the desired result! The
Court of Appeal felt unable to agree with this conclusion in *Re Bank of Credit
and Commerce International SA (No.8)*[556] and Lord Hoffmann himself, in the
subsequent appeal to the House of Lords,[557] acknowledged that it produced
anomalous results and was based on the peculiar wording of the guarantee.

*(2)   Deposit reinforced by personal guarantee payable on demand with no
principal debtor clause*

In this situation the surety is not a principal debtor and in the absence of demand   **7–98**
his liability is merely contingent. As we have seen, a contingent claim by the
company in liquidation against the solvent party was formerly not accelerated by
the liquidation, so that unless demand is made, converting the contingent claim
into a matured debt, no set-off could be invoked by the liquidator. In consequence
the liquidator could avoid the independent set-off by refraining from making the

---

[553] See para.8–33, below.
[554] The issue was clearly set out by Hoffmann L.J. in *MS Fashions Ltd v Bank of Credit and Commerce International SA (No.2)* [1993] Ch. 425, 430.
[555] *MS Fashions Ltd v Bank of Credit and Commerce International SA (No.2)* [1993] Ch. 425 at 431.
[556] *Re Bank of Credit and Commerce International SA (No.8)* [1996] Ch. 245; [1996] B.C.L.C. 204; sub nom. *Morris v Agrichemicals Ltd*. See para.7–95, below.
[557] *Re Bank of Credit and Commerce International SA (No.8)* [1998] A.C. 214 at 224–225.

requisite demand, thus maintaining the company's claim in full against the borrower without having to give credit for the sum that would have been treated as received from the surety in a balance of account had the set-off provisions been triggered. This would not now be the position, since the revised rr.2.85 and 4.90 impose set-off against contingent claims by the company, so that the creditor's liability is accelerated to the extent of the set-off,[558] although, unless the contingency has occurred before the date the account is taken, the amount of the set-off depends on the valuation of the debt by the liquidator or administrator.[559]

(3) Deposit not reinforced by any personal guarantee

7–99 This was the situation in the *BCCI* case mentioned above, where the facts were otherwise very similar to those in *MS Fashions*. Money was deposited with the bank by way of non-recourse collateral security[560] for a loan to the principal debtor. The bank then went into liquidation. The liquidator declined to resort to the security deposit and sought repayment from the principal debtor without giving credit for the deposit, leaving the depositor to prove as an unsecured creditor. The borrower and the depositor contended that credit should be given for the deposit. Among the various grounds advanced were: that the depositor as a non-recourse surety had a right to pay off the debt and to have his deposit utilised for that purpose; that the liquidator's approach would expose the borrower to a double liability, namely to repay the loan and to indemnify the depositor against the loss of his deposit through the bank's insolvency; that the bank's inability to repay the deposit discharged the borrower pro tanto from liability by reason of the bank's "loss" of the security in becoming insolvent and its consequent inability to return it; and that the deposit was paid to the bank on trust to be applied for a particular purpose, namely discharge of the principal debt, for which it should be used by the liquidator.

The House of Lords,[561] affirming the decision of the Court of Appeal,[562] had no difficulty in rejecting all these arguments. In the absence of any personal guarantee by the depositor it was not possible to set-off the deposit against the loan. The bank owed money to the depositor and the borrower owed money to the bank. The debts were therefore not due from the same parties, so that the mutuality which was essential to avoid a preference over other creditors was lacking. The proposition that the borrower was exposed to double liability was fallacious, since it rested on the assumption that the borrower was obliged to indemnify the depositor against the loss of his deposit, a proposition which was untenable. The surety's only right to indemnity was where he had paid off the

---

[558] See para.7–80, above.

[559] Insolvency Act 1986 s.322(3) (in relation to bankruptcy), r.2.81 in relation to administration (applicable to set-off by virtue of r.2.85(5) and r.4.86 in relation to liquidation (applicable to set-off by virtue of r.4.90(5)).

[560] The Court of Appeal, approving the decision of Millett J. in *Re Charge Card Services Ltd* [1987] Ch. 150, had held that it was conceptually impossible for a bank to take a charge over its own customer's credit balance and that the charge-back had purely contractual effect. The House of Lords had a different view. See para.3–12, above.

[561] *Re Bank of Credit and Commerce International SA (No.8)* [1998] A.C. 214.

[562] *Re Bank of Credit and Commerce International SA (No.8)* [1996] Ch. 245.

principal debt. Nor could the principle relating to loss of securities by the creditor avail the borrower or depositor. The deposit had not been disposed of or the depositor's legal entitlement to repayment impaired; the position was simply that the bank was unable to repay. In any event there was no basis for saying that the loss of a security provided by a surety discharges the principal debtor; at best it would discharge the surety. Finally, there was no evidence to show that the deposit had been impressed with a purpose trust. The bank was a mere debtor.

It was recognised that this result produced the paradox that a surety who gave no personal guarantee was worse off than one who gave a personal guarantee and thus had his liability extinguished by set-off. But that was inevitable if injustice to the general body of creditors was to be avoided. The point here is that what the depositor was seeking to do was to avoid the consequences of the bank's insolvency so far as he was concerned by requiring the bank to utilise the deposit to pay off the debt. But the deposit was an asset of the bank which under the pari passu principle[563] should be available for the general body of creditors. In the absence of any trust affecting it the depositor, as an unsecured creditor, had no right to give instructions to the liquidator as to the application of the deposit. By collecting repayment from the borrower the liquidator would cause the debt to be discharged, thus freeing the deposit from the security and entitling the depositor to repayment. In that situation the depositor should stand in the same position as other unsecured creditors.

One further issue which was left unresolved by the House of Lords in the **7–100** *BCCI* case was whether, if the depositor and the debtor were the same person, a charge created by the depositor in favour of the bank would break the mutuality necessary for insolvency set-off. Lord Hoffmann recorded the debate on this point but refrained from commenting.[564] The point is a difficult one, and of some practical significance. First, if insolvency set-off does apply, it applies automatically, and the chargee has no choice as to whether to enforce the charge or not, which he might wish to do if the timing of enforcement were critical, for example, if the debts were in different currencies. Secondly, if the charge were to be characterised as floating, the priority rules in relation to expenses, the prescribed part and so on would apply.[565] Thirdly, there is a possibility that it would have very serious consequences for the chargor were the chargee to become insolvent, as discussed below.

This issue can be analysed by separating out two issues. The first is whether insolvency set-off applies automatically if one of the parties holds security for the debt it is owed. As discussed earlier, the view taken here is that, although it applies where it is the insolvent party which is secured, when it is the solvent party, insolvency set-off does not apply, and that the secured creditor has a choice whether to enforce its security or to surrender its security and prove in the liquidation.[566] The second is the extent to which a charge over a debt breaks the mutuality required for insolvency set-off. It is clear that the chargee takes subject to any set-off arising in relation to that debt before the debtor has notice of the charge.[567] In applying these principles to a charge-back, let us first take the

---

[563] See para.7–90, above.
[564] *BCCI* [1998] A.C. 214, 225.
[565] See paras 5–68 et seq., above.
[566] See para.7–82, above.
[567] See para.7–70, above.

situation where the chargor is insolvent.[568] The fact that the chargee has security for the debt owed to it, means that insolvency set-off does not apply unless the chargee decides to prove. However, when the chargee took the charge, it took it subject to set-offs over the debt that it knew about: clearly here it knew of the set-off, which is inherent in the structure. Thus one can see the set-off which does apply as either contractual or an independent set-off. If this is the case, then, unlike insolvency set-off, it can be excluded by contract, and so the chargee (as debtor) could do this in order to give itself the freedom to enforce the charge by another means. If this is correct, then, if the chargor becomes insolvent, the chargee has the choice of enforcing the charge (by set-off or any other means) or choosing to prove in the chargor's insolvency, in which case insolvency set-off will apply.

Where the chargee is insolvent, the fact that it is secured will not prevent insolvency set-off arising.[569] However, where a debt owed by an insolvent party is subject to a security interest, this normally breaks the mutuality required for insolvency set-off between the debtor and the creditor.[570] The secured party, though, takes its interest subject to any (independent) set-offs arising before the debtor has notice of the security interest, so that the debtor's insolvency officer could choose, in theory, choose to rely on such a set-off against the secured party's proof, if it so wished (although this would not be insolvency set-off). Applying this analysis to a charge-back, it could therefore be argued that the security interest breaks the mutuality required for insolvency set-off, but that the chargee takes its security interest subject to the independent set-off. If this is correct, then this independent set-off could be contractually excluded, leaving the chargee's insolvency officer in a position either to choose to enforce the security (by book entry) or to sue the chargor for the debt it owes leaving the chargor to prove in the chargee's insolvency. This is potentially very detrimental to the chargor and an unsatisfactory state of the law. There are various arguments against this conclusion, none of which are clinching. The first is that any contractual exclusion of a set-off could be said to be inconsistent with the purpose of the charge-back, and would be ineffective. The second is that it would be unconscionable for the chargee to enforce in full without giving credit for the cross-claim, and so the situation is governed either by equitable set-off or by the rule in *Cherry v Boultbee*.[571] Thirdly, it could be said that a charge-back can only be effective if it is a mere charge (and not a mortgage), but that such a charge cannot break the mutuality required for insolvency set-off.[572]

(ii) Set-off in relation to executory contracts

7–101   It will be evident from the foregoing that where all the relevant contracts are executed and the claims on both sides are for money or are reducible to money insolvency set-off will rarely be a problem in English law. Set-off in relation to

---

[568] There is some rather weak authority for the proposition that mutuality is broken in this situation, see *In Re Hart Ex p. Caldicott* (1884) 25 Ch. D. 716.

[569] *Ex p. Barnett re Deveze* (1874) L.R. 9 Ch. App. 293. See para.7–82, above.

[570] See para.7–83, above.

[571] See R. Calnan, "The Insolvent Bank and Security over Deposits" (1996) J.I.B.F.L. 185.

[572] See H. Beale, M. Bridge, L.Gullifer and E. Lomnicka, *The Law of Security and Title-based Financing*, 2nd edn (Oxford: OUP, 2012), para.6.27.

existing liquidated claims, even if payable in the future, is straightforward. Unliquidated and contingent claims are valued (so far as capable of estimation) and become treated as the equivalent of liquidated claims for purposes of proof and set-off.

The one real danger zone is that occupied by executory contracts. Where the contracts on both sides are still in force and executory at the time of winding-up the solvent party is exposed to the risk of cherry-picking by the liquidator, who may seek to enforce the contract that is profitable to the estate[573] while disclaiming the unprofitable contract[574] and leaving the solvent party to prove in the winding-up for damages. In principle such damages cannot be set-off against the solvent party's liability under the other contract because of the principle that post-liquidation receipts derived from the activity of the liquidator and use of the company's resources do not belong to the company in its own right,[575] so that the requisite element of mutuality is lacking.[576] The solution is to provide in each contract that all executory contracts will automatically be rescinded, and the resulting money claims netted out, in the event of either party going into liquidation.[577]

(iii)   Preferential debts[578]

Where the creditor is owed both preferential and non-preferential debts, a set-off available to the company in liquidation for less than the total amount due is not to be applied exclusively to the preferential debts (thus benefiting the estate) or exclusively to the non-preferential debts (thus preserving the creditor's priority intact) but is to be applied to the two sets of debt rateably.[579]

7–102

(iv)   Voidable preferences

No question of preference can arise where the creditor collects payment by exercise of a right of set-off, for this does not require the consent of the company at all, let alone a desire on its part to improve the creditor's position. Payment by the company into an overdrawn account with its bank is likewise not capable of being a preference where the payment does not exceed the amount of a credit balance held by the company on another account to which the bank could have resorted by way of combination of accounts if the payment in question had not

7–103

---

[573] Which in principle he can do except where (a) the winding-up of the company can be regarded as a repudiatory breach; or (b) the court accedes to an application by the solvent party to rescind the contract under s.186 of the Insolvency Act 1986, which it will normally do only where the two contracts are so connected that it would be inequitable to allow the liquidator to enforce one contract if he is not prepared to procure the company's performance of the other.

[574] Under s.178 of the Act. See Goode, *Principles of Corporate Insolvency Law* (2011), paras 6–27 to 6–30.

[575] *Re Collins* [1925] Ch. 556; *Wilmot v Alton* [1897] 1 Q.B. 17.

[576] See Wood, *English and International Set-Off* (1989), paras 5–97, 7–145 et seq., for an exhaustive analysis with reference to typical transactions.

[577] See para.7–21, above.

[578] These are now limited in scope, see para.5–68, above.

[579] *Re Unit 2 Windows Ltd* [1985] 2 All E.R. 647. This would appear to apply equally to a combination of accounts not effected prior to the winding-up. See T. Shea, "Statutory Set Off" [1986] 3 J.I.F.B.L. 152, 154.

been made, for the effect of the payment is pro tanto to reduce the available amount of set-off against the account in credit, so that the position of other creditors is unaffected. Where, by virtue of an agreement between a company and its directors, the company has a contractual right to set-off against one director's credit balance amount due from another director, exercise of that right is not a preference of the first director, for it is for the company's benefit, not that of the first director.[580]

An assignment of a debt before the cut-off date is very unlikely to be set aside as a preference under s.239 of the Insolvency Act 1986, since the assignment is usually not "done" or "suffered to be done" by the insolvent debtor.[581] However, this is not an invariable rule, and it is still possible that an assignment could be a preference, if the relevant statutory requirements were met.

---

[580] *Re Exchange Travel (Holdings) Ltd (No.3)* [1996] B.C.L.C. 524.
[581] *Re Parkside International Ltd (In Administration)* [2008] EWHC 3554 (Ch).

CHAPTER 8

Some Aspects of Suretyship Law

We will turn to the last topic, namely that of suretyship guarantees.[1] First some   **8–01**
aspects of the general law on such guarantees outside insolvency will be
considered and then the rights of the creditor in respect of a guaranteed debt
where the debtor, the surety or both become bankrupt will be discussed. The term
"bankrupt" includes the liquidation of a company, as the rules governing
guarantees on a winding up or when a company is in administration are in all
material respects the same as those applicable in bankruptcy, except as otherwise
stated below.

1. GENERAL PRINCIPLES[2]

The suretyship guarantee as an accessory contract

A suretyship guarantee is an undertaking to be answerable for the debt or other   **8–02**
default of another. The obligation is triggered by the default of the principal
debtor. If the default is in payment of money, the surety's obligation is to pay
what is due; if it is failure to perform a non-monetary obligation the surety has
either to perform itself, if the contract so provides or permits, or to pay damages.
The essential point is that a suretyship guarantee is an accessory contract, not a
primary contract.[3] That is to say, the surety's obligations are co-terminous with

---

[1] The subject is bedevilled with problems of terminology. A traditional approach is to treat suretyship
as covering both guarantees and indemnities (see, for example, G. Andrews & R. Millett, *Law of
Guarantees*, 6th edn (London: Sweet & Maxwell, 2011), para.1.003 . However, in modern banking
and commercial usage the term "suretyship guarantee" denotes a guarantee triggered by default on the
part of the principal debtor, by way of contrast to "demand guarantee", which denotes an independent,
primary undertaking (see below). The suretyship guarantee is also contrasted with the contract of
indemnity, which is also a primary undertaking but differs from a demand guarantee in that typically
it is an undertaking to cover the creditor's loss rather than an undertaking to pay a specified amount or
maximum amount, so that the liability on an indemnity is unliquidated whereas that on a demand
guarantee is liquidated.
[2] The leading English textbook on guarantees is Andrews & Millett, *The Law of Guarantees* (2011).
See also *Rowlatt on Principal and Surety*, G. Moss & D. Marks (eds), 6th edn (London: Sweet &
Maxwell, 2011); J.C. Phillips & J. O'Donovan, *The Modern Contract of Guarantee*, 2nd English edn
(London: Sweet & Maxwell, 2010); K. P. McGuinness, *The Law of Guarantee*, 2nd edn (Toronto: The
Carswell Company Ltd, 1996).
[3] The typical bond given by an insurer in relation to a construction contract whereby the bond is
expressed to become void if the contractor fulfils its obligations is a suretyship bond, not an
independent obligation to pay the amount of the bond, and accordingly loss must be proved (*Trafalgar
House Construction (Regions) Ltd v General Surety & Guarantee Co Ltd* [1996] A.C. 199). The

those of the principal debtor, his liability does not arise until the principal debtor has made default and anything which nullifies, reduces or extinguishes the liability of the principal debtor has the same effect on the liability of the surety.[4] This cardinal principle may, of course, be qualified or displaced by the terms of the guarantee.

The question whether and in what conditions a surety may invoke a right of set-off which the debtor has against the creditor remains controversial. In principle, a transaction (or equitable) set-off available to the debtor should equally be available to the surety, on the grounds that he has a right in equity against the principal debtor to exonerate him, so the principal debtor cannot refuse to rely on the set-off.[5] Thus, if the creditor applies for summary judgment against the surety, the latter can obtain leave to defend, although this will be on the condition that the principal debtor is joined as a defendant to the action before full trial.[6] By contrast, it is generally considered that an independent (or statutory) set-off exercisable by the debtor is not available to the surety since this is a procedural defence which arises from a transaction independent of that to which the guarantee relates[7] and takes effect only at the point of judgment for any balance.[8] Against this it has been argued that any form of set-off, including independent set-off, is available so long as the debtor is joined in the proceedings.[9] But it may be questioned on what basis the debtor should be forced to have his right of independent set-off exercised in favour of the surety when it has nothing to do with the guaranteed debt.[10]

---

distinction between primary and accessory obligations is not always easy to draw. See, for example, the decision of the Court of Appeal in *Actionstrength Ltd v International Glass Engineering In.Gl.En Spa* [2001] EWCA Civ 1477; [2002] 1 W.L.R. 566, which reversed the decision of the judge at first instance. There was an unsuccessful appeal to the House of Lords [2003] UKHL 17, but not on the characterisation of the guarantee.

[4] See Andrews and Millett, *Law of Guarantees* (2011), paras 1.005, 6.018 et seq.; Phillips & O'Donovan, *The Modern Contract of Guarantee* (1996), para.1–22.

[5] *Bechervaise v Lewis* (1871–72) L.R. 7 C.P. 372, 377.

[6] See J. Phillips, "When should the guarantor be permitted to rely on the principal's set-off" [2001] L.M.C.L.Q. 383; R. Derham, *The Law of Set-Off*, 4th edn (Oxford: Oxford University Press, 2010), para.18.25.

[7] See Phillips, "When should the guarantor be permitted to rely on the principal's set-off" [2001] L.M.C.L.Q. 383, P.Wood, *English and International Set-Off* (London: Sweet & Maxwell, 1989), paras 10–216, 10–227; Phillips & Donovan, *The Modern Contract of Guarantee* (2010), paras 11–71 et seq.

[8] See para.7–35, above.

[9] Derham, *The Law of Set-Off* (2010), paras 18.10 and 18.27; also *Halsbury's Law of England* (London: Butterworths Law, 2008), Vol.49 para.1135, "On being sued by the creditor for payment of the debt guaranteed, a guarantor may rely upon any right of set-off or counterclaim which the principal debtor could set up against the creditor in reduction of the guaranteed debt in reduction of the claim against him under the guarantee," previous versions of which were cited with approval in *Hyundai Shipbuilding & Heavy Industries Co Ltd v Pournaras* [1978] 2 Lloyd's Rep. 502, 508–509; *Barclays Bank Plc v Gruffydd* Unreported October 30, 1992; *BOC Group Plc v Centeon LLC* [1999] C.L.C. 497; and see *Marubeni Hong Kong and South China Ltd v Government of Mongolia* [2004] EWHC 472 (Comm) at [232], although the distinction between transaction and independent set-off was not discussed in any of the cases, and it is not clear that any of them concerned an independent set-off.

[10] Even if an independent set-off is not a defence, the surety could join the principal debtor as a third party claiming an indemnity and the principal debtor could, if it wished, join the creditor as a fourth party on the cross-claim. This would also be possible if the cross-claim were a counterclaim and not a set-off, see Derham, *The Law of Set-Off*, (2010), para.18.30.

The suretyship guarantee is to be distinguished from the demand guarantee and the standby letter of credit, which are primary undertakings and are payable solely on presentation of a written demand and other specified documents and, in the case of a demand guarantee governed by the ICC's Uniform Rules for Demand Guarantees, a statement that the principal is in breach and the respect in which it is in breach.[11] Demand guarantees and standby credits are, like documentary credits, independent of the underlying transaction, so that in the absence of clear evidence of fraud the issuer has to pay even if there has been no default in performance by the principal (the debtor of the obligation). For the beneficiary to make a demand when there has been no default may well be a breach of its obligation to the principal but that is of no concern to the issuing bank, which has entered into a separate engagement to pay on presentation of documents and is not concerned with the underlying contract or with non-documentary factors. The present chapter is confined to suretyship guarantees.

(1) Requirement of evidence in writing

Contracts of guarantee are one of the few remaining contracts which under the Statute of Frauds are unenforceable unless evidenced in writing signed by or on behalf of the surety.[12] The statute does not apply to demand guarantees, indemnities and standby letters of credit, which as stated above are independent payment undertakings and are in principle enforceable whether or not there has been default in performance of the underlying contract. **8–03**

(2) Unilateral and bilateral guarantees

The typical guarantee is a unilateral contract, i.e. there is a promise by one party only, the surety. The creditor does not usually undertake to the surety that he will make an advance to the debtor; it is merely agreed that if the creditor makes an advance, the surety guarantees repayment. In contract law terms, the surety's promise is a continuing offer which is to be accepted by the offeree's conduct in making the advance, until which time there is no contract and the surety can revoke the guarantee unless this otherwise provides.[13] The fact that the prospective creditor may have committed itself to the prospective debtor to make an advance is irrelevant, for it remains the case that until the advance is made there is no acceptance of the surety's offer and no contract of guarantee. **8–04**

---

[11] Uniform Rules for Demand Guarantees art.15. See G. Affaki and R. Goode, *Guide to ICC Uniform Rules for Demand Guarantees* (International Chamber of Commerce (ICC) Publication, 2011).

[12] Statute of Frauds 1677 s.4. An email, or sequence of negotiating emails, will amount to a sufficient note or memorandum for the purposes of s.4, *Golden Ocean Group Ltd v Salgaocar Mining Industries Pvt Ltd* [2012] EWCA Civ 265. But it will not comply with the requirement of signature unless the guarantor's name appears at the bottom with the intention of this being a signature: the mere automatic insertion of the sender's email address is not enough, *Mehta v J Pereira Fernandes SA* [2006] EWHC 813 (Ch). The requirement under s.4 of the Statute of Frauds is strictly applied, even where the policy reasons behind it do not apply, and the mere agreement of the guarantor cannot amount to a representation sufficient to found an estoppel which would render the guarantee enforceable in the absence of writing (*Actionstrength Ltd v International Glass Engineering In.GL.en SpA* [2003] UKHL 17).

[13] *Offord v Davies* (1862) 12 C.B.N.S. 748.

However, if the consideration for the guarantee is indivisible, or entire, it is not necessary that the advance should be made in full in order for the surety to become bound. It is established that an offer to be accepted by performance ceases to be revocable once performance has begun.[14] So if the surety guarantees a prospective advance of £100 and in reliance on this the creditor commits itself to make such an advance but initially advances £40 as a first payment, the guarantee becomes irrevocable and the surety is committed not only for that advance but for further advances up to the balance of £60.[15] The position is otherwise if the consideration is divisible, as where the advance is to be made by five instalments of £20 each. In such a case each advance constitutes a separate acceptance and the surety can revoke his guarantee as to future instalments.

Where the guarantee is expressed to be given in consideration of the prospective creditor's agreeing with the creditor to make advances, the surety becomes committed to the creditor at the same time as the latter incurs a binding commitment to the prospective debtor, for that is the act of acceptance. If, by the terms of the guarantee, the prospective creditor also undertakes with the surety to make advances to the prospective debtor the guarantee is a bilateral contract and the surety becomes bound immediately.

Continuing guarantees

8–05   Similar considerations apply to a continuing guarantee, that is, a guarantee which is given not for a fixed advance but for all the debtor's obligations from time to time or for continuing advances on a current account, so that the surety in effect guarantees the ultimate debit balance.[16] In this case there is a separate acceptance of the surety's continuing offer each time an advance is made, so that the surety becomes committed as to all such advances but remains free to revoke the guarantee as to future advances.[17] A guarantee of obligations arising under a continuing contract between the debtor and the creditor, such as a factoring agreement, is impliedly terminated by the termination of the principal contract, since there are no future obligations under that contract to which the guarantee is capable of attaching, and this remains the case even if that contract is later restored. Accordingly in the absence of a fresh guarantee the surety's liability is limited to the obligations of the debtor under the principal contract prior to its termination.[18] Unless the guarantee is so revoked by notice to the creditor or is terminated by some legal event such as the surety's bankruptcy, the surety's liability continues until the debtor's account has been closed and the ultimate debit balance then struck and discharged.

The surety's ability to revoke a continuing guarantee is on the assumption that the consideration is divisible so that each advance is to be treated as a separate

---

[14] *Errington v Errington* [1952] 1 K.B. 290. The basis for this irrevocability is uncertain: for the possible analyses see G. Treitel, *The Law of Contract*, E. Peel (ed.), 13th edn (London: Sweet & Maxwell, 2011), para.2–053.

[15] If the creditor fails to fulfil its obligations the surety is not liable (*Errington v Errington* [1952] 1 K.B. 290).

[16] See below.

[17] *Coulthart v Clementson* (1879) 5 Q.B.D. 42.

[18] *Silverburn Finance (UK) Ltd v Salt* [2001] EWCA 279; [2001] 2 All E.R. (Comm) 438. See also *Close Brothers Ltd v Michael Roy Pearce* [2011] EWHC 298 (QB).

acceptance. Where, however, in reliance on the guarantee the creditor commits itself to allow the debtor a drawing facility up to a stated amount, then upon the first drawing being made the surety ceases to be able to revoke the guarantee even though the contract is unilateral, for the stipulated performance of an indivisible obligation has begun. The same applies to other types of indivisible obligation. For example, in *Lloyd's v Harper*[19] a father whose son was a candidate for underwriting membership of Lloyd's guaranteed all obligations of the son incurred in that capacity. The father later died and the question was whether notice of his death operated to revoke the guarantee. The Court of Appeal, upholding the decision of the trial judge, held that it did not. In contrast to the position in *Coulthart v Clementson*,[20] the consideration was an entire consideration given once and for all and there was no basis for limiting its scope to the lifetime of the surety or for treating the guarantee as revocable.

As before, if the creditor commits itself to the surety to give the drawing facility the guarantee is a bilateral contract and takes effect so as to bind the surety immediately.

So long as a continuing guarantee remains in force, the order of receipts and payments passing through the debtor's account is of little significance, for the surety's indebtedness relates not to a specific drawing by the debtor but to a balance of account, and the rule in *Clayton's Case*[21] does not apply. The position is otherwise where an event occurs which causes the guarantee to come to an end. Unless the guarantee otherwise provides,[22] termination of the guarantee fixes the moment at which the debit balance must be struck. The surety is not answerable for future drawings or advances. It is therefore important that the creditor should freeze the debtor's account when the guarantee comes to an end, and place all future receipts to the credit of a separate account.[23] If this is not done, or the rule in *Clayton's Case* otherwise excluded, further sums paid to the credit of the principal debtor's account will go in reduction of the earliest indebtedness first—that is, the indebtedness covered by the guarantee—whilst new drawings will be outside the guarantee. *Clayton's Case* thus has the effect of converting guaranteed indebtedness into non-guaranteed indebtedness, since the amount of the former is reduced by each payment to the credit of the account.

Although in principle a continuing guarantee of a current account is revocable at any time as to future advances, this is subject to any contrary provision in the guarantee. Bank guarantees commonly provide for a period of three months' notice to be given to terminate a continuing guarantee. Such a provision not only ensures that the bank is covered for transactions in course of processing at the time the notice is received but also provides the bank and the debtor with an

8–06

---

[19] *Lloyd's v Harper* (1880) 16 Ch.D. 290.

[20] *Coulthart v Clementson* (1879) 5 Q.B.D. 42.

[21] *Clayton's Case* (1816)1 Mer. 527.

[22] As in *Westminster Bank Ltd v Cond* (1940) 46 Com. Cas. 60, where a clause in the guarantee was held effective to exclude the rule in *Clayton's Case* despite the fact that pursuant to the clause the bank made no break in the account.

[23] In the absence of an effective appropriation of the payment by the debtor to the existing account, the creditor is entitled to open a new account for the crediting and debiting of receipts and payments unless the guarantee otherwise provides (*Re Sherry* (1884) 25 Ch.D. 692). But it is sensible to follow the usual practice of providing for this specifically in the guarantee (or otherwise excluding the operation of the rule in *Clayton's Case*), so as to avoid the possibility of an appropriation by the debtor to the existing account.

opportunity to procure a substitute security. Nevertheless several questions may arise. If the bank makes further advances during the currency of the notice, are these covered by the guarantee? Prima facie they are. Doubts have been expressed as to whether a bank which knows that its surety wishes to end the guarantee acts equitably in allowing further advances during the period of the notice, but in the ordinary way there seems no reason for equitable intervention. The parties have agreed on a specified period of notice, the surety's liability does not crystallise until the end of that period,[24] and to allow the surety to treat his liability as crystallised on receipt of the notice rather than on its expiry would enable him to call on the debtor to discharge the liability before expiry of the notice, which would be inconsistent with the bargain made by the parties.[25] A further question, deriving from the fact that a surety is not liable to pay until demand has been made, is whether the effect of expiry of the notice is simply to crystallise the surety's liabilities at that time or whether it is necessary that demand be made before such expiry. In *National Westminster Bank Plc v Hardman*[26] the Court of Appeal held that the surety was discharged if demand for payment was not made before expiry of the notice. The court may have felt that it was impelled to this result by the wording of the guarantee, which was expressed to remain in force until determined (inter alia) by notice but it could be said to run counter to the commercial sense of the transaction.[27] Moreover, since the liability did not crystallise until expiry of the notice it is hard to see how demand could have been made prior to that time. In *Bank of Credit and Commerce International SA v Simjee*[28] the Court of Appeal held, in relation to a somewhat differently worded guarantee, that no cause of action against the surety would arise until demand but that the demand could only relate to such of the obligations of the debtor at the time of expiry of the notice as still remained unperformed at the time of the demand. Expiry of the notice crystallised the surety's obligations but the guarantee continued in force as regards those obligations and there was no reason why demand could not be made thereafter. What these cases show is the importance of clarity in the drafting of continuing guarantees.

Limited guarantees

8–07   A guarantee may be limited in duration or in amount. It is, of course, necessary to state clearly what the specified time limit means. Professor Goode tells the story of, many years ago, being shown a guarantee by an overseas bank which provided that "this guarantee shall cease to have effect two years after the date thereof". He asked what it meant. Was it restricted to obligations maturing before the expiry of the period or did it cover obligations incurred before expiry though

---

[24] *Bank of Credit and Commerce International SA v Simjee* [1997] C.L.C. 135; *National Westminster Bank Plc v French* Unreported October 20, 1977, per Goff J.; *Morrison v Barking Chemicals Co Ltd* [1919] 2 Ch. 325.

[25] *Morrison v Barking Chemicals Co Ltd* [1919] 2 Ch. 325.

[26] *National Westminster Bank Plc v Hardman* [1988] F.L.R. 302.

[27] For a contrary view see Andrews and Millett, *Law of Guarantees* (2011), para.8–007.

[28] *Bank of Credit and Commerce International SA v Simjee* [1997] C.L.C. 135.

maturing afterwards?[29] Did the creditor have to make a demand within the two-year period? Issue a writ within that period? Serve the writ before the lapse of the two years? Or get a judgment within that time? He received a reply stating that in their 150 years of banking no one had ever raised the point. Nevertheless, they accepted his amendment!

Equal care needs to be taken in drafting a guarantee under which the surety's liability is to be limited in amount. In particular, it is necessary to distinguish the guarantee of a fixed sum, or of a part of an indebtedness, from the guarantee of the entire indebtedness with a limit of liability. If the debtor is to be advanced £10,000, a guarantee of £5,000 of the indebtedness may appear to be the same as a guarantee of the whole advance with a limit of liability of £5,000; but in law there is all the difference in the world. In the former case, the guaranteed part of the debt is treated as if it were a separate debt, so that on paying the £5,000 the surety discharges that notional separate debt and, unless otherwise provided by the guarantee, becomes entitled to share rateably in securities held by the creditor for the full indebtedness[30] and takes over the right to prove in the debtor's bankruptcy as regards the part so paid.[31] Where, on the other hand, the surety guarantees the whole indebtedness but with a limit of liability to £5,000, then whilst he cannot be sued for more than £5,000, the guaranteed indebtedness remains indivisible and the surety cannot take over securities or prove in the bankruptcy unless he discharges the entire indebtedness.[32]

Guarantees given at request of debtor and guarantees not so given

A distinction is also to be drawn between the case where the guarantee is given at the request of the debtor himself, in order to enable him to get the loan, and the case where it is given solely by arrangement between the creditor and the surety. Hire-purchase provides a neat illustration of the two forms of guarantee. A decides to acquire a car on hire-purchase through his local motor dealer, D, the hire-purchase agreement being concluded through the medium of D with a finance house, F. F may stipulate that A is to furnish a surety, and A arranges for his father, B, to guarantee his liability. F may also have an arrangement with the dealer, D, by which D undertakes recourse in respect of all transactions introduced by him. A is not involved in the furnishing of such a guarantee; indeed, it is extremely unlikely that he will know of it.

8–08

The importance of the distinction between the two forms of guarantee lies in the fact that where a guarantee is given at the debtor's request, he impliedly undertakes to indemnify the surety against all payments the latter has to make, whereas one who gives a guarantee without reference to the debtor has no right of indemnity as such,[33] but may have a right to be subrogated to the creditor if and when he, the surety, has discharged the full indebtedness.[34]

---

[29] For a detailed discussion, see Phillips & O'Donovan, *The Modern Contract of Guarantee* (2010), paras 9–026 et seq. For similar issues in relation to the termination of continuing guarantees, see para.8–06, above.

[30] *Goodwin v Gray* (1874) 2 2 W.R. 312.

[31] *Re Sass* [1896] 2 Q.B. 12. See para.8–18, below.

[32] *Re Sass* [1896] 2 Q.B. 12.

[33] *Owen v Tate* [1976] Q.B. 402, although this is subject to some exceptions. The test is "whether in the circumstances it was reasonably necessary in the interests of the volunteer or the person for whom

Nature of the surety's undertaking

8–09   The surety, in entering into the guarantee, undertakes responsibility for payment
of the principal indebtedness and for performance of all other obligations of the
debtor to which the guarantee relates. Of course, so far as the surety is concerned,
liability for breach of those other obligations has to be converted into monetary
terms. The surety's liability applies not merely to the debtor's primary payment
obligation but also to any secondary liability for damages which the debtor may
incur as the result of repudiating the principal contract. This was affirmed by the
House of Lords in *Moschi v Lep Air Services Ltd*[35]:

The appellant guaranteed the obligations of a company under an agreement by
which the company undertook to discharge his existing indebtedness to the
respondents by weekly instalments. The company having repeatedly failed to pay
the instalments due, the respondents treated the default as a repudiation and
terminated the agreement. The appellant's contention that this discharged him
from liability under the guarantee as being the equivalent of an unauthorised
variation of the agreement, was rejected. The House of Lords held that the
appellant's true liability as surety was not for payment of the instalments as such
but for performance of the company's obligations, so that the cause of action
against the appellant was not in debt but in damages, and this covered the
company's secondary liability resulting from its repudiation of the agreements, as
well as its primary liability for payment of the instalments.

Plainly the appellant's contention would have made a nonsense of the
guarantee, and the result of the case is to be applauded. However, one has to treat
with a degree of caution the rather sweeping statements in the speeches that a
claim against a surety sounds in damages, not in debt and that on acceptance of a
repudiatory breach all debt claims become converted into damages claims. The
first proposition is based on Lord Diplock's historical analysis of old forms of
pleading which has no relevance to modern pleading.[36] The second proposition is
true as regards future liabilities but is manifestly not the case as regards accrued
indebtedness. It is trite law (to use one of Lord Diplock's favourite expressions)
that termination for breach does not affect accrued liabilities nor, by the same
token, does it change their character. In *Lep* itself, for reasons which are not clear,
the claim seems to have been exclusively for damages, instead of being for
payment of the accrued instalments and damages for the value of the lost future

---

the payment was made, or both, that the payment should be made – whether in the circumstances it
was 'just and reasonable' that a right of reimbursement should arise" (ibid. at 409–410). See also
Chitty on Contracts, H. Beale (ed.), 31st edn (London: Sweet & Maxwell, 2012), para.44–124.

[34] There seems little doubt that the creditor would have a right of subrogation under the Mercantile
Law Amendment Act 1856 s.5, providing the conditions of that section are fulfilled. However, it is
much less certain that an officious surety has a right of subrogation under equitable principles. First,
such a right only arises where the surety's payment has discharged the debt, but this can only happen
if the debtor either consents to payment or ratifies it subsequently. Even if this is the case, there is a
persuasive argument that if equity denies the officious surety a right to an indemnity, it should
similarly deny him a right to subrogation. See P. Watts, "Guarantees undertaken without the request of
the debtor" [1989] L.M.C.L.Q. 7; Phillips & O'Donovan, *The Modern Contract of Guarantee* (2010),
para.12–279; Andrews and Millett, *Law of Guarantees* (2011), para.11–019.

[35] *Moschi v Lep Air Services Ltd* [1973] A.C. 331.

[36] See *Goode on Commercial Law*, E McKendrick (ed.), 4th edn (London: Penguin Books, 2010),
pp.890–892.

performance, and on this basis the surety's liability would equally be a damages liability. But it is evident that where a surety guarantees the payment of liquidated sums due under a contract which is later terminated for the debtor's repudiatory breach, then while the claim for the lost value of future instalments is a damages claim the claim for accrued indebtedness remains a claim in debt for which the surety is liable.[37]

In a subsequent decision of the House of Lords in *Hyundai Heavy Industries Co Ltd v Papadopoulos*[38] the majority of the House was in no doubt that the decision in *Lep* as to the character of the claim related to future sums payable, not to sums already accrued, and that nothing in that case was intended to displace the well-established principle, reiterated in *Chatterton v Maclean*,[39] that acceptance of a repudiatory breach does not affect accrued liabilities.[40]

8–10

In the decision in *Hampton v Minns*,[41] in which, curiously, there was no reference to *Papadopolous*, the deputy High Court judge nevertheless reached the correct conclusion that the surety's obligation in that case was a debt obligation and as such was outside the scope of s.1 of the Civil Liability (Contribution) Act 1978 and s.10 of the Limitation Act 1980. The learned judge drew a distinction between a promise by the surety to pay if the debtor did not pay and a promise to procure performance by the debtor. This distinction, though criticised in an earlier edition of this book, comes from the speech of Lord Reid in *Moschi v Lep Air Services Ltd*, where he describes two possible forms of agreement:

"A person might undertake no more than that if the principal debtor fails to pay any instalment he will pay it. That would be a conditional agreement. There would be no prestable obligation unless and until the debtor failed to pay. There would then on the debtor's failure arise an obligation to pay. If for any reason the debtor ceased to have any obligation to pay the instalment on the due date then he could not fail to pay it on that date. . ... On the other hand, the guarantor's obligation might be of a different kind. He might undertake that the principal debtor will carry out his contract. Then if at any time and for any reason the principal debtor acts or fails to act as required by his contract, he not only breaks his own contract but he also puts the guarantor in breach of his contract of guarantee. Then the creditor can sue the guarantor, not for the unpaid instalment but for damages. His contract being that the principal debtor would carry out the principal contract, the damages payable by the guarantor must then be the loss suffered by the creditor due to the principal debtor having failed to do what the guarantor undertook that he would do."[42]

---

[37] One explanation for the width of the pronouncement in *Moschi* is that the House of Lords were concentrating on liability for the future instalments (which was a damages claim) since liability for the accrued instalments was dealt with by another argument (which was dismissed by their Lordships as "an impossible argument" (per Lord Simon at 355). See *Hyundai Heavy Industries Co Ltd v Papadopoulos* [1980] 1 W.L.R. 1129, 1136–1137.

[38] *Hyundai Heavy Industries Co Ltd v Papadopoulos* [1980] 1 W.L.R. 1129.

[39] *Chatterton v Maclean* [1951] 1 All E.R. 761.

[40] This point was made and accepted in *Moschi v Lep Air Services* [1973] A.C. 331, 354–355, per Lord Simon; see also Treitel, *The Law of Contract* (2011), para.18–013 fn.85 in relation to the liability of the debtor. See also *Azimut-Benetti SpA (Benetti Division) v Darrell Marcus Healey* [2010] EWHC 2234 (Comm) at [34].

[41] *Hampton v Minns* [2002] 1 W.L.R. 1.

[42] *Moschi v Lep Air Services Ltd* [1973] 1 A.C. 331, 344–345.

Although in every case the true interpretation of the surety agreement will depend on its terms, this distinction has been used in a number of recent cases as an aid to interpretation.[43] The two types of obligation have recently been described in clear terms as follows:

"(1)   a 'see to it' obligation: i.e. an undertaking by the guarantor that the principal debtor will perform his own contract with the creditor;

(2)   a conditional payment obligation: i.e. a promise by the guarantor to pay the instalments of principal and interest which fall due if the principal debtor fails to make those payments".[44]

One particular consequence which flows from the characterisation of the surety's obligation concerns whether a creditor's bankruptcy petition can be presented against an individual surety under s.267 Insolvency Act 1986. Such a petition must be based on a debt for a liquidated sum.[45] If the surety agreement is of the "conditional payment obligation" type, then it is for a liquidated sum, and so falls within s.267. However, if the obligation is of the "see to it" type, it is for unliquidated damages, and so cannot form the basis of a bankruptcy petition, even though such a petition could have been presented against the principal debtor, and the liability of both was identical in financial terms.[46] This is an unfortunate result, and may lead to an incentive for courts to construe agreements as giving rise to the first type of obligation rather than the second.[47] However, as matters stand at present, it seems that the difficulty can only be addressed by legislative reform.

Another way of approaching the problem is to look at the nature of the performance required of the debtor. To the extent that this is an obligation to pay an ascertained sum of money the surety's obligation is to procure the debtor to make that payment or else pay himself and is therefore an obligation sounding in debt and not damages. Accrual of the debtor's payment obligation creates a debt due from the debtor and accordingly a debt due from the surety if the debtor defaults. It is only obligations unmatured at the date of termination for breach that become converted into damages, and this for the simple reason that because of the termination the innocent party is no longer able to tender the performance that will earn him the future money entitlements. The distinction between a claim for debt and a claim for damages is significant in that in the latter case the creditor has to prove his loss and is required to take reasonable steps to mitigate his damage whereas in the case of a debt claim the right to payment has accrued and

---

[43] In *Hampton v Minns* itself, the court held that the first construction was the most apposite (that of conditional obligation). In *Carlton Communications Plc v The Football League* [2002] EWHC 1650 (Comm) the court adopted the second construction (an undertaking that the debtor would carry out the principal contract). A similar conclusion was reached in *Barnicoat v Knight* [2004] EWHC 330 (Ch); *Nearfield Ltd v Lincoln Nominees Ltd* [2006] EWHC 2421 (Ch); and *Remblance v Octagon Assets Ltd* [2009] EWCA Civ 581 especially at [67]–[70].

[44] *McGuinness v Norwich and Peterborough Building Society* [2011] EWCA Civ 1286 at [7].

[45] Insolvency Act 1986 s.267(2)(b).

[46] *McGuinness v Norwich and Peterborough Building Society* [2011] EWCA Civ 1286 esp. at [19], [42].

[47] Andrews & Millett, *Law of Guarantees*, (2011), para.6–002, citing in particular the first instance decision in *McGuinness*.

neither proof of loss nor a duty to mitigate comes into consideration. This analysis particularly applies to the situation, as in *Hyundai Heavy Industries Co Ltd v Papadopoulos*, where there are both accrued liabilities at the time of termination of the debtor's contract and future unpaid sums. In that case, Lord Fraser characterised the agreement with the surety as including both of the types of agreement identified by Lord Reid.[48] In that situation, at least, it would seem that the nature of the performance required would govern the nature of the guarantor's obligation.[49]

Rights of the surety against the debtor

Where the guarantee was given at the request of the debtor, express or implied, the surety has a right to be indemnified by the debtor for liability incurred and payments made under the guarantee, and in particular is entitled to recoupment for each payment under the guarantee as it is made.[50]   **8–11**

Whether or not the debtor requested the surety to give the guarantee, the surety is entitled, on discharging the indebtedness, to be subrogated to the creditor's rights against the debtor and any securities held by the creditor.[51] For the purpose of protecting the surety, the guaranteed debt is considered notionally to remain in force and any securities given are likewise deemed to continue for the benefit of the surety notwithstanding that he has discharged the debt. As previously indicated, where the whole indebtedness is guaranteed, the right of subrogation arises only on complete payment of the debt; partial payment gives no right to pro rata subrogation.[52] The position is otherwise where the surety guarantees only part of the debt and then pays that part.

Finally, a surety is entitled, like anyone else, to purchase the debt from the creditor and to enforce it as assignee on giving notice of assignment to the debtor.

---

[48] *Hyundai Heavy Industries Co Ltd v Papadopoulos* [1980] 1 W.L.R. 1129, 1151. This construction was also used by Rix J. in *BOC Group Plc v Centeon LLC* [1999] C.L.C. 497, 508.

[49] The approach set out in this paragraph has been the subject of criticism, see Andrews & Millett, *Law of Guarantees* (2011), para.6–002.

[50] *Davies v Humphreys* (1840) 6 M. & W. 153. At law, the surety cannot claim this indemnity before payment. In equity, however, he may seek an order for indemnity on incurring the liability to pay as the result of the debtor's default, and the requisite order may be made even though, in the case of a guarantee callable on demand, the demand has not been made (*Thomas v Nottingham Incorporated Football Club Ltd* [1972] Ch. 596). The form of order in such cases is a declaration that the surety is entitled to be exonerated from liability, by payment by the debtor, and a direction to the debtor to pay or secure the debt (ibid.; *Tate v Crewdson* [1938] Ch. 869; *Watt v Mortlock* [1964] Ch. 84).

[51] Mercantile Law Amendment Act 1856 s.5 and/or under the equitable right to subrogation. See above fn.34 in relation to the situation where the debtor does not know of the guarantee. The right to subrogation applies whether or not the surety knew of the existence of the securities when giving his guarantee, and applies to securities taken by the creditor after as well as before the guarantee (*Forbes v Jackson* (1882) 19 Ch.D. 615).

[52] See para.8–07, above and para.8–18, below.

Rights of the surety against a co-surety

8–12   Contribution rights exist between sureties in the same degree. If one of two sureties pays more than his proportionate share of the indebtedness he is entitled to recover the excess from his co-surety.[53]

However, a co-surety, that is, a surety on the same level as the surety claiming contributions, is to be distinguished from one who may be termed a sub-surety, that is, who merely guarantees the obligations of the surety and undertakes no liability except on the surety's default. Contribution cannot be claimed from a sub-surety, for he is entitled to be indemnified by the surety for whom he gives his sub-guarantee.[54] The co-surety may have a right of set-off in respect of a cross-claim against the overpaying surety, but set-off cannot be asserted against a surplus payable to the overpaying surety from the proceeds of security which he acquired by subrogation as the result of his payment of the debt.[55]

Creditor's duty of care in the management of securities

8–13   As stated above, one of the rights enjoyed by a surety who pays off the debt is to be subrogated to securities held by the creditor. It follows that any act or omission of the creditor which impairs those securities (e.g. by failing to perfect them by registration)[56] or which leads to their being realised at less than a proper price potentially injures the surety's interests.[57] The creditor mortgagee[58] when enforcing its security is under a general duty to act in good faith.[59] Subject to this, a mortgagee is not under any duty to the mortgagor to enforce its security in any particular way, or, indeed, to enforce at all.[60] The general principle is that the

---

[53] *Deering v Earl of Winchelsea* (1787) 2 Bos. & Pul. 270. For the various methods of ascertaining the contribution in different situations, see Andrews & Millett, *Law of Guarantees* (2011), para.12.013; Phillips & O'Donovan, *The Modern Contract of Guarantee* (2010), paras 12–119 et seq.

[54] *Scholefield Goodman & Sons v Zyngier* [1986] A.C. 562.

[55] *Brown v Cork* [1985] B.C.L.C. 363. For a criticism of the decision, based on the operation of insolvency set-off, see Derham, *The Law of Set-Off* (2010) paras 8.49, 8.50; *Tolley's Insolvency Law Service* (London: LexisNexis), para.S-6055.

[56] *Wulff v Jay* (1872) L.R. 7 Q.B. 756. Under the legislation in force up to 2013, it was a criminal offence for a company, and its officers, to fail to register a registrable charge (s.860(1) of the Companies Act 2006, even though in practice most, if not all, charges were registered by a creditor). In *Brook v Green* [2006] EWHC 349 (Ch) the principal debtor (a company) had granted the creditor a charge which was never registered. The surety was managing director for the company. In a claim on the guarantee, the surety relied on the fact that the charge was unregistered as a defence, but it was held that he could not do so since he himself had committed an illegal act by failing to cause the company to register the charge. Under the new regime for registration of company charges introduced in 2013 (see Ch.2, above), the criminal sanction has been abolished, and there is no express obligation on the company to register a charge, although it is permitted to do so (as is the chargee or any person interested in the charge). It is unlikely, then, that a creditor could successfully make the argument made in *Brook v Green* where the 2013 regime applied to a company charge.

[57] Whether in fact it does so depends on the circumstances. The diminished value of the security may still be sufficient to ensure that the surety is recouped. Alternatively the debtor may be solvent, so that surety can recoup himself without the need to rely on the security.

[58] The duties are the same in relation to a chargee, *Downsview Nominees Ltd v First City Corp Ltd* [1993] A.C. 295, 311.

[59] *Downsview Nominees Ltd v First City Corp Ltd* [1993] A.C. 295, 317.

[60] *China & South Sea Bank Ltd v Tan* [1990] 1 A.C. 536, 545; *Silven Properties Ltd v Royal Bank of Scotland Plc* [2003] EWCA Civ 1409; [2004] 1 W.L.R. 997, 1003.

mortgagee is at liberty to act in its own self-interest. However, the law does offer some protection to the mortgagor, and also to others who might be harmed by a reduction in the value of the security, including sureties.[61] These duties are equitable, and not imposed at common law.[62] They are imposed on a mortgagee who takes active steps to enforce its security, either by taking possession or by selling the mortgaged assets.[63] For example, a mortgagee in possession must take reasonable steps to maximise the return from the asset, without taking undue risks.[64] He can, subject to the duty of good faith, choose whether or not to sell the asset and, if he decides to sell, he can decide when to do so.[65] However, if he does decide to sell, he must take take proper care whether by fairly and properly exposing the property to the market or otherwise to obtain the best price reasonably obtainable at the date of sale.[66]

What is interesting is that so far there appears to have been no case in which it was necessary to establish a positive duty on the creditor to the surety actionable in damages. Rather the effect of failure to hold the securities unimpaired has been to release the surety from its obligations to the extent of the impairment.[67] In Hohfeldian terms,[68] the surety's "rights" have so far been conceived as immunities and the creditor's breach of "duties" as imposing disabilities rather than as conferring an independent cause of action. However, one can readily envisage situations in which relief from liability would not be enough, as where the surety meets a demand for payment in full and then discovers that the security to which he has acquired rights by subrogation is worthless because it was not duly registered and has been displaced by a subsequent encumbrance. In that situation, can he recover any resultant loss in an action for damages for breach of the equitable duty? In principle, there seems no reason why he cannot. Damages (or equitable compensation) may be awarded for breach of the equitable duty of care and skill in just the same way as at law for negligence.[69] A similar situation to the one described above was envisaged in the recent case of *Barclays Bank v Kingston* (an application for summary judgment), where, on one construction of

---

[61] *American Express International Banking Corp v Hurley* [1986] B.C.L.C. 52, 61.

[62] *Parker-Tweedale v Dunbar Bank Plc* [1991] Ch. 12, 18–19; *Medforth v Blake* [2000] Ch. 86.

[63] For a full and recent account of the duties of a mortgagee, see *Silven Properties Ltd v Royal Bank of Scotland Plc* [2003] EWCA Civ 1409; [2004] 1 W.L.R. 997, 1003–1006; applied in the context of a guarantor in *Den Norske Bank ASA v Acemex Management Co Ltd* [2003] EWCA Civ 1559.

[64] *Palk v Mortgage Services Funding Plc* [1993] Ch. 330, 338; *Silven Properties Ltd v Royal Bank of Scotland Plc* [2003] EWCA Civ 1409; [2004] 1 W.L.R. 997, 1003–1004.

[65] *Cuckmere Brick Co v Mutual Finance Ltd* [1971] Ch. 949, 965; *Tse Kwong Lam v Wong Chit Sen* [1983] 1 W.L.R. 1349, 1355; *Raja v Austin Gray* [2003] EWCA Civ 1965; [2003] 1 E.G.L.R. 91, 96; *Silven Properties Ltd v Royal Bank of Scotland Plc* [2003] EWCA Civ 1409; [2004] 1 W.L.R. 997,1004; *Toor v State Bank of India* [2010] EWHC 1097 (Ch). For a recent discussion of the mortgagee's duty in relation to sale, see K. Loi, "Mortgagees exercising power of sale: nonfeasance, privilege, trusteeship and duty of care" [2010] J.B.L. 576.

[66] *Silven Properties Ltd v Royal Bank of Scotland Plc* [2003] EWCA Civ 1409; [2004] 1 W.L.R. 997, 1005; and see, in the context of a duty to a surety, *Skipton Building Society v Stott* [2001] Q.B. 261; *Potomek Construction Ltd v Zurich Securities Ltd* [2003] EWHC 2827 (Ch) at [40]; *Barclays Bank Plc v Kingston* [2006] EWHC 533 (QB) at [16], [18]–[20].

[67] *Skipton Building Society v Stott* [2001] Q.B. 261 at [21].

[68] See W. N. Hohfeld, *Fundamental Legal Conceptions as applied in Judicial Reasoning and other Legal Essays.*

[69] *Bristol and West Building Society v Mothew* [1998] Ch. 1, per Millett L.J. at 17, citing with approval the judgment of Ipp J. in *Permanent Building Society v Wheeler* (1994) 14 A.C.S.R. 109 at 157.

the guarantee, summary judgment would have had to be given against the guarantors for the whole amount due, and the guarantors could then have pursued their claim against the creditor for the difference between the sum actually realised and the sum that should have been realised.[70] This was the situation in *The Fedora*,[71] where summary judgment was indeed given, on the assumed basis that the cross-claims for damages were arguable.[72]

In the more usual case where the breach of duty is relied upon by a surety sued on the guarantee, the crucial question is the extent of the defence. Does the creditor's culpable behaviour discharge the surety entirely or only to the extent of the prejudice he has suffered? The answer to this question depends on whether the conduct in question constitutes the breach of a non-promissory condition of the guarantee,[73] in which case the surety is wholly discharged irrespective of whether he has suffered loss, or is merely a breach of the equitable obligation to respect the surety's interests (so far as is consistent with the protection of the creditor's own interests), in which case the surety is discharged only to the extent of his loss.[74]

Grounds of discharge of the surety

8–14 The law is very protective of sureties. The surety's liability is tailored to that of the principal debtor,[75] so that where the principal contract is void, voidable[76] or unenforceable or is discharged by the debtor's acceptance of the creditor's repudiatory breach[77] the surety is free from liability.[78] In addition, great importance is attached to the surety's rights of subrogation against the principal debtor and co-sureties. Accordingly any culpable act or omission of the creditor which alters or affects those rights is likely to discharge the surety, wholly or in part. As mentioned earlier, the exact impact of the creditor's improper behaviour on his rights against the surety depends on whether such behaviour constitutes a breach of an implied condition of the contract of guarantee itself or whether it

---

[70] *Barclays Bank Plc v Kingston* [2006] EWHC 533 (QB) at [11]. In fact, the preliminary issues as drafted did not address this situation.

[71] *The Fedora* [1986] 2 Lloyd's Rep. 441. In that case, the guarantee provided for payment "without set-off or counterclaim" and this was held to mean that the guarantor had to pay first and pursue his claim against the creditor afterwards.

[72] However, at the time of that case, it was thought that the mortgagee's duty might be a duty of care in negligence: this fallacy was exposed in *Parker-Tweedale v Dunbar Bank Plc* [1991] Ch.12, 18–19; *Downsview Nominees Ltd v First City Corp Ltd* [1993] A.C. 295, 315.

[73] The idea that the conduct could be a repudiatory breach of the contract of guarantee was regarded as possible in *Skipton Building Society v Stott* [2001] Q.B. 261 at [22], but this possibility is unlikely to arise with any frequency and was rejected on the facts in *Potomek Construction Ltd v Zurich Securities Ltd* [2003] EWHC 2827 (Ch) at [63].

[74] *Skipton Building Society v Stott* [2001] Q.B. 261.

[75] See para.8–02, above.

[76] And avoided. See Andrews & Millett, *Law of Guarantees* (2011), para.6.024.

[77] *Watts v Shuttleworth* (1861) 7 H. & N. 353. A non-repudiatory breach does not of itself discharge the surety (*National Westminster Bank Ltd v Riley* [1986] B.C.L.C. 268).

[78] He is also discharged, of course, where the creditor commits a repudiatory breach of the contract of guarantee (*Ankar Pty Ltd v Westminster Finance (Aust) Ltd* (1987) 70 A.L.R. 641) or fails to observe a non-promissory condition of the contract. This is a matter of general contract law, not a particular feature of the law relating to guarantees, though it is given particular force in guarantee law by the fact that it is an implied condition of the guarantee contract that no alteration will be made in the terms of the principal contract without the surety's consent. See below.

merely infringes the equitable right of the surety not to have his interests wantonly disregarded. In the former case the surety is discharged completely, irrespective of whether he has suffered prejudice. Into this category fall, first, those cases where the creditor fails to provide the consideration for which the guarantee was expressed to be given,[79] and, secondly, all cases where the creditor, without the consent of the surety,[80] varies the terms of the principal contract, so altering the basis of the surety's undertaking to guarantee the debtor's obligations.[81] So even if he suffers no loss the surety is fully discharged where, for example, the creditor releases the debtor,[82] concludes a binding agreement to give the debtor an extension of time for payment without reserving his rights against the surety,[83] releases the security, wholly or in part [84] or otherwise varies the terms of the agreement with the debtor without the surety's consent and in a manner capable of prejudicing him.[85] In effect, the maintenance of the terms upon the basis of which the surety gave his guarantee is a condition of the guarantee, and as in the case of any other breach of condition the court will not concern itself with the extent of the prejudice suffered as a result of the breach but will regard the breach as entitling the surety to regard himself as discharged.[86]

By contrast, where the creditor, without altering the basis of the bargain so far as the surety is concerned, carelessly impairs the surety's position, e.g. by failing to register a security or by realising it at an undervalue through careless acts or omissions, the surety is discharged only to the extent of his resultant loss.[87]

---

[79] *Scott v Forster Pastoral Co Pty Ltd* (2000) 35 A.C.S.R. 294; *Ankar Pty Ltd v National Westminster Finance (Aust) Ltd* (1987) 162 C.L.R. 549 (failure to give notice of events to the surety as provided by the guarantee).

[80] Consent means that there has to be an assent by the surety, probably communicated to the creditor, and mere knowledge is not sufficient, see *Polak v Everett* (1876) 1 Q.B.D. 669; *Wittmann (UK) Ltd v Willdav Engineering SA* [2007] EWCA Civ 824 at [27], although the Court of Appeal in the latter case declined to express a decided view on the point. For a discussion of the Australian authorities on this subject, see *Hickory Developments Pty Ltd v Brunswick Retail Investment Pty Ltd* [2012] V.S.C. 224 at [44]–[61].

[81] *Holme v Brunskill* (1878) 3 Q.B.D. 495, 505.

[82] *Commercial Bank of Tasmania v Jones* [1893] A.C. 313. This principle only applies to a traditional "see to it" guarantee (see para.8–10, above) and not to performance bonds or demand guarantees, see *Meritz Fire & Marine Insurance Co Ltd v Jan de Nul NV* [2011] EWCA Civ 827 at [21].

[83] *Webb v Hewitt* (1857) 3 K. & J. 438; *Swire v Redman* (1876) 1 Q.B.D. 536. The same is true when the creditor and debtor make a binding agreement that the debtor will pay earlier than originally agreed *St Microelectronics NV v Condor Insurance Ltd* [2006] EWHC 977 (Comm). The "time to pay" rule has been the subject of much criticism, see *Polak v Everett* (1876) 1 Q.B.D. 669, 673–674; *Associated British Ports (a company created by statute) v Ferryways NV* [2008] EWHC 1265 (Comm) at [87].

[84] *Pledge v Buss* (1860) John 663.

[85] The variation only needs to be capable of prejudicing the surety, so that the surety will only be held to his bargain when the creditor is able to show that the alteration can only be beneficial to the surety or cannot, by its nature, increase the surety's risk in any circumstances, *Ankar Pty Ltd v National Westminster Finance (Aust) Ltd* (1987) 162 C.L.R. 549, 559.

[86] *Smith v Wood* [1929] 1 Ch. 14.

[87] *Skipton Building Society v Stott* [2001] Q.B. 261; *Brueckner v Satellite Group (Ultimo) Pty Ltd* [2002] N.S.W.S.C. 378; *Wulff and Billing v Jay* (1872) L.R. 7 Q.B. 756; *Barclays Bank Plc v Kingston* [2006] EWHC 533 (QB) at [30].

Exclusion of duty of care and other grounds of discharge from liability

8–15   Almost invariably, standard-term guarantees contain provisions excluding the above rules. Typically, the guarantee will provide that the creditor's rights against the surety shall not be prejudiced or affected by the grant of any time or indulgence to the debtor or a co-surety or by the creditor's failure to take, perfect or hold unimpaired any security taken from the debtor or a co-surety. At common law such provisions are generally effective, although in each case the effectiveness of such a provision is a matter of interpretation of the contract.[88] There are now two lines of authority in relation to interpretation of guarantees, which the courts are still attempting to reconcile.[89] First, traditionally guarantees were interpreted strictly against the creditor, in order to protect the surety.[90] Secondly, the "modern" approach to interpretation of commercial contracts is that, in cases of ambiguity, the court will look for "what a reasonable person, that is a person who has all the background knowledge which would reasonably have been available to the parties in the situation in which they were at the time of the contract, would have understood the parties to have meant".[91] The current law in relation to guarantees steers a middle line between these two approaches. Generally, although clauses such as those referred to above will not necessarily be treated as exclusion clauses, and construed contra proferentem,[92] they will be construed as commercial documents in their factual matrix taking into account the need to protect sureties,[93] so that clear words will be necessary to derogate from the normal incidents of suretyship.[94] It is also commonplace for the guarantee to provide that the creditor may agree to vary the contract with the debtor without further reference to the surety. Although such a clause is usually effective to prevent the surety being released in the event of a variation, it may not have this effect if what is agreed is a new agreement rather than a variation,

---

[88] For an Australian example of an effective clause drafted in very wide terms, see *Hickory Developments Pty Ltd v Brunswick Retail Investment Pty Ltd* [2012] V.S.C. 224.

[89] For discussion of the two lines of authority, see *Meritz Fire, Marine Insurance Co Ltd v Jan de Nul NV* [2010] EWHC 3362 (Comm) at [55]–[62]; and *John Spencer Harvey v Dunbar Assets Plc* [2013] EWCA Civ 952 at [28]–[32]. In neither case did the court attempt a full reconciliation as this was not necessary to decide the case.

[90] *Blest v Brown* (1862) 4 De G.F. & J. 367.

[91] *Investors Compensation Scheme Ltd v West Bromwich Building Society* [1998] 1 W.L.R. 896, 912; and *Rainy Sky SA v Kookmin Bank* [2011] UKSC 50 at [14], [21].

[92] *Bauer v Bank of Montreal* (1980) 110 D.L.R. (3d) 424; *Barclays Bank Plc v Kingston* [2006] EWHC 533 (QB) at [29].

[93] This general approach to the interpretation of guarantees was approved by the Court of Appeal in *Static Control Components (Europe) Ltd v Egan* [2004] EWCA Civ 392 especially at [12] and [37]. See also *John Spencer Harvey v Dunbar Assets Plc* [2013] EWCA Civ 952, where the "modern" approach was followed: in that case there was no attempt to "derogate from the normal incidents of suretyship" at [32] nor was the wording of the agreement ambiguous at [44].

[94] *Trafalgar House Construction (Regions) Ltd v General Surety & Guarantee Co Ltd* [1996] A.C. 199, 208; *Liberty Mutual Insurance Co (UK) Ltd v HSBC Bank Plc* [2002] EWCA Civ 691 at [49], [59]; *Barclays Bank Plc v Kingston* [2006] EWHC 533 (QB) (where the interpretation sought would have imposed on the surety a liability greater than that of the debtor, as the debtor's liability was reduced by the creditor's sale of the security at an undervalue).

which imposes more onerous responsibilties on the surety.[95] Again, clear words are required for a clause to cover such a situation, although the safest course is for the creditor to obtain a new guarantee if the debtor's agreement is renegotiated to a significant extent.[96]

Another way to protect the creditor from rules which discharge the surety is to draft the contract as an indemnity or other primary obligation.

However, this might well be recharacterised as a guarantee,[97] and, in any event, may not be what the parties want to create. Therefore, another common method is to insert a "principal debtor" clause into a guarantee, which provides that the surety's obligations are expressed to be incurred as principal debtor. Such clauses are generally effective to insulate the creditor from the discharging effects of granting time or improperly releasing securities.[98] But it does not follow that the guarantee is to be treated for all purposes as an indemnity or other form of independent undertaking. It is necessary to construe the guarantee according to its terms.[99] So if the surety gives a guarantee of "the moneys hereby secured" and part of such moneys are irrecoverable as a penalty, that part is equally irrecoverable from the surety despite the use of a principal debtor clause.[100]

The efficacy of such clauses may be subject to the provisions of the Unfair Contract Terms Act 1977, if the clause is drafted in such a way that it can be construed as an exclusion or limitation clause[101] as regards a guarantee by a consumer or on standard written terms of business. The more wide-ranging provisions of the Unfair Terms in Consumer Contract Regulations 1999[102] are

---

[95] *Triodos Bank NV v Dobbs* [2005] EWCA Civ 630; see also Andrews & Millett, *Law of Guarantees* (2011), at para.4–025.

[96] *Triodos Bank NV v Dobbs* [2005] EWCA Civ 630. See also *Aviva Insurance Ltd v Hackney Empire Ltd* [2012] EWCA Civ 1716 at [71].

[97] For example, outside the context of banking there is a strong presumption against giving the words "on demand" the effect of creating an independent primary obligation, *Marubeni Hong Kong and South China Ltd v Government of Mongolia* [2004] EWHC 472 (Comm) at [30]; [2005] EWCA Civ 395 at [30]; *IIG Capital LLC v Van der Merwe* [2008] EWCA Civ 542. The presumption was not rebutted in the case of *Carey Value Added SL v Grupo Urvasco SA* [2010] EWHC 1905 (Comm); but in *Meritz Fire, Marine Insurance Co Ltd v Jan de Nul NV* [2010] EWHC 3362 (Comm), upheld on appeal at [2011] EWCA Civ 827; agreements entered into by an insurance company were held to be a performance bond.

[98] *National Westminster Bank v Riley* [1986] B.C.L.C. 268; see also *Heald v O'Connor* [1971] 1 W.L.R. 497, 503; *General Produce Co v United Bank Ltd* [1979] 2 Lloyd's Rep. 255, 259.

[99] *General Produce Co v United Bank Ltd* [1979] 2 Lloyd's Rep. 255. See also A. Berg, "Rethinking Indemnities" (2002) 10 J.I.B.F.L. 403.

[100] *Citicorp Australia Ltd v Hendry* (1985) 4 N.S.W.L.R. 1.

[101] This is unlikely to be the case unless it actually excludes the liability of the creditor to the surety, see *The Fedora* [1986] 2 Lloyd's Rep. 441 at 444; *Barclays Bank Plc v Kingston* [2006] EWHC 533 (QB).

[102] Unfair Terms in Consumer Contract Regulations 1999 (SI 1999/2083).

more likely to apply, but only as regards a guarantee by a consumer,[103] and only if the Directive, and therefore the Regulations, is held to apply to contracts of guarantee.[104]

2. BANKRUPTCY

8–16   We shall now turn to the impact of bankruptcy[105] on the rights of creditor and surety. The possibilities canvassed are the bankruptcy of the debtor, the bankruptcy of the surety and the bankruptcy of both debtor and surety. The discussion will then conclude with a brief analysis of the circumstances in which a guarantee may be set aside on the surety's insolvency as a transaction at an undervalue.

If the subject of fixed and floating charges seemed complicated, and the cases difficult to analyse, the going becomes harder still when we come to look at the case law on the impact of bankruptcy on suretyship guarantees. For some reason, conflicting authorities and obscure reasoning seem endemic in the earlier bankruptcy cases, and not infrequently one finds in the literature two quite inconsistent propositions placed one after the other, each being duly supported by authority, yet without a hint in the later case that it marks a departure from the earlier.

So anyone going into this field does so at his peril. What follows is an attempt to reconcile the apparently irreconcilable, to extract a consistent principle from seemingly conflicting cases and to discover and express a rational policy basis for some of the rules discussed later. That said, it is important to remember that bankruptcy law is one of the most technical and, in some respects, one of the most arbitrary branches of law, and that in the absence of a definitive ruling from the courts the answers to some questions remain conjectural.

(i)   Bankruptcy of the debtor

8–17   Three questions in particular arise where the debtor becomes bankrupt. First, on the assumption that the contract of guarantee is not vulnerable under bankruptcy law, to what extent do sums received by the creditor from the surety or from the realisation of security given by the surety or from a third party reduce the amount for which the creditor is entitled to prove or to maintain a proof already lodged? Secondly, in what circumstances does a payment by the debtor to the creditor

---

[103] The extent to which the Regulations apply to a contract of guarantee is somewhat uncertain, but the weight of authority is now in favour of their application, but of a narrow definition of "consumer", so that in none of the cases supporting the theoretical application of the Regulations was the surety held to be a consumer. See *Barclays Bank Plc v Kufner* [2008] EWHC 2319 (Comm); *Royal Bank of Scotland Plc v Chandra* [2010] EWHC 105 (Ch); *United Trust Bank Ltd v Dohil* [2011] EWHC 3302 (QB); and discussion in *Chitty on Contracts* (2012), paras 44–148 to 44–154.

[104] *Chitty on Contracts* (2012), para.44–136.

[105] This should be read as including corporate insolvency except as otherwise indicated. The rules in relation to proof of debts in a distribution by an administrator (if he decides to make such a distribution under Insolvency Act 1986 para.65 Sch.B1) are largely the same as those relating to liquidation and what follows includes such distribution unless otherwise indicated.

prior to the debtor's bankruptcy constitute a voidable preference of the surety? Thirdly, what is the impact of the debtor's insolvency on the position of the surety?

Receipts from surety or third party: the general rule

The general rule is that sums received from the surety, or from the realisation of **8–18** security taken from the surety, do not have to be deducted by the creditor from the amount of his proof, whether received before or after the bankruptcy has occurred[106] and, in the latter case, whether before or after proof, so long as the creditor does not receive in total more than 100 pence in the pound. Obviously, if the surety pays the entirety of the principal debt, the creditor cannot prove for it in the debtor's bankruptcy: in this circumstance the surety can prove either for an indemnity or under the right of subrogation. If the creditor does receive more than the amount of the principal debt, he holds the surplus in trust for the surety.[107] At first sight it seems surprising that, if the surety pays part of the debt the creditor should not have to give credit at least for sums received from the surety prior to the bankruptcy. But the rule has a sound policy base. It is a well settled principle of equity that until the creditor has received payment of the guaranteed debt in full the surety cannot prove in the insolvent debtor's estate for a sum paid by him to the creditor. The reason for this is that he has, expressly or by implication, undertaken to be responsible for the full sum guaranteed, including whatever remains due to the creditor after receipt of dividends by him out of the bankrupt's estate, and thus has no equity to prove for his right of reimbursement in competition with the creditor.[108] If the creditor were required to give credit for a pre-bankruptcy part payment by the surety, neither of them could prove for the amount of such payment and the general body of creditors would thus be unjustly enriched. Similarly, sums received by the creditor before the bankruptcy from the realisation of security furnished by the surety are not deductible in computing the amount for which he can prove.[109] A fortiori credit need not be given for sums received after bankruptcy and before proof, still less for receipts after proof. To

---

[106] *Ellis v Emmanuel* (1876) 1 Ex.D. 157; *Re Sass* [1896] 2 Q.B. 12; *Ulster Bank Ltd v Lambe* [1968] N.I. 161; *Re An Arranging Debtor No.A 1076* [1971] N.I. 96; *Westpac Banking Corp v Gollin & Co Ltd* [1988] V.R. 397, Tadgell J. (Supreme Court of Victoria); *Bula v Crowley* Unreported February 20, 2001 High Court, Ireland. In the last three decisions the court declined to follow an earlier Scottish decision, *MacKinnon's Trustee v Bank of Scotland* [1915] S.C. 411, in which it had been held that the creditor had to give credit for pre-bankruptcy payments received from the surety. It seems clear that whatever the position under Scottish law, *MacKinnon* does not represent English law.

[107] *Westpac Banking Corp v Gollin & Co Ltd* [1988] V.R. 397, 403.

[108] See cases cited fn.106, above. The rule against double proof (discussed at para.8–23, below) prevents the surety and the creditor from proving for the same debt, so that the creditor's right to prove for the whole debt without giving credit for a part payment received from the surety precludes both a proof for that payment by the surety and a set-off (*In Re Fenton Textile Association* [1931] 1 Ch. 85; *Barclays Bank v TOSG Trust Fund* [1984] A.C. 626, 643; *Secretary of State for Trade and Industry v Frid* [2004] UKHL 24 at [13]; [2004] 2 A.C. 506, 512; *Mills v HSBC Trustee (CI) Ltd*; sub nom. *Re Kaupthing Singer & Freidlander Ltd (In Administration)* [2011] UKSC 48 at [12]). In addition, the application of the rule in *Cherry v Boultbee* is precluded, see *Mills v HSBC Trustee (CI) Ltd* [2011] UKSC 48 at [53].

[109] It may be noted that for the purpose of bankruptcy a creditor is considered secured only where he holds security over an asset of the debtor. Security taken from a third party such as a surety does not fall to be treated as a security in the treatment of proofs in bankruptcy. This reflects the policy of

make assurance doubly sure it is common for guarantees to empower the creditor to place sums received from the surety which do not fully discharge the guaranteed debt to the credit of a suspense or "securities realisation" account.[110] But this procedure, though sensible as a matter of accounting practice, is not essential to enable the creditor to maintain his proof for the full sum owing to him.

The same is true where the creditor receives payment from a complete stranger. There is thus a general rule that only a payment by or on behalf of the party primarily liable (in the case under discussion, the bankrupt) has to be taken into account; payments from other sources are disregarded. As will be seen, a similar rule applies in the case where it is the surety who is bankrupt.

The same principle applies where the surety has guaranteed the whole indebtedness with a limit of liability. Since the guarantee covers the ultimate balance, the surety has no equity to prove in competition with the creditor until payment has been made in full, even though his liability under the guarantee is limited to a lower amount which he has paid.[111]

These principles have been challenged in a decision of the High Court in Auckland. In *Stotter v Equiticorp Australia Ltd (In Liquidation)*[112] Fisher J. held that a creditor's proof in the liquidation of the principal debtor had to be reduced by the amount received by the creditor from the surety before the onset of liquidation. His reasoning was based on the premise that if a surety pays part of the principal debt then, outside of insolvency proceedings, the creditor can only sue the principal debtor for the balance. Therefore, he said, the creditor should not be able, by general law or contract, to put himself in a better position in the debtor's insolvency than outside it. This reasoning seems doubtful, however. Although every case ultimately depends on the construction of the agreement, the general rule outside insolvency appears to be that a part payment by the surety does not prevent the creditor suing a solvent principal debtor for the whole amount of the debt. If the creditor recovers in full from the principal debtor, he is obliged to reimburse the surety. Support for this view comes from the Northern Irish case of *Ulster Bank v Lambe*,[113] where the debtor was solvent, as well as from dicta from the insolvency case of *Re Sass*.[114] In support of his view, Fisher J. cited the dictum of Dillon L.J. from *MS Fashions v BCCI* that "A creditor cannot sue the principal debtor for an amount of the debt which the creditor has

---

bankruptcy law that security should be brought into account only where, if given up, it would augment the debtor's estate (see *Re Dutton, Massey & Co* [1924] 2 Ch. 199).

[110] The effect of such a payment is to provide the creditor with a fund to which he can resort when he chooses. The payment constitutes a deposit by the surety which is withdrawable only if the creditor receives 100p in the pound. The creditor is entitled to appropriate the deposit in or towards the discharge of the principal indebtedness, but until he makes an appropriation the deposit does not constitute a payment of any part of the debt (*Commercial Bank of Australia v Official Assignee of the Estate of Wilson* [1893] A.C. 181).

[111] *Re Rees* (1881) 17 Ch. 98.

[112] *Stotter v Equiticorp Australia Ltd (In Liquidation)* [2002] 2 N.Z.L.R. 686. For further discussion, see Andrews & Millett, *Law of Guarantees* (2011), para.13–010.

[113] *Ulster Bank v Lambe* [1966] N.I. 161.

[114] *Re Sass* [1896] 2 Q.B. 12, 14: "I think that the common law right of the bank here was to sue the debtor for the whole amount that was due from him to them, irrespective of the sum which was paid by the surety, unless that sum amounted to 20s. in the pound", per Vaughan Williams J.

already received from a guarantor".[115] However, neither *Re Sass* nor *Ulster Bank v Lambe* were cited to the Court of Appeal in that case. The other case cited by Fisher J. is *Milverton Group Ltd v Warner World Ltd*.[116] In that case the Court of Appeal decided that payment of rent by a surety discharged the lessee's obligation to pay the same rent, but arguably this is not of more general application as first, in the landlord and tenant situation, there is a single set of obligations, to pay the rent and perform the covenants, owed by both tenant and guarantor[117]; and, secondly, it is at least arguable that the payment of the rent was payment in full of that particular obligation relating to that particular period.[118] If it is right that even outside insolvency, the creditor does not need to give credit for part payment by the surety when suing the debtor, the main plank of Fisher J.'s argument, namely that the rules should be the same outside and within insolvency, falls away.

Fisher J. also discussed the policy considerations set out above. He dismissed the argument that the creditor must prove for the whole as the surety cannot prove for any indemnity (because of the rule against double proof) as theoretical, since, given the likely deficiency in the debtor's estate, it will not normally make any difference to the surety whether the creditor proves for the gross or net amount: while in many cases this may be true there may be cases where the creditor eventually receives more than the net amount as a result of his proof for the gross amount, in which case he holds this on trust for the surety. Further, this ignores the windfall for the other creditors discussed above. The policy argument against the result in *Stotter* is also strong, since it creates a distinction between payments made by the surety before liquidation (for which the creditor has to give credit) and those made after (for which he does not).[119] Fisher J. deals with this argument on the basis that it is no more anomalous than other situations, for example, the position where the surety is insolvent and the debtor has made a payment.[120] However, as pointed out above, payments made by the person primarily liable do not fall within the rule in *Re Sass*.[121]

It is submitted, therefore, that the position in English law remains that partial payments by a surety do not reduce the amount for which the creditor can prove. By partial payments is meant payments of less than the total indebtedness to which the guarantee relates. If the creditor has misguidedly taken a guarantee covering only part of the debt, as opposed to a guarantee of the full indebtedness with a limit of liability, then on paying that part the surety becomes entitled to lodge a proof himself in respect of the part so paid[122]; and since two creditors cannot separately prove for the same debt— this is the so-called rule against

---

[115] *MS Fashions v BCCI* [1993] 1 Ch. 425, 448.

[116] *Milverton Group Ltd v Warner World Ltd* [1995] 2 E.G.L.R. 28.

[117] *Milverton Group Ltd v Warner World Ltd* [1995] 2 E.G.L.R. 28 at 31.

[118] *Milverton Group Ltd v Warner World Ltd* [1995] 2 E.G.L.R. 28 at 30.

[119] It should, perhaps, be pointed out that *Re Sass* deals with the latter situation, and so the decision in *Stotter* is not inconsistent with that authority.

[120] See para.8–31, below.

[121] *Re Blakeley Ex p. Aachener Disconto Gesellschaft* (1892) 9 Morr. 173; *Western Credit Ltd v Alberry* [1964] 1 W.L.R. 945; *Re Amalgamated Investment and Property Co Ltd* [1985] 1 Ch. 349.

[122] *Re Sass* [1896] 2 Q.B. 12, per Vaughan Williams J. at 15. It is a matter of interpretation of the contract as to whether the surety guarantees part of the debt or the whole indebtedness with a limit on liability, see *Barclays Bank v TOSG Trust Fund* [1984] A.C. 626, 644; *Re Butlers Wharf Ltd* [1995] 2 B.C.L.C. 43.

double proof—it follows that the creditor must reduce his proof (even if already lodged) by the amount paid by the surety in discharge of his guarantee. As stated earlier, the part of the indebtedness guarantee is treated as a separate debt for the purpose of the rules as to proof by a surety.

Receipts from surety or third party: negotiable instruments

8–19   For reasons which are not clear, negotiable instruments constitute an exception to the general rule.[123] Where, for example, the creditor is the holder of a bill of exchange accepted by the debtor and drawn or indorsed by a third party (whose position is thus analogous to that of a surety),[124] then although the creditor can prove in the debtor's bankruptcy for the full amount of the bill whilst concurrently pursuing a claim to full payment against the third party, yet if before lodging his proof against the debtor the creditor receives part payment from the third party he must reduce his proof by the amount of the payment.[125] Where, on the other hand, the payment is not received from the third party until after the creditor has lodged his proof, he can keep his proof for the full amount of the debt and need not give credit for the sum received.[126] The moral is obvious. Where one of the parties liable to you on a bill of exchange becomes bankrupt, lodge your proof as fast as you possibly can, and until then defer steps to recover from the other parties.

Preference of surety

8–20   Payments made or property transferred by a debtor prior to bankruptcy may in certain conditions be voidable on bankruptcy as a preference not only of the creditor but of a surety. Common cases are where an insolvent debtor reduces or discharges his loan account in order to procure the release of a relative or friend who has furnished a guarantee, and where moneys are paid into a debtor company's overdrawn account not simply because this is the natural depository of cheques and other sums paid to the company but with a view to reducing or extinguishing the suretyship liability of a director. The Insolvency Act 1986 makes separate provision for the avoidance of preferences in bankruptcy and in the administration or winding up of a company, and whilst the two are dealt with in almost identical fashion there are certain differences in detail which necessitate distinct treatment.

(1)   Bankruptcy

8–21   The statutory provisions as they affect sureties apply where an individual is adjudged bankrupt and he has at a relevant time given a preference to a surety, that is, has done anything or suffered anything to be done which puts the surety in a better position in the event of the debtor's bankruptcy than the surety would

---

[123] *Re Blackburne* (1892) 9 Morr. 249; *Re Houlder* [1929] 1 Ch. 205.
[124] *Duncan, Fox & Co v North & South Wales Bank* (1880) 6 App.Cas. 1; *Re Conley* [1938] 2 All E.R. 127, per Lord Greene M.R. at 133.
[125] *Re Blackburne* (1892) 9 Morr. 249.
[126] *Re London Bombay & Mediterranean Bank* (1874) L.R. 9 Ch. App. 686; *Re Houlder* [1929] 1 Ch. 205.

have been in if that thing had not been done.[127] The typical act of preference of a surety is a payment by the debtor to the creditor which reduces the surety's liability under his guarantee. The term "preference" is somewhat misleading, since whilst the earlier legislation was concerned with the preference of the surety over other creditors at the time of the payment or other act of preference, the new provisions apply where the surety's position is thereby improved on the debtor's bankruptcy, regardless whether the effect of the payment or other act in question was to favour the surety over other creditors at the time it was made or done. Where a preference is established the court is given wide powers to restore the status quo.[128]

In order for a preference to fall within the statutory provisions two conditions must be satisfied. First, in giving the preference the debtor must have been influenced by the desire to put the surety in a better position, in the event of the debtor's bankruptcy, than that in which he would otherwise have been.[129] Secondly, the preference must have been given at a "relevant time", that is, at a time in a specified period ending with the day of presentation of the bankruptcy petition on which the debtor is adjudged bankrupt, and the debtor must have been insolvent[130] at that time or have become insolvent in consequence of the preference.[131] Where the surety is an associate of the debtor[132] the period is two years; in other cases, it is six months.[133] The surety's exercise of a right of set-off is not a preference, for it does not involve the debtor's consent.

(2) Administration or winding up[134]

Similar provisions apply where the debtor is a company which has entered administration or which goes into liquidation,[135] but with the following modifications:

8–22

(a) instead of "associate" the provisions refer to a person connected with the company[136] otherwise than by reason only of being its employee[137];

(b) a "relevant time" is a time in the period of six months (or in the case of a connected person, two years) ending with the "onset of insolvency" (as defined by s.240(3) of the Act) or at a time between the making of an administration application in respect of the company and the making of an

---

[127] Insolvency Act 1986 s.340(1), (3).

[128] Insolvency Act 1986 ss.340(2), 342. See R. Goode, *Principles of Corporate Insolvency Law*, 4th edn (London: Sweet & Maxwell, 2011), paras 13–105 et seq. See also paras 8–29 and 8–39, below.

[129] Insolvency Act 1986 s.340(4). This is presumed where the surety was an associate of the debtor at the time (ibid., s.340(5)).

[130] For this purpose the debtor is insolvent if he is unable to pay his debts as they fall due or the value of his assets is less than the amount of his liabilities, taking into account his contingent and prospective liabilities (Insolvency Act 1986 s.341(3)).

[131] Insolvency Act 1986 s.341.

[132] As defined in s.435 of the Insolvency Act 1986.

[133] Insolvency Act 1986 s.341(1).

[134] For a fuller discussion, see Goode, *Principles of Corporate Insolvency Law* (2011), paras 13–71 to 13–107.

[135] Insolvency Act 1986 ss.238 (the ingredients of which are attracted by ss.239(1)) and 239–241.

[136] As defined by s.249 of the Insolvency Act 1986.

[137] Insolvency Act 1986 s.240(1)(a).

administration order on that application or at a time between the filing with the court of a copy of notice of intention to appoint an administrator under paras 14 or 22 of Sch.B1 to the 1986 Act and the making of an appointment under that paragraph[138];

(c)   instead of having to show that the debtor company was insolvent at the time of or in consequence of the preference, the liquidator or other office-holder attacking the preference has the much easier task of showing that at the time of or in consequence of the preference the company was unable to pay its debts within the meaning of s.123 of the Act.[139]

Proof by the surety

(1)   In respect of the guaranteed debt: rule against double proof

8–23   As mentioned above, there is a long-standing rule against double proof in respect of the same debt,[140] which, in a suretyship situation, means that, since the creditor is entitled to maintain his proof for the full amount of the debt existing at the date of the receiving order without giving credit for part payment by the surety, it follows that the surety himself has merely a contingent right to prove against the debtor's estate in respect of the guaranteed debt and cannot lodge a proof until the creditor has been paid in full.[141] As previously pointed out, the position is otherwise where the surety has guaranteed only part of the debt and paid that part.[142] However, where the right to indemnity is not by virtue of a liability incurred under a contract of guarantee *stricto sensu* but is that of a drawer or indorser under a bill of exchange, then if the drawer or indorser makes part payment to the holder before the latter has proved in the acceptor's bankruptcy, the maker of the payment can forthwith prove for it, for as mentioned earlier[143]

---

[138] As defined by Insolvency Act 1986 s.240(1).

[139] Insolvency Act 1986 s.240(2), which is much wider than the definition in s.341(3). For a recent discussion, in another context, of the test in s.123; see *BNY Corporate Trustee Services Ltd v Eurosail-UK 2007-3BL Plc* [2013] UKSC 28, applied in the context of s.240(2) in *In the Matter of Casa Estates (UK) Ltd* [2013] EWHC 2371 (Ch).

[140] For a full account of the rule and its background, see *Barclays Bank v TOSG Trust Fund* [1984] A.C. 626, 636, 643–644; *Re Polly Peck International Plc* [1996] 2 All E.R. 433, 441–443; *Mills v HSBC Trustee (CI) Ltd* [2011] UKSC 48 at [11]. See also *Re MF Global UK Ltd (In Special Administration)* [2013] EWHC 2556 (Ch)

[141] *Re Fenton* [1931] 1 Ch. 85. Set-off is precluded because of the rule against double proof (and non-provable debts cannot be subject to insolvency set-off, see *Re Glen Express Ltd* [2000] B.P.I.R. 456, para.7–82, above), but would not otherwise be precluded merely because the debt was contingent. This is the effect of the overruling of the reasoning of the Court of Appeal in *Re Debtor (No.66 of 1955)* sub nom. *Debtor, Ex p. v Trustee of the Property of Waite (A Bankrupt)* [1956] 1 W.L.R. 1226 by the House of Lords in *Re West End Networks Ltd; Secretary of State for Trade and Industry v Frid* [2004] UKHL 24. Rule 4.90 of the Insolvency Rules 1986 has been amended to reflect this so that the definition of "mutual debts" now includes contingent claims. The rule in *Cherry v Boultbee* (that equity requires that a person cannot share in a fund in relation to which he is also a debtor without first contributing to the whole by paying his debt) is similarly precluded, *Mills v HSBC Trustee (CI) Ltd* [2011] UKSC 48 at [53]. *Re SSSL Realisations*; sub nom. *Squires v AIG Europe UK Ltd* [2006] EWCA Civ 7 was disapproved on this point.

[142] See para.8–18, above. But his right to prove in competition with the creditor may be excluded by the terms of the guarantee. See para.8–24, below.

[143] See para.8–19, above.

the holder has to deduct such payment in calculating the amount of his proof, so that the problem of double proof does not arise.

(2) In respect of an independent liability of the debtor

The rule against double proof does not, of course, apply to a debt owed to the surety independently of that which he has guaranteed. If, for example, the surety has lent the debtor money, this is quite distinct from the debt to which the guarantee relates, and the surety is entitled to prove for it.

8–24

Most forms of bank guarantee provide that the surety is not to prove in competition with the bank until the bank's claim has been paid in full, the intention being to prevent the banker's dividend from being watered down by the surety's own claim. The non-competition clause has been standard for decades.[144] But the clause, far from protecting the interests of the creditor, is positively inimical to those interests, for its effect is to benefit not only the creditor himself but all other unsecured creditors.[145] To prohibit the surety from proving for an independent liability is thus not wisdom but folly, for it prevents the creditor from getting the benefit of a double dividend. What the well-drawn guarantee ought to provide is that the surety shall prove in the bankruptcy (with a power of attorney to the creditor to lodge a proof in the surety's name) and shall account to the creditor for any dividends he receives, to the amount necessary to discharge his guarantee liability, meanwhile holding such receipts on trust for the creditor.[146] Where such a provision is contained in two or more guarantees given to different creditors, then presumably the creditor holding the guarantee which is first in time prevails.

A clause encompassing both a non-competition clause and a clause providing for a trust as suggested above was considered by the Court of Appeal in *Re SSSL Realisations*; sub nom. *Squires v AIG Europe UK Ltd*[147] in the context of the liquidations of both the principal debtor and the surety, who were both part of the same group of companies. The non-competition clause did not appear to add anything to the trust clause in relation to the protection of the creditor, and the creditor in that case sought to waive its operation. The Court of Appeal, however, felt compelled to give the non-competition clause some meaning, which was that inter-company indebtedness was to be left out of account until the group debt to the creditor had been paid, and that since this was for the benefit of all the group companies as well as the creditor,[148] this had the effect that the clause could only be waived by the agreement of the liquidators of all the group companies and the

---

[144] A non-competition clause in such terms was considered by the Court of Appeal in *Cattles Plc v Welcome Financial Services Ltd* [2010] EWCA Civ 599, where it was held that the clause covered all liabilities of the debtor to the surety and not just those referable to the guarantee, despite the fact that this had a "disastrous" effect on the surety's bondholders, who would not then have the benefit of inter-company loans owed by the debtor to the surety.

[145] Previous editions of this book have recorded that this view came to Professor Goode one night while lying in the bath.

[146] This is a version of the turnover trust which is used extensively in subordinated debt (see para.5–60, above).

[147] *Re SSSL Realisations*; sub nom. *Squires v AIG Europe UK Ltd* [2006] EWCA Civ 7; [2006] Ch. 610.

[148] *Re SSSL Realisations*; sub nom. *Squires v AIG Europe UK Ltd* [2006] EWCA Civ 7; [2006] Ch. 610 at [64].

creditor. As drafted in the *SSSL* case, the non-competition clause seems self-defeating for the creditor, since in order to obtain the "double dividend" under the trust clause, he would always have to waive its operation. Therefore, at least from the point of view of a creditor, a well-drawn agreement will either just contain a clause providing that any dividend will be held on trust for him, or will include a non-competition clause on terms that the creditor can, in its discretion, instruct the surety to prove in the liquidation and hold any dividend on trust for the creditor.[149]

Is a trust of the dividends registrable as a charge on book debts? The view in earlier editions was that it was not, for the reasons that, first, the debt is not the dividend itself but the proved indebtedness which has given rise to the dividend and secondly, that the dividend payable in a bankruptcy or winding up is not a debt at all, for it is not recoverable by action against the trustee in bankruptcy or liquidator.[150] This view has been upheld in the *SSSL* case, partly relying on the first reason given above,[151] but mainly for the following reason. The trust only extended to such amount of the dividends as was necessary to pay the principal debt. It therefore exhibited none of the incidents of a charge[152] and would not be characterised as such.[153] Although not cited in *SSSL*, the idea that there can be a trust of part of a fund, being enough to cover a particular indebtedness, follows the reasoning in *Associated Alloys v ACN 001 452 106*.[154]

Surety's subrogation to creditor's rights

8–25   Upon paying the guaranteed debt in full the surety becomes subrogated to the rights of the creditor.[155] Accordingly: (1) the creditor is accountable to the surety for any further dividends received from the bankrupt's estate[156]; (2) the surety succeeds to securities held by the creditor; and (3) to the extent to which the

---

[149] This is the formulation suggested in Andrews & Millett, *Law of Guarantees* (2011) at para.13–012; and in Precedent 1 cl.6.4.This seems preferable to the formulation suggested by others that the non-competition clause is for the exclusive benefit of the creditor and can be unilaterally waived by it, see P. Walker, "Guarantees: do non-competition clauses work in insolvency?" (2007) 3 J.I.B.F.L. 167; A. Lenon, "Debt subordination in a group insolvency—the Save group case" J.I.B.L.R. 416.

[150] *Prout v Gregory* (1889) 24 Q.B.D. 281; *Spence v Coleman* [1901] 2 K.B. 199

[151] See the judgment at first instance, [2004] EWHC 1760 (Ch) at [54], approved by the Court of Appeal at [122]. This particular point is no longer relevant in relation to a charge created after April 6, 2013, since any charge created by a company would be registrable unless it fell under the FCARs, see Chs 2 and 6, above.

[152] See above and also generally H. Beale, M. Bridge, L. Gullifer and E. Lomnicka, *The Law of Security and Title-Based Financing*, 2nd edn (Oxford: Oxford University Press, 2012), para.4.24.

[153] *Re SSSL Realisations*; sub nom. *Squires v AIG Europe UK Ltd* [2004] EWHC 1760 (Ch) [50]–[51] approved at [2006] EWCA Civ 7; [2006] Ch. 610 at [122].

[154] *Associated Alloys v ACN 001 452 106* (2000) 202 C.L.R. 588. See L. Ho, "A matter of contractual and trust subordination" (2004) 19 J.I.B.L.R. 494, 496–498; L. Gullifer and J. Payne, *Corporate Finance Law: Principles and Policy* (Oxford: Hart Publishing, 2011), pp.214–215.

[155] Both in equity and under s.5 of the Mercantile Law Amendment Act 1856, see para.8–11, above.

[156] *Re Sass* [1896] 2 Q.B. 12.

creditor was a preferential creditor (whether directly or by subrogation to a preferential creditor), the surety becomes a preferential creditor for the like amount.[157]

Example

S guarantees D Company's overdraft with C Bank. D Company goes into liquidation by reason of insolvency. Part of its indebtedness to C Bank represents advances to pay wages which, if unpaid at the date of liquidation, would have ranked as preferential debts.[158] The bank, having advanced the wages, is by statute subrogated to the preferential claims of the employees concerned.[159] S later pays off the bank, and thus becomes subrogated to the bank's own subrogatory rights in respect of the wages. S can therefore prove as a preferential creditor to the extent to which the wages advanced by the bank were preferential. **8–26**

Impact of debtor's bankruptcy on surety's liability

(1)   In general, liability is unaffected

The bankruptcy of the principal debtor does not as a general rule affect the creditor's rights against the surety. The creditor may lodge a proof in the bankruptcy for the full outstanding balance of the debt and simultaneously sue the surety to judgment, and enforce such judgment to the extent to which the creditor has not received a dividend from the estate.[160] Even the discharge of the debtor does not affect the surety's liability. This is expressly provided by s.281(7) of the Insolvency Act 1986.[161] **8–27**

(2)   Interest accruing after bankruptcy order

Some care needs to be taken in regard to the interest clause in the guarantee. If interest is expressed to be payable "so long as any amount is due from the debtor", the right to charge interest to the surety apparently terminates with the debtor's bankruptcy, at which point the debt ceases to be legally recoverable from him.[162] This result can be avoided by stipulating that interest is to run against the surety "until payment" of the amount due from the principal debtor.[163] **8–28**

(3)   Invalidation of securities

What is the position of the surety where a debit balance on the debtor's account is cleared with a payment or the proceeds of a security which is later avoided, e.g. **8–29**

---

[157] *Re Lamplugh Iron Ore Co Ltd* [1927] 1 Ch. 308. Note that the categories of preferential creditors are now very limited, see para.5–68, above.

[158] Under the Insolvency Act 1986 s.386 and Sch.6.

[159] Insolvency Act 1986 Sch.6 para.11.

[160] For the position where the surety also becomes bankrupt, see para.8–33, below.

[161] For the effect on the surety of the entry of the debtor into a voluntary arrangement, see Andrews & Millett, *Law of Guarantees* (2011), para.9–014.

[162] *Re Moss* [1905] 2 K.B. 307.

[163] *Re Fitzgeorge* [1905] 1 K.B. 462.

as a preference under s.239 of the Insolvency Act 1986[164] or as a floating charge given by an insolvent company within s.245 of the Act or void for want of registration under s.874 of the Companies Act 2006? In the case of a preference the answer to this question, which was obscure under the previous law, is given by ss.239(3) and 241 of the Act. By s.239(3)[165] the court is required to make such order as it thinks fit for restoring the position to what it would have been if the company had not given the preference. Without prejudice to the generality of this provision, s.241 empowers the court to make an order providing for any surety or guarantor whose obligations were released or discharged (in whole or in part) by the giving of the preference to be under such new or revived obligations to the creditor as the court thinks appropriate.[166] The court may also order security to be provided for the discharge of any such obligation and for the obligation to be charged on any property, the security or charge to have the same priority as that released by the giving of the preference.[167] The effect of these provisions is to enable the court to restore the status quo existing before the giving of the preference. But unless and until it does so the preference by which the guaranteed debt was settled operates to discharge the surety and to release any security furnished by him to support his guarantee.

Where security subject to a floating charge—whether crystallised or uncrystallised—is realised and the proceeds utilised to discharge the debt, the surety is discharged and any security furnished by him is extinguished. The fact that the charge later becomes liable to avoidance for non-registration or on any other ground is irrelevant, for it is settled law that if the charge is enforced or payment collected prior to an event such as liquidation which avoids the charge, its effect is spent and its subsequent avoidance has no impact on the rights of the parties.[168]

(ii) Bankruptcy of the surety

8–30   It is now necessary to consider the converse situation where the debtor is still solvent (or at any rate not in bankruptcy or winding up), whilst the surety has become bankrupt, and to examine questions arising in relation to proof by the creditor and by a co-surety.

Proof by creditor

8–31   As in the case of the bankruptcy of the principal debtor, it is necessary to distinguish payments made by the principal debtor as the party primarily liable from those made by a third party such as a co-surety or a stranger. The creditor is required to deduct from the amount of his proof against the surety's estate sums received from the principal debtor prior to submission of the proof,[169] but not

---

[164] Or, in the bankruptcy of an individual, Insolvency Act 1986 s.340(1).

[165] In bankruptcy, Insolvency Act 1986 s.340(2).

[166] Insolvency Act 1986 s.241(1)(e). See also s.342(1)(e).

[167] Insolvency Act 1986 s.241(1)(f).

[168] See para.5–72, above.

[169] *Re Blakeley* (1892) 9 Morr. 173; *Re Amalgamated Investment & Property Co Ltd* [1985] Ch. 349. Note that the relevant date for taking account of payments by the principal debtor is the date the proof is submitted, not the date it is admitted (*Re Amalgamated Investment & Property Co Ltd*, above).

sums received after the proof has been submitted.[170] On the other hand payments received from a co-surety or other party not primarily liable for the debt do not have to be deducted even if received before proof.[171] The creditor cannot, of course, receive more than 100p in the pound.

Where the surety has guaranteed only part of the debt, then whether a payment by the principal debtor is to be attributed to the guaranteed part of the indebtedness or to the rest of the debt is a matter of appropriation as between debtor and creditor, and the surety's trustee has no right to require the payment to be applied in reduction of the part of the debt covered by the guarantee.[172]

Again, negotiable instruments are a special case. A creditor proving against a surety on a negotiable instrument must credit sums received before proof from any party liable on the bill, whether or not he is the party primarily liable on the bill,[173] but sums received after proof need not be deducted.[174]

Proof by co-surety

A co-surety who has paid more than his due proportion of the debt cannot prove   **8–32** for his right of contribution in the estate of the bankrupt surety until the creditor has been paid in full, for the creditor himself has the prior right of proof and the rule against double proof prevents the co-surety from proving for the same debt.[175] However, once the co-surety has paid in full he becomes subrogated to the rights of the creditor[176] and can prove in his name, or take over his proof if already lodged, for the full amount of the debt, not merely the amount of the contribution to which he is entitled, so long as he does not receive in total more than 100p in the pound.[177]

(iii)   Bankruptcy of both debtor and surety

The general rule

Where both debtor and surety become bankrupt, the creditor is in general entitled   **8–33** to maintain a proof in both estates for the full amount of the debt, and is not obliged to reduce his proof in one estate so as to give credit for dividends declared or received in the other,[178] so long as he does not receive in toto more than 100p in the pound.

---

[170] *Re Blakeley* (1892) 9 Morr. 173.

[171] *Re Blackburne* (1892) 9 Morr. 249; *Re Houlder* [1929] Ch. 205. See para.8–18, above.

[172] This is merely a particular application of the general rule that a surety has no right to dictate to what debt a payment by the debtor to the creditor should be appropriated (*Re Sherry* (1884) 25 Ch. D. 692).

[173] *Re Blackburne* (1892) 9 Morr. 249. The party primarily liable on a bill is the acceptor or, in the case of an accommodation bill, the drawer.

[174] *Re Blackburne* (1892) 9 Morr. 249; *Re London, Bombay & Mediterranean Bank* (1874) 9 Ch. App. 686.

[175] *Commercial Bank of Australia v Official Assignee of the Estate of Wilson* [1893] A.C. 181, 186 (discussion of position if the agreement had not been made).

[176] Both in equity and by virtue of s.5 of the Mercantile Law Amendment Act 1856.

[177] *Re Parker, Morgan v Hill* [1894] 3 Ch. 400.

[178] The same principle applies here as where only one of the parties is insolvent. See *Re Rees* (1881) 17 Ch. D. 98; *Re Sass* [1896] 2 Q.B. 12; and para.8–18, above.

Negotiable instruments

8–34   Where the debtor and the surety are both liable on a negotiable instrument, as where the debtor is the acceptor and the surety is the drawer or indorser of a bill of exchange held by the creditor, a different rule applies. In this case, when proving against one estate the creditor must give credit for sums received or dividends declared (whether or not paid) from the other estate before he lodged his proof in the former estate,[179] though he is not obliged to revise his proof lodged in one estate where the receipt from or declaration of dividend in the other estate does not take place until after the lodging of the proof in the first estate.[180]

Finally, mention must be made of the rule in *Ex p. Waring*.[181] Under this rule, where a bill is accepted for the accommodation of the drawer and the latter deposits money with the acceptor to meet the acceptances, then if the drawer and the acceptor become insolvent the holder of the bill is entitled to have the amount so deposited paid to him. The theory appears to be that as the deposit was made for the specific purpose of covering the acceptor's liability under the bill, it is impressed with a trust for that purpose and cannot be treated as an asset in the acceptor's estate.[182] In lodging his proof of debt, the holder must give credit for any sums received under the rule.[183]

3.   VULNERABILITY OF GUARANTEE AS TRANSACTION AT UNDERVALUE

The statutory provisions

8–35   Where a company in administration or liquidation has at a relevant time[184] entered into a transaction at an undervalue and is at that time unable to pay its debts as they fall due[185] or becomes unable to do so in consequence of the transaction, the Insolvency Act 1986 confers wide powers to restore the status quo.[186] Similar provisions apply on the bankruptcy of an individual.[187] It would seem that the giving of a guarantee is capable of constituting a transaction at an undervalue for the purpose of these provisions, though their application to guarantees is not free from difficulty.

---

[179] *Cooper v Pepys* (1741) 1 Atk. 107; *Re Stein Ex p. Royal Bank of Scotland* (1815) 2 Rosa 197; *Re Houghton* (1857) 26 L.J.Bcy. 58.

[180] *Re Fothergill* (1876) 3 Ch.D. 445; *Re London, Bombay & Mediterranean Bank* (1874) L.R. 9 Ch.App. 686.

[181] *Ex p. Waring* (1815)19 Ves. 345.

[182] *Ex p. Dever (No.2)* (1885) 14 Q.B.D. 611.

[183] *Re Barned's Banking Co* (1875) L.R. 10 Ch. 198.

[184] For the meaning of this see para.8–22, above.

[185] Within the meaning of s.123 of the Insolvency Act 1986, see fn.140, above.

[186] Insolvency Act 1986 ss.238, 240, 241.

[187] Insolvency Act 1986 ss.339, 341, 342. Note that it is necessary that the bankrupt person is insolvent at the relevant time or becomes insolvent as a result of the transaction.

What constitutes a transaction at an undervalue[188]

A company enters into a transaction with a person at an undervalue if:　　　　**8–36**

(a)　the company makes a gift to that person or otherwise enters into a transaction with that person on terms that provide for the company to receive no consideration; or

(b)　the company enters into a transaction with that person for a consideration the value of which, in money or money's worth, is significantly less than the value, in money or money's worth, of the consideration provided by the company.[189]

The general notion is clear enough. If a company makes a payment, transfers an asset or provides services or other things and receives in exchange either nothing at all or something less than the value of what it parts with or provides, it enters into a transaction at an undervalue. But how do the provisions apply in relation to a guarantee, which does not at the time it is given involve a payment, transfer or provision of any kind by the surety, merely the incurring of a contingent obligation to pay?

Guarantee as a transaction at an undervalue[190]

Let us take a typical case where a company gives a guarantee in respect of　　**8–37**
advances to be made to its parent by a third party. The giving of the guarantee confers a benefit on the creditor, and the advance of funds by the creditor to the parent may be expected to benefit the subsidiary in facilitating its support and development by the parent, but the value of the benefit in each case may be difficult to estimate. This brings us to a fundamental problem in applying the statutory provisions to a guarantee. Whether a transaction is a transaction at an undervalue has presumably to be tested as at the time it is entered into, not the time when performance of the obligations incurred under it is demanded or effected.[191] So in deciding whether a guarantee gives rise to a transaction at an undervalue the act which constitutes the transaction is the giving of the guarantee,

---

[188] See generally Goode, *Principles of Corporate Insolvency Law* (2011), paras 13–13 et seq.

[189] Insolvency Act 1986 s.238(4). The comparable provision in bankruptcy is s.339(3).

[190] See generally Goode, *Principles of Corporate Insolvency Law* (2011), paras 13–34 to 13–37. For discussion of this problem in the context of intra-group guarantees, see D. Spahos, "Lenders, Borrowing Groups of Companies and Corporate Guarantees: an Insolvency Perspective" [2001] J.C.L.S. 333.

[191] This does not seem to be affected by the House of Lords decision in *Phillips v Brewin Dolphin Bell Lawrie Ltd* [2001] UKHL 2. In that case, Lord Scott appeared to be advocating the use of hindsight in valuing a transaction; however, it is clear that the ex post facto events were only to be used to determine the value of the consideration at the time of the transaction, where this was itself uncertain, and a decline in the value as a result of the ex post facto events would not be relevant, see Goode, *Principles of Corporate Insolvency Law* (2011), paras 13–31 to 13–32; and L. Ho, "The common sense of transactions at an undervalue" (2004) 20 I.L. and P. 202. If this were otherwise, it would mean that almost every guarantee which is subsequently called upon would be a transaction at an undervalue, see R. Parry "Case Comment: *Philips (Liquidator of AJ Bekhor & Co) v Brewin Dolphin Bell Lawrie Ltd (formerly Brewin Dolphin & Co Ltd)* [2001] UKHL 2; [2001] 1 W.L.R. 143 (HL)" (2001) 2 Insolvency Lawyer 58.

not the creditor's subsequent call under the guarantee or payment by the surety in response to such a call; and the time as at which the benefit conferred by the creditor by the guarantee falls to be valued is the time the surety becomes bound by the guarantee,[192] not the time when payment under it is demanded or made. Similarly, the benefit derived by the surety from the prospective provision of funds to its parent must be valued at the date of the guarantee, not at the date the funds are actually provided to the parent or the date when the surety receives a benefit as the result of their provision. Hence the task is to assess the present value of the contingent right conferred on the creditor by the guarantee and then determine whether this is significantly greater than the present value of the contingent benefit to be received by the surety from the advance to the parent. The onus of showing this lies on the liquidator or other office-holder seeking to impeach the transaction.

The benefit conferred on the creditor by the giving of the guarantee varies inversely with the strength of the parent (the principal debtor). If the parent is solvent and there is little likelihood of default the guarantee has a correspondingly low value to the creditor. We cannot say that it has no value, for the guarantee relates to the future, and though the parent may be solvent when the guarantee is given it does not follow that it will still be solvent when repayment falls due. On the other hand, even if there is some prospect of default the value of the guarantee is not necessarily the full value of the debt, for against this must be set whatever part of the debt is likely to be recoverable from the parent as debtor and from any security furnished by the parent. It follows that whilst the benefit to the surety of an advance made to the parent will usually be considerably less than the amount of the advance, it will not necessarily be less or "significantly" less than the benefit conferred on the creditor by the guarantee.

The practical problems involved in valuing the contingent benefits received by the creditor on the one hand and the surety on the other, coupled with the fact that the onus is on the office-holder to prove an undervalue and the availability of the statutory defence referred to below, mean that in the ordinary way a guarantee is unlikely to be held a transaction at an undervalue unless there is both a serious risk of default and no benefit to the surety, as where the guarantee is taken to support an advance already made to the parent which the latter is unlikely to be able to repay.

---

[192] This will depend on the circumstances. Where the consideration for the guarantee is the creditor's counter-promise to make advances to the parent, the contract of guarantee is bilateral and comes into effect by the exchange of the promise and counter-promise. More commonly, however, the creditor makes no promise of any kind to the surety, and the consideration for the latter's promise is the actual making of the advance by the creditor. In such a case the contract of guarantee is unilateral and comes into existence only when the creditor accepts the surety's offer by making the advance, until which time the document is legally inoperative and the surety is free to withdraw from his guarantee. For this purpose it is immaterial that the guarantee is under seal, since as a purely accessory engagement it is intended to come into effect only on the furnishing of consideration by the creditor. See K. P. McGuinness, *The Law of Guarantee*, 2nd edn (Toronto: The Carswell Company Ltd, 1996), para.4.62. It follows from the above that the apparent difficulty of valuing a guarantee at the time it is given and before the creditor has either made his advance or undertaken to the surety to make it cannot arise, for until then the guarantee is not legally operative at all.

Defence in respect of bona fide business transactions

Even where it is established that the guarantee is a transaction at an undervalue, the court cannot exercise its powers of adjustment if it is satisfied:

(a) that the company which entered into the transaction did so in good faith and for the purpose of carrying on its business; and

(b) that at the time it did so there were reasonable grounds for believing that the transaction would benefit the company.[193]

8–38

Powers of court

Where the guarantee constitutes a transaction at an undervalue and the statutory defence referred to above is not available the court may make such order as it thinks fit for restoring the position to what it would have been if the company had not entered into the transaction[194] and without prejudice to the generality of this power may include in such an order provision for any of the matters listed in s.241(1) of the Act, subject to the restrictions imposed by s.241(2).[195]

8–39

---

[193] Insolvency Act 1986 s.238(5). There is no comparable provision for bankruptcy.

[194] Insolvency Act 1986 s.238(3). The comparable provision in bankruptcy is s.339(2).

[195] The bankruptcy equivalent is to be found in s.342(1), (2).

INDEX